THE CONGO TRIALS IN THE INTERNATIONAL CRIMINAL COURT

REVISED EDITION

This is the first in-depth study of the first three ICC trials: an engaging, accessible text meant for specialists and students, for legal advocates and a wide range of professionals concerned with diverse cultures, human rights, and restorative justice. It introduces international justice and courtroom trials in practical terms, offering a balanced view on persistent tensions and controversies. Separate chapters analyze the working realities of central African armed conflicts, finding reasons for their surprising resistance to ICC legal formulas. The book dissects the Court's structural dynamics, which were designed to steer an elusive middle course between high moral ideals and hard political realities. Detailed chapters provide vivid accounts of courtroom encounters with four Congolese suspects. The mixed record of convictions, acquittals, dissents, and appeals, resulting from these trials, provides a map of distinct fault-lines within the ICC legal code, and suggests a rocky path ahead for the Court's next ventures.

Richard Gaskins is Joseph M. Proskauer Professor of Law and Social Welfare at Brandeis University. He spent the past decade designing and directing student exchange programs in The Hague, which combined academic theory with hands–on practicums in courts and NGO's. He holds a Ph.D. (Philosophy) and J.D. from Yale University.

The Congo Trials in the International Criminal Court

Revised Edition

RICHARD GASKINS

CAMBRIDGE
UNIVERSITY PRESS

University Printing House, Cambridge CB2 8BS, United Kingdom

One Liberty Plaza, 20th Floor, New York, NY 10006, USA

477 Williamstown Road, Port Melbourne, VIC 3207, Australia

314–321, 3rd Floor, Plot 3, Splendor Forum, Jasola District Centre, New Delhi – 110025, India

103 Penang Road, #05–06/07, Visioncrest Commercial, Singapore 238467

Cambridge University Press is part of the University of Cambridge.

It furthers the University's mission by disseminating knowledge in the pursuit of education, learning, and research at the highest international levels of excellence.

www.cambridge.org
Information on this title: www.cambridge.org/9781009208772
DOI: 10.1017/9781009208772

First edition published 2020

Revised edition published 2022

A catalogue record for this publication is available from the British Library.

ISBN 978-1-009-20877-2 Paperback

For Elizabeth

The object of knowledge is not something with which thinking sets out, but something with which it ends: something which the processes of inquiry and testing themselves produce.

And so it is with mathematical knowledge, or with knowledge of politics or art. Their respective objects are not known till they are made in course of the process of experimental thinking. Their usefulness when made is whatever, from infinity to zero, experience may subsequently determine it to be.

John Dewey
Essays in Experimental Logic

Contents

Acknowledgments

This project started a decade ago, when I began leading intensive academic programs in The Hague for undergraduate students from a dozen US universities. These study programs (both semester-long and summer) were a collaborative venture between Brandeis University and Leiden University Law School and, most directly, with the Grotius Centre for International Legal Studies. I am grateful to Leiden Law Deans Carel Stolker and Rick Lawson for their cordial support over the years. Most especially, I want to thank Professor Carsten Stahn for sharing planning challenges and teaching duties, and also Martine Wierenga and Ioana Moraru for their constant assistance.

In each study program, the main themes went beyond international criminal law to include human rights, conflict resolution, and transitional justice. During these years, the Congo trials were on full display at the International Criminal Court (ICC); and other Hague courts and tribunals likewise opened their doors, along with NGO offices serving broader goals. My thanks to court officials, including judges and advocates, and to the dedicated network of justice experts throughout The Hague. In the midst of their own tribulations, they took the time and interest to enrich this student generation of global citizens, hosting court visits, informal discussion meetings, and on-site field practicums.

Teaching about new and dynamic systems of justice stimulated my research plans. It meant securing basic assumptions, making sure that core concepts were clearly understood, and then observing how bright undergraduates (both American and international students) responded to these extraordinary trials and projects spread across The Hague. I learned much from their questions and was inspired by their idealism. Global justice will be counting on their creativity to improve future systems.

Thanks also to my Brandeis colleagues, especially Melissa Stimell and Gregory Townsend, for their dedicated teaching. My fondest wishes to Hans and Loes van Waning, who hosted me in Leiden over the years, in their gracious home filled with warm feeling and fine music.

Beyond measure is my gratitude to Elizabeth Chadwick for sharing our joint logistical challenges, and whose support for this project made all the difference.

During this decade of collaborations and discoveries, I felt a growing sense of wonder about these three operatic trials of four Congolese men – which (at point of writing) remain the only ICC trials to see their final curtain, twenty years after the Rome Statute was approved. There is much to admire here, and even more to question. But it is this spirit of wonder that I invite my readers to share in exploring these historic trials.

November 2019

A Laboratory for Global Justice

In July 2002, after hasty renovations to an old Dutch telecom building on the margins of The Hague, the International Criminal Court (ICC) opened its doors to the world. Created by treaty in 1998, the ICC was a bold response to the hopes of many nations for a more compelling way to enforce the fundamental rights of humanity. A permanent international court would soon begin to prosecute suspects accused of mounting attacks on innocent populations – even if those accused were government officials, including heads of state. Amid investigations into more than a half-dozen global trouble spots, the ICC launched its first courtroom trials by charging a handful of men from the Democratic Republic of Congo. The following chapters tell the story of these pioneering trials, which dominated the ICC's first decade of operation.

Courtroom trials show us the law in action. The trial itself is not some quiet research survey or academic inquiry – even though courts do provide fruitful topics for researchers and scholars. In the core dynamics of a trial, out of the drama of adversarial testing, the outcome emerges as something greater than the sum of its parts. International trials are a kind of proving ground. And for new courts like the ICC, the initial trials unfolded like a brash laboratory experiment.

In the alchemy of the courtroom, trials set off reactions between legal norms in the statute book and concrete facts in the particular case. These frictional sparks signal the appearance of a new organic bond at the conclusion of the trial. In international courts the legal norms begin as grand abstractions, proclaiming broad humanistic ideals, while the concrete facts of individual cases are as raw and unpredictable as life itself.

From all these elements, the first ICC trials yielded a highly combustible mix. Unexpected twists and turns lengthened all the proceedings. Twenty years after the founding treaty was signed, the Court had completed just three full trials – in which two of four Congolese men were acquitted. These are the

Congo trials, and their close analysis will instruct us on the future of international criminal justice.

Criminal law takes action in many ways beyond the trials inside the courtroom. Crimes have to be investigated; cases and suspects have to be identified; charges need to be confirmed. Being new, international courts have to be created, and a dedicated professional staff must work out how to administer them. These tasks all manifest elements of politics, morality, and culture – another way of saying that legal systems belong to the larger human endeavor. It is up to the officials running this volatile system to conserve the defining marks of genuine criminal trials: the aspirations to objectivity and impartiality.

But can these noble qualities truly be realized in practice? Any account of the Congo trials must include tensions and doubts surrounding the legal process. Clearly this is no ordinary laboratory exercise. Courtroom inquiry needs to defend its core legal values in the face of political and moral pressure.

Inside the courtroom, where the law operates in a protected space, the process demands fair treatment and the rational scrutiny of facts and laws. But the courtroom is only one part of a larger institutional structure of inquiry, interacting with an array of global actors. These interactions too are regulated by law; but they must also enter into practical judgments extending outside the courtroom. When these external dealings go beyond the strict logic of legal process, they open themselves to critical attacks as political in nature. The legal experiment taking place in The Hague is itself a test of how Court officials manage the tensions between legal values and effective, pragmatic action. Their challenge is to avoid reducing the law to *mere politics*.

Another set of tensions arises when the legal process is surrounded by intense moral energy, going to the core purpose of the Court: to pass judgment on those responsible for committing mass atrocities. The legal experiment carried out in Hague courtrooms will be judged by how it balances the joint and several claims of law and morality. By adhering to strict legal practice, the Court earns its authority to declare justice in individual cases. But legality alone may not be enough to satisfy the moral demands of activists, particularly when initial trials end in acquittals, or in reduction of key criminal charges. Tensions between law and morality are present even inside the courtroom – in the passion of opening statements, but even more with the inclusion of crime victims as trial participants.

As crossroads for law, politics, and morality, international trials are often assessed in polarizing, all-or-nothing terms. This study of the first ICC trials avoids common rhetorical extremes – the skeptical reduction of law to politics or culture, or the true believer's zeal for collapsing legal rules into moral imperatives. Such strong reactions are always tempting with new and experimental trials – especially with the mixed results of the Congo trials. But here we steer a middle course between faith and skepticism, finding a balance in the play of legal process. Both inside and outside the courtroom, a critical approach to ICC trials opens up deeper connections to political, moral, and cultural realities.

Before studying any trial as a complex process, one might describe it more simply as a performance. Playwrights, novelists, and screenwriters have long known that courtroom trials hold the capacity for high drama. Legal actors may be cast in symbolic roles, as the trial becomes a proxy struggle between good and evil.

And surely, international trials ignite this ritual battle, starting with opening statements from Prosecutors – and sustained with impassioned commentary from observers outside the courtroom. But given the sheer length of the first ICC trials, the dramatic arc soon flattens out under the weight of time and tedium. On any given day, public visitors in The Hague are astonished by the ordinariness of it all: astonished by the dulled passions and subdued demeanor of the parties; by the fanatical tracking of documents down to the smallest filing details; by the seemingly bottomless descent into minutiae with witness testimony. Year after year, virtually every action in the courtroom, however minor, is verbally prefaced by invoking the precise legal or procedural code authorizing its occurrence.

In the Congo trials, there was little drama where good playwrights would have scripted it. But as a laboratory experiment, the surprising results, arising from masses of deeds and documents, have been deeply challenging. The following chapters explore these dynamic outcomes, observing closely as the ICC legal code began its long path to implementation.

TESTING A NEW COURT

> Even following the best part of a decade since [the ICC's] establishment, the strong feeling remains that so much is still in the process of being established . . .. There are successes and not a few problems, and the unexpected occurs almost on a daily basis.
>
> Each time a case is conducted in a particular way, the more difficult it is to break free from the trend of established precedent; yet it is dangerous for first-instance judges to use a serious war crimes trial as a laboratory experiment.
>
> ICC Judge Adrian Fulford
> "Reflections of a Trial Judge"

> And at this stage in the life of the Court we are still discussing our basic vocabulary.
>
> ICC Judge Christine Van den Wyngaert
> Bemba appeals hearing

> This is a game of ties and junctures, balancing contradictions and tensions.
>
> Alex Veit
> *Intervention as Indirect Rule*

A stranger settling into the public gallery at the International Criminal Court has to weave together a bundle of impressions, taking in far more than meets the eye. The legal code may be sitting there on the judicial bench, in thick binders; but the law itself comes alive only in the action taking place inside the courtroom. A criminal trial is a process of testing that can spread out over many years: finding ways to combine laws and facts, to reconcile competing stories from the Prosecution and Defense (among others), and to refine outcomes through procedures and proof standards. Culturally, the events inside the Hague courtroom could not be more distant from the underlying facts and circumstances – facts rooted in a distant place and time (central Africa in the years 2002 and 2003). These contrasts in culture and context must all be reimagined within the sterile confines of court proceedings.

Focusing on contrasts and tensions picks up the jagged rhythm of the Congo trials, as these troubled cases worked their way through the ICC. First there are tensions between what happens *inside* the courtroom and *outside* it. Then there are tensions between the strictly legal and the more elusive political ingredients of a trial. These differences open up further social dichotomies: between the distant culture where crimes allegedly occurred and the secure space in which trials take place; between the individual on trial and the shadowy groups through which his actions were implemented; between the social imperatives of local events and the legal norms enshrined in international law.

As these various contrasts are laid out, action inside the Hague Court starts to take on fuller meaning. The trials must reckon with mixed goals: on one side, a quiet confidence in the procedural neutrality of law; on the other, the moral angst of battling to end mass atrocities. Even after the courtroom spectacle has run for many years, it remains hard to measure the results in terms of winners and losers. Close observers come away from the trials with mixed satisfactions and concerns, with alternating moods of faith and skepticism about the entire venture.

This first glimpse into the ICC courtroom, anticipating the three Congo trials, introduces the contrasts and tensions that define the field of international criminal law. As in a lengthy trial, answers must be delayed until one finds the right questions, and until one explores the topic from various perspectives. Later parts of this book will offer in-depth studies about central African conflicts, about the history and design of the ICC, and about the ideas and philosophies that compete within its courtrooms. These first two chapters reveal some of the complications. They are meant to introduce key players and basic rules of the game, as a preview of central tensions that emerged within these historic first trials.

1

Spreading Justice to Distant Conflicts

1.1 INSIDE AND OUTSIDE THE COURTROOM

Trial Chamber: Day One

"All rise! The International Criminal Court is now in session." With this declaration from the Court usher – delivered on a brisk January morning in The Hague in 2009 – Trial Chamber I opened the case of *Prosecutor* v. *Thomas Lubanga Dyilo* – the first of the Congo trials and the very first trial conducted by this controversial new court.[1]

At center stage was Presiding Judge Sir Adrian Fulford. From his high judicial bench, Judge Fulford extended resonant greetings to all the participants in the crowded courtroom, identifying key players in the drama set to unfold. Down on the floor, to his left, was the Prosecution team, represented by the mercurial Luis Moreno-Ocampo and members of his office. Opposite the Prosecution, across the courtroom to the right, was the equally large Defense team, deep with seasoned Francophone advocates. Directly beneath the judges' bench sat a row of Court officers and legal assistants, including technicians ready to ensure that all computer systems were performing well – systems visible to those in the public gallery looking out onto a vast ocean of computer screens. There were also interpreters hidden away in cramped booths, waiting to ease the differences between the Court's two official languages, French and English, and to render into these languages the testimony yet to come in Swahili and Lingala, among other tongues. A keen observer would have noticed an additional lawyerly group, sitting between the judges' elevated bench and the Prosecution team: the Legal Representatives for

[1] Lubanga Trial Chamber, transcript, January 26, 2009, ICC-01/04-01/06-T-107-ENG. "Dyilo" is a customary post-name. It appears in official ICC records, while the trial transcripts and outside commentary generally used the family name "Lubanga."

Victims of specific crimes alleged to have occurred in the Congo. Ready to inject a compelling human story into these proceedings, they wore the same black gowns and ruffled white collars as the Prosecutors and Defenders; although their official role was unique, still to be tested.

In his celebratory round of introductions, Judge Fulford neglected to welcome the accused, Thomas Lubanga, an oversight he corrected most graciously at the outset of the second day. Lubanga's name had never previously figured in the headlines of leading European newspapers. He was a provincial player from Ituri district in the far northeastern corner of the Congo, forty-eight years old, who described himself simply as a "politician." Lubanga sat alone at a short desk in the far corner of the courtroom, flanked by two unarmed security guards and excused from any mandatory speaking role during the proceedings. From this angle, he could study the backs of his Defense team, sitting at two ranks of tables directly in front of him, staring ahead either at their computer screens or toward the judges at stage center. But Lubanga himself was easily seen from the public gallery, behind thick transparent, soundproof glass, where curious visitors from around the world took note of his dignified bearing – military in posture – as well as his deep ebony skin and lidless eyes. Many in the gallery were eager to speculate on what might be going through his mind as his trial unfolded.

Seated next to Judge Fulford that morning were two distinguished judges from Costa Rica and Bolivia, rounding out the membership of Trial Chamber I. Judge Fulford came from the United Kingdom, and, from his confident courtroom demeanor, one could sense his long legal experience, articulated in rich tones reminiscent of the classic BBC commentator. The polish of his diction and deportment fully matched that of his bald scalp, caught in the unnaturally bright light levels pervading this ultra-modern courtroom, reflecting off the blond paneling that covered every surface of wall and ceiling. On the bench, the three Caucasian judges were resplendent in dark gowns trimmed in royal blue. In the case of *Prosecutor* v. *Thomas Lubanga Dyilo*, they alone would hear the evidence, apply the law, and pass criminal judgment. At the International Criminal Court, there are no juries.

Background to the Congo Trials

The start of the Lubanga trial was but a ceremonial flourish in a longer-running legal drama. When the curtain rose on Monday morning, January 26, 2009, the basic scenery had barely shifted. Most of the actors in the courtroom that day had been rehearsing together for almost two years, laying the groundwork for this first trial – and indirectly for others to follow.

Thomas Lubanga had been delivered to The Hague three years earlier, in March 2006, after being bundled onto a French military plane, straight from his detention cell in the Congolese capital of Kinshasa. During his first year at the ICC, his status was managed by a different group of judges in a Pre-Trial Chamber, who scrutinized the conditions of his arrest, framed the charges against him that would be tested at trial, and set key ground-rules to ensure the fairness of that trial. The Trial Chamber took over in early 2007 and would remain tied to the case for more than five years. It finished its required tasks in late 2012, which included handing Lubanga a fourteen-year sentence, four months after releasing a massive written judgment (over 600 pages) detailing reasons for his conviction.[2] During this lengthy trial period, all three judges saw their judicial terms expire; but they stayed on to complete the work of this historic first case. In the end, two additional years ran off the calendar before the Appeals Chamber (involving yet another team of judges) sorted through various challenges to the trial judgment.[3] Altogether, starting from the Prosecutor's initial investigations in the Congo, the Lubanga case occupied more than a decade in the life of the ICC.

It was a rocky start for the new ICC, after its initial launch in July 2002, in accordance with its founding document, the 1998 Treaty of Rome. After the Treaty was initialed by the negotiating countries, following a contentious drafting process, friends of the Court were surprised by the speed with which it was formally ratified by sixty nations. This number was the legal threshold for opening the world's first permanent court dedicated to the prosecution of crimes linked to the very worst human atrocities. During its first ten years of operation, another sixty-plus nations joined the ICC – although not some of the very largest countries. China, India, Indonesia, Russia and the United States have not joined. The ICC's ambitious mission was driven by the twentieth century's appalling record of mass violence, including war crimes and genocide. But the Treaty (also known as the "Rome Statute") does not allow the Court to look backwards in time: its jurisdiction is strictly limited to events occurring after July 1, 2002. The Lubanga trial focused on events running for a twelve-month period (September 2002 to August 2003). Although this was only a small temporal slice of armed violence endemic in eastern Congo, it was a timely segment that handed the ICC the first opportunity to implement its historic mission.

By early 2008, as the Trial Chamber prepared for the groundbreaking Lubanga trial, the ICC pre-trial judges started picking up the pace. From the Congo there arrived two additional Ituri figures, erstwhile opponents of

[2] Lubanga Trial Judgment, March 14, 2012, ICC-01/04–01/06–2842.

[3] Lubanga Appeals Judgment, December 1, 2014, ICC-01/04–01/06–3121.

Lubanga in the same series of local conflicts taking place during the period 2002–03. The first was Germain Katanga in late 2007, to be joined in early 2008 by Mathieu Ngudjolo. The joint trial of these two figures would be the second trial undertaken by the ICC and would move at much the same pace as the first trial. For many months the Prosecutor had been searching other venues for suspects, including in Uganda, and in Sudan, where in 2009 he finally obtained an arrest warrant against President Omar al-Bashir for alleged crimes committed in Darfur. But gaining custody of suspects in those places proved elusive.

More fruitful was a case growing out of the Central African Republic (CAR), where the prime suspect was a well-known Congolese politician, Jean-Pierre Bemba, who had briefly crossed paths with local factions in Ituri district, prior to sending his personal militia into the CAR. In early 2008, Bemba's surprise arrest in Belgium opened the way for the third ICC trial. In all, these three groundbreaking trials of four Congolese nationals marked the ICC's emergence as a functioning tribunal – no longer just a lofty ideal. It was a sea change from a bold humanitarian promise to concrete legal reality. These three overlapping trials would leave no doubt that the new international court faced daunting challenges.

Much later, as the three Congo trials were winding down, another Congolese figure arrived in The Hague through a most surprising route. Having eluded arrest during the many years Lubanga sat in detention, Bosco Ntaganda had played a continuing role in conflicts persisting in Ituri and in volatile Congo provinces farther south. Like some other Lubanga associates, he found temporary refuge in the reorganized Congolese national army; but he was far more inclined to join rebellions and paramilitaries, some sponsored by neighboring countries. In early 2013 his luck finally ran out. Pursued by all factions in an armed standoff, he fled to the unlikely safe haven of the United States Embassy in Rwanda. Although Americans had expressed profound doubts about the ICC over the years since its creation, they quietly arranged for Ntaganda's immediate transfer to The Hague. Following a trial judgment in 2019, his conviction and sentence are currently under review by the Appeals Chamber.

Ituri and The Hague

As the trials played out over time, they drew worried responses from many of the ICC's ardent supporters. Had the Prosecutor chosen his first trials judiciously?[4] It was too late now to go back. When Moreno-Ocampo managed

[4] Of the many attempts to answer this question, one of the best informed comes from a Congolese human rights lawyer, who sees these suspects as "small fish." Pascal

to gain custody of his first four suspects, both he and the entire Court were soon tangled in an unforgiving web of local conflicts, involving a shifting group of militia factions with obscure links to outside sponsors. The microscopic details were already several years past. For the first two trials, these conflicts took place in Ituri, a small district in eastern Congo, which had been closely watched by global NGOs (non-governmental organizations), and where the United Nations had already sent peacekeepers. Reports on Ituri atrocities drew the ICC Prosecutor's attention, fueled by particular outrage from NGOs about widespread rape and sexual violence, along with the mass enlistment of child soldiers.[5] The stories of injustice in Ituri and the CAR were deeply shocking; but transferring that outrage into the courtroom proved much more difficult than the Prosecutor had imagined. Inside the courtroom, all that moral energy had to circulate through more restrained legal principles.

For more than a decade, the ICC was embroiled in a sustained and sobering examination of events in these remote areas of central Africa. Despite the ICC's impressive moral authority, inherited from outrage at all the atrocities afflicting nations and peoples throughout the twentieth century, the Congo trials served as a rude awakening from the early dream of implementing global justice. In retrospect, the trials were overwhelmed by conflicting stories about mass violence, amid growing uncertainty about the precise legal responsibility of suspects holding ambiguous roles inside shadowy organizations – loosely called "militias." Confronted by such complexity, the proceedings were slower and more expensive than anyone had imagined. Were these trials poorly planned by the Prosecutor, or poorly managed by the judges? Were the core rules just not clear enough? If the problems emanating from central Africa were so daunting, how will the ICC fare with future atrocities played out on a larger global scale?

Legal officials in The Hague were constantly surprised and challenged by the obscurities of events in Ituri. But for people who had spent their lives in this battered district, the very real chaos had been spreading since the 1990s – and would not stop during the tumultuous decade of the Congo trials. Moreover, as field researchers have confirmed, Ituri conflicts were embedded in the history,

Kalume Kambale, "A Story of Missed Opportunities: The Role of the International Criminal Court in the Democratic Republic of Congo," in Christian De Vos, Sara Kendall, and Carsten Stahn (eds.), *Contested Justice: The Politics and Practice of International Criminal Court Interventions* (Cambridge: Cambridge University Press, 2015), pp. 188–92. See also William A. Schabas, "The Banality of International Justice," *Journal of International Criminal Justice* 11 (2013), 545.

[5] Of particular note are Human Rights Watch (HRW), *Ituri: "Covered in Blood": Ethnically Targeted Violence in Northeastern DR Congo* (July 2003), and UN Secretary General, *Special Report on the Events in Ituri, January 2002–December 2003*, S/2004/573.

culture, and politics of the district. In the views of local and regional experts, the underlying causes went deeper than the criminal intent of specific actors who happened to fall into the hands of the ICC.[6] Eye-witness stories collected in Ituri were as diverse as the factions that regularly split away from brittle local organizations, political and military, all locked in fierce competition. This complexity posed the greatest challenge to the ICC during the Congo trials.

Equally obscure were events in the CAR, in and around the time Jean-Pierre Bemba's troops were present (the window for prosecution being October 2002 through March 2003). Here the context was a bloody political coup, with a band of Congolese troops sent to aid the doomed President, while their commander, Jean-Pierre Bemba, stayed behind. The violence in the CAR was horrendous, yielding heartbreaking stories from scores of victims.[7] But how much of it was related to the Congolese, and how did their actions filter back across the border to the man subsequently charged with responsibility? The stories veered off in multiple directions.

Of course, a courtroom is the natural home for competing narratives. The adversary system of conducting trials insists that judges shall hear alternatives to the dominant narrative told by the Prosecution. In these trials, where the Prosecution's story drew heavily on the narrative of injustice contained in reports from respected NGOs, it was even more urgent to bring such challenges into the courtroom. Moreover, the ICC goes farther than other international courts by including voices of the victims as a mandatory element. The Legal Representatives of Victims brought these local views from Ituri and the CAR into the proceedings, forever reminding the Court that the suffering itself was all too real. And yet these particular voices, while heartfelt from each victim, were but single threads in a dense tangle of narratives. The same was true for the live witnesses brought to the ICC courtroom from Ituri, whose testimony drew trial judges into a web of deception, ambiguity, and cultural confusion.

The ICC on Trial

The Congo trials took place in The Hague. But their twistings and turnings were dictated by opaque forces that can be understood only by closer study of

[6] Among field research studies, a good starting point is Koen Vlassenroot and Timothy Raeymaekers, "The Politics of Rebellion and Intervention in Ituri: The Emergence of a New Political Complex?" *African Affairs* 103 (2004), 385. The field literature is discussed in detail in Chapters 3 and 4.

[7] A key source on these CAR events was published by the Paris-based Fédération Internationale des Ligues des Droits de l'Homme (FIDH), *When the Elephants Fight, the Grass Suffers: Report on War Crimes in the Central African Republic* (February 2003).

actual conditions in places like Ituri. The same notion occurred to the judges in the second Congo trial, who decided to take a field trip, hoping to gain a concrete feel for the distant environment that had dominated their courtroom. That trip came after all the evidence had been presented at trial, and some eight years after the events being litigated. No one knows exactly how breathing the air and observing the landscape improved the judges' capacity to sort out conflicting tales told by witnesses, victims, and the legal parties to the case.[8] The desire to understand realities on the ground goes to the heart of challenges facing the ICC. Will it be possible, in future cases, for judges sitting in The Hague to engage with complex crimes coming to them from remote corners of the world? A close examination of the Congo trials may provide answers to this central question.

The first three trials of the ICC were nominally about the guilt or innocence of four Congolese nationals. The risk of prison terms fell on them alone. But it is even more compelling to see the Congo cases as a series of trials for the ICC itself. At stake was the moral capital already invested in this institution, funded by Nuremberg, and leveraged across atrocities in the Balkans and Rwanda, among other places. That fund of moral authority would face restrictions in the courtroom phase of proceedings.

At stake in these first trials is the future shape of global justice. After a detailed study of how the Congo trials unfolded, the final judgment lies with readers – and with all those who share the humane values guiding the ICC.

1.2 FROM MORAL IMPERATIVES TO LEGAL PROCESS

Putting Humanitarian Ideals into Practice

With the fortuitous arrival of Thomas Lubanga and other suspects, the Congo trials would dominate the ICC's first decade. During these trials, the judges began their historic task of implementing the ICC's legal code, known as the "Rome Statute" or the "ICC Statute." Starting from the bare text, these legal rules were interpreted by judges at three different procedural stages: pre-trial, trial, and appeals. Judges in future trials will inherit this process, moving further down paths marked out by the ICC's fateful encounters with Ituri.

8 In the Katanga Trial Judgment, the Chamber mentions several ways it applied local knowledge from the site visit to evaluate the credibility of witnesses: March 7, 2014, ICC-01/04-01/07-3436, paras. 106–08, 313, 1274.

One novel question facing the various judges dealt with the potential role of victims in the conduct of trials. The ICC Statute broke new ground in international criminal law by permitting victims of atrocities to participate in Court proceedings – under certain conditions. But who exactly are these victims? Do they include everyone among the tens of thousands of Iturians displaced by ongoing conflicts? Or only those who were allegedly victimized by Lubanga and his supporters? Once the class of victims has been properly narrowed, what limits should be placed on their participation in prosecutions? Can they request arrest warrants, or otherwise influence investigations on the ground? At trial, can they produce or cross-examine witnesses? These and many other practical questions emerge from the general language in the Statute:

> Where the personal interests of the victims are affected, the Court shall permit their views and concerns to be presented and considered at stages of the proceedings determined to be appropriate by the Court and in a manner which is not prejudicial to or inconsistent with the rights of the accused and a fair and impartial trial.

According to the Rome Statute, such views and concerns may be presented by the legal representatives of the victims where the Court considers it appropriate, in accordance with the Rules of Procedure and Evidence.[9]

This carefully hedged language indicates how much depends on the circumstances of each specific trial. The text acknowledges a range of trade-offs or tensions, all of which had provided topics for commentary by learned scholars.[10] When the first ICC trials took form, pre-trial judges began to implement Article 68(3) in the specific conditions arising from Ituri and the CAR. In a concrete trial, an "appropriate" balance depends on particular circumstances. Is it appropriate for survivors of rape and sexual slavery in Ituri to press the Trial Chamber to add these charges to the accusations against Lubanga? Are victims allowed to express their views on the credibility of specific witnesses offering live testimony?

[9] Article 68(3).

[10] The concepts here were derived from a key UN document: Declaration on the Basic Principles of Justice for Victims of Crime and Abuse of Power, UN General Assembly Resolution 40/34 (1985). This Declaration was further developed in 2005: Basic Principles and Guidelines on the Right to a Remedy and Reparation for Victims of Gross Violations of International Human Rights Law and Serious Violations of International Humanitarian Law, UN General Assembly Resolution 60/147. For a sympathetic vision of these provisions, see Mariana Goetz, "The International Criminal Court and Its Relevance to Affected Communities," in Royal African Society, *Courting Conflict? Justice, Peace and the ICC in Africa* (London: Royal African Society, 2008), pp. 65–72.

In a real trial, these questions are joined by Defense lawyers, speaking to the balance in the Statute between victim participation and the fair trial rights of the accused. The Court always starts from formal rules. But Article 68(3) itself requires the Court to make specific situational judgments. From these judgments comes an evolving sense of what *victim participation* will eventually mean in practice. After seeing what was appropriate for victims in Ituri, the potential victims in future cases may learn what to expect from the ICC Statute.[11]

It was inevitable that such questions would arise and need resolution in the initial ICC trials. Any newly functioning court must go through this formative process of implementing its legal code. As the trials took unexpected turns, judges were drawn into the smallest details of past events in far-off Ituri. These complex situations would test basic legal concepts and start to shape their future meaning.

The process of legal interpretation had to manage constant reminders of the ICC's institutional commitment to moral ideals. Much of what happened in the Congo trials revealed this critical gap between perplexity over concrete details and ardent certainty about moral ambitions. The breadth of those ambitions is manifest in the Preamble to the ICC Statute – identified here in **bold type**. According to the Preamble, the ICC was created to

> **ensure the effective prosecution** of certain **grave crimes**, including **unimaginable atrocities that deeply shock the conscience of humanity**. Such crimes can **shatter the delicate mosaic of cultural bonds**, undermining societies from within. Left unchecked, such crimes may further **threaten the peace, security, and well-being** of neighboring countries. An effective Court will **end impunity for those responsible for international crimes**, and **thus contribute to the prevention of such crimes.**[12]

With such high ambitions, it seemed unlikely that the first three trials would be rated a full success. But decisions taken in the courtroom will determine the practical future for international justice, as it shifts into operational mode.

The Legacy of Nuremberg

The larger vision of international justice had expanded several times across the twentieth century, notably in the aftermath of mass atrocities tied to

[11] An especially useful source is Christine Van den Wyngaert. "Victims before International Criminal Courts: Some Views and Concerns of an ICC Trial Judge," *Case Western Reserve International Law Journal* 44 (2012), 475.

[12] For all its soaring rhetoric, the Preamble to the Rome Statute does not have the same legal authority as the 128 Articles that comprise its substance. The Preamble language nonetheless enters into the interpretation of those Articles, seeking to bring moral ballast to the legal process.

international wars. The trials of Nazi officials at Nuremberg, following World War II, became a major inspiration for putting this vision into eloquent language.[13] Few writers can resist citing the words of the lead American Prosecutor at Nuremberg, Supreme Court Justice Robert H. Jackson, opening his case in November 1945:

> The privilege of opening the first trial in history for crimes against the peace of the world imposes a grave responsibility. The wrongs which we seek to condemn and punish have been so calculated, so malignant, and so devastating, that civilization cannot tolerate their being ignored, because it cannot survive their being repeated. That four great nations, flushed with victory and stung with injury stay the hand of vengeance and voluntarily submit their captive enemies to the judgment of the law is one of the most significant tributes that Power has ever paid to Reason.[14]

Jackson's rhetoric makes an extraordinary pivot between morally depraved crimes and the cool rationalism of legal principles in a proper courtroom. That same maneuver would become an everyday challenge at the new ICC. It was more difficult in The Hague. After all, the Nuremberg Tribunal was meant to perform a specific historical task. The victorious Allies won the conventional war, after which they moved to prosecute the aggressors, representatives of the Nazi state and close collaborators, for committing "crimes against the peace." Today, what stands out is that resolve "to stay the hand of vengeance,"[15] while the practical legal details of Nuremberg have been allowed to fade softly into history. Then and now, critics have drawn attention to troubling defects in the actual proceedings, noting gaps between grand ideals and implementation.[16] At the time, even more criticism was aimed at the Tokyo Tribunal[17] (the counterpart to Nuremberg in the Pacific theater)

[13] See the essays in Guénaël Mettraux (ed.), *Perspectives on Nuremberg* (Oxford: Oxford University Press, 2008). For creative histories of earlier twentieth-century influences, see Mark Lewis, *Birth of the New Justice: Internationalization of Crime and Punishment 1919–1950* (Oxford: Oxford University Press, 2014); William A. Schabas, *The Trial of the Kaiser* (Oxford: Oxford University Press, 2018).

[14] *Trial of the Major War Criminals before the International Military Tribunal* (Nuremberg: IMT, 1947), Volume II, proceedings of November 21, 1945 (Robert Jackson opening statement before the IMT).

[15] This phrase provides political scientist Gary Jonathan Bass with his theme for an informative history of war crimes tribunals, *Stay the Hand of Vengeance* (Princeton: Princeton University Press, 2000).

[16] A good overview is Richard Overy, "The Nuremberg Trials: International Law in the Making," in Philippe Sands (ed.), *From Nuremberg to The Hague: The Future of International Criminal Justice* (Cambridge: Cambridge University Press, 2003), chapter 1.

[17] Yuki Tanaka, Tim McCormack and Gerry Simpson (eds.), *Beyond Victor's Justice? The Tokyo War Crimes Trial Revisited* (Leiden: Nijhoff, 2011).

and to parallel military trials of hundreds of German nationals. But Nuremberg was not seeking to become a permanent court. Its operational side was not destined to guide a series of future cases. It could all be justified by the enormity and singularity of the historic moment.

Compared to Nuremberg, the idealism embedded in the Preamble to the Rome Statute is undiminished, but the institutional goals are different. The ICC seeks to become a permanent court to prosecute future crimes falling within its jurisdiction. How that ambition will fare in future decades depends on how the first ICC trials draw concrete meaning out of legal provisions in the Statute. The legal standards applied in the Congo trials were not built around a single global conflict; and immediately they were tested in culturally remote circumstances. As the trials slowed down and conjured with new circumstances, the tensions between morality and legality were increased. A criminal court steeped in moral commitments must put on a display of judicial restraint, for the very reasons offered by Justice Jackson in an earlier age. The courtroom is a place where legal principles are implemented using legal tools and procedures – and yet the whole enterprise will be measured from outside the courtroom by morally energized critics.[18]

Judicial implementation under the Rome Statute uses the principles contained in the 128 Articles – not the morally charged propositions of the Preamble. Restrained by the core principle of legality (Article 21), the first corps of judges had to test the formal legal rules against the facts of real-life cases. While not so tightly bound by precedents of their own making, these courts are nonetheless path-dependent in honoring the spirit of the law. Once the initial trials are completed and confirmed, it is increasingly difficult for later courts to circle back and lay out completely different legal pathways. Trails blazed in the initial proceedings eventually come to set the course for future cases.[19]

The complex details of first cases thus shape the evolution of legal meaning for future cases. In another contextual difference from Nuremberg, the ICC was presented with armed conflicts that differ in significant ways from the transnational wars of the past century.[20] The atrocities referred to in the

[18] Jonathan Hafetz, *Punishing Atrocities through a Fair Trial: International Criminal Law from Nuremberg to the Age of Global Terrorism* (Cambridge: Cambridge University Press, 2018).

[19] Article 21(2) says: "The Court may apply principles and rules of law as interpreted in its previous decisions," thereby providing for alternative paths beyond strict precedent. Nonetheless, the spirit of legality imposes a rhetorical burden on judges who would stray from the paths laid down in prior cases. A key dispute on this point came in the contentious Appeals Judgment in the Bemba case. See Bemba Appeals Judgment, Dissenting Opinion of Judge Sanji Mmasenono Monageng and Judge Piotr Hofmański, ICC-01/05–01/08-3636-Anx1, para. 5.

[20] On structural changes in armed conflict, see Martin van Creveld, *The Transformation of War* (New York: Free Press, 1991), which launched an extensive commentary on post-Cold War

Preamble to the ICC Statute are now more likely to occur in the cross-fire of civil strife, internal to a single national territory, where the main combatants are often non-state actors. Some weakened form of state authority may still play a role, but the conditions for such violence may stem from the collapse of state sovereignty, or from political corruption, electoral manipulation, or cross-border interference by elements (often rogue elements) within neighboring states. In the ICC Statute, the core legal doctrines derive from an age where armed violence conformed to fundamentally different social, economic, and political structures. The Congo trials have compelled the ICC to adapt these core doctrines, drawn from the age of interstate warfare, to the changed conditions of armed conflict in Ituri and the CAR.

Permanent Court versus Ad Hoc Tribunals

The ICC has judicial antecedents more direct than the Nuremberg trials. Most important are the ad hoc criminal tribunals created through initiatives of the United Nations in the early 1990s, during the period following the Cold War.[21] Even before these dedicated tribunals came along, some individual countries created special national courts or commissions to resolve, in various ways, the tensions of past injustice. South Africa and Argentina are two familiar examples.[22] At the international level, the United Nations was compelled to respond to extreme cases. In the 1990s, the breakup of Yugoslavia produced shocking visual images reminiscent of the worst atrocities from World War II. In Rwanda, the scale and ferocity of mass killings stirred global anxieties about ethnic genocide. In both cases, the United Nations Security Council (UNSC), acting in a period of post-Cold War harmony, used its global peacekeeping powers to encompass prosecutions, creating International Criminal Tribunals for the former Yugoslavia (ICTY) and Rwanda (ICTR). Still another brokered by the UN, the Special Court for Sierra Leone (SCSL) was established following the decade-long crisis in the

trends. Despite some optimism about declines in mortality in armed conflict over time (popularized by Steven Pinker, *The Better Angels of Our Nature* (New York: Penguin, 2011)), recent empirical studies show a return to late-Cold War violence levels in the 2010s. See Sebastian von Einsiedel, "Civil War Trends and the Changing Nature of Armed Conflict," UN University Centre for Policy Research, Occasional Paper 10 (March 2017), with its useful bibliography.

[21] For an overview, see William A. Schabas, *The UN International Criminal Tribunals: The Former Yugoslavia, Rwanda, and Sierra Leone* (Cambridge: Cambridge University Press, 2006).

[22] For a historical summary, see Pierre Hazan, *Judging War, Judging History: Behind Truth and Reconciliation* (Stanford: Stanford University Press, 2010), chapter 2.

West African state, which featured horrifying mutilations of civilians, and the particular abuse of women and children.

The Congo trials in the ICC arose after a global thaw had revived the idea of criminalizing extreme cases of armed violence.[23] The Preamble to the ICC Statute took this mission to a new level. Starting from principles framed in general terms, the ICC was created as a permanent court for prosecuting these grave crimes in future decades. The language cited in **bold type** (referenced in footnote 12) captures the main principles. Beyond its inspiring Preamble, the 128 Articles of the ICC Statute offer a procedural blueprint for building a fully operational justice mechanism. The cooler legal language in the Articles retains that moral mission as a directional force within the formal rules applied by judges.[24]

Implied in this history is the notion that global justice must adapt to concrete situations, while always remaining true to its core commitments. The classic tension between "law in the books" and "law in action" is well known to students of legal studies.[25] The ICC Statute faces practical challenges by embracing multiple legal principles that must then be reconciled in concrete cases. Thus, the overriding goals of ending impunity, ensuring effective prosecutions, and preventing future crimes are constrained, in practice, by equally strong legal principles limiting the ICC's jurisdictional scope, narrowing the definitions of crimes, and regulating the discretion of judges and court officials. Along with ending impunity, the ICC Statute is bound to core principles of legality, including such elements of fair trials as presumption of innocence and prohibition on ex post facto laws.

These key tensions in implementing the Court's humanitarian ideals have been manifest throughout the Congo trials. In putting its own principles to the test, the Court is expected to advance the international mission that runs back through the ad hoc international tribunals, on back through Nuremberg and beyond. An important part of the ICC's own story lies in this legacy of ambitious dreams;[26] but the future story of the ICC mission starts in the fateful encounter with Ituri. In the Congo, the ICC began the task of implementing

23 On the work of the International Law Commission in the years prior to the Rome conference, see James Crawford, "The Drafting of the Rome Statute," in Sands, *From Nuremberg to The Hague*, chapter 3.

24 Legal philosophers have difficulty accounting for such moral forces, to be discussed in Chapters 5 and 6. Theories of legal "positivism" tend to obscure the moral dimension behind crafted definitions and axioms.

25 The reference is to an article by US law professor Roscoe Pound (*American Law Review* 44 (1910), 12), a guiding apothegm of the law-and-society perspective in legal studies.

26 See Benjamin N. Schiff, *Building the International Criminal Court* (Cambridge: Cambridge University Press, 2008), chapter 1.

this noble experiment in international justice. The recoiling force of this impact would be felt in both locations.

1.3 COURTROOM NARRATIVES

Opening the Lubanga Case

The trial of Thomas Lubanga began with Prosecutor Moreno-Ocampo laying out his legal case about child soldiers. This would remain the only criminal charge against Lubanga, despite outside calls to tack on further crimes against Ituri civilians who were killed, raped, and pillaged by forces loyal to Lubanga. While the human context was a string of vicious attacks on civilian populations during a brutal twelve-month period, this first ICC case focused instead on a narrower question of military staffing. In the language of the ICC Statute, the Prosecution charged Lubanga with responsibility for *conscripting or enlisting children under the age of fifteen years into armed forces or groups or using them to participate actively in hostilities.*[27] These are three separate crimes (*conscripting* or *enlisting* or *using*), any of which would be enough to convict. Before endless complications and delays arose in this case, it might have seemed the simplest possible legal test for the ICC in its initial trial. For many years, international organizations had been documenting the presence of children under arms throughout the Congo.[28] The Statute offers a precise working definition of "children" – anyone under the age of fifteen at the time.

In his opening statement that morning, Moreno-Ocampo put his full emotions into his story. As he explained it, children under the age of fifteen were widely known to be present in the militia tied to Lubanga's main organization (known by the initials UPC (Union patriotique Congolais)). The UPC leadership made plans to abduct or induce children to join training camps, and used them not only in direct combat but often as bodyguards (the boys) and sex slaves (the girls). It was chilling to consider that, in addition to their own suffering and that of their parents, many of these children would, in turn, kill, rape, and pillage Ituri civilians, including even members of their own families.[29]

[27] Similar language appears in Article 8(2)(b)(xxvi) and Article 8(2)(e)(vii), but the former provision applies specifically to "national armed forces," while the latter applies more loosely to "armed forces or groups."

[28] See, for example, the website of UK-based Child Soldiers International, www.child-soldiers.org/democratic-republic-of-congo. See also Mark Drumbl, *Reimagining Child Soldiers in International Law and Public Policy* (Oxford: Oxford University Press, 2012).

[29] Lubanga Trial Chamber, Prosecution opening statement, January 26, 2009, ICC-01/04–01/06-T-107-ENG, starting at p. 4.

The graphic stories from these children were told even more powerfully by the victims' own Legal Representatives, who addressed the trial court immediately after the Prosecutor. While lawyers in The Hague understood the technical reasons why Lubanga's trial was delayed for so long, this was not true for the former child soldiers, set adrift in the harsh conditions of Ituri between 2003 and 2009. According to the Legal Representatives, these children were paying a lasting price, each and every day. In a district where human losses were still mounting, these children had lost their basic life chances. Taken from their families, there was often no place for them to return to. They had missed their education, and now had to cope with long-term medical and psychological effects. Girls who were victims of sexual abuse were often rejected by their families and communities.

Voices of Ituri Children

> Today is a day of hope, not only for the International Criminal Court, which hereby opens its first trial but also for them, for the thousands of victims of the Congolese conflict which seems to be without end, for these former child soldiers who are attempting to rehabilitate and rebuild their lives, for their families, and finally for those who today are still somewhere in the bush, filthy, exhausted, anxious, hungry, suffering aches and pains, crying themselves to sleep thinking of their old friends and their old school, and with just a bit of hemp to console them.[30]

Although the victims represented here, technically speaking, numbered just over 100, the message from the Legal Representatives was offered on behalf of a much larger class of children and families. Speaking through their appointed courtroom Representatives, what were these victims asking from the Court? A succession of requests was delivered orally to the Court that day in The Hague. First was the victims' desire for truth: for the ICC to establish beyond doubt the realities of their suffering, and the truth about who caused it. In this way, victims were relying on the Court's power to assign responsibility for such shocking crimes. They were yearning for justice – justice for the trial itself but even more for the communities affected by this period of chaos and heartbreak:

> International justice must bring an end to the impunity for the most serious crimes and also prepare the way for reconciliation. It must identify those who bear the greatest responsibility and those who followed, those who were

[30] Ibid., Victims' Representatives opening statement, p. 68.

> innocent and victims. Justice offers an alternative to stigmatization of whole communities as being guilty.[31]

By presenting the moral claims of Lubanga's child victims, the Legal Representatives began the process of implementing their innovative function outlined in Article 68(3) of the Rome Statute. Their stated aim was "to fill the gap that could take place between procedural establishment of facts and the truth itself." This formulation was prophetic. Within days, the new trial would encounter serious problems in establishing the most basic facts about alleged child victims. "The victims are independent actors in the proceedings before this Court. They have different concerns than the Office of the Prosecutor." These concerns are oriented to a special kind of *truth*, which the Legal Representative identifies less with evidence presented in court than with the anticipated judgment of guilt. It is this *judgmental truth* that would allow the victims to recover from the terror of their lives as child soldiers. Such truth restores the individual's sense of self-respect by publicly assigning personal responsibility to the real perpetrators, by "ending impunity," and thus restoring the endangered virtues of family, society, and community.[32]

A virtuous truth, a therapeutic truth – and a kind of truth with no ambiguities: such truth could make a dramatic difference in the turbulent world of Ituri. Such were the hopes for an active court that could establish this elusive moral clarity. Granted, the courtroom was far removed from the gritty details of enduring conflict; but perhaps that geographic leap was the necessary bridge to moral certainty. It is true that some local residents might distrust the ICC, or at least be suspicious of its strange authority, hidden behind mysterious rituals locked within a citadel, somewhere in northern Europe. But the ethical promise of the ICC came enshrined in the Preamble to the Rome Statute. As the ICC set out to operationalize that Preamble, by conducting its first Ituri-based trials, would it be able to meet such high expectations?

Doubts arose almost immediately. The Legal Representatives mentioned the gap between the judgmental truth of convictions and the slower "procedural establishment of facts." Before reaching judgment, a proper trial must invite the impartial exploration of conflicting stories and ambiguities. In a fully operational court, the only way to reach conviction is by rigorous testing of facts in the courtroom. For many reasons, the testimonies of child witnesses utterly failed to meet that test. Within minutes of starting his testimony, the first Prosecution witness started to backtrack on his much-anticipated story of

[31] Ibid.
[32] All quotes in this paragraph from ibid., p. 41.

abduction and abuse. Despite the confident stories told that first morning by the Prosecutor and by Legal Representatives of Victims, the first witness gave a more ambiguous story, and further inquiries led to mass confusion. Years later, when the judgment against Lubanga finally came down, it was based on other evidence; the testimonies from alleged child victims played no role whatsoever in convicting Lubanga. Similar difficulties would afflict the other Congo trials.

From the Congo, Discordant Voices

Soon after the Lubanga trial began, reporter Adam Hochschild visited the Congo. He was the author of a highly respected chronicle of Congo atrocities during the period of Belgian colonial rule. In late 2009, ending up in Bunia, the capital and major town in Ituri, Hochschild found himself sitting in a decaying schoolroom with several dozen Congolese youths. They were watching a video brought to Ituri by an ICC official as part of the Court's outreach program.

> We see the court's headquarters in Holland, in two high-rise towers with an all-glass sky bridge between them. We see, in the spacious, wood-paneled courtroom itself, every official or attorney sitting in a comfortable rolling chair in front of a computer screen. But computers are a luxury here in Bunia, and the few that can be found are hostage to erratic electricity.[33]

For a good reporter, the contrasts were stark and overpowering. With him in the room were former child soldiers. Some were having trouble with the language: the ICC official spoke Lingala but not Swahili, the language most accessible to his audience. But the visual images alone could provoke heated discussion, as the French-language commentary introduced pictures of Lubanga, wearing a trim business suit, sitting calmly in a plush Hague courtroom.

The group's sharp questions foretold the controversies that would emerge in court during the years the Lubanga case dragged on. Why was Lubanga singled out for prosecution? Yes, he was a leader well known to Ituri residents; but everyone also knew that his fortunes rested with distant, more powerful friends and foes, some in neighboring Uganda and Rwanda, some in the far-off capital of Kinshasa. And how could you distinguish *his* actions from those of rival leaders operating in the same cultural and economic milieu? Another thing: were these former child soldiers really conscripted by force? Or did they

[33] "The Trials of Thomas Lubanga," *The Atlantic*, December 2009, p. 80.

somehow volunteer (as several of the youths insisted in their own case), perhaps for tasks unrelated to combat – only to be swept up in revenge attacks, and seduced by charisma and magic spells? And exactly how old were they – did anyone know for sure?[34]

Yet there were other perspectives, even in Bunia, to offset Hochschild's skeptical reporting. He does not say, for example, whether his Congolese audience included any female "soldiers," whose abduction and sexual abuse by warring factions tell a very different story. These and other narratives were being collected and bundled by local and international NGOs, keeping the focus on innocent victims. (The Court's local investigators would come to rely heavily on these intermediaries.) But perhaps there were too many competing stories floating around town. Such widespread suffering and lasting destruction created mounting pressure to label injustice more clearly, and with unimpeachable authority.

It was indeed a chaotic period, dynamic and confused: a toxic brew of causation ranging from the smuggling of conflict minerals to ethnic rivalries. The destruction emerged from a dense web of micro-decisions taken by diverse local actors, and it was shaped by secret plans discussed in foreign capitals. The sheer scale of events was larger than could be encompassed in a roomful of restless young men. The truth about what happened could not be effectively established within just the group watching the video.

The leap from Ituri to The Hague makes sense if you anchor the connecting bridge in the linguistic space of universal justice. In these circumstances, the Hague courtroom offers a point of moral leverage for assigning responsibility for local atrocities. In a district where many thousands of innocent people have died, where endemic conflicts quickly reignite, and where the lives and fortunes of the next generation hang in the balance, hopes for improvement depend on finding solid moral ground. Justice wants to speak with an authoritative voice.

For less extreme conflicts, there might have been some resolution closer to home, if not in Ituri then in neighboring precincts. International organizations in the Congo were supporting national reconciliation programs. Given the desperate conditions throughout eastern Congo, some groups saw hope in peace negotiations brokered by neighboring countries. Here was a very large country in chaos, where the internal power vacuum encouraged meddling by willful neighbors, especially in the northeast region. Uganda had virtually taken over the administration of Ituri in the months prior to Lubanga's armed activities. Despite the vast distance to The Hague, where else could anyone

[34] Ibid.

seek resolution? International courts see their distinctive mission as ending impunity for sovereign leaders implicated in such atrocities, and for semi-sovereign leaders arising ad hoc within the vacuum of collapsing states. Distant courts would establish the baseline for accountability in the face of the most serious human rights offenses: a necessary (but not sufficient) foundation for local transitions to greater security, stability, and peace.

> But of course peaceful, clockwork, wealthy Holland, with its canals and bicycle paths, is a long way from Congo, where the national government barely functions, people speak several hundred languages, and a majority of the population is functionally illiterate and has no electricity, much less a radio or TV. The choice of Lubanga as the court's first defendant juxtaposes two worlds that, on the surface at least, could not be more different from each other.[35]

Can that distance provide the needed point of moral leverage? Despite the contrast, there may be positive connections: two worlds joined in distant embrace. Paradoxically, it is their differences that unite both locations – The Hague and Ituri – in ways that surprised and confounded actors situated at either end. The Hague Court had to absorb, within its dry legal discourse, the harsh facts and elusive dynamics on the ground in Ituri. In turn, the Court itself became a new player in those local dynamics, for better and for worse, in a region where conflicts continued to unfold with different principals.

For the ICC, this preoccupation with Ituri was no legal footnote. The ICC began its historic legal journey by traveling deep into the distant factual terrain of Ituri. By devoting its initial trials to the smallest details in this faraway district, the Court was forced to enter that bleak, forbidding landscape shared by human rights victims and the alleged perpetrators. In a paradox that unites both locations, the ICC could not avoid placing itself "on trial" during its formative years, testing its legal principles and guiding values in the chaos of Ituri. What the Court learns from this historic journey will shape its future direction.

1.4 BETWEEN FAITH AND SKEPTICISM

Will Criminal Trials Promote Global Justice?

Speaking days after the 1998 signing of the Rome Treaty, UN Secretary-General Kofi Annan expressed his hopes for the new ICC. There had been compromises, to be sure, but the drafters were confident that the power of

[35] Ibid., p. 78.

criminal prosecutions would become an important tool for advancing global justice.

> No doubt many of us would have liked a Court vested with even more far-reaching powers, but that should not lead us to minimize the breakthrough you have achieved. The establishment of the Court is still a gift of hope to future generations, and a giant step forward in the march towards universal human rights and the rule of law. It is an achievement which, only a few years ago, nobody would have thought possible.[36]

What exactly is this gift of hope? It offers something to future generations; and yet criminal prosecutions always look backwards: reliving past events, applying the remedy to past injustice. Annan's hopes for the ICC embraced this paradox of past and future, resting on a series of assumptions about how law influences future action.

It is often assumed, for example, that criminal prosecutions deter future crimes, to the extent that punishing past crime sends clear warnings to future lawbreakers. This power of deterrence is frequently asserted in domestic criminal law as well. It appeals to basic moral intuitions, although the empirical evidence behind it is often contested. Deterrence theory imagines crime as a product of individual choice, based on calculations of risk, including the risk of being caught and brought to trial. These calculations are difficult to model even in relatively stable, law-abiding societies. In the complex circumstances of armed conflict and social anarchy, these variables would be incomparably obscure. International justice embraces the challenge of deterrence in its mission "to end impunity" for the perpetrators of mass atrocities; but the ICC will never be able to prosecute more than a tiny fraction of those perpetrators.[37]

Hopes for the ICC rise well beyond some measure of deterrence. To advance the cause of global justice, criminal courts offer a mode of authority based on the integrity of the legal process. That process, defined by aspirations to impartiality and objectivity, is essential to the core task of determining the guilt or innocence of the accused. The same legal process can yield further by-products – exemplary findings on narrative facts and patterns of accountability – that may influence future peace discussions in conflict-ridden societies.[38]

[36] UN Press Release L/2890, July 20, 1998.

[37] See Beth Simmons, "Can the International Criminal Court Deter Atrocity?" *International Organizations* 70 (2016), 443. A more skeptical analysis is Immi Tallgren, "The Sensibility and Sense of International Criminal Law," *European Journal of International Law* 13 (2002), 561.

[38] On these broader products of court proceedings, see Gerry Simpson, *Law, War and Crime* (Cambridge: Polity Press, 2007), chapter 4 (on "Law's Promise").

In places as chaotic as Ituri, one cannot expect former combatants to agree easily on such basic questions as what really happened here, let alone who should be held responsible. But if the ICC has done its job well, the extensive testing of evidence in the courtroom may enrich these local deliberations. Ideally, courts will contribute to post-conflict justice by providing a descriptive and ethical baseline for future reconciliation. The courts have no power to impose moral intuitions; but their expertise in legality carries its own kind of authority. The rigorous testing of facts lends weight to judicial findings, quite apart from whether the trial ends in a judgment of guilt or innocence. Likewise, the special language of the law – terms like genocide, crimes against humanity, and war crimes – offers a precise set of labels for describing human contributions to mass atrocities. Such language finds powerful rhetorical uses in the broader discourse of human rights, with potential benefits for future generations.

The time and cost of legal proceedings may seem like a weakness of international courts. But the strict integrity of the courtroom testing process underwrites the courts' aspirations to speak with objectivity and impartiality. On this analysis, a fair trial is more than an individual right held by the accused;[39] it is also the gateway to a series of legal findings that can advance the cause of peace and justice. The hope for the ICC is that it will impart persuasive authority to its narratives of historical events, and to its description of criminal acts across a series of events. How these future possibilities play out remains to be seen. The Congo trials gave the ICC its first opportunity to test itself against these extraordinarily high expectations.

Balancing Purity and Practice

For some proponents of the ICC, these first halting steps toward implementing human rights principles would provoke a crisis of faith. Purity and practice do not mix easily, and proponents were justifiably nervous about diluting the ICC's humanistic mission. The Preamble of the ICC Statute conveys a special grandeur that would resist compromise. As the first trials unfolded, conditions in Ituri made for unexpected delays and tensions, leaving some of the Court's original supporters dissatisfied. For many, the dramatic acquittal of Mathieu Ngudjolo in the ICC's second trial was a rude surprise. Even more shocking was the Appeals Judgment that freed Jean-Pierre Bemba, after ten years in ICC detention. All the Congo trials fell short of sending the sharp categorical message so deeply desired by human rights activists.

39 Hafetz, *Punishing Atrocities through a Fair Trial*, p. 109.

But the unsettling of basic faith need not push toward an equally profound skepticism. The acquittals so early in the Court's experience could also be taken as affirming the primacy of fair trials. Acquittals may strengthen the future credibility of the Court, even if they slow the drive to end impunity.

The mood swings of critics need to be tempered by detailed analysis of what the Congo trials mean for future practice. Dealing with concrete trials moves the discussion away from abstract debates between purists and doubters. In real trials, the adversary method itself can be seen as a highly controlled contest between faith and skepticism – moderated by procedural rules and refereed by judges. In the context of trials, faith too can become operational and eventually strengthened by its bracing encounters with skepticism.

These are powerful challenges for any new institution. With the Congo trials, the ICC began its long and arduous legal experiment.

2

Balancing Politics, Morality, and Culture

2.1 ACTIONS AND REACTIONS

Reframing the Issues for ICC Trials

During its long first decade, the ICC cast an eye on numerous conflicts around the globe, opening formal investigations in some eight countries – all of them, as it happens, in Africa. Arrest warrants had gone out in several of these countries; but prior to 2013 the Court's active trials were limited to four Congolese figures.

Thomas Lubanga was introduced to the ICC in March 2006, when he made a brief Monday afternoon appearance to confirm his name and date of birth. The presiding pre-trial judge, the distinguished jurist Claude Jorda, was charmed by Lubanga's command of French, in an exchange that might have led, in some other setting, to deeper conversations on points of mutual interest.[40] After lengthy delays, Lubanga's trial commenced in 2009 and ended in 2012 with a conviction on charges concerning child soldiers. His conviction and fourteen-year sentence were then confirmed on appeal, with the case ending finally in 2014.[41]

Also from the Ituri district (via Kinshasa) were two accused, joined together in the ICC's second trial. Germain Katanga and Mathieu Ngudjolo were prosecuted as leaders of armed factions opposed to Lubanga's UPC organization. They faced a series of charges including murder, rape, and other inhumane acts. But the trial focused on a single attack, which started in the early morning hours of February 24, 2003 in the Ituri village of Bogoro. While limiting the facts to a single day might seem to streamline the prosecution,

[40] Lubanga Pre-Trial Chamber, transcript, March 20, 2006, ICC-01/04–01/06-T-3-FRA, p. 4.

[41] The Lubanga Appeals Judgment summarizes the earlier stages, December 1, 2014, ICC-01/04-01/06–3121.

this second trial experienced its own long delays. When, after three years, all testimony from both sides had been heard, the Court announced a surprising result. Separating the two accused, the Trial Chamber acquitted Ngudjolo and authorized his immediate release. Katanga remained in custody as the Chamber deliberated for another fifteen months, when the majority (two out of three judges) agreed to convict him on some – but not all – of the Prosecutor's original charges, and issued a twelve-year sentence. In a more controversial move, one that clearly salvaged the conviction, the majority applied a definition of legal responsibility different from what had been confirmed before the trial began.[42] The dissenting judge said later that even this modified definition of responsibility was not enough to convict, and added that she would have acquitted Katanga back at the same time as Ngudjolo.[43] It took the Appeals Chamber another two years to find a path through this contested legal terrain of crimes and responsibility.[44]

The third trial for Jean-Pierre Bemba did not deal with events in Ituri. Bemba had a much higher profile than the other three, who were often loosely described as "warlords" and "militia leaders." Bemba's more substantial political and military organization had intervened briefly in Ituri, but its scope ranged throughout the northern and eastern Congo during a period when the central Congolese government had almost collapsed. His broad business connections, family influence through his father, regional prominence in the north, and leadership during the Congo's period of near anarchy meant that Bemba was someone to be reckoned with at the national level.

Bemba became one of several Interim Vice-Presidents in the much-heralded political transition to national elections in 2006. But after finishing the Presidential race in second place, Bemba moved his family and considerable wealth to Portugal. In 2008 he was arrested in Brussels on an ICC warrant. The charges stemmed from actions by Bemba's militia troops, who had entered the neighboring country of the CAR. At trial, Bemba was charged with responsibility as a "commander" for crimes allegedly committed by his men in the CAR, while Bemba himself remained based in northern Congo.

Although Bemba was found guilty at trial, his convictions on all counts and eighteen-year prison sentence were overturned in 2018 by a divided Appeals

42 Katanga Trial Chamber, Decision on Implementation of Regulation 55, December 12, 2012, ICC-01/04–01/07–3319.

43 Katanga Trial Judgment, Minority Opinion of Judge Christine Van den Wyngaert, March 7, 2014, ICC-01/04–01/07–3436-Anx1, para. 320.

44 Ngudjolo Appeals Judgment, February 27, 2015, ICC-01/04–02/12–271. Katanga chose not to appeal his conviction.

Chamber of five judges.[45] They disagreed on the legal standards for assessing the responsibility of military commanders, as well as on important aspects of trial procedure. Quite apart from this late-innings drama, toward the end of the Bemba trial the Prosecutor brought a separate action against Bemba, his lead Defense attorney, and three others, charging them with witness-tampering. A sudden trial-within-a-trial consumed more time, ending in convictions for all five accused, all of which were upheld on appeal – although carrying only minor penalties.[46]

In 2013, the surprise appearance in The Hague of Bosco Ntaganda gave the Prosecutor another opportunity to revisit the Ituri conflicts. A former ally of Lubanga, Ntaganda was charged with various crimes against civilian populations, going back to the same armed struggles that wracked Ituri during the period 2002–03. Recalling the complex facts of that period, his trial shows the ICC stubbornly following the same conceptual templates from the Lubanga trial. In 2019, Ntaganda was found guilty on all counts, and his case is currently under appeal.[47]

Coming at Ituri from the direction of The Hague, it would almost seem that we were looking through the wrong end of the telescope. Inside the courtroom, the perspective on Congolese conflicts has been drastically narrowed. For all the complex events in this massive country, where for more than a decade human rights organizations had been documenting appalling violence affecting millions of people, the ICC came to concentrate its initial time and resources on two trials, prosecuting three persons from one very small district. The first trial was devoted exclusively to the use of child soldiers during a twelve-month period; the other dealt with a single armed attack, carried out on a single day in February 2003. This narrowing would allow the ICC to meet its own strict conditions for conducting an impartial legal process. By contrast, such limits would seem absurd in any local mediation process among disputing groups in this region of the Congo – a procedure so far without much record of success.[48]

In the Bemba trial, a similar process reframed the bloody (and successful) Presidential coup in the CAR, reducing issues there to questions about troop communications with a leader sitting across an international border. The trial spent time on evidence of atrocities in the CAR allegedly committed by Bemba's troops, but the main legal issue had to do with the technical responsibilities of a remote commander.

45 Bemba Appeals Judgment, June 8, 2018, ICC-01/05–01/08–3636.

46 Bemba *et al.* Appeals Judgment, March 8, 2018, ICC-01/05–01/13–2275.

47 Ntaganda Trial Judgment, July 8, 2019, ICC-01/04–02/06–2359.

48 Kris Berwouts, *Congo's Violent Peace: Conflict and Struggles since the Great African War* (London: Zed Books, 2017).

In focusing on such narrow legal questions, the Court managed to uncover important legal complications. Perhaps the most vexing challenge was to apply strict definitions of legal responsibility to suspects variously described as "warlords" or "militia leaders," acting through shadowy organizations that did not fit clearly into existing legal categories. Coming out of these trials, the most volatile portions of the ICC Statute are the parts dealing with *individual criminal responsibility* (Article 25). The Bemba trial featured diverse views of multiple judges on the related legal concept of *command responsibility* (Article 28). Meanwhile, the belated appearance of Ntaganda expanded the Court's reach to cover two further Ituri attacks, both within the same 2002–03 time frame as the other Ituri trials. In its 2019 judgment, the Ntaganda Trial Chamber embraced the paradigms and presumptions crafted by the Prosecution back in 2006.

Law and Politics in the ICC

The ICC is a legal institution. It is also a political institution, and the combination of these two distinct roles explains its power and its vulnerability. In practice, these elements of law and politics are separate but overlapping. It is a dynamic relationship, where the balance between law and politics changes across the main phases of the judicial cycle – pre-trial, trial, and appeals. As matters progress through this cycle, the distance between Ituri and The Hague seems to grow.

The legal role is vital to the Court's impact on promoting justice and resolving conflict. The political role enables the Court to engage on everyday terms with people and institutions at the global, national, and local levels. This is how the ICC becomes involved in specific conflicts, chooses individual suspects to prosecute, and collects detailed information from people on the ground. In managing the Ituri investigations prior to trials, the ICC Prosecutor tried to balance practical considerations against uncompromising legal constraints, overseen by the judges as cases moved through the system. In the two Ituri trials, judges faulted the Prosecution for its handling of local witnesses and evidence. In the Lubanga case, when these problems seemed to threaten the very possibility of a fair trial, the Trial Chamber halted the proceedings on two occasions and would have released Lubanga – until being overruled by the Appeals Chamber. Over the nine years of his tenure, Prosecutor Moreno-Ocampo's political and discretionary choices received mixed reviews.[49]

[49] For perspectives on the Prosecutor's performance, see David Bosco, *Rough Justice: The International Criminal Court in a World of Power Politics* (Oxford: Oxford University Press, 2014), especially pp. 151–53.

Once actual trials begin, after particular suspects are named and core issues are reframed in legal terms, the legal function takes firm control. The trial is closely contained within the courtroom as the guiding questions are both sharpened and narrowed, creating a controlled space for which the formal language of the ICC Statute provides the frame. Back in the Congo, many observers were confused and frustrated by these legal constraints, as when the Lubanga trial was confined solely to legal charges involving child soldiers.

Equally unsettling was the shift to the strictly legal processing of facts. In areas like Ituri, investigators from major human rights organizations as well as the United Nations (UN) had conducted extensive field investigations – and had already named names. Their information was clearly instrumental in the pre-trial phase, guiding the Prosecutor to the likes of Lubanga, Ngudjolo, and Katanga. But when trials start, the Court begins fresh with a factual blank slate. Facts are introduced in the form of trial evidence, much of it through live witnesses subject to cross-examination, all under the watchful eye of the Trial Chamber. Whereas in Ituri the conflicts themselves generated multiple stories, in the courtroom the Prosecutor creates a master narrative limited to certain key events. It then falls to the Defense to expose weaknesses in that narrative, often drawing on counter-narratives available from outside the courtroom.

The legal burden falls on the Prosecution to prove its case beyond a reasonable doubt.[50] When that burden is not met, the accused is acquitted; in the ICC (and in criminal law generally), acquittals do not require proof of innocence. Within this ritualized legal structure, it remains unclear to this day exactly how the victims, speaking through Legal Representatives, add to the stock or weight of evidence. Indeed, this was one of the difficult questions raised during the path-breaking Congo trials.[51]

At the close of the trial phase, the judges, in the absence of any jury, weigh the evidence against the legal charges, issuing a detailed judgment declaring the accused guilty or not guilty.[52] They complete their work, in cases of guilt, by pronouncing a sentence. The judgment and sentence then move on to an Appeals Chamber, where a different panel of judges reviews any contested interpretations of law and findings of fact. For both convictions and acquittals, the losing party may appeal. In unusual cases, the Appeals Chamber can even

[50] Article 66 places the legal burden on the Prosecutor and requires the "beyond reasonable doubt" standard for conviction. Judicial splits within Appeals Chambers for Ngudjolo and Bemba raised fundamental questions about the meaning of this standard.

[51] See Luke Moffett, *Justice for Victims before the International Criminal Court* (New York: Routledge, 2014).

[52] Article 74(2).

return the case to trial (with a new group of judges), looping all the way back to another round of courtroom evidence and argument. But once the Appeals Chamber has resolved matters raised by the parties on appeal, the legal outcome and meaning of the trial have been revealed. At that point, the Court has given its final judgment, from which there can be no further appeal. Amidst the welter of legal language, the world can see how the ICC Statute has been implemented and refigured.[53]

The fuller analysis of the Congo trials will uncover a set of deeper questions about the relationship of legal and political roles for the ICC. Some critics have challenged the Prosecutor's broad discretion in investigating and bringing charges, notwithstanding the chaotic political conditions present on the ground. When it comes to trials themselves, other critics have asked whether the courtroom can maintain its strict integrity, given pressures on the ICC to produce convictions as part of its humanitarian mission. Still others long to see the moral mission prevail over dry legal process.

2.2 INTO THE FIELD

The Impact of ICC Trials

The narrow focus on legal questions inside the courtroom is not an end in itself. It enables the ICC to make distinctive contributions to global justice. For some impatient observers, the scope of the Congo cases seemed excessively modest, given the Court's heavy investment of time and hope throughout its first decade.[54] But the special strength of legal institutions can be measured more by quality than by quantity. What underwrites the Court's unique authority is adherence to core legal principles. Strict practice empowers the Court to define "justice" with a pure, clear voice, one that can be heard above the conflicting claims of Congolese factions – and even above the moral clamor of human rights organizations. Over the years, ICC judges have insisted that their authority will not be compromised for the sake of expediency, despite pressures of time and money. With painstaking attention to the smallest details, along with excruciating delays and burdens on trial participants, ICC judges have jealously guarded their legal authority.

[53] Article 75 requires the Trial Chamber to deal further with issues of reparations for victims, which may lead to further appeals on specific reparations questions.

[54] William A. Schabas, "The Banality of International Justice," *Journal of International Criminal Justice* 11 (2013), 545.

The Court's larger goal is to project its legal power onto a global field. In the Congo trials, and also in other countries where the Court has considered legal actions, the aim is to strengthen justice in the interests of restoring peace. As part of a network of humanitarian institutions, the ICC's contribution lies with its power of criminal prosecution. Prosecutions mean to send strong warnings; the few exemplary cases seek to deter future perpetrators. According to the Preamble to the Rome Treaty, ending impunity is expected to "contribute to the prevention of such crimes." The Court's experience with the Congo trials has been a severe test of this heroic goal. In truth, it will be years (if not decades) before any preventive or deterrent effect can be adequately assessed. Critics have offered a range of opinions, both positive and negative, not only about the Congo but also about the Court's pre-trial actions in places like Uganda, Sudan (Darfur), Libya, and Kenya. The Court remains committed to its core ideals, even as the outcomes fade into the mist of events.[55]

For all its ambitions to end impunity, the Rome Treaty foresees a mix of relationships with national and international institutions. ICC prosecutions are intended as exemplary, just one dimension in a comprehensive network of criminal justice. The Preamble to the ICC Statute notes that "it is the duty of every State to exercise its criminal jurisdiction over those responsible for international crimes." More specifically, the Statute requires the Court to defer potential cases to national courts whenever possible, provided local courts are able and willing to prosecute serious crimes on their own.[56] By emphasizing this core principle of *complementarity*, the Court would come to occupy a particular niche within overlapping jurisdictions. Of course, local justice may have collapsed, along with other governing institutions, in the circumstances of grave crimes covered by the ICC Statute. Even then, when the ICC must step in and prosecute, its long-term goals may include improving local judicial systems, in cooperation with other groups active on the ground. As a political institution, the ICC joins in the difficult task of repairing societies torn by sustained armed conflict. It must conjure with real-world alternatives in the form of peace negotiations, truth commissions, and less formal means of restoring justice.[57]

55 For a political assessment of the Prosecutor's strategy in early situations, see Bosco, *Rough Justice*, chapter 6.

56 Article 1 mentions the principle of complementarity; relevant procedural issues surrounding this concept are dealt with in Article 17.

57 For an overview of these peace-building mechanisms, see Pierre Hazan, *Judging War, Judging History: Behind Truth and Reconciliation* (Stanford: Stanford University Press, 2010). On complementarity, see Carsten Stahn, *A Critical Introduction to International Criminal Law* (Cambridge: Cambridge University Press, 2018), section 3.5.1.

At a more concrete level, the ICC aims to improve the lives of the countless victims of serious international crimes. The growing movement within human rights to recognize victims found expression in the Rome Treaty, in language that was tested for the first time after the convictions of Lubanga and Katanga. The relevant provisions of the ICC Statute call for substantial measures "to establish principles relating to reparations to, or in respect of, victims, including restitution, compensation and rehabilitation." In this effort the Court is encouraged to consult with not just the victims but also "other interested persons or interested states." The Statute creates a dedicated Trust Fund for Victims (TFV) through which additional assistance may be provided beyond the scope of reparations tied to specific prosecutions.[58]

Selecting Cases for Trial

Law and politics combine when the ICC identifies individual countries and specific individuals for pre-trial investigations. In contrast to strict legal control inside the courtroom, there can be no prosecutions unless the ICC first enters into the highly negotiable world of national and local affairs – often in the midst of crisis.

When operating outside the courtroom, ICC representatives are still bound by the Rome Statute, regardless of complex conditions. Even in the most chaotic circumstances, there are limits on where and how the ICC can investigate. These rules are overseen by pre-trial judges when the Prosecution launches formal investigations, and even more when it begins to target individual suspects for possible trials. As the Congo trials will show, legal constraints on the Prosecution can generate serious tensions at trial.

When negotiators convened in Rome in 1998 to debate the draft ICC Statute, many voiced concerns about an overzealous Prosecutor with his or her own political agenda. Might the ICC go back and resurrect the atrocities of past decades? Would diplomats and heads of state avoid traveling to countries that joined the Rome Treaty, for fear of arrest by an aggressive Prosecutor? What emerged from Rome was a balanced structure: a set of rules limiting when and where the Prosecutor may look for cases.[59] How this plays out in practice will be looked at carefully in later chapters, but generally

[58] Articles 75(2) and 79 on the TFV. See Luke Moffett, "Reparations for Victims at the International Criminal Court: A New Way Forward?" *International Journal of Human Rights* 2 (2017), 1204.

[59] For the Rome negotiations, see William A. Schabas, *Introduction to the International Criminal Court*, 5th ed. (Cambridge: Cambridge University Press, 2017), especially chapter 1.

the initial fears have not been realized.[60] More than 120 countries have joined the ICC, thus opening their doors for scrutiny of conflicts within their borders, or wherever their citizens might be deployed across the globe. But some of the world's largest nations have not joined: namely, the United States, China, Russia, India, Indonesia, along with a number of Asian and Middle Eastern countries. The Congo was among the early nations joining the ICC, along with the CAR.

The principle of complementarity makes the ICC a secondary place for prosecuting international crimes, deferring to national courts that are *able and willing genuinely* to conduct prosecutions within their own systems.[61] In cases from the Congo and the CAR, the countries themselves invited the ICC to investigate crimes they felt could not be handled domestically. A fuller analysis of the Congo trials, along with conflicts in other countries investigated by the ICC, will highlight the difficulties in implementing this core principle.

The ICC prosecutes specific individuals, but its formal investigations officially begin at the level of entire countries. It is thus not surprising that the political concerns expressed in Rome were those of sovereign nations unwilling to compromise their national autonomy too far.[62] These political concerns gave rise to further legal restrictions on when the Prosecutor may launch an investigation, even within countries that have ratified the Rome Treaty. As practice has also shown, the Prosecutor is heavily dependent on cooperation from national and local authorities within conflict areas, with only limited ways to compel that cooperation from recalcitrant states. Even in countries like the Congo and the CAR, which invited the Court to intervene, investigations were hampered by problems of access to remote conflict areas, by security concerns for ICC staff and potential witnesses, and by self-serving local and national officials.

In light of sovereignty concerns, even on the part of member states, the ICC must meet certain conditions before asserting its power to prosecute the authorized crimes. The simplest condition is satisfied by a referral by one of the ICC member states. This includes self-referrals, as happened not only in

60 David Bosco has characterized the initial strategy as one of "caution and consensus." *Rough Justice*, chapter 4.

61 Article 17(1)(a).

62 In the particular case of referrals from the UNSC, the Prosecutor may be confined to a specific geographic area within a state. The Sudan referral was restricted to the area of Darfur and contained some other limitations on the Prosecutor's normal scope of seeking out individual suspects (UNSC Resolution 1593, March 31, 2005). The other UNSC referral, Libya, was not geographically restricted.

the Congo and the CAR but also in Uganda – the first three countries where the ICC opened preliminary examinations.[63]

The Prosecution can also launch its own investigation into a member country to explore possible crimes, but only with the approval of a Pre-Trial Chamber.[64] This process, known as a *proprio motu* action, was granted in the Kenya situation, with many complications and disputes about the spirit of Kenya's subsequent cooperation with the Court.[65] Pre-Trial judges have so far blocked the Prosecutor from moving to a formal investigation of crimes in Afghanistan.[66]

With respect to non-ICC members, the Prosecutor can start formal investigations only with the formal approval of the UNSC, as happened in both Sudan (Darfur) and Libya.[67] UNSC resolutions can be vetoed by any of the Permanent Five members, so this route to ICC investigations may prove to be rare. (Indeed, after 2013 Russia and China repeatedly blocked attempts to refer Syria to the ICC.[68]) And in any case, the lack of cooperation from non-

63 Article 13(a), Article 14. While any ICC member state can *refer* another member state, this did not actually happen until September 2018, when a number of Western Hemisphere member states referred Venezuela to the Prosecutor, who had already initiated a preliminary examination there on her own authority. The significance of these member-state referrals is to relieve the Prosecutor from the duty to seek authorization from a Pre-Trial Chamber before moving on to a formal investigation. See Statement by the Office of the Prosecutor, "On the Referral by a Group of Six States Parties Regarding the Situation in Venezuela," September 27, 2018.

64 Article 13(c), Article 15. Before opening a formal investigation authorized by one of these three mechanisms, the Office of the Prosecutor undertakes a preliminary examination to determine whether there is a "reasonable basis" for initiating such an investigation. In addition to familiar prosecutorial questions about potential legal violations, these ICC examinations also consider the "interests of justice" and the "gravity" of the alleged offenses. (Article 53 sets out the criteria; Article 15's *proprio motu* powers provide the basis for the Prosecutor's initial assessments.) See the "Policy Paper for Preliminary Examinations," ICC Office of the Prosecutor, November 2013. For competing tendencies in the process, see Carsten Stahn, "Damned If You Do, Damned If You Don't: Challenges and Critiques of Preliminary Examinations at the ICC," *Journal of International Criminal Justice* 15 (2017), 413.

65 Kenya Pre-Trial Chamber Decision Pursuant to Article 15 on the Authorisation of an Investigation into the Kenya Situation, March 31, 2010, ICC-01/09–19.

66 In April 2019 a Pre-Trial Chamber denied the Prosecutor's request to investigate potential crimes in the situation in Afghanistan (which potentially could have included crimes by Afghan national forces, the Taliban, and US/NATO military forces). Although the Prosecutor had shown sufficient evidence that crimes had been committed, and there was sufficient gravity, the Chamber ruled that likely limitations on local cooperation placed the investigation outside "the interests of justice." Afghanistan Pre-Trial Chamber, Decision Pursuant to Article 15 on the Authorisation of an Investigation into the Situation in Afghanistan, April 12, 2019, ICC-02/17–33. In March 2020 an Appeals Chamber reversed this ruling and authorized the Prosecutor to move forward.

67 Article 13(b).

68 See Shahram Akbarzadeh and Arif Saba, "UN Paralysis over Syria," *International Politics* (forthcoming 2019).

member states has frustrated the ICC's ability to move toward individual trials. Finally, non-members can officially request the ICC to investigate ongoing conflicts within their borders, as in the Ivory Coast, where a bloody Presidential transition polarized the country.[69]

Once these concerns of national sovereignty have been accommodated, under carefully monitored legal restraints, the Prosecutor acquires greater autonomy to investigate general conditions and to target specific individuals for possible trial. As the Court's early history shows, however, there remain all the practical problems of remote access, security for staff and witnesses, and national and local cooperation. And the Prosecution would consider the risk of offending national authorities in identifying suspects for individual arrest warrants, despite the invitation to investigate and bring charges.

In the language of ICC descriptions, countries that have been opened for preliminary examinations or formal investigations are called *situations*. Any subsequent focus on individual suspects leads to the creation of *cases*. Thus Uganda, the Congo, and the CAR were three early *situations* in which the ICC Prosecutor decided to launch investigations. While legally he had a free hand in naming specific suspects for ICC *cases*, many believe that he chose his targets with internal political considerations in mind. In the Congo, the choice seemed opportunistic when the Congolese government offered up first Lubanga, and then Katanga and Ngudjolo.[70]

But even before Lubanga showed up in The Hague, Prosecutor Moreno-Ocampo had already obtained arrest warrants in the neighboring country of Uganda, having launched an investigation into the *situation* in that country. For his first trials, he would have preferred to bring Joseph Kony and other members of the Lord's Resistance Army (LRA) to The Hague. In these cases, the charges behind the warrants included a range of war crimes and crimes against humanity. But the LRA proved elusive, finding refuge in remote areas of South Sudan, the Congo, and the CAR. Over time, as the LRA dwindled in numbers and its attacks came to fade, the Congo cases became the center of attention.[71]

[69] Article 12(3). See the Statement of the ICC Prosecutor in Relation to the Ivory Coast, April 6, 2011. The Ivory Coast later ratified the Rome Treaty.

[70] On the circumstances surrounding these three suspects and their detentions, see Pascal Kalume Kambale, "A Story of Missed Opportunities: The Role of the International Criminal Court in the Democratic Republic of Congo," in Christian De Vos, Sara Kendall, and Carsten Stahn (eds.), *Contested Justice: The Politics and Practice of the International Criminal Court Interventions* (Cambridge: Cambridge University Press, 2015), pp. 187–88.

[71] See Tim Allen and Koen Vlassenroot (eds.), *The Lord's Resistance Army: Myth and Reality* (London: Zed Books, 2010).

Unexpectedly in 2012, the odious profile of the LRA was reignited by an emotional video campaign that swarmed across the Internet.[72] Even more unexpectedly, in January 2015 the Court received LRA suspect Dominic Ongwen, included as a low-level figure in the Kony group but about whom very little was then known.[73] (As with Ntaganda, Ongwen's voluntary removal to The Hague was facilitated by US forces in Africa.) The Court's current Prosecutor, Fatou Bensouda, remains prepared to act should well-publicized efforts succeed in capturing Kony or other members of his gang.

The Congo suspects became the first to face trial because they were easier to find. In early 2006 Moreno-Ocampo got wind that Thomas Lubanga might be released from detention in the Congo capital of Kinshasa. In March, he quickly persuaded the Pre-Trial Chamber to issue the arrest warrant that would bring Lubanga to The Hague. While the full story remains obscure, Congolese authorities were in no hurry to prosecute Lubanga in their own courts, where a new amendment to the justice code set time limits for his continued detention without trial.[74] Katanga, similarly, was transferred to The Hague after lengthy detention in Kinshasa on various charges. Ngudjolo had been brought to Kinshasa to train for a position within the Congolese army – but he too proved expendable. By surrendering these suspects with roots in the far-off district of Ituri, Congolese authorities might have thought to distract the Prosecutor from investigating other conflict zones within their vast country, areas in which more prominent national figures could have been implicated.

Why Are There So Few Trials?

With so many conflicts in the world, it seems odd that the ICC found itself digging deeper into Ituri while taking no formal action in places like Sri Lanka, the Caucasus, Afghanistan, or other Middle East hotspots.[75] In addition to legal barriers restraining the Prosecutor, the lack of cooperation from national governments has delayed or hindered potential trials in places where the Court was fully authorized to bring cases, as in Libya, Sudan (Darfur), and Kenya. During the formal investigation phase, the Court becomes a local

[72] The video *Kony 2012*, produced by Invisible Children, Inc., went viral, enlisting US lawmakers and celebrities in the cause of capturing Kony and his band.

[73] See Office of the Prosecutor, Statement of the Prosecutor Following the Surrender and Transfer of Top LRA Commander Dominic Ongwen, January 21, 2015. Whether "top commander" is the right term was debated at trial, which was ongoing in 2019.

[74] See Benjamin N. Schiff, *Building the International Criminal Court* (Cambridge: Cambridge University Press, 2008), pp. 220–21.

[75] In addition to its announced preliminary examinations, the Prosecutor tracks developments in places like Syria, and receives extensive information from other sources.

player, seeking vital information and cooperation in places where public order may have broken down.

Eventually, the Prosecutor's exploratory outreach can be reviewed by pre-trial judges. But on the ground, the initiative belongs to the Prosecutor, operating less as a courtroom advocate than as a crime investigator. The ICC has an administrative wing (the Registry) that also contributes to this preliminary phase and that may handle direct negotiations with local political leaders, with neighboring ICC member states, and with the UNSC. During the years that the Congo trials were grinding along, the ICC continued investigations in at least eight separate *situation* countries – Uganda, Congo, CAR, Sudan, Kenya, Libya, Ivory Coast, and Mali. As many critics have noticed, all these countries are in Africa. In 2016, the Prosecutor received permission from a Pre-Trial Chamber of Judges to open a formal investigation in Georgia,[76] followed by Burundi and Bangladesh.[77]

The ICC has no police force and must rely on governments to honor its requests for cooperation. The Court needs access to remote places, security for its own staff and for potential witnesses, and reliable evidence for future use in trials. In conflict areas, local sources eager to speak to the Prosecutor may have self-serving reasons. In the Lubanga case, the Prosecutor's reliance on so-called "intermediaries" became an explosive issue, forcing changes in the way future investigations would be conducted.

Even before it became clear that prosecutions would be slow and difficult, the Prosecutor signaled that he would never expect to name all those individuals responsible for serious crimes – at best, it would be a sample of those "most responsible."[78] But these highest-profile suspects may be the hardest to capture, if they include sitting heads of state like Omar al-Bashir from Sudan. The Prosecution secured five arrest warrants in the UN-referred situation in Libya, but it has yet to bring a suspect to The Hague. The most prominent suspect, head of state Muammar Gaddafi, was killed in 2011. His son Saif al-Gaddafi and

[76] See the ICC press release from January 27, 2016.

[77] Even as a Pre-Trial Chamber turned down the Prosecutor's request to open an investigation in Afghanistan, an Appeals Chamber was reviewing the Prosecutor's twice-considered decision not to proceed (on grounds of "gravity") in the Situation on Registered Vessels of the Union of Comoros, Greece, and Cambodia. The situation concerns the May 2010 attack by Israeli Defense Forces against a flotilla of aid ships trying to reach the Gaza Strip. The Appeals Chamber ruled in September 2019 that the Prosecutor must (before December 2019) reconsider her decision not to proceed. Comoros Appeals Chamber, Judgment on Prosecutor's Appeal from the Pre-Trial Chamber Decision on the Application by the Government of the Union of the Comoros, September 2, 2019, ICC-01/13–98.

[78] ICC Office of the Prosecutor, Report on Prosecutorial Strategy, September 14, 2006.

two others remain at large. A fifth case was deferred to the Libyan courts under the principle of complementarity.[79]

In the case of Uhuru Kenyatta, who became President of Kenya after being summoned to The Hague for prior deeds, his voluntary appearance did not signal cooperation to the fullest satisfaction of the Court.[80] The Prosecutor's adventures on the front end of prosecutions are highly visible, controversial, and often impossible to control. Local perceptions of the ICC as a political actor are heavily influenced by these necessary roles outside the courtroom.

2.3 THE CULTURE OF THE COURTROOM: SEARCHING FOR TRUTH

Stories told in the courtroom are crafted narratives. By contrast, trained researchers in the field remain open to the diversity of stories on the ground. Indeed, under the terms of the ICC Statute, the Prosecutor's formal investigations in country situations must likewise remain open to all relevant evidence, being concerned equally with evidence of innocence as well as evidence of guilt.[81] In the courtroom, on the other hand, stories are strategically constructed in accordance with the adversarial approach to finding truth. For all the multiple causes behind the massacres and widespread suffering in Ituri, trial proceedings begin with the refined narrative brought by the Prosecutor: a story derived from the legal guilt of the accused. Despite such efforts to boil things down, the underlying complexities of the Ituri conflict managed to assert themselves, at times overwhelming the legal proceedings.

On the opening day of the Lubanga trial, the Prosecutor launched his narrative about child soldiers: the evidence will prove how "Lubanga's armed group recruited, trained and used hundreds of young children to kill, pillage, and rape."[82] The trial will explain how "[t]he defendant stole the childhood of the victims by forcing them to kill and rape. Lubanga victimized children before they ever had the chance to grow up into full human beings who could make their own decisions .... The children's feelings of complicity

[79] In 2014 the ICC Appeals Chamber upheld the Pre-Trial Chamber's decision deferring the case to Libyan courts. Appeals Judgment on the Admissibility of the Case against Abdullah Al-Senussi, July 24, 2014, ICC-01/11–01/11–565.

[80] Lorraine Smith van Lin, "Non-Compliance and Law and Politics of State Cooperation: Lessons from the Al Bashir and Kenyatta Cases," in Olympia Bekou and Daley J. Barkett (eds.), *Cooperation and the International Criminal Court* (Leiden: Brill Nijhoff, 2016), p. 114.

[81] Article 54(1)(a).

[82] Lubanga Trial Chamber, Prosecution opening statement, January 26, 2009, ICC-01/04–01/06-T-107-ENG, p. 4.

and shame will haunt them for the rest of their life."[83] The truth of all these matters would emerge at the end of the trial, based on the presentation of factual evidence through witnesses and extensive document collections. The case would lead off with live testimony from former child soldiers: "They will tell you the facts."[84] The Prosecution's evidence would establish truth in the rigorous environment of the Hague courtroom.

There was, of course, a background context for Lubanga's actions, thinly described in the opening statement. Ituri was part of the chaos affecting eastern Congo, in the aftermath of the Rwanda genocide, the breakdown of the Congolese state in 1997, and steady mischief emanating from Uganda and Rwanda. This much was common knowledge. But messy as it was in Ituri, the Prosecutor's evidence in the courtroom would insist that Lubanga was the author of his own destiny: a man steeped in deceit and lust for power, seeking to occupy the governance vacuum, driven by ethnic hatred, attacking his opponents' villages with no mercy for civilians. Yet this part of the story would be cut short, because Lubanga was facing no charges from the hundreds of civilian deaths linked to these militia attacks. The Prosecutor stated confidently that some 30 percent of Lubanga's armed forces were under the statutory age of fifteen. The world community has condemned this practice as criminal; and Lubanga's conviction must follow from the evidence to be presented in The Hague. "If convicted, Thomas Lubanga's sentence will send a clear message: The era of impunity is ending."[85]

***

For all their pathos, the Prosecutor's opening words could not match the power of the stories recounted by the Legal Representatives of Victims, who accurately advised the judges that "it is with much emotion that we take the floor today so the voice of victims is heard during the first trial before the International Criminal Court."[86] Distancing himself from the narrow legal framing of the charges, one of the Representatives informed the Court that "these documents can[not] make you hear the sobbing of these children as they were torn from their families, their fear as guns sounded on the front, the cries of their brothers, of their friends struck down by bullets . . . ."[87] Departing from the legal script about child soldiers, another speaker placed the Ituri conflict into a broader international stream, citing the "5 million Jews"

83 Ibid., p. 35.
84 Ibid., p. 5.
85 Ibid., pp. 34–36.
86 Ibid., Victims' Representatives opening statement, p. 37.
87 Ibid., p. 48.

exterminated during World War II, the Rwanda genocide that killed 800,000, and the Balkan massacre at Srebeniča with over 7,000 deaths. Suffering across the entire Congo was massive, and the Lubanga trial would remind the Court of such deep destruction, whatever the boundaries of Lubanga's arrest warrant.[88] At the end of a series of speeches from the Representatives, Judge Fulford reverted gently to these rhetorical flights, warning the Legal Representatives that they should confine their remarks to the specific charges under consideration inside the Lubanga courtroom.

But the Legal Representatives were not to be mistaken for the Prosecutor; they saw their mission in broader terms. The victims' suffering does not have to be proved with fresh evidence. It speaks eloquently for itself, and it now summons the Court to the larger humanitarian purpose for which these trials have been created. From this perspective, truth is not the contested product of a long adversarial trial. When the Legal Representatives spoke of the victims' "right to truth," they meant the right to have the moral truth of their suffering recognized by holding the main perpetrator accountable. "Given that there are victims, there must be people who are responsible, and that is why we must support our victims by giving them a voice, a voice to tell what they have been through. . . . To this end it should be established which adults were responsible. The responsibility of Thomas Lubanga Dyilo in particular should be recognized . . . ."[89] This approach to moral truth circumvents the presumption of innocence that binds the Prosecutor. It blocks any traction for the Defense and beckons the judges in their final determination.

The victims' stories will augment the normal kind of evidence that passes through the gauntlet of oral testimony and cross-examination. Through the Legal Representatives, the voices of victims will enable the Court "to fill the gap that could take place between procedural establishment of facts and the truth itself." As part of this deeper truth, punishing those responsible would finally allow the victims to "reconstruct their lives as adults because their childhood seems to have been denied, stolen from them."[90] As the victims are well aware, a conviction at trial opens the way to receiving monetary awards (reparations), which could support the difficult transitions they must still face. Of course, the trial would clearly be a long process, but the Legal Representatives were already looking past the trial, focusing on the future, "to help find a solution to bring to an end this practice of enlisting child soldiers in the Democratic Republic of Congo," a future that will not

[88] Ibid., p. 37.
[89] Ibid., p. 55.
[90] Ibid., p. 42.

come until the Court passes judgment on the accused.[91] As the final speaker summed it up that day for the Legal Representatives, the victims "merit respect. They have been disappointed, but they are not clamouring for vengeance. They ask to be recognized as victims. They want truth, justice, and reparations."[92]

***

But this was just the opening of the trial, not the closing. The Prosecutor still had a mountain of evidence to bring forward and was eager to get started.

> Mr. President, your Honours, the children will tell you the facts . . . .
> You will hear how a child soldier younger than 10 was shot by one of Lubanga's men because he lost his weapon.
> You will hear another boy telling what happened to those who tried to escape. I quote: "They caught him on the road, and they brought him back, and in front of everybody they killed him . . . . [T]hey said, 'In the army you are not supposed to run away, so he's here as an example . . . .'"
> Another child told us how during the fighting at Lipri the commanders ". . . really encouraged us to rape women, and the commanders will send to look for women. So we took them and brought them to the camp, and then we did those bad things."[93]

Stories told by the Prosecutor, in anticipation, on opening day in the courtroom are not the same thing as evidence. Two days later, Deputy Prosecutor Fatou Bensouda would begin offering evidence to support the main case, bringing her first former child soldier from Ituri to The Hague to tell his individual story. At around 11:20 a.m. on Wednesday, January 28, 2009, the ICC welcomed its first trial witness. The disaster that followed would instruct everyone involved in this case about the immense challenges of finding "the truth" about past events in Ituri – six years later in a Hague courtroom.

It started with some small glitches in administering the witness's oath to tell the truth, one of the common rituals in courtrooms around the world. "I solemnly swear to tell the truth, the whole truth, and nothing but the truth." When Judge Fulford asked the Court Officer to administer this standard oath, there was nothing from the witness table but a long silence. Judge Fulford asked for a second reading – and again, nothing but silence. In the midst of such anticipation, unaccountably, the witness's microphone was not responding, or at least it was not reaching the interpreters' booth so that the words

91 Ibid., p. 51.
92 Ibid., p. 69.
93 Ibid., Prosecution opening statement, pp. 8–10.

could be understood by those in the courtroom. Judge Fulford asked the Court Officer herself to try speaking into the witness's microphone. She tried once in English, once more in French. But the witness was speaking Swahili, and the words had to make their full circuit to the Swahili interpreter, so that they could come back swiftly, to listeners wearing earphones, in both English and French. Soon the technical problems were resolved and the witness's oath was heard by all.[94]

Among the few Swahili speakers on the courtroom floor that day was the accused himself, Thomas Lubanga, who would find troubling gaps in official translations made later during the afternoon session.[95] Inside the courtroom, Lubanga was able to hear the actual words spoken with their authentic sound. But for public broadcast the spoken words were distorted, so that listeners outside the courtroom could not detect the identity of the witness from his voice. For many witnesses testifying in The Hague, their visual images are mechanically distorted and their voices acoustically scrambled beyond recognition.

As it turns out, this episode with the oath was not just a comic interlude. When the witness broke down early in the questioning, he adverted to the solemnity of his oath. His testimony had started with an account of how soldiers from Lubanga's group (the UPC) abducted him and some of his school friends to take them off to a training camp. But, as Deputy Prosecutor Bensouda led him through this story, the witness suddenly stumbled, hesitated, and then recanted. Amid confusion in the courtroom, Judge Fulford stepped in and called for an immediate recess, out of concern for what might have been a panic attack for the witness.[96] After a long lunch break with time for the Legal Representatives of Victims to speak privately with the witness, the hearing resumed. But the witness was now even more adamant about backtracking on his initial statements, which had been given originally to ICC investigators several years before. He suggested now that he had been coached by an NGO worker to say things that were not true:

THE WITNESS: What I said previously did not come from me. It came from someone else. They taught me that over three and a half years. I don't like it. I would like to speak my mind as I swore before God and before everyone.

[94] Lubanga Trial Chamber, transcript, January 28, 2009, ICC-01/04–01/06-T-110-Red3-ENG, pp. 20–21. See also Tjitske Lingsma, *All Rise: The High Ambitions of the International Criminal Court and the Harsh Reality* (Utrecht: Ipso Facto, 2017), pp. 151–52.

[95] Lubanga Trial Chamber, transcript, January 28, 2009, p. 45.

[96] Ibid., pp. 36–37.

Judge Fulford then intervened to address the witness directly:

PRESIDING JUDGE FULFORD: I'm going to ask a question directly so that we can understand the position. This morning you told the Court about a time when you were going home from school when some soldiers from the UPC came and took you and your friends away. Was that story from you true or false?

THE WITNESS: That's not true.

PRESIDING JUDGE FULFORD: You can now have a break, Ms. Bensouda. Let us know, please, when you're ready.[97]

***

What was happening? In the confusion of the moment, it was impossible to sort out all the possibilities. Nor was this an isolated instance – coinciding by chance with the very first ICC witness. Throughout the entire Lubanga trial, all of the courtroom testimonies from child witnesses failed in some fashion. In its final judgment, the Trial Chamber went out of its way to say that it could not rely on any testimony from child witnesses as a basis for finding the truth of what happened.[98] Why did this go so badly? Over time, several explanations would emerge, but much of it has to do with the distance between Ituri and The Hague. In one sense, everyone simply knew that child soldiers were present in all the Ituri militias. But it became nearly impossible to prove it in court.

One factor certainly was the cultural dislocation of bringing young people from Ituri all the way to The Hague – a distance even greater in sensory impact than in actual miles traveled. In his opening remarks, Prosecutor Moreno-Ocampo had warned that these former soldiers were still fragile.

> We will be calling nine former child soldiers to take the stand .... Many of them have recently completed the high school exams, and yet even these nine would prefer not to speak about the details of what they saw and what they did .... For each of them, it is the first time in the courtroom, and the first time in a different country, away from their communities. These unfamiliar surroundings, the weather, everything, the formality of the process, when combined with the trauma they have already experienced in their short life make the prospect of testifying in court daunting .... All of these factors place

97 Ibid., pp. 40–41.

98 Lubanga Trial Judgment, March 14, 2012, ICC-01/04-01/06-2482, paras. 479–80.

> a particular challenge ... to ensure that the process of testifying is not re-traumatising them.[99]

Many theories about what had happened started spreading after this tumultuous first day of testimony. While visitors in the public gallery usually do not see the witness directly, and while video images shown to the world are often deliberately distorted, inside the courtroom, this first child witness had a direct line of sight with the accused, Thomas Lubanga. Did this sudden glimpse of Lubanga trigger a fright response, causing the witness to freeze? Very soon the Court erected a curtain that could be adjusted to block the witness's view of the accused.[100] There were many other concerns about the psychological state of child witnesses, based on assessments by professional counselors hired by the Court's own Victims and Witnesses Unit. The ICC quickly became aware of the problems encountered in many other courtrooms around the world with child witnesses, testifying to such traumatic events as abduction, torture, and sexual violence. But without the voices of child victims in the courtroom, the legal search for truth would be seriously restricted. Proof beyond a reasonable doubt means that the Court cannot gloss over a witness's troubled psychological relationship to the truth about what happened to them.

Judge Fulford had a different worry, which he had raised with the parties prior to the appearance of this first witness.[101] While child soldiers were introduced into this case as victims, it was plain that they could also be seen as perpetrators of atrocious crimes committed during the Ituri conflicts. The ICC Statute provides some legal protection for them, in that Article 26 explicitly prohibits the ICC from prosecuting anyone who was under the age of eighteen when crimes may have been committed. No matter what the evidence might say, the ICC has no jurisdiction to prosecute anyone who was underage. But this is not an easy concept to convey to ex-child soldiers who have been hearing about faraway courts and the workings of international justice. And no one in The Hague quite knew how Congolese criminal law might view the matter. Judge Fulford had previously asked the Legal Representatives to explain these arcane immunities to the victims; but when the first witness faltered, Fulford immediately saw the possible concern with self-incrimination. When he ordered the first emergency break (instantly interrupting Deputy Prosecutor Bensouda and calling for a recess), he asked the Legal Representatives to go back over this legal point with the witness. But when testimony resumed after lunch, the witness stated that

99 Lubanga Trial Chamber, Prosecution opening statement, January 26, 2009, pp. 34–35.
100 Lingsma, *All Rise*, p. 152.
101 Lubanga Trial Chamber, transcript, January 28, 2009, pp. 6–11.

his story of abduction and mistreatment was a lie, pressed upon him by NGO workers back in Ituri.[102]

Here, then, was yet another explanation for problems with the first Lubanga witness, and for problems that would raise questions about the reliability of all later child witnesses in this case. NGOs and the United Nations had started investigating crimes in Ituri as early as 2002, coinciding with the actual events under scrutiny in the later ICC trials. Reports on Ituri atrocities included eye-witness accounts; and the theme of child soldiers and their abuse seemed to resonate especially with the NGOs and their humanitarian support base. In addition to international bodies like Human Rights Watch (HRW), the International Crisis Group (ICG), and the United Nations, many local Congolese NGOs were digging hard for information, relying on local cultural knowledge and linguistic access. Some of these local intermediaries may have had their own roles and allegiances during the conflicts, which were still very much alive when Prosecutor Moreno-Ocampo began his formal investigation under ICC rules. Moreno-Ocampo's reliance on these intermediaries for enlisting witnesses backfired during the Lubanga trial, as the Defense raised devastating questions about their influence and reliability.

The first Lubanga witness, invoking his fresh oath to tell the truth, told the Lubanga trial that he had been coached to lie by intermediaries. This possibility haunted further testimony throughout the Lubanga trial. In its final ruling in the case, the Trial Chamber cited the problem of intermediaries in sharply criticizing the Prosecutor's investigative practices.[103] Similar issues spread into the overlapping trial of Katanga and Ngudjolo.

***

Whatever the problems for establishing truth inside the Hague courtroom, the fate of former child soldiers in Ituri remained troubling. The Legal Representatives mentioned the therapeutic value of convicting Lubanga, which could then help this lost generation to recover. In his opening statement, Prosecutor Moreno-Ocampo spoke to this lasting impact, citing the lament from one former soldier that had been recorded by ICC investigators in the field:

> "I was dreaming all the time and thinking about all the work, all the things that I had done. I was thinking about killing people all the time. Thoughts are coming to me now . . .." The children's feelings of complicity and shame will haunt them for the rest of their life. The past suffering, the present suffering, and the continued suffering that Lubanga inflicted will be a factor. Lubanga

[102] Ibid., p. 40.

[103] Lubanga Trial Judgment, paras. 482–83.

> affected not just one child. Lubanga affected an entire generation, and this must be reflected as a powerful aggravating factor in his sentence, if convicted.[104]

This was all part of the Prosecutor's opening story. Lubanga was eventually convicted, and his sentence of fourteen years was upheld on appeal five years after Moreno-Ocampo spoke these words in the ICC's first trial. But, for reasons that went well beyond the dynamics of the Hague courtroom, all of the evidence from alleged former child soldiers was deemed unreliable by the judges. And the same was true in the trial of Katanga and Ngudjolo, where the judges likewise determined that they could not rely on any evidence from child witnesses.

2.4 TENSIONS AND OPPOSITIONS

Challenging the Courtroom Narrative

The Defense team moves cautiously during the first days of an ICC trial. They see the time horizon of the trial differently from the Prosecutor or the Legal Representatives of Victims. The Prosecutor's master narrative sweeps in and dominates the trial process; but then it will be tested incrementally, scrupulously, remorselessly, in the grinding process of bringing evidence into the courtroom. Moving with the flow of the trial, the Defense finds the weakest points and begins to combine them into themes for leveraging doubt. As doubt builds up, potential counter-narratives come into view.[105] In the Lubanga trial, a counter-theme developed rapidly around the truthfulness of child witnesses.

Across the Congo trials, Defense teams never denied that atrocities had occurred, or that countless victims had suffered horrible deaths and unconscionable injuries, both physical and psychological – themes kept alive by the Legal Representatives of Victims. From the very first day at trial, the Legal Representatives seek to shorten the distance between all that suffering and the criminal responsibility of the accused. Their message always comes back to this quick, close link between suffering and guilt. By contrast, the Defense seeks to lengthen this distance, opening up space for explaining the violence as the product of other actors and other causes. Given the complexity of events in Ituri, this Defense strategy proved to be highly effective. Over time, the Prosecution's master narratives in all the Congo trials were significantly undermined.

104 Lubanga Trial Chamber, Prosecution opening statement, January 26, 2009, p. 35.

105 For a range of perspectives, see Colleen Rohan and Gentian Zyberi (eds.), *Defense Perspectives on International Criminal Justice* (Cambridge: Cambridge University Press, 2017).

Courtrooms operate differently from the realm of public opinion, which coalesces around surmises that "everyone just knows," and which is ready to assign fault and guilt. ICC trials, by design, put aside that common knowledge, allowing years for dissecting the Prosecutor's master narrative. The Defense role is dedicated to this process of organized dissecting: an adversarial approach to truth as the outcome of a contest over facts and law inside the courtroom. Adversarial truth is different from the moral truth asserted by the Legal Representatives for Victims, and from the narrative truth claimed by the Prosecutor for the master narrative. Tensions among these diverse conceptions of truth emerged over the course of the Congo trials.

For the Defense to do its job well, it must look outside the courtroom, finding complications in Ituri that open up new spaces within the master narrative for doubts and alternatives. But the Defense starts the process of investigating much later than the Prosecutor, and with far fewer resources. The ICC Statute addresses this problem head-on, by separating the Prosecutor's dual roles of investigating and prosecuting – a solution that proved highly problematic during the Congo trials. According to Article 54, "1. The Prosecutor shall: (a) In order to establish the truth, extend the investigation to cover all facts and evidence relevant to an assessment of whether there is criminal responsibility under this Statute, and, in doing so, *investigate incriminating and exonerating circumstances equally* . . ." (emphasis added).

Here the tension is resolved by a simple imperative statement: before formulating his narrative truth on the opening day of trial, the Prosecutor looks for "the truth" as an impartial investigator. Searching for truth (in any sense) in Ituri was no simple task in the period after mid-2003, when Prosecutor Moreno-Ocampo turned his attention to this region. As the methodology was often explained in the heated contention of trials, the Prosecutor's investigative teams try to separate all new evidence, depending on whether it is unfavorable or favorable to potential suspects – incriminating or exonerating. This process must be very difficult in practice, since investigations begin well before specific suspects have been identified. But after cases have been selected, and as the diverse Pre-Trial Chambers move to confirm legal charges in these cases, the exonerating evidence must be handed over to the Defense.[106] During the Congo trials, however, this system was the source of acrimony and delay. In the Lubanga case, the delay in disclosing exonerating

[106] The disclosure must occur "as soon as practicable"; Article 67(2). See Alex Whiting, "Disclosure Challenges at the ICC," in Carsten Stahn (ed.), *Law and Practice of the International Criminal Court* (Oxford: Oxford University Press, 2015), chapter 40.

evidence caused the case to break down entirely, until a pragmatic resolution was worked out. Later chapters will cover these intense battles over the disclosure of evidence gathered by the Prosecutor – and the vexed relationship to "the truth."

Interpreting Language and Culture

Cultural distance can be even more daunting than the geographic distance measured on a standard map. The language used inside the courtroom cannot escape these cultural gaps separating Ituri from The Hague. The complexities of Ituri would haunt the Congo trials through quite ordinary courtroom words like "militia" and "warlord," which carried obvious meanings to most speakers in The Hague. But under closer scrutiny, the armed groups and leaders active in Ituri did not fully match the standard definitions, and the differences would ultimately lead to the acquittal of Mathieu Ngudjolo and a split decision in the trial of Germain Katanga.

Cultural differences arise in such everyday matters as human relationships. Anthropologists often search the language of kinship for clues to cultural variations. In the Katanga trial, the simple word "brother," as used by a Defense witness, caused the Court to pause and reflect – aided, in this case, by the cultural insight of the Judge from Mali.

In early June 2011, fairly late in its case, the Defense for Germain Katanga called a witness to testify about Katanga's role in working with an armed group in one of the Ituri districts. In his testimony, this witness placed Katanga at some distance from the planning for a Bogoro attack, in contrast to the Prosecutor's master narrative. Following the lunch break, the Prosecution began cross-examination by suggesting that the witness might lack impartiality, pointing out that he had referred to Katanga as his "brother." Can we believe a witness who comes to The Hague to present favorable evidence on behalf of his own brother? The exchange occurred in French but referred to kinship relations that were beyond the imaginations of Europeans.

Q. Mr. Witness, I would like to start with a few questions on your family. Would it be right to say, Mr. Witness, that you have family ties to Germain Katanga?

A. I do agree that I could have family ties with Germain Katanga to a certain extent.

Q. You say "to a certain extent." Is it not right that you yourself consider him as your brother; would I be right to say that?

A. Katanga is a brother. First of all, in our place, when you come from the same group you become brothers. That is an African concept of relationship. We come from the same group, we come from the same tribe. So I would say Katanga is my brother.[107]

But the Prosecutor did not leave it just there. He had previously delved into the background of this witness, finding a connection that would, in the eyes of the Prosecutor, make this witness a maternal cousin of Katanga (the mothers of each being sisters).

Q. Essentially, Mr. Witness, Germain Katanga is your cousin; is that right?

Well, not quite right, because one sister was more like Katanga's stepmother – married to his father but not the mother of Katanga himself. The witness applied the word *marâtre* to this relative, not the more common *belle-mère*. The witness was confused by this line of questions. The chief Defense counsel, Mr. Hooper (an English barrister), stood up and pointed out that Katanga's father had more than one wife.

But it was Judge Diarra, from Mali, visibly impatient with the exchange, who intervened (in French) to put a stop to the Prosecutor's excursion into African kinship terms:

JUDGE DIARRA: Mr. Prosecutor, I understand completely what the witness is saying. He is talking about Katanga's step-mother, married to Katanga's father. But the witness does not use the usual word for "step-mother," but rather "marâtre," which is not well understood outside Africa .... Yes, in some sense they are cousins. But "brother" is something more than cousin, and he has already explained that they are brothers because they belong to the same group. I don't understand why you are pushing the matter.

PRESIDING JUDGE COTTE: Mr. Prosecutor, try not to split hairs with respect to family relations here.[108]

These kinship relations could not easily be mapped onto European structures and meanings. The relationship between the witness and Germain Katanga came more from their common membership in a group, which gave the word "brother" its social meaning in the cultural context of Ituri. Very little of this exchange managed to get into the official English transcript from that day.

[107] Katanga and Ngudjolo Trial Chamber, transcript, June 1, 2011, ICC-01/04–01/07–T-273-Red-FRA, p. 54.

[108] Ibid., p. 55.

The African listeners knew what was being said. It was a tiny incident in a mammoth trial that ran for years, but yet an example of communication difficulties across languages and cultures.

Finding Criminal Responsibility

The first day in the joint trial of Germain Katanga and Mathieu Ngudjolo was the second occasion for Prosecutor Moreno-Ocampo to launch a grand narrative into the courtroom. According to this story, the two accused belonged together in this trial because they were the respective supreme commanders of two Ituri militia groups – allies fighting against the UPC forces of Thomas Lubanga, among others. At the center of this story, the two commanders hatched a joint plan to launch a surprise attack on a large contingent of UPC soldiers in a strategic village. But the real goal of the plan, motivated by ethnic hatred, was to "wipe out the village of Bogoro," killing all its inhabitants and destroying houses, schools, and markets. According to this story, the war in Ituri was tied to ethnic conflict between Lendu and Hema ethnic groups. Katanga and Ngudjolo were leading the Lendu, while Lubanga and his allies were leading the Hema. (The Defense would soon challenge this ethnic characterization of the conflict.)

The attack on Bogoro began at 5 a.m. on February 24, 2003, as the villagers (and UPC soldiers) were still asleep. The joint Lendu forces, following the script prepared by Katanga and Ngudjolo as the two commanders, routed the UPC and massacred most of the civilian bystanders, tracking them down in the bush as they fled, carving people up with machetes to achieve slow, agonizing deaths. The violence was horrendous, including rapes and sexual torture, as recounted by the Legal Representatives of Victims on that first day of the second Congo trial.

These are the main facts of the Prosecutor's master narrative. The facts are trimmed and framed to fit the legal definition of "individual criminal responsibility," as provided in the ICC Statute.[109] Thus, the two supreme commanders jointly planned the attack, intending to "wipe out" Bogoro, knowing full well that torture and rape would occur as part of the attack, while exercising firm control, through their military command structure, over the soldiers who would carry out these crimes in the field. These key verbs – planning, intending, knowing, and exercising control – were words the Prosecutor needed to bring legal charges against Katanga and Ngudjolo as perpetrators of crimes against humanity and war crimes.

[109] Article 25(3).

The second Congo trial was a severe test for legal definitions of responsibility, which were difficult to apply to the complexities of armed conflict in Ituri. As the trial dragged on, and as the Prosecutor was pressed to prove the core elements of his story, it was no longer clear how either of the accused could be found criminally responsible.

The problem started with lack of evidence for the alleged "common plan" agreed between Katanga and Ngudjolo. Then it wasn't clear that either one was a recognized commander of troops that attacked Bogoro – nor even that these fighters were organized along strict military lines. As the master narrative started to unravel, it left a string of simple but urgent questions. In the chaotic world of Ituri, exactly what is a "militia"? What was the command structure in these various fighting groups? The realities on the ground did not match the conventional wisdom on standard warfare.

And who, really, were Katanga and Ngudjolo? Their particular stories would emerge as well. Germain Katanga was a young man of twenty-four years in the lead-up to Bogoro, viewed with respect by many in his local village of Aveba and drawn into the local self-defense units that had emerged throughout Ituri after a wave of violence up and down the district, fostered by Ugandan occupiers. Mathieu Ngudjolo, almost eight years older than Katanga, was trained as a practical nurse; and indeed, he explained to the Court that, on the day of the Bogoro attack, he was in a completely different village assisting with a complicated childbirth.[110]

The notion that both Katanga and Ngudjolo were acting as supreme commanders emerged only weeks and months after the Bogoro attack, during a volatile period when both men stepped forward, in the context of peace-building discussions, to represent the future interests of Lendu factions. Investigators from the United Nations were just arriving on the scene to document recent violence. These outsiders observed both Katanga and Ngudjolo, who may have indulged in some posturing to promote their own personal futures in a rapidly changing environment.[111]

Overall, the ICC's second trial (Katanga and Ngudjolo) produced far more questions than answers. It did not resolve the hardest questions about the Bogoro attack: exactly who planned it and exactly how it was conducted. But

[110] Sources on Ngudjolo are highly unreliable, as the ICC trial court discovered. The Trial Chamber had difficulty believing any of the witnesses regarding Ngudjolo's role, both Prosecution and Defense witnesses. The details are discussed fully in Chapter 8.

[111] As described in Chapter 8, there was a moment in Ituri when one's status at the peace table might be enhanced by claiming prior military exploits. For a balanced analysis (although not entirely free of credibility issues), see Henning Tamm, *FNI and FRPI: Local Resistance and Regional Alliances in North-Eastern Congo* (London: Rift Valley Institute, 2013).

the initial narrative told by the Prosecutor failed to meet the legal standard for fair trials at the ICC: confirmation by "proof beyond a reasonable doubt."

In December 2012, four years after the Trial Chamber first took custody of these cases, the judges acquitted Ngudjolo and ordered his immediate release.[112] For Katanga, two of the three judges considered that his actions in Aveba might still have contributed "significantly," if indirectly, to the Bogoro attack. They took an additional fifteen months before finding him guilty – as a mere contributor, not as a perpetrator – of only some of the crimes charged. Katanga's twelve-year sentence was widely interpreted as acknowledging the limited role that he may have played in the run-up to Bogoro. For Katanga, his nearly seven years in The Hague, awaiting the final outcome in his case, would be subtracted from the sentence.[113]

***

The trial of Jean-Pierre Bemba opened up another dimension of criminal responsibility, tied to the status of military commanders. Among the Congolese detainees brought to trial in The Hague, Bemba was far-and-away the most substantial figure, operating well beyond the parochial confines of local conflicts. Physically imposing, Bemba is a Big Man in every sense of the word: wealthy, educated, ambitious, and deeply implicated in Congolese power-politics.[114] His family was allied with the aging autocratic President Mobutu Sese Seko, holding a strong base in the northern Congolese province favored by Mobutu before his ouster in 1997. In the tumultuous aftermath of Mobutu's rule, after internal Congo factions gained armed support from neighboring countries, Bemba built his own militarized political movement, becoming a strong contender in the competition for national power.

As a skilled player on the national level, and responsive to international pressures for political reconciliation, Bemba gained a foothold as a Vice-President of the Congo from 2003 to 2006. He went on to lose the 2006 Presidential election by a popular vote margin of 58:42 percent. Two years later, living in self-imposed exile, he was arrested by Belgian police and

[112] Ngudjolo Trial Judgment, December 18, 2012, ICC-01/04–02/12–3.

[113] Katanga's sentence was soon reduced by one-third, which made him eligible for release in January 2016; Katanga Trial Chamber, Decision on Review of Sentence, November 13, 2015, ICC-01/04–01/07–3615. Weeks before his release date, however, he was voluntarily transferred to detention in the Congo, which promptly arrested him on domestic charges.

[114] See Ruben de Koning, "Big Men Commanding Conflict Resources: The Democratic Republic of the Congo," in Mats Utas (ed.), *African Conflicts and Informal Power: Big Men and Networks* (London: Zed Books, 2012), chapter 10.

brought to trial at the ICC for events that took place inside the Congo's northern neighbor, the CAR.

For five months from late 2002, a contingent of troops associated with Bemba's movement crossed the border to help defend the CAR's embattled President, who faced a serious – and ultimately successful – coup attempt from a long-time rival. After the coup, reports circulated about atrocities committed against CAR civilians by diverse groups, ranging from the ousted President's loyalists, down to Bemba's soldiers.[115] At the ICC, in the third Congo trial, the case against Bemba required the Prosecution to show that Bemba himself, while residing in the Congo, was responsible for actions of his marauding soldiers across the CAR border. Here, the conceptual distance between action and responsibility was being stretched even farther than in the other Congo trials. The physical distance between Congo-based Bemba and his CAR-based troops opened up a new dimension of legal accountability. On paper, Bemba was uppermost in the overall chain of command; but was this enough of a link for the ICC? The relevant section of the Rome Statute does not infer responsibility from the bare fact of an organization chart. But what more was needed? If Bemba did not personally direct his troops to commit violent acts, was he liable by way of sheer negligence – or must it be something stronger?

***

The Bemba trial played out the tension between moral and legal responsibility. The ICC courtroom became the laboratory for exploring these tensions, going to the heart of all the Congo trials. In each case, no one would deny that atrocities occurred – including the Defense. And the Legal Representatives of Victims were prepared to argue further that these actions were not just ordinary criminal acts. For the victims, all the rapes, mutilations, slayings, and pillaging were unique brutalities – with fatal or life-long consequences – and require no abstract reasoning to claim our sympathy. The harder questions in every trial had to do with responsibility.

The Rome Statute looks for larger patterns behind wartime violence. Soldiers operating in organized units may, for example, be ordered by their officers to commit brutal actions against protected civilians. If so, the ICC trial should seek to extend responsibility up the line to whoever gave that order. A campaign of planned terror thus implicates the planners and the organizers,

[115] The most influential report, *When the Elephants Fight, the Grass Suffers: Report on War Crimes in the Central African Republic* (February 2003), was issued by the Paris-based Fédération Internationale des Ligues des Droits de l'Homme (FIDH), based on investigations in November 2002 in the capital Bangui.

not just the soldiers on the ground. Someone must have planned it; but exactly who?

In the trials of Germain Katanga and Mathieu Ngudjolo, the ICC Prosecutor began with the position that both men, as supreme military commanders, formed a common plan directing their troops to attack civilians. When this narrative fell short of required proof, the main lines of responsibility were washed away. Ngudjolo was acquitted; Katanga was belatedly reclassified as a mere contributing agent. Ideally, international criminal law wants to pursue the core vectors of responsibility, aiming to discover who is "most responsible" for mass atrocities. In reality, the ICC courtroom has been a difficult place to document the fraught relationships of planning, ordering, and committing those multi-layered crimes that most concern the Court. The subtle contours of responsibility may be confidently expounded by moral philosophers; but they resisted the stubborn facts at the heart of the Congo trials.

At first, the ICC Prosecutor considered using the "planning" argument in Bemba's case.[116] Bemba must have planned these military misadventures in common with the besieged CAR leader, and the offending troops on-site were carrying out the details of that common plan. It was also possible that Bemba's troops had combined with CAR loyalist forces, still serving the master plan. Bemba was not on the scene; but his responsibility might have rested on some prior action as a planner.

Instead, the Prosecutor turned to a more indirect theory about the "responsibility of commanders and other superiors," codified in a separate section of the ICC Statute.[117] Even if Bemba had done nothing to order his troops to harm civilians, it would be enough, under this section, if he somehow knew what they were doing but did nothing to stop them. At trial, the Prosecution moved forward with this story, aiming to prove that Bemba, sitting in northern Congo, knew what was going on hundreds of kilometers away in the CAR. It was a theory of responsibility based on knowledge, not on Bemba's bare status as a commander – even if that status seems to create vague knowledge expectations, along with some capacity to act on that knowledge to control future actions.

At the ICC, the moral pressure from CAR victims was enormous, amplified by calls to action from international human rights organizations. The victims'

116 It was the Pre-Trial Chamber, at the confirmation stage, that asked the Prosecutor to shift the theory of responsibility from "indirect co-perpetration" (Article 25(3)(a)) to "command responsibility" (Article 28(a)). See Bemba Pre-Trial Chamber, Confirmation of Charges decision, June 15, 2009, ICC-01/05-01/08-424, para. 71.

117 Article 28(a).

suffering was graphically recounted, creating heart-stopping moments when the trial finally got underway. Numbering more than 5,000, their stories were introduced by the Prosecutor and by the Legal Representatives of Victims. Witnesses took the stand to recount their unimaginable pain and continuing burdens. Compared to the immediacy of these tragic individual stories, the legal inference to Bemba's mode of responsibility could be seen as an arid philosophical exercise. Terrible things happened in the CAR.

But, for the Court, the deepest challenge was to test the accountability link to Bemba. Even this approach looked uncertain as the Bemba trial advanced. The Prosecutor earlier meant to show that Bemba directly knew about actions taken by his distant troops, only to encounter heavy resistance from Defense arguments. On closer reading, however, the Rome Statute offered the Prosecutor a safer route with a more permissive notion of responsibility: even if Bemba did not know what was going on, it was still possible that, "under the circumstances at the time, [he] *should have known*."[118] Just as the Katanga trial lurched forward by modifying the Prosecution's theory of responsibility late in the trial, the same thing happened with Bemba. Both Trial Chambers pressed forward, despite strenuous objections from the Defense.[119]

The lessons gained from these early trials were unsettling to the Prosecution, as it struggled to apply formal definitions of criminal responsibility. Justifying these practical applications would haunt all the Congo trials, leaving question marks for future cases. By the time the belated Ntaganda trial got underway, the Prosecution simply threw up its hands and applied all the liability definitions at once, hoping the trial judges would find something persuasive.

2.5 JUDGING THE CONGO TRIALS

The stage has now been set for a comprehensive study of the first trials conducted by the ICC. This analysis will shift, as necessary, between the distant locations of Ituri and The Hague. On the Hague side, it will dwell inside the courtroom, but it will also consider the ICC's expanding roles beyond the courtroom – in a balance of legal and political roles. It will expand on the history and purpose of the ICC, including legal situations beyond the

[118] Citing Article 28(a) (emphasis added). Bemba Trial Chamber, Decision Giving Notice of Possible Change in Legal Characterization of Facts under Regulation 55(2), September 21, 2012, ICC-01/05-01/08-2324.

[119] In the Trial Judgment, Bemba's convictions (later overturned on Appeal) were nonetheless based on the narrower knowledge standard; March 21, 2016, ICC-01/05-01/08-3343, paras. 717–18.

Congo. And it will place the ICC within a network of global justice institutions as the Court establishes its competence in the field of prosecutions. Throughout this study, the contrast with Ituri provides a critical dimension, using Ituri as a testing ground for gauging the dynamic possibilities – and limits – of international justice. These contrasts and tests have been introduced in the opening chapters. Readers are now invited to observe, to analyze, and to judge for themselves what the future may hold for the ICC.

There is nothing scandalous in underlining the tensions and dynamics within a set of high legal principles. Indeed, one might say that the life of the law is the interplay of principles and practice.[120] And, like the broader interplay of faith and skepticism, legal dynamics tend to fluctuate between extremes.[121] Certainly there are life-or-death issues at stake in the deeper values of global justice – the practice of international criminal law is no dry exercise in data gathering.

But the operational side of law must have its day. Through the adversary structure, courtroom trials provide a unique formula for applying legal principles to concrete cases. This is not just an exercise in logic; rather, it is a discursive process in which legal principles are seen to evolve – if sometimes in retrospect. The confrontation between Prosecution and Defense serves as a proxy struggle enabling this evolution of legal principles.

Polarized rhetoric is still present, but it is contained mainly in opening statements and summarizing flourishes. In the ICC, these polarities may be amplified through the participation of Legal Representatives of Victims. But the rhetoric in trials, while grand, is also balanced and checked by the imperative to reach a concrete result in each specific case. This process carries its own default rules of impartiality, fairness, and the presumption of innocence. Under these operating norms, the ICC asserts its authority to speak on behalf of moral values inscribed in the Preamble to the Rome Treaty. The Court would thus aspire to declare justice, end impunity, and ensure the future where mass violence is replaced by peaceful resolution of disputes. It would deter the violence that has destroyed far too many lives and life chances.

The Congo trials were the initial step toward achieving this promise.

120 Recalling the famous comment of US Judge Oliver Wendell Holmes, Jr., who argued that "the life of the law has not been logic; it has been experience." *The Common Law* (Boston: Little, Brown, 1881), p. 1.

121 On the dialectic of faith and skepticism, see Michael Oakeshott, *The Politics of Faith and the Politics of Skepticism* (ed. Timothy Fuller) (New Haven: Yale University Press, 1996).

BACK IN ITURI

There are no history books yet written on Ituri. Those involved in this trial have not had the advantage of being able to read themselves into the subject through reliable histories and documentation .... Most of the background information we have is second-hand, often based on a partisan view, scattered through various documents, often unsourced.

Katanga Trial Defense
Closing Brief (2012)

Throughout these proceedings I had the feeling that in this Court, so far from Ituri, nobody could understand what really happened. Nobody could understand these young people, fleeing massacres and organizing their defense. Nobody could understand what I was doing – or did – in the middle of them all .... What makes me despair in these proceedings, your Honour, is the incomprehension, a massive incomprehension against which my sincerity and good faith crash like waves against a sea cliff – a wall of incomprehension.

Thomas Lubanga
ICC appeals hearing (2014)

Mr. President, your Honours, we may be far away from Ituri, we may be far away from those sufferings. And those mysteries and those distances, physical as well as in time, culture and history call for the greatest caution on your part – caution and fairness, which must take into account the fair share of ignorance that we may have.

Jean-Marie Biju-Duval
Lubanga Defense (2012)

In a different universe, the first two ICC trials should have been quick and easy. Instead, they followed a maze of twisting paths, subjecting the ICC to a decade-long obstacle course, tangled in the bottomless complexities of the Congo district of Ituri. Untangling that history requires venturing far beyond the Hague courtroom.

When the Prosecutor initiated these cases, the international humanitarian gaze had recently fallen on Ituri, peering through layers of raw facts on the ground. But, in truth, NGO investigators only scratched the surface of hard realities in this outpost of a turbulent nation. And as these trials progressed, they also revealed strains within a legal process facing its own Hague-based realities – creating a parallel turbulence inside the courtroom.

The next chapters take a sharp turn away from criminal law, into the thick of Ituri's recent history. Chapter 3 maps the overlapping forces (international, regional, and national) that held this single district in their grip. The Prosecutor wanted to narrow the focus, cutting everything down to basics suitable for the courtroom – constructing a tight narrative in which the named suspects were the central players. He needed his suspects to be masterminds of Ituri violence, so that he could apply legal concepts of criminal responsibility. The Prosecutor's tunnel vision was in sharp contrast to field studies conducted during this same period by social scientists and geopolitical experts. That analysis starts in the late 1990s with the collapse of the corrupt Congolese state, instigated by regional neighbors Uganda and Rwanda, who remained a dominant presence in the eastern districts. The macro view includes the rise of national rebel groups in the Congo, tied to regional sponsors by proxy relations, while exerting their own gravitational pull on local Ituri actors. The further role of international peacekeepers (both the United Nations and European donors) strengthened the grip of national rebels, who entered into power-sharing arrangements within a new state-building scheme. The Prosecutor's local Ituri masterminds were pawns in these larger dynamics.

Chapter 4 focuses on Ituri's internal conditions, especially local actors and their diffuse network structures – exploring the micro level where all these complex layers came together. In contrast to trial concepts of tightly structured militias and commanding warlords (concepts linked to historic paradigms of armed conflict going back to the prior century), this analysis relies on field research and comparative studies about armed conflict across Africa and other global hotspots. The available research on Ituri economic, social, and political structures contrasts sharply with the Prosecution's presumptions about military command structures, ethnic hatreds, and omnipotent local masterminds. The research cited in this chapter contains no definitive conclusions about what happened in Ituri in 2002–03, but it does provide a nuanced alternative to ICC Prosecution narratives, all of which encountered difficulties under the stress of trial conditions.

To explain these local dynamics is not to excuse anything that happened in Ituri. The purpose is rather to understand the legal developments in the first two Congo trials. Later chapters will engage fully with legal blame and criminality. As the trials will show, the complexities of blaming stem from the complexities of real conditions on the ground. The view from Ituri provides an essential angle of vision on what happened inside the ICC courtroom.

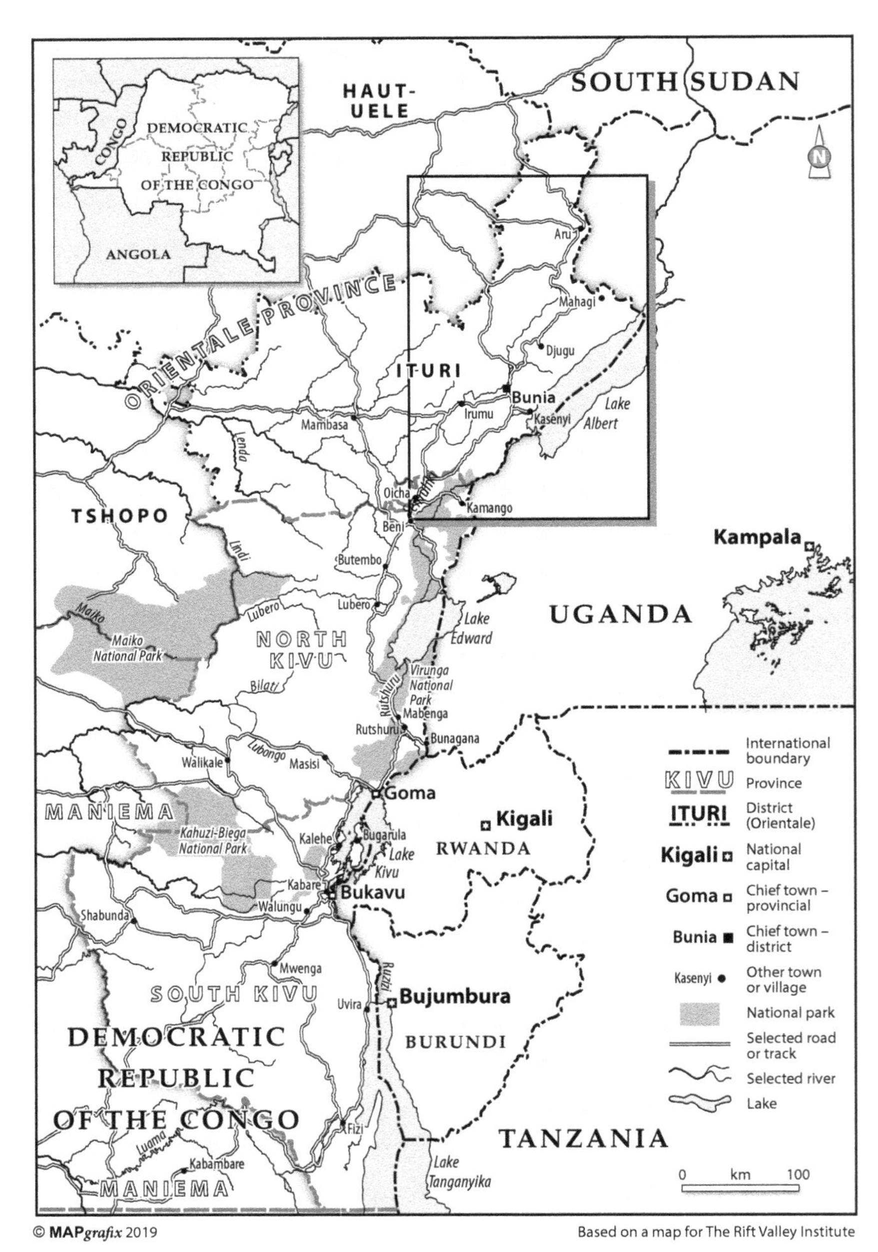

Congo: Eastern Provinces and Borders

3

Ituri in the Web of Chaos: The Macro View

It was on the ninth of August 2002 that Governor Jean-Pierre Molondo Lompondo was chased barefoot out of Bunia, the capital of Ituri district in the far northeast Congo. Lompondo, an improbable outsider from distant Kasai Province, at the opposite end of this massive country, had been installed just months before by a rebel faction that had been calling the shots in eastern Congo.[122] Upon exit, there was no time to find his shoes.

Elsewhere, during 2002, conditions in the Congo seemed to be improving, as the largest rebel groups sat down to peace negotiations with the weak national government. They were angling for a share in rebuilding the central state, as part of a transitional arrangement brokered by international donor countries. In this context, in the eyes of some local Ituri elders, the hapless Lompondo had become the front man for a possible return to weary patterns of corruption, recalling prior decades of autocratic misrule from the distant capital.[123] But it was the Ugandan occupiers who sent him fleeing.

Lompondo's fall became a flash point for the district, touching off a fresh surge of violence, fed by an inflow of weapons, leading to more killings, torture, rape, and dislocations in the civilian population. Lompondo's rebel-group sponsors retreated over the border to their stronghold in North Kivu province, from which they continued to intervene in Ituri conflicts. On the margins of national peace talks, Ituri churned from within. Older enmities were giving way to new strategic opportunities in

[122] Filip Reyntjens, *The Great African War: Congo and Regional Geopolitics, 1996–2006* (Cambridge, Cambridge University Press, 2009), pp. 207–31.

[123] Alex Veit, *Intervention as Indirect Rule: Civil War and Statebuilding in the Democratic Republic of Congo* (Frankfurt: Campus Verlag, 2010).

the flux of national renewal. Continued meddling by Uganda and Rwanda added more fuel to the fire. Locally, dozens of startup groups and would-be leaders took turns at political formation, military action, and cutthroat rivalries. The result was deeper instability and fragmentation. After May 2003, with the arrival of outside peacekeeping forces, the violence continued under new dynamics.

There was a period of ten months between Lompondo's ouster and the appearance of international forces: August 2002 to May 2003. By coincidence, this time period happened to fall within the jurisdiction of the new ICC, which was ready for business after July 1, 2002. During the Court's initial decade, the first ICC trials would dwell deeply, and almost exclusively, upon this intense period of disorder in Ituri.

To be sure, the crisis in Ituri had been gathering over some years.[124] By 1999 it flared up in fresh tensions between competing local networks of patronage and paramilitary violence. Under the influence of national rebel factions, the scale of violence expanded. The weapons and larger sponsorship came from regional powers – Uganda and Rwanda – as fallout from their central roles in toppling the Mobutu national regime. Global networks of illicit trade guaranteed that the financial pipelines were flowing smoothly. These multiple forces all came together in Ituri, fatefully and tragically, with horrifying impact. After May 2003, despite weak gestures at pacification, local fighting continued apace. Ituri remained volatile during the long years when the Congo trials unfolded in The Hague.[125]

In June 2015, when the ICC contemplated traveling to Ituri to hold opening statements in yet another Congo trial, it determined that security conditions there were too unsettled.[126] The Court would stay home; that trial would open in The Hague.

3.1 INVESTIGATING THE CONGO

Stumbling across Ituri

Ituri lies at the far corner of the northeast Congo – somewhat smaller than the state of Maine in a nation as large as the entire Eastern United

[124] Koen Vlassenroot and Timothy Raeymaekers, "The Politics of Rebellion and Intervention in Ituri: The Emergence of a New Political Complex?" *African Affairs* 103 (2004), 385.

[125] Kris Berwouts, *Congo's Violent Peace: Conflict and Struggle since the Great African War* (London: Zed Books, 2017).

[126] ICC Presidency, Decision on Holding Part of the [Ntaganda] Trial in the State Concerned, June 15, 2015, ICC-01/04–02/06–645-Red.

States, up to the Mississippi River. The heavily populated areas along the Congo's long eastern border, more than a thousand miles away from the capital Kinshasa, had been set adrift in the 1990s by the collapse of central power in a country long known as Zaire. Regional tensions flared in 1994 with the Rwanda genocide, when over a million Hutu refugees set up long-term camps across the border in the Congo's Kivu provinces, which stretch southward from Ituri. The continuing ethnic battle between fleeing Hutu extremists and their Tutsi antagonists became endemic in the Kivus, merging with an overload of local grievances and rivalries.[127]

The leaders of Rwanda and another intrusive neighbor, Uganda, exploited these conditions to manipulate local and national factions. In 1996–97, Rwanda and Uganda spearheaded the demise of the long-time Congo dictator Mobutu Sese Seko, supporting a rebel movement that swept from the east across the entire Congo, all the way to Kinshasa.[128] The Congolese figurehead in this rebellion, Laurent-Désiré Kabila, became the new Congo President in 1997.

A year later, when Kabila turned against Rwanda and Uganda, they responded by launching a second powerful insurgency from within the eastern districts.[129] This time, however, the movement stalled well short of victory, ending in a territorial stalemate and partition that dragged on until 2003. These power struggles, involving three or more rebel groups and their regional sponsors, ignited a patchwork of local armed conflicts across the whole country, with its (then) 50 million inhabitants, belonging to more than 200 distinct ethnic groups, and speaking at least that many local languages.

The extreme brutality of these conflicts drew worried attention from the United Nations, based on field reports from international NGOs like HRW, Amnesty International (AI), and the ICG. While the Congo remained a sovereign nation in theory, its implosion left a power vacuum to be filled by regional and local forces, even as international organizations sought to broker practical solutions. Global ties remained economically

[127] Gérard Prunier, *Africa's World War: Congo, the Rwandan Genocide, and the Making of a Continental Catastrophe* (Oxford: Oxford University Press, 2009). Under new legal reforms, Ituri became a province in 2015.

[128] In addition to works already cited by Reyntjens and Prunier, see Jason K. Stearns, *Dancing in the Glory of Monsters: The Collapse of the Congo and the Great War of Africa* (New York: Public Affairs, 2011).

[129] Georges Nzongola-Ntalaja, *The Congo from Leopold to Kabila: A People's History* (London, Zed Books, 2002), chapter 6.

important, considering that Ituri and the Kivu provinces to its south were commercially aligned more with East Africa than with the distant capital of Kinshasa. In the midst of chronic disorder, global trade networks passing through eastern neighbors found ways to profit from traffic in natural resources, especially gold, diamonds, and coltan, all present in abundance in the resource-rich district of Ituri and throughout the eastern Congo.[130]

In two decades after 1996, international organizations have documented massive human suffering in conflicts across the entire Congo nation. According to some sources, population mortality and displacements in the Congo between 1996 and 2007 reached levels unseen anywhere in the world since World War II. (Estimates vary from 3.9 million to 5 million excess deaths.[131]) The underlying causes were a combustible mix of political, historical, economic, and cultural factors. Over time, international NGOs and UN agencies decried the scale and intensity of violence throughout the Congo, violence that found a ready label in the Preamble to the Rome Statute: "unimaginable atrocities that deeply shock the conscience of humanity." It was for precisely these conditions that the ICC was created, with a mandate to prosecute "the most serious crimes of concern to the international community."[132]

Prosecutorial Choices: Why Ituri?

Considering the grim toll from atrocities committed over such a vast land mass, it is necessary to ask how the ICC came to focus on a narrow set of criminal suspects and events within the small peripheral district of Ituri. ICC Prosecutor Luis Moreno-Ocampo's broad mandate for the Congo investigation would have allowed him to name individual suspects from anywhere in the country.[133]

[130] Tom Burgis, *The Looting Machine: Warlords, Tycoons, Smugglers, and the Systematic Theft of Africa's Wealth* (London: William Collins, 2016), chapter 2.

[131] Estimates are from International Rescue Committee (IRC), *Mortality in the Democratic Republic of Congo: An Ongoing Crisis* (New York: International Rescue Committee, 2008). Excess deaths include deaths from disease and malnutrition, which outnumber combat deaths by 4:1. For cautionary views on Congo mortality, questioning the IRC methodology, see Human Security Report, *The Causes of Peace and the Shrinking Costs of War* (Oxford: Oxford University Press, 2011), chapter 7. See also Michael Deibert, *The Democratic Republic of Congo: Between Hope and Despair* (London: Zed Books, 2013), p. 127.

[132] Rome Statute Preamble.

[133] Rod Rastan, "The Jurisdictional Scope of Situations before the International Criminal Court," *Criminal Law Forum* 23 (2012), 1; see Part II on the DRC, especially references cited on p. 4.

This question has no easy answers, and it relates partly to timing, and partly to international pressures. As for timing, the ICC's governing rules restrict the Court's jurisdiction to those events occurring only after July 1, 2002.[134] The ten-month period in Ituri, between the fall of Governor Lompondo and the arrival of outside military forces (August 2002 through May 2003), fell neatly within this temporal mandate of the new Court. During 2003, international observers were shifting attention to Ituri, confronting local events in terms demanding legal action. In March 2003, the UNSC declared the unrest in Ituri as a threat to international peace; and in September 2003, UN forces assumed peacekeeping duties in Ituri, in an all-out effort to end the fighting.[135] This attention from international observers may explain why, in July 2003, the newly appointed ICC Prosecutor Moreno-Ocampo chose Ituri as the site for his first preliminary examination, worldwide.[136]

The international community saw Ituri as one more area slipping into savagery, extending the Congo's long misery.[137] By contrast, on the national level, peace negotiations were coming together by late 2002, when the largest rebel groups operating across the Congo signed accords with Kinshasa, pledging to abandon military struggle and to rebuild the national state.[138] It was not yet understood that these peace accords would themselves create fresh incentives for splinter groups to keep fighting – as indeed fighting continued for another decade, especially in the eastern

[134] The Court's temporal jurisdiction over specified crimes began only when the underlying Statute "entered into force" shortly after formal ratification by the first sixty countries (Articles 11(1) and 126). As a result, only those crimes committed after July 1, 2002 can fall within the Court's authority.

[135] UNSC Resolutions 1468 (March 20, 2003) and 1493 (July 28, 2003).

[136] ICC Press Release, July 16, 2003 (Prosecutor would "closely follow the situation in the DRC"). Moreno-Ocampo started work on June 16, 2003, following his election on April 21. In September, Moreno-Ocampo indicated a readiness to use his *proprio motu* powers to launch a formal investigation. After pressure from international sponsors and negotiations with Moreno-Ocampo, Congo President Joseph Kabila made the self-referral in April 2004. Benjamin N. Schiff, *Building the International Criminal Court* (Cambridge: Cambridge University Press, 2008), pp. 212–13. See Thierry Cruvellier, "ICC Joins the Congolese Chess Game," *International Justice Tribune* 8 (July 5, 2004). David Bosco reports, on the basis of anonymous interviews, that the Prosecutor's zeal for an Ituri investigation struck some staff associates as overly hasty: *Rough Justice: The International Criminal Court in a World of Power Politics* (Oxford: Oxford University Press, 2014), pp. 90–91.

[137] Séverine Autesserre discusses the international fixation on Ituri in *The Trouble with the Congo: Local Violence and the Failure of International Peacebuilding* (Cambridge: Cambridge University Press, 2010), pp. 207–09.

[138] Reyntjens, *The Great African War*, pp. 252–61.

zones.[139] The more natural assumption was that violence would subside as the largest rebel groups entered into national governance. Ituri was an outlying district, threatening this fragile campaign for national peace-building. And now Ituri was "covered in blood,"[140] according to one influential report from HRW: only forceful intervention by the UN could pacify the district. For the ICC Prosecutor, Ituri presented a neat, self-contained target. In a large country of deep complexity, it was a tempting focus for ICC attention.[141]

Criminal investigations inside active war zones face obvious difficulties. They require state cooperation in providing physical safety for ICC staff, and long-term protection measures for witnesses. Although Ituri was a perilous field for investigations, the expanding UN mission in 2003 was designed to stabilize conditions, especially in the capital of Bunia. With the UN and other international organizations already thick on the ground, the ICC Prosecutor would count on their active assistance – although in ways that ultimately raised questions about the integrity of trial evidence.[142]

As it turned out, Ituri was not pacified, even as the structure of local violence evolved toward guerrilla opposition to the UN, which was seen by some as an ally of corrupt national forces. Meanwhile, throughout the eastern Congo, the process of nation-building would prove to be far more complicated than expected. Like Ituri, some other parts of the country saw the continuation of local conflicts. Fresh confrontations emerged, as former rebel leaders redoubled their competition for favored slots in the ranks of national politics and military security. In retrospect, Ituri was perhaps not so exceptional, as violence persisted throughout the eastern Congo.[143]

139 Veit, *Intervention as Indirect Rule*, Part IV; Koen Vlassenroot and Timothy Raeymaekers, *Conflict and Social Transformation in Eastern DR Congo* (Ghent: Academia Press, 2004), pp. 58–59.

140 HRW, *Ituri: "Covered in Blood": Ethnically Targeted Violence in Northeastern DR Congo* (New York, 2003). The forensic impact of this document will be discussed in detail in Chapter 5.

141 See Patryk I. Ibuda, "The ICC in the Democratic Republic of Congo: A Decade of Partnership and Antagonism," in Kamari M. Clarke, Abel S. Knottnerus, and Eefje de Volder (eds.), *Africa and the ICC: Perceptions of Justice* (Cambridge: Cambridge University Press, 2016), pp. 277–300.

142 Pascal Kalume Kambale, "A Story of Missed Opportunities: The Role of the International Criminal Court in the Democratic Republic of Congo," in Christian De Vos, Sara Kendall, and Carsten Stahn (eds.), *Contested Justice: The Politics and Practice of International Criminal Court Interventions* (Cambridge: Cambridge University Press, 2015), pp. 188–92.

143 Autesserre, *The Trouble with the Congo*.

With all this troubled history yet to emerge, it seems likely that Ituri's outlying status in 2003 increased its attraction for the ICC Prosecutor. Ituri could be seen as a safe remove for testing out new legal definitions of mass atrocities, with little threat to the state-building aspirations of Congolese leaders and their international supporters. Criminal inquiries in Ituri were the least likely to implicate emerging leadership in the Congolese army or the ruling regime.[144] In short, any ICC investigation in Ituri was bound to stay in Ituri. Whether it would drift eastward into Uganda and Rwanda would not have bothered the Kinshasa government.[145]

Another possible distinction for Ituri has to do with amnesties, built into local peace documents involving broader rebel groups and Kinshasa officials. As peace negotiations brought prior military competitors into a transitional phase, leading up to national elections projected for 2006, the parties looked to mutual exoneration as a condition for cooperation. Impunity was the "glue" of the whole peace process, according to Jason Stearns.[146] While ICC principles could have superseded such internal grants of immunity, any ICC moves against peace negotiators would have greatly complicated the ICC Prosecutor's efforts. There were reports that an ICC investigator assured US Embassy officials that the search for cases would not touch the peace process.[147]

Why These Suspects?

Even in the small world of Ituri, the Prosecutor still had to choose potential suspects from among dozens of candidates within the tangle of upstart militias. In 2003, a discussion paper from the Office of the Prosecutor set some tentative priorities: "to focus its investigative and prosecutorial efforts and resources on those who bear the greatest responsibility, such as leaders of the state or organization allegedly responsible for those crimes."[148] By the years 2006–08, when the ICC took custody of its first three Congolese suspects, *chance* would come to play a much larger role than *choice*. The ICC gratefully accepted three suspects who had already spent periods in

[144] See Phil Clark, "Law, Politics and Pragmatism: The ICC and Case Selection in Uganda and the Democratic Republic of Congo," in Nicholas Waddell and Phil Clark (eds.), *Courting Conflict? Justice, Peace and the ICC in Africa* (London: Royal African Society, 2008).

[145] Kambale, "A Story of Missed Opportunities," pp. 173–76.

[146] Jason Stearns, "Congo's Peace: Miracle or Mirage?" *Current History* 106 (2007), 202, quoted in Theodore Trefon, *Congo Masquerade* (London: Zed Books, 2011), p. 22.

[147] Bosco, *Rough Justice*, p. 101.

[148] ICC Office of the Prosecutor, Paper on Some Policy Issues (2003), p. 7. See Schiff, *Building the International Criminal Court*, p. 118.

Kinshasa detention. This happened at a time when the Court had failed to capture any of the five suspects already named in its Uganda investigations – the elusive Joseph Kony and other members of the LRA. By contrast, Lubanga, Katanga, and Ngudjolo were already known to Congolese authorities. Lubanga and Katanga were moving slowly through a dysfunctional military justice system. Ngudjolo had emerged from earlier legal scrapes and was training with the national army, while remaining known to authorities. Congolese leaders were eager and able to deliver this particular trio to The Hague.[149]

During this same time, there was another ICC warrant outstanding for the arrest of Bosco Ntaganda, an ally of Lubanga, and an ethnic Congolese Tutsi, born in Rwanda and active in the Kivu districts as well as Ituri. Initially, the ICC pre-trial judges doubted whether Ntaganda was senior enough to merit attention – and in reality he remained beyond their reach.[150] Having briefly joined the national army, in 2005 he fled Kinshasa and returned to the eastern provinces – until his dramatic surrender to the ICC in 2013. The question about Ntaganda's relative seniority was never fully answered. The more obvious target for ICC prosecution would have been his superior in the military chain of command, Floribert Kisembo. But Kisembo had already abandoned his Ituri colleagues in late 2003. Enticed by the head of the UN Bunia office, Kisembo shifted his loyalties to Kinshasa. He was a prime example of suspects the ICC would deliberately avoid.[151] Additionally, by 2005 HRW had singled out Bosco Ntaganda as a field commander during several massacres in 2002–03, although its evidence would ultimately be given little credibility in the courtroom.[152]

[149] On Lubanga and Katanga, see Schiff, *Building the International Criminal Court*, pp. 220–26. Kambale describes the circumstances of Congolese detentions for all three suspects; "A Story of Missed Opportunities," pp. 179–85.

[150] DR Congo Pre-Trial Chamber, Decision on the Prosecution's Application for a Warrant of Arrest, February 10, 2006, ICC-01/04–02/06–20-Anx2, para. 89. This was overturned on appeal: Appeals Decision on the Prosecutor's Application for a Warrant of Arrest, July 13, 2006, ICC-01/04-169, para. 74. For background on Ntaganda, see Jason Stearns, *Strongman of the Eastern DRC: A Profile of General Bosco Ntaganda* (London: Rift Valley Institute, 2013), written prior to Ntaganda's voluntary surrender in The Hague.

[151] There are reports that Kinshasa made explicit promises to protect Kisembo from prosecution, although this pledge would not have been formally binding on an unencumbered ICC Prosecutor. See Henning Tamm, *UPC in Ituri: The External Militarization of Local Politics in North-eastern Congo* (London: Rift Valley Institute, 2013), pp. 37–38. Tamm notes that Kisembo's erstwhile Ituri colleagues were meanwhile being arrested by UN peacekeepers. Kisembo was reportedly killed in Ituri in April 2015.

[152] In addition to *Ituri: "Covered in Blood,"* see the June 2005 HRW report, *The Curse of Gold*, which implicates "Bosco Taganda" in a series of civilian attacks (see Part V). The author of

Some years after the ICC received its first three Congo suspects, the Court issued further arrest warrants for two Congo-based leaders of the displaced Rwandan Hutu refugees, still active in North Kivu long after the 1994 genocide. A 2010 warrant named Callixte Mbarushimana, who was arrested in France but released by the ICC in 2011 for lack of evidence.[153] In 2012, there was a warrant for Sylvestre Mudacumura, who remains at large somewhere in the Kivus. If any other Congo warrants were approved, they had not been made public as of 2019.[154]

Framing the Investigation

Even within the microcosm of Ituri, the violence in 2002–03 contains a degree of complexity that severely tested the ICC's trial capacity. The underlying causes were multiple and contested. Key local actors were tied to dense networks spreading out in many directions. The proliferation of armed groups was encouraged in obscure ways by the conduct of national political reforms and regional peace initiatives. To an eager Prosecutor, the task of fitting these Ituri conflicts into the legal categories of the Rome statute required extensive narrowing and reframing of the underlying facts.[155]

How far does one need to go with this narrowing process in order to reach the descriptive level where men like Lubanga, Katanga, and Ngudjolo emerge as leading players?[156] The first steps down this road came in 2001, as NGOs began describing local events in Ituri in broad

these two reports consulted with the ICC Prosecutor in the lead-up to arrest warrants in the Congo investigation. See Ntaganda Trial Chamber, transcript, June 23, 2016, ICC-01/04–02/06-T-108-ENG, pp. 8, 22 (testimony of Anneke van Woudenberg). The prior day, the Presiding Judge indicated that her reports, based on anonymous sources, had "little relevance" to the trial proceedings. Ntaganda Trial Chamber, transcript, June 22, 2016, ICC-01/04–02/06-T-107-ENG, p. 58.

[153] Mbarushimana Pre-Trial Chamber, Confirmation of Charges decision, December 16, 2011, ICC-01/04–01/10–465-Red.

[154] See Phil Clark, "Chasing Cases: The ICC and the Politics of State Referral in the Democratic Republic of the Congo and Uganda," in Carsten Stahn and Mohamed M. El Zeidy, *The International Criminal Court and Complementarity: From Theory to Practice* (Cambridge: Cambridge University Press, 2011), chapter 38.

[155] For a sympathetic view on framing as a kind of "hypothesis building," see Paul Seils, "Putting Complementarity in Its Place," in Carsten Stahn (ed.), *The Law and Practice of the International Criminal Court* (Oxford: Oxford University Press, 2015), pp. 318–20.

[156] Kambale considers this narrow script entirely unpersuasive; "A Story of Missed Opportunities," p. 184.

humanitarian terms – although it was not until mid-2003 that they linked that analysis to specific crimes in the Rome Statute.

One storyline resonating with NGO observers centered on local military recruitment, notably the presence of child soldiers in combat units (military groups that were assumed to fall under conventional command structures). Another common theme, in response to violence directed against Ituri civilians, was one of bitter hatred between ethnic groups, in particular the Hema and the Lendu (both groups together comprised 40 percent of the Ituri population). Some observers found analogies with Tutsi–Hutu conflicts in Rwanda and applied the term "genocide." Further reports documented the appalling record of sexual violence carried out on civilians.[157]

Building on these core themes, over time NGOs moved to identify representative leaders of discrete armed groups, meaning to impute atrocities to specific individuals acting with criminal intent. In this way, complex events were gradually reframed in terms inviting ICC prosecutions. In their brutality, the Ituri conflicts were described as a systematic campaign of ethnic cleansing, with dominant Hema ethnic groups trying to drive out the less-organized Lendu – but provoking strong resistance and counterattacks. (The term "ethnic cleansing" had arisen in the context of Balkan wars from the previous decade, and was widely featured in cases being heard in the early 2000s before the ICTY.[158]) When prosecutions eventually opened up in The Hague, the ICC Prosecutor's narrative was built around this set of themes. The facts on the ground would need to fit this specific template.[159]

By July 2003, immersed in the legal constructs of the Rome Statute, NGO observers described not just a war zone but a crime scene: notable for its violence against women and children.[160] The physical violence was graphic – even grotesque – in a series of documented attacks by armed groups, described confidently as militias under the strict military control of specific commanders, who were determined to destroy their ethnic

[157] For a critical perspective on storylines in describing Congo violence, see Séverine Autesserre, "Dangerous Tales: Dominant Narratives on the Congo and Their Unintended Consequences," *African Affairs* 111 (2012), 202.

[158] That tribunal was officially known as the International Criminal Tribunal for the former Yugoslavia (ICTY) based in The Hague. Regarding this tribunal as a response to "ethnic cleansing," see David Scheffer, *All the Missing Souls* (Princeton: Princeton University Press, 2011), chapter 1.

[159] Chapter 5 provides an overview of NGO reports on Ituri violence.

[160] This shift to ICC legal terms was the pivotal contribution of *Ituri: "Covered in Blood"* (July 2003).

adversaries at any cost. As courtroom trials unfolded, this simple framework began to weaken, slowly but surely, as plausible alternative explanations were allowed to emerge.

The courtroom discourse broke through the Prosecutor's narrow framing, as facts on the ground reclaimed some of their initial complexity. Once the evidence was seriously tested, and once several counter-narratives emerged, the initial take on Ituri violence lost its sharp contours. Simply keeping track of shadowy armed groups proved difficult enough. Their structure and leadership were volatile, highly diverse, with a tendency to fragment into rival camps. Over time, groups split off to form new alliances, linked to shifting sponsors across territorial borders.[161] These stubborn facts about weak, fragmented local networks challenged the tighter narratives developed by NGOs and taken over by the Prosecutor. In response to courtroom surprises, the Prosecutor doubled down on the theme of ethnic hatred.[162]

Beyond the Courtroom

In contrast to these ICC courtroom narratives, there was still another perspective from the Congolese capital of Kinshasa – on the opposite side of this vast country. The Kinshasa perspective held that Ituri and the eastern provinces of North and South Kivu had fallen under the sway of hostile leaders in Rwanda and Uganda. Indeed, Ituri district was effectively occupied by Ugandan army forces from 1999, continuing past the historic moment in July 2002 when ICC jurisdiction came into effect (shortly before the ouster of Governor Lompondo). In geopolitical terms, for Kinshasa the problems in Ituri would need to be addressed at a broader level – first by reducing the meddling by Rwanda and Uganda, and second by reconciling the domestic rebel forces sponsored by these two predatory neighbors.[163]

161 Vlassenroot and Raeymaekers, "The Politics of Rebellion," pp. 397–98.

162 The Prosecutor's emphasis on ethnic conflict was embraced by the respective Pre-Trial Chambers: Lubanga Pre-Trial Chamber, Confirmation of Charges decision, January 29, 2007, ICC-01/04–01/06–803, para. 4; Katanga and Ngudjolo Pre-Trial Chamber, Confirmation of Charges decision, September 30, 2008, ICC-01/04–01/07–717, para. 4.

163 On the Congo press view of Rwanda and Uganda, see Kambale, "A Story of Missed Opportunities," p. 193. The Kinshasa regime had already brought a claim under international law against Uganda in the International Court of Justice. Case concerning Armed Activities on the Territory of the Congo (*Democratic Republic of Congo* v. *Uganda*), Judgment of 19 December 2005.

Between 1998 and 2003, in the volatile Kivu provinces south of Ituri, the Rwandan-supported rebellion against the Kinshasa government had taken hold under the name "Rally for Congolese Democracy" (RCD). Western governments pressured Kinshasa to share power with the RCD, which eventually broke into two warring factions (one linked to Rwanda, one to Uganda). Included in these national discussions was yet a third powerful political-military group, Jean-Pierre Bemba's home-grown "Movement for the Liberation of the Congo" (MLC), which gained Ugandan sponsorship. During the 2002 national peace talks, these large rebel factions agreed on a power-sharing arrangement, in transition to national elections planned for 2006.[164]

Excluded from these peace talks were countless localized factions in Ituri and the Kivu provinces, considered too insignificant to merit a share of national power. In the margins of Ituri, prior to 2003, Lubanga was one among several dozen players starting to gain the attention of international observers, while Ngudjolo and Katanga were still undetected by international radar. Lubanga appeared as a mid-level powerbroker in mid-2002, shortly before Governor Lompondo was ousted from Bunia. With his university degree in psychology, Lubanga seemed rather more of a political figure than a military one – one among many upstart personalities in Bunia and surrounding Ituri precincts.[165] Possible roles for Ngudjolo and Katanga in the 2003 fighting were ascribed only much later – well after key events had occurred, for which they would ultimately stand trial. Their alleged roles in armed conflicts were extrapolated from post-conflict interviews and reconstructions, based on observers' assumptions about how Ituri violence must have been organized.[166]

In late 2003, when the Kinshasa government warmed to the ICC's investigations in these liminal insurgent areas, it found a Prosecutor eager

[164] Stearns, *Dancing in the Glory of Monsters*, provides an overview of RCD and MLC in chapters 14 and 15.

[165] On Lubanga's background, see Tamm, *UPC in Ituri*, pp. 19–20. Kambale criticizes the Lubanga prosecution as settling for "small fish," describing Lubanga as a "mid-level actor" among many other comparable players ("A Story of Missed Opportunities," p. 179).

[166] Henning Tamm, *FNI and FRPI: Local Resistance and Regional Alliances* (London: Rift Valley Institute, 2013); Koen Vlassenroot and Timothy Raeymaekers, "The Politics of Rebellion and Intervention in Ituri: The Emergence of a New Political Complex?" *African Affairs* 103 (2004), 385. Tamm's sources (ten years after the events in question took place) are a mix of anonymous interviews and references to ICC evidence. The attribution of combat roles for these two accused would become a major point of contention at trial, as discussed in Chapter 8.

to implement his new mandate.[167] Under the circumstances, his focus on Ituri reduced the chance of stumbling across wrongdoing by Congolese government forces. Indeed, the Ituri investigations would cause far greater discomfort for Kinshasa's opponents in Kampala (Uganda) and Kigali (Rwanda). Any member country referring its own troubles to the ICC cannot put geographic limits on the Prosecutor's investigation within the country-wide *situation*. But the Prosecutor would have realized that success depended on close cooperation from Congolese authorities for access to combat areas, for the execution of arrest warrants within the Congo, and for other assistance with crime investigations. When the time came for the Prosecutor to arrest his first suspects anywhere, Congolese authorities in Kinshasa could easily put their hands on Lubanga, Katanga, and Ngudjolo. The ICC focus on Ituri thus offered mutual advantages to both the Congolese government and the ICC Prosecutor.[168]

3.2 UNGOVERNED SPACES?

The Hobbesian Dread

Well before President Mobutu was deposed in 1997, he had lost his grip on the eastern districts. In a huge country with a decaying transportation infrastructure, there was no longer a central sovereign power that could reach into Ituri or the Kivu provinces. For many Western observers, this power vacuum was the root cause of violence and disorder. The point was forcefully stated by Adam Hochschild toward the end of his bestselling book on the Congo's violent history, as shaped by colonialism. Speaking of the late 1990s, Hochschild concludes:

> For the Congo, the combination of being a great mineral treasure house and in effect having no working government has been catastrophic. When there is no money in the public till, armies become self-financing networks of miners and smugglers. When there are few schools or jobs, they can easily recruit children. When the millions of small arms circulating in Africa can be bought at street bazaars or from policemen who've received no pay, there are guns for all.[169]

[167] For an analysis of Moreno-Ocampo's broader strategy during this period, see David Bosco, *Rough Justice: The International Criminal Court in a World of Power Politics* (Oxford: Oxford University Press, 2014), chapter 4.

[168] See Kambale, "A Story of Missed Opportunities," pp. 179–85; and also pp. 185–86 on formal cooperation agreements between Kinshasa and the ICC Prosecutor.

[169] *King Leopold's Ghost* (Boston: Houghton Mifflin, 1998), p. 301.

As with other parts of the Congo, the eastern zones qualified as lawless regions, zones of state failure – sometimes referred to as "ungoverned spaces."[170] Following a Hobbesian line of inference, the loss of sovereign power allowed for a nasty, brutish series of conflicts, for which the only remedy was the restoration of central power. Violence bubbled up from the base elements of human nature. It could be halted only through intervention by superior force, followed by political reconstruction of the central Congolese state. This sovereignty agenda, coming from the international humanitarian community, matched the assessment from global NGOs that wholesale human rights violations were inevitable in such ungoverned spaces.[171]

But there were more nuanced explanations for violence in places like Ituri. Africa researchers had already explored a range of spaces beyond effective sovereign power, finding key patterns within the chaos. Instead of the Hobbesian void, they identified new modes of privatized governance, operating in the shadows of traditional sovereign power. State failure of various kinds had long eroded security conditions across many parts of Africa, going back to the 1970s. By the 1990s, however, several developments came together into a new figuration. The end of the Cold War reduced great-power sponsorship of states and rebel groups. Efficient (and often lawless) global markets in natural resources provided localized groups with sustainable financing, reducing the need for civilian support in their immediate locality. The availability of cheap weapons and new communications technology allowed for upstart movements to mobilize more handily. In parts of Africa, one saw a willingness of some entrepreneurial national officials to meddle in the rebellions of neighbors. For all this, armed groups were generally short on payments, opening up the trend to fill out the ranks with child soldiers.[172] In short, the same factors mentioned by Hochschild could also be taken as the formula for a new, more violent, social configuration.

170 For scholarly responses to this image, see Anne L. Clunan and Harold A. Trinkunas, *Ungoverned Spaces: Alternatives to State Authority in an Era of Softened Sovereignty* (Stanford: Stanford University Press, 2010), especially chapter 3 by William Reno on African examples. See also the work of the Africa Borderlands Research Network in Benedikt Korf and Timothy Raeymaekers (eds.), *Violence on the Margins: States, Conflict, and Borderlands* (New York: Palgrave Macmillan, 2013).

171 Séverine Autesserre, "Hobbes and the Congo: Frames, Local Violence, and International Intervention," *International Organizations* 63 (2009), 249.

172 On youth options in stressed economies, see Timothy Raeymaekers, "Captured Lives: The Precarious Space of Youth Displacement in Eastern DRC," in Amanda Hammar (ed.), *Displacement Economies in Africa* (London: Zed Books, 2014), pp. 230–49.

According to Crawford Young, a long-standing Congo expert:

> A sea change in the world order in the 1990s has altered the basic texture of the linkages between Africa and the global system of states as well as the international normative domain. At the same time, a gradual weakening of the fabric of stateness occurred in many African countries, a product of the prolonged economic crisis beginning in the 1970s and the delegitimation of patrimonial autocracy as a mode of rule.
>
> These broad transformations have increased the vulnerability of African states to civil conflict. Meanwhile, armed challengers to public order have acquired new capabilities in the 1990s.[173]

The common term "warlord" calls up the strongman who commands some measure of control over private power networks, balancing across political, economic, cultural, and military objectives. Unlike rebels opposing the established government on ideological grounds, warlords tend to thrive in these ungoverned spaces, pursuing vague or improvised political agendas. In the Congo, such upstart leaders would arise in the 1990s by taking over segments of black-market networks abandoned by Mobutu and his minions, who had lost control of their corrupt patronage system with the waning of the Cold War.[174] By the end of the decade, in the eastern districts of the Congo, further variations would emerge.

Improvised Governance: "Parochial" Authority

Outside the bounds of formal sovereignty, patrimonial networks take on a life of their own. From the remnants of prior state-run patronage, more diffuse power structures emerge, whether or not some dominant "warlord" takes charge. Local elites, sometimes referred to as "parochial leaders," come to dominate illicit markets, working in the shadows of black economies where natural resources are in high demand, linking through mediators to global markets.[175] In the Congo, after the end of state-controlled

[173] "Contextualizing Congo Conflicts: Order and Disorder in Postcolonial Africa," in John F. Clark (ed.), *The African Stakes of the Congo War* (New York: Palgrave Macmillan, 2002), p. 28. Young's essay anticipated the next decade of research on patterns of African conflict. Among later texts developing these themes, see William Reno, *Warfare in Independent Africa* (Cambridge: Cambridge University Press, 2011); Paul Williams, *War and Conflict in Africa* (Cambridge: Polity Press, 2011). Reno had previously discussed political patterns in weak states in *Warlord Politics and African States* (Boulder: Lynne Reiner, 1998).

[174] David van Reybrouck, *Congo: The Epic History of a People* (New York: HarperCollins, 2014), chapter 11.

[175] Reno, *Warfare in Independent Africa*, chapter 6 (on "Parochial Rebels").

mining in the 1980s followed by new liberalized global trading rules, private networks for exporting natural resources were able to expand. Economic returns allowed parochial elites to establish relative dominance. But life in such networks was inherently unstable. Fragile patronage systems are too strapped to provide even minimal social and administrative services, failing to win any widespread local support (beyond those inside the network). But where they are the only game in town, civilian populations have little choice but to endure.[176]

The following analysis avoids the term "warlord" for local Ituri leaders, in favor of William Reno's term "parochial leaders."[177] In the broader Congo, one might well apply the warlord label to large rebel groups like Wamba's RCD (and to the later RCD-ML breakaway faction), or to Bemba's MLC.[178] Within Ituri, however, this degree of personal dominance was never really possible – despite the high ambitions of local actors. Power could not be monopolized by any single individual. Later interpretations from NGOs would assign this elevated status – however briefly – to Thomas Lubanga, a view inherited by the ICC Prosecutor. And while some local Ituri groups sought the trappings of formal governance, they were forced to rely on stronger patrons within national rebel groups or regional command centers. This complex pattern of fragmented governance would haunt later ICC investigations, which relied on NGOs' ungrounded theories about local power configurations.

3.3 NATIONAL DYNAMICS: REBEL FACTIONS IN TRANSITION

Reconstructing the State

What was the violence in Ituri all about? Experts on the Congo have explored this question for years without coming to easy conclusions. At the very least, one can say that home-grown actors like Lubanga, Ngudjolo, and Katanga did not, by themselves, create the violent conditions in which they came to play supporting roles. Violence inside Ituri

176 Ibid., pp. 206–08. See also Patrick Chabal and Jean-Pascal Daloz, *Africa Works: Disorder as Political Instrument* (Bloomington: Indiana University Press, 1999), chapter 3.

177 Reno, *Warfare in Independent Africa*, chapter 6. For "warlords," see also Mark Duffield, "Post-Modern Conflict: Warlords, Post-Adjustment States and Private Protection," *Civil Wars* 1 (1998), 65.

178 Ruben de Koning, "Big Men Commanding Conflict Resources: The Democratic Republic of the Congo," in Mats Utas (ed.), *African Conflicts and Informal Power: Big Men and Networks* (London: Zed Books, 2012), chapter 10.

increased after 1999 with the steady growth of political and armed groups, variously organized and guided. During this period, local dynamics in Ituri were manipulated by regional powers – notably Uganda and Rwanda, as a sideline to their sponsorship of broader national insurgencies. Their interventions in eastern Congo filled part of the political vacuum after the demise of long-time Congolese ruler Mobutu Sese Seko. Uganda and Rwanda fostered the rebellion that swept Mobutu from power in 1996–97, leading to more protracted meddling. Virtually all observers agree that the complexity of violence inside Ituri comes from this interplay of local, regional, and national forces.[179]

During 2002, as violence intensified in Ituri, national discourse in the Congo was turning to reconciliation and rebuilding.[180] After the inconclusive rebellion of 1998, international observers saw vast sections of the country fall into lawlessness. Their preferred remedy was to reconstruct the national political system, with the hope that local affairs could also be brought under better control. A formal peace initiative started up in 2001 and would soon be hosted by South Africa under the name Inter-Congolese Dialogue.[181]

Political institutions in the Congo had been rotting for more than a decade when outside attention became focused on the region. At the beginning of the 1990s, with the end of the Cold War, autocrats like Mobutu lost their Western support under pressure to abandon one-party rule – the dominant political style since the early days of independence.[182] This sudden opening to multi-party politics in the Congo would stir local ethnic tensions throughout the country, as rival factions rushed to build electoral coalitions in a culture with little democratic experience.[183] After Mobutu was deposed in 1997, and as the ensuing struggle for leadership threatened to partition the country among rebel factions, Western governments and international agencies pushed for national political renewal. The answer to internal bloodletting would be to strengthen central state authority, with the strongest rebel groups transitioning into rival political parties.[184] The Congolese military would expand to integrate insurgent forces into national ranks. A return to centralized power would hasten the

[179] See van Reybrouck, *Congo*, chapter 12.
[180] Reyntjens, *The Great African War*, chapter 8.
[181] Ibid., pp. 252–61.
[182] Deibert, *The Democratic Republic of the Congo*, pp. 36–41.
[183] Vlassenroot and Raeymaekers, "The Politics of Rebellion," p. 390.
[184] See van Reybrouck, *Congo*, pp. 467–71.

exit of Rwanda and Uganda from the eastern zones. UN monitors would help maintain internal peace.

When the Inter-Congolese Dialogue began, the national government was in the hands of Joseph Kabila, son of the first post-Mobutu President. Earlier, in January 2001, the elder Kabila was assassinated in his Kinshasa headquarters, reportedly by a member of his own security team – a former child soldier (*kadogo* was the Swahili term) from the first rebellion of 1996–97.[185] The elder Kabila, in turning against his Rwandan sponsors, had enlisted military support from southern neighbors Angola and Zimbabwe, which provided enough firepower to battle the second Rwandan-led rebellion to a standstill in 1998–99. But the nation was severely weakened and divided. The inexperienced younger Kabila, just twenty-nine years old when he assumed office, was ready to heed the global call for political compromise. In return, the international community stipulated the younger Kabila's "special status" as the transitional custodian for Congolese sovereignty.[186]

The South African peace talks brought the Kabila government into a weary dialogue with large rebel factions and national opposition political parties.[187] The 1998 invasion had broken the country into partitions. In the east, the Rwandan-sponsored RCD insurgency split into two warring factions linked separately to former allies Rwanda and Uganda. Both RCD factions would cooperate in the internationally brokered South African talks, along with a small number of localized armed groups.[188] Also joining the Inter-Congolese Dialogue was the powerful internal MLC rebellion led by Jean-Pierre Bemba, the scion of a wealthy Congolese family with dominance in the northern province of Équateur, the stronghold for Mobutu's former network. Along with his broad local support base, Bemba's organization gained the sponsorship of Uganda, now openly competing with Rwanda for influence in the Congo negotiations.

Indeed, in early 2002, the South African talks produced a tentative power agreement between just Bemba and Kabila, excluding both

185 Details remained mysterious. See Prunier, *Africa's World War*, pp. 249–55, with background on the role and dynamics of *kadogo*. Trefon also discusses this event, mentioning that son/successor Joseph Kabila "was once commander of the infamous army of child soldiers." *Congo Masquerade*, pp. 20–21.

186 Stearns, *Dancing in the Glory of Monsters*, pp. 314–18, explaining Joseph Kabila's deference to international donor nations and to erstwhile military allies.

187 Prunier, *Africa's World War*, pp. 265–77, explaining that "all the parties started to scramble in various directions to take care of their special interests, hoping to fit them into the general framework before it was too late" (p. 274).

188 Reyntjens, *The Great African War*, chapter 8.

branches of the RCD.[189] But negotiations were later expanded to include all three rebel groups, yielding a transitional path toward shared power, pointing toward a national election in 2006. In that election Bemba would lose the Presidential vote to Joseph Kabila by a margin of 58 percent–42 percent.[190]

Two years later, Bemba was arrested in Belgium and transported to The Hague on charges that his MLC troops, while under Bemba's remote command, committed international crimes in the CAR back in 2002–03. Bemba would not be the only losing presidential candidate to find himself, soon after defeat, facing prosecution at the ICC.[191]

A Post-Conflict Mindset

Ituri in 2002–03 was an annoyance to international players who had watched the chaos from the twin insurgencies in 1996 and 1998. They had successfully imposed a power-sharing mandate on young Joseph Kabila, after his father's assassination in January 2001. The Inter-Congolese Dialogue, joined by major rebel groups (but excluding any representatives from Ituri armed groups), reached a Global and Inclusive Accord in December 2002, to be followed by an agreement among cooperating factions for the period of transition to elections between 2003 and 2006. Former rebels would become aspiring politicians; their organizations (Bemba's MLC and a fragmented RCD) would take on national portfolios, their leaders Vice-Presidential titles.

Other brokered peace talks aimed to protect the Congo central state from its intrusive neighbors. After the stalemated 1998 insurgency, launched from the eastern regions by Rwanda and Uganda, but halted by armies from Angola and Zimbabwe, the Lusaka Peace Agreement signed in July 1999 called for the withdrawal of foreign troops. And while Rwanda and Uganda remained firmly within the eastern districts, in late 2002, both

[189] Stearns, *Dancing in the Glory of Monsters*, pp. 316–17.

[190] Prunier, *Africa's World War*, pp. 309–15. Prunier mentions Bemba's vote-fraud challenge, rejected by the Supreme Court, followed by Bemba's withdrawal from the capital.

[191] Bosco, *Rough Justice*, p. 173. The other electoral casualty was Laurent Gbagbo, defeated for reelection in the Ivory Coast and handed over to the ICC in November 2011 by his successor. After years of detention, Gbagbo was acquitted and granted conditional released by the Trial Chamber in January 2019, in a split vote deciding that the Prosecution's case against him was too weak to require a Defense. Soon afterwards, a divided Appeals Chamber overruled his release, pending an appeal by the Prosecutor. ICC Press Release, "ICC Appeals Chamber Maintains Laurent Gbagbo and Charles Blé Goudé," January 18, 2019.

countries renewed their pledge to withdraw.[192] In Ituri, where Uganda had been a dominant influence since 1999, both countries would continue to sponsor armed factions into 2003 and beyond.

UN peacekeepers began arriving in the Congo in late 1999. Both the UNSC and the Secretary-General followed events closely, through monitors on the ground and in cooperation with concerned European nations. An extensive mapping operation was charting the patterns of violence throughout the Congo, documenting levels of mortality that exceeded those in other large global eruptions, going back to World War II.[193] Reports in 2002 of fresh violence in Ituri, seeming to perpetuate ethnic patterns seen in the Rwanda genocide, came as a profound shock, just as the impetus toward peace was appearing to yield results. The international community had striven mightily to drag the Congo into its post-conflict stage. Thus, the response in Ituri was more muscular intervention after May 2003, first with a European strike force in June, followed by a massive UN presence in September. From the Ituri side, however, peacekeeping efforts were largely ineffective, as conflicts continued within a new configuration of power centers.[194]

Thus, a further explanation arises for the ICC special focus on Ituri suspects. After years of turmoil, the weakness of the central Congolese state was finally being addressed, thanks to the dogged intervention of the international community. Rebel groups were more or less cooperating through agreements on transitional terms, pointing to new national elections. Suffering from "Congo fatigue," donor countries were ready to pin the "post-conflict" label on the whole country, whose struggles had been so thoroughly mapped by outside experts. As Séverine Autesserre described it, a "peacebuilding culture" had "shaped the intervention strategy in the Congo": "International peacebuilders have their own world, with its own rituals, its own customs, its own beliefs, its own roles, its own stars, its own villains, its own rules, its own taboos, its own meeting places – in brief, its own culture."[195] The ICC Congo trials grew out of this culture, eager to project a norm of stability that resonated with all the idealism that had

[192] The peace talks put international pressure on Rwanda and Uganda to withdraw, and their continued presence increased the finger-pointing by international NGO's. Prunier, *Africa's World War*, pp. 269–77.

[193] Office of the High Commissioner on Human Rights, *Report of the Mapping Exercise, March 1993–June 2003* (June 2010).

[194] On the tendency for power-sharing arrangements to perpetuate violence, see Denis M. Tull and Andreas Mehler, "The Hidden Costs of Power-Sharing: Reproducing Insurgent Violence in Africa," *African Affairs* 104 (2005), 375.

[195] Autesserre, *The Trouble with the Congo*, p. 1, on the peacekeeping culture.

brought so many countries together in the 1998 Rome Treaty. The Congo trials put this peacebuilding culture to the test. In Hague courtrooms, however, it seemed that this culture had glossed over complex local dynamics and unresolved tensions – still festering in Ituri but endemic to the eastern provinces, and even elsewhere in the Congo.

3.4 REGIONAL DYNAMICS: RWANDA AND UGANDA

The prospects for nation-building were constrained by neighboring Rwanda and Uganda. The pattern was set in the late 1990s, with two invasions aimed at regime change. By 2002, national reconstruction would need to contend with these regional players, who were supporting the main rebel organizations. Both countries, by selecting allies within rebel ranks, were deeply implicated in the upsurge of local violence in the eastern Congo.

The Congo is so large that it fairly points in many directions. To the east, the country opens out to the Great Lakes region, including Uganda, Rwanda, and Burundi, all of which share borders with the Kivu provinces just south of Ituri. The Ituri violence of 2002–03 grew out of the prior decade of turbulence throughout the eastern provinces, especially the heavy-handed intervention by Rwanda. North and South Kivu provinces were profoundly affected by the fallout from genocidal conflicts in Burundi and Rwanda – epic conflicts among populations divided along ethnic lines, Hutu and Tutsi. Hutu refugees started streaming into the Kivu provinces after the 1993 civil war in Burundi, followed the next year by over a million Hutu from the catastrophic events in Rwanda during summer 1994. The battle-hardened Tutsi-led government in Rwanda, having just ended the genocide in that country, was determined to root out hardline Hutu militants among the refugees, launching military strikes within Congolese territory. These events set the stage for Rwanda and Uganda to sponsor the invasions of 1996 and 1998, both of which sought regime change for the entire Congo. When progress stalled in the second of these invasions, the eastern RCD rebels remained as a proxy force for Rwanda, which continued its aggressive battles with unrepentant Hutu adversaries.[196]

To complicate matters, the Kivus were already home to large numbers of indigenous Congolese with ancestral links to Rwanda, both Tutsi and Hutu – from an era, going back to the nineteenth century, when these

[196] These events are laid out in Prunier, *Africa's World War.*

classifications were less contentious. The surge of refugees after 1993–94, followed by Rwandan military intervention and joint sponsorship of the invasion, ignited strong ethnic divisions inside the Congolese population.[197] There were obvious tensions between those Congolese who shared kinship links with either Hutu or Tutsi. But other local groups in the east were ready to attack anyone of Rwandan heritage – even those whose families had lived in the Congo for generations. Rwandan militancy sharpened these local enmities. As the Rwandan army expanded operations, Hutu militants vowed to return to Rwanda to finish off their Tutsi antagonists. Local Kivu communities were caught in the crossfire and armed themselves for self-defense. Eventually they would mount their own retaliatory attacks. For the time being, these conflicts remained in the Kivus, not yet reaching northward into Ituri.[198]

Alongside these tensions in eastern Congo, local conflicts spread throughout the country following the 1998 invasion, as stalemated rebel groups struggled to hold territory. With its deep ties to Rwanda, the RCD rebel faction brought grassroots conflicts to the surface, as would eventually happen in Ituri. While these conflicts had political and economic origins, they also ignited local ethnic tensions.[199] The international community was quick to assume that ethnic hatred was a major source of such conflicts, based on the model of Tutsi–Hutu conflict in Rwanda. But each area had its own specific dynamics – just as Ituri would provide its own variations. Ethnic rivalries would generally count as both cause and effect of emerging violence.[200] The major rebel organizations were battling for control of Congolese sovereignty, but also for control of lucrative patronage networks, and for enough military strength to protect those networks. These were the greater ambitions that drove Jean-Pierre Bemba's MLC rebel movement, as well as Congolese groups drawn to the RCD movement. In trying to maintain their hold under pressure, these larger organizations learned to exploit ethnic tensions in local affairs.

197 Mahmood Mamdani, *When Victims Become Killers: Colonialism, Nativism, and the Genocide in Rwanda* (Princeton: Princeton University Press, 2001), chapter 8.

198 Reyntjens, *The Great African War*, pp. 207–15.

199 Local dynamics in the Kivu provinces would soon spill over into Ituri. These developments are covered by Vlassenroot and Raeymaekers, *Conflict and Social Transformation in Eastern DR Congo*.

200 Vlassenroot and Raeymaekers, "The Politics of Rebellion," p. 390; Veit, *Intervention as Indirect Rule*, p. 144. See also Johan Pottier, "Displacement and Ethnic Reintegration in Ituri, DR Congo: Challenges Ahead," *Journal of Modern African Studies* 46 (2008), 1; Pottier, "Representations of Ethnicity in the Search for Peace: Ituri, Democratic Republic of the Congo" *African Affairs* 109 (2010), 23.

The international community was slow to question the motives behind Rwandan military ventures, even as the Rwandan armed forces pursued and massacred tens of thousands of Hutu refugees, searching out the perpetrators of the 1994 genocide.[201] Western nations supported the ouster of Mobutu and then rallied behind Joseph Kabila in the negotiations on transitional power-sharing, leading up to the 2006 national elections. After 1999, the United Nations became involved, beginning what would become the largest deployment of UN peacekeepers in any one nation. Officials from the UN, the United States, and Europe all decried the brutality and scale of violence throughout the country, but their solutions remained heavily focused on rebuilding the national political framework. From 1999 to 2003 they pursued peace negotiations to promote reconciliation among national factions, and eventually to end foreign military involvement. In these key discussions, the lowly parochial factions were ignored – leaving many local leaders with few alternatives but to continue fighting.[202]

The Rwandan-sponsored RCD rebel group had a turbulent record during the period 1998–2003. While it began with the strategic goal of ousting Laurent-Désiré Kabila and restoring Rwanda's influence over Congolese affairs, the military stalemate left the RCD struggling to consolidate its hold on the eastern third of the country. As fighting became entrenched, many local Kivu communities armed themselves for self-defense, sometimes cooperating with Hutu forces, and eventually launching counterattacks of their own. Rwanda regarded the RCD presence in eastern Congo as vital to its national security. But militancy came at the expense of popular support, and RCD thus became a polarizing force targeted by local groups.

By 2000, some local resistance groups in the Kivus were being armed and coordinated by elements of the Kinshasa-based national army, taking the fight against Rwandan invaders into the east. The Congolese army, having fended off Rwanda's military challenge with the help of troops from Angola and Zimbabwe, was able to put the RCD and Rwanda on the defensive by allying with Hutu militants among the hundreds of thousands of refugees from Rwanda and Burundi. It drew further support from local defense groups known as Mai-Mai.[203] These were not formal

201 Judi Rever, *In Praise of Blood: The Crimes of the Rwandan Patriotic Front* (Toronto: Random House Canada, 2018).

202 Veit, *Intervention as Indirect Rule*, pp. 146–51.

203 Jason Stearns, *Mai-Mai Yukutumba: Resistance and Racketeering in Fizi, South Kivu* (London: Rift Valley Institute, 2013). See also René Lemarchand, *The Dynamics of Violence in Central Africa* (Philadelphia: University of Pennsylvania Press, 2009), pp. 229–46.

military campaigns, but more rogue operations conducted by elements of the national army. Civilians became easy targets in these struggles, and many local communities took up arms against both Rwandan and Congolese sponsors.

Fostering large rebel movements was likewise a strategic goal for Uganda. Finding itself in open competition with Rwanda after the 1998 invasion got bogged down, Uganda successfully split off a portion of the RCD rebel group and imposed it on Ituri in 1999. Early on, Uganda also embraced Bemba's MLC rebel group as a counterweight to the Rwanda-backed RCD and the national Congolese government. Uganda had its own security concerns inside Congolese borders, as some Ugandan insurgent groups were alleged to have found refuge in the Kivus and in Ituri. Remnants of the dreaded LRA, led by the ruthless Joseph Kony, were holing up across borders from Uganda's northern regions. But some Ugandan officers also saw opportunities to profit from the rich natural resources in the northeast Congo. From 1999, the Ugandan army operated as an occupying force in Ituri, behaving in undisciplined and often contradictory ways. When disorder finally engulfed Ituri with the ouster of Governor Lompondo in August 2002, Uganda tried, with little success and much hypocrisy, to manage the unfolding conflict.[204]

3.5 INTERNATIONAL DYNAMICS: PEACEKEEPERS AS POWERBROKERS

Groups inside Ituri had their own scores to settle. But they did so under a heavy burden of constraints imposed from outside. The Congo trials tended to narrow the frame in such a way that three Ituri men stood at the center of violence and disorder. Yes, there was a broader context; but ICC legal doctrines required a particular angle of vision – one in which these three men standing trial were the authors of events within their field of action.

But the fields of action in Ituri turned out to be more complex and multi-layered. While Chapter 4 will analyze that local complexity in detail, it all remains inseparable from the many layers of pressure coming from outside. Local events reflect the larger agendas of nation-building and regional

[204] On Uganda in the Congo, see John F. Clark, "Museveni's Adventure in the Congo War," in Clark (ed.), *The African Stakes of the Congo War*, chapter 9; on Uganda in Ituri, see Koen Vlassenroot and Sandrine Perrot, "Ugandan Military Entrepreneurialism on the Congo Border," in Utas (ed.), *African Conflicts*, chapter 1.

meddling. A further layer came from international peacekeepers themselves, whose arrival in Ituri in June 2003 opened a new phase of local conflicts, following ten months of disorder. The peacekeepers were expected to spread the post-conflict spirit to this chaotic corner of the country. Instead, it reconfigured the conflict in new ways, in which the peacekeepers themselves became unwitting brokers for new forms of violence.[205] Their arrival, along with the inflow of international NGOs, ignited conflicting narratives about exactly what had taken place between August 2002 and May 2003. The very dynamics of post-conflict administration opened a new phase of posturing by the weary survivors, quickly adjusting to new conditions. Along with new alliances and new violence, scores were being settled under the watchful eye of outside monitors. Stories would be told; fingers would be pointed. It was all part of the continuing struggle played according to outside rules.

The United Nations had already sent peacekeepers into the Congo after the 1999 chaos that followed the ouster of strongman Mobutu Sese Seko. Known as Mission des Nations-Unies au Congo, or "MONUC," it was to become the largest UN mission ever mounted in a single country.[206] From 2002, with a focus on Ituri, the UN strengthened its mission, eventually invoking its Chapter VII powers of military engagement to enforce the peace. Launching that outside military element in Ituri was left to a vanguard of troops authorized by the European Union ("Operation Artemis"), arriving in Ituri in June 2003. The attention of the UNSC and the UN Secretary-General had been focused on Ituri as a pocket of violence threatening the larger national movement toward political reconstruction across the Congo.[207] One UN expert had warned of ongoing "genocide" in the district, sharpening the call to action. Eager to replace the regional influence of Uganda and Rwanda in this district far from the capital Kinshasa, UN and EU military authorities welcomed an infusion of international NGOs ready to assist in pacification and reconciliation.

Despite some short periods of relaxed tensions, MONUC brought with it a new layer of complexity to local conditions in Ituri. When it replaced Uganda and Rwanda as potential sponsors, it became the new focus for diverse local groups jockeying for position. Indeed, the power stakes with MONUC

205 Veit, *Intervention as Indirect Rule*, pp. 146–51.

206 Emily Paddon, *Perils of Peacekeeping without Politics: MONUC and MONUSCO in the DRC* (London: Rift Valley Institute, 2013).

207 Vlassenroot and Raeymaekers, "Politics of Rebellion," p. 400; Veit, *Intervention as Indirect Rule*, pp. 151–63. UNSC Resolution 1493 (July 28, 2003) placed the UN presence under Chapter VII.

became even greater than with mere regional forces. MONUC became the conduit through which ambitious local players might engage with national politics, at a moment when a new transitional power-sharing plan was being rolled out.[208] More immediate prospects for advancement came through the MONUC-brokered demilitarization campaigns. Through MONUC there emerged the prospect of new military opportunities in the Congolese armed forces.[209]

And when these constructive operations failed to deliver, MONUC became the target of new militarized struggle. The UN had authorized MONUC to fight back in its mission to restore order in Ituri. At the extreme, MONUC became another usurping power – perceived as serving the interests of corrupt national politicians. Its superior supply of armaments meant that opposing MONUC would require new alliances using guerrilla tactics.[210] Fifteen years after MONUC established a firm base in Ituri, the district remains wracked by violence. Along with similar disorder in the Kivu provinces to the south, Ituri is still unpacified. Despite the investment from UN coffers, the toll on innocent civilians continues to increase.[211]

208 Veit, *Intervention as Indirect Rule*, p. 185. Jason K. Stearns, "Can Force Be Useful in the Absence of a Political Strategy? Lessons from the UN Missions to the Congo," Congo Research Group, December 2015.

209 Christopher Vogel and Josephat Musamba, *Recycling Rebels? Demobilization in the Congo* (London: Rift Valley Institute, 2016).

210 Veit, *Intervention as Indirect Rule*, pp. 173–80.

211 Jason Stearns, "The Trouble with the Congo: Local Violence and the Failure of International Peacekeeping," *Review of African Political Economy* 40 (2013), 163.

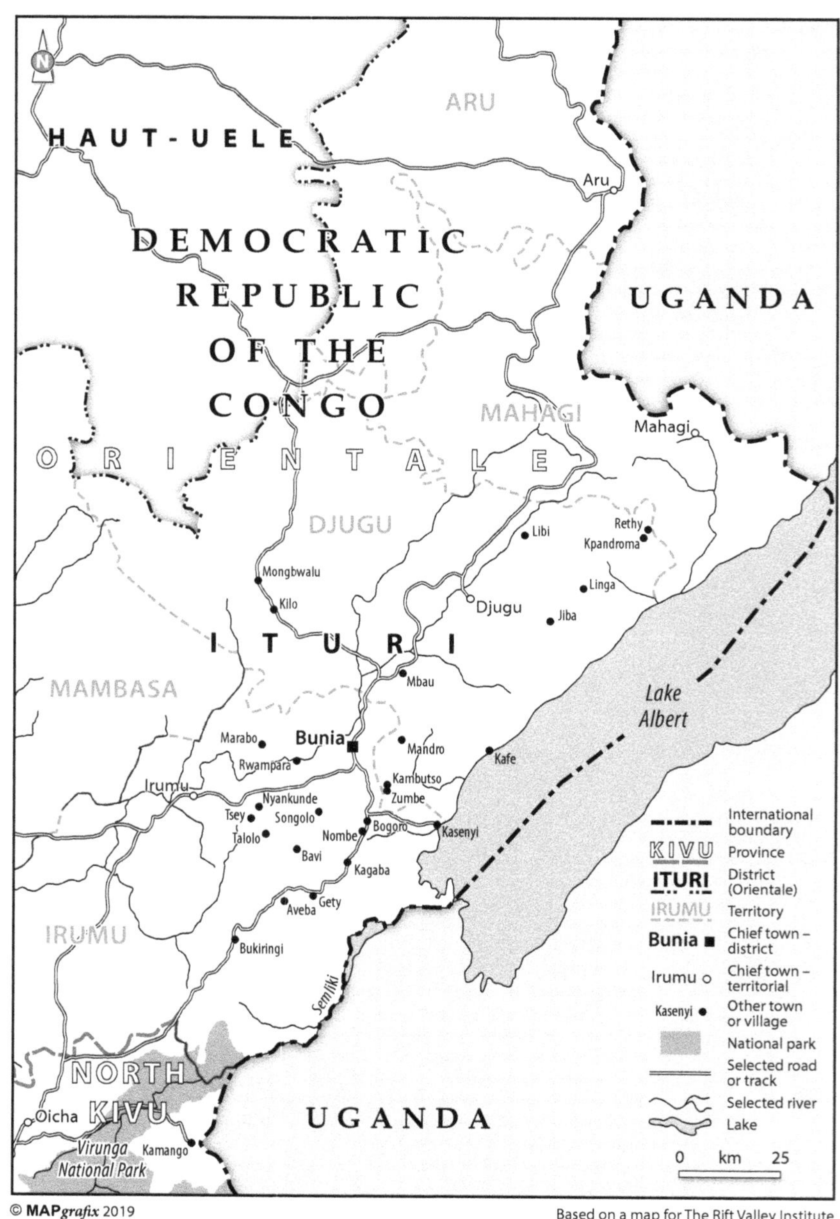

Based on a map for The Rift Valley Institute

Congo: Ituri District

4

Structures of Local Conflict: The Micro View

4.1 RECONSTRUCTING LOCAL EVENTS: THE MYTH OF EQUILIBRIUM

The array of forces outside Ituri determined the scale and scope of conflicts inside the district, especially during the period of interest to the ICC. But those forces alone were not the only ones that mattered. It was their fateful interaction with local dynamics that produced such traumatic effects on the lives and fortunes of everyday Ituri civilians. Local tensions and conflicts contributed their own synergies, giving shape to new patterns of behavior and new structures of violence.

Understanding local factors behind Ituri violence is no easy task. It means reconstructing past events – five, ten, twenty years after the fact – from the further distance of place and culture. At the outset, it is important to lay aside certain simplifying myths about micro-level social events. The myth, for example, that certain peoples are inherently violent, gains little credit these days.[212] To the extent that it survives in international commentary, it feeds on

[212] This line of cultural argument was sometimes used by skeptics of international humanitarian intervention in the 1990s Balkan crisis. In the words of Timothy Garten Ash,

> ... there is a whole regiment of arguments from cultural prejudice. Here are the old saws about ancient hatreds and atavistic tribes. We can't stop people who want to kill each other, I recently heard a senior EU official say. Here is the view that, after all, what else can you expect of the Balkans? This is a view particularly associated in the United States with the work of Robert Kaplan (Balkan Ghosts), but implicit in many other analyses and commentaries.

"Bosnia in Our Future," *New York Review of Books*, December 21, 1995. The same cultural stereotypes might also be used for opposite purposes: to justify the presumption that criminality was the source of widespread violence in the Balkans and in Rwanda – the two places that prompted UN ad hoc tribunals in the 1990s. For the Rwandan case, moving beyond the presumption of criminality, see Scott Straus, *The Order of Genocide* (Ithaca: Cornell University Press, 2008).

the Hobbesian dread of statelessness – a theory cited in Chapter 3 as one justification for international state-building interventions in the Congo during the period 2002–03.

There is also a contrasting myth derived from rationalistic models in social science, found variously in mainstream economics, structural-functional sociology, and cultural criminology: the myth that societies either start from a steady equilibrium state, or are generally tending toward it. In its criminological form, this myth supposes that typical societies observe a strict set of social norms, with any disturbances classified as criminal deviations – coming from within or without. The necessary response is to condemn the criminal acts and restore the norms. Identify and eliminate the alien criminal elements, and societies can return to their natural equilibrium.[213]

Overly facile approaches to war and peace use the same self-adjusting model: peace is the equilibrium state, interrupted one dark day by disruptive war; for which the remedy is to stanch the war and restore the peaceful order. Most studies of war and peace, for both local and global wars, know to complicate these formulas. Especially with internal wars, the deeper causes may reveal fundamental imbalances in the social order. Restoring order begs the question of what the future order should be, if it is to be worth restoring. The rich literature on restorative justice has wrestled with these problems across a vast range of complex cases.[214] The pioneer cultural anthropologist Émile Durkheim identified the central flaw in social and moral equilibrium:

> Every society embodies conflicting factors, simply because it has gradually emerged from a past form and is tending toward a future.[215]

For Ituri – emerging and tending toward an unknown future, driven by local conflicting factors, even as external cyclonic winds were bearing down – these were the dynamic conditions during the critical years 2002–03. It was a twisting path through the dense forest, trodden by diffuse local entities as *alliance*

[213] Gerry Simpson treats this view as "the evil man view" of history: "War crimes trials describe a world of bad men doing evil deeds. The problem is the man: 'no man, no problem . . .'"; *Law, War and Crime* (Cambridge: Polity Press, 2007), p. 157. For a close critique of the equilibrium thesis, see Stathis N. Kalyvas, Ian Shapiro, and Tarek Masoud (eds.), *Order, Conflict, and Violence* (Cambridge: Cambridge University Press, 2008), especially the opening chapter by the editors, asserting that "order and violence are inextricably intertwined," and that under some circumstances "violence is used to create order, to maintain it, and to uphold it in the face of challenges."

[214] Pierre Hazan, *Judging War, Judging History: Behind Truth and Reconciliation* (Stanford: Stanford University Press, 2010).

[215] Émile Durkheim, *Montesquieu and Rousseau* (Ann Arbor: University of Michigan Press, 1960), p. 59 (originally published in 1953 based on Durkheim's 1892 Latin dissertation).

networks, working from the parochial group formations found in the district. The unpredictable outputs from these fragile networks differed sharply from what one would expect in societies moving through the sunshine toward efficient equilibrium. For Ituri, the standard legal paradigms and presumptions found little to work with. The resulting complexity provoked a series of crises in each of the Congo trials.

It was surely the hope of understanding this complexity that prompted the wistful plea from judges in the trial of Germain Katanga and Mathieu Ngudjolo. After it became clear (to all but the Prosecution) that Katanga and Ngudjolo did not fit the original template of violence "masterminds," the Chamber must have realized that there was much more about Ituri society and culture it wanted to know – indeed *needed* to know. Its curiosity spilled over in questions from the bench, even if the witnesses in court might lack the experience or impartiality to speak fully. "In fact, much of the socio-cultural framework was discussed in response to the Chamber's questions. In the Chamber's view, this material should have been discussed at the beginning of the Prosecution's presentation of its evidence so as to prompt a more informed debate from the start."[216]

4.2 INVESTIGATORS IN THE FIELD

Reconstructing conditions during this period in Ituri requires close attention to sources. The ICC faced practical challenges in trying to understand Ituri local dynamics, despite the mountains of evidence introduced in court. For observers today, the challenge is even greater, after such a great tangle of local facts have passed through the funnel of protracted court proceedings. After the severe Prosecutorial narrowing of the case, followed by the vigorous adversarial response throughout the Congo trials, a forensic haze now hangs over this contested terrain. Even today, tracking down former combatants in Ituri is likely to elicit partisan truths. International criminal justice may seek to create a definitive historical record of past traumatic events. But in the case of the Congo trials, the short-term result has been to deepen the mystery of that faraway place.

During 2003–04, only a handful of academic field researchers were on the ground in eastern Congo (mainly in the Kivus), taking observations close to the same moment that humanitarian and adversarial voices were digging into their local sources. Using models built up over the prior decade of research in Africa and Asia, they sought to explain how the violence flared up and how it

[216] Ngudjolo Trial Judgment, December 18, 2012, ICC-01/04-02/12-3, para. 123.

was organized. The underlying dynamics were starkly different from the Prosecution story about tightly run organizations, led by supreme commanders, guided by detailed planning documents, and fixated on criminal goals. It is these contrasting research findings that will be featured in this chapter, independent of the discourses that animated the trials themselves.[217]

By contrast, the ICC Prosecutor, preparing to frame the Congo cases, was inspired by a separate group of experts on the ground in Ituri. Knowledgeable and resourceful, these investigators were rhetorically bold and passionately committed to the humanitarian ideals of global NGOs. They knew what they wanted to hear, and then leapt to sweeping conclusions. Their powerful reports created the conceptual bridge to the ICC Prosecutor's cases, using the paradigms and presumptions featured in the courtroom. Their work will be examined separately in Chapter 5.[218]

For field investigators in an active conflict zone, the search for objective or impartial witnesses is indeed daunting. After March 2003, Ituri (and especially the capital city of Bunia, virtually the only place safe enough for outsiders) was filled with witnesses saying highly contradictory things about recent conflicts, often for self-serving reasons. The humanitarian NGOs built much of their argument on the testimonials of individual victims – whose voices would later resonate in the courtroom during the Congo trials. Once these NGO reports were published, and certainly after the Congo trials began, some commentators have come to treat humanitarian sources and court findings as established facts. As time goes by, this way of reconstructing history can become an echo chamber for lofty ideals. Carried to the extreme, it misses important reasons why the Congo trials hit a series of brick walls.[219] The research used in this

[217] Among these studies from Ituri, the closest in time was published in 2004 by two Belgian researchers: Koen Vlassenroot and Timothy Raeymaekers, "The Politics of Rebellion and Intervention in Ituri: The Emergence of a New Political Complex?" *African Affairs* 103 (2004), 385. Vlassenroot visited Bunia in summer 2003 and conducted interviews with recent combatants. At some points the analysis relies on NGO reports, including the HRW report cited in the following footnote.

[218] The key work was HRW, *Ituri: "Covered in Blood": Ethnically Targeted Violence in Northeastern DR Congo* (2003). The July publication of this report (to be discussed in Chapter 5) shifted the international discourse on Ituri into terms taken from the Rome Statute. With its vivid eye-witness accounts and willingness to point fingers, this report has become a standard reference for Ituri violence, along with contemporary UN documents.

[219] This tendency clouds the work of Jim Freedman, *A Conviction in Question: The First Trial at the International Criminal Court* (Toronto: University of Toronto Press, 2017). An anthropologist with his own field experience in Ituri, Freedman projects his broad humanitarian commitments onto the Prosecutor's narrative. When it comes to explaining the numerous crises of the Lubanga case, Freedman faults the arid formalism of courtroom procedure, while lamenting the amoral tenacity of defense attorneys and the personal quirks of the presiding trial judge. Freedman's analysis will be discussed in Chapter 7.

chapter has generally sidestepped these activist perspectives on Ituri, to explore new accounts and explanations.

Local tensions contributed decisively to the maelstrom of Ituri violence. Interacting with broader trends, it was local economics, living conditions (including land use), and competition between networked alliances that shaped the critical months of 2002–03. At the center of overlapping forces on multiple levels, what emerged in Ituri was a particular structure of localized violence, following patterns identified by researchers in other parts of Africa. The applicable research raises important alternatives to the standard narrative used by the ICC Prosecutor in the Congo trials.

Political Dynamics in Ituri: Three Phases

A short chronology of events will bring these multiple layers of causation down to local realities of Ituri, starting from the 1999 upsurge of conflict. Local actors and adversaries confronted each other through diffuse networks of influence, marking out new forms of conflict that diverged from traditional models of warfare. These new and unfamiliar structures would cause the ICC serious distress, when they failed to fit comfortably within legal templates descended from military campaigns in twentieth-century Europe. Over the first decade of ICC proceedings, the Congo trials brought these important structural differences to the surface.

RCD-ML in Ituri (November 1999–August 2002)

While Rwanda remained dominant in the Kivu provinces, Ituri fell under the sway of Uganda. Uganda kept a close watch on Ituri affairs through a steady flow of military officers, operating independently from their superiors in Kampala. In late 1999, the Ugandans welcomed to Bunia the breakaway RCD rebel group known as RCD-ML as the nominal government. Uganda would make passing attempts to lure Bemba's MLC rebel group to Ituri as well, including a short-lived plan to create a grand coalition of national rebel groups.[220] Ituri was caught in the web of these proxy dynamics, and the road to violence in 2002–03 was prepared by RCD-ML's failure to provide effective governance, amidst falling out with Ugandan sponsors. With its kinship ties to ethnic Nande trading networks, RCD-ML leadership alienated Ituri's main business elites, while manipulating ethnic tensions in a losing effort to extend its hold on the district. From the time of its arrival in Bunia, the RCD-ML was

[220] David van Reybrouck, *Congo: The Epic History of a People* (New York: HarperCollins, 2014), pp. 439–58.

prone to fragmentation and defection.[221] The polarization of Ituri groups had many other causes too, but it was heightened by RDC-ML's vain effort to survive.

The RCD-ML faced limited options when it staggered into Bunia in 1999. This splinter group emerged in the frustration of military objectives after the original RCD rebel advance toward Kinshasa was repulsed in early 1999 by forces of the national Congolese army, backed up by assistance from Angola and Zimbabwe. RCD also met with stiff competition from Jean-Pierre Bemba's MLC rebel movement. Under these circumstances, tensions within RCD broke out between Rwandan and Ugandan sponsors, resulting in the two separate factions. The Ugandan-backed RCD-ML, when it moved to Ituri in late 1999, was led by former history professor Ernest Wamba dia Wamba, who came originally from the far-Western Congo, near the capital Kinshasa, by way of Tanzania and Kalamazoo in the United States. His next-in-command, Antipas Mbusa Nyamwisi, came from a family of Nande traders, an ethnic group from North Kivu whose commercial ambitions were resented by Ituri's indigenous elites. The RCD-ML was now constrained by their Rwandan-backed RCD rivals to the south, and by Bemba's MLC armies to the west. Meanwhile the Congolese national army was encroaching on the eastern Congo, as it started recruiting among local self-defense groups, and stirring up Mai-Mai and Hutu militants in the Kivu provinces. In concert with RCD-ML, Kinshasa would soon foster similar alliances with Lendu groups in Ituri.[222]

Between 1999 and 2002, the RCD-ML failed to establish a stable administrative regime in Ituri. The leadership was caught up in constant rivalries, and its links to Ugandan patrons were generally freelance business connections, granting access to natural resources. Within the RCD-ML, rival leaders found independent support through competing ethnic ties, including links to local Hema business elites.[223] Feeling its own ambitions, the Hema faction grew suspicious of RCD-ML's increasing focus on Nande elites in North Kivu, on Lendu armed groups in Ituri, and (before long) on elements of the Congolese national army.[224]

[221] Alex Veit, *Intervention as Indirect Rule: Civil War and Statebuilding in the Democratic Republic of the Congo* (Frankfurt: Campus, 2010), pp. 114–25.

[222] Jason K. Stearns, *Dancing in the Glory of Monsters: The Collapse of the Congo and the Great War of Africa* (New York: Public Affairs, 2011), chapters 14–15.

[223] Filip Reyntjens, *The Great African War: Congo and Regional Geopolitics, 1996–2006* (Cambridge: Cambridge University Press, 2009), pp. 241–43.

[224] Vlassenroot and Raeymaekers, "The Politics of Rebellion," p. 396.

The first signs of fracture within the organization occurred in mid-2000, when a group of mainly Hema military officers within the RCD-ML's armed units mutinied against their superiors. They approached Uganda President Museveni to voice their grievances, choosing Thomas Lubanga as one of their spokesmen. Lubanga, a university graduate, had been working as a vegetable trader in Bunia's main market; but his education made him a useful representative. The Ugandans started playing both sides: imposing a temporary truce on RCD-ML while cultivating this Hema group, offering them special military training, including some time spent with Bemba's forces in Équateur Province.[225]

By the end of 2000, the professorial Wamba was ousted as RCD-ML leader by his deputy, the Nande outsider Mbusa Nyamwisi, who in turn appointed as his deputy an ethnic Hema, John Tibasima. As a former director of important mining operations in Ituri, Tibasima was adept in facilitating commercial ventures for Ugandan patrons. In a strategic gesture, during 2001 they played along with Uganda's wild hedge in proposing a grand alliance with Jean-Pierre Bemba's MLC group. But Nyamwisi was soon building strategic ties to the national Congolese government. In early 2001, he had already traveled to Kinshasa to meet with Joseph Kabila, not long after Kabila's father's assassination. Nyamwisi tried to sell himself as "Kinshasa's man in the north-east" as part of the shift toward reconciliation.[226] By 2002, both Nyamwisi and Tibasima were spending time in South Africa on the fringes of the Inter-Congolese Dialogue, hoping to gain a foothold in power-sharing negotiations. The Dialogue would eventually offer rebel leaders like Nyamwisi the prospect of some national political role, with the understanding that joining early would bring rewards.

None of this went over well back home in Ituri. The mutinous RCD-ML Hema officers, now more confident after additional military training facilitated by Uganda, challenged Nyamwisi over his military alliances with Lendu armed groups and his links to larger influence networks in North Kivu and Kinshasa. They saw the appointment of the improbable Governor Lompondo as a further insult. In June 2002, they managed to take over half of the city of Bunia, setting off alarms in surrounding precincts.[227]

This time Uganda's intervention made matters worse. Desperate to maintain its hold on Ituri, it was still playing both sides. Uganda pretended to seek

225 Henning Tamm, *UPC in Ituri: The External Militarization of Local Politics in North-Eastern Congo* (London: Rift Valley Institute, 2013), pp. 17–20.

226 Ibid., p. 25.

227 Ibid., pp. 23–26.

reconciliation between Nyamwisi's RCD-ML and the mutinous officers. After inviting the mutineers to Kampala, the Ugandans clumsily proceeded to arrest several of them, including Thomas Lubanga and Bosco Ntaganda. While Lubanga was packed off to Kinshasa for a couple of months – and thus absent from Ituri during this critical period – the military officers formed a guerrilla cell. With heavy weapons support from Uganda, they staged a final push against Nyamwisi, driving him back to North Kivu, along with his despised front-man Governor Lompondo – now shoeless. With backing from network patrons, members of the mutineers made secret contact with Rwanda as an alternative to their unreliable Ugandan patrons. But for the moment, when it came time to dispatch Nyamwisi and Governor Lompondo, the Ugandan military was happy to assist. Uganda was not ready to accommodate the national Congolese dialogue, and wanted to maintain its dominance in Ituri under any circumstances.[228]

UPC in Ituri (September 2002–March 2003)

Out of this matrix of alliances, ambitions, corruption, and betrayals, Bunia faced a moment of anarchy. Hema-dominated commercial interests found common cause with the mutineers and their civilian allies, fostering a new political group known as the Union patriotique Congolais (UPC). Entering a political vacuum, and as an organization founded in crisis – short on affirmative goals – the UPC declared their mission as protecting Ituri from the predations of Kivu-based opportunists.[229] At this point the RCD-ML, from its North Kivu base, had thrown in its lot with the South African political agreements, hoping to gain national standing. The UPC could now introduce themselves locally as the only hope for Ituri self-rule, while at the same time trying to project the image of a robust organization – angling to be included in the national reconciliation talks.

But in the end, the coalition of UPC figures could not shed their patronage relations to Ugandan generals, to their clandestine Rwandan handlers, and to the Hema elites in Bunia and surrounding districts who had fostered their creation. As a candidate for inclusion in national talks, the UPC aspired to be a vanguard movement for protecting all of Ituri; but their more immediate mission was sheer survival. Their tenuous effort at governance lasted just a shade beyond seven months. During this time, they would host the desperate

[228] Ibid.

[229] A series of mission statements shifted among themes of Ituri self-determination, protection of civilians, and the right to representation in national reconciliation talks. Vlassenroot and Raeymaekers, "The Politics of Rebellion," pp. 396–97.

ambitions of local figures, including Thomas Lubanga, who was named as UPC President, acceptable both to the commercial elites and to the ex-mutineers. From the beginning, UPC held together several factions, with diverse leaders ready to go their separate ways.[230]

As with similar groups in other parts of the Congo, it has been difficult to pin down the structure and capabilities of the UPC. They were a mixed blend of "parochial groups" and "militarized politics," combining (however ineffectively) functions of local governance and armed conflict. Neither the political wing nor the military wing matched up with textbook models of their respective functions. But this kind of hybrid parochial organization was becoming the norm in the unsettled conditions of the Congo.[231]

In response to its unstable environment, the UPC wrestled with multiple and conflicting goals. On the one hand, they would champion Ituri's local autonomy, standing up to the Ugandan occupiers, to nationalist Congolese bullying, and to power-sharing ambitions of Kivu-based elites. On the other hand, there were deepening tensions within Ituri, after ethnic Lendu communities created their own village-based armed defense groups, fearing the dominance of Ugandan-supported ethnic Hema in Ituri affairs. In short, the UPC was caught in a dilemma between governance and security. Their governance ambitions would require stable cooperation across all the ethnic communities of Ituri – which contains upwards of fifteen ethnic groups. During their short period of control, they made numerous gestures toward ethnic reconciliation. On the other side, the UPC's military requirements depended on strict solidarity with the Hema business elites and with trained

[230] Ibid. There is considerable controversy about when the UPC was "founded," an overly precise concept given the rapidly shifting strategic circumstances. In an effort to present themselves as serious players, the mutineers in September 2000 issued documents using the UPC name – leading to the conclusion that this date marked the beginning of a stable organization (a view supported by NGOs and the ICC Prosecutor). Further programmatic statements were issued after April 2002, as the conflict with RCD-ML came to a head and the mutineers wanted to be taken seriously. It was not until September 2002 (after Lubanga returned from detention in Kinshasa) that any real structures were put in place, including the integration of an armed wing. Functionally, this was the moment when the UPC tested its own strength as a coherent alliance of forces. The otherwise independent expert Henning Tamm specifies September 2000 as the moment of creation (*UPC in Ituri*, p. 20). But Tamm also notes that others place the date in mid-2002, considering the earlier date as marking the creation of a loose "discussion group." Vlassenroot and Raeymaekers specify July 2002 (p. 396). More important than any starting date is the time analysis of structures and capacities, which were inchoate (at best) prior to September 2002 and highly brittle thereafter.

[231] On "parochial" groups, see William Reno, *Warfare in Independent Africa* (Cambridge: Cambridge University Press, 2011), chapter 6, summarizing prior decades of research across Africa. The concept is developed further in Paul Staniland, *Networks of Rebellion: Explaining Insurgent Cohesion and Collapse* (Ithaca: Cornell University Press, 2014).

mostly Hema military officers, opposing the broad alliance of suspect groups led by RCD-ML. They could not disguise strong internal pressures for ethnic mobilization. During the critical period from September 2002 to March 2003, these dilemmas marked the realities facing UPC President Thomas Lubanga, his associates, and his numerous rivals.[232]

The brief UPC initiative in Ituri ended in massive failure after just seven months. Given the conflicting goals and unforgiving environment, their prospects were never strong. But when failure came, it was rooted in all three levels of region, nation, and locality. Regionally, the UPC could not balance their dual dependence on rivals Uganda and Rwanda. Ugandan strongmen were still powerful in Ituri precincts, unwilling to abandon lucrative access to natural resources. Uganda never gave up control of the Bunia airport, forcing the UPC to use provincial airfields whenever they wanted to shield their movements from the Ugandans. The Rwandan connection had been created out of desperation, but it would damage the UPC's political strength, given local distrust of Rwandan ambitions.

By January 2003, Uganda retaliated against the UPC by peeling off key political and military associates, setting up rival proxies in an increasingly chaotic environment. The Rwandans had little interest in Ituri beyond exploiting natural resources, and by March of 2003 they were no longer willing to underwrite the UPC's tenuous hold on Bunia. By February, the UPC military arm came under sustained attack, as Uganda lent its support to a military alliance spearheaded by RCD-ML, augmented by national Congolese army units, and with the cooperation of Lendu armed groups. In March 2003, the UPC were driven out of Bunia, finished off by the Ugandans.[233] Amid the chaos of this period, and after Uganda suddenly withdrew its own forces during April, the UPC (supported once again by Rwanda) would return in mid-May for a two-week final stand. But by late May 2003 the UPC were done with governing. Preceded by a European emergency strike force, the UN would expand its Congo mission to bring Ituri back – ever so slowly – into the national framework.

At the national level, the UPC were too obscure to qualify for power-sharing discussions, which were completed in late 2002. Just as the UPC was losing its grip in Bunia in 2003, the internationally brokered national dialogue cobbled together its power-sharing plan, combining the Kabila national government and the two largest rebel groups, Bemba's MLC and the Rwanda-backed branch of RCD, whose leaders became transitional Vice-Presidents. The

[232] Veit, *Intervention as Indirect Rule*, pp. 124–43.
[233] Vlassenroot and Raeymaekers, "Politics of Rebellion," pp. 397–98.

smaller rebel groups (including Nyamwisi's RCD-ML, still based in North Kivu) were encouraged to compete as political parties in elections projected for 2006. The failure to include the local Ituri groups was barely noted in 2003.

A separate process – also internationally supported – would promote an Ituri Pacification Commission, in which all contending Ituri groups might participate.[234] It was a moment when previous network alliances and ethnic ties would unravel and find new configurations. But from March 2003, some deposed UPC figures saw little advantage in this process and remained on the sidelines, thus distancing themselves further from the national drift toward reconciliation. Later initiatives would offer former rebels the opportunity to integrate with the Congolese national army, in a formal demobilization process. The UPC remnants, including Thomas Lubanga, remained on the periphery of these demobilization efforts too, at least for a while.

MONUC (September 2003–June 2010[235])

Ituri politics and society had broken down utterly within a period of four years, beginning in 1999. That final year was toxic for Ituri civilians, particularly those in Bunia and in surrounding districts with militarized villages. National political reconciliation had no immediate impact here in the far corner of the country. When the UPC was ousted from Bunia for the last time in late May 2003, the UN faced the same anarchic conditions. Uganda had finally withdrawn during the month of April. The European strike force had stabilized the capital by early June. This allowed time for the UN to expand its Congo mission, known as MONUC, with additional troops arriving in September.[236]

The countryside remained dangerous, with continuing waves of violence beyond the reach of MONUC. Over time, alongside continued ethnic score-settling, still different patterns started to emerge, with local fighters from a mix of ethnic groups banding together to challenge the joint UN/Congolese mandate in Ituri. Some leaders of former Lendu units joined with those

[234] The Ituri Pacification Commission, formally launched in February 2003, grew out of the September 2002 Luanda agreement between Uganda and Congolese national authorities. That agreement's call for withdrawal of Ugandan troops was clearly ignored. See Gérard Prunier, *Africa's World War: Congo, the Rwandan Genocide, and the Making of a Continental Catastrophe* (Oxford: Oxford University Press, 2009), pp. 292–93.

[235] The UN mission remained in the Congo after this date with a new acronym – MONUSCO. See UNSC Resolution 1925, May 28, 2010.

[236] See Emily Paddon, *The Perils of Peacekeeping without Politics: MONUC and MONUSCO in the DRC* (London: Rift Valley Institute, 2013); Veit, *Intervention as Indirect Rule*, chapter 4; Denis M. Tull, "Peacekeeping in the Democratic Republic of Congo: Waging Peace and Fighting War," *International Peacekeeping* 16 (2009), 215.

from former Hema units, teaming up with other ethnic groups, including Congolese Tutsi commanders like Bosco Ntaganda. Ethnicity lost its strategic importance in this new configuration of local resistance.[237]

Ituri pacification was nonetheless a high priority for UN officials, backed by the UNSC. Although local groups were not part of the national power-sharing scheme, Ituri fighters were given the opportunity to lay down arms and join the national Congolese army. It was during this process that various men emerged from the shadows, presenting themselves as former commanders, even when their roles in previous fighting could not be easily verified. There was a moment in March 2003 when NGO staff on the ground first encountered Mathieu Ngudjolo and Germain Katanga, among others claiming to have masterminded attacks by Lendu groups carried out in preceding months. It may have been boasting for the sake of gaining attention and status, with an eye to the well-funded demobilization process. But it was enough to supply evidence to the ICC Prosecutor years later, who would try to reconstruct these obscure armed coalitions.

4.3 ALLIANCE NETWORKS IN ITURI

Parochial Formations

During the period August 2002–May 2003, the conflict in Ituri was intense. But the underlying conditions had been taking shape from at least 1999. Early on, the militarized status of region and nation encouraged the formation of local armed groups, originally aimed at self-protection. As in other parts of the Congo, some Ituri groups received more advanced weapons from outside sponsors, evolving from spontaneous self-defense forces, moving up to joint attacks on nearby enemy camps, often with dire consequences for the civilians living in the midst. Local defense groups gained support from social, economic, and political networks. In turn, these under-resourced networks sought ties to national rebel groups, and through them – or even more directly – with regional powers Rwanda or Uganda.

The conflicts grew increasingly brutal with civilian killings, sexual violence against women, and conscription of children – perpetrated by all the warring groups. Similar upgrades in localized violence were occurring elsewhere across the Congo – including the Kivus, where village-based self-defense groups, including the Mai-Mai, joined the carnage.[238] These patterns had

[237] Veit, *Intervention as Indirect Rule*, p. 174.

[238] Koen Vlassenroot, *South Kivu: Identity, Territory, and Power in the Eastern Congo* (London: Rift Valley Institute, 2013).

already been seen in earlier conflicts, going back to 1996, involving Rwandan and Ugandan-sponsored insurgents, as well as the MLC rebels and the Congolese national army.[239] As military assistance permeated the microcosm of local groups, more violence descended to the village level, killing, maiming, and displacing large numbers of innocent civilians.

In the shadow of national and regional patronage systems, the purely local dynamics within Ituri remain difficult to classify. Much commentary by NGOs, the courts, and even academic researchers relies on stock terms like "militias" and "warlords" to cover a diverse range of local organizations and leaders. The reality on the ground deserves a more nuanced description.[240] Popular wisdom attributes extreme events to psychological motives at the level of ethnic hatred and personal greed.[241] In reality, the destruction in Ituri was coordinated through diverse networks of group action, as rival players exploited brittle alliances to achieve multiple, often conflicting goals. In the decades since Ituri's most violent period, the rush by commentators to assign personal blame has had the effect of obscuring these essential but diffuse network structures. Rights advocates tend to turn things around, starting from legal paradigms and moral outrage in search of classic criminal perpetrators, working through more familiar organizational structures. At the end of any analysis, to be sure, there must be plenty of blame to go around. To explain events in their full complexity is not to justify the actions of anyone involved – something that must wait, in the fullness of time, for the process of courtroom trials to unfold.

Rival Alliance Networks

Just as the main conflicts were centered more in the Kivu provinces than in Ituri, it was the same with social scientists in the period 1998–2003. Starting with a thin representation of humanitarian aid workers in Bunia throughout 2002, more rights investigators would make their way slowly to Ituri during the final days of the 2002–03 cycle of events. A few social scientists were able to assess conditions in Ituri very close to this period, beginning with a 2004 article

239 Jason Stearns, Judith Verweijen, and Maria Eriksson Baaz, *The National Army and Armed Groups in the Eastern Congo* (London: Rift Valley Institute, 2013); Jason Stearns, "Causality and Conflict: Tracing the Origins of Armed Groups in Eastern Congo," *Peacebuilding* 2 (2014), 157.

240 See Mats Utas (ed.), *African Conflicts and Informal Power: Big Men and Networks* (London: Zed Books, 2012).

241 On this tendency, see the essays in Karen Ballentine and Jake Sherman (eds.), *The Political Economy of Armed Conflict: Beyond Greed and Grievance* (Boulder: Lynne Reiner, 2003).

by Belgian researchers Koen Vlassenroot and Timothy Raeymaekers.[242] Their theories built on empirical studies of armed insurgencies elsewhere in Africa and around the world.[243]

According to Vlassenroot and Raeymaekers, the key structural units during this period in Ituri were loose alliance networks – highly adaptable, diversified, but fatally prone to defections. As a "new political complex," these alliances emerged from older patronage networks used extensively in the black-market economy of the Mobutu era, expanding into the fragmented political environment of the 1990s.[244] These networks combined multiple identities (social class, ethnic group, political party; often all three together) as a strategy for survival under harsh conditions.[245]

In Ituri around 1999, one dominant patronage network was composed of landowners and business elites from the Northern Hema (Gegere) ethnic group. This group began with many social advantages as far back as the colonial period: better access to education, more government cronies, and preferred links to commercial ventures, including exploitation of rich natural resources.[246] Their major competitor was the Nande patronage network, based in Beni in North Kivu but active in Ituri, particularly at the trading borders with Uganda.[247] Thus a further challenge for the Hema network was to compete for attention from Ugandan military elites, who had their own

242 "The Politics of Rebellion."

243 For the Kivus in the early 2000s and broader applications, see Zacharia Mampilly, *Rebel Rulers: Insurgent Governance and Civilian Life During War* (Ithaca: Cornell University Press, 2011), especially chapters 6 and 8.

244 This pattern is elaborated by Paul D. Williams, *War and Conflict in Africa* (Cambridge: Polity Press, 2011), chapter 3 on "Neopatrimonialism." For eastern Congo see Koen Vlassenroot and Timothy Raeymaekers, "The Formation of Centres of Profit, Power, and Protection," Occasional Paper of the Centre of African Studies, University of Edinburgh, January 2005. See also the references to "mutuelles" as economic/ethnic networks in the Kivus, in René Lemarchand, *The Dynamics of Violence in Central Africa* (Philadelphia: University of Pennsylvania Press, 2009), chapter 13.

245 See Mark Duffield, "War as a Network Enterprise: The New Security Terrain and Its Implications," *Cultural Values* 6 (2002), 153. The network concept is discussed extensively in Duffield's book *Global Governance and the New Wars: The Merging of Development and Security* (London: Zed Books, 2001).

246 Vlassenroot and Raeymaekers, "The Politics of Rebellion," p. 396.

247 On the Nande network, see Koen Vlassenroot and Timothy Raeymaekers, *Conflict and Social Transformation in Eastern DR Congo* (Ghent: Academia Press, 2004), chapter 2. See also Ruben de Koning, "Big Men Commanding Conflict Resources: The Democratic Republic of the Congo," in Mats Utas (ed.), *African Conflicts*, p. 236. De Koning analyzes the post-1998 eastern Congo war economy as a hybrid structure "between warlordism and network enterprise" (pp. 232–42). For an economic assessment, emphasizing brokerage elements of trading networks, see Timothy Raeymaekers, *Violent Capitalism and Hybrid Identity in the Eastern Congo* (Cambridge: Cambridge University Press, 2014).

commercial ambitions in Ituri. With the Ugandans playing both sides, the struggle between patronage networks caused inevitable tensions within the RCD-ML rebel faction during 2002, as the Nande leader Mbusa Nyamwisi ultimately lost the struggle against the mutinous set of Hema fighters who went on to form the UPC.[248]

Just as networked patronage structures operate differently from normal commercial enterprises, so are networked military organizations different from self-standing armies or militias. Under the conditions studied by Vlassenroot and Raeymaekers, alliance networks in Ituri required both political and military extensions, in a district where political authority was weak and security was heavily threatened. Any political or economic initiative in Ituri had no choice but to find support within established networks. The same was true with security concerns at the local level – including the ubiquitous self-defense units that popped up in small Ituri villages, which needed economic and social backing from stronger networks. In Ituri, as in most other places in the Congo, military action was thus inextricably linked to political ambitions; and politics was invariably militarized.[249]

Comparative studies from other parts of the globe provide insights into how such structures may have operated in the Congo. In general, parochial groups seek to project a sense of organizational solidity. Out of weakness, parochial leaders must address the symbolic elements of political authority. An alliance network may adopt an impressive organizational name; associates may assign each other political/military titles like President, Chief of Staff, Commander in Chief. Parochial leaders – who function more as network "brokers" – may draft organization charts (often fanciful) that imply more grassroots support than they can reliably count on. They may build tenuous, fleeting alliances with rival groups. These pseudo-organizations may also invent prior histories; they may institute rituals of statecraft or military prowess; they may seek publicity from local or regional news outlets. Using new media technologies, they may video themselves in training camps, carrying out military drills, breaking out in patriotic song. For parochial patronage networks, broad gestures of governance may include some or all these strategies.[250]

[248] Henning Tamm, *UPC in Ituri*, pp. 17–23.

[249] Anthropologist Danny Hoffman speaks to "the militarization of a social network rather than . . . a military organization"; "The Meaning of a Militia: Understanding the Civil Defence Forces of Sierra Leone," *African Affairs* 106 (2007), p. 639.

[250] See Staniland, *Networks of Rebellion*, especially pp. 30–32 on the symbolic functions of organization charts, and brokerage models of leadership. See also Zacharia Mampilly, "Performing the Nation-State: Rebel Governance and Symbolic Processes," in Ana Arjona, Nelson Kafsir, and Zacharia Mampilly (eds.), *Rebel Governance in Civil War* (Cambridge: Cambridge University Press, 2015), chapter 4.

The fact remains that such bootstrap patronage networks are inherently fragile. To strengthen vertical ties, ethnic solidarity can provide some degree of internal loyalty. But the problem with parochial alliance groups is their weak horizontal ties among principals, where minor disagreements and setbacks ignite fresh disputes, internal revolts, and the formation of competing networks. Despite their pretensions to govern, the overriding challenge for parochial groups is sheer survival.[251]

Network structures have special characteristics, straddling the common social science variables of "structure" and "agency."[252] The actions of such alliances cannot be imputed to single individuals, independent of positional roles within fluid structures. As a result, action outcomes are nonlinear, spontaneous, and "emergent" – where the collective sum is larger than its individual components. Individual network actors may be assumed to have rational intentions, but their range is constrained by relational factors outside their control. Plans of some kind may have been articulated early on; but the complex results cannot be used to infer back to what those original plans must have been. Outputs bear little direct relationship to the prior choices or intentions of individual network actors, even for people situated near the center of an evolving system.[253]

Applying these field research models to conditions in Ituri during the period 1998–2003, it is possible to see some deeper coherence in the chaotic flow of events. This analysis differs from interpretations coming from leading NGOs, which will be fully explored in Chapter 5. Within the complex environment of Ituri, the purpose here is to articulate the distinctive governance model through which local actors were constrained to operate: a fragile system of parochial alliances, based on remnants of patronage. Events in Ituri were especially complex, as this local pattern was augmented by links to national rebel coalitions (RCD and MLC) and by regional links to Uganda and Rwanda. The Ituri action networks sought leverage within these broader, more powerful movements, only to find new pressures for fragmentation.[254]

In addition to such powerful external forces, parochial networks face a series of challenges from internal competition and local roadblocks. When they

[251] Staniland explores the strains of managing weak horizontal ties, which, in turn, can reduce the comparative strength of vertical ties linking different layers of cooperating units. Ethnic links may bring the various layers together, but they do not preclude feuds and defections at the upper layers. *Networks of Rebellion*, pp. 49–55.

[252] Duffield, *Global Governance*, pp. 146–47.

[253] For a technical analysis of "emergence," see Jeffrey Goldstein, "Emergence as a Construct: History and Issues," *Emergence* 1 (1999), 49.

[254] Vlassenroot and Raeymaekers, "The Politics of Rebellion," p. 397.

establish temporary dominance in each area, their impact can be substantial for ordinary civilians living in the shadows of improvised governance. When these networks rely on ethnic ties, the structure of opportunities may be tightly constrained for the general population – especially those who find themselves cast in the position of ethnic rivals or outsiders. In urban areas like Bunia in Ituri, economic opportunity depended on one's capacity to enter into prevailing or rival networks.[255] When the inevitable rivalries ignite back-and-forth attacks, all hope for escaping violence will have vanished. The pressure to defend one's network leads to an escalation of mutual destruction.

Command structures operate differently in such diversified networks, even if individual members insist on using traditional titles like President, Commander, or Chief of Staff. Strategic decisions cannot be reached independently of network sponsors, for whom economic concerns remain central.[256] At the other end of the influence spectrum, it is reported that both Ugandan generals and Rwandan generals regularly inserted themselves into command roles for UPC military engagements, superimposing their own demands on UPC forces.[257]

These differences account for many of the problems weighing on the Congo trials at the ICC. Most of the legal apparatus in the Rome Statute, especially war crimes, comes from European experience, including armed forces command structures operating in developed countries up through World War II. As has now been widely recognized, since that distant era the organization of armed conflict has changed markedly, as conflict arenas shift from transnational to localized battles. In local conflicts around the globe, military action occurs within civil wars, insurgencies, insurrections, and pillaging gangs. As a result, the boundaries between combatants and civilians become harder to define.[258]

Parochial alliance networks are specially adapted to advancing group interests under tight economic and political conditions. They offer opportunities for survival, sometimes for ephemeral success. But lacking strong horizontal loyalties, they also have an innate tendency to fragment. Rivalries,

[255] Veit, *Intervention as Indirect Rule*, p. 103.

[256] Stearns, Verweijen, and Baaz, *The National Army*, p. 13.

[257] Pascal Kalume Kambale, "A Story of Missed Opportunities: The Role of the International Criminal Court in the Democratic Republic of Congo," in Christian De Vos, Sara Kendall, and Carsten Stahn (eds.), *Contested Justice: The Politics and Practice of International Criminal Court Interventions* (Cambridge: Cambridge University Press, 2015), p. 180. The author provides no documentation for this claim, which is evidently something he and other Congolese NGO leaders believed to be common knowledge.

[258] A classic source is Martin van Creveld, *The Transformation of War* (New York: Free Press, 1991). Additional insights can be found in Duffield, *Global Governance*.

breakdowns, defections within fragile networks describe the constant struggle in Ituri between 1999 and 2003; and they are critical to comprehending the violence between 2002 and 2003. Whenever network solidarity was threatened, sometimes the only countervailing pressure came from ethnic mobilization. "Playing the ethnic card" can always be seen as evidence of personal hatred and genocidal ideologies; but it may also be a rational (if reckless) strategy for preserving crumbling networks. Within networks, other ties and defections may still eclipse ethnicity alone.[259]

Finally, the Ituri networks with local roots had to connect with national rebel groups and regional power brokers, which had swarmed into Ituri after 1996. Vlassenroot and Raeymaekers, in their research findings on Ituri between 1998 and 2003, describe this pattern as "the emergence of a new political complex."[260] Pressures within local networks are difficult to survive, accounting for the reflexive turn to ethnic solidarity as a cohesive force. But it is even more difficult to incorporate links to Ugandan generals, who import their own patronage networks, usually illicit, with global traders. Still other network options came from national rebels like Jean-Pierre Bemba, or from bellicose Rwandan proxies, some of whom were already flirting with national reconciliation talks. During this tumultuous period, Ituri was torn by multiple competitive struggles, all taking place in an economically depressed African district – but a district blessed with rich deposits of natural resources.

Writing a decade after these events, another group of researchers elaborated on the previous study by Vlassenroot and Raeymaekers:

> Over time the Congo Wars changed the nature of armed groups, as locally rooted rural militias became enmeshed in networks led by business and political elites. These militia networks drove and were driven by the development of a war economy, which thrived on illegal taxation, smuggling, and racketeering. While this economy allowed for the quick enrichment of some, millions of civilians depended on it for survival, leaving them little choice but to collaborate with armed groups.[261]

[259] Vlassenroot and Raeymaekers, "The Politics of Rebellion," p. 411. See generally Paul D. Williams, *War and Conflict in Africa*, chapter 6 on "Ethnicity." From a somewhat different angle, in a retrospective comparative study, two political scientists found that ethnicity was often a weaker influence than economic survival, in conditions leading to violent insurgency; see James D. Fearon and David D. Laitin, "Ethnicity, Insurgency, and Civil War," *American Political Science Review* 97 (2003), 75.

[260] Vlassenroot and Raeymaekers, "The Politics of Rebellion," pp. 410–12.

[261] Stearns, Verweijen, and Baaz, *The National Army*, p. 21.

Activating Networks: Economic Pressures

Attempts to pinpoint the escalation of Ituri violence tend to focus on incidents in 1999, following on years of Hema manipulation and defense of land titles. Pressures on land use had figured in a long history of conflict between Hema and Lendu populations in Ituri. This early history helps explain the origins of particular alliance networks active during the 2002–03 period. In the tumult of the 1990s, the better-connected Hema elites, supporting commercial agriculture and pastoral land practices, took advantage of arcane provisions in a Congolese property-rights regime adopted in the 1970s. The results, if fully implemented, would have excluded as many as 200,000 Lendu from land used for their own subsistence agriculture. Based on incidents reported by news agencies in 1999, picked up later by MONUC, and referenced by Vlassenroot and Raeymaekers, the initial purpose of ethnic-based paramilitary units was to enforce land claims (Hema) and to protect small communities from land-exclusions (Lendu).[262]

Speaking about the Kivu provinces, Stearns and his colleagues note the similar development of grassroots community self-help groups during the 1990s, which later became the basis for electoral mobilization, but also for settling disputes over land and for regulating the authority of customary leaders. The existence of such rural "militias" spread rapidly across the region. "Many of today's armed group commanders began their careers during this period . . . ."[263]

From here it was necessary for local armed groups to adapt to the economic, political, and regional pressures that fell on Ituri after 1999. Facing competition, armed groups needed the resources and political access that could come only through larger networks. These networks, in turn, needed to back up their

[262] Vlassenroot and Raeymaekers, "The Politics of Rebellion," pp. 391–92, with references to armed conflicts in June 1999. UN sources picked up an earlier incident in April 1999, which is frequently referenced as the "start" of Hema-Lendu armed action. (UN Secretary-General, *Special Report on the Events in Ituri, January 2002–December 2003*, S/2004/573, July 16, 2004, pp. 9–10.) But Vlassenroot and Raeymaekers note alternative views on how these conflicts began, including a preexisting alliance between the Lendu and units of the Congolese national army. Researcher Dan Fahey, who visited relevant sites in 2012 and spoke with informants, tends to accept that Lendu were the aggressors in this episode: "This Land Is My Land: Land Grabbing in Ituri," in An Ansoms (ed.), *Losing Your Land: Dispossession in the Great Lakes* (London: Boydell & Brewer, 2014), pp. 36–57. See also Joost van Puijenbroek and An Ansoms, "A Legacy from the Past Hindering the Future: Land Conflicts in Ituri (DRC)," in An Ansoms and Stefaan Marysse (eds.), *Natural Resources and Local Livelihoods in the Great Lakes Region of Africa* (London: Palgrave Macmillan, 2011), pp. 49–67.

[263] Stearns, Verweijen, and Baaz, *The National Army*, p. 19.

actions with credible military power. As the entire Congo was wracked by national rebellions, no political group could function without an "armed wing." And later, as national reconciliation talks assigned status to rebel groups according to the strength of their military forces, these armed wings expanded in alliances far beyond the parochial circle of a single ethnicity.

> Urban-based provincial and national politicians and businessmen have, in some cases, stronger influence on armed groups than the military leaders in the field, providing and organizing crucial financial, political, and logistical support. It is simplistic to think of armed groups as purely military organizations standing apart from society: they are embedded in civilian social networks, and inputs from elites and communities are often essential for their survival.[264]

4.4 STRUCTURES OF VIOLENCE

Challenge and Response

UN sources recounted a common story, showing how micro-level forces in Ituri might have combined to foster violence. The story conveniently points to an originating moment in 1999. There was a time when Hema elites tried to exclude a large number of Lendu farmers from disputed land in Djugu district north of Bunia, with lethal consequences. In response, Lendu armed groups joined together and destroyed or occupied some of the disputed estates. "Some Lendu traditional authorities created self-defense units. Believing that a Hema conspiracy existed against them, the Lendu militias began attacking Hema villages mainly on account of their ethnicity. They also benefited from external support to organize themselves, from either the Congolese [Government, rebel movements,] or individual Ugandan officers."

The Hema landowners did not take long to react.

> Under the leadership of the [Hema] Savo family, the *concessionaires* [Hema landowners] began to organize militias around Fataki. They imposed a fund-raising system on the Hema/Gegere businessmen. Two prominent Hema/Gegere businessmen who were opposing the fund-raising were murdered. As the collegial [*sic*] leadership of this militia was expecting violence, all of the Hema *concessionaires*, by the end of May 1999, contracted squads of UPDF [Ugandan] soldiers to protect their land. On 29 May 1999 important Hema families reportedly paid Captain Kyakabale, the UPDF sector commander,

[264] Ibid., p. 13.

> the alleged amount of $12,000 for a punitive action to be undertaken against the populations occupying the concessions and surrounding areas in the *collectivité* Walendu Pitsi . . .. UPDF carried out its first attacks on the village of Loda . . . in the night of 29 to 30 May 1999, burning it down and burning alive several elderly persons and women locked in their houses.[265]

Whatever the status of this precise report, events of this kind surely set the stage for polarized network-building in Ituri. By late 1999, the breakaway branch of RCD-ML rebels had arrived in Bunia, under the leadership of Ernest Wamba dia Wamba and his deputy Mbusa Nyamwisi. Friction between these two men was based on Wamba's alleged tilt toward emerging Lendu groups, whose weak ties within Ituri had to be compensated for by joining national rebel networks, and ultimately by allying with the Congolese government. Wamba was a well-placed broker with access to these broader networks, as were some individual Ugandan officers. Nyamwisi undermined Wamba by skillfully managing the ambitious Hema who initially joined with RCD-ML in great numbers, including the group of restless officers placed in the "armed wing." But it was this group who had already mutinied against Wamba in 2001, and then mutinied for good in 2002 against Nyamwisi. By this time, Nyamwisi himself had jumped networks, moving openly to the national stage by participating in the Inter-Congolese Dialogue in South Africa.

The final shove came in August 2002, when Nyamwisi and Governor Lompondo were driven out of Bunia, and the Hema economic-paramilitary network were left holding the reins in Ituri. Their favored spokesperson, Thomas Lubanga, had been arrested in Kampala and sent to Kinshasa during the final push; but he came back to Bunia in September 2002 to serve the Hema network using the title President of a newly repurposed UPC group. Neither Lubanga nor his network fared well during the coming months.[266]

Networks of Violence: Fragmentation, Disorder, and Survival

The particular structures of Ituri violence were not fully investigated by ICC Prosecutors, whose working models came through NGO reports. These cultural realities were indeed challenging for Western human rights activists, relying on more familiar templates. As Carsten Stahn notes:

> International criminal trials involve inquiries into cultures and societies that are often foreign to judges or prosecutors. The judicial process relies on

265 UN Secretary-General, *Special Report on the Events in Ituri*, p. 9.
266 These events are summarized in Tamm, *UPC in Ituri*, pp. 17–21.

> certain social ideal types (i.e. ideas of organizations, formation of plan and policy, use of command) to categorize violence. This representation may not always offer a proper fit to social reality. [Courts] may treat fundamental socio-legal or anthropological questions ... as matters of 'common knowledge', rather than testing them through scientific inquiry. The underlying picture is often constructed through mediated knowledge, i.e. information from states, NGOs or international organizations that have a normative interest in the use of specific labels and their connotations.[267]

Above all, network structures are loosely organized. They come in many shapes and are subject to constant change. They are different from organizations with stable defined hierarchies and lines of reporting. Only recently have field researchers studied how these networks perform generally in armed rebellions and insurgencies. Conditions in Ituri and the eastern Congo can be compared to similar patterns found in other parts of the world. These patterns became increasingly prominent in the period after 1990, in armed conflicts involving mainly non-state actors, where goals are driven less by ideology than by material and political ambitions of diverse network members – and by the sheer need to survive.[268]

The action frameworks appearing in Ituri after 1999 were cobbled together out of necessity and opportunity. Both the extended Hema network in Ituri and the RCD-ML rebel network (centered in nearby Beni in North Kivu) were built from a core of ethnic business elites (Hema and Nande, respectively), acting through ambitious brokers able to do their bidding. Rivalries within the network were endemic, even among those with the same ethnicity, as landowners and resource entrepreneurs jostled for advantage, and politically ambitious leaders competed for dominance.[269] With nothing to solidify their relationships – not the old ideologies of anti-colonialism, nor Marxism, nor even religious fundamentalism – the social ties within this ethnic core were never strong enough to counter the uncertainties of their environment. Networks depend less on formal hierarchies and more on reciprocal bonds of trust and loyalty. Within months of finding themselves nominally in control

[267] *A Critical Introduction to International Criminal Law* (Cambridge: Cambridge University Press, 2018), pp. 172–73.

[268] See Paul Staniland, *Networks of Rebellion*, chapter 3, with theory and data on the morphology of parochial networks. For a research overview, see Elisabeth Jean Wood, "The Social Process of Civil War: The Wartime Transformation of Social Networks," *Annual Review of Political Science* 11 (2008), 539.

[269] Vlassenroot and Raeymaekers, in *Conflict and Social Transformation*, emphasize that power from these networks flows less from leaders than from elite economic brokers and intermediate trade brokers (p. 38). More generally, see Mark Shaw, *The Middlemen: War Supply Networks in Sierra Leone and Angola* (The Hague: Clingendael Institute, 2002).

in Bunia, the UPC leadership group had splintered into four separate branches – rivals pried apart by the machinations of former Ugandan allies.[270]

The Ituri Hema network included fragile ties to the two main regional powers. In its successful takeover of Bunia in August 2002, it had the assistance of Ugandan fighters, participating out of short-term interest. But distrust had already clouded any stronger relationship. Just one month before, when Uganda invited the restless Hema military officers to Kampala, it arrested their spokesman Thomas Lubanga (who remained in custody in Kinshasa until September). After driving RCD-ML leaders all the way back to their North Kivu base, this Hema network reached out to Rwanda. These links paid off briefly in terms of military training and supplies, with economic rewards accruing to Rwanda from Ituri goldfields.[271] But in 2003 it proved to be just one more weak link, when Uganda increased cooperation with the RCD-ML network, while Rwanda bowed to international pressure to back off. To fill the network holes of these unreliable regional allies, Lubanga and his internal rivals kept a close eye on the Inter-Congolese Dialogue in South Africa, hoping for a seat at the bargaining table. (Their rival RCD-ML had beaten them to it, blocking their path.) While unrealistic, the distant possibilities of political recognition and future military integration were enough to sharpen rivalries within the Hema brokerage circle.

***

The most opaque links within the Ituri networks were military. At the ICC Congo trials, probably the central difficulty for the Court was comprehending the shape and strength of alliances among the diverse armed groups in Ituri between August 2002 and March 2003. As the 1999 disputes in Djugu over land possession made plain, local action networks needed armed groups to advance their socio-economic claims under otherwise lawless conditions. On paper both the Hema and RCD-ML networks would declare armed wings, complete with military titles and the appearance of standard military structure. Their recruits included, notoriously, the Ituri youth, sent from their respective villages – boys and girls; under eighteen, and under fifteen years of age; voluntary, abducted, and everything in between. But there were also weaker links with random armed groups, still based in village units with their respective ethnic bonds. It is thought that the Hema network did a better job of integrating their disparate groups; although some evidence suggests that, by early 2003, certain Hema units

270 Tamm, *UPC in Ituri*, pp. 35–40.

271 Vlassenroot and Raeymaekers, "Politics of Rebellion," p. 398, n. 47.

still operated autonomously.[272] Inside the RCD-ML network, Lendu armed groups maintained a far looser alliance than their Hema counterparts. Judging from the evidence of destructive attacks, this alliance strengthened during the period 2002–03, event-by-event, with shifting combinations of local Lendu groups, diverse Mai-Mai groups from the Kivus, an RCD-ML armed wing, stray troops from the national Congolese army, and even roving groups of armed Hutu refugees.[273]

For all three Congo trials, the ICC Prosecutor assumed that he was dealing with more conventional armed units, organized by battalions and brigades, led by a professional officer corps, following a strict military chain of command. He was focused on troop sizes and hierarchies. The NGOs who provided information thought along similar lines. Early in his investigations, vast deposits of documents (mostly from UPC, but a few from Lendu-based groups) were acquired from the UN (which had confiscated documents from armed groups during 2003 and acquired still more from Congolese police shortly thereafter). But when it seemed that the official documents and figures might be unreliable – that they were created in part to convey a display of military weight – the Prosecution had to make some choices. It tended to accept at face value those documents that were consistent with conventional military structure: organization charts, brigade numbers, recruitment figures listed in typed reports. It dismissed as propaganda those documents that told a different story about patchwork staffing, commanders making up their own battalion numbers, and troops who might "self-deploy" by simply dropping out and returning to their home villages.[274]

The precise facts and events were difficult enough to reconstruct during the trials themselves and are now nearly impossible to check. The Congo trials have provided lengthy testimonies of two accused, Germain Katanga describing the Lendu operations, and the even more extensive testimony of Bosco Ntaganda, describing nearly two years' worth of UPC operations. Katanga testified for some sixty hours, including cross-examination; Ntaganda for double that amount. Further details will be discussed in the chapters devoted to particular trials.

Both Katanga and Ntaganda were witnesses defending themselves against serious criminal charges, telling the Court what would be in their own self-interest. But much of their testimony about daily life in Ituri military actions

[272] Vlassenroot and Raeymaekers, "Politics of Rebellion," p. 399.

[273] Henning Tamm, *FNI and FRPI: Local Resistance and Regional Alliances in North-Eastern Congo* (London: Rift Valley Institute, 2013), pp. 16–21.

[274] These choices were manifest in the extensive cross-examination of Bosco Ntaganda. See, for example, Ntaganda Trial Chamber, transcript, July 19, 2017, ICC-01/04-02/06-T-228-ENG, pp. 35–36, regarding the circumstances with battalion numbers.

introduced reasonable alternatives to the more conventional templates of the Prosecution. In the comparatively looser structures of the Lendu combatants, Katanga offered extensive information about overlapping structures of authority: local village commanders, village elders and chiefs (not always in agreement), allied professional groups providing weapons and uniforms. In Katanga's world, one of his co-combatants would be given the military title S3 (in charge of "operations") because he had a bicycle and knew how to repair it.[275] From Ntaganda, who was Deputy Chief of Staff in a more structured military environment, there were stories of reaching distant locations on foot; or if there was a vehicle available (and not in the repair shop), digging it out of the mud in remote spots. When the UPC was on the ropes in Bunia in May 2003, Ntaganda missed the call from his superior – under devastating attack by international forces just outside Bunia – because he was outside watering the cattle.[276] At another juncture, when challenged by the senior prosecutor as to whether his secretary had drafted a note, he explained that he hadn't had a secretary for months. More such examples will be given close examination in later chapters. And it remains the case that courtroom testimony must be carefully evaluated. But the practical realities of these military environments fit much better with the alliance network model, rather than more conventional patterns.

***

The texture of everyday life in Ituri, leading up to the conflicts of 2002–03, included local defense committees embedded in villages and towns. As cited earlier, Stearns and his colleagues addressed these structures: "It is simplistic to think of armed groups as purely military organizations standing apart from society; they are embedded in civilian social networks, and inputs from elites and communities are often essential for their survival."[277] Because of land disputes, these local committees were initially directed to protecting local economic interests, standing up to elite-driven trading networks, generally ethnically based. These shadow committees of self-protection were also a collecting point for displaced youth, in areas lacking any neutral outlets for employment or advancement. Vlassenroot and Raeymaekers studied such formations in South Kivu, and then found similar backgrounds to the patterns of violence in Ituri.[278]

[275] Katanga Trial Chamber, transcript, October 11, 2011, 01/04–01/07-T-320-FRA, p. 57.
[276] Ntaganda Trial Chamber, transcript, July 11, 2017, ICC-01/04–02/06-T-222-ENG, p. 15.
[277] Stearns, Verweijen, and Baaz, *The National Army*, p. 13.
[278] Vlassenroot and Raeymaekers, *Conflict and Social Transformation*, pp. 92–96; "Politics of Rebellion," pp. 391–92.

At the grassroots level, armed fighters within these networks found a measure of stability, offsetting the fear and general lawlessness pervading Ituri in the period after 1999. While the land disputes that helped form the militant Hema network originated in Djugu district (an area of Hema and Lendu population centers to the north of Bunia), by 2001 the killing and pillaging had spread south to Irumu district, south of Bunia – and indeed into Bunia itself. In a process that was sadly familiar throughout the Congo, villages in these parts of Ituri organized self-defense units, generally with small arms obtained through Ugandan intermediaries. Within these localized groups, the line between civilians and combatants would not be clearly drawn.

As violence escalated, local groups needed more fighters, supplies, information – the kinds of resources available through external networks of sympathetic allies. For civilians under these conditions, linking in some fashion to the two dominant networks in Ituri was only a matter of time. One key benefit of network alliances was recruitment beyond the intra-village level. It is beyond dispute that all sides in these conflicts brought young children into the battle. The use of children (certainly under the age of eighteen, and often under fifteen) in armed conflict was familiar throughout this region of Africa.[279] In the first rebellion that toppled Mobutu from power, Laurent-Désiré Kabila himself spoke fondly of his *kadogo* – the underaged fighters surrounding him, some of whom remained in his service after he became President of the Congo in 1997, and one of whom reportedly assassinated him in January 2001.

If local self-defense groups needed reinforcements, young men in Ituri were also in search of structure and opportunity, some kind of lifeline in a forbidding environment. At a time when opportunities were collapsing, when basic services moved beyond their grasp – education, healthcare, and even security – armed networks provided a default option. This is not to ignore the many instances of abduction, forced conscription, and cruel treatment surrounding the insertion of children into Ituri's brutal struggles. In no way does it explain or excuse the barbaric treatment of girls, including sexual enslavement and torture. Despite these cruel practices in Ituri and other rural localities throughout the Congo, military conscription provided a structure and occupation for young men with no other realistic options. Within Ituri there were compelling reasons why ordinary people might join such groups voluntarily, or at least adapt quickly, after abduction, to military structure and purpose.

279 Williams, *War and Conflict in Africa*, p. 45.

Of course, these decisions are difficult to comprehend from any distance. They are also highly ambiguous in their consequences, encompassing both real opportunity and cruel mistreatment. But there is ample evidence from field researchers in the Congo, and in places like northern Uganda, that loosely networked armed groups managed to motivate and retain effective fighters, at least over short periods of time.[280] It has sometimes been argued that "ethnic entrepreneurs" would foment ethnic hatred to enlist local fighters in the barbaric cause. While not ruling out this possibility, it seems plain that a critical number of armed fighters found themselves adapting to prevailing networks of opportunity. Under such extreme circumstances, the pressure of armed conflict has the potential to create situational bonds of cooperation. But those bonds can disappear just as quickly, as with all the other weak links within such fractious networks.[281]

***

Conflicts in network-dominated districts like Ituri were manifestly able to inflict appalling atrocities on local civilians, including even close neighbors. As a result, Ituri drew international comparisons with other serious cases in central and West Africa, including nearby Rwanda. True, in all these conflicts, the lines between combatants and civilians were more difficult to draw than in conventional warfare. The sharp distinctions found in the 1949 Geneva Conventions may be hard to apply in practice. But even allowing for some ambiguity, the Ituri conflicts produced a heavy toll of civilian killings, torture, sexual abuse, and similar trauma, along with massive population displacements. The victims included a disproportionate number of women, children, and elderly, all of whom stood well outside the legal boundaries of network-linked combatants.

For observers inside and outside these local events, the reasons behind all the violence remain mysterious. Without some more practical explanation, such events open the door to speculative macro-explanations: ethnic hatred, hardened criminality, tribal irrationalities, the demonization of "outsiders," and even hallucinogenic drugs and magic spells. These explanations assume that massive atrocities could have been caused only by depraved or criminal mentalities. It is an assumption found, explicitly or tacitly, in most NGO reports about Ituri and the Congo, and it feeds into the string of presumptions

[280] Reno, *Warfare in Independent Africa*, pp. 208–09; Staniland, *Networks of Rebellion*, pp. 48–51.
[281] Vlassenroot and Raeymaekers, *Conflict and Social Transformation*, pp. 54–55, 89–90.

about criminal plans, supreme commanders, and strict military efficiency that found their way into the ICC.[282]

In the past two decades, researchers have paid closer attention to the micro-sociology of local violence, identifying more diffuse causes in small-group dynamics and particular localized practices – generally interacting with national or regional pressures. The large-scale 1994 killings in Rwanda have received the most attention, but the overall research program includes comparative studies in other parts of Africa, Asia, Eastern Europe, and beyond. These approaches may be relevant to the networked violence found in the Ituri conflicts.[283]

Studying the micro-behavior of mass violence has a particular aim. It is not meant to identify perpetrators for prosecution, but rather to discover how such appalling events can be humanly possible, especially in situations where ethnic groups have previously lived in proximity. While not excluding the search for larger criminal elements, the goal of micro-analysis is to find the informal, everyday structures through which ordinary populations are drawn into the maelstrom of mass violence.

In the Congo trials, Prosecutorial narratives favored modes of explanation that matched the templates of individual criminal responsibility: typically searching for master-planners with iron command over robot-like foot soldiers, who obeyed higher orders without question.[284] The research focus on micro-causes provides alternative explanations for large-scale violence, focusing on highly localized structures and small-scale dynamics. For the Congo trials, these alternative perspectives create reasonable doubts about alleged patterns of behavior, challenging the standard ICC legal templates for individual criminal responsibility. In all the Congo trials, serious questions surrounded the legal process of moral attribution, which relied on weak factual evidence about presumed hierarchical structures for organizing and committing crimes.

Although micro-sociological studies of Ituri in the period 2002–03 are lacking, some useful comparisons can be found in community studies from

[282] The best-known example is HRW, *Ituri: "Covered in Blood."* This report and others from NGOs will be discussed fully in Chapter 5.

[283] A prominent example of this research is Scott Straus, *The Order of Genocide*, building on earlier work by Stathis N. Kalyvas: "The Ontology of 'Political Violence': Action and Identity in Civil Wars," *Perspectives on Politics* 1 (2003), 475; and *The Logic of Violence in Civil Wars* (Cambridge: Cambridge University Press, 2006).

[284] This template is discussed in detail in Chapters 7 and 8. As Neha Jain has written, ICC individual crimes are "crimes of obedience," "acts carried out under explicit instructions from makers of official policy"; *Perpetrators and Accessories in International Criminal Law: Individual Modes of Responsibility for Collective Crimes* (Oxford: Hart, 2014), p. 3.

Rwanda. There, researchers have attempted to reconstruct the mobilization of violence that struck swiftly and with unimaginable intensity, back in 1994. The research builds on interviews with past participants at the level of districts and villages, and in even smaller action groups in rural parts of the country. While Rwanda also had political leaders in the capital city actively directing widespread genocidal attacks on Tutsi, much of the actual killing took place in rural communities through small groups of ordinary citizens. Even though many actual killers lacked clear genocidal intent, they nevertheless joined in exterminating local neighbors and former friends.

In her studies of such local groups, anthropologist Lee Ann Fujii suggests the importance of small-group dynamics in implementing Rwandan violence, proposing a "social interaction thesis" of group behavior.[285] Under normal circumstances, the collective experience of killing one's neighbors would have been unimaginable. But under conditions of extreme anxiety and uncertainty, the group's willingness to take decisive action allowed the interacting individuals to inhabit new social identities, offering a momentary sense of power and clarity, as a mode for their own survival. These deeds are atrocious in every way, but their collective performance provides group members with a semblance of order, confirmed through the process of social interaction.

According to Fujii, appalling atrocities like those in Rwanda were a byproduct of small-scale social interactions, carried out for the immediate purpose of confirming the social connectedness of group members. Fear may be a cause for joining a killing group – but it is not simply fear of the victims, but also fear of distance within one's own group, and from powerful allies weakly tied to one's group.[286] Under the extraordinary circumstances of savage conflicts, participating in small-group action allows members "to know who to be and how to act."[287] The hate comes later; and in Fujii's view, for everyday Rwandan killers, "ethnic hatred was a consequence of the genocide, not a cause."[288] Other researchers have reached similar results from looking at slightly broader social interactions. Straus and other micro-sociologists conclude that the existence of a state policy to exterminate the Tutsi was not a sufficient explanation for how the Rwandan genocide happened.[289] The ordinary killers in local conditions were intent on maintaining social bonds in an environment of deep uncertainty. By carrying out their lethal work, the

285 *Killing Neighbors: Webs of Violence in Rwanda* (Ithaca: Cornell University Press, 2009). For the social interaction thesis, see pp. 19–21, 185–89.

286 Ibid., p. 183.

287 Ibid., p. 179.

288 Ibid., p. 183.

289 Straus, *The Order of Genocide*, pp. 11–12.

killers would confirm their sense of belonging through group action. (Western readers might consider the virulent subcultures that persist on the Internet, even in peaceful, stable social conditions.[290])

Ituri in 2002–03 was not Rwanda in 1994. In some ways, Ituri may offer a simpler case for the social interaction thesis, where highly networked social structures could allow for more differentiated moments of group expression. In Rwanda, there was an overriding state policy for carrying out the genocide, generated in the capital and disseminated to rural areas by state agents.[291] And Rwanda may also have had a cultural disposition toward social conformism, based on widely diffused historical labor practices.[292] In Ituri, layered networks contained a mix of strong and weak ties, where bonds of trust were constantly being tested. These conditions created opportunities for spontaneous assertions of group solidarity – enhancing the core network imperative of survival with a transitory sense of personal fulfillment. More than Rwanda, Ituri's social structure of weak horizontal ties fits with Fujii's social interaction dynamics.

At the very least, considering the fragile and non-hierarchical network ties for members of Ituri armed groups, it was not necessary for observers to impute genocidal ideologies and master plans to "wipe out" certain groups and villages. Over time in Ituri, patterns of violence show a striking variety of targets and outcomes. In most documented Ituri attacks, civilian killings went beyond members of just the Hema or Lendu ethnic groups. And erstwhile allies in one massacre might change sides for the next (as with the Bira between attacks in Nyankunde and Bogoro). Violence may be endemic in such extreme conditions, but the patterns of civilian violence might depend less on waves of mass hatred or irrationality, and more on interactive local structures, which mutate according to time and place.

Especially in cases where local armed groups joined with more professional forces (such as the RCD-ML, and the trained elements within the UPC), the

[290] Americans have been haunted by experiments with US university students going back to the 1960s, exploring the interactive environment favoring cruelty to strangers. Best known are Stanley Milgram's experiments at Yale, followed by Philip Zimbardo's prison-guard simulations at Stanford. See Milgram, *Obedience to Authority* (London: Tavistock, 1974); Zimbardo, *The Lucifer Effect: Understanding How Good People Turn Evil* (New York: Random House, 2007).

[291] While such master plans existed, Straus emphasizes that implementation passed through diffuse mechanisms, not strict hierarchy. *The Order of Genocide*, pp. 10–12.

[292] Straus examines this thesis as well, focusing on the labor policy known as *umuganda* (ibid., pp. 109–10). Gérard Prunier speaks of an "almost monstrous degree of social control" in Rwandan society, in *The Rwanda Crisis: History of a Genocide* (New York: Columbia University Press, 1995), p. 3.

killing of civilians could have been opportunistic sequels to ordinary battles between conventional forces. Such paroxysms do not invariably require a superstructure of criminal plans and hierarchical execution. In looser network systems, such violence can emerge from purely local dynamics, where spontaneity provides its own purpose. Individual members become endowed with a sense of solidarity and meaning inside the cooperating group – a mode of survival tied to the moment. After mid-2003, the sudden willingness of some Hema and Lendu to join in new armed alliances, targeting the MONUC regime, suggests the brittleness of former networks and their surprising adaptability to new conditions.

***

Unlike earlier guerrilla networks that could persist for decades, the Ituri networks could not survive the destructive pressure from regional, national, and international levels. The two main local networks arising after 1999 were essentially finished by mid-2003. Based on their observations in the eastern Congo during 2003, Vlassenroot and Raeymaekers note the similar fate of "militia" groups throughout the region: "Most militia leaders have lost control over the rank-and-file militia members. As a consequence, most militia groups are disintegrating into loose gangs of social bandits, highly increasing the level of violence against the rural population."[293] The mutation of networks did not mean that peace would return to Ituri. Indeed, quite different networks arose almost immediately, this time cutting across ethnic boundaries to include both Hema and Lendu officers, even some who had been fighting against each other in prior years. These developments raise serious questions about the presumption of ethnic hatred as the root cause of Ituri violence, which figured heavily in the first two Congo trials.

From 2003 to the present day, armed networks remain active in Ituri and eastern Congo, still fractious, still mutating, still violent, and still driven by local tensions and frustrated ambitions. Ituri was not in fact isolated from larger forces operating in the Congo. These upstart networks could not survive without external sponsors; but external links became their downfall. Under international pressure in 2003, Uganda and Rwanda would start planning their exit from Ituri. Alongside political transition, there were new initiatives for demobilizing armed groups and integrating fighters into the national Congolese army – a patronage system that offered far greater rewards than local ethnic fighting.[294]

[293] Vlassenroot and Raeymaekers, *Conflict and Social Transformation*, p. 188.

[294] Christopher Vogel and Josephat Musamba, *Recycling Rebels? Demobilization in the Congo* (London: Rift Valley Institute, 2016).

The UPC's network architecture was easily pulled apart. Once Uganda determined that the UPC had gotten too close to Rwanda, it found ways to dismember the UPC's fractious leadership. In December 2002, the leader known as Yves "Chief" Kahwa defected – a Southern Hema who was never part of the inner circle of Northern Hema (Gegere). Kahwa ingratiated himself with Uganda and then Kinshasa, and soon would head up a new armed alliance with Lendu groups, and with groups from Alur and Lugbara ethnicities in the far northern part of Ituri. Another UPC ally from the northern districts, Jérôme Kakwavu, defected in March 2003 and brought his own fighters into the growing alliance to oust the UPC from Bunia. In another sign of fickle alliances, Chief Kahwa shifted back to the UPC in May for a brief return to Bunia.[295]

But by May 2003 the UPC was an empty shell. As Vlassenroot and Raeymaekers discovered:

> The increasing fragmentation eventually resulted in an unstable mosaic of non-state actors, in which militia leaders lost most of their control over their roaming recruits. While Lubanga, chief Kahwa and other rebel leaders continued to portray themselves to the international community as the chief representatives of their suffering communities, uncontrolled armed groups of Gegere, Hema and Lendu combatants were roaming across the local countryside, preying on the local population. Simultaneously, the continued arming of the warring militias by the region's great powers in Kigali, Kampala, and Kinshasa constituted a major obstacle to achieving a peaceful resolution to this conflict.[296]

***

At this point, groups were jockeying mainly for position at local peace talks that had started in March 2003. The Ituri Pacification Commission had been floated as part of the 2002 Luanda peace accord, when Uganda pledged to withdraw its military remnants from northern and eastern portions of the Congo.[297] For the international community, the Pacification Commission was a noble idea, providing a place for Ituri factions to resolve their differences peacefully. For the fractious groups in Ituri, it opened up another competitive struggle for leverage. A figure like Chief Kahwa, rather than occupying a small node in the Northern Hema network, could step out onto a broader stage – a leader in his own right,

[295] Veit, *Intervention as Indirect Rule*, pp. 129–32.
[296] "The Politics of Rebellion," p. 399.
[297] Prunier, *Africa's World War*, pp. 292–93.

whose signature would have as much space on the final document as Thomas Lubanga's.

For some combatants, the Ituri Pacification Commission offered the first step toward higher aspirations. Throughout 2003, one's place at the local peace table would depend on one's prior battlefield success – or at least one's reputation for past success.[298] Reconstructing the past year's conflicts – sorting out fact from fiction – was no simple project.

Speaking with some of the loosely allied Lendu groups, observers from humanitarian agencies started compiling stories about military organizations with previously unknown names, mysterious acronyms, dog-eared organization charts, and leaders cross-claiming responsibility for past attacks – on the reasonable assumption that such roles would entitle them to sign peace documents. Based on these retrospective stories, two figures would later end up at the ICC: Mathieu Ngudjolo and Germain Katanga. Ngudjolo was linked to a group of Northern Lendu belatedly identified as FNI. Katanga was associated with a Southern Lendu consortium now identified as FRPI. (Some hasty documents would conflate these two acronyms, projecting an even grander coalition of Lendu militias.[299]) Years were then spent in The Hague, debating whether these two men had really served and conspired as seasoned militia commanders, coming in from the cold – or, rather, whether they were desperate boasters, seeking advantage in the post-conflict deliberations.[300]

The effort to reconstruct Lendu organizational patterns proved especially difficult at the ICC trials for Ngudjolo and Katanga. During March–May 2003, after the UPC grip on Bunia had been broken, military charts compiled by global NGOs quickly entered into humanitarian commentary, on their pathway into Prosecutorial briefs. Sidestepping this body of self-referential commentary, the best impartial effort to untangle this mass of Lendu links came a decade later, in the sober histories produced by the Rift Valley Institute. Drawing on mostly anonymous interviews (possibly from the same figures who testified at ICC trials) as well as ICC testimony, author Henning Tamm sketches a rudimentary history for FNI and FRPI. But his most telling comment, referring to the March 2003 moment in Bunia when

298 As Emeric Rogier wrote, "Greedy warlords indeed managed to shoot their way to the table"; "The Inter-Congolese Dialogue: A Critical Overview," in Mark Malan and João Gomes Porto (eds.), *Challenges of Peace Implementation: The UN Mission in the Democratic Republic of the Congo* (Pretoria: Institute for Security Studies, 2004), p. 39.

299 These confusing acronyms were dutifully catalogued in HRW, *Ituri: "Covered in Blood,"* pp. 15–17. As David van Reybrouck noted, the Congo was "rich in abbreviations," *Congo*, p. 451.

300 See Kambale, "A Story of Missed Opportunities," pp. 182–85.

Lendu figures came forward with personal stories, is that "confusion prevailed."

Ten years later, interviewees gave Tamm conflicting accounts of these supposed organizations and who staffed them. According to some of Tamm's sources, it was not until late 2002 that Katanga first heard the term FRPI, while leading a group from his hometown Aveba to the headquarters of Nande sponsors in Beni. He and others went home and started using this acronym to win Kinshasa's support for existing armed groups. Meanwhile, at the very end of 2002, some Northern Lendu began using the name FNI, in the process of seeking recognition for the upcoming Ituri Pacification Commission. They did so, however, without building any "political or military structures." Speaking generally, Tamm concludes: "[T]he regional alliance shifts that occurred between mid-2002 and mid-2003 gave the decentralized Northern Lendu and the fragmented Ngiti [Southern Lendu] militias each a common name and provided them with weapons, but they did not fundamentally alter their organizational structures."[301] By early 2003, national power-sharing talks were entering their implementation phase. Coveted Vice-Presidential positions would go to Bemba (MLC) and to the leader of the Rwanda-backed RCD faction. But the lower ministries in the transitional government were available to former combatants of lesser consequence. RCD-ML would be included at this level. Such opportunities were coveted among the more obscure Ituri groups. Thomas Lubanga boycotted the Ituri Pacification Commission throughout the early part of 2003, demanding that the UPC should first be recognized with a place at the table in South Africa. Later in 2003, after Lubanga and other Ituri fighters agreed to meet in Kinshasa, they would openly compete for favor from the national government. Lubanga lost this competition to his UPC Chief of Staff, Floribert Kisembo. In late 2003, Kisembo bolted and set up yet another rival UPC faction, reportedly with the support of MONUC and the Kinshasa government.[302] In 2005, Kisembo was appointed general in the national army, while Lubanga found himself detained in Kinshasa, months away from becoming the first accused to arrive at the International Court in The Hague.[303]

[301] Tamm, *FNI and FRPI*, pp. 25, 26, 30. As will be discussed in Chapter 8, both Mathieu Ngudjolo and Germain Katanga testified at length about these same developments, presenting views contrasting with Tamm's sources. Tamm traces these groups through later years, especially from 2004, when they finally developed organized political and military capabilities.

[302] Tamm, *UPC in Ituri*, pp. 39–40.

[303] In 2015 there were reports that Floribert Kisembo had been killed in Ituri, after deserting his National Army position. Broadcast from Radio Okapi, transcribed May 1, 2015.

4.5 SEQUEL

Move forward now to June 2005, to a fine hotel on the shore of Lake Victoria in Jinja, Uganda. Across the distant border in Ituri, the UN peacekeeping force MONUC was nominally in control, with backup from the national Congolese Army. With limited success, MONUC was trying to integrate former Ituri combatants into either civilian life or the Congolese military. Among other problems, former leaders from some militias strongly resisted making their fortunes in Kinshasa (or had tried doing so, before scrambling back to Ituri out of fear). And it was precisely these former leaders who came together at the Uganda hotel, in 2005, to announce the formation of a new resistance group: the Mouvement revolutionnaire Congolais (MRC), with goals that could have been lifted from the old paper declarations of 2002 and 2003.

More surprising than this reprise of militancy was the ethnic mix of participants sitting around the table. They included Mathieu Ngudjolo, a Northern Lendu who would later stand trial at the ICC for atrocities committed against Hema civilians; and Bosco Ntaganda, former Chief of Staff in the UPC armed wing, who would later stand trial at the ICC for atrocities against the Lendu. Also attending was another former UPC member, Mbuna Gombi, along with representatives from former Lendu groups and from the Lendu-allied RCD-ML in North Kivu.[304]

The very fact of this meeting suggests that ethnicity had played a mainly strategic role in Ituri violence, subject to change when MONUC arrived and provided a unified target for opposition. At the very least, this meeting supports the impression that Ituri remained complex, difficult to explain, calling for deeper understanding.

. . . Also Present

Moving even farther forward to 2007, old Ituri figures crossed paths in even more unlikely circumstances. Antipas Mbusa Nyamwisi, the wily leader of RCD-ML, had been driven out of Bunia in August 2002, along with his frontman Governor Lompondo. From his stronghold in North Kivu, Nyamwisi built strategic alliances with Lendu armed groups, to the point of specifically enlisting Germain Katanga in November 2002.

Nyamwisi also continued his dalliance with national peacekeeping talks. And there he managed to achieve some success: initially a candidate in the

[304] Veit, *Intervention as Indirect Rule*, pp. 174–75, citing Reuters and BBC sources.

2006 national presidential elections, he wisely stepped aside in favor of Joseph Kabila, and later joined the government of Kabila's Prime Minister Antoine Gizenga. Nyamwisi's term as Congolese Foreign Minister included the period when Germain Katanga (October 2007) and Mathieu Ngudjolo (February 2008) were surrendered to The Hague to face criminal charges.

THE BRIDGE TO THE HAGUE

Human beings suffer,
They torture one another,
They get hurt and get hard.
No poem or play or song
Can fully right a wrong
Inflicted and endured . . . .

History says, don't hope
On this side of the grave.
But then, once in a lifetime
The longed-for tidal wave
Of justice can rise up,
And hope and history rhyme.

So hope for a great sea-change
On the far side of revenge.
Believe that further shore
Is reachable from here.
Believe in miracle
And cures and healing wells . . . .

Seamus Heaney
The Cure at Troy

But let judgment run down as waters, and righteousness as a mighty stream.

Amos 5:24 (King James Version)

Everyone had ideas, variously grandiose, minimal, punitive, reconciliatory, dissuasive, and, above all, contradictory. No one knew for sure. But everyone was certain of one thing: justice must be done.

Thierry Cruvellier
Court of Remorse

Missing from this discussion of Ituri are personal stories from the victims. For too many years, horrific conflicts in the Congo had produced a grim toll of death, torture, rape, misery, displacement, and lost chances. At various times, the same patterns were reported from across the entire country. This chronicle of human suffering would remind the world why the ICC itself was created.

From 1993, violence in the Kivu provinces followed the arrival of Hutu refugees from Burundi and Rwanda. The 1996–98 invasions (led by Rwanda and Uganda) spread destruction to most parts of the country. In late 2002, international attention shifted northward from the Kivu provinces to the district of Ituri, where humanitarian workers on the ground perceived an ethnic bloodbath with echoes of the Rwandan genocide. With the surge in international peacekeepers from June 2003, there began a determined campaign to halt the carnage, document the toll, and seek accountability. The ICC Prosecutor was monitoring the results.

Victims gained a powerful voice through advocacy networks of global NGOs. Pleas on behalf of *victims' justice* were eagerly picked up in The Hague. There the victims' moral claims would resonate inside the courtroom, confronting skeptics who would dismiss ICC justice as mere *victors' justice*. For the most ardent believers, ICC trials held out the promise of *final judgment* in the righteous struggle against impunity.

The new ICC gained custody of these extravagant hopes, inheriting the historic task of creating an enduring institutional structure. But the precise terms had to be negotiated among founding nations signing onto the Rome Treaty. Compromises were inevitable. There were limits on the Court's power to preempt national trials; limits on prosecutorial zealotry; limits on any attempt to go back and revisit past atrocities (prior to July 2002).

The legal rules of the Rome Statute had to be launched into the dynamic process of the courtroom, relying on an extensive administrative support network. Two decades of practice have tested rules of jurisdiction, crime definitions, and the subtle mechanisms for attributing individual criminal responsibility. Many of the specifics were left to judges to figure out, based on conflicting signals and unresolved tensions.

The test for all these foundational concepts would unfold in concrete trials, guided by a cadre of judges organized in a self-corrective matrix of decision-making. The outcomes constitute new working principles of legality, where justice meets factual complexity, and hope endures the rigors of fairness and human capacities.

5

Battling Impunity in Ituri

5.1 ITURI COVERED IN BLOOD: REPORTS FROM THE VICTIMS

Within the Congo, Ituri was not exceptional in the extent of death and human destruction. But the organization of violence somehow seemed more sinister. For some time, the Ugandan military had been a destabilizing presence, much like Rwanda in the Kivus.[305] In the middle of 2002, something changed – just as the ICC, far off in The Hague, was opening its doors. News sources told of ethnic massacres, reporting stories from Ituri coming from international organizations. By late 2002, the fear was contagious.[306]

Already, in 2001, the *New York Times* had reported a story from Bunia, calling up Hollywood B-film images of "Lendu warriors, armed mostly with spears and machetes." Reporting directly from the heart of darkness, the story opened with a horrific street scene: "The head was hacked off a young man who was quite small, witnesses said. It was then skewered on the top of a spear and paraded on the back of a white pickup truck."[307] Behind such grisly sights there must be deep underlying causes. On the surface, such barbarism surpasses understanding; but the reporter gave vivid accounts of where it all came from. Among the causes were the land disputes in Djugu, notably the 1999 stand-off between Hema and Lendu, and its lethal consequences. The *Times* article left little doubt: with any semblance of political order, the problem could have been contained. Instead, greedy Ugandan generals were fanning

[305] Gérard Prunier, *Africa's World War: Congo, The Rwanda Genocide, and the Making of a Continental Catastrophe* (New York: Oxford, 2009).

[306] United Nations Office for the Coordination of Humanitarian Affairs (OCHA), *DRC: Special Report on the Ituri District, northeastern DRC*, published December 18, 2002 on the IRIN network.

[307] Ian Fisher, "Congo's War Turns a Local Spat into a Blood Bath," *New York Times*, January 29, 2001. Shortly thereafter the European Union issued a statement, "Declaration of the Presidency on behalf of the European Union on the Hema-Lendu conflict in northeastern DRC" (Brussels, February 1, 2001).

the flames. With no political restraints, core human drives of greed and hate led the descent into ethnic savagery.

The *Times* writer took his background information from an investigator for HRW, who was completing an exposé of Uganda's double role in Ituri as "firefighter and arsonist."[308] By late 2002, after the ill-fated Governor Lompondo had fled Bunia along with Mbusa Nyamwisi and the RCD-ML rebel group, NGO attention shifted to the local Ituri elite, who were unable or unwilling to maintain public order. Global NGOs like HRW warned of another genocide if the world stood idly by.[309] They called for stronger UN intervention, demanding action to stop the violence. It was unacceptable for Ituri to collapse into chaos, just as the rest of the country was awakening to a new power-sharing peace agreement – a new dawn of political stability. The everyday civilians of Ituri were suffering beyond all measure. Someone must be held responsible.

It was not easy for NGOs to convey the true scale of suffering to their constituents in Europe and the United Nations. Indeed, there was some risk of Congo fatigue, at a time when the major rebel groups, weary after years of struggle, had finally agreed on a path to political normalcy. At the close of 2002, the UN published the astonishing estimate of 50,000 people killed in Ituri in less than three years (in a population of around 4 million).[310] Although this estimate seems high (in light of later, more detailed surveys in the region), it was a big round number that was easily quoted. A few months later, in July 2003, HRW published its densely researched report *Ituri: "Covered in Blood,"*[311] compiling first-hand reports from victims of the carnage, sparing no details about massacres, impalings, cannibalism, sexual torture and rape, and abduction of child soldiers.

During these months, the world community was otherwise focused on the American–British led invasion of Saddam Hussein's Iraq, launched in mid-March. According to HRW, however, there was no time to spare: the UN

[308] HRW, *Uganda in Eastern DRC: Fueling Political and Ethnic Strife* (March 2002); a lengthy report authored by Suliman Baldo.

[309] The references to genocide were prompted by comparisons with Tutsi-Hutu conflicts in Rwanda and the Kivus. The first HRW mention of Hema-Lendu conflict, alleging that members of each group identified with the Rwandan groups, was a short unattributed document *Background to the Hema-Lendu Conflict in Uganda-Controlled Congo* (January 31, 2001). The UN *DRC: Special Report* prominently mentioned "ethnic cleansing" and cited an AI statement about genocide, but remained non-committal on that term (pp. 1, 6, 10).

[310] UN, *DRC: Special Report*, p. 1.

[311] HRW's *Ituri: "Covered in Blood": Ethnically Targeted Violence in Northeastern DR Congo* (July 2003), written by Anneke van Woudenberg.

needed to stand up immediately in Ituri, where only an outside show of force could end the violence. With stability, the international community could then concentrate on documenting atrocities in full detail, preparing the way for legal action. Responding quickly to this call, in July 2003 the ICC Prosecutor signaled his focus on Ituri.[312]

Earlier HRW reports had described thick waves of violence, as local players in Ituri latched on to rebel patrons RCD and MLC, and to the erratic sponsorship of Uganda and Rwanda.[313] Adding to the melee were rogue units of the national Congolese army, alongside roving armed bands from the Kivus. "*Covered in Blood*" solidifies the narrative that fierce ethnic conflict between Hema and Lendu "began" with the 1999 confrontation over land in Djugu. Egged on by outsiders, the local conflicts pivoted on ethnic hatred.

Beyond this history, HRW describes lurid details about key local actors, emphasizing the time frame of August 2002 to May 2003 – the same time parameters for the future ICC Congo trials. As happens so effectively in such reports, the many voices are first-hand accounts.

In a long struggle at the Mongbwalu gold mines, in the western part of Djugu district, all ethnic groups were counted among the victims. A Lendu man related his own experience to HRW investigators:

> I was taken to the prison and could see out the window of my cell. The Hema militia were killing people from particular groups. They were especially looking for Lendu. They would pick out prisoners to kill. They took them one by one to question them, then they released them or killed them. They shot people in front of other prisoners. They tied their arms behind their back with wires. They slashed their heads with knives. They made them sit down and then they shot them. They also shot any who tried to escape, including some boys I knew from my neighborhood. I even saw them kill two Pygmies – a man and a woman. Another woman came to the prison to look for her son. They asked her why she had come there and then they killed her. They beat us with whips and ropes .... I managed to escape the following day ... and I hid so they wouldn't see me. I saw holes, like graves on the edge of town. They were freshly dug and covered with earth ....[314]

The town of Nyankunde experienced one of the worst massacres. This town lies south of Bunia in the Irumu district and has a high concentration of Hema and Bira inhabitants. In September 2002, some combination of Lendu armed

[312] It was Prosecutor Luis Moreno-Ocampo's first Press Conference, held at ICC headquarters on July 16, 2003. In his PowerPoint presentation, he confirmed: "The Prosecutor has decided to closely follow the situation in Ituri" (ICC Press Release, July 24, 2003).

[313] *Attacks on Civilians in Ugandan Occupied Areas in Northeastern Congo* (February 13, 2002).

[314] "*Covered in Blood*," p. 25

groups and RCD-ML troops killed more than a thousand people in Nyankunde. Patients in the district hospital were systematically slaughtered, room-by-room. RCD-ML soldiers managed to help some medical staff escape on foot, all according to HRW:

> They left behind a destroyed hospital, hundreds dead, and some of their friends and colleagues held prisoners. "As we walked out, the Ngiti [southern Lendu] combatants carefully looked over the whole group still searching for the enemy," said one person who made the trek. "On the road we saw the body of a man whose throat had just been slit. It was a sad reminder of what could happen to us. We were all so quiet and sad."[315]

Those held prisoner at Nyankunde faced torture and death:

> At about 5:00 p.m. on Sunday Colonel Khandro arrived. He was angry because we were all still being held as prisoners. He said all the people in the prisons should be killed. One of the prisoners was a Rwandan Hutu girl, Kasima, aged about eighteen. Khandro was very cross. He said, "Why are you still holding the hostages?" He whipped the guards, and then killed Kasima himself with a double-edged knife. I saw him kill her. I ran away.[316]

Elements of the supernatural and cannibalism would end any readers' doubts about the need for international rescue.

> One day in October they arrested a woman who was accused of being a witch. But she was Hema and that was the real reason. There were about ten Lendu combatants with machetes and knives. They took her from her house, stripped her and then cut her all over – they cut off her arms and then cut her genitals. Then they killed her near the central marketplace and burned her body. About fifteen of us witnessed this . . . .[317]

In Mongbwalu, an RCD-ML commander started to reprimand one of his own men for killing an allied Lendu combatant. But the Lendu soldiers took matters into their own hands. According to one eye-witness account:

> They took [the accused] to the central area of Mongbwalu and called everyone to come and see. [He] was tied up and completely nude. They made him sit on the ground and then a Lendu fighter sat on a chair behind him, holding the man's head between his legs. He cut the soldier's throat with a quick cut of his knife. Another Lendu fighter came up with a big machete and cut open his chest and took out his heart. They gave the heart to their Chief – Maitre

315 Ibid., p. 33.
316 Ibid., pp. 33–34.
317 Ibid., p. 35.

> Kiza – who took the heart and washed it in a bowl of water they had prepared. He then placed the heart on the fire. He put a little bit of salt and oil on the heart and then roasted it. They had two large bowls of cassava ready near the fire. As the heart cooked, the other Lendu combatants took the remainder of the body and placed it on the wood and then placed other hot pieces of wood on the top so the body was roasting as well. The Chief and his entourage then ate the heart with the cassava while the rest of the Lendu fighters ate the body. They even offered the crowd some of the meat.[318]

Sexual violence was an especially wrenching theme in these testimonies. International tribunals were beginning to recognize gender crimes as a distinct category of offense. Investigators in the Congo documented an onslaught of violence directed against women, including rape, sexual torture, and sexual slavery, especially for young girls abducted with other child soldiers. But it was directed not only to women: men and boys were also victims of sexual violation and torture. Their lives too were ruined.

As part of the cruelty at Nyankunde, sharper ethnic lines were being drawn:

> At about 4:00 in the morning they made us walk to the nurses' compound. They made us go into the first house and continued to hit us. There were about nine combatants – four of them had guns, others had machetes, spears, and axes. They made us strip and then they raped us. Two men raped me, three men raped each of the other girls – it lasted about an hour and a half. I knew the men who raped me. They were people from Nyankunde. One said to me that he had liked me before but that my parents wouldn't let him marry me. He said he could do whatever he wanted to me and that I didn't have a word to say about it. He even said he could kill me if he wanted to.
>
> After they had finished raping me they said I could put on some of my clothes and that I should go to check on my son – he was just twelve years old. My son had a Lendu father, so he was Lendu, although I am considered Hema .... I looked everywhere for my boy that night but couldn't find him. I heard that they had taken him to transport their goods to Songolo and it was only much later that I heard from a friend that he had died.[319]

These stories grab us with their unimaginable cruelty. Investigators were keen to collect them, documenting the precise events and perpetrators with enough detail to bring war crimes charges – knowing that the ICC was created for just this purpose.

[318] Ibid., pp. 35–36.
[319] Ibid., p. 45.

Soon after this report was prepared, and just as MONUC peacekeepers were arriving in force, a broader group of NGOs expanded its presence in Bunia. Starting from May 2003, the respected Médecins Sans Frontières (MSF) provided much-needed medical services in the main center. It also kept careful records, compiling a systematic appraisal of violence during the period 2003–07. When the old networks of 2002–03 were dissolved in the face of international intervention, the violence in Ituri resumed with scarcely a pause. New alliances – this time without the sharp ethnic boundaries – ensured that Ituri's civilians would remain in constant danger.

Focusing on sexual violence, MSF summed up the record over four years. During that time, each month saw 50 to 300 victims reporting sexual assault. Some of this may have been due to the utter breakdown of social order, with an increase in victims below the age of twelve, which MSF thought included an increase in non-combat violence, implicating the "private and domestic sphere." MSF also reported that 2 percent to 4 percent of sexual abuse was reported by men or boys. "The specific nature of [sexual] violence risks having a lasting impact on the whole community, as men are not spared from this type of abuse."[320] With the changed military dynamics after 2003, the very process of "pacifying" the rural areas had itself generated its share of victims among the civilian population, both from the Congolese national army and from domestic violence in camps for displaced civilians.

Providing professional treatment for sexual violence was important for reasons of health and community-building.

> The medical treatment protocol for sexual violence at Bon Marché Hospital encompasses both prevention of sexually transmitted diseases (gonorrhea, chlamydia, syphilis) and prevention of tetanus for all victims. It also includes AIDS prevention for victims attending the hospital within 72 hours of the last assault, prevention of pregnancy as a result of rape (within 5 days of the assault) and a hepatitis B vaccination (within 3 months) . . . . At present, there are few health facilities in Ituri that offer quality health care to carriers of the HIV virus, and it is acknowledged that the rate of seropositivity in armed groups is high, in a context in which rapes have taken place on a massive scale.[321]

Such close medical analysis of violence – especially sexual violence with its physical, psychological, and social aftermath – added complexity to the task of computing the human toll of Ituri's conflicts. There was the challenge of

[320] Médecins Sans Frontières, *Ituri: "Civilians Still the Victims": Permanence of Sexual Violence and Impact of Military Operations* (Geneva: October 2007), p. 18.

[321] Ibid., p. 22.

finding adequate resources for treating (and, if possible, rehabilitating) the victims, even as their social and economic opportunities remained grim. With any cessation of violence, there would remain enormous humanitarian challenges that could take years to address.

An additional challenge was to find adequate legal terminology – which would have to be created, if necessary – to express fully the nature of these offenses, especially sexual crimes, as a route to full accountability. By investigating Ituri's conflicts in detail, NGOs were anticipating new opportunities for legal redress should the ICC decide to bring charges.

5.2 ADVOCATES FOR HUMAN RIGHTS

A Muddy Path

The world order has seen a proliferation of actors in the past half-century, reaching below and beyond traditional nation-states. New constituencies and structures challenge the dominance of national sovereignty, riding on a wave of human rights. With its appealing universal values, the human rights agenda is still under development, and its potential must still be tested in forums like the ICC.[322] But something fundamental has changed in the links between sovereign rulers and their diverse populations.

The connection between human rights, seen as a broad movement, and the ICC has been described in various metaphors. Benjamin N. Schiff imagines a mighty river, fed over the centuries by obscure tributaries, gaining special strength in the twentieth century. It all started in antiquity with rational ethics and just-war theory, moving on through a transitional phase of chivalric fortitude. The flow picked up in 1474 in the trial of Peter von Habenbach for offenses against civilians in Alsace. The great Dutch theorist Hugo Grotius opened the floodgates. The historical streams joined forcefully in the aftermath of World War II at Nuremberg, followed by the ad hoc tribunals founded in the 1990s. It all disgorges into a sea of righteousness with the founding of the ICC in 1998.[323] Updating Schiff's image, the area in question is now safely secured inside a sculpted moat, fortified by imported

[322] For a balanced overview, see Kenneth Cmiel, "The Recent History of Human Rights," in Akira Iriye, Petra Goedde, and William I. Hitchcock (eds.), *The Human Rights Revolution: An International History* (Oxford: Oxford University Press, 2012), chapter 1.

[323] *Building the International Criminal Court* (Cambridge: Cambridge University Press, 2008), chapter 1. Schiff's playful conceit pays homage to the "norm cascade" propounded by fellow political scientist Kathryn Sikkink. He is the first to admit that "The river metaphor has its limits, too" (p. 15).

sand dunes, on a street called Oude Waalsdorperweg in the northeast part of The Hague.

There is just about everything wrong with this image. Its whiggish triumphalism seems premature, at least until the Court finishes a few more trials. Above all, it obscures the elements of human agency and contingency, not to mention the many tensions and contradictions that surrounded most of the historical precursors of the ICC. The phrase "Nuremberg to The Hague" collapses decades when global justice was swimming upstream. One hopes for a more nuanced history sensitive to differences in culture and society.

Scholarly attention has uncovered a score of early blueprints for international criminal courts, looping back well before Nuremberg to Versailles, and even farther into the nineteenth century. Despite the temptation to see them all as anticipations of today's ICC, on closer examination the details point more to fragments and dead ends. In surely the most extensive survey of these efforts, historian Mark Lewis traces multiple "strands of international legal movements" with such a diversity of purposes and proponents that the strands "did not converge in one legal agenda," while the arguments, ideas, and plans led off into conflicting projects.[324] In a mixed assessment, William A. Schabas looks back at trail-blazing figures who preceded the Nuremberg trials, whose accomplishments were to map "some of the unfordable streams, the precipices, and the *culs-de-sac*, leaving blazes and waymarks to show the trails to be avoided as well as the way forward. . . . This inchoate phase in the history of international justice left the half-formed trail, muddy and soon rather overgrown," that would ultimately open out into Nuremberg.[325]

This overwrought history of international justice calls for some humility. One cannot rule out that Oude Waalsdorperweg is just another muddy path. The larger movement for human rights may someday reassess whether a permanent ICC remains a high priority. For the moment, however, the link remains strong. The hundreds of NGO members represented in Rome played a major role in shaping its outcome.[326] Several years before the Rome meetings, new coalitions of international NGOs were formed, seeking to build networks of local civil society groups around the world who

[324] *The Birth of the New Justice: The Internationalization of Crime and Punishment, 1919–1950* (Oxford: Oxford University Press, 2014), pp. 5–9.

[325] *The Trial of the Kaiser* (Oxford: Oxford University Press, 2018), pp. 1–2.

[326] Marlies Glasius, *The International Criminal Court: A Global Civil Society Achievement* (New York: Routledge, 2005).

would push for ratification of the Treaty in their home countries – and push further for domestic implementation.[327]

Mobilizing Civil Society

Human rights norms draw sovereign authority down to earth, redefining state authority by declaring the state's responsibility to respect the expanding rights of ordinary citizens. By qualifying sovereign power, human rights finds countervailing authority in transnational alliances, reaching across borders, forming global networks of moral persuasion.[328] While some skeptical critics question the sources and coherence of the human rights movement,[329] others have celebrated its breadth, analyzed its novel mechanisms, and pushed for stronger institutions to enforce human rights.[330]

These emerging human rights fill an expanding rhetorical space in public discourse, confronting traditional claims by nation-states to speak with the single voice of supreme authority. Diversity among and within modern states promotes a greater plurality of voices – individuals and groups – with ties extending to like-minded groups across the community of mankind. Horizontal rights alliances have become fresh conduits of power and authority, strengthening dissenting voices inside each nation. Global rights networks concentrate moral pressure on target states.[331]

The rise of human rights was a response to the twentieth century's painful experience with totalitarian regimes, both at the end World War II and again during the Cold War. Also important was the global anticolonial struggle from the 1950s, when the ideal of self-determination was advanced by restless nationalists as a universal human right, over against colonial powers.[332] A further chapter in the story of human rights began at the end of the Cold

[327] The group formally became the Coalition for the International Criminal Court, which remains a powerful source of support and critical commentary on the ICC's performance. See David Bosco, *Rough Justice: The International Criminal Court in a World of Power Politics* (Oxford: Oxford University Press, 2014), pp. 39, 68. Also influential was the worldwide coalition Parliamentarians for Global Action.

[328] On the networked structure of global connections, see Anne-Marie Slaughter, *A New World Order* (Princeton: Princeton University Press, 2005).

[329] For two different rhetorical styles, see Stephen Hopgood, *The Endtimes of Human Rights* (Ithaca: Cornell University Press, 2013); and Samuel Moyn, *The Last Utopia: Human Rights in History* (Cambridge: Harvard University Press, 2010).

[330] Ruti G. Teitel, *Humanity's Law* (Oxford: Oxford University Press, 2011).

[331] Margaret E. Keck and Kathryn Sikkink, *Activists beyond Borders: Advocacy Networks in International Politics* (Ithaca: Cornell University Press, 1998).

[332] Roland Burke, *Decolonization and the Evolution of International Human Rights* (Philadelphia: University of Pennsylvania Press, 2010); Pierre Hazan, *Judging War, Judging*

War, with sudden attention to places in the developing world where conventional state power had collapsed. Such state weakness would present a dual threat to local human rights and to the security of neighboring states.[333]

It was this condition in the Congo, with its calamitous human toll, that captured the attention of human rights advocates. Their response focused on two broad remedies: restoring order by rebuilding central political institutions and serving justice by holding accountable those responsible for "atrocities that deeply shock the conscience of humanity."[334]

After World War II, an overriding motive in founding the United Nations was to rein in future aggression among nation-states.[335] Shortly after the UN was created, a broad coalition of countries drafted and approved the Universal Declaration of Human Rights – a non-binding framework for future transnational norms. It would take another thirty years for rights networks to codify these principles in treaties with the intended force of international law.[336]

Contemporary with the Universal Declaration was the 1948 Convention on Genocide, which defined, denounced, and criminalized the wholesale extermination of populations, including at the hands of their own governments. Rounding out this foundational period, the 1949 Geneva Conventions restated past international laws governing the conduct of war, advancing human rights by expanding the protection of combatants and civilians in times of war. Whereas earlier agreements had been limited to conventional wars between states, the 1949 treaties added new language for conflicts involving non-state militarized groups.[337] The Geneva

History: Behind Truth and Reconciliation (Stanford: Stanford University Press, 2010), chapters 3–4.

333 Mark Duffield, *Global Governance and the New Wars: The Merging of Development and Security* (London: Zed Books, 2001).

334 Alex Veit, *Intervention as Indirect Rule: Civil War and Statebuilding in the Democratic Republic of Congo* (Frankfurt: Campus, 2010); Séverine Autesserre, *The Trouble with the Congo: Local Violence and the Failure of International Peacekeeping* (Cambridge: Cambridge University Press, 2010).

335 Mark Mazower, *Governing the World: The History of an Idea* (New York: Penguin Press, 2012) provides a skeptical view alongside a comprehensive history. On the longer history of campaigns against aggression, see Oona Hathaway and Scott J. Shapiro, *The Internationalists: How a Radical Plan to Outlaw War Remade the World* (New York: Simon and Schuster, 2017).

336 See Daniel Moeckli and Helen Keller (eds.), *The Human Rights Covenants at 50* (Oxford: Oxford University Press, 2018).

337 See William I Hitchcock, "Human Rights and the Geneva Conventions of 1949," in Iriye, Goedde, and Hitchcock, *The Human Rights Revolution*, chapter 4.

Conventions (and subsequent Protocols) thus brought the later Congo conflicts into the web of legal responsibilities binding on state and non-state perpetrators. Legal protections for individual victims of internal violence became part of the expanding arena for human rights.[338]

How are these rights and duties enforced under international law? The formal treaty mechanisms were notoriously weak. And the sovereign power of oppressive states, when openly challenged, would usually win out against the softer rhetorical tools available to non-governmental proponents of human rights.[339] It was this contest that brought to prominence our best-known global NGOs. Beginning in the 1970s, these organizations began to mobilize public opinion against the persecution of individuals and groups.[340] Eventually, the rhetorical power of human rights, fully articulated and amplified through global NGO networks, might presume to blunt the worst abuses – or at least shame tyrannical governments into softening (or hiding) their baleful practices. Shaming would include the naming of individual perpetrators.[341]

There was remarkable energy in this approach, as global NGOs coordinated their advocacy with international aid policies of Western governments. They engaged as well through the outreach functions of international organizations like the UN, and with regional interstate organizations in Latin America, Africa, and Europe. For all these efforts, sovereign prerogatives in predatory states remained strong enough to ward off most threats of "humanitarian intervention" from outside. But in the 2000s, new pressure would arise from an international legal principle known as "Responsibility to Protect" (or R2P). It was the idea that sovereign power could retain its privileges only so long as it successfully fulfilled its duty to protect the human rights of its citizens. Failure to meet this burden could shift responsibility to the international community.[342]

It was not necessary to apply R2P to the Congo, since the regime of Joseph Kabila clearly acknowledged its weakness, asking for outside help in

[338] Philippe Sands, *East West Street: On the Origins of "Genocide" and "Crimes Against Humanity"* (New York: Knopf, 2016).

[339] Christian Tomuschat, *Human Rights: Between Idealism and Realism* (Oxford: Oxford University Press, 2014).

[340] For an important case study, see Barbara Keys, "Anti-Torture Politics: Amnesty International, the Greek Junta, and the Origins of the Human Rights 'Boom' in the United States," in Iriye, Goedde, and Hitchcock, *The Human Rights Revolution*, chapter 9.

[341] For more case studies, see Lilian A. Barria and Steven D. Roper (eds.), *The Development of Institutions of Human Rights: A Comparative Study* (New York: Palgrave Macmillan, 2010).

[342] See Thomas G. Weiss and Ramesh Thakur, *Global Governance and the UN: An Unfinished Journey* (Bloomington: Indiana University Press, 2010), chapter 10.

rebuilding central political authority. In contrast to his father's resistance, young Joseph had little choice but to accept global assistance to maintain some semblance of governance. International aid was essential for maintaining the budgets of not just the Congo but also Uganda and Rwanda.[343] NGOs embraced this cooperation, while remaining skeptical about chances that the Congo would be able to improve its abysmal human rights record, anytime soon.

Adding Accountability to Human Rights

Global NGOs drew further strength in the 1990s with the creation of international criminal tribunals dealing with mass atrocities in the Balkans, in Rwanda, and eventually in Sierra Leone.[344] In the period following the Cold War, these tribunals provided a mechanism for the international community to hold rights violators accountable, up to and including the highest leaders of offending states. Along with conducting prosecutions, these tribunals offered rights advocates a powerful new legal language: a detailed code for classifying and condemning the most serious atrocities. At last there would be institutions for confronting the impunity that had allowed rights violators to flourish – states oppressing minorities, but also non-state groups slaughtering civilians.[345] The signature conflicts of the 1990s included widespread ethnic cleansing, genocide, sexual crimes, and the abuse of children. Global NGOs played a central role, leading up to the 1998 Rome Conference to create the ICC.[346] They remain committed to fulfilling the promise of the ICC, sometimes challenging the Court to live up to its human rights ideals. Starting in 2003, NGO investigations in the Congo helped set the stage for the first trials entering the Hague tribunal.

[343] For background on NGO roles in reshaping the international debt regime, see Thomas M. Callaghy, "Networks and Governance in Africa: Innovation in the Debt Regime," in Thomas Callaghy, Ronald Kassimir, and Robert Latham (eds.), *Intervention and Transnationalism in Africa: Global-Local Networks of Power* (Cambridge: Cambridge University Press, 2001), chapter 6.

[344] See William A. Schabas, *The UN International Criminal Tribunals: The Former Yugoslavia, Rwanda and Sierra Leone* (Cambridge: Cambridge University Press, 2006); Milena Sterio and Michael Scharf (eds.), *The Legacy of Ad Hoc Tribunals in International Criminal Law: Assessing the ICTY's and the ICTR's Most Significant Legal Accomplishments* (Cambridge: Cambridge University Press, 2019).

[345] Aryeh Neier, *The International Human Rights Movement: A History* (Princeton: Princeton University Press, 2012), chapter 11.

[346] Schiff, *Building the International Criminal Court*, chapter 5.

5.3 NGO INVESTIGATIONS IN THE CONGO

Converging on Ituri

Chaos in the Congo posed a timely challenge for human rights advocacy. The permanent international court opened up a new path toward strengthening human rights. One powerful idea behind the ICC was that atrocities would spread in the absence of legal mechanisms for punishing perpetrators. In the Congo, where sovereign power and judicial authority had broken down, the masterminds of violence were likely to escape with impunity. The justice vacuum allowed mass murder and sexual violence to become standard practice. Ituri attracted larger national rebel groups, as well as violence entrepreneurs from Uganda and Rwanda. This critical analysis emerged fully in HRW's Ituri report in July 2003, which addressed its recommendations directly to the new ICC.[347] The ICC Prosecutor would immediately heed these calls, opening up a path to The Hague as the venue where impunity would be checked. ICC prosecutions alone might not solve the Congo's massive human rights problems. But without ICC action, there would be less hope for nation-building, truth-finding, and ethnic reconciliation. First, of course, the United Nations would need to mount a strong show of force, putting an end to local barbarism in Ituri.

Soon after the 1998 insurrection, when Rwanda and Uganda tried unsuccessfully to topple their earlier protégé Laurent-Désiré Kabila, the United Nations authorized its first Congo mission (MONUC). Its initial purpose was to help implement an exit agreement reached among the outside combatants, which also included Zimbabwe and Angola.[348] But such efforts were in vain, given bad faith among these neighboring states and within the older-Kabila's government. After his father's assassination, the young Joseph Kabila had little choice but to accede to international demands. As a token stand-in for national sovereignty, Joseph Kabila played his role dutifully, as the Inter-Congolese Dialogue lurched toward a transitional plan in March 2003. During this lead-up to the 2006 national elections, MONUC pursued a more forceful agenda. The initial MONUC challenge came in Ituri, where NGOs on the ground warned that ethnic violence was burning out of control. Disarming the Ituri fighters (on the way to ending impunity) would cement the alliance between UN peacekeepers and international

[347] *"Covered in Blood,"* p. 4. All the other recommendations speak to judicial and criminal remedies in other forums.

[348] See Emily Paddon, *The Perils of Peacekeeping without Politics: MONUC and MONUSCO in the DRC* (London: Rift Valley Institute, 2013).

NGOs. At least, this was the hope in mid-2003, when HRW published its "*Covered in Blood*" analysis.

Before that publication, HRW, along with AI, the ICG, and other NGOs, had kept close track of conflicts throughout the Congo, going back to the overthrow of Mobutu in 1996–97. Initially, the main focus was on the eastern districts, where Rwanda's post-genocidal vengeance set off waves of local ethnic violence. Publications after 1999 described the rise of RCD and MLC as national movements backed respectively by Rwanda and Uganda, accusing both rebel groups of massive human rights violations. The Kivus remained the epicenter of violence, even after Ituri started to draw some attention. The ICG kept the focus on the Kivus, although it recognized the difficulties of bringing lasting change to all areas.[349]

By 2002, as word of ethnic conflict in Ituri started to grab more attention, this relatively small district on the edge of the Congo had become a microcosm for problems affecting the entire nation. A UN Report issued in December 2002, based on observations by UN staff in Bunia, established the core narrative frame, starting from the ouster of Governor Lompondo in August.[350] At that moment, the UPC, said to be a tightly structured organization with Thomas Lubanga as its President (also presumably in charge of its armed wing), seized control and proceeded to settle ethnic scores. This was now homegrown Ituri violence, with Uganda fading into ineffectiveness, amid rumors that Lubanga was shifting his allegiance to Rwanda. More rumors – which would come to pass – suggested that even a powerful warlord like Lubanga faced pressure within his own ranks. And indeed, as events unfolded between March and May of 2003, these predictions of anarchy came true. By July 2003, when HRW issued its landmark report, Ituri had been "covered in blood" for almost a year; and now it might finally claim the attention of the ICC.

Anticipating ICC Action

Before "*Covered in Blood*," NGO reports on Ituri focused primarily on external sources of conflict: the national rebel groups and regional interlopers. The UPC, whose very existence remained obscure until the middle of 2002, was seen as a pawn in the larger struggle. The main source of violence was Uganda, while national rebel groups like RCD and MLC were exploiting local

[349] See, for example, HRW, *Eastern Congo Ravaged: Killing Civilians and Silencing Protest* (May 2000); ICG, *The Kivus: The Forgotten Crucible of the Congo Conflict* (January 2003).

[350] UN, *DRC: Special Report* (December 18, 2002).

conflicts in their competition for the national spotlight. According to these early Ituri reports, the Congo government was doing little to advance peace, while supporting Mai-Mai groups and Hutu refugees in the Kivus. The preferred solutions remained national power-sharing and the transitional plan for restoring full Congolese national sovereignty.[351] There were legal obligations on all the parties, coming from international humanitarian law (mainly the 1949 Geneva Conventions and later Optional Protocols). Breaches of these laws were the responsibilities of countries like Uganda and Rwanda, providing reasons for the UN to increase its strength on the ground.

Just one month before "*Covered in Blood*," the ICG issued a lengthy analysis of the Ituri crisis, adopting the time frame from the UN Report (December 2002) that began with the August takeover of Bunia, with the ousting of the RCD-ML and Governor Lompondo. ICG closed this time frame with the arrival of French peacekeepers in late May 2003.[352] But local Ituri figures like Lubanga appear as shadow proxies for foreign patrons. The report wants Uganda to live up to its agreement to discipline its forces and to leave Ituri, but first to prepare the way for a robust UN force to take over. The ICG remained more worried about the Kivus and argued that Ituri might be a test case for solving the more intractable problems farther south. Their report mentions the ICC in passing but does not describe Ituri events in the language of the Rome Statute.

Another respected organization with researchers into the field, AI, followed a similar cycle. Its Ituri report from March 2003 makes no mention of the ICC or the Rome Statute as a source of applicable law. The main driver of events is Uganda, in conjunction with the chief rebel groups and factions MLC and RCD-ML.[353] Drawing on the December 2002 UN Report, AI mentions UPC as the local challenger to those larger rebel groups. It mentions Lendu armed groups, but so far it does not have organizations or acronyms, or leaders whose names are known. Uganda bears the main responsibility, and the legal framework remains traditional Geneva law.

By fall 2003, however, the lessons from "*Covered in Blood*" had been universally adopted. An October report from AI was subtitled "Ituri: A Need for Protection, a Thirst for Justice," and leads with the idea that ICC prosecutions "will send an important signal":

[351] See HRW, *Chaos in Eastern Congo: UN Action Needed Now* (October 2002); ICG, *Storm Clouds over Sun City: The Urgent Need to Recast the Congolese Peace Process* (May 2002).

[352] ICG, *Congo Crisis: Military Intervention in the Congo* (June 2003).

[353] AI, *Democratic Republic of Congo: A Neglected Human Rights Tragedy in Ituri Province* (March 20, 2003).

> There will be no peace and reconciliation in Ituri without justice. Impunity must not be sanctioned in the name of national unity. The cycle of brutal reprisals, of attacks and counter-attack will not stop unless impunity is ended for all abuses . . .. For years Ituri has been the scene of plunder, pillage and massive human rights abuse, while the world watched in silence. This must not be allowed to happen ever again. International attention must be converted into effective action to protect the human rights of the people of Ituri.[354]

In July 2003, "*Covered in Blood*" changed the discourse in NGO reports by highlighting the promise and the language of the Rome Statute. This was not the first mention of the ICC in HRW Congo reports. One year earlier, a special report on sexual violence in the Kivus quoted sections of the Rome Statute, but it was devoted more to describing the legal scope of sexual crimes, along with practical problems from lack of medical treatment.[355] Prior to "*Covered in Blood*," HRW reports focused on "the humanitarian crisis" rather than prosecutable crimes. In these prior reports, which alternate their attention between Ituri/Uganda in one report and the Kivus/Rwanda in the next, the preferred remedies are UN intervention.[356] Mention of the Hema–Lendu ethnic conflict goes back to early 2001, around the same date as the *New York Times* article cited at the beginning of the chapter. Prior HRW reports on ethnic violence call on the President of Uganda to contain his troops, thus smothering the flames ignited by rogue officers.[357] Construing the conflict as the responsibility of a foreign army fits with duties laid out in the Geneva Conventions, which focus on state violations of the laws of war.

[354] AI, press release, October 21, 2003.

[355] HRW, *The War within the War: Sexual Violence against Women and Girls in the Eastern Congo* (June 2002), Appendix I. The report uses terms like "impunity" and "crimes against humanity," which become commonplace in and after "*Covered with Blood*."

[356] The HRW report *Chaos in Eastern Congo: UN Action Needed Now* (October 2002) speaks to "humanitarian crises" (p. 7) rather than a crime scene; it stresses the need for protecting civilians rather than prosecuting perpetrators (p. 2); it treats Ituri as part of the larger disorder in the Kivus (p. 2); it sees Uganda and Rwanda as the main players, with Lubanga mentioned briefly as a minor local player (p. 5); it draws generally on international humanitarian law rather than invoking Articles in the Rome Statute, more aligned with notions of state responsibility than with individual criminal responsibility (p. 3). Lubanga's hold on Bunia after August 2002 is described as tenuous; his main opponent is the RCD-ML group led by Mbusa Nyamwisi – not the Lendu group as such. Although ethnic violence is obviously present, the report mentions victims among the Bira and other ethnicities beyond the Lendu; and the violence is described as reciprocal (p. 5). Nande outsiders like Nyamwisi share the blame for chaotic conditions (p. 4). This report, released October 31, 2002, is the last HRW report on the area before the July publication of "*Covered in Blood*."

[357] This call was made in all the HRW reports before 2003.

HRW reports through early 2002 do not mention any Ituri militia groups by their later acronyms; nor is the UPC mentioned as an organization, let alone Thomas Lubanga. The main agents of violence are Ugandan military officers, who encourage Ituri groups loosely identified by ethnicity.[358] In October 2002, the last HRW report on Ituri prior to *"Covered in Blood"* contains no mention of the Rome Statute – although it references UN reports on the conflict in Bunia, the local UPC ouster of RCD-ML, and Thomas Lubanga as leader of the Hema faction.[359] There is no suggestion, in late 2002, that Lubanga and his group should bear any criminal burden, let alone that he should become the primary figure to stand trial before the ICC. But after March 2003, as NGO investigators arrived in greater numbers, the response to Ituri events underwent a major transformation. The process of framing and narrowing the conflicts started in earnest with *"Covered in Blood"* and would culminate in the 2006 ICC arrest warrant for Thomas Lubanga.

Of course, *"Covered in Blood"* repeats certain themes carried over from earlier reports. It repeats earlier concerns about national rebel groups (Bemba's MLC, Nyamwisi's RCD-ML), along with Uganda, in fostering the Ituri conflicts. But *"Covered in Blood"* brings a different tone and uses a different language. It describes the massacres as crimes; it seeks to name the leaders who should be held accountable; and it insists that unrest in the Congo will not stop until the courts put an end to impunity. In effect, this analysis speaks directly to the newly elected ICC Prosecutor: here, Sir, is your first case!

In the prefatory section on Recommendations, *"Covered in Blood"* addresses some sixteen recommendations to local governments, rebel groups, Ituri groups, the United Nations, donor nations, and, finally, the ICC Prosecutor.[360] All sixteen are directed to punitive legal remedies, going beyond past reports that had concentrated instead on strategies of national state-building. Governments are admonished to investigate and punish violations of war crimes laws by their respective armies (failure to do so could itself become a punishable offense at the ICC). The Congolese government and the United Nations are encouraged to set up judicial mechanisms for prosecuting offenders, including an ad hoc tribunal through the UNSC to punish offenses committed before July 1, 2002 that fall outside the

[358] HRW, *Attacks on Civilians in Ugandan Occupied Areas in Northeastern Congo* (February 13, 2002).
[359] HRW, *Chaos in Eastern Congo: UN Action Needed Now* (October 31, 2002).
[360] *"Covered in Blood,"* pp. 3–4.

jurisdiction of the new ICC.[361] MONUC resources should be used to investigate Ituri rights violations to ensure that evidence is available for criminal prosecutions. Donor governments are asked to amplify the NGO message about ending impunity by investigating crimes and denouncing criminal acts such as the recruitment of child soldiers.

Organizations and Accountability

In its resolve to label groups and name individuals, "*Covered in Blood*" established the now familiar catalogue of acronyms, assigning local Ituri groups to labeled organizations. Atrocities on this scale do not happen by random accident. One must infer a degree of planning and structure, and investigators on the ground were ready to attribute massacres to organizations that must bear accountability – through their declared leaders. The UPC had already emerged as the name chosen by rebellious Hema members of the RCD-ML in August 2002, shortly before they sent Governor Lompondo packing.[362] "*Covered in Blood*" characterizes the UPC as "a government that purported to control Bunia and the rest of Ituri." It eagerly names some of the new ministers in this self-proclaimed government, including "Bosco Taganda" as Assistant Minister of Defense.[363] As a government, the UPC failed to carry out its legal responsibilities.

For UPC officers to be held accountable for unlawful acts, it helps to regard this organization as a coherent, effective governing body – its coherence being the favored explanation for its criminal effectiveness. Having an internal constitution, organization chart, ministerial appointments, and a tight chain of command – all of these characteristics allow for justice systems to assign criminal liability to people acting within the organization. Thus, if one portion of the UPC expressed extreme anti-Lendu rhetoric, their actions

[361] The history of this proposal goes back at least to October 2001, according to Pascale Kalume Kambale, "A Story of Missed Opportunities: The Role of the International Criminal Court in the Democratic Republic of Congo," in Christian De Vos, Sara Kendall, and Carsten Stahn (eds.), *Contested Justice: The Politics and Practice of International Criminal Court Interventions* (Cambridge: Cambridge University Press, 2015), p. 175, n. 10.

[362] There remains confusion about the origins and status of the UPC as an organization. Henning Tamm provides valuable background, even though one might differ from his conclusions. *UPC in Ituri: The External Militarization of Local Politics in North-Eastern Congo* (London: Rift Valley Institute, 2013), p. 20. The UN Secretary-General's 2004 update on Ituri described the UPC as "an embryo" in 2001 and noted that its "official" beginning was not until mid-2002. UN Secretary-General, *Special Report on the events in Ituri, January 2002–December 2003* (July 16, 2004), p. 47.

[363] "*Covered in Blood*," p. 10.

could become the legal responsibility of persons in charge, including leaders like Thomas Lubanga.[364]

Similarly, the report assumes a tight connection between political and military functions, imputing still more responsibility to the UPC and its hierarchical leadership. Although the field history from 1999 suggests the decentralized, networked structure of local armed groups, the HRW report lumps together all Hema "militias" as simply "UPC/Hema."[365] This structural elision led to the conclusion that massacres of Lendu were carried out by a unified Hema command, even placing Lubanga himself on the battlefield.[366]

Indeed, as arguments later emerged at the ICC, the prosecution seemed to presume a cross-cultural analogy between the military structure of the UPC and the military command structure of the Nazis during World War II. These comparisons will be discussed more fully in the analysis of the two Ituri trials. "*Covered in Blood*" is a fully researched document, aware of qualifications surrounding the inferred structure of UPC.[367] In later retellings, however, most of these qualifications got lost in the rush to assign blame. In this framing and narrowing of events, there is a steady loss of cultural details that distinguish Ituri armed violence from that of more familiar European models.

While the UPC's inflated governing claims were allowed to confirm its organizational reality, the references to Lendu armed groups in "*Covered in Blood*" are more cautious. At times, these groups are described as "militias," without specifying any particular degree of unified command. The report acknowledges that Lendu groups worked in loose alliances, often cooperating with the RCD-ML and with Congolese national forces, among others. In most cases, the report distinguishes between actions taken by Southern Lendu (Ngiti) armed groups, based in Irumu, and those taken by Northern Lendu (Bale) groups in Djugu.[368]

But the report goes much farther in an influential summary table of "Who Is Who – Armed Political Groups in Ituri" as of May 2003. Here, the two Lendu coalitions are named as unified organizations – although it is not clear

364 Ibid., p. 21.
365 Ibid., p. 17.
366 HRW, *The Curse of Gold* (June 2005), in part V (see the mysteriously sourced n. 57), in the context of UPC attacks on Mongbwalu. At the time of the Congo trials, no evidence was presented in court that Lubanga commanded any military operations.
367 The lead author, Anneke van Woudenberg, held local interviews with key figures (Lubanga, Nyamwisi) during February 2003, weeks before other NGO investigators arrived. It was her first HRW assignment, although she had previously spent several years in the Congo (including Ituri) with OXFAM-GB.
368 Ibid., p. 30.

whether they are two separate organizations, or one combined organization. In this table, their prominence is fully equal to the UPC, and equal also to larger national rebel groups like Nyamwisi's RCD-ML and Bemba's MLC.[369] Once named in this handy table, the Lendu alliances instantly became organizational realities, even though the report's detailed information about both "political parties" remained sketchy.[370] One called itself the Front for National Integration (FNI), under which "Lendu militias are reportedly being organized" in a military wing. These are presumably Northern Lendu, because the table lists separately the "Patriotic Force of Resistance in Ituri" (FRPI), based in North Kivu and fostered by RCD-ML, which is "meant to bring together Ngiti militias with traditional leaders in a single force against the UPC."[371]

Published in July 2003, this summary table may be the first mention in European publications of FNI and FRPI as self-standing organizations. In the body of the report, their status is still quite cloudy. Yet their appearance in an influential table and their inclusion in an accompanying schematic diagram of alliance webs in Ituri begged the question of whether their structure was anything like that of the UPC, let alone RCD-ML. In the table, FNI and FRPI are two organizations; while in the schematic diagram they are fused: FNI/FRPI/Lendu occupies a single box, similar to the UPC/Hema box.[372] As investigations of past violence gained momentum among NGOs during the remainder of 2003, FNI and FRPI (sometimes fused, sometimes separated) became standard explanatory terms – providing the symmetrical counterpart on the Lendu side to the Hema-led UPC.

Lendu figures themselves helped to promote this retrospective view. After all, having been the "commander" of an organized militia might earn you a future place at the table for the Ituri Pacification process. When Mathieu Ngudjolo stepped out of the shadows in March 2003, he freely invoked both organizations. In his subsequent trial, however, it was heavily disputed exactly how the FNI was organized, and just when Ngudjolo played any major role in it. *"Covered in Blood"* also picked up an incidental mention of "Commander

369 Ibid., p. 16.
370 Ibid., p. 30.
371 Ibid., p. 17. The schematic diagram was much reprinted, providing beginners to the topic with a presumptive *dramatis personae* of Ituri history. The summary table became the basis for a slightly expanded version in the July 2004 UN Secretary-General, *Special Report*, pp. 47–50. NGOs quickly established an acronym-based discourse on the dynamics of Ituri violence, leading one historical commentator to observe: "Congo was rich not only in raw materials, but also in abbreviations"; David van Reybrouck, *Congo: The Epic History of a People* (New York: HarperCollins, 2010), p. 451.
372 *"Covered in Blood,"* p. 17.

Germain" as a "key commander in the newly formed FRPI," allegedly present at the September 2002 Nyankunde massacre.[373] This appears to be the first mention of Germain Katanga in NGO reports, but certainly not the last. In his trial, Katanga denied any role in Nyankunde, and his relationship to FRPI remained obscure. The judges dropped any reference to FRPI in their final judgment on his guilt.[374]

Proving individual criminal responsibility would become a major obstacle in the Congo trials, for reasons explored in later chapters. By contrast, HRW and other NGOs were able to reach immediate assessments: naming perpetrators and demanding accountability. If you knew what you were looking for, it was relatively easy to rest such judgments on anonymous interviews gathered in the wake of mass violence. But the ICC courtroom has more stringent standards for evidence. Reports like "*Covered in Blood*" are assigned the lowest level of relevance, in the words of the Presiding Judge in the Ntaganda trial.[375] But the deeper impact of this and other reports came much earlier in the trial process, as the ICC Prosecutor borrowed heavily from NGO paradigms and presumptions in building his master narratives for the Congo trials.

5.4 THE POWER OF VICTIMS' JUSTICE

Victims Imply Perpetrators

Arriving in the midst of near-anarchy, waiting for international peacekeepers to disarm the hold-out combatants, NGOs like HRW, AI, FIDH, and ICG were investigators with an urgent agenda. Different from social scientists like Vlassenroot, Raeymaekers, Veit, and Autesserre, their inquiry into *What Happened?* was linked to the imperative to determine *Who Was*

[373] Ibid., p. 34. Note that in the July 2004 UN Secretary-General, *Special Report*, Commander Germain was assigned his last name Katanga (p. 49).

[374] These matters are discussed fully in Chapter 8.

[375] Ntaganda Trial Chamber, transcript, June 22, 2016, ICC-01/04–02/06-T-107-ENG, p. 58. HRW's research methodology was dissected during the Ntaganda trial cross-examination of Anneke van Woudenberg, the author of "*Covered in Blood*" and the later *Curse of Gold* report from June 2005. Van Woudenberg defended her methods with boundless confidence, while the Defense cross-examiner pointed to potential weaknesses. It happened, for example, that "*Covered in Blood*" mistakenly connects Bemba's MLC troops with the UPC action in Mongbwalu in November 2002, when in fact Bemba's forces were engaged farther west in Ituri. See Ntaganda Trial Chamber, transcript, June 23, 2016, ICC-01/04–02/06-T-108-ENG, pp. 14–21. As mentioned above, *The Curse of Gold* questionably places Thomas Lubanga on the battlefield in Mongbwalu during the November 2002 action. This report provided core theories for Prosecution charges later brought against Bosco Ntaganda.

Responsible? Their investigations produced the essential narrative that would dominate ICC courtrooms for more than a decade.

In the Congo trials, the strict requirements for legal accountability, as framed by the ICC Prosecutor, would be challenged by the Defense argument that *What Happened?* was actually far more complex than first appeared, and simply did not match up with the Prosecutor's prior answer to the question *Who Was Responsible?* The acquittal of Ngudjolo and the late modification of charges against Katanga will be studied in later chapters, illustrating the gap between the start and finish of the Prosecutor's respective cases. As in the Lubanga trial, there were difficulties finding trustworthy witnesses who would confirm, in Court, some of the things "everyone just knew" in the field. This was especially true with former child soldiers, none of whom were deemed credible enough by the judges to have their evidence taken seriously.

World War II prompted new doctrines of accountability for conditions of war and mass destruction. Early on, the Nuremberg precedent swept aside the excuse that military staff (and others) could hide behind the state apparatus – that they were merely "following orders." The human toll of such conflicts gave rise to a new criminal lexicon, moving beyond the standard legal definitions of murder, assault, and theft. These enhanced terms included genocide, crimes against humanity, and war crimes.[376] They were tested from the 1990s in the UN ad hoc criminal tribunals, in response to violence in the Balkans, in Rwanda, and in Sierra Leone.

As part of the human rights revolution, a new world order would recognize the fundamental dignity of individual persons – not just the sovereignty of separate states. It was individuals themselves who deserved protection under these new rules – reaching the inevitable conclusion that perpetrators of these new offenses could just as well be internal actors, and not always foreign military. This enhanced individualism would pierce the veil of sovereignty surrounding past uses of international law: recognizing, within the global system, human beings as such; treating them, for the first time, as subjects within the reach of international legal concepts.[377]

[376] Carsten Stahn points to the fluid nature of the core crimes, which have "evolved over time" in response to changing notions of human rights, causing "a lot of confusion." "In many instances, crimes have been developed beyond their historical context through jurisprudence or institutional practice. The process of gradual adaption and normative expansion remains a source of friction . . . ." *A Critical Introduction to International Criminal Law*, pp. 32, 15.

[377] The human rights influence is emphasized by Hitchcock, notably the expansion of non-combatant protections, under the Fourth Geneva Convention, to include all civilians; "Human Rights and the Geneva Conventions of 1949," in Iriye, Goedde, and Hitchcock, *The Human Rights Revolution*, chapter 4.

The same focus on individual persons would ultimately reach not just those who are victims but also those who must be held accountable. It was different at Nuremberg, where the individuals accused were carefully chosen to represent diverse parts of a criminal state system, as reconstructed by the Allies.[378] The UN ad hoc tribunals consciously defined their targets as individual persons. Under the influence of human rights concepts, just as individual victims gained new status for protection, the focus turned to individual perpetrators within state systems, as targets of criminal prosecution.

This view of perpetrators as individuals was on full display at the ICTY. The ICTY Prosecutor, Carla Del Ponte, introduced her high-profile case against the former President of Serbia Slobodan Milosevic, declaring this new direction in international criminal trials:

> The accused in this case, as in all cases before the Tribunal, is charged as an individual. He is prosecuted on the basis of his individual criminal responsibility. No state or organization is on trial here today. The indictments do not accuse an entire people of being collectively guilty of the crimes, even the crime of genocide. It may be tempting to generalize when dealing with the conduct of leaders at the highest level, but that is an error that must be avoided. Collective guilt forms no part of the Prosecution case.[379]

Days before, speaking to the court directly, Milosevic had denounced the trial as a politically motivated act by enemies of Serbia. The justice on offer in The Hague was not an ordinary trial, but an example of *victors' justice* – an act of retribution by states that had intervened in the Balkan crisis, acting through the United Nations: "I wish to say that the entire world knows that this is a political process. So we are not here speaking about legal procedures that evolve into political ones. This is a political process to begin with, and as far as what I would prefer, I would prefer the truth."[380] Milosevic was by no means alone in dismissing international trials as political stunts. Virtually every defendant appearing in 1990s tribunals made similar points, playing up one of the deepest anxieties about international justice: that the

[378] Taking his title from one of the iconic phrases used at Nuremberg, namely that "crimes are caused by men and not by abstract entities," Gerry Simpson explores the impact of this focus on the development of international criminal law; "Men and Abstract Entities: Individual Responsibility and Collective Guilt in International Criminal Law," in André Nollkaemper and Harmen van der Wilt (eds.), *System Criminality in International Law* (Cambridge: Cambridge University Press, 2009), chapter 4.

[379] International Criminal Tribunal for the former Yugoslavia (ICTY), Milosevic Trial transcript, February 12, 2002, p. 4.

[380] Ibid., January 30, 2002, p. 352.

process itself was tainted by state power dynamics. The scorn for *victors' justice* challenged the legitimacy of the whole trial system.[381] To be sure, the international judges themselves came from a diverse group of nations. The legal rules and procedures were all drafted in a neutral idiom. But suspects could still deride the prosecuting authorities in these novel courts, who were seen picking and choosing their way through a turbulent world to find a small subset of targets. The curse of victors' justice is virtually impossible to refute on its own terms.

For drafters of the Rome Statute, the inclusion of victims in trials can be seen as one response to such anxieties about the neutrality of international prosecutions.[382] Nor is it just a token response – providing mere courtroom space for Legal Representatives of Victims, dressed in the same lawyerly garb as advocates for Prosecution and Defense. Rather the presence of victims is meant to remind the Court of its overriding mission: to hear the literal cries of victims and pursue justice on their behalf. *Victims' justice* becomes the contemporary answer to a half-century of doubt about victors' justice. As one advocacy group expressed it, the new role of victims is the "grand beacon of international justice." Later commentators worried lest the expectations should run too high: "If the ICC is not thoughtful, prudent, and practical about how it manages these expectations, it could end up digging its own grave with the spade of good intentions."[383]

The testimonies of victims, as collected by NGOs like HRW, were powerful in persuading the ICC Prosecutor to take seriously the deep suffering of innocent civilians in Ituri. While these testimonies were not formal evidence – or at least not yet, pending the commencement of the trial – they promised to inject moral urgency into the courtroom. It was the victims' plight, after all, which demanded justice from the Congolese chaos. The moral vibrancy of victims' justice would insulate the ICC from skeptical attacks tied to the Court's *political* vulnerabilities.

[381] See Martti Koskenniemi, "Between Impunity and Show Trials," in Jochen Frowein and Rüdiger Wolfram (eds.), *Max Planck Yearbook of United Nations Law*, Vol. 6 (The Hague: Brill Nijhoff, 2002), 1.

[382] See "Law's Anxieties: Show Trials," in Gerry Simpson, *Law, War and Crime* (Cambridge: Polity Press, 2007), chapter 5.

[383] These quotes are (respectively) from the NGO known as Redress, and the academic Eric Stover, both cited in Sergey Vasiliev, "Victim Participation Revisited: What the ICC Is Learning about Itself," in Carsten Stahn (ed.), *The Law and Practice of the International Criminal Court* (Oxford: Oxford University Press, 2015), chapter 45, footnotes 10 and 11. Vasiliev reviews the major debates and cites relevant sources. For other commentary, see Sara Kendall and Sarah Nouwen, "Justified and Abstract Victimhood," *Law and Contemporary Problems* 76 (2013), 235.

Ending Impunity: The Bridge to The Hague

As legal scholar Gerry Simpson has written: "In war crimes trials, bad men are tried for gross crimes but, at the same time, the prosecuting party often is attempting to clear itself of tyranny."[384] For the ICC, victims' justice advances both agendas. It is on behalf of the victims, not some political goal, that the Court does its work. This approach also benefits from its association with what Simpson calls the "evil men" view of history,[385] which insists on identifying individual agents deemed responsible for atrocious crimes.

No matter how complex the underlying conditions, the victims' stories confirm the reality of harms defined by law as *war crimes* and *crimes against humanity*. The unalterable truth of victims creates a moral imbalance: until perpetrators are found and punished, the victims' world – and ours – is haunted by impunity. The dyad of *victim and perpetrator* personalizes the generic link between *injury* and *impunity*. The *injury* side is fully present, indeed self-validating with the testimonials collected from victims by international NGOs. From a moral perspective, *impunity* is the natural corollary of such injuries, setting off moral demands: obliging the international community to take steps to end impunity.

From a moral perspective, the demand for action cannot be weakened by the difficulty or obscurity of the task. Indeed, the task only gains in nobility, by virtue of its raw challenges. The activist spirit among delegates at the 1998 Rome Conference can be understood in this sense of mission. In the words of the Preamble, the very existence of "unimaginable atrocities that shock the conscience of humanity" creates two imperatives for ICC States Parties: "**Affirming** that the most serious crimes of concern to the international community as a whole must not go unpunished . . .; **Determined** to put an end to impunity for the perpetrators of these crimes . . .." For compelling reasons, the drive against impunity follows an elevated path from places like Ituri back to The Hague. Yes, the testimonies of victims originate in Ituri and must be collected there. It is then up to professional legal representation to see that their stories ring out in the Hague courtroom. But identifying perpetrators, especially during an ongoing brutal conflict, requires more capacity than the Ituri environment itself can provide. International justice offers a vocabulary to describe these enhanced kinds of crime. Even more, it provides a methodology for attributing responsibility to specific individuals, caught in the web of complex actions. As an outgrowth of Nuremberg and

384 Simpson, *Law, War and Crime*, p. 89.

385 Ibid., p. 191, n. 28. Echoing Hannah Arendt, Simpson elaborates: "War crimes trials describe a world of bad men doing evil deeds. The problem is the man: 'no man, no problem'" (p. 157).

1990s courtroom innovations, the ICC Statute was designed to codify modes of "individual criminal responsibility," even when complex actions are leveraged through layered organizations, or permitted by the omissions of command from military officers and other superior leaders.[386]

The suffering of victims discloses the real-world condition of impunity. Justice to the victims means defeating that impunity, using the language and exemplary procedures of Hague-based criminal trials. True, the ICC principle of *complementarity* says that the preferred location for combating impunity should rather be in local courts – especially if domestic legal reform has expanded the criminal code to include the special crimes covered by the Rome Statute. But complementarity requires that local courts be "willing and able genuinely" to put an end to the impunity defined by international criminal law. For countries like the Congo in its years of disorder, the route of morality follows that bridge to The Hague.[387]

Victims and Restorative Justice

The goal of ending impunity inspires the ICC, providing the moral substance to defeat the inevitable skeptics of international justice. But other ways of regarding victims' suffering may push the Court in different directions. A different moral response – but equally passionate – would demand practical steps to reduce or relieve human suffering, at least for survivors trying to make their way under difficult circumstances. Quite aside from prosecutions, the existence of victims and their straitened prospects can also demand more practical remedies: to relieve the present suffering and to prevent a similar fate befalling future victims. Tragically, it is now too late for those who lost their lives. It may also be too late to literally "restore" family and community life, once the foundations have been ripped away. But saving lives and rebuilding communities are compelling goals, precisely in the face of widespread suffering. In this alternative, *victims' justice* centers on improving the quality of life for victims – whatever may happen to perpetrators. The punishment function

[386] Articles 25, 28.

[387] In its ruling on the admissibility of the Katanga case, an ICC Appeals Chamber adopted a broad definition of the national judiciary's "unwillingness" to prosecute, to include the circumstances where the Congo was simply inactive in pursuing the perpetrators of the Bogoro violence (the basis for the ICC case against Katanga). If the Congolese courts' inactivity were to bar the ICC prosecution, said the Appeals Chamber, then "impunity would persist unchecked, and thousands of victims would be denied justice." Katanga Appeals Chamber, Decision on Admissibility, September 25, 2009, ICC-01/04-01/07-1497, para. 79.

can thus be distinguished from a rehabilitative or restorative purpose for the community of victims.[388]

This expansive approach to victims may seem far removed from trial proceedings. And indeed, judges in the courtroom were often forced to select among potential classes of victims. Thus, the more practical challenges *outside the courtroom* fell to other parts of the Court, inventing new capabilities and forming new alliances.

When the first trials began at the ICC, opinions varied about the definition of victims as a class. At the core were specific persons whose suffering was tied to the direct criminal actions of the accused on trial – or of his varied associates. In the case of Lubanga, where the charges were restricted to child soldiers, this meant that the victims were restricted to children (then) under the age of fifteen who were recruited, conscripted, or used in Lubanga's military operations. In terms of ethnic groups, these victims were predominantly Hema – the same ethnicity as Lubanga and his allies. Under this restrictive definition, the far more numerous targets of Lubanga's actual attacks (understood mainly as Lendu) would not count as victims. This obtuse result comes from the limited way in which the ICC Prosecutor, choosing his first "cases" in the Congo, chose to address the problem of impunity. After Lubanga was convicted at trial, this restrictive definition of victims was upheld by the ICC Appeals Chamber.[389]

A more inclusive concept of crime victims, advanced by global NGOs, was the much larger group of people injured by Lubanga's forces, not just the direct victims of highly specific crimes charged by the Prosecutor. An even broader concept would have included all those who suffered from the violence in Ituri, approaching the scale of suffering that had prompted international groups to intervene. Borrowing ICC language, one might describe this larger group as *victims of the situation* rather than victims of the specific *case* that was being handled at trial. The gap between these two classes of victims reflects tensions in the juridical purpose of placing victims at the center of international justice. The moral power of victims' justice offers new criminal courts a vital defense from charges of partisanship. The inference from victimhood to impunity of perpetrators was the key pivot – giving the ICC its moral edge. Yet prosecutorial strategies for attacking impunity, including limiting the charges at trials, had the unintended boomerang effect of shrinking the category of victims.

388 Hazan, *Judging War, Judging History*, chapters 1–2.

389 Lubanga Appeals Decision on the Principles and Procedures to Be Applied to Reparations, March 3, 2015, ICC-01/04-01/06-3129, para. 8.

Victims of the *situation* might include the vast majority of people living in Ituri during these years of turmoil, starting with those killed, maimed, sexually assaulted, displaced – where the survivors faced ruined lives and shattered hopes. Indeed, the ICC concept of the *situation* applied not just to Ituri but to the entire Congo. The suffering of survivors everywhere in the country was neither less nor greater depending on whether the ICC Prosecutor had selected particular *cases* that would put distinct perpetrators on trial. At this level of vision, it was clear that most of the population needed some kind of restorative assistance, whether or not their afflictions could be connected to a specific crime.

Justice at this most comprehensive level exceeds the technical bounds of criminal courts. Indeed, the contrast is common between the "retributive" justice of legal prosecutions and the "restorative" justice of aid programs on a national scale. At times this discussion veers into a facile dichotomy between goals of justice versus goals of peace – only to be tempered by the more realistic position that prosecutions can, under proper circumstances, be an integral part of the peace process.[390]

It is important to note that the ICC has found various creative solutions to the unmet needs of victims' justice. While not abandoning the duty to fight impunity, the Prosecutor acknowledged the broader perspective in a 2007 Policy Paper on the Interests of Justice.[391] According to Conor McCarthy's reading of this document, the Prosecutor "noted the existence of alternative forms of justice in respect of mass atrocities other than individual punishment," and expressed openness to "alternative justice mechanisms including national reparations programmes," especially "'in dealing with large numbers of offenders and in addressing the impunity gap.'"[392]

Before the Court began its first trials, it encouraged new initiatives by its small staff administering the TFV. This Fund is mentioned in Articles 75(2) and 79, although many questions remained to be settled about its mandates, both in relation to paying reparations to "victims of the case" at the conclusion of ICC trials and also in relation to broader, community-based groups of victims. And while the Lubanga case ended up narrowing the classification of victims for purposes of case-related reparations, it seemed to liberate the TFV to cultivate independent ways of channeling assistance to communities in conflict areas, in cooperation with NGOs and other aid providers.

390 See Priscilla Hayner, *The Peacemaker's Paradox: Pursuing Justice in the Shadow of Conflict* (New York: Routledge, 2018).

391 Office of the Prosecutor, Policy Paper on the Interests of Justice (September 2007).

392 "The Rome Statute's Regime of Victim Redress: Challenges and Prospects," in Stahn, *Law and Practice of the ICC*, chapter 46, p. 1213.

A balanced assessment of the ICC, with respect to its recognition of victims, requires looking both inside and outside the courtroom.[393]

Indeed, in June 2018, just days after the Appeals Chamber reversed the conviction of Jean-Pierre Bemba, thus dashing hopes for court-assigned reparations to more than 5,000 registered "victims of the case," the TFV announced an immediate increase in aid directed to distressed communities in the CAR.[394]

5.5 THE CALL TO JUDGMENT

The Language of Legality

Moral truth yearns for final judgment. The energy stirred by victims' testimonies drives a hard battle against impunity. But there can be no victory until a court pronounces its judgment of guilt. International aid may alleviate suffering, but a judicial ruling carries unique moral weight in the larger balance of justice.

The struggle against impunity brings the victims' demands all the way to The Hague. But there, upon arrival, a different kind of spirit prevails. These trials will be conducted in a court of law, following principles of legality laid down in the Statute. The difference is easily overlooked, in the same way as it is possible to meld the Preamble into the 128 Articles of the Rome Statute – which alone have the force of law. To be sure, the authors of the Statute explicitly framed their legal mission with the high moral language of the Preamble, in a bold flourish performed by a combination of legalists and NGO activists. When the Prosecution's case gets launched, the moral imperative commands the rhetorical ramparts of courtroom discourse. Invoking the victims' moral claims gives the Prosecutor a vital opportunity to project good faith.

Once the trial starts in earnest, it follows the overarching principle of legality, with its insistence on the integrity of a fair trial. Legality re-channels the founders' idealism along new paths. It answers the inevitable question: why do we need to go through the time and expense of a trial, when we know that such evil men are guilty? It was Churchill, reportedly, who initially

393 A compendium of issues relating to victims and reparations principles was issued in 2019 by the Lubanga Appeals Chamber. See Judgment on Appeals on Setting the Size of the Reparations Award, July 18, 2019, ICC-01/04–01/06–3466.

394 ICC Press Release, Following Mr Bemba's Acquittal, Trust Fund for Victims at the ICC Decides to Accelerate Launch of Assistance Programme in Central African Republic (June 13, 2018).

dismissed the Nuremberg legal project as an extravagant diversion – when the obvious solution was to take Nazi officials out behind the building and shoot them.[395] The principle of legality in international criminal law found its voice rather in Chief Prosecutor Robert Jackson's famous phrase: that the Allies would send a message of fairness and reason, and would "stay the hand of vengeance."

The contrary image haunting legalists during the Nuremberg period was the Soviet "show trials" of the preceding decade. The popular image of these Soviet dramas decried the cynical corruption of the trial's whole essence. What seemed to happen in the courtroom had already been scripted in advance: the formal trial was but a pre-arranged spectacle. Later on, in the 1950s Eastern European trials, if the accused should suddenly fail to make the anticipated confessions, there were stand-by tape recordings of prior confessions, ready to sound out in the courtroom.[396]

The anxieties about show trials went still deeper: anxieties about the subjective limits of conventional moral philosophies. In Soviet Marxist practice, the humanistic perspective was overridden in the larger moral sweep of materialist history.[397] The simulated trial was ostensibly aligned with this objective morality, even if the particular details were not accessible to the moral conscience of the individual spectator – or perpetrator. In reviling show trials, international criminal courtrooms elevate the accessible values of impartiality and the rule of law.

Law between Morality and Politics: The Hope of Finality

Nuremberg showed how the principle of legality might carry the burden of moral crusade. It featured the display of moral restraint, supported by legal tools of fair process and impartial fact-finding. This notion of legality found its way, with modifications, into the Rome Statute. Though steeped in moral

395 Gary Jonathan Bass, *Stay the Hand of Vengeance: The Politics of War Crimes Tribunals* (Princeton: Princeton University Press, 2000), pp. 185–86.

396 George H. Hodos, *Show Trials: Stalinist Purges in Eastern Europe, 1948–1954* (New York: Praeger, 1987), p. 82, with reference to the 1952 Czech trial of Rudolf Slánský. See also Anne Appelbaum, *Iron Curtain: The Crushing of Eastern Europe 1944–56* (New York: Doubleday, 2012), chapter 12 on "Internal Enemies."

397 The prime witness to this moral dichotomy is Arthur Koestler's 1940 novel *Darkness at Noon* (reprinted, New York: Scribner's, 2019). A recently discovered original version of Koestler's text has been released in English: *Darkness at Noon (Rediscovered Manuscript)* (New York: Vintage Classics, 2019). Maurice Merleau-Ponty wrote a 1947 philosophical analysis, taking issue with Koestler, published in English in 1969 as *Humanism and Terror* (new translation, New York: Routledge, 2017).

outrage at unspeakable atrocities, the ICC builds on the Nuremberg manner of speaking and acting inside the courtroom. There is a path to final judgment in individual cases, provided trial judges adhere to the canons of legal fairness. At trial, the evidence from prior investigations is to be thoroughly tested in the system of adversarial justice. Putting aside all preconceptions, the final judgment about guilt is based solely on evidence tested at trial, using legal principles subject to review within the trial framework. In the end, a judgment of guilt would require "proof beyond a reasonable doubt," given these significant ground-rules.

Chapter 6, covering the legal provisions of the ICC, reviews the main principles of legality written into the Rome Statute, drawing on common understanding among negotiators from multiple nations, multiple cultural backgrounds, and multiple moral persuasions.

As the Congo trials will show, this juridical turn remains vulnerable to challenge from contrary perspectives – political and moral. As the ICC faced difficulties in the initial trials, critics were quick to revive the skeptical attack on victors' justice, based on the broader critique of international justice as fundamentally political in nature. The ICC rejoinder, based on the countervailing notion of victims' justice, has thus far shown limited strength in quieting these challenges. The dual nature of the Court as a political institution *and* a legal institution means that this critique will always find plenty of traction.

From the moral perspective, legality runs the risk of diluting moral imperatives. Going back to Hannah Arendt's famous analysis of the Eichmann trial in 1961, the ultimate fear of moral purists is that legal institutions fail to grasp the full magnitude of human evil. Indeed, the whole legal enterprise is conducted in strictly neutral terms. In trials, criminal judgment must be based solely on legally qualified evidence. This means that the trial is compelled to reject laws drafted ex post facto, relying instead on the prior definitions of crimes to carry the moral weight. In the end, findings of guilt must survive the test of reasonable human doubt.

Legal processes are a part of the human enterprise. There are no assurances that trials held under legal rules will fully certify themselves. And they will certainly not answer critics from all directions, given the deep passions surrounding Hague trials. Whether these critiques seek to reduce law to just one more form of politics, or whether they fault the law for moral blindness, the fragile medial status of ICC justice guarantees future criticism.

6

ICC Structures, Dynamics, Tensions

6.1 BUILDING THE LEGAL FAITH

The Alchemy of the Courtroom

Victims' stories were brought from Ituri and the CAR to The Hague – to the venue where, in a final reckoning, justice might be achieved. Some stories were told directly in live testimony. More often they were retold by learned representatives fluent in the idioms of international law. As the first ICC cases unfolded, the question was whether the justice being sought was the sort of justice this new court could deliver. The final judgments rendered in the Congo cases would underscore these concerns.

Putting justice into action means creating new institutional structures, testing the original purity of vision. In theological terms, international criminal justice cannot remain an abstract faith, locked in sacred tablets. It must be incarnated in the terrestrial realm, to which its tenets are explicitly directed. The battle against impunity performed this leap with the Rome Treaty, specifying the courtroom as its transformational realm.[398]

The ICC courtroom is a legal space, governed by the dynamics of law as a human process. Within these confines, the first ICC trials released strong tensions that had been held in check during the high optimism of creation. The Court's founding creed was reconfigured within legal boundaries. Moral

[398] In March 2003, at the ICC's ceremony swearing in the inaugural group of eighteen judges, the sanctity of the courtroom was invoked by the French ICC official Bruno Cathala: "The first act of the judiciary in every society has always been to set aside an area, to delineate a physical form in which to dispense justice. The judicial area is sacred and by its very existence defines the lay area. It is commonly symbolically protected by the presence of a 'bar' or barrier in the courtroom, which ensures that the law cannot be attacked." Cited in David Bosco, *Rough Justice: The International Criminal Court in a World of Power Politics* (Oxford: Oxford University Press, 2014), pp. 85–86.

values in the Preamble were compressed into a legal code, organized within the rule of law. Humanitarian principles were embedded in legal definitions of crimes, with special mechanisms developed to channel moral responsibility into particular modes of individual liability.

The printed legal codes looked imposing on paper – part of the law's claim to legitimacy. But change and adaptation are fundamental to a set of laws being asked to do bold and experimental tasks. The ICC's evolving standards were joined with a set of process values carrying their own intrinsic dimensions of faith: impartial trials, the presumption of innocence, and a prohibition on ex post facto rules. The whole legal apparatus needed to show how it would carry the weight of moral expectations, in responding to new and unusual circumstances.[399]

Outside the courtroom, Court officials scrutinize local conflicts – while keeping a close eye on global politics. But overt politics are put aside once an individual trial begins, with its emphasis on rigorous testing and balanced judgments. The strict rules and procedures of trial courts serve as a rejoinder to skeptical suspicions arising from the Court's inescapable role in practical affairs.[400] Overall, the challenge inside the courtroom is to construct a mediating realm, inspired by moral values, informed by politics, and conserving the faith in legal process values. The courtroom seeks to avoid the pathologies of moral self-certainty (delivering raw moral judgments) and of political self-dealing (choosing whose interests are being served). In the struggle between faith and skepticism, the law recognizes something of both elements within its crafted design.

The idealism behind the legal process is revealed in its universal reach. As Robert Jackson expressed it during the Nuremberg trials:

> We must never forget that the record on which we judge these defendants today is the record on which history will judge us tomorrow. To pass these defendants a poisoned chalice is to put it to our own lips as well. We must summon such detachment and intellectual integrity to our task that this Trial will commend itself to posterity as fulfilling humanity's aspirations to do justice.[401]

399 Tim Meijers and Marlies Glasius, "Trials as Messages of Justice: What Should Be Expected of International Criminal Courts?" *Ethics and International Affairs* 30 (2016), 429.

400 Leila N. Sadat, "International Criminal Justice: The Journey from Politics to Law," in David M. Crane (ed.), *The Founders: Four Pioneering Individuals Who Launched the First Modern-Era International Criminal Tribunals* (Cambridge: Cambridge University Press, 2018), chapter 1.

401 *Trial of the Major War Criminals before the International Military Tribunal* (Nuremberg: IMT, 1947), Volume II, proceedings of November 14–November 30, 1945, pp. 98–102, cited in

It is a stern test; and some have noted that Jackson himself contrived to avoid using the term "genocide" in his closing arguments – sensitive perhaps to well-known brutal aspects of American history.[402] The universalism of legal norms has prompted spirited attacks against the hypocrisy of Western countries, particularly the former colonial masters.[403]

Across the post-Cold War decade of the 1990s, it seemed possible that global society was entering a new phase based on a foundation of universal legal norms.[404] In the spirit of Jackson's Nuremberg remarks, the supremacy of law means avoiding contamination by mere politics – quieting the charges of hypocrisy. Of course, the norms embodied in the Rome Statute required the consent of sovereign states, so that their universality rests – paradoxically – on the same state-centered authority that dominated the twentieth century. But there was now "an aura of utopia"[405] about international justice: that it might ultimately free signatory nations from the skeletons hidden in back closets.

Outside the Courtroom: Before and After Trials

In The Hague, at the sprawling permanent ICC headquarters, not far from the beaches of the North Sea, three stunning courtrooms fill the glass-walled central tower. These lofty chambers rise above more faceless office compounds laid out in surrounding wings. But trials themselves do not rise up out of thin air. The Court's nearly two decades of practice show the importance of its supporting parts, operating from their earth-bound office rows. Before trials can take place, the ICC must first immerse itself in selecting cases, conducting investigations, negotiating with other international bodies (such as the United Nations), and engaging with national authorities. At times it must take the plunge into the local dynamics of armed conflicts.

Such varied functions, down on the ground, prepare the way for conducting full trials high inside the courtroom tower. The ground-level buildings are

Pierre Hazan, *Judging War, Judging History: Behind Truth and Reconciliation* (Stanford: Stanford University Press, 2010), p. 15.

402 Philippe Sands, *East West Street: On the Origins of "Genocide" and "Crimes Against Humanity"* (New York: Knopf, 2016), pp. 332, 189.

403 Roland Burke, *Decolonization and the Evolution of International Human Rights* (Philadelphia: University of Pennsylvania Press, 2010).

404 The high point of celebration was Francis Fukuyama, *The End of History and the Last Man* (New York: Free Press, 1992). On a less celebratory note, see Jürgen Habermas on the thin bonds in European structures: *Zur Verfassung Europas* (Berlin: Suhrkamp, 2011).

405 Hazan, *Judging War*, p. 61. See also Jens David Ohlin, "Meta-theory of International Criminal Procedure: Vindicating the Rule of Law," *UCLA Journal of International Law and Foreign Affairs* 14 (2009), 77.

likewise concerned with what happens after trials are finished, regarding long-term restorative goals from a human rights perspective. To the extent that trials themselves are a means to larger ends, the ICC must consider their impact on social change beyond the Hague courtrooms. While the first ICC trials took many years to complete, the time horizon extends even farther when it comes to ending impunity and mitigating future conflict. To this day, the violence in Ituri and the CAR continues to spread, in the midst of social, economic, and political breakdown. It remains to be seen how and when finished trials, conducted in The Hague, might have any measurable impact in the everyday world, however scrupulously those trials are conducted.[406]

For some Court observers, this dose of realism suggests that the ICC's long-term mission cannot be confined to simply conducting trials. The goal might even be to *avoid* ICC trials, if the alternative exists to strengthen national justice systems.[407] The ICC's signature doctrine of *complementarity*, built into its founding treaty, declares The Hague to be the second-best venue for conducting criminal trials, assuming national systems can do their job. Taking this policy of deferral to the next stage, the Court's larger mission may require strengthening local judicial capacities within its member states.[408] Considering the Court's mixed performance in the Congo trials, conducted inside its own courtrooms, the idea of building up alternative forums must be approached seriously, if modestly.[409]

Complementarity was originally seen as a limitation on ICC judicial power – the result of compromises among treaty negotiators in Rome. In particular, member states with developed legal systems should be able to block Hague-based trials, minimizing the impact on their own nationals. But there was another side to complementarity: the responsibility to improve

406 See Carsten Stahn, "Legacy in International Criminal Justice," in Margaret M. deGuzman and Diane Marie Amann (eds.), *Arcs of Global Justice: Essays in Honour of William A. Schabas* (Oxford: Oxford University Press, 2018), chapter 14.

407 Moreno-Ocampo famously argued that "the absence of trials led by this court as a consequence of the regular functioning of national institutions would be its major success." ICC Press Release, Election of the Prosecutor, Statement by Mr. Moreno-Ocampo, April 22, 2003.

408 See Jo Hyeran, Mitchell Radtke, and Beth A. Simmons, "Assessing the International Criminal Court," in Theresa Squatrito, Oran R. Young, Andreas Føllesdal, and Geir Ulfstein (eds.), *The Performance of International Courts and Tribunals* (Cambridge: Cambridge University Press, 2018), chapter 6.

409 Payam Akhavan, "Complementarity Conundrums: The ICC Clock in Transitional Times," *Journal of International Criminal Justice* 14 (2016), 1043.

internal justice mechanisms that needed help. Court officials and critics have explored this approach under the rubric of "positive complementarity."[410]

Another long-term initiative was to flesh out the Court's responsibilities to victims, beyond their participation in Hague trials.[411] In addition to creating that framework for participation, the Lubanga trial demonstrated that a crime-centered approach to victim reparations would have little impact on larger populations in the Court's main conflict areas. The more ambitious initiatives belong to the TFV, perhaps the Court's most creative branch among its outlying functions.[412] In the end, advancing restorative justice may be more demanding than conducting exemplary trials. The evolving nature of the ICC must include its capacity to shape what happens outside the courtroom, as well as inside. Contemplating both dimensions, the ICC must ultimately assess how its fortunes might be divided between its legal and restorative functions. Performance from the Court's first two decades needs to inform this long-term calibration.[413]

Both inside and outside the courtroom, the ICC initiated its mission in a series of central African conflicts that departed significantly from familiar twentieth-century military models. The major concepts of international criminal law still bear the stamp of historic conflicts between traditional sovereign states. The ICC crime definitions retain this orientation to state-centered practice, in ways that complicated the Congo trials.[414]

Already, in the decade leading up to the Rome Conference, the international legal community had been wrestling with new kinds of conflict, both in the Balkans and in Rwanda. The Congo situation added further anomalies: endemic violence between non-state actors; looser forms of military structure; globalized economic networks. When legal concepts embedded in the ICC criminal code were tested in the Congo trials, the Ituri and CAR conflicts seemed like an uncomfortable fit. The same challenges will complicate the

[410] Carsten Stahn, "Complementarity: A Tale of Two Notions," *Criminal Law Forum* 19 (2008), 87.

[411] M. Cherif Bassiouni, "International Recognition of Victims' Rights," *Human Rights Law Review* 6 (2006), 203.

[412] On the early development of the Trust Fund, see Benjamin N. Schiff, *Building the International Criminal Court* (Cambridge: Cambridge University Press, 2008), pp. 183–86. See also Tom Dannenbaum, "The International Criminal Court, Article 79, and Transitional Justice: The Case for an Independent Trust Fund for Victims," *Wisconsin International Law Journal* 28 (2010), 234.

[413] An important reckoning with these issues was issued by the Lubanga Appeals Chamber, Judgment on Appeals on Setting the Size of the Reparations Award, July 18, 2019, ICC-01/04–01/06–3466.

[414] See William A. Schabas, "State Policy as an Element of International Crimes," *Journal of Criminal Law and Criminology* 98 (2007–08), 953.

ICC's future mission outside the courtroom as well. The complementarity concept, especially its positive version of building localized judicial capacity, has proved especially hard to implement in conflicts lying outside the conventional framework of sovereign states.[415] The Court's long and frustrating decade in the quagmire of Ituri would spotlight future implementation challenges, both inside and outside the courtroom.

A Dialectic of Faith and Skepticism

The flame of justice flickered ominously during the years of the Congo trials. Keepers of that flame would express understandable skepticism about the wisdom of entrusting their moral agenda to ICC structures. At times, the self-enclosed legal authority seemed to ignore its humanitarian roots, especially in the acquittals of Ngudjolo and Bemba, and the dropping of sexual violence charges against Katanga. The structural skepticism built into the adversary process would provoke a higher skepticism among NGO critics, faced with setbacks suggesting that international justice was losing its way.

The unavoidable gaps between promise and fulfillment inspire even more hyperbolic doses of skepticism among academics, skilled in managing the dilemmas of faith and skepticism. At this level, the process-centered faith in legality becomes a mask for more odious agendas. With enough polemical zeal, it is possible to unmask the whole international legal enterprise as inherently, incurably *political*. With its moral aspirations thus deflated, law descends into *legalism*. A classic source for this argument was political theorist Judith Shklar, whose doubts about post-war criminal trials presupposed a strict divide between practical, situated action and moral truth.[416] By puncturing law's pretensions to moral purpose in high-profile trials, Shklar

[415] Kris Berwouts, *Congo's Violent Peace: Conflict and Struggles since the Great African War* (London: Zed Books, 2017).

[416] Shklar acknowledged some positive effects of post-war trials but was mainly concerned to deny the moral triumphalism. Later critics would embrace this skeptical style, including Shklar's coyness in revealing the source of moral energy behind her critique. Shklar hinted at some deontological principle of personhood or voluntarism in her own position; but her rhetorical method would allow for a wide range of doctrines to reside within that Kantian space. See *Legalism: Law, Morals, and Political Trials* (Cambridge: Harvard University Press, 1964), with the hard reductionism all happening in chapter 1 on "Law and Ideology," and the whiff of "transcendence" appearing on the final page (p. 221). Gary Jonathan Bass's insightful work follows a similar logic, in the ease with which it finds hypocrisy throughout the trial process, and not just tensions, uncertainties, or mistakes. The ad hoc tribunals for Yugoslavia and Rwanda would not have been necessary if only "the West managed to summon the political will to stop the slaughters in Rwanda and Bosnia"; *Stay the Hand of Vengeance: The Politics of War Crimes Tribunals* (Princeton: Princeton University Press, 2000), p. 283.

allows moral rectitude to regain its purity. If law is utterly political, then it cannot also represent morality; and moral virtue remains safe for other potential uses. Shklar's Neo-Kantian resoluteness is the likely basis for her lasting appeal, both for moral traditionalists on the right and for progressive critics on the left. Her rhetorical flair delivers uncompromising critique, sharp and provocative – along with a flash of moral perfectionism, itself insulated from doubt.[417]

Having escaped contamination under false cover of legality, morality may simply retreat into its hermetic realm of virtue . . . presumably to await other modes of implementation. Skeptical critics of current legal institutions may be content to wrap their prey into deconstructive knots; or they may declare quite different moral agendas as a counterweight. It could be said, for example, that a Court obsessed with African violence might better apply its energy to Western states and their particular modes of violence. Why deal only with crimes surrounding armed violence, and not the forces of historical oppression and global inequality? Behind the wave of skepticism, one senses the frustration of moral ambitions that have little prospect of being implemented in an imperfect world. Those frustrations accompany sharp, insightful, sometimes world-weary theories and meta-theories – often in painstaking historical deconstructions of the present. As one wry commentator wrote: "On the verge of losing faith in our ability to distinguish right from wrong, we find solace in theory and method, for they appear to relieve us of the pain of decision-making."[418] But certainly not all skeptical critiques vanish into esoterica. The reduction of law to politics can be softened by the strategy of regarding law as a unique manner of doing politics. The reduction can then be more-or-less forgotten, as legalists map the structures and dynamics of justice institutions in naturalistic terms, with particular openness to tensions, contextual oppositions, and inconsistencies.[419] It is possible to reach well below the surface of law's formal patina to find dynamic challenges, including law's

[417] Shklar's approach finds current echoes (with a variant moral agenda) in Samuel Moyn's polemical treatment of human rights movements and international criminal prosecutions. In addition to *The Last Utopia: Human Rights in History* (Cambridge: Harvard University Press, 2010), see his essay "Anti-Impunity as Deflection of Argument," in Karen Engle, Zinaida Miller, and D.M. Davis (eds.), *Anti-Impunity and the Human Rights Agenda* (Cambridge: Cambridge University Press, 2016), chapter 2.

[418] Aleksi Peltonen, "Theodor Meron and the Humanization of International Law," in Immi Tallgren and Thomas Skouteris (eds.), *The New Histories of International Criminal Law: Retrials* (Oxford: Oxford University Press, 2019), p. 235.

[419] An example is Gerry Simpson, who brings historical and reflective depth to analyses of international criminal law. For the heuristic of law as a distinct mode of doing politics, see *Law, War and Crime* (Cambridge: Polity Press, 2007), pp. 23–25.

uneven stewardship of moral purpose.[420] In practice, criminal tribunals may be charged with hypocrisy and self-deception; but these are not the only possible verdicts, under fair adjudication.

Back in the gritty architecture of The Hague, on the verge of the North Sea, the operational systems created for the ICC have soldiered on, despite the many doubts and concerns coming from all directions and persuasions. In practical terms, ICC structures and dynamics aim to build reflexiveness into the working realities of legal process through a variety of cross-cutting functions and roles. The descriptions that follow stay below the meta-theoretical radar, focusing on a robust scheme of institutional checks and balances. The effects of this scheme will be assessed further in the context of the Congo trials.

6.2 CASTING THE LEGAL NET: CASE SELECTION

Investigating New Conflicts: Uganda, Congo, and the CAR

The twelve months following July 2002 were fateful for the new ICC. At the Court's original, makeshift building (a repurposed telecommunications high-rise on the southern outskirts of The Hague), the doors officially opened on July 1. The first courtroom trial – in the case of Thomas Lubanga – was more than six years away. During this period of relative calm in The Hague, the conflicts in Ituri burned out of control, the details of which would have to be reconstructed years later in ICC courtrooms. And it was not only Ituri setting the Court's future agenda. During these same months, conflicts in the CAR would eventually draw the ICC's attention to Congolese political heavyweight Jean-Pierre Bemba.

Additionally, this same time period saw yet another burst of trauma in northern Uganda (across the lake from Ituri) centering on a long-standing, elusive armed group called the Lord's Resistance Army (LRA). Ugandan national forces had spent several years trying to suppress the LRA and capture its zealous, erratic leader Joseph Kony, who was attacking civilians in his own ethnic territory. But Kony was masterful in fading across the border into the Congo or Sudan, and the Ugandan army was itself unpopular in the northern region of the country.[421] In December 2003, Ugandan President Yoweri

[420] The works of Martti Koskenniemi are a notable source of critical and historical insight. While not much concerned with "the bureaucratic bustle at The Hague," his writings provide important models for legal reflection, addressing foundational issues often missing from conventional legal commentaries. See, for example, "The Politics of International Law: 20 Years Later," *European Journal of International Law* 20 (2009), 7.

[421] For background, see Tim Allen and Koen Vlassenroot (eds.), *The Lord's Resistance Army: Myth and Reality* (London: Zed Books, 2010).

Museveni invited the ICC to help bring Kony and his group to justice, and the Court began to engage with the details of specific crimes. The atrocities in Ituri, the CAR, and northern Uganda were among the first such events worldwide to reach the action agenda for the new ICC Prosecutor.

In April 2003, when Luis Moreno-Ocampo began his nine-year term as Prosecutor, his task was to implement one of the Court's most controversial functions: deciding how and where to apply the new legal code in particular conflicts. Fear of the crusading prosecutor had led the Rome delegates to impose a series of constraints, laid out in the Rome Statute, which then had to be tested in practice.[422] Under pressure of events, the succinct formal rules would open out into a wide range of variations.

In addition to constraints, there had to be prudential limits; the battle against impunity could not be waged on all fronts at once. There would be no lack of possibilities. One month before the Prosecutor was elected, the Americans had gone in search of Saddam Hussein's weapons of mass destruction, turning Iraq upside down. The NATO mission in Afghanistan was little more than a year old, in the aftermath of the September 11 attacks. Long-term insurgencies were wreaking havoc in Colombia, Sri Lanka, the Caucasus, and elsewhere. The Great African War had drawn a half-dozen countries into the maelstrom of the collapsing Congo. The Prosecutor needed to make a start.

Legitimacy Mixed with Complementarity

Courts are designed to dispense justice; but they must gain their own authority from higher sources. In national systems, this source can be a Constitution, setting forth the powers and limitations of a judicial branch. Within this framework, lawmakers specify particular crimes or offenses brought before the courts, setting clear limits on judicial power and scope. These procedural and jurisdictional boundaries, prescribed in advance, lay down the conditions under which courts provide impartial justice – in harmony with the broader *rule of law*: the ideal of law as the highest secular authority.

International courts are exceptional because they do not fall under the constitution of a particular nation state. Instead, their legal authority comes

[422] The time period featured crusading judges and prosecutors in European countries determined to hold foreign leaders accountable under universal jurisdiction. The arrest of the former Chilean dictator Augusto Pinochet occurred in Britain (acting on a Spanish warrant) three months after the Rome Treaty was signed. See Bosco, *Rough Justice*, p. 60; Philippe Sands, "After Pinochet: The Role of National Courts," in Philippe Sands (ed.), *From Nuremberg to The Hague* (Cambridge: Cambridge University Press, 2003), chapter 3. The bursting dam of prosecutions became the liberating theme for Kathryn Sikkink's history, *The Justice Cascade: How Human Rights Prosecutions Are Changing World Politics* (New York: Norton, 2011).

from existing institutions, such as the United Nations, acting in accordance with the UN Charter (which, in turn, was agreed to by the sovereign nations that comprise the UN).[423] Although UN groups played an active part leading up to the Rome Conference,[424] the ICC is not a UN organization – unlike the earlier ad hoc and hybrid tribunals. Rather, it was constituted by a separate treaty, voluntarily accepted by sovereign states, who thus become members of the ICC. By 2019, more than 120 states had ratified the Rome Treaty.[425]

The principle of complementarity establishes a form of partnership between the new ICC and its members. It is a fragile collaboration, where disputes can fall between the ICC's claim to judicial supremacy and the residual power of national sovereignty.[426] Conflicts with non-member states are even more intractable, even in cases where the UNSC has played a role. The Rome Treaty structure for constituting authority does not put an end to all disputes.

The governing authority for the ICC is the Assembly of States Parties (ASP), composed of all member states, with responsibilities for key appointments, for legal amendments, and for funding.[427] While the burden of funding is spread unevenly among ICC members, within the ASP the democratic principle assigns each member state an equal voice. For the past decade the number of member states has remained fairly stable. Two members, Burundi and the Philippines (both targets of Prosecutorial attention), exited the Rome Treaty in 2017 and 2019, respectively, during which time Malaysia has joined. Despite additional threats from several African countries, the exodus seems to be limited.[428]

423 See Nobuo Hayashi and Cecilia M. Bailliet (eds.), *The Legitimacy of International Criminal Tribunals* (Cambridge: Cambridge University Press, 2017).

424 In 1989 the UN General Assembly created a study group for establishing a permanent international criminal court, in the specific context of dealing with drug trafficking, among other crimes. This was the catalyst for a series of draft proposals throughout the 1990s. See Schiff, *Building the International Criminal Court*, pp. 37–39.

425 See Frederica Gioia, "State Sovereignty, Jurisdiction, and 'Modern' International Law: The Principle of Complementarity in the International Criminal Court," *Leiden Journal of International Law* 19 (2006), 1095.

426 Disputes arose when a number of ICC member states raised the Court's ire by hosting the fugitive Sudanese President Omar al-Bashir, in a contest between the Court's eagerness to gain custody of a high-status suspect, and the obligations felt by some countries to recognize immunity for heads of state. In 2019 the ICC Appeals Chamber confirmed a finding that Jordan had violated its member-state obligations to the Court but declined to uphold sanctions against the Jordan regime. Appeals Chamber Judgment in the Jordan Referral re Al Bashir Appeal, May 6, 2019, ICC-02/05–01/09–397.

427 For an overview, see Jonathan O'Donohue, "The ICC and the ASP," in Carsten Stahn (ed.), *The Law and Practice of the International Criminal Court* (Oxford: Oxford University Press, 2015), chapter 6.

428 See the essays in Kamari M. Clarke, Abel S. Knottnerus, and Eefje de Volder (eds.), *Africa and the ICC: Perceptions of Justice* (Cambridge: Cambridge University Press, 2016), in particular Abel S. Knottnerus, "The AU, the ICC, and the Prosecution of African

Missing altogether are several very large countries that were unwilling to take on the responsibilities of ICC membership: the United States, Russia, China, India, Indonesia. Most countries from the Middle East are not members, including Iran, Saudi Arabia, and Israel. Three conspicuous non-members are permanent members of the UNSC: the United States, Russia, and China. Particular hostility to the ICC from the United States has ebbed and flowed.[429]

Checkpoints for the Prosecution

Among the first group of countries ratifying the Rome Treaty were Uganda, the Congo, and the CAR.[430] Membership opens each country and its citizens for possible ICC investigations, but only under a series of qualifying steps. When a member country *refers* a serious conflict matter to the Court, it triggers potential action by the ICC Prosecutor, including the identification of individual suspects.[431] The Prosecutor can choose to go forward with a full investigation, after confirming that the matter falls within the legal parameters of ICC jurisdiction and "admissibility" (a term relating to the principle of complementarity).[432] Further on, prior to making any individual arrests, the Prosecutor must gain approval from a panel of pre-trial judges.[433] The Prosecutor's failure to observe these constraints can spark legal challenges when issues eventually reach a judicial panel.

Presidents" (chapter 8). For a view favorable to the ICC, see Brendon Cannon, Dominic Pkalya, and Bosire Maragia, "The International Criminal Court and Africa: Contextualizing the Anti-ICC Narrative," *African Journal of International Criminal Justice* 2 (2016), 6.

[429] For an account by the US Representative to the Rome Conference, see David Scheffer, *All the Missing Souls: A Personal History of the War Crimes Tribunals* (Princeton: Princeton University Press, 2011), chapter 7. In the early years of George W. Bush's presidency, a moderate distance from the Court was maintained by the State Department: John B. Bellinger III, "International Courts and Tribunals and the Rule of Law," in Cesare P. R. Romano (ed.), *The Sword and the Scales: The United States and International Courts and Tribunals* (Cambridge: Cambridge University Press, 2009), chapter 1, part C. The contrasting view from Bush's later UN Ambassador (and President Trump's former National Security Advisor) John Bolton is aptly titled, "No, No, No to International Criminal Court," *Human Events* (August 21, 1998). For detailed coverage of US efforts to blunt possible ICC jurisdiction over US personnel, see Bosco, *Rough Justice*, pp. 71–76.

[430] All three had been financially dependent on European donor nations, at a time when the ICC was seeking enough members to get launched. The Congo was among a group of ten states ratifying the Rome Treaty in April 2002, thereby crossing the numerical threshold of signatories that began the countdown to July 2002.

[431] Articles 13(a) and 14. These triggers authorize the "exercise of jurisdiction" by the Court.

[432] Article 17.

[433] Article 58.

Although not much discussed during the Rome Conference, there was no apparent reason why a member country could not refer *itself*, inviting the ICC Prosecutor to enter and investigate. Self-referrals may have political roots, but they can also ease the Prosecutor's practical burdens, when investigations invariably require local assistance.[434] In the ICC procedural scheme, referrals (including self-referrals) allow the Prosecutor to set his or her own pace, always assuming that legal requirements of jurisdiction and complementarity have been met. The Prosecutor's first three (self-)referrals were in the Congo, Uganda, and the CAR (all in 2004).[435] The trigger itself does not guarantee that the Prosecutor will advance the case, which also depends on statutory provisions as to the "gravity" of the matter, and the overall "interests of justice."[436] The Prosecutor must constantly decide how to manage scarce resources.

Beyond referral by a member state, two other triggers allow the ICC Prosecutor to undertake investigations. The UNSC, acting under its powers laid out in Chapter VII of the UN Charter, can refer a country to the ICC Prosecutor, including countries that are not members of the ICC.[437] Although the ICC was not established under the legal authority of the UN, its structure includes a line of cooperation with the UNSC.[438] Under Chapter VII, the UNSC has the authority to respond to "threats to international peace," including the authority to intervene militarily.[439] Referring a non-member country to the ICC may accompany UNSC-authorized military intervention (as in the case of Libya in 2011[440]), or stand on its own (as in the case of the Darfur region in Sudan in 2005[441]). After the UNSC makes a referral, the ICC Prosecutor must still determine independently whether to launch a formal

434 See Harmen van der Wilt, "Self-Referrals as an Indication of the Inability of States to Cope with Non-State Actors," in Stahn, *Law and Practice of the International Criminal Court*, chapter 9.

435 The Court's first state-party referral that was not a self-referral came in September 2018, when a number of Western Hemisphere member states referred Venezuela, where the Prosecutor had already initiated a preliminary examination.

436 Articles 53(1)(c), 53(2)(c).

437 Article 13(b).

438 In addition to Article 13(b) and provision for a formal agreement between the Court and the UN in Article 2, the Preamble imagines "an independent permanent International Criminal Court in relationship with the United Nations system." The UNSC, acting under Chapter VII, may suspend ICC investigations or prosecutions for periods of twelve months (Article 16).

439 United Nations Charter, Chapter VII.

440 UNSC Resolution 1970, February 26, 2011.

441 UNSC Resolution 1593, March 31, 2005. See Robert Cryer, "Sudan, Resolution 1593, and International Criminal Justice," *Leiden Journal of International Law* 19 (2006), 195. For limitations on the ICC's scope in Sudan, see Bosco, *Rough Justice*, pp. 112–14.

investigation. Whatever kind of working relationship was envisioned between the ICC and the UNSC, this second trigger might have generated more referrals, if it were not for the veto-power of five permanent members. For example, Russia and China routinely blocked UNSC efforts to refer Syria to the ICC.[442] Of course, without UN intervention in egregious cases, the alternative could be unilateral "humanitarian intervention," as happened in 1999 with the NATO push in the Balkans on behalf of Kosovo. The Rome discussions of 1998 took place in the shadow of such controversies.

A third, more controversial trigger for investigations comes from the ICC Prosecutor's own inherent authority. At all times, the Prosecutor scrutinizes events throughout the world, informed by NGO reports, by reports supplied by member states, and by an active staff within the Office of the Prosecutor (OTP). The Prosecutor may engage in preliminary inquiries, with the threat of eventually opening an investigation as a potential peace-making strategy.[443] The Prosecutor's own authority (or *proprio motu* power) becomes its own trigger, in the absence of a referral from either an ICC member state or the UNSC.[444] But to keep this source of power in check, the Prosecutor, acting *proprio motu*, cannot proceed to a formal investigation without prior approval from a pre-trial judicial panel.[445]

This third trigger process was tested in the wake of electoral violence in Kenya (2010) and the Ivory Coast (2011), and later in Georgia (2016), Burundi (2018), and Bangladesh/Myanmar (2019); and it will continue to provoke controversy.[446] The Kenya matter would become a long agony for the ICC, until the cases were finally abandoned. *Proprio motu* investigations by two successive ICC Prosecutors met strong resistance from the Kenyan government (an ICC member state), particularly after two suspects named by the first Prosecutor were subsequently elected President and Deputy President of the

442 See Shahram Akbarzadeh and Arif Saba, "UN Paralysis over Syria," *International Politics* (forthcoming 2019).

443 His apparent strategy in Colombia was to use the threat of formal investigation to change the behavior of national officials. See Bosco, *Rough Justice*, pp. 121–23 and references cited. Prior to initiating a formal investigation, the Prosecutor is given several criteria to evaluate (Articles 53(1)(a)–(c)). See Office of the Prosecutor, Policy Paper on Preliminary Examinations (November 2013).

444 Article 15(1).

445 Article 15(3). The Prosecutor's request in the Kenya situation was approved by majority but drew a strong dissent from Judge Hans-Peter Kaul. Kenya Pre-Trial Chamber, Decision Authorizing an Investigation in Kenya, March 31, 2010, ICC-01/09–19, Dissent from Judge Kaul.

446 Lorraine Smith van Lin, "Non-Compliance and Law and Politics of State Cooperation: Lessons from the Al Bashir and Kenyatta Cases," in Olympia Bekou and Daley J. Barkett (eds.), *Cooperation and the International Criminal Court* (Leiden: Brill Nijhoff, 2016), p. 114.

country.[447] The Ivory Coast initiative, by contrast, came with the active cooperation of that country's government (prior to becoming an ICC member). Here, too, the political context was contentious, with both the electoral winner and the loser implicated in the violence. The Prosecutor's investigation seemed to reach a pause after the defeated Ivorian President was readily offered up to The Hague, along with one of his close allies, by his victorious opponent. The political context of such *proprio motu* situations reflects the fraught ground conditions in which the ICC must attempt to fulfill its mandate.[448]

These three trigger mechanisms indicate the diverse ways in which the ICC can lawfully insert itself into particular global and local controversies. Long before any courtroom trials begin, the Prosecution must acquire its lawful authority to investigate, circumscribed by these legal constraints – all much debated at the 1998 Rome Conference.[449] Key tensions in the Rome debates surrounded these precise restraints on investigations. The three triggers provide an escalating scale of checks and balances on the Prosecutor's discretion. While the first trigger – referral by a member state – could itself prove highly contentious, the special case of a *self-referral* appears to simplify matters. But while self-referrals may seem easy under conditions of normal state sovereignty, countries experiencing intense internal conflict raise doubts about who is referring whom.[450] The ICC's first three self-referrals illustrated all these difficulties.[451]

Narrowing the Field: Naming Suspects

When President Museveni invited the ICC to open an investigation in Uganda, the Prosecutor saw an easy path toward his first ICC investigation.

[447] Uhuru Kenyatta and William Ruto were elected to these positions, respectively, in March 2013, two years after receiving summonses to appear as suspects at the ICC. Charges against Kenyatta were dropped in 2014, and the Ruto trial was halted in 2016 by the Trial Chamber at the close of the Prosecution's case.

[448] Although a non-member at the time, Ivory Coast invited ICC intervention under Article 12(3), which the Prosecutor accepted under *proprio motu*. In early 2019, the Trial Chamber aborted the prosecutions of Laurent Gbagbo and his associate Charles Blé Goudé, leading the Prosecution to appeal. Ivory Coast (who in the meantime ratified the Rome Treaty) decided not to surrender Gbagbo's wife despite an ICC warrant, prosecuting her in local courts in 2015.

[449] Bosco, *Rough Justice*, pp. 44–48.

[450] Outside the politics of election violence, self-referrals may direct the Prosecutor's attention to non-state actors, especially when any prosecutions will depend on host-state cooperation and protection. See Frédéric Mégret, "Is the ICC Focusing Too Much on Non-State Actors?" in deGuzman and Amann, *Arcs of Global Justice*, chapter 10.

[451] Bosco, *Rough Justice*, pp. 95–101.

An invitation from an African leader (then highly respected in the West) was an unexpected gift, sparing the ICC the potential friction that would come from referral by another state, let alone either of the other trigger mechanisms. Moreno-Ocampo already had his eye on the Congo, Uganda's immediate neighbor, having announced in July 2003 that he would "closely follow" events in Ituri (stirred by reports from NGOs and the UNSC). By September 2003 he seemed ready to approach a panel of ICC judges, under the *proprio motu* trigger, to authorize the Ituri investigation.[452] In such an investigation, it was not inconceivable that the Ugandan President might himself become a target.

President Museveni's invitation may even have been a way to discourage that possibility. In any case, it offered the Prosecutor a quick trigger for exploring a new situation, avoiding the legal and political complications of *proprio motu*. The self-referral suggested that the ICC Prosecutor would actually be welcomed and assisted.[453] In March 2004, Congolese President Joseph Kabila followed suit, self-referring his country to the Prosecutor – likely under international pressure from donor countries pushing the Congo for national reforms.[454] By the middle of 2004, both situations were assigned to respective panels of Pre-Trial Judges, and the Prosecutor signaled that he was ready to proceed with formal investigations.[455]

The Prosecutor's journey toward making specific individual arrests must pass through several stations. The three triggers authorize the Prosecutor to

[452] See Schiff, *Building the International Criminal Court*, pp. 212–13.

[453] See Payam Akhavan, "The Lord's Resistance Army Case: Uganda's Submission of the First State Referral to the International Criminal Court," *American Journal of International Law* 99 (2005), 403. In advance of the referral, Akhavan had met with the Prosecutor on behalf of Museveni to discuss the more delicate aspects of the matter. See also Bosco, *Rough Justice*, p. 97.

[454] ICC, "Prosecutor Reviews Referral of the Situation in the Democratic Republic of Congo," April 19, 2004. Bosco mentions the "quiet intervention by European officials," *Rough Justice*, p. 98. More details can be found in William W. Burke-White, "Complementarity in Practice: The International Criminal Court as Part of a System of Multi-Level Global Governance in the Democratic Republic of Congo," *Leiden Journal of International Law* 18 (2005), 563. Pascale Kalume Kambale reports that the Congolese transitional government had agreed to the referral as early as September 25, 2003; "A Story of Missed Opportunities: The Role of the International Criminal Court in the Democratic Republic of Congo," in Christian De Vos, Sara Kendall, and Carsten Stahn (eds.), *Contested Justice: The Politics and Practice of International Criminal Court Interventions* (Cambridge: Cambridge University Press, 2015), p. 176.

[455] As discussed in Chapter 3, the Prosecutor's focus on the Congo's peripheral Ituri district was least likely to threaten Congolese authorities engaged in transitional justice talks. The ICC investigator reportedly assured US embassy officials that this would be the case. See Bosco, *Rough Justice*, p. 101.

move beyond preliminary examinations, pending a decision on whether to open a formal investigation (assuming, in the case of *proprio motu*, prior approval by pre-trial judges[456]). The trigger means that a new country-wide *situation* has been established, opening up broad-ranging inquiries into complex matters, pursued in an impartial fashion.[457] A formal investigation may end inconclusively, or it may result in the selection of individual suspects. Much depends on the quality of cooperation from leaders and local officials in the *situation* country. Moving from the general situation to specific cases activates a host of additional constraints on the Prosecutor – jurisdiction, crime definitions, and individual criminal responsibility.[458] Approval from a pre-trial judicial panel is necessary before individual arrest warrants can be issued.

In the CAR situation, the Prosecutor did not open a formal investigation until 2007, more than two years after the self-referral trigger and four years after he received the first ground reports on CAR victims from Paris-based Fédération Internationale des Ligues des Droits de l'Homme (FIDH). Those reports were detailed and chilling, especially accounts of sexual crimes. Jean-Pierre Bemba's name was included along with the names of several others deemed responsible by the NGO report.[459] The new CAR regime was pushing for action, fast-tracking a finding from the CAR judiciary that confirmed their inability to try these cases in national courts. Still the Prosecutor held back, resisting pressure to act from a Pre-Trial Chamber, being egged on by FIDH and others. During this time, the Prosecutor was focusing intensively on Darfur, following the UN referral in 2005. But there may also have been hesitation about naming Bemba, who was on the 2006 Presidential ballot in the Congo in a period of fragile nation-building, in which many Western governments held a large stake. But soon after Bemba lost the election, Moreno-Ocampo formally opened his investigation in 2007.[460]

456 Article 15.

457 Article 54(1).

458 On the choices confronting Prosecutors, see Carsten Stahn, "Damned If You Do, Damned If You Don't: Challenges and Critiques of Preliminary Examinations at the ICC," *Journal of International Criminal Justice* 15 (2017), 41; also David Bosco, "Discretion and State Influence at the International Criminal Court: The Prosecution's Preliminary Examinations," *American Journal of International Law* 111 (2017), 395.

459 FIDH News Release, "War Crimes in the Central African Republic: FIDH Formally Brings Its First Case before the International Criminal Court" (February 13, 2003). The FIDH investigative report was *When the Elephants Fight, the Grass Suffers: Report on War Crimes in the Central African Republic* (February 2003).

460 For background, see Marlies Glasius, "'We Ourselves, We Are Part of the Functioning': The ICC, Victims, and Civil Society in The Central African Republic," *African Affairs* 108 (2008), 49.

The naming of individual suspects (and whether to name any) rests entirely with the Prosecutor, working independently after one of the trigger mechanisms first opens the situation for scrutiny. When it comes time to seek a court summons or arrest warrant for specific cases, the Prosecutor must be ready to characterize that person's role in committing crimes within the Rome Statute, covering both facts and law. The Prosecutor's policies indicate a search for those who are "most responsible" for the relevant crimes.[461]

From this brief summary, the Prosecutor's movement from situations to cases passes through a gauntlet of legal requirements. The politics of each situation may be quite diverse. Levels of cooperation from situation-countries may be different, although even in self-referrals that cooperation may well remain self-interested. In 2019, ICC judges were asked to rule on two politically charged controversies surrounding investigations. In the situation in the Comoros Islands, responding to a self-referral, and after a years-long period of scrutiny, the Prosecutor declined to proceed with a formal investigation. The self-referral came from several member states with registered ships that participated in an aid flotilla sent to the Gaza Strip in 2010, in support of besieged Palestinians. The ships were intercepted at sea by Israeli Armed Forces and were turned away after a brief but lethal engagement. Prosecutor Fatou Bensouda based her decision on the insufficient "gravity" of the events, given a small number of victims.[462] For several years she resisted pressure from the Pre-Trial Chamber to pursue the matter further. But in September 2019 an Appeals Chamber ordered the Prosecutor to reconsider her decision before the end of the year.[463]

In a mirror situation, the Prosecutor wanted to proceed *proprio motu* in Afghanistan (a member state), seeking to launch a formal investigation after a decade of preliminary examination. The potential targets for individual cases would have been not just Afghan and Taliban forces but also US/Coalition

[461] See the Office of the Prosecutor, Paper on Some Policy Issues before the Office of the Prosecutor (ICC, 2003), stating the priority "to focus its investigative and prosecutorial efforts and resources on those who bear the greatest responsibility, such as leaders of the state or organization allegedly responsible for those crimes," p. 7. Critics have lamented the Prosecutor's lack of transparency and apparent caution in confronting major powers. See William A. Schabas, "Prosecutorial Discretion v. Judicial Activism at the International Criminal Court," *Journal of International Criminal Justice* 6 (2008), 731.

[462] See Susana SáCouto and Katherine Cleary, "The Gravity Threshold of the International Criminal Court," *American University International Law Review* 23 (2008), 807.

[463] Comoros Appeals Chamber, Judgment on Prosecutor's Appeal from the Pre-Trial Chamber Decision on the Application by the Government of the Union of the Comoros, September 2, 2019, ICC-01/13–98. This was an appeal from a decision by the Pre-Trial Chamber, which had been authorized to review the Prosecutor's decision under Article 53(3).

troops. But her requests were turned down by the Pre-Trial Chamber as contrary to "the interests of justice," with reference to the likely problems of gaining local cooperation for meaningful investigations. Any investigation that might come close to targeting Americans was certain to bring powerful political pressure to bear on the Court; but, of course, this dynamic was not explicitly mentioned in the judicial ruling.[464]

One can see why self-referrals held some practical advantages for both the Prosecutor and the country making the self-referral.[465] But Uganda and Congo may not have understood the extent to which they opened themselves to ICC scrutiny. In Uganda, for example, the self-referral could have put President Museveni and his army under suspicion. In late January 2004, Museveni and Moreno-Ocampo appeared jointly at the Intercontinental Hotel in London to announce the historic first ICC referral – featuring the unexpected novelty of a self-referral. Museveni's remarks left no doubt that his own intended target was the LRA leadership, pure and simple. His own national Ugandan forces had just fought an inconclusive military campaign against the LRA, driving Kony and his group across the porous borders of Sudan, Congo, and the CAR. It was not clear how Museveni expected the ICC Prosecutor, who has no police force and commands no military power, to capture LRA fugitives who had eluded Museveni's own efforts. Nonetheless, on this London occasion, Museveni seemed to embrace Moreno-Ocampo as a legal/military ally in his battle to neutralize the LRA. It was also possible that Museveni understood full well the limitations of the ICC's police powers and was staging this handover of the LRA mess as a way to gain international favor and perhaps also some internal Ugandan sympathy.

It was up to Moreno-Ocampo (somewhat awkwardly, under the celebratory circumstances) to remind the press that ICC investigations were conducted impartially and objectively.[466] This meant that an ICC investigation into the *situation* in Uganda could target anyone in the country. Left unsaid was the possibility that such targets could include Museveni's own armed forces, following the brutal northern campaign against the LRA and other fractious groups. Global NGOs were already urging the Prosecutor to examine possible crimes on both sides. But when it came time for the Prosecutor to seek

464 Afghanistan Pre-Trial Chamber, Decision Pursuant to Article 15 on the Authorisation of an Investigation into the Situation in Afghanistan, April 12, 2019, ICC-07/17–33. In March 2020 an Appeals Chamber authorized the Prosecutor to proceed.

465 Bosco believes that Moreno-Ocampo openly signaled his desire for self-referrals. *Rough Justice*, p. 96.

466 On this episode, see Schiff, *Building the International Criminal Court*, pp. 199–201. At the time, NGOs criticized Moreno-Ocampo for appearing to accommodate Museveni.

Ugandan arrest warrants from ICC judges, it turned out that the only names on the list were LRA members.

In general, after arrest warrants have been issued and before suspects have been apprehended, the political complications can be heightened by circumstances unforeseen by the Court. In a much-studied episode, there was a moment in 2006 when the Ugandan government planned reconciliation talks with Joseph Kony and the LRA.[467] Meetings were scheduled to take place in Juba, across the border in Sudan (now South Sudan); but Kony balked at exposing himself to possible ICC liability. Under enormous pressure to bury the warrants as part of a larger bargaining process with Kony, the ICC held to its policy of rejecting all such grants of immunity. As a case study, various researchers have come to opposite conclusions about whether this ICC stance was a fatal blow to the negotiations – which never occurred – or whether the process was doomed from the start, for other reasons. The episode gave rise to broad speculation about possible dilemmas between promoting peace or justice, in the context of protracted conflicts. As it happened, the LRA faded in significance as a disruptive force in Uganda. The ICC kept its powder dry, until the surprise appearance of Dominic Ongwen in 2015.

6.3 SECURING THE LEGAL FRAME: JURISDICTION

When, Where, Whom?

Courts declare the law but must themselves behave lawfully. A bedrock restraint on judicial power is the concept of *jurisdiction*. Jurisdictional limits are especially critical for criminal courts, given their power to incarcerate those lawfully found guilty. The jurisdiction of the ICC is spelled out in the

[467] For an overview, see Marieke Wierde and Michael Otim, "Courts, Conflict, and Complementarity in Uganda," in Carsten Stahn and Mohamed M. El Zeidy (eds.), *The International Criminal Court and Complementarity* (Cambridge: Cambridge University Press, 2011), chapter 37; Tim Allen, *Trial Justice: The International Criminal Court and the Lord's Resistance Army* (London: Zed Books, 2006), chapters 4–5, 8. See also Matthew Brubacher, "The ICC Investigation of the Lord's Resistance Army: An Insider's View," in Allen and Vlassenroot (eds.), *The Lord's Resistance Army*, chapter 14. A more recent analysis is Anna Macdonald, "'In the Interests of Justice?': The International Criminal Court, Peace Talks, and the Failed Quest for War Crimes Accountability in Northern Uganda," *Journal of Eastern African Studies* 11 (2017), 628. For contemporary press reports, see Bosco, *Rough Justice*, pp. 128–31. On both Uganda and Sudan, see Sarah Nouwen and Wouter G. Weimer "Doing Justice to the Political: The International Criminal Court in Uganda and Sudan," *European Journal of International Law* 21 (2010), 941.

opening Articles of the Rome Statute.[468] Tensions among negotiators in Rome meant that defining jurisdictional powers and limits would require both compromise and imagination. All dimensions of jurisdiction came under close scrutiny: time periods, geography, classes of suspects, and a specific list of prosecutable crimes.[469]

When?

At the outset, the ICC was bound by a strict initial date of July 1, 2002.[470] The ICC would have no power to prosecute crimes committed before this date, no matter how horrendous. Moving forward, the starting dates might vary, depending on when a particular country joined the Rome Treaty. For later adopters, a host of special arrangements might delay the start of jurisdiction for certain crimes[471]; or a non-member of the ICC could invite the Court to investigate during a specified period (but in no circumstances before July 2002).[472] In the situations of the Congo and the CAR, everything after July 1, 2002 was fair game; and for Uganda that date was September 1, 2002. In the Congo, where violence permeated the entire nation during the invasions of 1996 and beyond, the Court came along too late for a truly comprehensive role. In both the Congo and the CAR, the Prosecutor was guided by NGO reports describing atrocities and naming perpetrators.[473] The period of critical ICC interest, from July 2002 until the middle of 2003, coincided with one cycle of Ituri violence, although in retrospect it was just one of many cycles. It remains unknown whether serious atrocities in Ituri occurring after 2003 have received the Court's further attention. The Bemba case fell within the same time frame. But when completely different conflicts emerged years later in the CAR, there was a second self-referral in 2014, and in 2019 two suspects were placed in ICC detention.[474]

[468] Article 5 speaks to crimes "within the jurisdiction" of the Court; Article 12 contains the limits discussed in this section as "preconditions to the exercise of jurisdiction"; and Article 13 lists the conditions (informally called "triggers") that permit the "exercise of jurisdiction."

[469] For details on the negotiations, see M. Cherif Bassiouni and William A. Schabas (eds.), *The Legislative History of the International Criminal Court*, revised expanded edition (Leiden: Brill Nijhoff, 2016).

[470] Article 11(1).

[471] Articles 126(2), 124.

[472] Article 12(3). This invitation is a special grant of jurisdiction regarding time and place and must be accepted by the Prosecutor under the *proprio motu* trigger.

[473] In addition to FIDH's CAR report of February 2003, the key document for the Congo was from HRW: *Ituri: "Covered in Blood": Ethnically Targeted Violence in Northeastern DR Congo* (New York, 2003).

[474] ICC Press Release, "ICC Pre-Trial Chamber II Joins Yekatom and Ngaïssona Cases" (February 20, 2019).

Where? Whom?

The geographical scope of ICC jurisdiction is bound up with the question of persons. Assuming that the time frame is valid, the ICC has jurisdiction over people who are nationals of ICC member states (or possibly other states referred by the UNSC), or people from any state who commit crimes on the actual territory of a member state.[475] Thus, potential suspects are defined by either their nationality or the location where relevant crimes were committed. In the Uganda situation, there was little reason to quibble: LRA members were Ugandan nationals allegedly committing crimes in Ugandan territory. So were the other combatants in the battle to control the LRA, not to mention other armed groups operating in Uganda. In Ituri, the networks of violence were more diverse, with both Ugandan and Rwandan nationals allegedly operating on Congolese territory. (In the event, arrest warrants for Ituri were directed against only Congolese suspects.) In the CAR, the grounds for jurisdiction were the atrocities committed on CAR territory, while a second source was the nationality of the Congolese troops and their Congolese leader Jean-Pierre Bemba, working from his residence in the Congo.

What Crimes?

The Rome Conference tested the negotiating skills of participating countries and NGOs. Perhaps the greatest challenge in Rome was to compile a code of crimes that would keep pace with the steady evolution of human rights over the past half-century. While the scope of human rights is constantly expanding, a countervailing force in criminal law leans in a more conservative direction. As in most national legal systems, the Rome Statute restricts prosecutions to crimes clearly labeled and fully articulated in the formal text. No novel offenses can be brought to the court that go beyond the published code. This is the venerable principle of *nullum crimen sine lege*, which includes the common prohibition on crimes defined "ex post facto."[476] All international courts have struggled with tensions between the dynamic growth of human rights for victims, on the one hand, and strict principles of fair notice to defendants, on the other. Some predecessor courts to the ICC resolved this tension by creative lawyering at the appellate level, shielding impressive degrees of innovation behind a conservative rhetoric of legal interpretation.[477] The rules already in place

475 Articles 12(2)(a) and (b).

476 Article 22(1).

477 See Shane Darcy and Joseph Powderly (eds.), *Judicial Creativity at the International Criminal Tribunals* (Oxford: Oxford University Press, 2011). As Carsten Stahn noted: "Over past decades each of these crimes has been adjusted to fit new contexts through the practice of

were thus allowed to yield steady growth. By this artful approach, *plus c'est la même chose, plus ça change.*

The Preamble to the Rome Statute invokes no limitations. It condemns "unimaginable atrocities that deeply shock the conscience of humanity." But the detailed criminal code (Articles 6–8 in the Rome Statute) provides the necessary details. The Rome Statute followed the pattern fixed during the 1990s of recognizing three rubrics: *genocide, crimes against humanity, and war crimes.* These are "the most serious crimes of concern to the international community as a whole," couched in a language that derives from the most destructive twentieth-century wars.[478]

All three crimes are defined as modes of collective action – implicating states or state-like organizations in the scale and scope of patterned violence. Down in the fine print, one finds more familiar criminal concepts like murder, rape, destruction of property. But an ordinary murder case, or random acts of sexual violence, or property damage are not what the Rome Statute has in mind. The massacres, torture, sexual violence, ethnic cleansing, and wholesale destruction of villages must all be translated into the rubrics listed above.

The Rome Statute took special efforts to elaborate crimes of sexual violence, building on two decades of evolution through human rights networks.[479] Articles 7 and 8 include as specific offenses "rape, sexual slavery, enforced prostitution, forced pregnancy, enforced sterilization, or any other form of sexual violence of comparable gravity."[480] As a context for these categories of crime, the Rome Statute acknowledges the concept of "gender" as a cultural construct, not merely a biological datum.[481] The discussions at Rome went beyond crime definitions to address gender balance in appointments at the ICC, including judges. As the Congo trials unfolded, they became a test for the ICC's capacity to address sexual crimes within its mandate – everything from investigations to criminal charges to final judgments. As later chapters

international criminal courts and tribunals"; *A Critical Introduction to International Criminal Law*, p. 32.

478 See Sands, *East West Street: On the Origins of "Genocide" and "Crimes Against Humanity."*

479 A pioneering work published just prior to the Rome Conference was Kelly Askin, *War Crimes against Women: Prosecution in International War Crimes Tribunals* (Leiden: Martinus Nijhoff, 1997). The Rome negotiations included the participation of an active Women's Caucus for Gender Justice (later renamed Women's Initiatives for Gender Justice, based in The Hague). See Louise Chappell, *The Politics of Gender Justice at the International Criminal Court: Legacies and Legitimacy* (Oxford: Oxford University Press, 2016).

480 Article 7(1)(g). A similar list with some modifications, including "Committing outrages upon personal dignity, in particular humiliating and degrading treatment," was built into Articles 8 (2)(b)(xxi) and (xxii), and 8(2)(c)(ii) and (d)(vi).

481 Article 7(3). "For the purpose of this Statute, it is understood that the term 'gender' refers to the two sexes, male and female, within the context of society."

will show, the results from the Congo trials were disappointing, despite the extensive documentation of sexual crimes by NGOs in the field.[482]

There are potentially many other crimes that might fit the Preamble's conditions. Terrorism is one such possibility. Others include human trafficking, as well as drug trafficking. Long-term damage to the environment might also be included. The Rome Statute does not preclude amendments for adding these crimes, all of which were discussed in the 1998 conference. These and other serious crimes have already been addressed in separate international treaties, and individual countries may provide a national forum for prosecuting such offenses. Another controversial topic was the crime of aggression, a concept reaching back to the early decades of the twentieth century, which played a catalytic role in the post-World War II trials at Nuremburg. The Rome Treaty placed the crime of aggression within ICC jurisdiction but deferred its exercise until further negotiations on definitions and procedures.[483] But aggression was not an issue in the ICC's first situations in central Africa.

Genocide (Article 6)

Understanding genocide, crimes against humanity, and war crimes requires both a legal dictionary and a historical atlas. Even the dictionary must reflect historical roots, as each of these broad terms arose in the aftermath of escalating violence during the past century. *Genocide* is the most emotionally charged of all three crime groups, even though it has seen limited application in cases at the ICC. Associated now with the mass killings of Jews and other religious, ethnic, racial, or national groups, before and during World War II, the legal definition of genocide has remained faithful to its original wording in the 1948 treaty known as the Genocide Convention.[484]

Invoking painful memories of twentieth-century mass killings, the word "genocide" captures one notably extreme element, going beyond a series of murders: the deliberate attempt to exterminate an entire population group. Although the term genocide is still commonly invoked by human rights

482 For a critique, see Niamh Hayes, "*La Lutte Continue*: Investigating and Prosecuting Sexual Violence at the ICC," in Stahn, *Law and Practice of the International Criminal Court*, chapter 32. In June 2014, the Office of the Prosecutor issued a new Policy Paper on Sexual and Gender-Based Crimes.

483 Article 5(2) in the original version of the Statute.

484 Convention on the Prevention and Punishment of the Crime of Genocide, adopted by the UN General Assembly on December 9, 1948. See William A. Shabas, *Genocide in International Law: The Crime of Crimes*, 2nd ed. (Cambridge: Cambridge University Press, 2009); Payam Akhavan, *Reducing Genocide to Law: Definition, Meaning, and the Ultimate Crime* (Cambridge: Cambridge University Press, 2015).

advocates, there are as yet no ICC trials where the definition has been tested.[485] The killings seen in the Congo, Uganda, and the CAR are certainly "unimaginable atrocities," but they point toward different legal categories. Though extreme in other ways, current conflicts in central Africa are not designed to exterminate entire populations, even when they are said to target civilian victims by ethnicity. The 1994 Rwandan massacres of some 800,000 Tutsi were treated as genocide, based on a fairly close legal judgment that Tutsi victims were in fact a separate ethnic group from the Hutu perpetrators.[486] But here the intent to exterminate was established in court.

Crimes Against Humanity (Article 7)

Growing out of the human rights movement (and with roots going back more than a century), this category of international crimes derives from official state violence directed against civilian groups, starting with that state's own citizens. The growth of this concept tracks the declining prerogatives of sovereign rulers – who may no longer act legally entirely as they wish within their own national borders. Historically, crimes against humanity modify the customary legal principle that "the sovereign can do no wrong."[487] And where sovereigns venture beyond their own borders, civilians in neighboring territories are equally protected.[488]

In the context of the Congo and Uganda, the violence in question was coming not from state sovereigns (or at least not predominantly or directly). It was rather the product of diverse armed groups, operating under more-or-less stateless conditions. To qualify under Article 7, killings, ethnic cleansings, mass rapes, extermination, and related atrocities must be sufficiently

485 The definition of genocide was considered in charges brought against Sudanese leader Omar Hassan al-Bashir. ICC Office of the Prosecutor, Prosecutor's Statement on the Application for a Warrant of Arrest against Omar Hassan Ahmad al Bashir (July 14, 2008). Initially the Pre-Trial Chamber rejected the genocide charge, altering its view only after the Prosecutor's request was upheld by the Appeals Chamber. Judgment on the Appeal of the Prosecutor for a Warrant of Arrest against Omar Hassan Al Bashir, February 3, 2010, ICC-02/05–01/09–73. On the controversy, see Claus Kreß, "The ICC's First Encounter with the Crime of Genocide: The Case against Al Bashir," in Stahn, *Law and Practice of the International Criminal Court*, chapter 27.

486 See Payam Akhavan, "The Crime of Genocide in the ICTR Jurisprudence," *Journal of International Criminal Justice* 3 (2005), 989.

487 See Roger S. Clark, "History of Efforts to Codify Crimes Against Humanity: From the Charter of Nuremberg to the Statute of Rome," in Leila Nadya Sadat (ed.), *Forging a Convention for Crimes Against Humanity* (Cambridge: Cambridge University Press, 2011), chapter 1.

488 For an overview, see M. Cherif Bassiouni, *Crimes Against Humanity: Historical Evolution and Contemporary Application* (Cambridge: Cambridge University Press, 2014).

"widespread" or "systematic" attacks. Moreover the "attack" must be "pursuant to or in furtherance of a State or organizational policy to commit such attack."[489] These qualifications prompted some artful inferences to permit action against non-state actors, upstart militias, and other organizations seemingly able to inflict violence, either widely or systematically. The long history of LRA violence in Uganda persuaded ICC judges that Joseph Kony's group could be held accountable under this test. But in the Congo trials, applying this same definition to armed groups proved to be more difficult.[490]

War Crimes (Article 8)

War has changed over time, but regrettably not the infliction of harm on helpless combatants or civilians caught in the crossfire. This category of offense has a longer history than the others, going back to the mid-nineteenth century. The much older concept of "just war" was an earlier effort to reconcile the conduct of war with legal constraints – a challenge that increased over time as the scale and methods of warfare changed.[491] Prevailing agreements on these constraints were codified and strengthened after World War II in the consolidated Geneva Conventions (1949). There have been supplementary treaties approved widely, if not universally, by major nations.[492] For purposes of the Rome Statute, the list of war crimes provides an expansive set of protections for civilian victims.[493] Some actions classified as crimes against humanity – civilian killings, sexual violence, torture, and persecution – can also be war crimes, and are not excused by the context of lawful armed conflict. In both Uganda and the Congo, persistent armed

489 Article 7(2)(a).

490 On the general concepts, see Claus Kreß, "On the Outer Limits of Crimes Against Humanity: The Concept of Organization within the Policy Requirement," *Leiden Journal of International Law* 23 (2010), 855.

491 For the history of "just war" theorizing, see Daniel R. Brunstetter and Cian O'Driscoll, *Just War Thinkers: From Cicero to the 21st Century* (New York: Routledge, 2017). On current developments, see Christopher M. Ford and Winston S. Williams (eds.), *Complex Battlefields: The Law of Armed Conflict and the Dynamics of Modern Warfare* (Oxford: Oxford University Press, 2019).

492 For an overview of changes in the Geneva system, in the face of evolving modes of conflict, see Dapo Akande, "Classification of Armed Conflicts: Relevant Legal Concepts," in Elizabeth Wilmshurst (ed.), *International Law and the Classification of Conflicts* (Oxford: Oxford University Press, 2012), chapter 3. Other legal prohibitions on means of conducting war derive from the Hague Peace Conferences of 1899 and 1907.

493 The lengthy and elaborately structured list of war crimes in Article 8 preserves the historical complexity. There had been some early hope that Rome delegates would reshape the field, starting with eliminating the divide between "international" and "non-international" armed conflicts. See ibid., p. 34.

conflicts meant that civilians lived amidst a state of perpetual war, however unconventional by historical standards. Evolving definitions of war crimes stigmatize particular practices, such as the conscription and use of child soldiers in armed combat. The first ICC trial, the case of Thomas Lubanga, dealt exclusively with the use of child soldiers as a war crime.

Aggression (Article 8*bis*)

The delegates at Rome agreed to postpone defining this concept, which fit poorly with the other crimes on their list. It was not until a scheduled Review Conference in 2010 that something was hammered out: a crime that belonged to the early twentieth-century global order of sovereign state actors, awkwardly updated for the contemporary focus on individual responsibility.[494] The abhorrence of aggressive war had been the foremost concern of legalists who plotted initiatives after World War I, and for those who founded the United Nations after World War II.[495] At the ICC Review Conference, the quixotic desire to legislate a pacifist future scored a diplomatic victory, finding ingenious compromises on paper. But it only increased the gap between "law in the books" and "law in action," already present across the Rome Statute as a whole.

Needless to say, this crime played no formal part in the Congo trials, where the charges were fixed prior to the 2010 Review Conference. But the new definition brought its own special jurisdictional rules and bureaucratic limitations. It applies only to countries (ICC member states) who choose to opt-in to the system; it does not protect a signatory country invaded by a non-signatory, even when the harm occurs on the territory of the attacked nation. It explicitly requires that aggressive acts be attributed both to a state entity and to a particular individual acting within the state structure. For findings that a state has engaged in acts of aggression, it defers to definitions and practices of the UNSC. Applying the crime of aggression may require unprecedented ICC proficiency in political and diplomatic relations – more proficiency than anything shown thus far by ICC prosecutors, judges, and staff. Perhaps the whole crime definition is far ahead of its time and will reveal its strengths in

494 Claus Kreß and Stefan Barriga, *The Crime of Aggression: A Commentary* (Cambridge: Cambridge University Press, 2016). For personal accounts of the negotiations, see Niels Blokker and Claus Kreß, "A Consensus Agreement on the Crime of Aggression: Impressions from Kampala," *Leiden Journal of International Law* 23 (2010), 889.

495 On the idea from these legalists, see Oona A. Hathaway and Scott J. Shapiro, *The Internationalists: How a Radical Plan to Outlaw War Remade the World* (New York: Simon & Schuster, 2017). The "radical plan" in question was the 1928 Kellogg-Briand Pact.

future decades. For the moment, it looks more like a faith-based solution to a historical conundrum.

Individual Criminal Responsibility (Articles 25 and 28)

Even if international crimes have been proven, the ICC cannot win convictions unless it can attribute individual criminal responsibility to the accused sitting in the courtroom. All three Congo trials stumbled over this challenge, exposing the most serious fault-lines in the Rome Statute. Victims and witnesses testified to the personal impact of serious crimes, but the ICC mechanisms for attributing responsibility were not equal to the demand for victims' justice.[496]

The statutory crimes are embedded in collective action, but they run up against the old Nuremberg doctrine that crimes are committed by men, not by abstract entities. And yet the focus on individual criminal responsibility was central to the movement toward an ICC. The moral realities of violence and victims found their remedy by pivoting from victims to named perpetrators; and it was this imperative that drove the faith in criminal punishment as a means of deterring mass atrocities. But it is more than international courts can ably accomplish by simply examining factual evidence. Squaring this circle requires judicial resort to paradigms and presumptions, superimposed onto dry legal categories.

The ad hoc and hybrid tribunals had operated with liability doctrines adapted from national criminal law systems, commonly used for domestic crimes policed by every law-abiding society. There was a core distinction between principals and accessories, sometimes broken down into further sub-categories. But the experience of applying these concepts to collective behavior proved difficult. At Nuremberg, to make it work, the indictments borrowed doctrines of conspiracy from Anglo-American law. The Yugoslav Tribunal wrangled a controversial doctrine of *joint criminal enterprise* (JCE).[497]

[496] An early critic of this process questioned "the ideology of a disciplined, mathematical structure of responsibility [which] serves as a relieving strategy to measure the immeasurable. The seemingly unambiguous notion of guilt creates consoling patterns of causality in the chaos of intertwined problems of social, political, and economic deprivation surrounding the violence." Immi Tallgren, "The Sensibility and Sense of International Criminal Law," *European Journal of International Law* 13 (2002), p. 561.

[497] For an uncompromising defense of JCE doctrine, see Michael P. Scharf. "Joint Criminal Enterprise, the Nuremberg Precedent, and the Concept of 'Grotian Moment,'" in Tracy Isaacs and Richard Vernon (eds.), *Accountability for Collective Wrongdoing* (Cambridge: Cambridge University Press, 2011), chapter 4.

Determined to improve on those concepts, the Rome Statute developed a more intricate set of categories, still derived from the state-centered wars of the twentieth century.[498] But it was anyone's guess how these more detailed categories would match the ICC's first cases from central Africa. In the Lubanga case, the first Pre-Trial Chamber to contemplate the matter devised a secondary layer of theory, imported from German law, to strengthen the Rome Statute concept of perpetration.[499] A detailed analysis of the Congo trials shows the limitations of this baroque apparatus when applied to the cultural and structural conditions in Ituri. There was never any doubt, both in Ituri and in the CAR, that violence was severe, consisting of murders, rapes, and other forms of brutality: the victims and the crimes were real. But attributing responsibility to the accused individuals, in these specific circumstances, could be done only by forcing leadership paradigms cribbed from the previous century's history books.

As with the hard-fought definition of the crime of aggression, the Rome Statute provisions for individual criminal responsibility bore the marks of diplomatic compromise and virtuoso legal drafting. But it was clearly not enough; and the judges themselves had to devise a further layer of legal theory to try to make it work. But even that imported theory needed help from the inevitable paradigms and presumptions, allowing the pre-selection of helpful facts. It was the experimental conditions of actual trials that exposed this weakness within the Rome Statute.[500]

Naming Perpetrators: Finding the Right Suspects

The Prosecutor's particular challenge is to find the right suspects in a situation: "those responsible for international crimes," in the words of the Preamble – and

[498] Articles 25(3)(a)–(d). Liability for "command responsibility" appears in Article 28(a).

[499] For a review of developments in the tribunals, the ICC, and domestic legal systems, see Neha Jain, *Perpetrators and Accessories in International Criminal Law: Individual Modes of Responsibility for Collective Crimes* (Oxford: Hart, 2014). In a carefully balanced assessment, Carsten Stahn describes "the crystallization of the principle of individual criminal responsibility," and notes that it is "widely hailed as one of the major achievements of the twentieth century." But there are "darker sides": "The legal framework remains somewhat detached from social reality"; *A Critical Introduction to International Criminal Law*, p. 157.

[500] Even before Lubanga arrived in The Hague, commentary had already predicted the difficulties to come. See Kirsten Ainley, "Responsibility for Atrocity: Individual Criminal Agency and the International Criminal Court," in John T. Parry (ed.), *Evil, Law and the States: Perspectives on State Power and Violence* (Amsterdam: Rodopi, 2006), chapter 11. Ainley anticipates the judicial turn to "inferences and legal fictions" to fill the gaps in legal concepts (p. 147).

preferably those who are "most responsible."[501] Naming suspects is difficult enough; apprehending and bringing them to The Hague poses even graver challenges. With the LRA in Uganda, after brief investigations the Court named five suspects, but it had no effective way to capture them, somewhere in the border regions of Uganda, the Congo, and Sudan. Still, the very existence of ICC arrest warrants played a secondary role in local negotiations among stakeholders in the region, complicating efforts to bring LRA leaders to the peace table, as mentioned earlier. One year after the Uganda warrants, the Prosecutor made his move in the Congo situation. There, with so many potential targets of suspicion, the Prosecutor took a contrasting approach: biding his time and eventually requesting warrants for several persons who were already in state custody or had recently been there. Thus, the very first suspects brought to The Hague were in some sense thrust upon the ICC by circumstances.[502]

As the Congo trials unfolded over the next decade, plagued with procedural, evidential, and legal complications, the haunting question was whether the Prosecutor had indeed named the right suspects – quite apart from the fact that he knew where to find them.[503] The stories told by prosecutors about the accused – who they were, what roles they played within complex groups – were strenuously challenged and had to be modified in key respects. The prosecutors used the Congo cases to flex their hard-won legal categories, both the definitions of crimes and the modes of action through which individual players were assigned responsibility, in accordance with the Rome Statute. But applying these categories to the realities of Ituri raised a host of new questions. Suddenly, the legal categories themselves seemed to be put on trial.

Much remains obscure about the search for cases in the CAR. While Bemba's name was prominent in reports from NGOs at the time of the coup-related violence in 2002–03, there were other commanders implicated in the same chaotic circumstances, not to mention both the defeated CAR President and his successor, François Bozizé. But by the time that Moreno-Ocampo opened his formal investigation in 2007, the other foreign commanders had gone back to their home countries; the ousted President was making overtures of reconciliation; and President Bozizé might have wanted to be rid of the

[501] Office of the Prosecutor, Paper on Some Policy Issues (2003). A skeptical response to the question about getting the right suspects can be found in William A. Schabas, "The Banality of International Justice," *Journal of International Criminal Justice* 11 (2013), 545.

[502] Patryk I. Labuda, "The ICC in the Democratic Republic of Congo: A Decade of Partnership and Antagonism," in Clarke, Knottnerus and de Volder, *Africa and the ICC*, p. 277.

[503] See Kambale, "A Story of Missed Opportunities," pp. 179–85. See also Phil Clark, "Chasing Cases: The ICC and the Politics of State Referral in the Democratic Republic of Congo and Uganda," in Stahn and El Zeidy, *The International Criminal Court and Complementarity*, chapter 38.

powerful Bemba, whose stronghold was just across his southern border. From the CAR standpoint, selecting Bemba as the one and only suspect in CAR violence was an ideal solution, fulfilling the hopes of the self-referral.

The Debates Continue

Once the ICC Rome Statute was finalized, the long negotiations over draft codes came to a close and the implementation phase was about to begin.[504] While it was no small feat for diverse countries to agree on formal articles of jurisdiction, it fell to the ICC's own staff to apply these rules under the rigors of courtroom trials. The Congolese suspects chosen by the Prosecutor were the only accused to face trials in the Court's first decade. During this time, ICC legal concepts had to mix with the distant environments of Ituri and the CAR.

The Court's jurisdictional framework set the legal parameters for the first trials. To be sure, that framework was a political product, based on compromise among the drafters in Rome. But resolving such tensions, on paper, produced a clean legal slate once the ICC became operational. Strict rules of jurisdiction underwrote the lawfulness of the Court's own operation. The terms for exercising jurisdiction, including the three triggers, supplied a public checklist of rules the Court must strictly observe – and must be seen to observe.

As the ICC put its plans into motion, the prior debates lived on in academic seminars and law journals, where veterans and students of Rome continued to parse the coherence of jurisdictional standards, exploring anomalies and ambiguities.[505] Gradually, inside ICC courtrooms, the existential tensions buried in these codes were destined to emerge; and their consequences soon became manifest. Some novel practices of the ICC had to be generated from spare statutory outlines – notably, the role of victims in the trials, and their legal representatives. Specific questions arose from procedural compromises

[504] In the gap between 1998 and the 2003 appointments of judges and Prosecutor, operating plans were developed by a Preparatory Committee (PrepCom), with participation from member states and NGOs. PrepCom drafted the Rules of Procedure and Evidence, Elements of Crimes, and early regulations for the Office of the Prosecutor, as well as preparing the agenda for the first ASP meeting in February 2003. United Nations Preparatory Commission for the International Criminal Court, "Road Map Leading to the Early Establishment of the International Criminal Court" (September 26, 2001). See Schiff, *Building the International Criminal Court*, pp. 104–12. The legal basis for PrepCom was a "Final Act" approved at the Rome Conference. United Nations Diplomatic Conference of Plenipotentiaries on the Establishment of an International Criminal Court, Section F (July 17, 1998).

[505] Beyond a dozen or so active journals, the anthologies grow in weight each year. A recent comprehensive overview of the field is Stahn, *A Critical Introduction to International Criminal Law*, with an extensive list of references.

papered over in the statute – such as whether judges could modify, on their own authority, some of the charges against the accused, after the trial had begun. Other practical questions emerged from conflicting legal standards for oversight of the Prosecutor's investigations. Trial-by-trial, the numerous fault-lines would register seismic tremors, making their presence felt.

6.4 TURNING THE LEGAL WHEELS: TRIAL DYNAMICS AND MESHING JUDICIAL FUNCTIONS

All this apparatus had to prove itself in practice. The raw facts came from far-distant Ituri and the CAR, and it fell to the ICC judiciary to turn the wheels of justice. As stewards of legal norms, the eighteen ICC judges met their responsibilities by diversifying their roles, which are designed to be complementary, even oppositional. The ICC judicial structure is a dynamic system of self-imposed, self-policing prescriptions for how laws are applied. Trial outcomes constitute legal justice, provided this self-correcting system shows it was conducted with fidelity to the legal process.

ICC legal norms are laid out primarily in the Rome Statute.[506] Alongside the detailed definitions of crimes, other Articles in the Statute address trial dynamics, supplemented with published Rules and Procedures. Some provisions work to restrain authority, including the triggers for Prosecutorial action, limits on jurisdiction, and the unique restraint of *complementarity* between international and national justice systems. Looming over these provisions were still larger principles of adjudication: specifying the transparency and constancy of legal standards and assigning the burden of proof to the Prosecution.[507]

Altogether, these norms represent "the law on the books." ICC judges are the ones who set this machine into motion: applying the printed norms to the contingencies of real cases brought before the Court. In that process, by legal alchemy, "the law in action" may alter the appearance of the original norms by enriching their content in concrete cases. The norms themselves remain the same, while the things to which they apply come from all directions, unscripted and often unexpected. The dynamics of courtroom trials mean to regulate this combustible mix of norms and facts.

506 According to Article 21(1), there are circumstances under which ICC judges can turn to further sources of law, beyond the Rome Statute.

507 In addition to the principle of *nullum crimen sine lege* (Article 22(1)), other principles include the presumption of innocence (Article 66) and the rights of the accused (Article 67).

Pre-Trial Chambers (PTC)

The trial process overflows that single phase – inside the courtroom – where Prosecution and Defense present their cases (supplemented by Legal Representatives of Victims). Effective courtroom trials presuppose that certain initial conditions have already been vetted: situations and cases have been lawfully identified; suspects are present in The Hague; criminal charges and surrounding circumstances are now clearly defined; witnesses are accessible, while receiving proper protection; victims have been properly certified and granted effective representation; parties have exchanged relevant information allowing both sides to prepare for trial. While criminal justice systems around the world use various means to meet these pre-trial conditions, at the ICC the process is overseen by a set of judges (usually three) forming a Pre-Trial Chamber (PTC). They meet with the parties inside courtrooms, although their concerns include the prior political entanglements of building valid cases.

At the far end of the trial process, there is an outflow of legal issues that fit the parameters for appeals. This calls for yet another set of judges (usually five) – the Appeals Chamber (AC) – to hear appeals from either side at the conclusion of a trial, in addition to resolving interim disputes on legal interpretations during the course of trial. Appeals are yet another process for checking and balancing the work of fellow judges in the pre-trial and trial phases of a case. At the ICC, both the PTC and the AC enlist different judges from those (normally three) who sit in judgment at the trial itself, forming the Trial Chamber (TC).

The very first ICC trials allowed the PTC to test its statutory powers over against the Prosecution.[508] By design, the PTC balances the Prosecutor's authority by monitoring and confirming the lawfulness of the Prosecutor's discretionary pre-trial duties. Important control points include the approval of *proprio motu* formal investigations,[509] and the approval of individual arrest warrants or summonses to appear.[510] At the ICC, the Prosecutor proposes formal legal charges against the suspect, but the PTC must confirm those charges in a written judgment of its own, known as the *Confirmation of Charges* decision.[511] Even at this early stage, there is Defense representation, although it may not yet constitute the Defense team that will go to trial. But it is enough to raise early questions about the Court's jurisdiction, about the lawful confinement of the suspect, and even about complementarity.

508 Article 57 sets out the "functions and powers" of the PTC.
509 Article 15(3).
510 Article 58.
511 Article 61.

This balance of functions between Prosecution and the PTC was the product of yet another compromise at the 1998 Rome meetings. Legal systems represented at Rome recognize different structures for handling pre-trial investigations and preparations for formal trials. The major divide is between common-law legal systems and civil-law systems, often described as polar opposites, even though, in practice, these gaps may be closing.[512]

The PTC strategy at the ICC found a midpoint between these two systems. It stops short of civil law practice, which brings the judiciary into the investigative process, thus reducing the independence of the Prosecutor. Nor does the ICC conform with common-law practice, where a stronger Prosecutor shapes the criminal charges with minimal oversight. This latter system was used in the ad hoc tribunals – the Yugoslav and Rwanda Tribunals. The PTC system adopted at Rome assigns investigations solely to the Prosecutor, unlike the civil law system. But the ICC Prosecutor needs more from pre-trial judges than the common law requires: the PTC conducts a formal hearing to test the Prosecutor's background evidence, with the possibility that charges will be rejected, or returned for revision, or that the proceeding will be adjourned to give the Prosecutor more time to make a case.[513]

The Congo trials were a testing ground for these new dynamics. In the Lubanga case, the PTC was especially active in its pioneer role, launching itself into relationships with victims, poking its nose into investigations, and raising stubborn questions about the arrest warrant.[514] In confirming the war crimes charge against Lubanga for the offense relating to child soldiers, the PTC embellished the concept of perpetration as a mode of individual criminal responsibility, supplementing it with an elaborate meta-theory imported from German criminal law.[515] Although the Presiding Judge in the Lubanga TC thought this intervention was unnecessary and unhelpful,[516] the new doctrine proved to be popular with the Prosecution and later PTCs. The

[512] For comparative analysis and for trends toward convergence in practice, see John D. Jackson and Sarah J. Summers, *The Internationalisation of Criminal Evidence: Beyond the Common Law and Civil Law Traditions* (Cambridge: Cambridge University Press, 2012).

[513] Article 61(7). Schiff describes the ICC regime as tilting toward a more even balance between the two systems, in contrast to the ad hoc tribunals. *Building the International Criminal Court*, p. 11. Carsten Stahn concludes: "Overall, there has been a strong trend toward the hybridization of procedures"; *A Critical Introduction to International Criminal Law*, p. 272.

[514] Schiff, *Building the International Criminal Court*, pp. 217–19. On PTC efforts to influence the Lubanga investigation, see Michela Miraglia, "The First Decision of the ICC Pre-Trial Chamber: International Criminal Procedure under Construction," *Journal of International Criminal Justice* 4 (2006), 188.

[515] Article 25(3)(a); Jain, *Perpetrators and Accessories*, covers these developments.

[516] Lubanga Trial Judgment, March 14, 2012, ICC-01/04–01/06–2842, Separate Opinion of Judge Adrian Fulford, paras. 7–11.

PTC for Katanga and Ngudjolo fully embraced the new approach – even though it eventually had to be abandoned at trial. But the Bemba PTC forced the Prosecutor to shift the liability mode from *perpetration* (under Article 25(3)(a), supplemented by the Germanic theory) to *command responsibility* (under Article 28(a)). This shift fundamentally altered the theory of the case.

The Confirmation of Charges process is a moment for pre-trial judges to abort a case they believe should not go forward to a full trial, based on the legal merits.[517] While all agree that the PTC does not conduct a "mini-trial," and that the standard of proof is something less than proof beyond a reasonable doubt, it is still possible for the PTC to reject the Prosecutor's proposed charges, ordering the release of suspects.[518] One of the first such circuit-breaking decisions occurred with the Congolese suspect Callixte Mbarushimana, where the PTC determined that the evidence presented at the Confirmation hearing was insufficient to go forward.[519]

The first PTC in Lubanga was quickly overwhelmed with new issues, practical and legal, ranging from creating a regime for victims, to concerns about witness protection, and to the disclosure of evidence held by the Prosecutor. Each of these issues meant that the PTC had to wrestle with practical conditions on the ground in conflict-ridden Ituri; and yet the judges themselves were operating at some distance in The Hague. Working through the ICC Registry was one necessary option; although this branch of the Court had its own issues of competition with the Prosecution, and in any case was obligated to act lawfully. These and other pre-trial issues require a judicial capacity to engage with complex conditions in the field – including bargaining, finding compromises, and accepting practical solutions that fall short of perfection. And much of it happens beyond the scrutiny of other actors in the system, let alone actors outside the system.

517 Volker Nerlich, "The Confirmation of Charges Procedure at the International Criminal Court," *Journal of International Criminal Justice* 10 (2012), 1339 (discussing cases that were blocked at this stage). For an extended assessment, see American University War Crimes Research Office, *The Confirmation of Charges Process at the International Criminal Court: A Critical Assessment and Recommendations for Change* (Washington, D.C., October 2015).

518 Another option used by PTCs is to withhold the confirmation of charges, granting time for the Prosecutor to investigate charges further, under Article 61(7)(c)(i). This option was used for cases in the Kenya situation and the Ivory Coast situation.

519 Mbarushimana Pre-Trial Chamber, Confirmation of Charges decision, December 16, 2011, ICC-01/04–01/10–465, finding deficiencies in the evidence from NGOs and UN reports (paras. 112–20, 239). The decision was upheld on Appeal, May 30, 2012, ICC-01/04–01/10–514. Similar wariness of NGO evidence was a factor in the initial PTC adjournment of the Confirmation Decision for Laurent Gbagbo in the Ivory Coast Situation. Gbagbo Pre-Trial Chamber, Decision on Adjournment, June 3, 2013, ICC-02/11–01/11–432, para. 35.

Another axis of concern for the PTC is the balance between Prosecution and Defense, leading into the trial phase. That balance includes ensuring that the Defense gains access to information needed to prepare an effective case at trial. The Prosecution has the time advantage in conducting its investigations but faces legal obligations to share the results. In a gesture derived from civil-law procedure, the Prosecutor is legally required to expend equal effort gathering incriminating and exculpatory evidence – and all the latter must be disclosed at the earliest practical time.[520] Overseeing information exchange was difficult enough for the PTC, but it became uniquely complex when the Prosecution asserted the need to withhold information to protect the safety and confidentiality of Ituri witnesses and other sources. This problem became one of the main constraints blocking the Lubanga pre-trial and trial phases.

Yet another core function of the PTC is to set conditions for the conduct of trials, starting with utter clarity (and finality) about the criminal charges. The pre-trial phase must also lay out the essential facts of the offenses charged, giving the accused enough notice and specificity to mount an effective defense at trial. This requirement is echoed in a key section of Article 74, providing that the trial court's final judgment shall "not exceed the facts and circumstances described in the charges and any amendments to the charges."[521] This provision proved to be pivotal in all of the Congo cases, where the experience of years-long trials put pressure on trial judges to venture beyond the original PTC-confirmed charges and liability modes, and to put a different spin on the core facts anchored to that confirmation.

Trial Chambers (TC)

Trials are the main focus for this book. They are one phase in a continuous judicial cycle, between pre-trial and appeals functions on either end. But the trial begins with a fresh slate of evidence – opening statements by the parties, presentations by the Legal Representatives of Victims, and a parade of witnesses. In the end, the results must be measured against the confirmed charges, which loom over the trial proceedings. In the Congo trials, the reference point of confirmed charges, along with the underlying *facts and circumstances* from pre-trial documents, imposed serious constraints on the TC's flexibility. Each of the Congo trials pushed hard against these constraints. Trial judges had to balance

520 Articles 54(1), 64(3)(c), and 67(2). Schiff reports that the Office of the Prosecutor was quick to mix investigators with prosecution team members in the field, in the initial screening of situations. According to Deputy Prosecutor Fatou Bensouda, the Prosecution division was involved in investigations "from the get-go"; *Building the International Criminal Court*, p. 120.

521 Article 74(2).

a mix of goals: seeking to fulfill the moral destiny of the Court, while strictly observing the canons of procedure.

The TC takes possession of the case once the PTC has completed the Confirmation process. But this does not mean that a trial will begin promptly. Delays involving pre-trial issues may well carry over into the next phase of courtroom action. In the Lubanga case, the Confirmation process was completed almost a year after Lubanga arrived in The Hague; but his trial did not see its opening day for nearly two more years. Long delays also occurred in the other Congo trials. At stake were some basic issues central to the conduct of fair trials: disclosure of evidence by the Prosecutor to the Defense, protection of witnesses, and lingering issues of jurisdiction. Trial judges must also vet applications from victims seeking to participate. By the time an ICC trial begins, the judges, the parties, and the court officials are thoroughly accustomed to working together.

Once the trial finally begins, it feels like a new beginning, with a heightened formality surrounding the witnesses and other forms of evidence. With many practical issues relegated to pre-trial judges, the trial courtroom is exorcised of political spirits. In this ideal setting all preconceptions are laid aside; fresh evidence enters into a factual vacuum. The accused is treated with elaborate courtesy. Even though he may have arrived at Court under armed guard from the ICC detention facility, in the courtroom he enjoys the presumption of innocence. Judicial demeanor suggesting otherwise would jeopardize the crafted atmosphere of neutrality.

The biggest surprise to American spectators in the public galleries is the absence of juries. Aside from the many cultural, political, and practical reasons why juries have no place in ICC trials, their absence has profound implications for the legal process. In common-law criminal prosecutions, the use of juries marks a sharp distinction between legal and factual elements of a trial. Here, indeed, is the dynamic core of the trial system: when norms in the statute confront the unique factual evidence of a case at trial. If juries are present, they determine the facts, which they insert into legal categories defined by the presiding judge. The resulting judgment may be challenged on the basis of facts or law; and their separation can mean breaking open an organic bond. Appeals judges generally defer to juries (seen as block-box decision-makers) on the facts, while focusing their attention on more abstract legal categories.

The TC carries responsibility for findings of facts and decisions of law, addressing both dimensions in a final written judgment. Especially when the legal categories are previously untested, the TC has immense flexibility in bonding facts and law. The results have created tensions with the appeals phase, setting off broad jurisprudential inquiries into the nature of facts, the flexibility of legal categories, and the operation of proof standards. The Congo trials became the laboratory for self-analysis on all these points.[522]

When judges rather than juries hear trial evidence, they have less concern about the prejudicial nature of some categories of evidence. Hearsay is generally disfavored when juries evaluate the evidence; but trial judges at the ICC expect to hear most everything, professing confidence in their ultimate abilities to assign precise weight to whatever evidence comes in. In the context of Ituri and the CAR, their confidence was at times met with skepticism in the appeals phase. On the surface, this skepticism focused on the TC's failure to develop its reasoning with sufficient detail to allow appellate scrutiny.[523] In trials of this nature, "finding facts" always means constructing complex judgments. These are not raw sensory observations. The various metaphors used by fact-finding judges imply a struggle for visual clarity, backed by the inner convictions of personal psychology. But on appeal, what matters are the inference patterns that give facts their practical significance in the overall judgment. Suppressed or tacit inferences may insulate the judgment from appeal, depending on the degree of appellate scrutiny.

Apart from the role of victims, the Congo trials in the ICC followed a conventional common-law adversarial pattern. The Prosecution presents its case through documents and witnesses, obliged to use live testimony where possible, rather than written submissions. Witnesses are cross-examined by Defense attorneys, with different styles of questioning allowed for direct-examination and cross-examination. Once the Prosecution has concluded its case, it is the turn of the Defense, which brings its own witnesses. The accused may testify on his own behalf, but otherwise is not required to speak under oath. Following closing statements, the trial judges retire to compose a written judgment. This last process took many months, and judgments ran for hundreds of pages.

But this is not a pure common-law model. Advocates from common-law systems are sometimes surprised by the active involvement of TC judges. There are, of course, the usual legal objections from the advocates, followed by rulings from the bench. But trial judges also pose questions directly to witnesses, sometimes interrupting the advocates. TC members come from a range of domestic legal systems, including those where judges themselves actually lead the questioning. The record of the Katanga case shows an especially assertive

[522] These developments are discussed fully in the chapters on the three Congo trials.

[523] The most severe challenge came in the Bemba Appeals Judgment, June 8, 2018, ICC-01/05–01/08–3636 (Majority opinion).

judge, whose questions may have influenced the TC's decision to alter the original charges at the conclusion of the trial. This particular episode, while controversial, was never put to the scrutiny of appeals judges.[524]

While unusual in a standard adversary process, this moment from the Katanga trial was a reminder that TC judges hold considerable discretion about the overall conduct of the trial process. How far that discretion might extend is still unclear. The Rome Statute leaves the door open, saying only that the TC shall "[c]onfer with the parties and adopt such procedures as are necessary to facilitate the fair and expeditious conduct of the proceedings."[525] In practice, if a TC were to depart significantly from the conventional adversarial model, it might jeopardize the appearance of fairness and impartiality. In the Congo trials, no radical experiments in trial procedure were broached.

TC functions are concluded, if the accused is found guilty, with a sentencing hearing and imposition of the sentence. The TC also deals with victim-specific reparations, entering into an unaccustomed practical domain. For convicted persons serving a sentence, the TC retains a set of oversight responsibilities – although over time, as judges complete their terms, a different TC may need to be formed for the individual case.

Appeals Chambers (AC)

The final phase of the trial process belongs to a panel of five judges, different from those who might have served in the PTC or the TC. The practice of using multi-judge panels, at all phases, acknowledges the complexity and novelty of the many inferences – large and small – that drive the whole trial process. A separate appeals phase increases the multiplicity of judging, in a manner familiar in most criminal justice systems. It is a recognizable form of balancing judgments by the TC, contributing to the overall goal of fairness and impartiality of the legal process.

The AC has a broad mandate, including the review of TC findings of both facts and law (the juries of other systems having been replaced by TC judges as finders of facts). The depth in which the AC reviews factual findings became an issue in all the Congo trials, especially in the Bemba case. There the AC acquitted Bemba by a split chamber, in which two judges in the minority faulted their colleagues for lacking proper deference for the factual findings of the TC.[526] As later chapters will show, judgments of both facts and law in ICC trials contain

[524] This aspect of the trial is discussed in Chapter 8.

[525] Article 64(3)(a).

[526] Bemba Appeals Judgment, Dissenting Opinion of Judge Sanji Mmasenono Monageng and Judge Piotr Hofmański, June 8, 2018, ICC-01/05–01/08–3636-Anx1, paras. 2–18.

complex inferences patterns; and the normal line between raw facts and complex legal judgments lost its sharpness.

As dissenting judges and outside commentators have noted, the AC in Bemba may have followed a course that later ACs will modify. This raises a general point about the status of internal ICC judicial rulings, including the AC: later chambers at all levels are not tightly bound by the prior decisions of the other chambers. Officially, there is no strict system of *stare decisis* – or the requirement of "following precedent" from prior cases. With reference to the AC, even its lengthy decisions do not freeze the evolving law into a rigid doctrinal block. Later cases will offer opportunities for other judges to place different weights on legal principles that always stand in close proximity to each other, allowing the tensions to resolve into new patterns. In these early years of the Court's jurisprudence, it is difficult to foresee where this interpretive freedom might lead. The axioms of legal process favor stability in the rules, even as they adapt and evolve over time.[527]

Most important about the AC: it marks the final stage or *instance* in a lengthy, self-reflective and self-defining process of legal judgment. The AC has the final word, at least for the particular case at hand, and it has the potential to shape the path down which later trials will travel. Finality of judgment plays a special role in the drama of legal principles. While so much else speaks to checks and balances, to the division of labor, and to the ability to revise and revisit preliminary decisions, the purpose of a legal trial is to reach final judgment.

Finality here means the final stage of the process; it thus becomes a legal surrogate for the more grandiose notion of final truth in an uncompromising moral theory. In a revealing aphorism, one US Supreme Court justice in the 1950s noted that, as a court of last instance on Constitutional matters, "we are not final because we are infallible; but we are infallible only because we are final."[528] The legal process cannot perform its function if appeals extend into an endless future. The needs in law are different from those in experimental science, where a determined lack of closure keeps the process of discovery moving toward a bottomless horizon.

[527] The dissenters on the Bemba Appeals Chamber quote a previous Appeals Chamber's holding that "absent 'convincing reasons' it will not depart from its previous decisions"; ibid., para. 5 (quoting from an interlocutory order on victims' participation in the Gbagbo case). The Bemba Appeals majority clearly thought that it had "convincing" reasons for exercising more active scrutiny of the Bemba Trial Chamber's factual judgments.

[528] The source of this famous quote is the same Robert Jackson who served as the Chief Prosecutor for the Allies at Nuremberg. See his concurrence in *Brown* v. *Allen*, 344 U.S. 443, 540 (1953).

While powerful moral aspirations hover over the whole ICC enterprise, the ultimate prize is the finality of legal judgments. Without this guarantee of final resolution, the process would be too exhaustive and too disruptive to sustain. It means, of course, that the final outcome in a case may be to acquit the accused. Outside critics – those with deep investments in waging the battle against impunity – may yearn to keep litigating the case in public opinion. Critics often see themselves as yet a further appeals body, readjusting the findings of facts and law, extending the legal edifice of the Rome Statute in ways they believe will lead to further victories in the moral struggle. But the legal process cannot function with a proliferation of self-appointed appeals chambers, piling instance upon instance until the case achieves victory in some larger forum.

The ICC can be seen as an experimental exercise, testing and recasting the original language in the Rome Statute. The process chosen for this purpose is that of legality, which demands closure at the end of appeals. Time will tell whether legal procedures, strictly observed, can hold up under the inevitable criticisms. As the case studies will show, the first ICC trials magnified tensions between moral and legal principles.

6.5 CONSERVING LEGAL PRINCIPLES

Legality in Practice

Under the Rome Statute, it is a war crime for someone in an armed group to "use [children under the age of fifteen years] to participate actively in hostilities."[529] Although there could be questions in a courtroom, years later, about the precise ages of such children at the time, there are larger problems in applying this criminal category. What about children being used to wash the laundry back in camp? Or to cook the food in an urban posting? And, more pointedly, what about young girls "used" to provide sexual and domestic services for male commanders? The generic term "participating actively in hostilities" does not tell us which specific cases should fall under its umbrella. There are always new examples at the margins.

The Congo trials, like many other international trials, were filled with novel problems requiring judges to make sharp classifications. Either the sexual services fall within the definition, or they do not. In moral terms, this exploitation of girls may seem even more heinous than sending young boys off to fight

[529] Article 8(2)(e)(vii).

with sticks and machetes. But this is not a moral question; rather, a legal one: how should a neutral steward of the law classify this particular behavior?

The Rome Statute provides some relevant legal guidelines, including the venerable principle of *nullum crimen sine lege*:

> 1. A person shall not be criminally responsible under this Statute unless the conduct in question constitutes, at the time it takes place, a crime within the jurisdiction of the Court.
>
> 2. The definition of a crime shall be strictly construed and shall not be extended by analogy. In case of ambiguity, the definition shall be interpreted in favour of the person being investigated, prosecuted or convicted. . . .[530]

Is the sexual services case inside or outside the statutory charge? The definition mentions using children "to participate actively in hostilities," a general action category that does not specify individual examples. Is it therefore "ambiguous"? If so, then the principle tells judges to go slow, to err in the direction of excluding borderline cases. Or is it sufficiently open, as a general category, to allow judges to determine objectively – through some impartial manner of reasoning – that sexual services for commanders fall within the scope? Does the moral gravity of the act, independent of the statute, play any role in this reasoning?

TC judges in the Lubanga case came up with different answers. Only Judge Odio Benito concluded that sexual services came under the war crimes definition; and thus the issue was left in a dissenting note to the final Lubanga judgment.[531] Another approach might have been to revert to the original confirmed charges, adding an additional charge as a better match with the evidence at trial: perhaps an offense of "sexual slavery," or even "other inhumane acts of a similar character intentionally causing great suffering . . .."[532] But strict principles of stability within the Rome Statute work against such late changes, whatever might have been revealed in trial testimony. The TC judgment must be limited to "the facts and circumstances described in the charges . . .."[533] Despite the complex possibility for amending charges, there remains the barrier of the PTC *facts and circumstances*.[534]

530 Article 22.

531 Lubanga Trial Judgment, March 14, 2012, ICC-01/04–01/06–2842, Separate and Dissenting Opinion of Judge Odio Benito.

532 Note that the latter offense appears in the Rome Statute not under war crimes (Article 8) but under crimes against humanity (Article 7(1)(k)), raising issues that would not have been addressed previously by either the Prosecution or the Defense.

533 Article 74(2).

534 Chapter 7 will describe more fully why, in the Lubanga Trial Chamber, proposed changes along these lines were rejected on appeal, based in part on the pre-trial *facts and*

Any final TC judgment will have made a large number of such classification decisions, while navigating through a turbulent sea of other legal tensions. The final result (putting aside dissenting views) will speak with authority, organically changing the relationship between general legal categories and the concrete things coming into their orbit. What makes the final judgment *legal*, as well as *final*, is not just the conclusion but the contested process through which it was reached. The presence of an adversary system at trial draws out alternative views on the precise meanings of legal terms, on the legal classification of behavior, and on many further tensions within the statutory structure. Legal proceedings must be open to alternative views, even at the risk of upsetting conventional wisdom.

These issues of interpretation in no way suggest that there was anything defective in the drafting process for the Rome Statute. "Laws in the books" inhabit general concepts and categories, awaiting the moment of application. Moreover, the legal text is not designed for dry exercises in formal logic. The whole system of active judging – self-reflective, self-corrective, and multilayered – is meant to give dynamic effect to the goals behind the text. Legal language is formulated in declarative sentences, but its contents include the larger purposes the Statute was meant to serve. Giving effect to statutory purpose is as much a part of judging as observing the stability and transparency of the law. Balancing the tension between these legal functions is the task for judges – acting together in teams, reviewing each other's work, interacting with advocates whose role is to ensure that even unpopular views are considered in the courtroom.

In a long-established court, with thousands of prior cases, it is likely that judges would find more definitive guidance for matching concrete behavior (using girl soldiers for sexual services) and statutory categories (using children to participate actively in hostilities). This same exercise is repeated for many of the fact patterns brought to the floor of the courtroom. Even the broader principles of legality – such as *nullum crimen sine lege* – require close interpretation, when they employ concepts like "ambiguity" to designate the main points on which that principle pivots. Similar balance is built into other core principles that call for openness, fairness, impartiality – all of which must be tested under practical conditions of concrete cases.[535]

circumstances standard. Lubanga Appeals Chamber, Judgment on Regulation 55, July 14, 2009, ICC-01/04-01/06-2049, para. 97.

535 For the doctrines of fairness, see Yvonne McDermott, *Fairness in International Criminal Trials* (Oxford: Oxford University Press, 2016); Jonathan Hafetz, *Punishing Atrocities through a Fair Trial: International Criminal Law from Nuremberg to the Age of Global Terrorism* (Cambridge: Cambridge University Press, 2018).

The principle on burden of proof is no exception. The Rome Statute follows other criminal systems by requiring the proof of the accused's guilt to be judged "beyond reasonable doubt." Just how problematic this term can be was fully displayed in all the Congo cases, particularly at the AC level. Split decisions in the Ngudjolo and Bemba AC judgments dwelt at length on alternative ways to apply this suggestive metaphor. Within any group of three judges, any one judge's "reasonable doubt" could have implications for the entire group. Imagine this lone judge making the following argument: *I am a reasonable person; I have doubt about the guilt of the accused; therefore, his guilt cannot be placed beyond reasonable doubt*. While compelling in an everyday sense, this syllogism does not require the other two judges to defer, if they do *not* harbor *reasonable doubt*. Even the core standard-of-proof principle can be the topic of lively interchange among judges. Strict logic is necessary in law, but never sufficient.

Legal Process and the Anxiety of Politics

Legality should not feel embarrassed by the presence of indeterminacy in applying legal rules. Nothing else could be expected, especially in a new court dealing with untested norms, and working in culturally diverse environments. It is the role of trial judges to foster debate on all such points, and to resolve interpretive problems in an impartial manner. The presence of multiple judges, and multiple levels of judging, aims to counteract individual bias along the way. Issues of fact and law spend months testing the reasoning prowess of the Appeals Chamber, and the detailed judgment will underwrite the finality of their decision. The final word will have reckoned with the most serious alternative views. The final appeals decision, if not "infallible," must win its legitimacy by being responsive to reasonable alternatives.[536]

Trials in the ICC can be analyzed along multiple dimensions. One dimension concerns the accused and his fate: guilty? and, if so, of what, and based on what evidence? These questions occupy center stage at all levels of the ICC

[536] In a retrospective mood, Martti Koskenniemi explores the implications of viewing legal argument as inherently unsettled and dynamic, moving beyond the strategy of unmasking law as simply "political" and searching for alternative ways to reflect on experience with international tribunals ("Politics of International Law: Twenty Years Later"). In a similar spirit, the venerable notion of "responsive" law integrates critique with reflexive elements of legal reasoning. A classic treatment of this concept left many questions unanswered: Philippe Nonet and Philip Selznick, *Law and Society in Transition: Toward Responsive Law* (New York: Routledge, 2017) (originally published in 1978). The problem of what law should be "responsive to" remains a significant challenge for an international system in transition.

judicial system. Another concern looks to a farther horizon: the constant reweaving of legal standards embedded in the statute. Courtroom encounters with cases and facts – brought from such faraway locations as Ituri and the CAR – change the weight and nuance of both legal text and legal purpose. The formal statute remains the same, but tensions within the body of law are exposed, scrutinized, and recalibrated, as a result of being tested in concrete situations. The trials analyzed in the coming chapters will consider these shifting dynamics.

Are these all-too-human judgments truly part of the legal process? At what point do they cross over into the alien territory of politics? Anxiety over these questions hangs over courts in general, but especially over new courts, and even more so international criminal courts. In legal proceedings, a political decision is to be abhorred if it means that judgments are guided by anything more than the legal norms embodied in the founding statute.[537] Thus "being guided by norms" becomes an elusive defense against the scourge of politics. The Congo trials in the ICC became the years-long testing ground for this essential phase of legal process.[538] If dynamic implementation is both natural and necessary, so too are the anxieties that surround the progression of law: any unexpected, unwelcome results can be attacked as alien to the original law, belonging instead to a flawed process. Criminal trials heighten these anxieties by their reflexive structure – and by their self-conscious scrutiny of real-time decisions. Formal adversarial procedures adopted by the ICC institutionalize self-doubt. A gauntlet of anxiety awaits the pristine ideals agreed at Rome.

The implementation phase of any new legal code is an inescapable ordeal for core legal principles. At the ICC, once the whole chain of triggers, situations, jurisdiction, and individual arrest warrants opens up the flow of legal process, the work of the ICC takes on a new dimension: more dynamic and fluid than the pure legal text. Like any professional legal code, the Rome Statute fully anticipates this active dimension, by specifying precisely who is authorized to make each kind of implementation decision. It also ensures anxiety by insisting that core legal concepts must be conserved at the end of the process. The Congo trials give us the mixed results of this heroic venture.

537 Michael J. Struett, "Why the International Criminal Court Must Pretend to Ignore Politics," *Ethics and International Affairs* 26 (2012), 83.

538 As Carsten Stahn concludes: "Critiques relating to fairness remain a central concern of international criminal justice"; *A Critical Introduction to International Criminal Law*, p. 276.

THE CONGO TRIALS

Is it possible to extract from this tangled web one element, to isolate it, to subject it to legal analysis . . .?

ICJ Judge Pieter Kooijmans
DRC v. *Uganda* (2005)

[T]he underlying facts are often more complex than revealed through evidence and testimony at trial. The judgment is constrained by this. It relies on constructed chains of causality or fiction. It is controversial to what extent it may serve as an authoritative account of facts. Often, a differentiated vision emerges only through a sequence of trials.

Carsten Stahn
A Critical Introduction to International Criminal Law

A trial, especially one that lasts as long as those before the UN tribunals, can be a numbing process. To guarantee their impartiality, the proceedings must take place under the anesthesia of rules of procedure and legal decorum. Form and codes are all-important. The vocabulary is abstruse and disembodied. The dynamics of the legal battle between the parties emphasize this cold distancing of what is really at stake, shifting it to a place shielded from emotion and feeling. The product of the trial – the judgment of an individual – can also, therefore, appear to be technical, as though it were necessary to downplay the toll it takes on a person's life.

Thierry Cruvellier
Court of Remorse

[A]nd slowness is part of justice, so long as everything does not become mired.

Assingambi Zarambaud
Victims' Representative, ICC Bemba trial

[A] trial should never last more than eighteen months total.

ICC Judge Claude Jorda

The third Congo trial cleared its final hurdle in June 2018, some fifteen years after the Prosecutor announced his interest in the Ituri conflicts. By the following month, on the twentieth anniversary of the Rome Statute, these were the only ICC trials to reach the end of the judicial process. Another (belated) Ituri-based Congo conviction currently awaits appeal, following a Trial Chamber Judgment in July 2019.

The slow pace was excruciating for all concerned, punctuated with surprises and procedural fixes that laid the course for future trials. Surprises inside the courtroom reflected systematic problems on the outside: launching investigations, finding and protecting witnesses, and vetting potential courtroom evidence. Starting with the Lubanga case, the Trial Chamber demanded a stronger role in overseeing prosecutorial behavior, while appointing itself as the custodian of fair trial rights for the accused. In all three Congo trials, the Chamber's authority reached its own limits in controversial efforts to change the pre-trial legal characterization of facts. New procedures for victim participation required extensive, ongoing attention.

Witness testimony brought the challenges of Ituri and the CAR into the courtroom. From the first witness in the Lubanga trial, on through months and years to follow, doubts about credibility loomed large. The Defense used its own investigations to undermine a significant number of central witnesses. Overall, much of the evidence submitted was circumstantial in nature, testing the Trial Chamber's fact-finding capacity. Disputes arose over methods used by trial judges to lever weak evidence into findings the judges deemed persuasive. Standards and burdens of proof were drawn into these disputes.

The broadest experiment lay in stretching inherited crime definitions to fit the diffuse forms of armed conflict taking place in central Africa. The pivot to individual criminal responsibility called forth a chain of bold judicial inferences, resting on a series of paradigms and presumptions imported from culturally distant settings.

Across all three Congo trials, the cumulative rulings produced a fractious dialogue. The mixed tally (two convictions and two acquittals) does not capture the full diversity of perspective. Split panels, dissenting opinions, and appellate reversals tell a much broader story of judicial conflicts over key principles. These differences reach the most fundamental concepts of legality: fair trials, the presumption of innocence, and proof beyond reasonable doubt.

Thomas Lubanga enters the courtroom on the opening day of his trial, January 26, 2009. ©ICC-CPI/Michael Kooren

7

The Trial of Thomas Lubanga

7.1 THE TYRANNY OF FACTS

From Facts to Evidence

The trial centered on a single criminal charge about child soldiers. It lasted more than three years, from opening arguments in January 2009 to the delivery of the Trial Chamber's Judgment in April 2012. It began nearly three years after Lubanga first arrived in The Hague; and by the time his appeals were exhausted in December 2014, he had lived more than eight years in ICC detention. That time was subtracted from his fourteen-year sentence, which was completed in March 2020.[539]

There is a provision in international law for the reduction of time served, based on good behavior and discretion of the judges. The Trial Chamber denied Lubanga's petition for early release in late 2015 and again with subsequent requests.[540] Having asked to serve out the remainder of his sentence in the Congo, Lubanga was released with the hope he would assist future peacekeeping goals in Ituri.[541] Meanwhile, the ICC spent more years debating ways to implement reparations principles for victims associated with this case, reaching a complex resolution in 2019.[542]

[539] Lubanga Trial Judgment, March 14, 2012, ICC-01/04–01/06–2842; Lubanga Sentencing Judgment, July 10, 2012, ICC-01/04–01/06–2901; Lubanga Appeals Judgment, December 1, 2014, ICC-01/04–01/06–3121.

[540] Lubanga Appeals Chamber, Decision Concerning Reduction of Sentence, September 22, 2015, ICC-01/04–01/06–3173; Second Decision Concerning Reduction of Sentence, November 3, 2017, ICC-01/04–01/06–3375.

[541] ICC Presidency, Decision Regarding a State of Enforcement, December 8, 2015, ICC-01/04–01/06–3185. Lubanga was transported to the Congo on December 19.

[542] Lubanga Appeals Chamber, Judgment on Appeal of Reparations Award, July 18, 2019, ICC-01/04–01/06–3466.

The trial is about the guilt or innocence of the accused. But in the case of the ICC, other legal frames and broader objectives are equally at stake. The trial is also about the victims and what kind of justice they may receive at the end of the process. And it is about the legal norms that are suddenly mobilized – about testing them, articulating them in concrete terms, and seeing them interact with faraway facts brought into the courtroom. Thus was the ICC experiment set in motion.

The criminal charge might be simple, but the underlying facts arose from a conflict steeped in complexity. In the Lubanga trial, this complexity posed an immanent challenge, overwhelming the Court with a series of crises over its management of trial evidence. Amid multiple stories about all that had happened, the courtroom was wracked by conflicting and contradictory accounts – sometimes from the same witness. It was from this tangled web that the Trial Chamber needed to extract reliable threads that could then be connected to relevant legal categories. The legal process speaks of "finding facts," but in these trials it was not as simple as stumbling across something ready-made. The raw facts had to be converted into *evidence*, entering into a structure of judgment. It all had to be actively reconstructed, inside the courtroom, and with a conspicuous show of objectivity. Things that "everyone knew" were distressingly difficult to establish in the courtroom – starting with the true ages of witnesses said to be former child soldiers.

Much of the evidence came into the courtroom through live witnesses. As in other international criminal tribunals, the cognitive distance between the Court and the underlying conflicts created special burdens for the Trial Chamber. Even with the best intentions, any testimony from victim-witnesses had to pass through layers of psychological trauma, endemic to local conditions.[543] But ICC judges also faced copious inconsistencies, contradictions, and allegations of witness manipulation, all of which were difficult to separate from opaque cultural barriers. Staring across wide language gaps, judges could rely, only at their peril, on customary ways of assessing demeanor, candor, and even coherence of what they heard, what they read, and what they saw.[544]

543 Lee Ann Fujii, "Shades of Truth and Lies: Interpreting Testimonies of War and Violence," *Journal of Peace Research* 47 (2010), 231.

544 Similar assessment issues have been studied in the ad hoc tribunals by Nancy Amoury Combs, *Fact-Finding without Facts: The Uncertain Evidentiary Foundations of International Criminal Convictions* (Cambridge: Cambridge University Press, 2010), chapter 3. Combs's book has received mixed reviews: compare Beth S. Lyons, "Enough Is Enough: The Illegitimacy of International Criminal Convictions," *Journal of Genocide Research* 13 (2011), 287 (a generally positive review, extending Combs's analysis to account for the

For witnesses, the cultural barriers were mutual. As strangers from Ituri, the protocols and expectations of the Hague courtroom lay far beyond their lived experience. The rhetoric of cross-examination surpassed imagination. The very notion of truth-telling before a neutral judge could be a cultural and emotional stretch.[545] Ituri witnesses came from a fractious social environment, where loyalties were constantly being subverted, and where neutrality was in short supply. Speaking to investigators could put their personal safety at risk, leading the Court to move some witnesses into protective programs – even to the point of starting new lives in distant communities. The Lubanga testimony came six to eight years after the relevant events, well after positions taken during the conflict had both hardened and metastasized.

And then there were documents, including a selection of videos. Those criminal jurisdictions using juries filter such evidence through a system of strict restraints. Not so the trials conducted by the ICC. Early on, the Lubanga Pre-Trial Chamber declared a wide readiness to receive evidence with few traditional limits. No matter that documents might have been seized illegally under Congolese law, or that allegations came in as anonymous hearsay.[546] Provided it had some potential connection with truth, it should all come into the courtroom – where judges were prepared, for whatever material seemed relevant, to exercise precise judgment about the weight and probity of each individual item. Something in the videos might catch the judges' attention. This was essential for a Court designed to end impunity for the worst criminal atrocities, which could not afford to ignore any morsel of truth.[547]

Faced with mountains of evidence, the judges themselves would sort it all out – first in the pre-trial Confirmation decision, and then more definitively in the formal Trial Judgment. This sorting out process, powerful but obscure, would constitute a distinctive legal truth. This truth would rise up

extensive use of presumptions and inferences in international criminal trials); and Ward Ferdinandusse, "Fact-Finding by and about International Criminal Tribunals," *Journal of International Criminal Justice* 11 (2013), 677 (pointing to methodological weaknesses, including an overly rosy view of how fact-finding works in national criminal systems).

545 This reciprocal cultural factor is discussed, with useful bibliographical references, by Tim Kelsall in his study of the Special Court for Sierra Leone, *Culture under Cross-Examination* (Cambridge: Cambridge University Press, 2009), pp. 13–17.

546 Lubanga Pre-Trial Chamber, Confirmation of Charges decision, January 29, 2007, ICC-01/04–01/06–803, paras. 84–90, 99–103 (interpreting Article 69(4) and 69(7) of the Rome Statute).

547 For formal rules on admissibility of evidence at trial, see Article 69(4), with further provisions in the Rules of Procedure and Evidence.

out of the internal convictions of each judge – an opaque source expressed in rich metaphors of personal struggle.[548] This performative nature of legal fact-finding created unique problems for appeals judges, when it came time for review. Overall, the Congo trials would shine a harsh light on the mechanics of reaching final trial judgments. Across all three trials, the mysteries of judicial fact-finding were deepened by stark dissents and dramatic reversals.

The first ICC Trial Chamber expected a vigorous adversarial contest. But nothing prepared it for the open contradictions, confessions of lying, and signs of witness-coaching by corrupt intermediaries. It began on the trial's opening day, in late January 2009, when the first witness blurted out a strange tale about being asked to lie. His story about being abducted on the way home from school "came from someone else. They taught me that over three and a half years. I don't like it."[549] But this remarkable tale was subject to various explanations – perhaps it was just nervous shock from being in a courtroom with strange rules, and with "Monsieur Thomas" sitting over in the far corner. For most of the Prosecution's case presentation, other child witnesses told their stories much as forecast in the Prosecutor's opening statement. Even that first witness returned and spoke again of his abduction: this time without flinching.[550]

Then, in June 2009, another child witness told the Court that he had lied about his name and circumstances, saying he had been coached to deceive.[551] Once more the Prosecution glossed over the damage in what was being said, with the Senior Attorney rapidly changing the subject, embarking (in the chiding words of Judge Fulford) on a discursive "voyage of discovery." This testimony was heard in closed session, and only a brief summary caught the eye of careful trial monitors among the public.[552]

548 The position that moral authority resides in a single individual's satisfied conscience can be traced to John Locke and followed through Montesquieu and Enlightenment sources. Its career in law includes the Napoleonic endorsement of *le principe de la preuve morale*, for which proof is a function of the judge's conscientious decision, relatively unencumbered by formal rules of evidence. John D. Jackson and Sarah J. Summers, *The Internationalisation of Criminal Evidence: Beyond the Common Law and Civil Law Traditions* (Cambridge: Cambridge University Press, 2012), pp. 34, 62–65.

549 Lubanga Trial Chamber, transcript, January 28, 2009, ICC-01/04–01/06-T-110-Red-ENG, p. 40.

550 Lubanga Trial Chamber, transcript, February 11, 2009, ICC-01/04–01/06-T-123-Red-ENG, pp. 19–25.

551 Lubanga Trial Chamber, transcript, June 16, 2009, ICC-01/04–01/06-T-192-Red3-ENG, pp. 4–6.

552 Ibid., p. 7.

It was not until the Defense case started in early 2010 that the reliability of all child witnesses came under withering attack. Reverting to that first-day child witness, allegations of coaching and deception burst into the court record through the very first Defense witness. In a rapid flow of testimony, the Defense offered a crushing response, raising doubts about whether any of the Ituri witnesses could be free of suspicion. The judges had already heard the Prosecution's full case, organized according to the master narrative, only now to confront the rupture presented by the Defense.[553]

This heavy reliance on live testimony in the Congo trials invites comparisons with conditions noted some years before at the Rwanda Tribunal (ICTR). A French journalist who covered those trials extensively recalled the first ICTR trial, regarding killings in a rural district in 1994. "There was no material evidence. Events in this small commune in Central Rwanda from April to June 1994 were reconstructed solely on the basis of witness testimony. There is nothing more abundant than human testimony. There is also nothing more fragile and more easily influenced."[554]

In Ituri there were random documents – indeed thousands of pieces of paper, much of it scooped up by the UN after the March 2003 turmoil in Bunia. But documents do not always speak for themselves. They purport to "document" facts and relationships, but their purpose may also be strategic. In the *parochial network* structures of Ituri, titles like "commander" and "minister" could not simply be taken at face value. Behind such documents were the hidden dynamics of factions and defections that punctuated the critical months of 2002–03. The contrast is greatest with a regime like Nazi Germany, where acres of credible documents were dutifully produced by a robust German bureaucracy. At the Yugoslav Tribunal (ICTY), Serbian national politicians and their Bosnian allies left similar paper trails, which played an important role in those trials.[555]

553 Lubanga Trial Chamber, transcript, January 27, 2010, ICC-01/04–01/06-T-236-Red2-FRA.

554 Thierry Cruvellier, *Court of Remorse: Inside the International Criminal Tribunal for Rwanda* (Madison: University of Wisconsin Press, 2006), p. 20.

555 The existence of UPC documents helped to persuade Bernard Lavigne (lead ICC investigator in the Congo) that the UPC was a worthy criminal target. Other groups, some splintered off from the UPC, had no documents or tangible policies at all, and thus did not fit the mold for perpetration. See Lavigne's oral deposition, November 16, 2010, ICC-01/04–01/06-Rule68Deposition-Red2-FRA, pp. 28–32. Lavigne also received information from the local Bunia magistrates and prosecutor, who at the time were being paid not by the Congolese state but by international NGOs (ibid., p. 70). Further references will be to "Lavigne Deposition" with the date, and page references in the French version.

The Lubanga Pre-Trial Chamber had been generous in allowing Prosecution documents into the evidence pool, granting them a presumption of authenticity,[556] including would-be birth records that were later shown to be contrived. They left all the evaluation to future judges, to determine the probative value for each bit of evidence – as needed, reasoning item-by-item, keeping in mind the larger purpose of the Court. This lack of gatekeeping added to the complexity of later fact-finding. It left the Defense to guess what might find its way into final judicial deliberations. But the Court had its reasons: "The Chamber recalls that in the fight against impunity, it must ensure an appropriate balance between the rights of the accused and the need to respond to victims' and the international community's expectations."[557] In the Ituri conflicts, virtually any document might serve some extrinsic purpose. Statements of principles, lists of cabinet members, charts of military organization – all would require some kind of secondary support to be taken at face value. The trial judges discounted several written orders issued by Lubanga for the demobilization of children from armed groups, treating them as self-serving propaganda.[558] But then what about the organization charts: did they really prove the paradigm of a tight bureaucratic structure? When these documents were prepared, the leadership group in the UPC organization sat atop multiple fault-lines and would gradually splinter into competing camps. Whatever else was happening, factions and individuals were posturing early-on for roles in upcoming peace talks – locally in Ituri, and nationally as part of the Inter-Congolese Dialogue. Many were also angling for positions in the Congolese national army. These larger dynamics would eventually sort winners from losers within the crumbling UPC, the umbrella organization associated with Lubanga. The general atmosphere of decay was articulated by the Defense, well after the Prosecution's master narrative had been presented.

Video evidence was introduced by the Prosecution with the assurance that it would strike the judges as self-evident.[559] Largely through work by the Defense, key ambiguities would emerge, even here. The main point of contention was the Prosecution's position that these films depicted "soldiers" who were manifestly younger than fifteen. Not all of them, of course, but certain ones who would ultimately catch the judges' eye. For the judges, these visuals seemed to carry great weight. They could see this specific evidence for

556 Lubanga Confirmation of Charges decision, para. 97.
557 Ibid., para. 86.
558 Lubanga Trial Judgment, para. 1348.
559 Lubanga Trial, Prosecution opening statement, January 26, 2009, ICC-01/04–01/06-T-107-ENG, pp. 11, 17–18.

themselves, whatever doubts surrounded the documentary and witness testimony.[560]

After the conclusion of the trial, and notably at the sentencing hearing, the Defense had a strange fixation on one video scene of a young-looking recruit watching a giant insect crawl up and down his arm. While observers in the Public Gallery were perplexed by this journey of the wayward bug, captured in slow-motion, the trial judges lost patience and shut down the presentation. Eventually the purpose was revealed: the young-looking "child" in this drama was simultaneously poised to speak to the Court, by satellite, declaring that he had been older than fifteen at the time of his filmed encounter with the insect. On his arm, next to the bug and visible to the camera, was an identifying tattoo: he was *that* person. If it was a mistake to take *him* for a child, then how could any observer trust his or her visual intuitions? The Defense was provoking reasonable doubt. But the Chamber felt that it was wasting its time, months after the Trial Judgment, watching slow-motion replays.[561]

The Master Narrative

The Prosecutor's Ituri investigations started sometime in 2004, when field staff got no closer than Kinshasa, more than a thousand miles away. It was there that the ICC investigating team started collaborating with the United Nations and international NGOs.[562] The UN had only a tiny force in Bunia during the conflict, with most NGO personnel arriving near the chaotic close of the period covered in the Lubanga trial (from March 2003), when Lubanga's network had already broken apart and Lubanga himself was on the run. It was in this retrograde environment, according to testimony from the chief ICC investigator, that the Prosecution formed its core template: framing the recent conflict as a battle between two ethnically defined militia groups. That template was cribbed from the HRW report *Ituri: "Covered in Blood"* (July 2003), with its influential roster of military organizations.[563] The report

560 Lubanga Trial Judgment, paras. 644, 1262, 1278.

561 Lubanga Trial Chamber sentencing hearing, June 13, 2012, ICC-01/04–01/06-T-360-Red2-ENG, pp. 26–27. For a description of the dynamics in the courtroom, see Tjitske Lingsma, *All Rise: The High Ambitions of the International Criminal Court and the Harsh Reality* (Utrecht: Ipso, 2017), pp. 158–59.

562 Lavigne Deposition, November 16, 2010, pp. 19–20.

563 HRW, *Ituri: "Covered in Blood": Ethnically Targeted Violence in Northeastern DR Congo* (New York, 2003). The listing of organizations is on pp. 15–17. The lead author of this report, Anneke van Woudenberg, held interviews in Bunia and North Kivu starting in February 2003. Also influential were two UN reports: United Nations Office for the

presented a quick history of armed groups but directed most of its attention to HRW's characteristic first-person accounts from victims. The appended diagram of Ituri militias – shortened to acronyms – inspired the master narrative in Lubanga, as well as the ICC's second trial of Katanga and Ngudjolo.

After March 2003, information in intrigue-ridden Bunia was coming from all directions: from a wide number of fragmented groups, with few (if any) members counting as objective or disinterested. The arrival of European peacekeepers in early June, followed in September by MONUC reinforcements seeking to fill the power vacuum, gave new focus for local strategic actors adjusting to a new hegemon. Offering eye-witness accounts might get you killed; but it could also earn you new life-chances, whether joining the national Army or simply assisting Western NGOs.[564]

Along with its famous militia charts, "*Covered in Blood*" pioneered a new NGO style of description, connecting the witness narratives to relevant legal categories drawn from the Rome Statute, clearly meaning to attract the attention of the ICC Prosecutor. In this new idiom, NGO facts were being *legally characterized*, speaking to the personal responsibility of those named as commanders. Such legally characterized facts were meant to interpret Ituri violence after July 1, 2002. Reports from HRW and similar groups polished up the narrative themes of tightly controlled military organizations, dominated by supreme commanders; of ethnic hatred and the solidarity of armed groups on two sides of an ethnic divide. Also present in these reports was the presumption that events so appalling could be explained only as the implementation of a prior master plan. This inferential leap allowed the pivot to ICC concepts of individual responsibility.

From mid-2003 to 2005, the rumor mills in Ituri never ceased. From 2005, as renewed violence increased in Bunia and kept the rural areas beyond reach, it became even more difficult for the ICC to investigate. The Rome Statute envisions an open-minded process, obligating the Prosecutor to search "equally" for "incriminating and exonerating circumstances."[565] Before

Coordination of Humanitarian Affairs (OCHA), *DRC: Special Report on the Ituri District, northeastern DRC*, published December 18, 2002 on the IRIN network; and UN Secretary-General, *Special Report on the Events in Ituri, January 2002–December 2003*, S/2004/573, issued July 16, 2004.

564 See Emeric Rogier, "The Inter-Congolese Dialogue: A Critical Overview," in Mark Malan and João Gomes Porto (eds.), *Challenges of Peace Implementation: The UN Mission in the Democratic Republic of the Congo* (Pretoria: Institute for Security Studies, 2004), pp. 25–42.

565 Article 54(1)(a). From the beginning, investigators and prosecutors were integrated in team visits to the Congo, a practice built into policies in the Office of the Prosecutor. Benjamin N. Schiff, *Building the International Criminal Court* (Cambridge: Cambridge University Press, 2008), p. 120 (citing an interview with then-Deputy Prosecutor Fatou Bensouda).

individual suspects were even identified, this obligation must have been especially difficult. But NGO assessments, following *"Covered in Blood,"* had already started naming organizations and imputing liability to individual leaders, connecting complex facts to legal paradigms of individual responsibility. The storylines were converging: real alternatives were swept aside.

At the start of the Lubanga trial in 2009, the Prosecutor's master narrative gathered threads found within these NGO reports, creating a fresh pattern radiating out from a central focus on Thomas Lubanga – the man then sitting in the far corner of the Hague courtroom. By this time some of Lubanga's erstwhile associates and/or rivals had been identified, even interviewed. Their relationships were configured so that all lines of responsibility converged with Lubanga. A similar focus would also make Germain Katanga and Mathieu Ngudjolo into the primary actors in their chapter of the Ituri drama – a single attack on Hema soldiers and civilians in February 2003.

By these accounts, Ituri was properly understood as a crime scene; figures like Lubanga seized control over events through strong military command over armed troops; Lubanga's purpose was to gain raw political power; he and his lieutenants were motivated by ethnic hatred of the Lendu population. As for the distinct war crime regarding child soldiers, it was one inevitable element in a conscious military strategy – for which Lubanga was a master planner, and someone who could have stopped it had he wished. The trial process would be simple, because everyone in Ituri could plainly observe the presence of children under fifteen in various military roles.

From this master narrative, the Prosecutor allocated facts-on-the-ground into a series of templates or reinforcing scripts, marking the conversion of raw facts into courtroom evidence. Since much evidence would come in through live testimony, witnesses were brought to strengthen each narrative element. Of course, there were risks, if some witnesses managed to sow confusion on key elements. A witness's credibility on one point could always be challenged if he or she deviated from the script on other points. The judges, as finders of fact, had to weigh it all in the balance, demarcating the boundary lines of doubt.

The obvious missing chapter in this narrative was a focus on sexual violence in Ituri, which had been the subject of several NGO reports. Near the end of the Prosecution case in 2010, urged on by Victims' Representatives and outside commentators, the Chamber was briefly persuaded to assert its limited authority to expand the charges against Lubanga. The reasons why this effort was abandoned will be explained in Section 7.6; but the Prosecution case doubled down on sexual exploitation of girls among the child soldiers. The children themselves would come to The Hague to present their stories, including female soldiers.

Early versions of the master narrative are found in the Prosecution's 2006 request for Lubanga's arrest warrant. In a heavily redacted transcript, the Senior Trial Attorney for the Prosecutor answered pointed questions from the pre-trial judges. Question: How could Lubanga be responsible for an uprising in Bunia at a time when he was incarcerated a thousand miles away in Kinshasa? Answer: The Prosecution knew that his control over his loyal lieutenants was so great that he found ways to direct their actions from his distant jail cell. Question: Given the instability of the area, is it possible to see Lubanga's UPC organization as an effective, powerful unit? Answer: The UPC had a stable command structure with Lubanga as the supreme leader, and it was the prime cause of disorder in Ituri. Question: With all the external forces swirling around Ituri (such as Uganda generals), did Lubanga have much impact of his own? Answer: Lubanga's UPC organization was a powerful independent actor, calling the military shots in Ituri when it came to ethnic conflict. These assurances were sufficient for purposes of granting an arrest warrant, persuading the pre-trial judges that the Prosecution had a fully elaborated theory of the crime.[566] Its truth was constituted by the coherence of the narrative.

Once Lubanga had appeared in The Hague, the Pre-Trial Chamber went further in proposing its own structural improvements to the evolving master narrative. From German law, it imported an arcane theory to tighten up the paradigm of individual responsibility: the doctrine of a mastermind, at the pinnacle of an efficient organization, guiding the actions of foot soldiers. This part of the story will have its own treatment in Section 7.4. The Chamber also moved to subtract Uganda and Rwanda from the overloaded causal engine for Ituri violence. Thomas Lubanga alone would be on trial; not the shadowy forces of neighboring countries, and certainly not the furtive interlopers from Kinshasa.[567]

566 Lubanga Pre-Trial Chamber hearing of February 2, 2006, ICC-01/04-01/06-48 (redacted version issued March 22, 2006), pp. 26–31. Part of this dynamic was due to unresolved competition between the Prosecution and the pre-trial judges for managing the actual investigations. See Michela Miraglia, "The First Decision of the ICC Pre-Trial Chamber: International Criminal Procedure under Construction," *Journal of International Criminal Justice* 4 (2006), 188.

567 Although the Ituri conflict seemed to be international in scope, with clear roles for Uganda and Rwanda, the Pre-Trial Chamber split the time period, designating the period from July 2002 to June 2003 as "international" and from June 2003 to December 2003 as "non-international." But for purposes of applying the child-soldier provision against Lubanga, the Chamber simply disregarded the distinction, because not to do so would "undermine the object and purpose" of the Rome Statute (Confirmation of Charges decision, para. 281). This conflict-within-a-conflict theory proved cumbersome at trial, and finally the Trial Chamber

The Cloud of Doubt

The trial process puts the Prosecutor's master narrative to the test. The testing process may begin slowly through cross-examination of initial Prosecution witnesses, along with any questions from the bench. The Defense stirs doubt about the courtroom evidence, creating a cloud, however small, to hang over the proceedings. The Prosecution plans its narrative to resist that buildup: with discrete segments meant to contain any stray doubts within watertight compartments, all the time maintaining enough redundancy in testimony to compensate for the failure of any single witness. The Prosecution wants to maintain the coherence of its master story, while the Defense points to a realm of alternatives, moving outside the narrative.

A large, dense cloud of doubt alters the capacity of trial judges to reach a point of internal conviction, each in the depths of his or her own personal reflection about the accused's guilt *beyond a reasonable doubt*. The impetus for doubt may begin with uncertainty, which surrounds virtually all complex human affairs, and notably across distances of time and culture. The pause for uncertainty crystallizes into doubt with the emergence of reasonable alternatives to the core narrative. These alternatives shift the judicial task toward a deliberative process, interpersonal and discursive rather than purely internal and subjective.

The emergence of *doubt* advances the dynamic elements of judging. Courtroom doubt arises within a structure of reasoning, revealing tacit inferences and legally inflected facts. In this whole exercise, the master narrative may introduce itself as the default truth, to be rendered plausible through the testimony of Prosecution witnesses. The doubt that matters – what starts the formation of a cloud – is anything that undercuts that narrative, including layers of uncertainty opened up by the Defense. These layers produce alternatives to challenge the integrity of the original narrative.

Under such challenges, the master narrative may suddenly lose its default status. It would be different for some ordinary story told in everyday discourse that can stay afloat by polite inertia, even in the face of skepticism.[568] But in the courtroom, the structure of defaults is subject to the presumption of innocence. Under that vital principle of legality in criminal law, the

reduced the whole matter to a "non-international" armed conflict. These issues will be explored in Section 7.5.

568 On conversational defaults in contrast to courtroom narratives, see Hans V. Hansen, Fred J. Kauffeld, James B. Freeman, and Lilian Bermejo-Luque (eds.), *Presumptions and Burdens of Proof: An Anthology of Argumentation and the Law* (Tuscaloosa: University of Alabama Press, 2019).

appearance of reasonable alternatives changes the rhetorical balance. And the stronger the doubt, the greater the burden on the Prosecution to keep its narrative intact.

Courtroom doubt operates on multiple levels of law and fact, down to such concrete facts as the true age of the child witness. "Fact-finding" becomes a process of complex judgment: sifting through faulty school records, multiple and conflicting identification cards, vague memories of families and relatives, all in addition to visual assessments of the particular person. Under the structure of defaults, the Prosecution's original statement loses its inertial force; the process is rhetorically driven by the presumption of innocence.

The reckoning comes at the end of the trial, when the Chamber prepares its final judgment. In all the Congo trials, beginning with Lubanga, judicial declarations of facts came cloaked in various idioms. They were often reduced to psychological terms, rising up from each judge's personal conviction, closing off further deliberations. These subjective reports dismissed some doubt-based alternatives as simply "unpersuasive." The resulting opacity of factual judgments created tensions within the appellate review process.

The opportunity to build up sources of doubt falls to the Defense as it launches its independent case. But doubts can emerge sooner, with early chinks in the master narrative, as when Prosecution witnesses suddenly go off-script. When Lubanga's lead Defense counsel opened her case in January 2010, her statement made its own flourishes. All of the child witnesses were lying, she announced, and the Defense would present new witnesses to undermine them.[569] Picking up on early warnings from two errant Prosecution child witnesses, she presented the theory that the deception was systematically hatched by shadowy intermediaries freely used by the Prosecution. Adult witnesses testifying about Lubanga's organization and its planning were likewise tainted – or at least that possibility must be rigorously considered. After presenting new witnesses, including perhaps the impugned intermediaries themselves, the Defense would ask the Chamber to drop the entire case, owing to the Prosecution's "abuse of process." With evidence of serious witness corruption, there came a tipping point: so much false testimony invites suspicion that none of the Prosecution witnesses could be safely relied on.[570]

[569] Lubanga Trial Chamber, transcript, January 27, 2010, ICC-01/04-01/06-T-236-Red2-FRA, pp. 22–23.

[570] Ibid., pp. 24–25.

This was not the first international trial to pose questions about the integrity of witness testimony. A sustained challenge to fact-finding at the ICTY and the ICTR had just been published. It followed an earlier critique of evidence introduced before the SCSL.[571] Both critics argued that complex facts from the field had breached the narrow confines of the Prosecution's master narrative. These alternatives shifted the burden of reasoning out of its initial default comfort zone.

In the Rwandan and Sierra Leonean cases, the loose organization of violence cast doubt on the narrative theme of strict military planning, which was derived from conceptual models dating back to twentieth-century conflicts. Gaps of time and culture put undue constraints on judges, as they cobbled together their judgments, working within legal paradigms of individual responsibility. These published critiques anticipated the argument from Lubanga's Defense team. But for Lubanga there were additional factors, including the corrupt intermediaries spreading deception before the Court. The Defense would not be drawn into saying that there were no child soldiers present in the Ituri conflicts. Their job was to convince the judges that the Prosecution evidence on this point, given its systematic flaws, had failed to establish a credible link to Lubanga himself.

In their final judgment, the judges removed vast swaths of testimony from consideration. All nine child witnesses were deemed unreliable.[572] Moreover, the groundbreaking testimony of three victims, speaking as special witnesses, was likewise tainted and dismissed (and their status as registered victims was rescinded).[573] The Prosecution was roundly scolded for its investigative methods, which threatened the fair trial standard, not to mention wasting the Court's valuable time.[574]

The aura of doubt grew still further, after two sketchy intermediaries testified during the Defense phase, along with the Prosecutor's field director in the Ituri investigations.[575] The Trial Chamber granted Defense requests – over strenuous opposition from the Prosecution and the Victims' Representatives – to bring this counter-narrative of corrupt evidence squarely into the courtroom. But the Chamber was not prepared to throw the case out entirely. It rejected the last-ditch Defense motion to condemn the Prosecution's "abuse of process." Bad as it was, it did not exceed the

[571] Combs, *Fact-Finding without Facts* (2010); Kelsall, *Culture under Cross-Examination* (2009).
[572] Lubanga Trial Judgment, para. 480.
[573] Ibid., para. 484.
[574] Ibid., para. 482.
[575] Intermediary 321 testified before the Chamber in late June and early July 2010; Intermediary 316 and the Prosecution field director appeared later in November.

Chamber's capacity to sort things out in the end. "Given the ability of the Court to resolve all the relevant factual issues in due course," the Chamber assumed the burden of calibrating the precise value of each witness's testimony, all in its final judgment.[576] The climate of doubt was stifling, but the remedy of ending the trial was a step too far. The Trial Chamber would ultimately make all the tough decisions. Its task would be gargantuan, but somehow it would prevail.

Under the circumstances of the Ituri conflicts, doubts in the trial were inevitable – indeed, quite serious doubts. The challenge to the Court was to manage this shape-changing mass of evidence: to encompass both the whole and the various parts, and to find a clear path to reasoned judgment. This would be the ICC's first attempt in a full-blown trial.

7.2 DISCLOSURE AND INTERMEDIARIES

Information Flows

Before the Trial Chamber could deliberate on the charges, it was forced to spend months scrutinizing its own procedures. The truly path-breaking contributions of the Lubanga trial turned on matters of evidence. It was the weighing not only of evidence inside the courtroom but also of the larger flows of whole blocks of potential evidence, moving through the hands of Prosecution, Defense, and the Trial Chamber. The Lubanga trial saw two particular moments when the Trial Chamber, exasperated with the Prosecution's handling of its massive stock of information, halted the proceedings and ordered Lubanga's release. Each time the Appeals Chamber intervened, and the problems with evidence flows were ultimately resolved. In the end, the Trial Chamber asserted its dominant power to manage the mountains of information generated by the parties.

The first breakdown over disclosing Prosecution evidence occurred months before the trial finally opened in January 2009. The second one came in mid-2010, at a key moment in the Defense phase, amid allegations that "intermediaries" working for the Prosecution had corrupted the witnesses and their stories, already presented by the Prosecution. In both breakdowns, the challenge went beyond the everyday capacity of judges to weigh the truthfulness of specific evidence brought into the courtroom. The question was whether the Prosecution's management of evidence at the wholesale level was consistent

[576] Lubanga Trial Chamber, Decision on "Abuse of Process" Application, March 11, 2011, ICC 01/04–01/06–2690-Red2, para. 197.

with fundamental fairness. In both crises, with backing from the Appeals Chamber, the Prosecution was compelled to cede greater authority to the Trial Chamber.

A third crisis threatened the trial later in 2010, when the Defense asked the Trial Chamber to abandon the case because of the Prosecution's failure to vet its own evidence, amounting to an "abuse of process." It was an extension of the previous breakdown over intermediaries, forcing the Trial Chamber to decide, yet again, whether a fair trial had become impossible. Whereas the two previous breaks were a struggle for dominance between the Prosecutor and the Trial Chamber (won in both cases by the Chamber), the "abuse of process" motion questioned the judges' innate capacity to deliberate on evidence, in the face of so much deception and uncertainty. In rejecting this Defense motion, the Chamber again asserted its dominance, confident in its own extraordinary power to reach a final trial judgment on the merits.

In sum, the procedural crises inside the Lubanga trial strengthened the power and ambitions of the Trial Chamber.[577] In its duels with the Prosecution, the Chamber articulated sections of the Rome Statute dealing with investigations and the handling of evidence. Rejecting the ultimate protest of the Defense, it declared itself the guardian of fair trial rights for ICC accused. These results acknowledged clear tensions within the statutory framework and procedural rules. The Chamber's pivotal role – overseeing the flow of evidence into the courtroom – yielded working principles for later trials.

How the Court Investigates

Before evidence can enter into the courtroom, there must be a process of digging, sorting, and vetting the raw information found in the conflict zone – perhaps even as the conflicts continue. This kind of work was started in Ituri by international NGOs, who arrived in Bunia near the end of the time period scrutinized in the Congo trials. There had been a small UN presence in August 2002, when the rebel group RCD-ML and Governor Lompondo were ousted and the UPC assumed a dominant presence in the main city. A large European force arrived in early June 2003, followed by a substantial buildup of MONUC peacekeepers in September. It was a time of failing

577 This dynamic is discussed by Christian De Vos, who sees it as a shift toward civil law procedure, in strengthening evidentiary responsibilities of the judiciary; "'Someone Who Comes between One Person and Another': *Lubanga*, Local Cooperation, and the Right to a Fair Trial," *Melbourne Law Journal* 12 (2011), 230.

networks, of posturing for seats at the peace table, of infiltration from national Congolese circles, and of continuing interference from neighboring countries. During this time, competing narratives circulated throughout Bunia.

The Congo trials had to collect their streams of evidence from people working in this turbulent environment. On their first visit, the ICC investigators remained in Kinshasa, unable to reach Ituri for security reasons. The ICC team received assurance of cooperation, realizing that they would need to rely initially on local informants, searching through distant memories, second-hand accounts, and rumors about potential witnesses. According to the team director Bernard Lavigne, there was major work to be done. Despite the ICC-friendly focus of NGO groups, there was still "a gap between the assessment of the human rights groups and the [legal] evidence." For one thing, the courtroom creates space for cross-examination. The Court investigator must therefore dig deeper. This view was echoed by prominent human rights activist William Pace, who told the *Wall Street Journal* that "human rights and humanitarian organizations are lousy criminal investigators. They are not producing forensic evidence that can be used by a prosecutor."[578]

Although the investigators had already modeled their conception of the conflict on legal characterizations by these same NGOs, they knew they would have to find witnesses who could offer live testimony. Searching for them would take place under severe security risks, affecting the safety of potential witnesses and investigators alike. On the ground in Bunia in 2005, the investigation was narrowed by the Prosecutor's decision to focus on child soldiers. In this context, the ICC team came to rely on local informants who would serve as "intermediaries" in finding potential witnesses – including former child soldiers and perhaps member of their families. At first this activity was sporadic, and it was not until 2006 – after Lubanga was already detained in The Hague – that the Ituri field office became fully operational.[579]

The intermediaries were "the only solution to the security problem," according to Nicolas Sabire, a member of the investigating team.[580] Lack of security and lack of prior knowledge of the conflict zone created the opening for local "militant activists" to spearhead the ICC search for potential

[578] Both quotes are referenced in the Lubanga Trial Judgment, paras. 130–31.

[579] Lavigne Deposition, November 16, 2010, p. 76. For a critical view of the Prosecutor's Congo investigations, written by a member of the Katanga Defense team with her own Congo experience, see Caroline Buisman, "Delegating Investigations: Lessons to Be Learned from the *Lubanga* Judgment," *Northwestern Journal of International Human Rights* 11 (2013), 30.

[580] Cited in Lubanga Trial Judgment, para. 413.

courtroom evidence.[581] According to the Trial Chamber's summary, it was these activists who provided the ICC with names of potential witnesses. It was they who interacted with MONUC and who went to the villages outside of Bunia. At the time, Lavigne said that he was not aware of problems, already noted by the UN, concerning children falsely claiming to have served in the militias, and who were now seeking aid and rehabilitation.[582] He seemed equally unaware that the ICC's chosen intermediaries might themselves be pursuing personal interests in Bunia during 2006.

After a painstaking review of the integrity of the Prosecution's main evidence, the Trial Chamber's ultimate verdict was blunt:

> The Chamber is of the view that the prosecution should not have delegated its investigative responsibilities to the intermediaries in the way set out above, notwithstanding the extensive security difficulties it faced .... The Chamber spent a considerable period of time investigating the circumstances of a substantial number of individuals whose evidence was, at least in part, inaccurate or dishonest. The prosecution's negligence in failing to verify and scrutinise this material sufficiently before it was introduced led to significant expenditure on the part of the Court. An additional consequence of the lack of proper oversight of the intermediaries is that they were potentially able to take advantage of the witnesses they contacted.[583]

After hearing courtroom testimony from two intermediaries, the Trial Chamber prodded the Prosecution to explore legal action against them for deceiving the Court.[584]

581 Lavigne Deposition, November 16, 2010, pp. 51–52 ("militants activistes").

582 Lavigne Deposition, November 17, 2010, ICC-01/04–01/06-Rule68Deposition-Red2-FRA, pp. 17–18. Concerning these false claims, the Lubanga Trial Chamber noted that they were common knowledge at the time among UN and NGO groups, which were supporting Lavigne's investigation. Lubanga Trial Judgment, para. 147.

583 Lubanga Trial Judgment, para. 482. For an extended analysis of the Prosecution's approach, see *Investigative Management, Strategies, and Techniques of the International Criminal Court's Office of the Prosecutor*, American University (Washington College of Law), War Crimes Research Office (2012).

584 Lubanga Trial Judgment, paras. 483, 1361. The Prosecutor later reported commissioning an external review, on the basis of which she decided to take no further action under Article 70. But there was no public access to that review, and a Defense motion to disclose it was denied by the Appeals Chamber (Decision on the Defence Request in Relation to Investigations Pursuant to Article 70, June 17, 2014, ICC-01/04–01/06–3114). In 2012, the Defense team for Germain Katanga noted that Intermediaries 143 and 316 received benefits of Court-financed relocation. Katanga and Ngudjolo Trial Chamber, Second Corrigendum to the Defence Closing Brief (Katanga), June 29, 2012, ICC-01/04–01/07–3266, paras. 500, 504. In March 2014, the Office of the Prosecutor released a policy paper on the use of intermediaries, perhaps a belated acknowledgment of past problems.

Disclosing Trial Evidence

In the contrived setting of the courtroom, where *facts* in the everyday sense give way to *evidence* in the strategic confines of a criminal trial, much depends on the custody and flow of that evidence. How it is collected, whether it is vetted in advance, and how it is shared between the parties – all these dynamic issues are laid out in procedural articles of the Rome Statute and in the supplementary Rules of Procedure and Evidence.[585] The Trial Chamber holds the final responsibility for managing those flows, although this might not have been clear at the outset of the Lubanga trial. Seen as a kind of laboratory experiment, the Lubanga case tested relevant parts of the Rome Statute and the Rules of Procedure and Evidence. Tensions in the rules forced the trial to its sequential stops and starts, setting the path for later cases.

The crisis over intermediaries underscored the absence of a police force for conducting pre-trial investigations. Nor did the ICC architects in Rome assign the task of oversight to a magistrate judge, as in some legal systems. In a series of provisions, the Statute assigns that role to the Prosecutor, awkwardly separating that task from the downstream function of the Prosecutor as advocate.

Article 54 (Duties and Powers of the Prosecutor with respect to investigations) sets out the initial mandate for non-adversarial, impartial investigations:

> 1. The Prosecutor shall:
>   (a) In order to establish the truth, extend the investigation to cover all facts and evidence relevant to an assessment of whether there is criminal responsibility under the Statute, and in doing so investigate incriminating and exonerating evidence equally . . ..

Further provisions in Article 54 stipulate that investigations shall be "effective" while respecting the interests of security and privacy for witnesses and victims – with particular note of sexual crimes. In this context, Article 54 imagines real-world negotiations over evidence with states and organizations, including a passage that figured heavily in the first Lubanga trial stoppage:

> 3. The Prosecutor may . . .
>   (e) Agree not to disclose at any stage of the proceedings, documents or information that the Prosecutor obtains on the condition of confidentiality and solely for the purpose of generating new evidence, unless the provider of the information consents . . ..

[585] See Article 51 on the status of this important document.

The grandiose truth aspirations in Article 54 spread confusion across all the Congo trials. The goal is a *non-partisan truth*, which is nonetheless a *legal truth* – understood as the outcome of a process of judicial deliberation. In launching this whole process, the Prosecutor is expected to search for facts and evidence relating to courtroom applications of criminal statutes. These facts and evidence are like the legally characterized facts collected by HRW in its influential report *Ituri: "Covered in Blood,"* and not the broader corpus of data used by social scientists like Vlassenroot and Raeymaekers. The ICC is not a scholarly forum, and the Prosecutor is not expected to explore academic models of networked violence. If there is something in these theories that could challenge presumptions built into the statutory framework, the burden of finding it and introducing it would fall, by default, to the Defense. The Prosecutor's search for legal truth is constrained by tacit presumptions about the world, baked into international criminal rules.

The lead investigator for the ICC, Bernard Lavigne, realized that reports like *"Covered in Blood"* could be submitted directly to the Court's evidentiary base. These reports were skillfully designed to convert raw data on Ituri atrocities into statutory terms. Lavigne might search in a non-partisan way for further facts and evidence, but the underlying framework was there from the beginning: the main pillars of the Prosecution's master narrative supported the search for legally relevant facts – some incriminating, and perhaps others exonerating.

It would then be a contest between these two categories, already separated according to the adversarial method of testing. The shift came in an awkward transition from impartial investigations to adversary trial, with the first rehearsal coming in the Pre-Trial Chamber. In making this shift into the courtroom, the Rome Statute stipulates rights for the accused, which require legal representation, the opportunity to question witnesses, and other legal supports, such as translation services.[586]

On top of this minimal list, Article 67(2) requires the Prosecutor to disclose to the Defense the exonerating evidence, mentioned previously in Article 54(1)(a) as the duty of the Prosecutor to collect during the investigations phase. Along with these broad requirements for disclosure of evidence in the Prosecutor's possession, Rule 77 of the Rules of Procedure and Evidence expands the domain of disclosure to include all documents and similar objects, for the purpose of allowing the Defense to prepare its case. Significantly, this Rule contains the same exceptions as stated in Article 54(3)(e), when the source of that information has requested confidentiality.

586 Article 67.

A further provision in Article 69(3) gives the Trial Chamber judge authority to request "all evidence that it considers necessary for the determination of the truth." This mix of rules and exceptions set the stage for the June 2008 shut-down, before the Lubanga trial officially opened.

The struggle over disclosing exonerating material took a long time to develop. With hints of such undisclosed evidence already present in the Pre-Trial Chamber, the confrontation first came to a head in September 2007 between the Prosecutor and the newly appointed Trial Chamber.[587] As several deadlines then came and went for disclosure, the Prosecutor protested that UN officials were unwilling to release confidentiality on nearly 200 documents. Unimpressed by Prosecution pledges to provide some kind of "analogous" evidence in lieu of these actual documents, the Trial Chamber halted proceedings on June 13, 2008.[588] The Trial Chamber insisted that it must itself review the disputed evidence directly, rather than relying on the Prosecutor – at this stage of an adversary proceeding – to revert to the impartial, even-handed custodian of information. To indicate the seriousness of the stay in proceedings, the Trial Chamber prepared the order to release Thomas Lubanga.

As a quick Appeals process unfolded, Lubanga stayed in detention; but the maxim of judicial supremacy ultimately won out. Supporting the Trial Chamber, the Appeals panel sought to reconcile potential conflicts within the Rome Statute. The provision for confidentiality of sources was only an "exceptional" measure, heavily outweighed by the rights of the accused to prepare a Defense.[589] The potential threats to anyone's personal safety, as a result of disclosure, were for the Trial Chamber to judge for itself. The ICC had a unit dedicated to witness protection, for just this purpose. During the Appeals process, as it happened, the UN sources relented, and the materials at issue were soon in the hands of the Trial Chamber, on the way to the Defense.

Throughout this controversy, the Prosecutor presented his actions as necessary to protect vulnerable sources in a conflict zone. Whatever his responsibilities as a seeker of truth, the circumstances required some margin of appreciation: without the full confidence of potential sources, the entire system of information might suffer.[590] In some cases, according to the

[587] Lubanga Trial Chamber status conference, September 4, 2007, ICC-01/04–01/06-T-50, as well as the November 9, 2007 Decision Regarding the Timing and Manner of Disclosure, ICC-01/04–01/06–1019.

[588] Lubanga Trial Chamber, Decision on the Consequences of Non-Disclosure, June 13, 2008, ICC-01/04–01/06–1401.

[589] Lubanga Appeals Chamber, Judgment on the Appeal from the Trial Chamber's Decision on the Consequences of Non-Disclosure, October 21, 2008, ICC-01/04–01/06–1486.

[590] For additional background, see Larry D. Johnson, "The Lubanga Case and Cooperation between the UN and the ICC," *Journal of International Criminal Justice* 10 (2012), 807.

Prosecutor, the alleged exonerating information was itself weak, or could be conveyed just as effectively through indirect sources. Fair trials were obviously essential, but they encompass more than just rights of the Defense. The very ability to gather evidence was itself tied to fairness. The language of the Statute and Rules of Procedure seemed to recognize this complexity.

In the end, however, the Trial Chamber insisted on striking its own case-by-case balance among competing information interests. That dominance was necessary, in functional terms, to preserve the rights of the Defense in gaining access to the fruits of an impartial investigation. While the Court could not compel the United Nations to waive confidentiality for the documents in question, its decision to suspend the trial produced the desired result. Within weeks the documents were made available, ending the crisis. The Prosecution was on notice that its conduct of investigations was subject to judicial oversight.[591]

The Role of Intermediaries

By the time the next shutdown crisis occurred, the dynamics of the trial had shifted dramatically. The early dispute over disclosure had happened well before any testimony was introduced into the courtroom. Months later, when the Prosecution began its case, a faltering first witness said that he was asked by third parties to lie before the Court. The Prosecution considered this episode a mere bump in the road, likely caused by the witness's general fear in the presence of Lubanga. The Defense saw it differently: the reference to someone coaching in the background set off alarms. According to the witness, the story of abduction was not his. "It came from someone else. They taught me that over three and a half years. I don't like it."[592] Other child witnesses mentioned intermediaries, whose names were all redacted by the Chamber (and were thus unavailable to the Defense at this stage). But the clues were certainly there.

The Defense then had some further information fall into its lap. Several weeks into the trial, in March 2009, the Defense noticed a pattern of certain intermediaries helping prospective victims complete the ICC enrollment forms. One particular intermediary (code-named "143") had been especially

[591] For concerns that this balance puts too much emphasis on fairness issues and too little on ending impunity, see Christodoulus Kaoutzanis, "A Turbulent Adolescence Ahead: The ICC's Insistence on Disclosure in the Lubanga Trial," *Washington University Global Studies Law Review* 12 (2013), 263.

[592] Lubanga Trial Chamber, transcript, January 28, 2009, p. 40.

active with victims but had also been mentioned in an early pre-trial witness interview, taken all the way back in January 2008.[593]

Responding to these suspicions with caution, in early 2009 the Trial Chamber was not yet prepared to order disclosure of intermediaries' names. But it did require the Prosecution to supply a chart of interactions between code-named intermediaries and all the witnesses. As the judges summarized it in March 2009, the Defense "wished to explore the possibility that certain people have participated in preparing false evidence for alleged former child soldiers." A few weeks later the Court removed redactions on the name for Intermediary "321," who had been in contact with the Prosecution's first errant child witness.[594]

Two months later, when another child witness went off-script in June 2009, the name of Intermediary "316" was revealed in his testimony. This witness asserted what the Defense was eager to explore:

> My name is REDACTED. This is contrary to the statement given to the [Prosecution] and that's why I wanted to make the statement and explain why I came here. That's why I met the [Prosecution's] intermediary who told me the following. He said, You have to change your name, you have to change your identity. Don't give the true story that took place; in other words, there was a story that they were telling to the witnesses. And I say that they're crooks . . . and swindlers. . . .[595]

As a result of these deviations from the Prosecution script, Defense investigations in the Congo went on to produce dramatic results. In early February 2010, the first witness called by the Defense offered specific testimony about Intermediary 321. This man (whom he knew well) went around recruiting children, promising them money if they gave false stories to the ICC about being child soldiers. They were to use false names and lie about their parents.

> [Intermediary 321] did not have any secrets . . .. He talked about money. He told them they would be given money. He said that the child had to claim to have served as a child soldier in order to get money. He went all over town recruiting children, and he would tell you what you had to say. He told the

593 See the historical discussion in Lubanga Trial Chamber, Redacted Decision on Intermediaries, May 31, 2010, ICC-01/04–01/06–2434-Red2, paras. 15–16.

594 Ibid., para. 19.

595 Lubanga Trial Chamber, transcript, June 16, 2009, ICC-01/04–01/06-T-192-Red3-ENG, p. 6 (redacted text released in February 2012). In its assessment of Intermediary 316's utter lack of credibility, following his testimony in the trial, the Lubanga Trial Chamber also noted his admitted relationship to Congolese national intelligence services. It strongly criticized the Prosecution for ignoring that link (Lubanga Trial Judgment, paras. 366–68).

children to claim that they had served as child soldiers, but I knew that the child had never been a child soldier.[596]

This testimony changed the courtroom atmosphere substantially. Ten months earlier, the Chamber had resisted the Defense request to learn the names of multiple intermediaries. In the face of the Prosecution's insistence on maintaining protective confidentiality, the Defense was then invited to lay a deeper foundation before the balance could swing in their direction.

In 2010, their very first witness did the trick. The judges responded swiftly in an email to the Prosecutor: "Following the reference to an intermediary in court yesterday, the Chamber wishes to receive comprehensive information on all the intermediaries."[597] This order included anyone involved in facilitating contact with potential witnesses, regardless of whether they were mentioned in court. To its astonishment, within days the Chamber also learned that the Prosecution had conducted its own private review of Intermediary 321, prompted most likely by disclosure from the Defense about upcoming Defense witnesses. The Chamber demanded a copy of the sixty-page long interview, done in January 2010.[598]

What was the Prosecution thinking? Would it silently revisit its links to some or all of the twenty-three intermediaries? Would it disclose these interviews to the Defense under the provision of Article 69(2)? Would it call some of these intermediaries to The Hague for questioning inside the courtroom? And was it planning to reveal their names to the Defense? During these early days of February 2010, more Defense witnesses came forward to testify about further misdeeds. Through it all, the Prosecution never lost faith in its nine child witnesses. Under siege from the Defense narrative of corruption, the Prosecutor reiterated the many challenges facing any ICC investigation: security concerns for staff and witnesses, protective measures for informants. Probing the intermediaries might satisfy Defense curiosity; but it put at risk the broader aims of the investigation. If there were specific questions about particular intermediaries, the Prosecution would certainly follow up; but there was "no basis to impugn the integrity of the intermediaries on a wholesale basis."[599]

596 Lubanga Trial Chamber, transcript, February 2, 2010, ICC-01/04–01/06-T-239-Red3-ENG, p. 34.

597 Lubanga Trial Chamber, Redacted Decision on Intermediaries, para. 30.

598 Ibid., para. 77.

599 Lubanga Trial Chamber submission by Prosecution, February 22, 2010, ICC-01/04–01/06–2310-Conf-Corr., para. 23.

The Trial Chamber's confidence in the body of Prosecution evidence was eroding. Late in 2009, as the second Congo trial was getting ready to start, the Defense teams for both Ngudjolo and Katanga pressed their Trial Chamber for disclosure on intermediaries, including names.[600] The same Prosecution investigation strategies were being used for both trials; the same intermediaries had been searching out witnesses. In the face of resistance on revealing the name of Intermediary 143, the Lubanga Trial Chamber took its firm stand. Allowing time for protective measures to take hold first, it demanded the name of 143, invoking its power under Article 69(3): "The Court shall have authority to request the submission of all evidence that it considers necessary for the determination of the truth."

In an order dated May 31, 2010, the Trial Chamber demanded five things from the Prosecution:

1) disclosure to the Defense of Intermediary 143's name;
2) disclosure to the Defense of short background summaries for 143 and two others;
3) calling those two other intermediaries to The Hague to testify in the trial;
4) calling the ICC's lead investigator to testify in the trial;
5) full disclosure to the Defense of all contacts between 23 intermediaries and all witnesses[601]

The Prosecution's resistance on the matter of Intermediary 143 triggered the shutdown crisis. Citing his duties to protect the personal safety of its contacts, the Prosecutor based his opposition on the Statute itself. But, as with the earlier crisis, the Trial Chamber prevailed on the grounds that tensions among the legal articles were for the judges to reconcile. Like the controversy over disclosure of evidence, the Trial Chamber came out of this crisis with the preeminent role for determining what weight to give to the fair trial rights of the accused.

The second shutdown ended after three months. Lubanga was not released. The Prosecutor complied with the Trial Chamber's order to reveal the name of Intermediary 143, and then stood back while the focus of the Lubanga trial shifted to the gritty details of the Prosecutor's investigations.

During these early weeks of 2010, when the Prosecutor was under siege, the spirit inside that office was defiant. Their mood was well captured in a public

600 Katanga and Ngudjolo Trial Chamber, Defence Closing Brief (Katanga), paras. 473–74. See Buisman, "Delegating Investigations," p. 43.

601 Lubanga Trial Chamber, Redacted Decision on Intermediaries, para. 150.

interview granted to one of the leading NGOs by Ms. Béatrice Le Fraper du Hellen, who was then Head of the Jurisdiction, Complementarity, and Cooperation Division inside the Prosecutor's domain. In that interview, Ms. Le Fraper du Hellen characterized the intermediaries as "fantastic and committed people," advancing international justice with their dedication. She rejected all complaints about the Prosecution's record of compliance with disclosure duties. After blaming the confusion of child witnesses on courtroom antics by Lubanga himself, she predicted that the trial would end by putting him away for a very long time.[602]

Further goading the Trial Chamber, which declared its exception to these published comments, the Prosecution then filed an unsolicited submission doubling down on these claims.[603] Far from apologizing, the new submission defended the interview, noting that the Prosecutor "considered that it was important to clarify its policy on intermediaries." These remarks were the occasion for the Trial Chamber to muse about the "public" aspirations of the fair trial ideal. The Defense case was being heard largely in closed session, and evidently the NGO public was getting nervous, as the trial seemed to be deviating from the question of guilt for the accused. Certainly, the long procedural delays – while also impinging on what the Rome Statute calls a trial "without undue delay"[604] – caused the anti-impunity lobby to worry about the Court's direction. The Prosecutor was serving notice that he would look to this group to shore up his standing, under attack by the Defense.[605]

The Trial Chamber put the interview aside, after scolding the Prosecution and warning that any repeat performance would not be tolerated. The push-back from the judges was to salvage their authority to decide the case on their own terms, beyond the glare of public opinion. It was scurrilous for Ms. Le Fraper du Hellen to spread false information about Lubanga's demeanor in the courtroom. But it was utterly unacceptable for the Prosecutor to launch a press campaign predicting the outcome of the trial. The Trial Chamber's reprimand came from jealous protection of its own capacity to see its way through the fog of doubt – to resolve the complex factual questions and reach a legal result.

602 This matter is summarized by the Lubanga Trial Chamber, Decision on the press interview with Ms. Le Fraper du Hellen, May 12, 2010, ICC-01/04–01/06–2433.
603 Ibid., para. 25.
604 Article 67(1)(c).
605 See Jim Freedman, *A Conviction in Question: The First Trial at the International Criminal Court* (Toronto: University of Toronto Press, 2018), pp. 142–49, for an assessment (by a Prosecution insider) of the strategy behind the letter.

Abuse of Process?

The Lubanga trial, coming out of conditions in Ituri, tested the limits of legal proceedings under the novel rules of the ICC. The experiment began in a recognizable way, with a master narrative advanced by the Prosecution (after the matter of evidence disclosure had been dealt with by the Appeals Chamber). But then the Defense case changed the Court's focus to a meta-narrative about faulty investigations and corrupt evidence. It was a counter-narrative not about the innocence of the accused; rather, about the misconduct of the prosecuting authority. What had begun as a conventional adversarial trial had shifted into a process for scrutinizing the Prosecution's performance. The larger question of whether Lubanga and his associates recruited or otherwise used child soldiers in armed conflict was buried for the moment in self-reflective motions and remedial measures.

The Prosecution's reaction to this dramatic turn could be seen in the provocation from Ms. Le Fraper du Hellen. In its courtroom submissions, the Prosecution countered that Defense witnesses might themselves be lying. And furthermore, that the former Prosecution witnesses (those who now recanted) could be lying right now. With such polarized evidence, and with the meta-narrative of prosecutorial corruption, the overriding question was whether the Court could conduct its business as originally planned. The Defense argued that enough is enough: the Court should declare the trial broken beyond repair. For the very first ICC case, let alone the future of the ICC, the stakes could not get any higher.

This was the third cessation of normal business in the Lubanga trial, enough to ignite a countervailing imperative that the show must go on – whatever stumbling blocks might appear. The first two confrontations saw the Trial Chamber using its leverage to gain a dominant position, over against the Prosecution, on matters of evidence. This time was different, as the push for Trial Chamber dominance now served to keep the trial going. Serious as the Defense accusations might be – even taken at their worst – the Trial Chamber would hew to its core function. With all the immodesty that goes with the exercise of final legal authority, the Chamber insisted that it would settle all disputes about truth and truthfulness in its Trial Judgment.

In the words of the Appeals Chamber, which had reversed the July 2010 stay of proceedings in the matter of Intermediary 143, halting the trial is an extreme measure that should be a last resort.[606] Other steps might be taken to enforce

[606] Lubanga Appeals Chamber, Judgment on the Appeal of the Prosecutor against the Decision of 8 July 2010 regarding Intermediary 143, October 8, 2010, ICC-01/04-01/06-2582, para. 46.

a court order, or to punish one of the adversarial teams (including financial penalties); but the Trial Chamber's job is to assert its competence up to the very limit. A two-part test grew out of these crises: (1) would continuing the case be "odious" or "repugnant" to the administration of justice? and (2) have the accused's fair trial rights been breached to the point of impossibility? The answers were judgment-calls by the judiciary itself, emanating from the oracular depths, based on existential circumstances in the moment.[607]

By this standard, according to the Appeals Chamber, the Trial Chamber's stay of proceedings back in July 2010 had been premature. Pressure on the Prosecution could be applied without upending the whole process of declaring justice. Under that same standard, the Trial Chamber felt empowered to reject the "abuse of process" motion. In doing so, it issued to the Defense – and equally to the victims and to the world – a promissory note: everything would be sorted out in the final judgment. Once all the evidence was in, however complicated and self-referential, the Trial Chamber would sort it all out, witness-by-witness, point-by-point.[608] The trial would grind on for a few more months.

7.3 PROVING THE CRIME

Defining the Charges

After the "abuse of process" episode, the trial returned to its original purpose: judging the evidence on whether Lubanga was guilty as charged. For the better part of 2010, the trial had teetered on the brink of losing that focus, as the Defense scrutinized the methods used by the Prosecution. The entire legal process was being tested and stretched, pushing the judges to consolidate their authority as managers of evidentiary flows, custodians of the accused's fair trial rights, and oracles of legal truth – the core elements of finality that would vindicate years of mind-numbing deliberations over procedure.

The single charge against Lubanga concerned child soldiers, an offense codified for the first time in the Rome Statute, evolving out of human rights campaigns over several decades.[609] An ICC trial assumes the prior confirmation of explicit charges, resting on specified facts and circumstances, coming out of the Pre-Trial Chamber. During the trial itself, controversy arose concerning this charge, as confirmed. After the months-long presentation of

[607] Lubanga Trial Chamber, Redacted Decision on the Defence Application Seeking a Permanent Stay of the Proceedings, March 7, 2011, ICC-01/04-01/06-2690, paras. 168, 169.

[608] Ibid., paras. 197, 198.

[609] For background see Roman Graf, "The International Criminal Court and Child Soldiers: An Appraisal of the Lubanga Judgment," *Journal of International Criminal Justice* 10 (2012), 945.

evidence for the Prosecution, a groundswell of opinion from the NGO sidelines, amplifying voices of the victims, pushed for an expansion of charges to include crimes of sexual violence.[610] The collapse of this campaign will be described in Section 7.6, including disagreement between a majority of the Trial Chamber and the Appeals Chamber.

Another question about the confirmed charge grew out of an anomaly under international legal rules that required the Pre-Trial Chamber to specify whether the child soldiers charge occurred in the context of an armed conflict that was either *international* or *non-international* in scope. The context was important because the Rome Statute followed historical models in associating some crimes with actions taken by states and the conscription of children into "national armed forces." It was an awkward configuration in the Statute. And, given the complexity of Ituri violence during this period, this choice was especially difficult, with either solution resting on facile assumptions. This controversy, too, will have a brief section of its own (Section 7.5).

The final judgment on Lubanga was divided into two parts, representing a core structural feature of international law. The Trial Chamber addressed (1) whether the criminal offenses occurred in fact and (2) whether the accused held individual responsibility for them. This structure captures the moral pivot, central to the evolution of international criminal law, from the plight of victims to the battle against impunity. The justice system needs to perform this pivot effectively if it wants to provide a legal response to the suffering of victims.

In all three Congo trials, judges were pushed to the limits on both parts, but with particular strains in ascribing individual responsibility. These pressures confounded and discouraged many trial observers, who started from the common understanding that serious atrocities had occurred in Ituri and in the CAR. The violence was obviously real; NGOs had been documenting it for years leading up to the ICC's own investigations, which drew generously from NGO sources.[611] The whole purpose of prosecution was to apply the label of responsibility. But the Congo trials were different from an NGO area report. The process was not about impunity at large, but about proving the

610 See the letter to the Prosecutor from August 2006 expressing "grave concerns at the narrow charges being brought by the OTP in the case of Thomas Lubanga Dyilo," described in Louise Chappell, *The Politics of Gender Justice at the International Criminal Court: Legacies and Legitimacy* (Oxford: Oxford University Press, 2015), pp. 111–12. Chappell also reports an interview in which Moreno-Ocampo suggested that he was unsure about proving the link between crimes against humanity and the requirement that such crimes must be "pursuant to or in furtherance of a State or organizational policy" (ibid.).

611 See Freedman, *A Conviction in Question*, p. 122.

legal responsibility of the particular accused, sitting in the courtroom. The moderating spirit of legal process imposed certain limits on all elements of the trial. Imperatives of a fair trial, including the presumption of innocence, changed the way that routine facts about violence were measured and balanced. The result would need to meet the standard of proof beyond reasonable doubt.

The single legal charge against Lubanga came out of the pre-trial confirmation process. The text for this charge appears in Art. 8(2)(e)(vii): "Conscripting or enlisting children under the age of fifteen years into armed forces or groups or using them to participate actively in hostilities."[612] But there was more from the pre-trial stage: a set of *facts and circumstances* attached to the charge, circumscribed for the purpose of allowing the Defense a meaningful opportunity to prepare its case. Given the difficulties of defending charges like those in the Congo trials, this contextual requirement would prove to be both elusive and controversial. Elusive, because the precise *facts and circumstances* are hard to pinpoint. They may be annexed to pre-trial filings by the parties; prescribed in confirmation judgments by the Pre-Trial Chamber; or elaborated in auxiliary summaries of evidence provided by the Prosecution. And they become controversial when they impose limits on judicial action – when judges are not allowed to exceed their contents. Such problems arose in all three Congo trials.

The pre-trial confirmation stage must also specify the mode of legal responsibility, drawing from a set of definitions contained in Articles 25(3) and 28. In this instance, Lubanga was charged as a *co-perpetrator* of the crime involving child soldiers. The word itself sounds technical, and it comes encumbered with history from other international courts. As it happens, the Lubanga Pre-Trial Chamber borrowed from academic legal theory to import an array of presumptions and inferences, seeking to operationalize these dry legal terms. Imposing a general paradigm on armed groups in Ituri became problematic, both in the Lubanga trial and in the second Congo trial for Ngudjolo and Katanga.

In sum, the Trial Chamber derives its overall mandate from three legal elements: a formal criminal charge under the Rome Statute, a constraining background of Ituri-specific *facts and circumstances* (anchoring that charge), and a particular definition of individual responsibility (also part of the original

[612] The Trial Chamber reduced the charges to this single section, identified with non-international armed conflicts, using its power under Regulation 55 to recharacterize the original charge (these issues will be discussed in detail in Section 7.6). For most purposes, the ICC considered that these were three separate charges ("conscripting"; "enlisting"; "using . . .") under the same statutory umbrella.

charge). Through all the procedural crises spread out across four years, these elements gave the Lubanga trial judges their baseline standards against which to measure the evidence introduced in the courtroom.

At many points during these four years, of course, the victims saw the Lubanga trial in much broader terms. They brought a wider selection of stories about local violence, going beyond the limited scope of the *facts and circumstances* of the confirmed charge. Their recollections were compiled in NGO reports, following the pattern of HRW's "*Covered in Blood.*" Their suffering inspired the pivot to legal responsibility, on the assumption that so much violence meant that someone must be responsible. In a years-long legal trial, many observers grew impatient with the narrow focus of trial judges, as they stuck to their assigned tasks.[613]

Rescuing the Evidence: The Declaratory Power of Trial Judges

In its formal judgment, the Trial Chamber reached a dramatic conclusion about the nine child witnesses: it would disregard them all! After reviewing the extensive Defense case, especially the role of intermediaries, the judges reasoned their way through all nine witnesses. None of their evidence was reliable enough to factor into the deliberations on the core crime.[614] The coherence of the master narrative was shattered.

What else was left? In the evidence summaries submitted by the Prosecution at the outset of the trial, the nine child witnesses had occupied center stage – arguably the entire stage. Under this plan, the Court would hear directly from nine witness-survivors of Lubanga and his group: first-hand evidence of forced conscription and military exploitation, speaking directly to the single charge. Going back to the *facts and circumstances* stipulated at the pre-trial stage, there were only incidental mentions of other sources of corroboration. And because the child witnesses were the Prosecutor's prime evidence, he never gave up on them. Through it all, the Prosecutor's final brief to the Trial Chamber stood by its child witnesses.[615] Meanwhile, the Defense, recognizing the centrality of these witnesses, focused its own investigations on them.

613 Freedman, *A Conviction in Question*, chapter 5; Niamh Hayes, "*La Lutte Continue*: Investigating and Prosecuting Sexual Violence at the ICC," in Carsten Stahn (ed.), *The Law and Practice of the International Criminal Court* (Oxford: Oxford University Press, 2015), chapter 32.

614 Lubanga Trial Judgment, para. 480.

615 Lubanga Trial Chamber, Prosecution's Closing Brief, June 1, 2011, ICC-01/04–01/06–2748-Red, Section 10.2.

With those witnesses gone, what remained was an assortment of circumstantial evidence, much of it originally directed to other aspects of Lubanga's actions. There were up to ten adult witnesses, originally called to speak to other matters, who had offered opinions (with varying degrees of persuasion) about the presence of children younger than fifteen years in Ituri military roles, including Lubanga's UPC. Some of these witnesses had themselves been contacted through the impugned intermediaries. Some belonged to factions hostile to Lubanga, and some others provided inconsistent statements. There was also a handful of documents that the Court considered in the final determination of facts.

During the early days of the trial, the Prosecution called its own expert witness for background on political and social conditions in the Congo, with special reference to Ituri. The noted French Africanist Gérard Prunier disclaimed any first-hand knowledge of Ituri events, having done no research there during the period covered by the trial. But he warned the Court about the reliability of witness testimony, coming years after the underlying events: "[I]t is impossible to know without being present in the field, without speaking to people during the time of the events, because as soon as everything is over the entire history is reconstructed . . . ."[616] Another Prosecution-friendly source, and former UN advisor in Bunia, writing after the trial, acknowledged the extreme conditions in Ituri from March 2003, which cast doubt on the truthfulness of any testimony.

> [Some NGOs] were there expressly to work with child soldiers. There was money and clothes on offer for the child soldiers, the *kadogos*, and cash to pay for their schooling as long as they could prove they had fought in the wars and could hand in a gun. A fledgling market emerged for those looking for a piece of the post-war peace-building funds.
>
> Getting help from any of them was always a negotiation . . . . If someone served in the army, that was an asset, and there were hopefuls who had served but maybe not in the right way to qualify. They might have to change their story about who they were or what happened to meet a certain requirement. If a young man came in who claimed to be a soldier but had no gun to give up, he would have to make up a story to explain it. Parents might inflate the number of their children they care for to get more from a feeding program . . . . A boy soldier who had been contacted by someone from the International Criminal Court would not hesitate to claim he was younger than he really was, just to make his own case stronger.

[616] Lubanga Trial Chamber, transcript, March 26, 2009, ICC-01/04–01/06-T-156-FRA (revised), p. 45. Further references will be to "Prunier Testimony" with the date, and page references in the French version.

> … For many of them, truth had become a liability. There was nothing wrong if they embellished the reasons that brought them there. It meant there were lies … simply because they were trying to recover a life lost to war.[617]

Back to Prunier, it was hard to imagine how, in retrospect, so many victims today could pinpoint the complex source of their misery: "But to know that one group felt threatened, it's necessary to be present in the field. It's necessary to speak to the people involved while the events in question are unfolding. This can't be done subsequently."[618] And yet, this is precisely what the Trial Chamber was trying to reconstruct – using conventional legal methods of evaluating witness credibility and reliability, grounding conclusions deep in their own psychological recesses. To declare the whole exercise as impossible, as Prunier seemingly suggested, would mean sacrificing the larger goals of the new ICC, here in the very first trial.

The most intriguing evidence came from a series of ten videos, several of which were of sufficient quality to show closeups of young-looking recruits in a military training camp. With no live testimony from children to draw on, here, at least, was *some* evidence that the judges could see and feel with direct intuition. The Prosecutor had promised that the videos would speak for themselves – and that may well have been prophetic.

The Trial Chamber was sobered by the need to rescue some kind of evidence. It was the first ICC trial, and the single charge was quite specific and straightforward. There was a hardened faith – outside the courtroom – that *all* the Congo militias used underage children in abundance. Could it possibly be, given all the resources poured into this trial, that the Chamber would be unable to reach a conclusion? On the other hand, there was also the solemn duty to respect – even to constitute – the fair trial rights of the accused. The Defense had vindicated its demands for early disclosure of evidence, considering the zeal behind its own investigations: tracking down school records, uncovering false identities, interviewing family members whose names had been suppressed. Evidence produced by these efforts had raised a cloud of reasonable doubt.

But the Defense was not running the trial. The "abuse of process" application had gone too far, if there was still some chance that the Chamber could eke out a result. Nor would the Chamber be pushed around by the

[617] Freedman, *A Conviction in Question*, pp. 131–33.
[618] Prunier Testimony, p. 45.

Prosecution – not by the defiant observations of Ms. Béatrice Le Fraper du Hellen, nor by the self-serving moralism of the Prosecution's unsolicited submissions. What emerged instead was a pledge to proceed with eyes wide open – an approach steeped in psychological caution. "Given the undoubted differences in personal perception as regards estimates of age and, most particularly in the context of this case, the difficulties in distinguishing between young people who are relatively close to the age of 15 (whether above or below), the Chamber has exercised caution when considering this evidence."[619] Caution and mindfulness became the modal response for the Chamber's reconstructive survey of witnesses and evidence. Ambiguities in testimony or texts were resolved by exercising "great care." Sketchy backgrounds of some witnesses required the Chamber to show "particular care"[620] in assigning inscrutable weightings to each statement – not to mention assessing the complete scope of a witness's testimony.

The wild card here was the psychological readiness of each judge to grant credibility to some or all of what each witness said. At times this internal green light extended to accepting the witness's reliability as well – the likelihood that his or her credible beliefs told the Court something true about the world. It was not too late to secure a conviction, supported by patterns of coherence found within the shards of remaining testimony. The trope of circumspection strengthened the hermetic force of psychological conviction. Perceived coherence would become the touchstone of credibility and the basis for inferring reliability.

In its general treatment of oral testimony, the Trial Chamber gave notice that it had weighed each and every nuance, all possible weaknesses, any conflicting or supportive strains from all the other testimony.

> The Chamber has made appropriate allowance for any instances of imprecision, implausibility or inconsistency, bearing in mind the overall context of the case and the circumstances of the individual witnesses .... There are ... reasons why a witness's evidence may have been flawed and the Chamber,

619 Lubanga Trial Judgment, para. 643.

620 "Care," "caution," "circumspection" – these are all terms scattered throughout the Trial Judgment (ibid.), sometimes preceded by qualifiers such as "particular." ("Caution" see para. 643; "great caution" see para. 476; "considerable caution" see para. 724; "care" see para. 422; "particular care" see para. 393.) In many cases, diffuse factors affecting belief are simply "borne in mind" (para. 114). On the positive side, consistency seems to open a path to judicial belief, where "convincing" equates with "internally consistent" (paras. 284, 348, 698). Some witnesses are "entirely credible" (para. 1036); other witnesses are "sufficiently reliable" (para. 1031); while still others are simply lying. When all else fails, the Chamber advances by building its internal belief structure "case-by-case" (para. 628). These examples could be multiplied many times over.

> when assessing his or her testimony, has taken these considerations into account and they are reflected in its overall assessment of the account in question.[621]

Would there be some independent reality-test for this cascade of subjective judgments? In its grim self-confidence as a master calculator of testimonial weight and probity, the Chamber wanted its diverse findings to leverage one other, leading up to a whole greater than the sum of its parts. "This Judgment is based on the entire proceedings and the Chamber's evaluation of the evidence .... The Chamber has assessed the reliability of individual pieces of evidence and their probative value in the context of any other admissible and probative material."[622] Did this mean that the Chamber would provide a public accounting of its evidentiary ledgers, so that others might check its sums and test its factoring of testimonial weights? Not really, because the total summation must be intuited on an issue-by-issue basis. "The extent to which a piece of evidence, standing alone, is sufficient to prove a fact at issue is entirely dependent on the issue in question and the strength of the evidence. Accordingly, once again the Chamber has adopted a case-by-case approach."[623] Ultimately, the decisions came down to each judge's *intime conviction*, where the French expression locates final authority within the sphere of interior privacy. While still part of the French criminal code today, this phrase is a philosophical relic traceable to Cartesian rationalism and Locke's notions of "moral certainty" and the "satisfied conscience."[624] Empirical facts meet with truth, not on their own public level but only in the soul of the beholder. Legal truth is

[621] Ibid., para. 103.

[622] Ibid., para. 94.

[623] Ibid., para. 110.

[624] *Code de Procédure Pénale*, article 353, which concludes: "La loi ne leur fait que cette seule question, qui renferme toute la mesure de leurs devoirs: 'Avez-vous une intime conviction?'" See Mark Klamberg, "Epistemological Controversies and Evaluation of Evidence in International Criminal Trials," Stockholm University Faculty of Law, Research Paper Series no. 65 (2019), p. 6 (forthcoming in Kevin Jon Heller *et al.* (eds.), *Oxford Handbook of International Criminal Law*). On the philosophical history of *intime conviction*, see Jackson and Summers, pp. 211–12, who discuss the hold of these classic solipsisms on both common law and civil law traditions, both for findings of facts and for broader legal principles. Written into the Napoleonic Code, the *intime conviction* formulation replaced Roman formal proofs, and became part of the juror's oath. See James M. Donovan, *Juries and the Transformation of Criminal Justice in France in the Nineteenth and Twentieth Centuries* (Chapel Hill: University of North Carolina Press, 2014), pp. 35–36. Simon de Smet explores "a number of serious problems" with this subjective standard, in the context of the Congo trials; "The International Criminal Standard of Proof at the ICC: Beyond Reasonable Doubt or Beyond Reason?" in Stahn, *Law and Practice of the International Criminal Court*, pp. 866–70.

a private experience, not a collective, social, or interactive project – according to this image.

From the standpoint of modern legal process, this withdrawal into rational-psychological authority brings a premature end to discursive, deliberative judgments about public matters of fact. The assessment of evidence turns into an opaque, declaratory exercise – a report on the shifting states of mind of the triers of fact, steeped in a dialectic of "care" and "caution." The warrants for judgments of fact operate beyond public scrutiny – all part of an oracular style that would eventually be challenged by appeals judges in the Bemba trial.[625]

It may seem like a natural element of the judicial function: that judges should be sincerely convinced in their belief. Judges in the civil law tradition may see it simply as part of rendering decisions, as well as a guarantee of finality in legal judgments. If the alternative is to surrender the judge's personal conviction to the workings of smart algorithms – that is certainly a step too far. But the issue in international trials is not whether the *intime conviction* is necessary, but whether it is sufficient. It might well be sufficient in a system where personal judgment is the standard for legal truth; but it may not go far enough in a system geared to the presumption of innocence, and to proof beyond reasonable doubt. Not only must these further legal principles be applied sincerely; they must also be manifest in their application, open to scrutiny by others. That scrutiny may come both in appeals decisions and in the comprehension of outside observers.

Across all the Congo trials, related jurisprudential concerns emerged in judicial split decisions, dissents, and reversals. In all these cases, one challenge was to balance an extraordinary degree of complexity (factual and legal) with the imperative to reach a decision, on the path to legal finality. The psychological standard of judgment was confusingly mixed with a separate analytical controversy about "holism" and "atomism," where the need for composite judgments was elided with the subjective theory of judgment. This whole subjective epistemology was mobilized to handle critical challenges in the Congo trials, including the interpretation of large pools of circumstantial evidence (mixed in with dodgy witnesses) and the use of interpretive

[625] Bemba Appeals Judgment, June 8, 2018, ICC-01/05–01/08–3636 (Majority Opinion). This judgment and the spirited dissent will be discussed in Chapter 9. The most elaborate defense of this oracular mode of fact-finding came in the Ngudjolo Appeals Judgment, likewise in a dissent – defending the authority of factual judgments based on their conscientious emergence, in which caution, circumspection, "holism," and case-by-case conclusions play the dominant roles. Ngudjolo Appeals Judgment, February 27, 2015, 01/04–02/12–271 (Majority) and Annex A (Dissent). This judgment will be discussed in Chapter 8.

paradigms and presumptions in establishing individual criminal responsibility. It became a favored weapon in the fight against impunity, especially when the alternative might be another acquittal.

More will be said about these disputes in each of the trial chapters, but the declarative or oracular mode of judicial fact-finding came to light first in the Lubanga Trial Chamber's assessment of witnesses. Thus, it was no barrier, when it turned out that Prosecution Witness 0038 had been in contact with the sketchy Intermediary 316. He was found to be "generally reliable and credible."[626] This inner judicial revelation builds a presumptive belief – requiring some unknown degree of contrary evidence to dislodge. By default, it was for the Defense to provide enough evidence to dissuade the Chamber from its declared assessment of Witness 0038. The presumption of innocence and reasonable doubts could be deferred to the very end, where they would be weighed in the final intuitive calculus. Driven by this confident inner light, the oracular judicial style would prove especially useful in validating the grand paradigms of individual responsibility – a topic considered in Section 7.4.

Appealing the Findings of Facts

These self-certifying determinations of facts complicated the process of review on appeal. Across all the Congo trials, Appeals Chamber judges conducted an intense commentary among themselves on the appropriate methods for reviewing factual findings at the trial level. In most national legal systems, and especially where juries are being used, findings of fact are granted a measure of deference, unless they are clearly unreasonable; and the appeal focuses instead on more professional questions of legal interpretation. Four out of the five Appeals Chamber judges in the Lubanga case chose to observe this deferential style of review. In dismissing a long list of challenges by the Lubanga Defense, the Appeals Chamber accepted nearly all the individual findings of fact as "not unreasonable."

For example, when it came to the question of video evidence as self-validating proof that children under fifteen were to be found in UPC military settings, the Appeals Chamber was satisfied that the Trial Chamber had taken appropriate psychological care in reaching its conclusion – even if the individual elements remained opaque. The Appeals Chamber had no means for testing these judgments but preserved them out of respect for their personal sincerity.

626 Lubanga Trial Judgment, para. 690.

> The Appeals Chamber considers that the Trial Chamber was indeed aware of the limitations of determining age on the basis of physical appearance, including video images and expressed caution with regard to age assessment on that basis .... The Appeals Chamber notes that the Trial Chamber indicated that it applied a large margin of error and made findings as to the age of the children only where the children were, in its assessment, "clearly under the age of fifteen years." The Appeals Chamber considers that such an approach is not unreasonable, even though the reasoning of the Trial Chamber in that regard could have been more extensive, which, in the view of the Appeals Chamber, could have facilitated appellate review.[627]

The default authority assigned to trial court findings creates new presumptions within the appeals process. The strength of these presumptions can be seen in one notable example, when the Lubanga team challenged the Trial Chamber's confidence in its ability to assess the "size and general appearance" of persons in one of the videos, and to conclude that some were under the age of fifteen.

> In the view of the Appeals Chamber, the Trial Chamber's approach was not unreasonable .... [I]t provided reasons as to why it considered these individuals to be under the age of fifteen years, focusing on their size and also on their "general appearance." The Appeals Chamber considers that the size of an individual, when compared to the other individuals present in the video excerpt, can be a determining factor for finding that the person is under the age of fifteen years, if considered in connection with their general appearance. Mr. Lubanga has not made any arguments as to why the Trial Chamber's reliance on size and general appearance in relation to the video excerpt at issue was unreasonable and the Appeals Chamber therefore dismisses this argument.[628]

Lubanga's supporting brief to the Appeals Chamber had already protested against this shift in de facto proof burdens, both in general terms and in the specific case of videos used as evidence. In echoes of prior battles over disclosure of Prosecution evidence, Lubanga's team pointed out that it had no advance knowledge of precisely which persons in the video would draw the trial judges' attention and would meet their subjective sense of belief. "This reversal of the burden of proof is particularly unfair to the Appellant, insofar as until judgment was handed down, he was precluded from determining which excerpts the Chamber might rely on. The video excerpts run to several hours and show several hundred individuals. No information as to their identity or

[627] Lubanga Appeals Judgment, December 1, 2014, ICC-01/04-01/06-3121, para. 222.
[628] Ibid., para. 229.

age was imparted by the Prosecutor at trial."[629] In this context, the Appeals Chamber had to address the curious insect episode, which was extracted from a video deemed compelling evidence for conviction in the Trial Judgment.[630] It happened that the Defense team knew the identity of the youth who was caught on camera laughing as the insect moved up and down his arm. Yes, it was too late to influence the Judgment, but the Defense had hoped to play the video at Lubanga's sentencing hearing and to supplement it with a voice feed from Ituri with two witnesses who would establish that this young man had been older than fifteen at the time. The Trial Chamber had allowed the Defense presentation to ramp up the presentation, delaying the sentencing hearing for a couple of hours. But the Chamber then abruptly shut it down in mid-crawl, as the meandering insect seemed to mock the courtroom.

Months later, the Appeals Chamber reopened the matter, allowing the insect's journey to be presented in full – an extraordinary moment for an appellate hearing. But in its written Judgment, the Appeals Chamber declared this material inadmissible, on the grounds that the Defense should have offered all its evidence back at the trial stage.[631] The Rome Statute gives judges the discretion to admit any "evidence that it considers necessary for the determination of the truth."[632] And, on this basis, large amounts of undigested documents get submitted during the trial, from which the Trial Chamber can choose its points of emphasis. But now the trial was over, and the search for truth in a court of law had to observe time constraints, in the interests of legal finality.

The Lubanga Trial Chamber did not escape some appellate second-guessing around the edges. In the case of three witnesses (out of ten), the Appeals Chamber decided that the Trial Chamber's reliance on their testimony, concerning the presence of children under fifteen in the UPC, was indeed *not reasonable*.[633] But there was no impact on the overall conclusion,

629 Lubanga Appeals Chamber, Defence Brief against the Trial Chamber Judgment, December 3, 2012, ICC-01/04–01/06–2948-Red, para. 153.

630 See Lubanga Trial Judgment, para. 1278. With regard to the video from which the insect portion was excerpted, the Trial Chamber had coyly indicated that it had independently confirmed the appearance of children under fifteen in that video, "to the extent that it is possible to draw a safe conclusion based on their appearance" (paras. 718, 711).

631 Lubanga Appeals Chamber hearing, May 19, 2014, ICC-01/04–01/06-T-362-ENG. The Appeals Chamber rejected this evidence in its final Judgment, para. 81. The Lubanga Defense position was that it did not know, until it read the Trial Judgment, what weight was being given to single individuals in this video. Lubanga Appeals Chamber, Defence Application to Present Additional Evidence (Third Defence Request), May 23, 2014, ICC-01/04–01/06–3105, para. 24.

632 Article 69(3).

633 Lubanga Appeals Judgment, paras. 361, 417.

given the remaining proportion of the Trial Judgment that was *not unreasonable*.

In its own defiant statement of the matter, the Trial Chamber had already signaled its embrace of "caution," after the near-death experience of losing the nine child witnesses. On the bright side, the Trial Chamber took comfort that "the sheer volume of credible evidence ... relating to the presence of children below the age of 15 within the ranks of the UPC/FPLC has demonstrated conclusively that a significant number were part of the UPC/FPLC army. An appreciable proportion of the prosecution witnesses ... testified reliably that children under 15 were within the ranks of the UPC/FPLC."[634] Following this logic, the rules for transforming evidence into judicial belief run up against the simple laws of mathematics. For the string of ten or so witnesses found credible enough by the Trial Chamber, most had some kind of discount applied to at least some parts of their testimony. Multiply any fraction by another fraction – and the product is necessarily an even lower number. In the world of objects, compounding fractional shares is a game of diminishing returns.

But in the realm of subjective belief, the strength of personal conviction may be lifted by its own bootstraps.[635] This distinctive legal-psychological calculus was something the Appeals Chamber warmly approved of. What mattered, on appeal, was the constant exercise of caution, care, and vigilant close scrutiny. The results were not to be tampered with, so long as they were not unreasonable.

The Trial Chamber's openly "cautious approach" became an insulating, self-protective factor. On appeal, only Judge Ušacka questioned whether the lower chamber's caution had been exercised consistently, and in accordance with the general presumption of innocence.[636] In a comprehensive dissent, in which she concludes that she would have acquitted Lubanga, she argued further that the decisive evidence about child soldiers exceeded the *facts and circumstances* as defined back at the pre-trial confirmation stage.[637] Echoing

634 Ibid., para. 643.

635 There is a branch of subjective probability theory, derived from Bayesian perspectives, that supports this bootstrap logic, where the increase accrues to the subjective certitude of the believer. See Yvonne McDermott, "Strengthening the Evaluation of Evidence in International Criminal Trials," *International Criminal Law Review* 17 (2017), Part 4.1.

636 Lubanga Appeals Judgment, Dissenting Opinion of Judge Anita Ušacka, December 1, 2014, ICC-01/04–01/06–3121-Anx2, para. 44.

637 Her overall conclusion was that "Lubanga's right to be informed in detail of the nature, cause, and content of the charges against him was violated by his conviction for charges formulated in impermissibly vague terms" (para. 22). Chapter 9 will discuss in detail a similar principle that contributed to the acquittal of Jean-Pierre Bemba.

suggestions in the Defense appeals brief, Judge Ušacka examined the Prosecutor's Document Confirming the Charges (in its amended form), along with the Summary of Evidence marking preparation for the trial phase. In these documents, the Prosecution explicitly narrowed its evidentiary base to the nine specific child witnesses. While it mentioned other forms of evidence in passing (part of the background context), these elements were not specified in a way that allowed the Lubanga Defense team a reasonable chance to prepare its case. Moreover, the video evidence was not reasonably taken as self-evident, as the Trial Chamber seemed to think (even with its declared "caution"); and dismissing the insect video was an example of constricting Lubanga's fair-trial rights.[638]

Hers was a minority view; but such views remain part of the legal process, even when they do not affect the outcome for the accused. Over time, concerns raised in dissents may come back in later trials.[639] Indeed, similar points to those raised by Judge Ušacka would drive the majority decision in the Bemba appeal, setting Bemba free.

Interpreting the Crime: Using Children in Hostilities

The protection of child soldiers was part of a long-standing legal campaign. It marked the convergence of two branches of international law: the human rights protection of children, and the protection of vulnerable groups in the context of armed conflict.[640] Human rights protections under recent treaties had aimed to protect persons under the age of eighteen. The Rome Statute was the first to stipulate criminal penalties for this specific rights violation, although by compromise the age was reduced to fifteen years. The legal regulation of armed groups comes from the tradition of international humanitarian law, represented most prominently in the revised Geneva

638 She identified weaknesses in the analysis of ten videos (ibid., para. 67), while regarding the insect video as the strongest evidence for conviction. Thus, Lubanga's attempt to respond (following the Trial Judgment) should have been allowed. "In addition to challenging the Trial Chamber's specific findings on the basis of these ... video excerpts, he seeks to also attack the Trial Chamber's application of the cautious approach because the additional evidence demonstrates that it was impossible to determine the age based on appearances" (para. 34).

639 Judge Ušacka's perspective on the specificity of charges and the judicial treatment of indirect evidence would resonate across the Congo trials, recognizable in dissenting views and reversals.

640 On the evolution of this crime, see Matthew Happold, "International Humanitarian Law, War Criminality and Child Recruitment: The Special Court for Sierra Leone's Decision in Prosecutor v. Samuel Hinga Norman," *Leiden Journal of International Law* 18 (2005), 283.

Conventions of 1949. This branch of international law was designed to regulate the armed forces of nation states, setting boundaries for permissible military action in armed conflict between nations. Part of the 1949 renewal of the Geneva Conventions anticipated the evolution of armed conflict to include internal rebellions, guerrilla actions, and other military hostilities within a single state.[641]

The architects of the Rome Statute wanted to apply the same prohibition on child soldiers in all armed conflict, whether between nations or internal to a single country. But the Statute also maintained the structure of the Geneva Conventions in separating out these two kinds of conflict and ended up with two separate lists of prohibited war crimes in the lengthy text of Article 8. It made a point, however, of formulating the prohibition on children under fifteen in similar language for both kinds of conflict. One provision applied to children in "national armies" in international conflicts; while the other applied to children in "armed forces or groups" in non-international conflicts.

In the Lubanga case, the stories originally told by the nine direct victim-witnesses included details of forced conscription. But with the Trial Chamber's rejection of all testimonial evidence from these victims, it was left with indirect observations, from other witnesses, that children under fifteen were somehow present in Lubanga's UPC organization. The way the law is written, it does not really matter exactly how such children ended up in military service; the crime of "using" children "to participate actively in hostilities" was enough for conviction, whether these children arrived by way of voluntary enlistment or forced conscription. But this left open the interpretive question of what was covered under "active participation in hostilities." The children observed by the remaining Lubanga witnesses were described in a variety of roles: some in background support positions, some simply in training. The fate of young girls, once inside the militias, was likely to include sexual violence, domestic slavery, and other exploitation in non-combat roles.

It was the Court's first opportunity to interpret the scope of the rule – what it meant "to participate actively in hostilities." The Trial Chamber devised an expansive definition, broad enough to include some of the non-battlefield roles that were essential for upstart militias, such as moving supplies, carrying communications, conducting surveillance. The Chamber wanted to generalize on this breadth, encompassing tasks with personal risks comparable to

641 William I. Hitchcock, "Human Rights and the Geneva Conventions of 1949," in Akira Iriye, Petra Goedde, and William I. Hitchcock (eds.), *The Human Rights Revolution: An International History* (Oxford: Oxford University Press, 2012), chapter 4.

active combat.[642] The term "participation" is used elsewhere in the laws of war to determine when ordinary civilians may lose protection under the Geneva Conventions, by joining in combat ("active participation"). But in Rome, the criminal rule was designed to protect a vulnerable population. The Lubanga court was nonetheless cautious, sensitive to the criticism that it might be expanding the scope of the law retroactively – a practice prohibited by Article 22. In the end, the Chamber recommended a case-by-case determination of "participating actively in hostilities" under specific circumstances of each victim.[643] This cautious approach protected the rulings behind the veil of judicial self-certitude.

Judge Elizabeth Odio Benito from Costa Rica tried to push her colleagues further, on the sensitive matter of counting as "active participation in hostilities" the girls who were subject to sexual abuse and domestic exploitation by militia combatants. The sentiment among external supporters of the ICC favored this interpretation, particularly after the Appeals Chamber rejected the move to amend formal criminal charges against Lubanga to include crimes of sexual violence. Her reasons were articulated in a dissent to the Trial Judgment.[644]

7.4 LUBANGA'S INDIVIDUAL RESPONSIBILITY

Paradigms and Presumptions

For international trials, the central challenge surrounds the legal pivot from victims to perpetrators. The moral framework of international justice depends on perfecting this turn from documenting atrocities to banishing impunity. Construing the harm to victims as *crimes* creates the license to prosecute individuals as legally responsible. The underlying social conflict may not be ripe for resolution; but pursuing justice in the courtroom can be an important step in that direction.

Inside the courtroom, the battle against impunity requires a high-caliber conceptual apparatus – a set of working paradigms – to guide the inference from collective violence to individual responsibility. These paradigms are forged in historic courtroom battles, going back to World War II and beyond. In the 1990s, the ad hoc tribunals updated this arsenal, allowing creative presumptions and inference patterns. The Rome Statute was a further call to arms.

642 Lubanga Trial Judgment, para. 628.
643 Ibid.
644 Ibid., Separate and Dissenting Opinion of Judge Odio Benito, para. 17.

A preview of this humanitarian battle came in NGO reports, along the lines of HRW's "*Covered in Blood.*" But the decisive battle must unfold within the courtroom, where judges hold singular authority to apply key paradigms and presumptions, on the way to final judgment. In this respect, the Congo trials turned into hard-fought campaigns. The outcomes were mixed – considering two acquittals out of four accused. And even the victories were fragile. In the battle against impunity, the ICC needs to learn from these three trials, if it is to fulfill its destiny as the permanent, preeminent foe of impunity.[645]

The paradigms of responsibility rest on intuitions inherited by survivors of twentieth-century conflicts. The core intuition is that widespread harm to victims cannot be treated as a random string of calamities. Such harms are rather the outcome of insidious plans, hatched within powerful organizations, inspired by commanding leaders. The responsibility for mass atrocities must extend all the way to these leaders. En route, the path of justice must battle its way through protocols and organizations, notwithstanding their scale and complexity, until reaching the commanders at the top. Moral attribution cannot get sidetracked along this path: it must surmount any and all obscurities to nail the presumed masterminds behind the mayhem. They are the ones "most responsible" for the "unimaginable atrocities that shock the conscience of humanity." Their prosecution is imperative "for the sake of present and future generations."[646]

Outside the Paradigm: Staying the Hand of Attribution

As a product of twentieth-century European experience and anxieties, the long battle against impunity met its match in central Africa in the early years of the twenty-first century. Conditions in Ituri were far removed from the core paradigm, which had universalized a Weberian model of rational planning, organizational bureaucracy, and charismatic leadership. Earlier chapters in this book described the contrasting structures operating in Ituri during the period 2002–03, derived from recent social research models, putting aside the legally characterized facts of international NGOs. Yes, there were "organizations," loosely speaking. But their diffuse, networked structure promoted fragmentation rather than bureaucratic efficiency. They

[645] It remains to be seen what patterns survive in the final appeals stage of the Bosco Ntaganda trial, which was a replay for the Prosecution of the Lubanga case, but with a host of additional charges. The Trial Chamber found Ntaganda guilty on multiple counts, drawing on the same Ituri events and presumptions (even the identical time frame) as the Lubanga case. Ntaganda Trial Judgment, July 8, 2019, ICC-01/04–02/06–2359. An appeal will be heard in 2020.

[646] Rome Statute Preamble.

might differ substantially from structures projected in contemporary documents and manifestos – often the strategic outputs of hard-pressed opportunists.

Yet it was the goal of the ICC to bring such complex events under the mandate of the Court, including the vital process of moral attribution. From the outset it was a mismatch. Not because violence in central Africa somehow stands beyond moral judgment, but because the paradigms of attribution used by the Court were anachronistic, tied to radically different cultures and conditions.

Stepping outside the conventional paradigm for a moment, it is possible to see just how much is lost in the reductions favored by the Court's code of moral attribution. During 2002–03 in Ituri, most of the active players were already caught up in a web of preexisting circumstances. There was no historical moment that could serve as a point of moral equilibrium – no clear beginning to the dynamics in which actors like Lubanga were embedded. By April 2002, when the Inter-Congolese Dialogue was advancing in distant cities, and when a group of restless (mostly Hema) officers in Bunia mutinied against the RCD rebel leadership, control over local conditions in Ituri eluded everyone's grasp. Lubanga and his adventitious allies started using the UPC label, but they were already mired in circumstances offering virtually no room for calculation or control.

Their environment was overdetermined in a convergence of distinct causes: the long-standing land tenure rules and practices from the Mobutu years, the adventurism of Ugandan generals and freebooters, globally inflected trading networks, and military stalemate among national rebel groups like the RCD and Bemba's MCL. Maybe the ground was starting to shift with the first whiff of national power-sharing negotiations; but no one knew how this would work out. The best and only strategy was simply to dig in, hold on, and adapt at the margins where possible. Rwanda's continuing interference – with the lure of fresh sources of military supplies – added to the array of new centering forces.

What about children under the age of fifteen in some kind of armed service? Surely, they were already part of the amalgamating military structures prior to 2002, and their continuing presence can be taken as one of many contingent facts, at the same moment when Lubanga was moving closer to the center of events. Military forces were built up continuously from loosely organized village self-defense groups, coalescing into hybrid structures. In addition, families and children might follow these local combatants into new camps and deployments, especially after being displaced themselves by violence. They might participate in ways large and small, including the looting that followed successful armed campaigns.

In August 2002, when the UPC sought to fill the power vacuum in Ituri (although Lubanga was still incarcerated in Kinshasa), his associates found themselves with monumental challenges and little means of control. Months later, when NGOs warned Lubanga and others about international legal constraints regarding children under fifteen, his options were limited by the realities of a fractured organization, using its limited resources to survive in conditions approaching anarchy. Perhaps the demobilization orders issued in his name were not expected to have much impact – like so much else during this chaotic phase, where symbolic action could be the least awful option. Under the circumstances, bad (or weak) faith may have been all that Lubanga (or anyone) had to offer, in a failing structure from which key players were defecting.

When the shift in hostilities finally came in June 2003, soon thereafter a general child-soldier demobilization campaign created further confusion.[647] By late 2003, any child, even one with a borrowed weapon, might qualify for benefits by presenting himself or herself as a former combatant. Despite the best efforts of UN human rights workers, it was already too late to make accurate counts of underage children connected to ephemeral groups and factions. Among the difficulties was separating small village-based defense units from more systematic forces – with much of the fighting hovering close to the lower threshold for defining "armed conflicts," for purposes of Article 8 war crimes.[648]

It was these fraught conditions on the ground that made the Hague courtrooms virtually impotent in documenting a practice widely condemned by NGOs and emerging international law. The first two Congo trials produced no credible first-hand testimony from purported child soldiers, all of their testimony having been dismissed by the respective Trial Chambers. Even though the Rome Statute conveniently blurred the distinct categories of enlistment, recruitment, and simply using children in armed conflict – framing the law so that *all* such practices were illegal – it was never clear to what extent the UPC operated on the level of policy design and choice. The children were already there, increasing their numbers as village units got absorbed into larger networks. The question for the UPC was whether to use its limited resources to bend these realities. As in most other strategic guises, its

[647] The outlines of MONUC-supported efforts to demobilize child soldiers from area militias are summarized in UN Secretary General, *Special Report on the Events in Ituri*, pp. 44–45.

[648] Under Article 8, war crimes provisions do "not apply to situations of internal disturbances and tensions, such as riots, isolated and sporadic acts of violence or other acts of a similar nature" (Article 8(2)(f)). The legal interpretation of this lower threshold will be discussed in Section 7.5.

overwhelming purpose was survival. Under these conditions, even having policies (let alone altering them) was a luxury they could scarcely afford.

By 2003, and then over time, it was possible to see Lubanga's position in highly circumscribed terms. At first, he had been chosen to speak for the mutinous Hema officers in the RCD, as they took their grievances to Kampala for greater leverage. Lubanga was among the few with a university education; he spoke fluent French; he gained the trust of network brokers and was potentially useful to other ambitious men, at a time when calculations often failed to look beyond the shortest of short terms. In 2002, with the decay of the RCD interlopers, the diverse action networks in Ituri could not exist without militarized units – in which local self-defense groups sought links to groups like the Hema mutineers – rising from the remnants of dead-end rebel campaigns. The process of militarization was impossible without the cultivation of Ugandan occupiers – and eventually their Rwandan rivals. For men like Lubanga, opportunities and choices were constrained by these formidable, loosely coordinated elements. For UPC figures, facing constant pressure from defections in the key months after filling the power vacuum in Bunia, any moral agency was embedded in weakened action networks. The legal pivot to individual responsibility would require extensive use of broad presumptions.

The Individual Responsibility Paradigm

The Lubanga Trial Chamber would not venture outside the standard paradigm inherited from prior international tribunals and reengineered by the Lubanga Pre-Trial Chamber.[649] Any time spent outside this paradigm would only have stirred deeper doubts, putting more pressure on the already thin stock of evidence (most of it circumstantial) that survived the trial process. Rather than actively considering plausible alternatives to the Prosecution narrative, the Trial Chamber stayed within the four corners of the standard model.

The Court's pivot to individual responsibility rests on a series of presumptions and inferences, shaped by the components of the Pre-Trial Chamber's *control over the crime* theory of perpetration.[650] These presumptions interact

[649] For a comprehensive analysis, see Neha Jain, *Perpetrators and Accessories in International Criminal Law: Individual Modes of Responsibility for Collective Crimes* (Oxford: Hart, 2014).

[650] See Elies van Sliedregt and Lachezar Yanev, "Co-Perpetration Based on Joint Control over the Crime," in Jerôme de Hemptinne, Robert Roth, and Elies van Sliedregt (eds.), *Modes of Liability in International Criminal Law* (Cambridge: Cambridge University Press, 2019), chapter 5.

with the complex evidence base through broad inferences that convert circumstantial evidence into usable facts. This pattern of reasoning reverses the conventional flow between facts and law: instead of independent facts looking for legal categories, it is the legal categories that look back and select necessary facts. Individual criminal responsibility is not a contingent fact but a prior assumption, serving the imperatives of moral attribution. When reprocessed as a fact, the finding of responsibility resides within the subjective conscience of the judge, resting on oracular authority.

The paradigms and presumptions that power this process are not spelled out in Articles 25(3) and 28 of the Rome Statute. Rather, they are baked into the judicial application of those Articles, in a series of practices that constitute the most remarkable – and the most controversial – features in all three Congo trials. The judicial use of moral paradigms deserves close study, including its interplay with judicial fact-finding. The power of paradigms was not unlimited. In the hands of diverse judges, the paradigms of individual responsibility crossed with conflicting judicial philosophies, as seen in the split decisions, dissents, and sudden reversals in the second and third Congo trials. The ICC's judicial struggles reached their greatest intensity in this quest for moral attribution. Across all three trials, significant tensions rose to the surface.

The roadmap of moral presumptions was already laid out in the advocacy of international NGOs and absorbed into the ICC Prosecutor's master narratives. In the Lubanga case, some of the background documents seized by MONUC in Ituri helped launch the main paradigm. The existence of some documents bearing the facsimile of Western organizations seemed like presumptive proof of the preconceived model. These documents may well have persuaded the first ICC investigator in Ituri to focus attention on Lubanga and the UPC, when virtually none of the other armed groups had any documents to speak of.[651]

From March 2003, when Bunia was in a state of anarchy, international NGOs arrived on the scene, transcribing stories from armed remnants about tight military organizations (with impressive initials), supreme commanders, and meticulously planned campaigns, formulating the surmises that coalesced into the first ICC preliminary examination in a *situation*. Armed groups projected the façade of effective organizations ("militias"), hoping to earn a spot at the local peace table in Ituri, if not at the national level. In later skirmishes in Ituri, during the period 2004–07, when the ICC investigations took hold, these groups desperately brandished their corporate initials: UPC, FRPI, FNI, which were retroactively treated by the ICC Prosecutor as the

[651] Lavigne Deposition, November 16, 2010, pp. 28–32.

same continuous organizations, for which Lubanga, Katanga, and Ngudjolo were the respective masterminds during 2002–03.

For anyone outside the ICC universe – anyone trying to figure out, without a preconceived script, what was happening in Ituri – it became virtually impossible to comprehend the raw structure of Ituri violence, leading up to March 2003. Going back to the testimony of Prosecution expert Gérard Prunier in the early days of the Lubanga trial, any possibility of finding neutral witnesses vanished before the observers and investigators arrived: "[I]t is impossible to know without being present in the field, without speaking to people during the time of the events, because as soon as everything is over the entire history is reconstructed ...."[652] And one of the main ways in which "everything is over" is when NGOs arrive with their armory of moral paradigms. As humanitarian advocates start building the bridge to The Hague, the demand for accountability reconfigures the landscape of facts. The moral imperatives of international justice selected the relevant facts on the ground, which were now legally characterized. In the words (previously cited) of the Lubanga Pre-Trial Chamber, "the Chamber recalls that in the fight against impunity, it must insure an appropriate balance between the rights of the accused and the need to respond to victims and the international community's expectations."[653] No balance would be appropriate without due regard for moral imperatives.

This approach to individual responsibility came to the ICC from prior judicial practice. Earlier international tribunals used roughly similar formulas to validate legal judgments against defendants, but with idiomatic variations. In Nuremberg, the American legal concept of "conspiracy" performed its versatile role of allowing the actions of any one group member to be attributed to all the others. The ad hoc tribunals embellished their respective statutes with a new liability tool, pulled from customary international law, finding collective culpability among all those united in a "joint criminal enterprise" (JCE).[654] In these historic instances, the physical crimes were typically committed not by the high leadership but by lowly foot-soldiers and bureaucratic subordinates; yet the responsibility needed to revert back to the leaders. Both

[652] Prunier Testimony, March 26, 2009, p. 45.

[653] Lubanga Confirmation of Charges decision, para. 97.

[654] A full-bodied defense of this doctrine comes from Michael P. Scharf. "Joint Criminal Enterprise, the Nuremberg Precedent, and the Concept of 'Grotian Moment,'" in Tracy Isaacs and Richard Vernon (eds.), *Accountability for Collective Wrongdoing* (Cambridge: Cambridge University Press, 2011), chapter 4. The contrasting view played with alternative meanings for the initials "JCE": see, among many examples, Mohamed Elewa Badar, "Just Convict Everyone!" *International Criminal Law Review* 6 (2006), 293.

military and civilian/political commanders were responsible for planning the violence – for creating rational, efficient organizations that operated as killing machines. The lower-echelon killers were mere cogs in that machine. The greatest responsibility fell on those who built it.

Originally, these paradigms supposed that criminal planning occurred within the structures of sovereign states. The violence was typically state violence, unleashed against external foes and internal enemies. By the 1990s, the global evolution of armed conflict had become apparent.[655] There was state violence within the context of a fragmenting state (the breakup of the former Yugoslavia), a genocide in Rwanda that overlapped in inscrutable ways with a political transition, a civil war inside Sierra Leone but with involvement of neighboring state leaders.

The Rome Conference was influenced by these transitional conflicts, as it chose to modify some older crime definitions to reach new agents and structures. Thus, "crimes against humanity" may be committed by states or by non-state actors; although in the latter case there is still a requirement of "widespread or systematic" violence, as well as some semblance of a "state or organizational policy." War crimes are divided into two separate lists, depending on whether the conflict is between nation states or inside a single state territory. The belatedly activated ICC crime of "aggression" applies to actions by conventional states and to individuals acting within their auspices.[656]

While ICC crime definitions were moving cautiously in new directions, the treatment of individual criminal responsibility remained firmly tied to familiar moral paradigms. In Rome, the previous statutory formulas grew more robust: spelling out a series of organizational roles with matching modes of individual liability. Thus, "ordering" others to commit crimes had its own formulation, as did the role of "aiding and abetting," as well as a residual category of "contributing in any other fashion." Under Article 25(3) these were liability modes (b), (c), and (d), respectively. The top of the list was Article 25(3)(a): "committing" the crime, with variations allowed for joint perpetration ("co-perpetration") and perpetration through others ("indirect perpetration"), and even a composite of these two ("indirect co-perpetration).

This list caused great anguish among the judges in the Congo trials, who were left with the task of making it operational. Some judges saw the categories as overlapping (e.g. "ordering" and "indirect perpetration"). Some saw a stark

[655] See Martin van Creveld, *The Transformation of War* (New York: Free Press, 1991); Mark Duffield, *Global Governance and the New Wars: The Merging of Development and Security* (London: Zed Books, 2001).

[656] Articles 7, 8, and 8*bis*.

moral hierarchy between the first mode ("perpetrator") and the other three, which also seems to have been the Prosecutor's view. The Congo suspects brought to The Hague were initially assigned to the top category. All would be brought as "perpetrators," although only Lubanga ended his legal process with that label firmly applied.

Applying the Paradigm: Doctrinal Imports from German Law

The Pre-Trial Chamber in the Lubanga case made the first interpretive move, seeking to operationalize the concept of "perpetration" in the case of international crimes. According to the model imported from German law, the essence of individual responsibility lay in the defendant's iron "control" over the circumstances of systematic crimes. This liability model creates a space for moral agency – enabling a key axiom of legal proceedings: that, above and beyond the sheer complexity of physical causes, there must exist a pinnacle of moral responsibility. In its application, this *control over the crime* paradigm had to be shored up with presumptions about how the world works, with loads of circumstantial reasoning, with furtive assumptions about risk-taking, and with subtle shifts in the burden of proof. In the end, if international justice is to have the tools it needs to end impunity, it must impose some such practical system of moral attribution.[657]

Academic critics have raised the question of whether the Lubanga Pre-Trial Chamber, by importing this German concept, exceeded the scope of the Rome Statute.[658] And Judge Fulford, in the Lubanga Trial Judgment, filed a lone dissent to the new theory.[659] In the Katanga and Ngudjolo cases, a trial judge raised more fundamental objections.[660] But across the range of judicial decisions in the Congo trials, the *control over the crime* doctrine has permeated the concept of "perpetration."[661]

657 Lubanga Trial Judgment, para. 976.

658 In the view of Joseph Powderly, it was the indeterminacy of Article 25(3) that seemed to drive the Lubanga Pre-Trial Chamber toward supplementary theories. He found it "difficult to tally" this doctrinal innovation with "the prevailing textual approach to interpretation mandated by Articles 21(1)(a) and 22(2)"; "The Rome Statute and the Corseting of the Interpretive Judicial Function: Reflections on Sources of Law and Interpretive Technique," in Stahn, *Law and Practice of the International Criminal Court*, p. 468.

659 Lubanga Trial Judgment, Separate Opinion of Judge Adrian Fulford, paras. 6–12.

660 Ngudjolo Trial Judgment, Concurring Opinion of Judge Christine Van den Wyngaert, December 18, 2012, ICC-01/04–02/12–4, para. 64; Katanga Trial Judgment, Minority Opinion of Christine Van den Wyngaert, March 7, 2014, ICC-01/04–01/07–3436-Anx1, paras. 279–81.

661 See Thomas Weigand, "Indirect Perpetration," in Stahn, *Law and Practice of the International Criminal Court*, chapter 22.

Nothing, however, could be further from the conditions of complex action in Ituri and the CAR. Chapter 8 will explore the collapse of the second trial, which went overboard in stretching the *control* theory of perpetration to a pair of "indirect joint perpetrators" – two quite marginal figures, lost in the fog of uncertainty surrounding a February 2003 attack on the Ituri village of Bogoro. Neither accused man in that case could be considered a "mastermind" of the attack, at a point in time when the Lendu armed groups were far removed from the tight organizational efficiency of the German Nazis, or the East German Stasi. Bemba's connection to the CAR violence was quickly seen as falling into a completely different pattern; although in the end that connection was not sufficient, even for the attenuated mode of responsibility contained in Article 28 ("command responsibility"). All three Congo trials had difficulty finding their way through the moral maze created by this conceptual web.

The *control over the crime* theory had an appealing history, as it was reconstructed by academic commentators on the ICC trials.[662] The instigation for this German law comes from the famous Adolf Eichmann trial of the 1960s, as well as the domestic prosecutions of former East German officials.[663] In both cases, according to the theory's creator Claus Roxin, the moral/legal responsibility of organizational superiors must not be diluted by the fact that orders were carried out by subordinates in Hitler's concentration camps, or at East German border crossings. The controlling decisions by commanders must be presumed to move in a frictionless way through highly efficient organizations, so tightly controlled that deviations could never happen. If one subordinate had decided, as a matter of conscience, to defy an order, there was a presumed endless supply of replacement servants ready to do the deed. The true perpetrators are those formulating the plans, standing at the head of efficient organizations, whose decisions pass through the gauntlet of physical causes with no loss of moral turpitude.

A remarkable supplement to this theory was proposed by American academic Mark Osiel, commenting on the acceptance of Roxin's model in the first two Congo trials. Other critics had posed the simple question (but without further analysis)[664] of whether the Roxinian doctrine had much to say about

[662] See Jens David Ohlin, "Co-Perpetration: German *Dogmatik* or German Invasion?" in Stahn, *Law and Practice of the International Criminal Court*, chapter 21.

[663] Claus Roxin, "Crimes as Part of Organized Power Structures," *Journal of International Criminal Justice* 9 (2011), 193. This translated article draws its contents from the larger work *Täterschaft und Tatherrschaft*, 9th ed. (Berlin: de Gruyter, 2015).

[664] Hints had cropped up in writings of Elies van Sliedregt: see her essay "Perpetration and Participation in Article 25(3)," in Stahn, *Law and Practice of the International Criminal Court*, p. 514.

African social realities. Osiel acknowledged that the assumption of tight organizational systems may not apply to loosely structured armed "militias," with their tendency to fall into factions. His conclusion was to rescue the moral imperative behind the *control* theory, boosting it with a fresh metaphor. Inside Roxin's "organizational apparatus of hierarchical power," the mastermind at the top pulls the levers that set mass atrocities in motion. In Roxin's words, "... the person behind the scenes at the controls of the organized structure presses a button," and the order will inevitably be fulfilled. On the front lines, "[i]ndividuals who refuse to commit crimes are dismissed and replaced," and are no more than cogs in a bureaucratic machine (citing Hannah Arendt's well-known views on Eichmann).[665] But this was not the way things worked in central Africa.

Osiel points to contrasting non-Weberian organizational structures – "more informal, unsystematic, and decentralized." They may be seen as "bizarre motivational-organizational hybrids," and they might allow a clever Defense team to distinguish its case from the pure Roxinian model. Osiel's solution was to reboot the *control* model with an African update. In his view, during the early stages of armed action by groups in places like central Africa, there exists a tight bond of social solidarity within "tribal" groups, even if it falls apart over time. Borrowing tacitly from Durkheim rather than Weber, Osiel postulates "intense camaraderie and other, equally intangible elements of 'social capital.' The group's members coordinate spontaneously in response to their comrades' immediate cues, which are often unobservable (much less intelligible) to outsiders." To round out these Westernized views of how African networks operated, Osiel quotes a like-minded commentator: "[T]hey make football passes blindly because they always know where the other players will be."[666]

For Osiel, these organizations cannot rely on machine-like efficiency in the later execution of common plans. It is enough, morally speaking, during the phase of customary solidarity based on "tribal affiliation," if they create a powerful watch-work mechanism that can then run according to its own mechanical power. Using this model, Osiel posits "a village watchmaker who constructs a little clock, then winds it up and walks away, without looking back. In the present cases he has also attached that clock to a bomb, of course, which detonates well after he has left the room."[667]

665 Mark Osiel, "Ascribing Individual Liability within a Bureaucracy of Murder," in Alette Smeulers (ed.), *Collective Violence and International Criminal Justice: An Interdisciplinary Approach* (Portland: Intersentia, 2010), chapter 5, pp. 108–09.
666 Ibid., p. 116.
667 Ibid., p. 117.

The African perpetrator of mass crimes is like this watchmaker, who creates a plan that will tick-tock on its own, long after the maker has picked up and moved his tent to the next hunting camp. The autonomous watch is the criminal plan, originating in the close embrace of tribal solidarity but then allowed to float freely on its own. Such a tightly wired plan will have consequences (unless hijacked by some interloper), and its creators can be deemed responsible for setting the stage for the resulting atrocities. The watchmakers assume the risk that the intended bomb will go off. They can be held responsible on the basis of foreseeable harms that would materialize sometime in the future, and for sheer recklessness in simply crafting inherently dangerous plans. The perpetrators may not *control* the final application of their plans, but their responsibility lies in assuming risks that the plan will eventually unfold. "The evidentiary burden may even shift toward the defendant, requiring him to show that he could no longer control his forces, rather than requiring the prosecutor to show that the accused continued to control them right up to the very moment when, and in the very situs where, they performed their deeds."[668] The Lubanga Trial Chamber did not have the same academic license to craft new liability metaphors on the spot. And Judge Fulford himself remained dubious about the standard *control* theory. But the other two judges seemed to anticipate the path later described by Prof. Osiel, through skillful judicial management of presumptions and inferences. In particular, the Lubanga Trial Chamber pursued the logic of liability for assuming risks, along with strategic shifts in proof burdens. Similar patterns prevailed in the later judgment against Germain Katanga.

Applying the Mastermind Theory to Lubanga

"The Statute sets out the modes of liability in Articles 25 and 28, and they should be interpreted in a way that allows properly expressing and addressing the responsibility for these crimes."[669] Two Lubanga trial judges accepted the *control of the crime* doctrine as the proper expression of Article 25(3)(a). Certainly, an attraction of this theory is that it transforms a seemingly remote leader into a front-line perpetrator, provided certain rigors of the theory are observed. Judge Fulford was not convinced and thought that any of the liability modes listed in Article 25(3) would send a strong enough message, even if it meant that Lubanga had simply "ordered" the crime to be committed by others, or "aided and abetted" their criminal actions. He thought further

[668] Ibid., p. 119.
[669] Lubanga Trial Judgment, para. 976.

that the Teutonic approach to co-perpetration placed too many burdens on the Prosecutor.[670]

Fulford may have underestimated the power of timely presumptions in easing the path to individual responsibility. As a co-perpetrator linked to political and military associates under the umbrella of an *organization* known as UPC, Lubanga's responsibility would extend to their actions as well, when they fall under a *common plan* agreed to collectively. This plan need not be memorialized on paper; it may be inferred from what happened in Ituri during the months when the UPC was active. With such destructive events, the presumption is that they must have been centrally planned. Such a presumption is the necessary first step toward finding the master planner, who can then be held responsible.

A presumed plan need not include a plank calling for enlisting, recruiting, or using child soldiers actively in hostilities. It was enough (like Osiel's evil watchmaker) to count such events as *foreseeable risks* implied by the master plan. A presumed plan thus includes a series of presumed risks – all of them attributed back to the master planners. Within this chain of inferences, a leading figure like Lubanga can be presumed to contribute to the plan's implementation – if only because he was in fact a *leader*. As a leader of the imputed organization, he must have performed a variety of leading tasks, or perhaps failed to halt a variety of actions by others. All that was required to complete this circle was a presumption that Lubanga (as a leader) would have been powerful enough to stop the integration of child soldiers, but (based on inferences from events) evidently chose not to do so. It was these imputed actions and omissions that could be presumed to play an essential part in implementation – when the results were so utterly foreseeable.

The Lubanga Trial Chamber expected the Prosecutor to show that implementation of the common plan embodied a sufficient "risk" that – other things being equal – the crime will occur. This showing "involves consideration of the concepts of 'possibility' and 'probability,' which are inherent in the notions of 'risk' and 'danger.'"[671] But the Appeals Chamber was unwilling to accept even this meek reference to contingency, especially when it was so easy for judges to simply infer a kind of "virtual certainty" that the child-soldiers crime would emerge from the common plan. And if the judges could do so, then plainly Lubanga *should* have done so.[672] This style of "normative assessment" was essential for the legal fight against impunity.[673] Waffling on the presence

[670] Ibid., Dissent of Judge Fulford, paras. 7, 3.
[671] Ibid., paras. 984, 1012.
[672] Lubanga Appeals Judgment, para. 449.
[673] Ibid., paras. 465–66.

of risk began with the Lubanga Pre-Trial Chamber, in a form received cautiously and evasively by the Trial Chamber. Later Pre-Trial Chambers tried various ways to reconcile elements of risk with the general "knowledge" standard of Article 30. Even if perpetrators do not quite intend for criminal acts to happen, they *know* such things *will* happen – since the world is an orderly place where things happen "normally." Some commentators argued that more explicit risk analysis would be a healthy addition to ICC judgments, even though the drafting history of the Rome Statute suggests some wariness, especially for the siren call of *dolus eventualis*.[674]

As part of this structure of presumptions, the paradigm of absolute leadership was central. In all three Congo trials, the crimes were prosecuted as crimes of leadership, in several guises. For Lubanga, this translated into a type of criminal responsibility contained in the top echelon of Article 25(3), under the term "co-perpetration." For Katanga and Ngudjolo, the term changed to "indirect co-perpetration," but the structure of legal presumptions was the same, starting from the presumed leadership positions of the two accused within their respective organizations. (It turned out that neither one was a plausible leader, at least at the time the crimes were committed, and so the original theory of responsibility had to be abandoned.) For Bemba, the leadership label survived, but the military venture at the heart of that case could not be forced into the mold of the *control over the crime* theory. Indeed, the moral duties assigned to Bemba's leadership position were so attenuated that a majority of the Appeals Chamber reversed his conviction.

The Lubanga trial judges were fully aware of a contrary line of argument about Ituri organizations, even as they stuck to the presumptions of Weberian structures. The expert witness Gérard Prunier was invited by the Prosecution to comment on the situation in Ituri. Speaking of groups like the UPC, the image he offered, instead of a tightly controlled hierarchical organization, was that of "an amoeba. It divides, it regroups, and all the people spent their time infighting, fighting with each other."[675] The same analysis can be found in the

[674] These pre-trial developments are discussed in Mohamed Elewa Badar, "Dolus Eventualis and the Rome Statute Without It?" *New Criminal Law Review* 12 (2009), 433. Badar believes that accepting *dolus eventualis* (associated with tort-like foreseeability) would strengthen the battle against impunity, and that justice to the victims (based on the correct judicial inferences) will be improved (p. 467). See also Mohamed Elewa Badar and Sara Porro, "Rethinking the Mental Element in the Jurisprudence of the ICC," in Stahn, *Law and Practice of the International Criminal Court*, chapter 26. For the view that the Lubanga Trial Chamber "confused matters by importing the principles of *dolus eventualis* but simply dropping the controversial label," see Ohlin, "Co-Perpetration," p. 534 (with citations to the Lubanga Trial Judgment).

[675] Prunier Testimony, March 26, 2009, p. 49.

work of Vlassenroot and Raeymaekers, speaking to the period in late 2003: "[M]ost militia leaders have lost control over the rank-and-file militia members. As a consequence, most militia groups are disintegrating into loose gangs of social bandits, highly increasing the level of violence against the rural population."[676] Plenty of evidence in the Lubanga trial could have supported this notion. Operating within the general presumption of innocence, the Trial Chamber might have seen its duty as reckoning with the many reasonable alternatives to the Prosecution's glib presumptions. But instead the Trial Chamber found just enough weight and probity in scattered testimony to support the chain of presumptions leading to individual responsibility. Further parts of Prunier's testimony would challenge the remaining presumptions as well.

To be successful in prosecuting Lubanga on the child-soldiers charge, the Prosecution needed to describe the UPC as a tightly structured, effective organization, in which the unified common plan of the co-perpetrators would be fully and faithfully executed by those in the lower echelons. The very existence and nature of such a plan and its probabilistic relationship to the use of child soldiers were all presumptive elements in the struggle to find Lubanga individually responsible for the child-soldier crime.

Selecting the Evidence: The Power of the Paradigm

International criminal law was created to meet the humanitarian resolve to find those "most responsible" for large-scale atrocities. It is a heroic task, given the wide metaphysical gap between empirical facts and moral responsibility – between "is" and "ought." Outside the courtroom, raw facts cannot produce, on their own, a conclusion about moral right or wrong. But inside the courtroom, using normative principles embedded in legal statutes, there is a framework for connecting trial evidence with *legal* responsibility. That framework or paradigm opens up a system of connected presumptions that guides the judicial search for *confirming* evidence. Uncertainties on the ground would be superseded by a judicial truth, constituted by coherence, anchored in the psychological recesses of the satisfied judicial conscience.

Judges referred to this method of reasoning as "normative assessment."[677] It follows a subtle logic for testing evidence, rooted in the oracular authority of judicial fact-finding, and sheltered by the deferential mode of appellate

[676] Koen Vlassenroot and Timothy Raeymaekers, *Conflict and Social Transformation in Eastern DR Congo* (Ghent: Academia Press, 2004), p. 188.

[677] See, for example, Lubanga Appeals Judgment, paras. 465–66.

review. Across the three Congo trials, this method allowed for a conviction in the Lubanga case – but came under withering fire in the remaining cases. As a method driven by presumptions, it holds a fugitive relationship to the legal presumption of innocence, and to the legal standard of proof beyond reasonable doubt. From one point of view, "normative assessment" greatly simplifies the search for proof; but all it takes is a sudden shift in presumptions to undermine it – as seen in later Congo trial dissents and appeals.

Factual evidence (mainly circumstantial) was available to support the chain of judicial inferences. In this quest for accountability, the evidence does not select the paradigm; rather, the paradigm selects the evidence, endowing it with moral salience. In each section of the Lubanga judgment, the Trial Chamber found credible precisely those scraps of evidence that tended to confirm the presumptions derived from their legal paradigm. It started with the principle that mass atrocities do not happen like natural disasters: somewhere, there is a perpetrator who must be understood as a mastermind, manipulating an efficient organizational structure such that the destruction caused by underlings depends fully on the actions (or omissions) of those at the top. Without that framework firmly in place – you have no case for conviction.

Amidst conflicting testimony about the nature of the UPC as a traditional hierarchical, military organization, the Trial Chamber found enough evidence to satisfy the inner convictions of its individual members. "[A]t least from September 2002, the accused as President of the UPC-RP endorsed a common plan to build an effective army to ensure the UPC/FPLC's domination of Ituri, and he was actively involved in its implementation."[678] Was the military mission tightly connected to the political goals espoused by the UPC? "[T]here is a clear dispute as to the nature of the UPC's aims prior to late August/early September 2002. The UPC's founding documents describe a political programme as well as the organization's military ambitions. Other contemporary documents ... indicate the UPC-RP was a 'political-military movement' ... which had taken up arms against the RCD-ML."[679] Among these documents (taken at face value by the Trial Chamber) was a retrospective history of the UPC written in June 2004, well after the group had dispersed into rival networks, when the remnants had morphed into a political party still angling for influence within the ongoing peace negotiations. At trial, a Defense witness had testified that this document was not an accurate history; but the Trial Chamber gave it full credit, because Lubanga

678 Lubanga Trial Judgment, para. 1134.
679 Ibid., para. 1107.

once possessed an annotated copy, and he failed to register any complaints at the time it was written.[680]

The judges defined this assumed common plan at a high level of generality: it presupposes an organization with both political and military aims, locked in a struggle with an equally armed enemy. But the coherence of the organization is itself inferred from circumstantial facts. In accordance with the *control of the crime* theory, organizational coherence is simply an inference from these imputed goals and need not be proven down to the last detail. "[C]o-perpetration does not require that the agreement or common plan is explicit in order for the individual conduct of each co-perpetrator to be connected. Finally, although direct evidence of the plan is likely to assist in demonstrating its existence, this is not a legal requirement. The agreement can be inferred from circumstantial evidence."[681] Throughout lengthy reckonings of divergent testimony about the UPC as an organization, the Trial Chamber clung tenaciously to the view that this group was a coherent, powerful, efficiently run enterprise with a military mission. If specific members of the leadership came to their roles through anomalous histories and allegiances, such distinctions were dissolved in the common purpose ascribed to the inferred plan. It does not matter if some members of the cabal were more actively involved in recruiting child soldiers, while others attended to other concerns.

> [T]he Chamber agrees with the conclusions ... of the Pre-Trial Chamber that criminal liability in this context is "not limited to those who physically carry out the objective elements of the offence, but also include(s) those who, in spite of being removed from the scene of the crime, control or mastermind its commission because they decide whether and how the offence will be committed."[682]

The mastermind theory is clearly broad enough to encompass the idea of a mastermind committee – even though the composition, personal relationships, and goals of that committee are based on inferences, drawing on conflicting and circumstantial evidence. But did this organizational model seem plausible in the context of Ituri? Was it the only reasonable model, or were there others on offer?

For each of the presumptions used in this case, the Chamber heard strong contrary possibilities. As an alternative to the masterminded, efficient military organization, there was a very different image introduced by Prosecution expert Gérard Prunier. Professor Prunier's expertise was the whole sweep of

680 Ibid., paras. 1096–97.
681 Ibid., para. 988.
682 Ibid., para. 1003.

history in the turbulent eastern Congo provinces, and his grasp of specific conditions in Ituri was not based on his own field research at the appropriate times. But he apprised the Court of local dynamics that ran directly counter to the Roxinian theory. In his view, an armed group like the rebel RCD was not comparable to a functioning government; rather, it was "like an amoeba. It divides, it regroups."[683] Driving these shape-changes were the actions of Ugandan occupiers, and also the prospect of national power-sharing, opened up in April 2002 with the beginning of the Inter-Congolese Dialogue. At precisely the moment when the Trial Chamber saw the UPC as an established masterminded organization, Prunier stressed the fragile character of armed groups in Ituri:

> Don't forget that we are talking about ... militias. We are not talking about a regular army whose commanders are able to ensure some discipline within the ranks. Very often, after a military defeat ... many people just dispersed. They go away, and they may return to or they may come back together again later on, but most of the time they just disperse.[684]

Was there a conflict of standard armies in Ituri after August 2002? According to Prunier, it was less a clash of organized armies than a period of "anarchy, because groups confront each other. Everybody tries to give themselves a respectable name to try ... to have the trimmings of an institution, but it was nothing more than a confrontation of armed groups."[685] What unfolded in Ituri was the product of this anarchy:

> It wasn't a diabolical strategy that had been calculated, intelligently planned, but the situation was such a violent one that even groups that weren't players created militia to protect themselves because an ... ethnic group that finds itself in a combat zone and has no fighters ... is literally like a beast faced with a predator. So it's more of a result of the disintegration of authority. It is a Hobbesian situation as there's no authority, everyone tries to do as best they can.[686]

The UPC was not to be taken seriously as a hegemon in Ituri but was posturing for attention in peace negotiations. "So the UPC was trying to have a little seat somewhere. They weren't looking for an important role, but they were trying to find a role within the framework of Congolese negotiations .... I just don't see the UPC as being resolutely, monolithically, powerfully organized in favor

683 Prunier Testimony, March 26, 2009, p. 49.
684 Ibid., p. 54.
685 Ibid., pp. 58–59.
686 Ibid., p. 67.

of secession, no."[687] As for the published UPC manifestos, "Since when do political people say clearly what they want to do and when did we start taking them literally?"[688]

And finally, what about the children? In Prunier's view, the extreme environment made soldiering a natural choice for any youth interested in survival. "[A]ll the victims were civilians, and actually . . . with this kind of civil war, not only in Ituri but elsewhere too, the safest place is to be an armed militia man. Anybody carrying a weapon incurs much less risk."[689] While this view may not count as a *defense* under the statute, it is an alternative way of seeing the emergence of armed groups in Ituri – as resulting from something other than a masterplan by top leaders.

In the end, Prunier's expert testimony was simply one more bit of evidence, which the Trial Chamber was entitled to treat with caution and circumspection. He came to the ICC at the invitation of the Prosecution, as an authority on Congolese history and politics, and he spoke as a researcher outside the conventions of the courtroom. His vision of chaotic conditions and amoeba-like organizations was in stark contrast to the framework of presumptions adopted by the Trial Chamber. Prunier's approach would make it virtually impossible, in a court of law, to find anyone, let alone Thomas Lubanga, responsible (legally or morally) for the destruction in Ituri.[690]

As between these two overarching visions of Ituri conflict, the Trial Chamber was not able to choose on the basis of trial evidence alone. Among the stockpiles of submitted evidence, there were some facts at trial to support either vision; neither one stood outside the realm of plausibility. But the Trial Chamber selected witnesses and documents that allowed the *control over the crime* doctrine to prevail. It found these witnesses credible enough, despite the

687 Ibid., p. 92.
688 Ibid., p. 90.
689 Ibid., p. 42.
690 An anthropologist studying expert witness testimony at the ICTY, near the end of his project, overlapped briefly in The Hague with Prunier's ICC testimony. Without immersing himself in the larger issues of the Lubanga case (still in the Prosecution phase, before doubts about witnesses were confirmed), Richard Ashby Wilson detected in Prunier's words "relativism bordering on cynicism," filled with "grandiose generalizations about Africa and beyond," also suggesting that Prunier was pontificating under pressure from the Defense. But it was also possible that the hyperbolic doubt behind Prunier's testimony was meant to challenge the narrow construction of events contained in the Prosecution's master narrative. In the moment, Wilson focused on tensions between Prunier and Defense counsel, although the greater challenge of his remarks went against the Prosecution that had brought him into the courtroom. See *Writing History in International Criminal Trials* (Cambridge: Cambridge University Press, 2011), pp. 199–209. Prunier is among the most respected scholarly authorities on conflicts in the eastern Congo and Great Lakes area.

sorts of flaws and red flags that might otherwise lead to a state of reasonable doubt.

It found confirming evidence in testimony from a group of Prosecution witnesses (and a few Defense witnesses) with sketchy pasts: defectors from Lubanga's circle (referred to by code numbers: 0012, 0055), people who were not physically present in Ituri during critical periods (0014), witnesses brokered by the impugned intermediaries (0030, 0038), witnesses who had become close to the Congolese government (0016). The Trial Chamber exercised its signature "caution" and "particular care" to parse each witness's contribution, rejecting some parts as not reliable; while not ruling out other parts. The Appeals Chamber found the Trial Chamber's judgments on this testimony as "not unreasonable," with but a few awkward exceptions (selected portions of 0012, 0014, 0055). For any more robust challenge to the Trial Chamber's conclusions, it was up to Lubanga to persuade the Appeals Chamber that the decision below breached a recognized rule of law.[691]

Under the Roxinian view, Lubanga's co-perpetrators were those men who held important organizational titles. They were counted as Lubanga's co-perpetrators, and their actions – particularly in recruiting child soldiers – would be treated as Lubanga's responsibility, once the existence of a common plan was inferred. But nearly all this inner circle would defect from Lubanga in the coming months, confirming the inevitable fault-lines of networked organizations. Chief Kahwa, with several others, broke away in February 2003; Jérôme Kakwavu in March 2003, and Floribert Kisembo in December 2003. All these men were ambitious for themselves and for their own sub-networks, in a period of time (after mid-2002) when the Inter-Congolese Dialogue might offer rewards for going their own way. It was not a frictionless organization through which Lubanga's own wishes would be automatically fulfilled.

Beyond Reasonable Doubt

Reaching the end of an endless trial proceeding, the Chamber could look back on a series of nearly fatal crises. In the disputes over disclosure and intermediaries, it had stood up to the Prosecution on behalf of Lubanga's fair trial rights – even to the extent of twice threatening to abort the whole proceeding. The Chamber showed its seriousness about evidence by refusing to credit any of the nine witnesses that had been introduced as central to the Prosecution's case. This trial had been called a "nightmare" by one of the Court's most

691 Lubanga Appeals Judgment, para. 175.

distinguished academic commentators.[692] But, through it all, the Chamber fulfilled its pledge (in rejecting the Defense motion on "abuse of process") to see it all the way to the end.

The verdict on Lubanga was utterly clear: he was the man in charge – whatever else was happening.

> Military leaders dealing with forces on this scale will not be involved in all aspects of the decision-making process. The evidence demonstrates that there was a hierarchy within the army and a functioning structure that would have enabled an appropriate degree of delegation, certainly as regards routine operational decisions. This conclusion does not diminish the extent to which the accused was aware of what was happening within the armed forces or his overall responsibility for, or involvement in, their activities. Instead, it is an inevitable result of his position as the overall commander. The Chamber is persuaded beyond reasonable doubt that the evidence demonstrates that Thomas Lubanga was the ultimate authority within the organization . . ..[693]
>
> The Chamber concludes beyond reasonable doubt that the accused, by virtue of his position as President and Commander-in-Chief . . . was able to shape the policies of the UPC/FPLC and to direct the activities of his alleged co-perpetrators.[694]
>
> Viewed in its entirety, the evidence demonstrates that the accused and his alleged co-perpetrators ... worked together and each of them made an essential contribution to the common plan that resulted in the enlistment, conscription and use of children under the age of 15 to participate actively in hostilities.[695]

Despite the sketchy evidence from flawed sources, the Chamber found a way to fulfill the moral ambitions of the Court's founders. But its conviction of Lubanga depended heavily on a set of stereotypes, drawn from another century and another culture, that was a poor match for Ituri. It was aided by subtle reversals of proof burdens, insulating the outcome from doubts that gave rise to reasonable alternatives. Those alternative views were part of the trial record; but instead the Trial Chamber picked out the incriminating facts.

The paradigm employed by the Lubanga Trial Chamber allowed the judges to reach agreement on conviction, overcoming the tribulations of their long journey. In the end Judge Fulford dissented from adopting wholesale the

692 Professor William Schabas, as quoted in *New York Times*. November 22, 2010, p. A12 ("For International Criminal Court, Frustrations and Missteps in Its First Trial").
693 Lubanga Trial Judgment, para. 1219.
694 Ibid., para. 1270.
695 Ibid., para. 1271.

control over the crime paradigm. Nonetheless, he endorsed most of the reductive inferences that established Lubanga's starring and decisive role in the events themselves, including the crime involving child soldiers. As later trials would show, however, it does not take much to unsettle the faith behind these paradigms, which can shift quickly into a cascade of skepticism. A slight shift back in the onus of proof allows reasonable doubts to emerge. Plausible alternative explanations might not be so easy to ignore. In the next Congo trials, the record of dissents and reversals on appeal would show the fragile status of the Lubanga Trial Chamber's judicial style.

7.5 THE SHAPE OF ARMED CONFLICT

Considering the many active players in Ituri during the years 2002–03, operating on multiple levels, there was plenty of responsibility to pass around. Outside the courtroom, the norms of attribution are broad enough to cover diverse modes and degrees of responsibility for complex events. Starting with a macro perspective – focusing on national Congolese machinations, alliance brokering by major rebel groups, and interventions by Uganda and Rwanda – it was possible to compile a long list of perpetrators, promoters, and facilitators implicated in mass atrocities, during the critical months covered by the Lubanga prosecution. These actors all intersected with local players – taken at the micro level – whose range of action depended on fragile alliances with external sponsors.[696]

Inside the courtroom, tracing responsibility calls for a different process, operating within much narrower margins. Here, the strictly legal attribution of blame is regulated by codes and procedures contained in the Rome Statute and associated Rules – starting with Articles 25(3) and 28. By restricting its prosecution targets to single individuals, even in the face of complex webs of violence, the Court must simplify the sweep of moral attribution. Its task is to reduce the moral landscape to the level of individual behavior, even though much of the trial evidence extends to organizations, leadership groups, and interactive networks.[697] To meet this challenge, judges in the Congo trials needed to impose a series of paradigms and presumptions, reducing the complexities of armed conflict down to core factors of master plans, master planners, and hierarchically structured military organizations.

[696] For background, see Filip Reyntjens, *The Great African War: Congo and Regional Geopolitics, 1996–2006* (Cambridge: Cambridge University Press, 2009); Alex Veit, *Intervention as Indirect Rule: Civil War and Statebuilding in the Democratic Republic of the Congo* (Frankfurt: Campus, 2010).

[697] See generally Jain, *Perpetrators and Accessories in International Criminal Law.*

The broader landscape of armed conflict became a factor in the Lubanga Trial Chamber's deliberations. Article 8 in the Rome Statute divides war crimes into two branches, depending on whether actions occurred in the course of an *international armed conflict* or a *non-international conflict*. For the crime involving child soldiers, the two statutory provisions are identical, except that one provision dealt with inductions into "national armed forces," the other into simply "armed forces or groups." The dry details of the distinction were the preserve of legal specialists, drawing on classic Red Cross definitions and legal precedents in the ad hoc tribunals.[698] Wading into these details, judges in the Lubanga case came up with contrasting answers, reflecting the hybrid realities. When it first brought the Lubanga case, the Prosecution described the entire conflict as *non-international*.[699] The Pre-Trial Chamber then decided to straddle the difference, carving out the time period (up to June 2003) before Uganda formally withdrew its forces from Ituri, which the Chamber regarded as an overall *international* conflict.[700] Confusingly, they allowed for a *non-international* conflict to coexist, within this time period, as a distinct conflict within a conflict.[701] In the Lubanga Trial Chamber's final Judgment, the whole time period was reclassified as a *non-international* conflict from start to finish.[702]

Behind the subtle legal analysis of this arcane debate, several aspects of the controversy merit brief attention. First, the decision to exclude network links with Uganda and Rwanda from the analysis served to reduce the complexity of

[698] The International Committee for the Red Cross, in its compendium of customary international humanitarian law, notes in a foreword that, while the written law surrounding "non-international armed conflict falls short of meeting the protection needs arising from these conflicts," current "State practice goes beyond what those same States have accepted at diplomatic conferences, since most of them agree that the essence of customary rules on the conduct of hostilities applies to all armed conflicts, international and noninternational." Foreword by ICRC President Jakob Kellenberger, in Jean-Marie Henckaerts and Louise Doswald-Beck, *Customary International Humanitarian Law Volume I: Rules* (Cambridge: Cambridge University Press, 2005), p. xvi. This convergence through custom was famously anticipated in the ICTY Tadič case, Decision on the Defence Motion for Interlocutory Appeal on Jurisdiction, IT-94-1-AR72, October 2, 1995, para. 119.

[699] See Lubanga Pre-Trial Chamber, Document Containing the Charges, August 28, 2006, ICC-01/04–01/06–356-Conf-Anx1, para. 7.

[700] Lubanga Pre-Trial Chamber, Confirmation of Charges decision, January 29, 2007, ICC-01/04–01/06–803, para. 220, based on the dominance of Uganda in Ituri affairs up until June 2003.

[701] Ibid., para. 293. In a tortured chain of reasoning, with reference to the ICTY Tadič decision, and a declaration that the fight against impunity should not be lost because of this technical distinction, the Pre-Trial Chamber concluded that the child soldiers crime itself took place within a comparatively non-international portion of the larger conflict.

[702] Lubanga Trial Judgment, para. 567.

moral attribution. Second, the basic distinction may itself be seen as a historical anomaly – to the extent that central African conflicts in 2002–03 outgrew the traditional categories of international law. And third, by recharacterizing the conflict in its Trial Judgment, the Lubanga Trial Chamber tested out its intriguing power under Regulation 55,[703] a power that would feature prominently in all the Congo trials, causing significant controversy. This section provides an overview of these three topics.

Reducing the Scope of Moral Attribution

Although the nature of armed conflict comes before the Court as a problem in legal classification, it alters the more fundamental task of mapping the moral landscape. If the Ituri conflict is ruled to be *non-international* in scope, then the search for responsible actors does not have to leave the territory of Ituri. By excluding actors and motivations based outside Ituri, it was easier for the Court to embrace the Prosecutor's theme of ethnic hatred between Hema and Lendu groups as the root cause of Ituri violence, into which child soldiers had been invidiously drawn.

The story was told differently in the early NGO reports, including HRW's *Ituri: "Covered in Blood,"* which worked from a much broader map.[704] In these accounts, the years of occupation by Uganda, along with national Congolese assistance to the RCD rebels, added substantial fuel to the fires of local conflict.[705] The particular violence against civilians may have been guided by local forces, but that did not excuse the role of outsiders in instigating, assisting, and joining with local groups in actual combat. During the period of investigations, it would have been possible for the Prosecutor to identify more suspects and to frame the whole case within a set of overlapping causes and lead players, extending far beyond Ituri.

The Lubanga Pre-Trial Chamber found it impossible to ignore these multiple layers of causation, at least during the months that Uganda military personnel remained physically based in Ituri. But the Prosecution had already restricted its case to just one Ituri-based suspect, and the Pre-Trial Chamber still confirmed that case as falling within a restrictive field: a secondary *non-international* conflict subsisting within the context of an *international* conflict. Such artificial boundaries required the Pre-Trial Chamber to presume the

[703] *Regulations of the Court.*

[704] *"Covered in Blood,"* pp. 6–8. This report was authored by Anneke van Woudenberg.

[705] This was the extended argument in HRW, *Uganda in Eastern DRC: Fueling Political and Ethnic Strife* (March 2002), a lengthy report authored by Suliman Baldo.

existence of a limited field of action, in which the search for responsible masterminds might plausibly culminate in the person of Thomas Lubanga. Later on, the Trial Chamber saw little point in accepting this "conflict-within -a-conflict" theory – and simply recharacterized the Ituri violence as a local one – for purposes of reaching a judgment about the particular accused present in the courtroom.

Current Relevance of the International/Non-international Distinction

Given the ease with which different panels of judges reached opposite conclusions, it is fair to ask whether this distinction had outlived its historical function.[706] Many commentators admired the subtle ICTY jurisprudence, which artfully blurred the distinction in favoring prosecutions.[707] But the Rome Statute nonetheless codified two distinct lists of war crimes in Article 8, reflecting a history that has been slow to extend protections to civilian victims in non-conventional types of warfare.

From the core definition of war as a conflict between two sovereign states, legal conventions since World War II have steadily expanded to include comparable protections for civilians in situations like civil wars, anti-colonial insurrections, or other forms of internal rebellion.[708] These changes can be seen in the 1949 codification the Geneva Conventions, and in later international Protocols added to these Conventions. Even these developments do not quite reach the relevant conflicts in central Africa, where a collapsed state had ceded the field of sovereignty, replaced by a mélange of parochial armed groups.[709]

The battle against impunity brought the ICC into the forefront of these developments. The campaign to reach all acts of violence – especially gender violence and victimization of young children – pushes against the inertial distinctions and limitations built into Article 8. While some war crimes (such as the one relating to child soldiers) are defined in the same words for both segments of Article 8 – others contain minor differences, reflecting the specific

[706] See Emily Crawford, "Unequal before the Law: The Case for Elimination of the Distinction between International and Non-international Armed Conflict," *Leiden Journal of International Law* 20 (2007), 441.

[707] For a comprehensive overview, see Dapo Akande, "Classification of Armed Conflicts: Relevant Legal Concepts," in Elizabeth Wilmshurst (ed.), *International Law and the Classification of Conflicts* (Oxford: Oxford University Press, 2012), chapter 3.

[708] See Hitchcock, "Human Rights and the Geneva Conventions of 1949."

[709] For a perspective on how evolving Congolese conflicts fit into prevailing categories, see Louise Arimatsu, "The Democratic Republic of the Congo 1993–2010," in Wilmshurst, *International Law and the Classification of Conflicts*, chapter 6.

legal conventions out of which they arose. Considering the mission of expanding the Court's reach over gender violence, these small verbal differences may limit the scope of prosecution, depending on how the underlying conflict is classified. A further condition lurking in Article 8 is the threshold requirement that all such conflicts must rise above the minimal level of small disturbances and transitory forms of unrest.[710]

History thus casts a shadow over legal categories that the ICC wants to apply freely to a range of new conflicts, recognizing changes in patterns of warfare. In the Lubanga case, judges managed to press Ituri events into available paradigms, thus allowing the application of war crimes law. Given this ease and flexibility of judicial interpretation, the structural distinctions in Article 8 may now seem dated.

Regulation 55

When the Lubanga Trial Chamber first took control of the litigation, after the pre-trial Confirmation of Charges, one of its first announcements was notice to the parties that it might change the characterization of the conflict – making it *non-international* from start to finish.[711] The Trial Chamber advised the parties to prepare their respective cases with both possibilities in mind, serving notice in particular to the Defense that it could not gain any traction from challenging the Pre-Trial Chamber's "conflict-within-a-conflict" approach.

Regulation 55 played a much more controversial part in this trial the following year, near the end of the Prosecution's case. This episode is described in Section 7.6, as a preview of still more expansive uses of Regulation 55 in later Congo trials. In its first application of Regulation 55, the Lubanga Trial Chamber sought to change very little by recharacterizing the legal significance of stable background facts about the Ituri conflicts. In a technical sense, it meant dropping the child-soldiers charge that applied to international armed conflicts (Article 8(2)(b)(xxvi)) and maintaining the comparable charge under Article 8(2)(e)(vii), which applied to non-international armed conflicts.[712] The Lubanga Defense remained skeptical of this change, suspecting that it would obscure the moral complexity of the Ituri conflicts,

[710] Article 8(2)(f). For discussion of this standard, see Antony Cullen, *The Concept of Non-international Armed Conflict in International Humanitarian Law* (Cambridge: Cambridge University Press, 2010), p. 187 (arguing that this threshold should be interpreted in a way that promotes "the protection of victims").

[711] Lubanga Trial Chamber, Decision on the Status of Evidence and Decisions of the Pre-Trial Chamber in Trial Proceedings, December 13, 2007, ICC-01/04–01/06–1084, para. 49.

[712] Lubanga Trial Judgment, para. 568.

obscuring the overall context in which Thomas Lubanga and his associates went about their work.[713] In its final Judgment, the Trial Chamber (by Majority) embraced the paradigm of individual responsibility wrapped up in the Prosecution's master narrative. In its determination, the child-soldiers crime was a risk entirely foreseeable as part of the master plan attributed to Lubanga and his Ituri associates. Lubanga had the presumptive power to block that consequence of the plan, had he chosen to do so.

7.6 NEW CHARGES FOR SEXUAL CRIMES? THE LIMITS OF REGULATION 55

The Lubanga Trial Chamber's second encounter with Regulation 55 blew up in its face. There had been little controversy about recharacterizing the type of armed conflict. Indeed, the circumstances of Ituri never fit neatly into one legal category or the other. Characterizing these events as a *non-international conflict* was not manifestly unreasonable, even if it denied the most obvious realities visible to observers outside the courtroom. This first episode gave no indication of how far later judges would push their discretion under Regulation 55.

The second appearance of Regulation 55 brought yet another rupture in the Lubanga case, including a suspension of the trial, pending appellate review. Months later, the Appeals Chamber halted the whole experiment.[714] These events began with a petition to the Trial Chamber from the twin teams of Legal Representatives of Victims, filed near the end of May 2009, when the Prosecution case had been sailing along (despite its problems back on the first day of testimony).[715] The Victims' petition asked the Chamber to impose more substantial criminal charges on Lubanga, in light of the Prosecution's evidence, still emerging at trial, that child soldiers had endured unconscionable levels of hardship and personal suffering. In particular, the female child soldiers had been harmed through sexual exploitation amounting to torture and inhumane treatment, also fitting the legal definition of sexual slavery. New charges were drawn from the list of war crimes (Article 8) and crimes against humanity (Article 7). The argument expressed a passion for fair and full labeling of the initial crime

[713] Lubanga Trial Chamber, Defence Closing Submissions, July 15, 2011, ICC-01/04–01/06–2773, paras. 20–26.

[714] Lubanga Appeals Chamber, Judgment on Appeal from Trial Chamber Notice under Regulation 55, December 8, 2009, ICC-01/04–01/06–2205.

[715] Lubanga Trial Chamber, Joint Application of the Legal Representatives of the Victims for the Implementation of the Procedure under Regulation 55, May 22, 2009, ICC-01/04–01/06–1891.

brought by the Prosecutor, which had mysteriously stopped short with the lone charge about child soldiers.

The Prosecutor had already faced withering criticism from NGOs for boiling down the case against Lubanga to a single count involving child soldiers.[716] What was implicit from the pre-trial hearings, and even more patent from the Prosecution's trial evidence, were the associated injuries to exploited children, especially for girl soldiers. The Rome Statute had been conservative in drafting its criminal code provisions – notably in the cumbersome division of Article 8 into two sections linked to different types of armed conflict, but also in its cautious association of Article 7 crimes against humanity with state-like organizations and policies.[717] The Lubanga trial was an opportunity to recognize deeper manifestations of violence conducted in stateless conditions – regardless of international intervention. The frameworks of Article 7 and 8 were still shedding their anachronistic links to state-sponsored violence, closer to concerns of the twentieth century than those of the twenty-first. But now it was possible for the ICC to act boldly by recognizing new offenses appearing in recent human rights treaties. Rights violations through gender violence and sexual slavery had been picked up by the drafters of the Rome Statute and woven into lists found in Articles 7 and 8.

In effect, the victims and the NGOs were daring the Trial Chamber to ramp up more charges at the midpoint of trial proceedings. Their extraordinary request won the support of two out of three judges.[718] For Judges Odio Benito and Blattmann, it was an opportunity to extend judicial power to manage the proceedings more comprehensively, even to the point of supplementing the role of the Prosecutor in amending the original charges. They looked to Regulation 55 as a source of judicial power, liberating them from the cramped scenario passed on from the Pre-Trial Chamber. They were opposed by the Prosecutor, who was likely sensitive (and not forthcoming) about the reasons why such broader charges against Lubanga had

[716] In addition to the NGO letter of August 2006, described in Section 7.3 (footnote 610), see the Open Letter from Women's Initiatives for Gender Justice to Mr. Luis Moreno-Ocampo, September 20, 2006, available at ICC-01/04–313-Anx1.

[717] On the Lubanga case, Louise Chappell reports an interview in which Moreno-Ocampo suggested that he was unsure about proving the link between crimes against humanity and the requirement that such crimes must be "pursuant to or in furtherance of a State or organizational policy." *The Politics of Gender Justice at the International Criminal Court: Legacies and Legitimacy* (Oxford: Oxford University Press, 2015), pp. 111–12.

[718] Lubanga Trial Chamber, Decision on Notification concerning Regulation 55, July 14, 2009, ICC-01/04–01/06–2049.

not been proposed from the beginning.[719] They were opposed by the Defense, which was just a few months away from launching its part of the trial, hoping for a quick checkmate of the Prosecution's main evidence on child soldiers.[720] They were opposed by Presiding Judge Fulford, who took a narrower view of what was possible for ambitious trial judges under Regulation 55.[721] And, in the end, they were opposed by the Appeals Chamber, which unanimously struck down their effort to expand the charges.

Further adventures of Regulation 55 in the second and third Congo trials will feature more details about specific applications.[722] For the Lubanga case, the overriding question was about adding new charges against an accused almost midway through the trial – which was the ambition of this radical proposal coming from the victims and their NGO allies. Under skeptical pressure from Judge Fulford and both adversarial parties to the case, the two activist judges scaled down their first projection of judicial power. It soon became clear that Regulation 55 did not preempt the Prosecutor's power to amend the charges, as provided in Article 61(9) of the Rome Statute. But it was still possible for these judges to insert new charges as less than formal *amendments*, and more as logical elaborations of the Prosecutor's original charge. In their view, the crimes of inhumane treatment and sexual slavery were fully implied in the core crime involving child soldiers – especially as the trial evidence revealed how female recruits had been subjected to sexual exploitation.[723]

The spirit of this initiative came from a profound sense that the battle against impunity would require greater empowerment of judges to advance the ideals of the Rome Statute to their farthest limits.[724] Even though the pre-trial process is meant to sort through the basic facts emerging from the Prosecutor's investigations, much of the detailed evidence in the case comes

719 Lubanga Trial Chamber, Prosecutor's Application for Leave to Appeal the Notification concerning Regulation 55, August 12, 2009, 01/04–01/06–2074.

720 Lubanga Trial Chamber, Defence Application for Leave to Appeal the Notification concerning Regulation 55, August 11, 2009, ICC-01/04–01/06–2073.

721 Lubanga Trial Chamber, Second Corrigendum to Minority Opinion on the Decision on Notification concerning Regulation 55, July 31, 2009, ICC-01/04–01/06–2069-Anx1.

722 For critical commentary, see Kevin Jon Heller, "'A Stick to Hit the Accused With': The Legal Recharacterization of Facts under Regulation 55," in Carsten Stahn (ed.), *The Law and Practice of the International Criminal Court* (Oxford: Oxford University Press, 2015), chapter 39.

723 Lubanga Trial Chamber, Clarification and Further Guidance to Parties, August 27, 2009, ICC-01/04–01/06–2093.

724 See Sienna Merope, "Recharacterizing the Lubanga Case: Regulation 55 and the Consequences for Gender Justice at the ICC," *Criminal Law Forum* 22 (2011), 311.

in only during the trial itself. Instead of treating judges as passive bystanders, while evidence is mounted by the adversarial parties, it would behoove the search for justice if judges could actively refine the Prosecution's case in real time. The Latin maxim *jura novit curia* reminds us that *the judges know the law*. They also know the evidence, and thus they know how to adapt available legal concepts to fit the evolving measure of events. If the evidence shows that the accused committed further crimes, judges should have the power to hold him responsible.

This gambit led Court observers to parse the three sections of Regulation 55. Regulation 55(1) puts restrictions on the Trial Chamber's scope *at the point of writing its final judgement*. Before that point, it allows some room for the Chamber to select new legal categories to match the facts in evidence (to "recharacterize" those facts); but these newly operative facts cannot exceed "the facts and circumstances described in the charges and any amendments to the charges." The phrase *facts and circumstances* would cause future trial chambers endless trouble, but it was plain that the pre-trial statement of underlying facts and circumstances set some legal boundaries that a Trial Chamber could not ignore. Conscious of this sense of limits, the Lubanga Majority struggled to say that its proposed changes – the addition of several criminal charges from Articles 7 and 8 – built "a procedural unity" with the pre-trial facts and circumstances, although not explicitly contained in those pre-trial sources.[725]

Sensing the weakness in this part of the argument, the Lubanga Majority took a radical position about the remaining two sections of Regulation 55. It confined the troubling boundaries set out in 55(1) as applicable only when judges waited to the very end to make changes, at the point of writing the final judgment. Before that moment, the Majority found a much greater freedom in 55(2), which listed a set of procedures to be used anytime during the course of the trial, whenever the Trial Chamber first anticipates a change of legal characterization. These second and third sections of Regulation 55 require the Trial Chamber to notify the parties and take particular care to see that the fair trial rights of the Defense are not compromised, even if it means altering the course of proceedings, allowing the recalling of witnesses, and allowing further time for Defense investigations. The Lubanga Majority seemed to think that any infringements on Defense rights could be rectified by this device of giving formal notice. Provided it all happened prior to the end of trial, *prior to the writing of the final judgment* as invoked by 55(1), then

[725] Lubanga Trial Chamber, Decision Adjourning the Evidence in the Case and consideration of Regulation 55, October 2, 2009, ICC-01/04–01/06–2143, para. 41.

the judges could ignore the boundaries set by pre-trial *facts and circumstances*.[726]

The Appeals Chamber agreed with Judge Fulford that all three sections of Regulation 55 needed to be read as a unity. The regime for protecting fair trial rights of the Defense must be found in all three sections. The pre-trial facts and circumstances are an integral part of the entire Regulation. The Defense must know the extent of the charges in advance, and may reasonably build a Defense strategy with the clear understanding that any adjustments in the charges will stay within the same factual boundaries discussed at the pre-trial stage. The limits on trial judges laid out in 55(1) apply *at any point in the proceedings*, whenever the Trial Chamber anticipates making changes under Regulation 55. Not only must it announce its intentions in a timely fashion, and not only must it grant additional scope for the Defense to do some additional preparation; but, in the final reckoning, its findings cannot change the fundamental nature of the case as it was confirmed by the Pre-Trial Chamber.[727]

The full mysteries of Regulation 55 were obviously not resolved by this controversy. Indeed, they returned in greater force in the next two Congo trials, driven by the pressure on trial judges to rescue proceedings that had taken unexpected turns. Regulation 55 seems to invite judges to be bold and creative, based on evidence they hear in the courtroom. But the same Regulation also puts limits on that creativity, allowing only marginal changes – keeping the case within boundaries set by the Pre-Trial Chamber. As it developed, the phrase *facts and circumstances* proved to be a most porous boundary.[728] The Lubanga case awakened this dynamic force, even though the eager Majority of the Trial Chamber overplayed its hand.

Not impressed by these arcane legalisms, NGO advocates pushed back. For Lubanga, these further offenses were not wholly new – they should have been on the tips of the tongues of the pre-trial judges – if only they and the Prosecutor had been paying adequate heed to the Court's mandate to attend carefully to such crimes.[729] In a new and experimental kind of prosecution, there should be more freedom and a sense of trials as a learning process led by impartial judges – not just a gladiatorial contest between adversarial parties.

The Prosecutor opposed ceding his charging authority to the Trial Chamber and had no appetite for expanding the charges in this particular

[726] Lubanga Trial Chamber, Decision on Notification concerning Regulation 55, paras. 27–32.

[727] Lubanga Appeals Chamber, Judgment on Appeal concerning Regulation 55, para. 109.

[728] See ibid., para. 97.

[729] See Niamh Hayes, "*La Lutte Continue*: Investigating and Prosecuting Sexual Violence at the ICC," pp. 809–10.

case. But he promised to raise gender issues in a prominent way at the time of sentencing, assuming Lubanga was convicted on the child-soldiers charges. When he did so at the sentencing hearing, he was soundly reproved by the Trial Chamber in the Sentencing Judgment.[730]

7.7 BUILDING A REPARATIONS REGIME

Following its arduous journey to judgment and sentencing, the Lubanga Trial Chamber faced one further mandatory task: settling the legal claims of victims. The larger role for victims in ICC proceedings had prompted intense debate over implementation, once the real trials began. Along the way, administrative wings of the Court developed new programs for identifying, protecting, and representing victims as participants in the trial process.[731] But there remained the function of adjudicating reparations under a distinct mandate.[732] Like so much else in this pioneering trial, it was left to the first Trial Chamber to propose ways to balance the tensions lurking in the Rome Statute.

The polarities of choice were daunting. The Statute stipulates some categories of individual claims: restitution, compensation, and rehabilitation.[733] But everything about this mandate required a whole new reckoning: defining the class of victims, measuring and verifying individual claims, providing notice and opportunity for adversarial contention by the Defense, not to mention the mechanics of holding and disbursing funds (if any). Since reparations were defined as a direct responsibility of persons convicted for ICC crimes, the further question was how these efforts would be funded in the aftermath of the Congo trials. While Bemba's assets may not have been completely used up for his own Defense, there was nothing to be squeezed out of Lubanga or Katanga.

Putting aside the matter of funding, the Statute includes possible roles for the TFV as a specialized body for handling individual disbursements.[734] In the Rules of Procedure and Evidence, the Trust Fund was given its own separate

[730] Lubanga Trial Chamber, Judgment on Sentencing, July 10, 2012, 01/04–01/06–2901, paras. 60, 75.

[731] Building on Article 68, the ASP has maintained a strategy document on initiatives relating to victims. See Report of the Court on Implementation of Revised Strategy for Victims, October 11, 2013, ICC-ASP/12/41. In its first years, the Registry established the Victims and Witnesses Unit, the Victims Participation and Reparations Section, and the Office of Public Counsel for Victims.

[732] Article 75.

[733] Article 75(2).

[734] Article 75(2), Article 79.

authority to provide assistance to individuals and communities in the Court's situation areas, independent of the reparations mandate.[735] This *assistance mandate* had already been the source for TFV outreach activities in places like northern Uganda and eastern Congo, before any Trial Chambers had issued verdicts. Donations to the TFV from member states meant that the assistance function of the TFV began to take hold before the Court's first criminal convictions. The TFV's programs spread to populations in need, often in cooperation with other aid groups, to the benefit of individuals and whole communities.[736] In light of this flexibility for assistance, the reparations regime came to consider dividing its payments between individuals and larger communities, given the likelihood of limited funds.

Tensions in the ICC's Responsibilities to Victims

The conflicts in Ituri created a complex environment for articulating the reparations mandate. Parameters depended on the Prosecution's original choices in framing and narrowing the conflicts for purposes of bringing individual cases to trial. The scope of a local figure like Lubanga (while still significant for victims) would be less than the scope of a national or regional figure like Museveni in Uganda. The scope of the charges against Lubanga had been limited to child soldiers, excluding possible counts of sexual crimes and other forms of violence against the Lendu populations of Ituri. The victims of crimes for which Lubanga was convicted were thus restricted to child soldiers (direct victims) and some immediate family members (indirect victims) – all of whom were likely of Hema ethnicity. The class of victims for Katanga would consist largely of Hema.

It is hard to imagine a greater gap between "victims of the case" and "victims of the situation." The NGO reports that prompted the Prosecution's focus on Ituri spoke of widespread violence and destruction, leading to population displacements, loss of life chances, plundering of natural resources, poverty, and disease.[737] Aid agencies monitoring this region of the Congo would use all these categories for their needs assessments. And it was more than just Hema

[735] *Rules of Procedure and Evidence*, Rule 98. See also *Regulations of the Trust Fund for Victims*, Regulation 47.

[736] For a summary, see TFV, *Overview of Activities* (covering both Reparations and Assistance Mandates), updated periodically on the Trust Fund website, www.trustfundforvictims.org/en/what-we-do/.

[737] See, for example, Andrea Durbach and Louise Chappell, "Leaving Behind the Age of Impunity: Victims of Gender Violence and the Promise of Reparations," *International Feminist Journal of Politics* 6 (2014), 543.

and Lendu, which (combined) constitute less than half the Ituri population. A holistic perspective would assess needs in collective terms, turning to everyday notions of equity in allocating scarce funds among groups and individuals.[738]

But this was not the regime envisioned by the ICC. Early in the Lubanga case, the Appeals Chamber narrowed the definition of victims, after Confirmation of Charges,[739] requiring a close nexus between the individual victim's harm and the particular crimes charged. The victims of the situation were thus dropped from the victim pool that would hang on (many years later) to qualify for reparations, post-conviction.[740] After the Lubanga Trial Judgment came down, the Trial Chamber sought a broader scope by targeting reparations to communities, in which affected victims would derive benefits along with others. Recognizing the need for equitable distribution on a collective basis, and soberly acknowledging that the money would not be coming directly from Lubanga, the Trial Chamber proposed to turn the entire distribution function over to the TFV.[741] The TFV would manage questions of individual eligibility and size of awards. The funds would come from TFV's resources, derived from voluntary contributions by ASP member states, and Lubanga himself would play no role in the disbursement process.[742]

It took a later Appeals Chamber well over two years of review to strike down this pragmatic approach.[743] Rather than see the whole reparations regime absorbed into the TFV's assistance mandate, the Lubanga Appeals Chamber insisted on keeping the judiciary at the center of the reparations process. The concept of reparations was different from general assistance to war-torn communities. It was instead the recognition of a juridical relationship between perpetrator and victim, mediated by the specific charges behind the conviction. The nexus with perpetrators meant that reparations

738 For this approach, emphasizing the human rights element, see Luke Moffett, "Reparations for Victims at the International Criminal Court: A New Way Forward?" *International Journal of Human Rights* 21 (2017), 1204.

739 Lubanga Appeals Chamber, Judgment on Appeal against Trial Chamber Decision on Victims' Participation, July 11, 2008, ICC-01/04–01/06–1432, paras. 58–66.

740 On the classes of potential victims and related issues in the Congo trials, see Christine Van den Wyngaert, "Victims before International Criminal Courts: Some Views and Concerns of an ICC Trial Judge," *Case Western Reserve Journal of International Law* 44 (2011), 475.

741 Lubanga Trial Chamber, Decision Establishing Principles and Procedures for Reparations, August 7, 2012, ICC-01/04–01/06–2904, para. 266.

742 See the TFV First Report on Reparations, September 1, 2011 (public redacted version at ICC-01/04–01/06–2803-Red).

743 Lubanga Appeals Chamber, Judgment on Appeals against the Decision on Principles and Procedures for Reparations, March 3, 2015, ICC-01/04–01/06–3129.

awards by trial chambers fell under the adversary process, in which the convicted perpetrator retained fairness rights to participate in – and challenge – the allocation of funds. The fact that a perpetrator might be indigent was inconvenient, but not sufficient for outsourcing the overall legal function to the Court's TFV.[744] The trial judges would not be finished with their work until they wrestled with the claims of qualified individual victims. The reparations award would need to assign a total monetary figure to the liability of Thomas Lubanga.

From the General to the Specific, and Back Again

It took seven years from the Lubanga Trial Chamber's initial reparations judgment until yet another Appeals Chamber approved the revised award. The original judges had long-since left the bench, but their successors managed to forge an approach that could allocate as much as US$10 million to programs fulfilled by the TFV. One-third of this amount is earmarked for the approximately 425 victims individually certified by the Trial Chamber; and two-thirds have been set aside for future claims from similarly affected individuals who have yet to file claims.[745] The TFV will still need to find two-thirds of this money from voluntary sources.[746]

The long delay in authorizing individual reparations is one further indication of how courts operate inside their closed legal realm. The pace of legal action remains unaffected by real-world contingencies but is dictated by the necessity of finding and following correct legal procedures. The trials themselves spent years moving at this hermetic pace; and the task of building a reparations regime could not be hurried. From the standpoint of victims' needs, the clock had started running in 2002, quickly switching to crisis mode, as acute losses turned into chronic conditions. A fourteen-year-old child soldier in 2003 would now be turning thirty, reaching an age in the depressed conditions of Ituri where life chances have already passed by. For some victims, along with the general population, there had been some aid assistance along the way, including modest

[744] For commentary, see Carsten Stahn, "Reparative Justice after the Lubanga Appeal Judgment," *Journal of International Criminal Justice* 13 (2015), 806, 812 (noting the issue of funding).

[745] Lubanga Appeals Chamber, Judgment on the Appeals against the Decision Setting the Size of Reparations, July 18, 2019, ICC-01/04–01/06–3466, para. 7.

[746] By late 2019 the TFV had identified US$3.5 million and faces the task of raising the remaining funds, in addition to serving its other priorities. See the website, www.trustfundforvictims.org/en/what-we-do/reparation-orders.

rehabilitation programs funded by the TVF.[747] Even so, the shortages spread across the population were immense, in a district where most people had been affected in serious ways by armed conflicts. Just as the Congo prosecutions had yet to register any impact on deterring future conflicts, so the reparations function of the Court had made virtually no difference in the lives of victims.

From the standpoint of justice and legality, the Court's embrace of victim participation had sent signals of hope beyond just the Congo cases that went to trial. The unprecedented embrace of victims was meant to provide a beacon for victims everywhere, even though the first trials would understandably deal with only a small fraction of the affected population. Of course, it was tempting to interpret the Court's embrace of victims as aiding the self-justification of the Court's own existence, where the appeal to *victims' justice* would drown out any protest against *victors' justice*. But that calculation all happened on the front-end of the planning process. The ICC's moral capital would have started to accrue with the festivities at Rome; while the realities confronting victims would not be assessed until years later (some twenty years later when it came to the Lubanga trial), and likely for decades to come.

The victims in question were the "victims of the case" as clarified in the first of several Appeals Chamber decisions narrowing the Lubanga pool.[748] Their nexus to the Court was through the specific charges made against Lubanga at trial – where wider charges would have qualified a greater number of victims than the specific charges concerning child soldiers. In the words of one influential commentary, these limited numbers were "juridified" victims, their common link being the juridical concept of specific charges confirmed at the pre-trial stage.[749] The process for juridifying victims was driven not by victims' own needs but rather by the contours of crime definitions. The purpose of insisting on such legal links, as Carsten Stahn has indicated, is "expressivist" in nature: reparations complement the Court's punitive function by attaching a cost figure to the crimes for which a convicted person is found responsible.[750] To the

747 The TFV assistance programs for the Congo ran from 2008 to 2017, covering demonstration projects in Ituri and the Kivu Provinces, reaching some 230,000 beneficiaries. See TFV, *Overview of Activities*.

748 Lubanga Appeals Chamber, Judgment on Victims' Participation, July 11, 2008, paras. 58–66.

749 Sara Kendall and Sarah Nouwen, "Representational Practices at the International Criminal Court: The Gap between Juridified and Abstract Victimhood," *Law and Contemporary Problems* 76 (2014), 235.

750 Stahn, "Reparative Justice," p. 806.

extent that such assessments impose real burdens on the convicted person (someone well-funded, perhaps through a state entity), these payments may perform an additional deterrence role. It seems to have been this symbolic tie to long-term impact and legacy that drove the 2015 Lubanga Appeals Judgment to insist on a tight juridical link between the crime and an eligible victim. Lubanga played a part in this tableau, represented by lawyers who challenged the specific assessment levied against their client, as well as the specific qualifications of victims themselves under judicial criteria.

Just as decisively, however, the Trial Chamber's revised implementation decision beat a hasty retreat in the direction of generalized terms. Under adversarial pressure, the criteria for reparations started to blur. Was the victim's misfortune specifically caused by Lubanga, or is the relation between injury and crime more diffuse? And what about the presumption of innocence and burden of proof? And what about all those long inference chains that connected Lubanga himself to crimes through the fraught modes of liability? A victim's injury may in fact have been the result of multiple causes, traceable to diverse sources beyond Lubanga. Two-thirds of the victims covered in the final implementation order have yet to be identified – if they even come forward.

Under pressure from such arguments, the sharp focus on specific crimes has evolved into a much softer focus on more general concepts. The causation link is less exacting than in the criminal phase of the trial; the proof standards are reduced; the specifics of responsibility are drawn further into the shadows of liability.[751] Under these conditions, Lubanga and his team might lose interest in pursuing the details of reparations. It will be left to present and future trial chambers (with a changing composition of judges) to divide the labor of formal approval with the TFV's resourcefulness in assessing present victims and recruiting future ones. Compared to the Lubanga trial itself, where all nine would-be child witnesses were held to be unreliable, the practical system for vetting and calibrating victim awards will experience far less adversarial scrutiny.

[751] On the softening of trial doctrines, see Stahn, "Reparative Justice," p. 808. The Katanga reparations order determined that it would apply a proportional level of responsibility for reparations, reducing Katanga's share of the total $3.7 million assessment to US$1 million. Katanga Trial Chamber, Order for Reparations Pursuant to Article 75, March 24, 2017, ICC-01/04–01/07–3728, para. 264. Soon afterwards the TFV signaled its ability to meet that US$1 million liability, based on its authority to "complement" payment of individual and collective reparations for indigent convicted parties. See Notification of TFV Decision to Complement Payment, May 17, 2017, ICC-01/04–01/07–3740.

By the time the Lubanga reparations order crossed its final appeals hurdle in 2019, the ICC had already completed its third Congo trial. There had been just one other surviving Congo conviction, Germain Katanga, as well as a guilty plea in the case of destruction of monuments in Timbuktu.[752] But in the trials themselves, there were stark disagreements among judges about such trial concepts as the required specificity of charges, the weighing of factual evidence, and the treatment of proof burdens. In 2018, when the Bemba Appeals Chamber cleared Bemba of all his convictions, setting him free, the reasons had to do with the overgeneralized formulation of his crimes. As the metaphors in that case would suggest, it was the old problem of confusing the forest and the trees; and the Appeals Chamber interpreted the crimes in accordance with specific criminal acts, rather than broad criminal categories. Insisting on greater levels of specificity, two judges in the Majority of that Appeals Judgment cited the need to clarify the scope of future reparations awards.[753]

The same two judges spoke separately to the disappointment of more than 5,000 victims who had already been qualified in the Bemba case, which was the only Congo trial where the accused might have had some assets left over by the end of his criminal appeals. The fact that Bemba victims would receive no reparations was regrettable, but it could have no impact on the pure judicial function of upholding principles of legality on appeal. The logic of "expressivism" works in counter-intuitive ways; and it was not to be confused with empathy or moral obligations.[754] In the end, what was left for those victims was the TFV assistance mandate, joined with the ongoing efforts of other international aid groups.

752 For updates on these few awards, see TFV, *Overview of Activities*. In July 2019, Bosco Ntaganda was found guilty by the Trial Chamber and awaits an appeal sometime in 2020.

753 Bemba Appeals Judgment, Separate Opinion of Judges Van den Wyngaert and Morrison, June 8, 2018, ICC-01/05–01/08–3636-Anx2, para. 29.

754 Ibid., para. 77.

Germain Katanga receives his twelve-year sentence on May 23, 2014. ©ICC-CPI

Mathieu Ngudjolo hears that his acquittal was confirmed on appeal, February 27, 2015. ©ICC-CPI

8

The Trial of Germain Katanga and Mathieu Ngudjolo

8.1 COLLAPSE OF THE MASTER NARRATIVE

Surprises in The Hague

The opening of the second trial at the International Criminal Court – November 24, 2009 – was greeted by Presiding Judge Bruno Cotte as "a very important date for this Court and beyond that for international criminal justice."[755] One of the Victims' Representatives went even farther: it was "a high point in the story of this Court and the history of the world."[756] Some three years later, the trial took an utterly unexpected turn. In late 2012 (more than a year after hearing closing arguments), the Trial Chamber severed the two cases, acquitted Mathieu Ngudjolo,[757] and served notice that it would keep working on the case of Germain Katanga – likely judging him by a softer mode of individual responsibility, different from what had been confirmed by the Pre-Trial Chamber.[758] After still another fifteen months, in March 2014, two members of the Trial Chamber found Katanga guilty, holding him responsible (under that other mode) for some of the crimes originally charged – but not all.[759]

The original case had clearly collapsed. It was salvaged by the Trial Chamber itself, exercising managerial control and probing the outer limits of fair trial rights. The story of the second Congo trial covers two distinct phases: a conventional adversarial trial, held under the terms prescribed by the

[755] Katanga and Ngudjolo Trial Chamber, opening statements, November 24, 2009, ICC-01/04–01/07-T-80-FRA, p. 6.

[756] Ibid., p. 42 (following what the English interpreter heard) (ENG p. 39).

[757] Ngudjolo Trial Judgment, December 18, 2012, ICC-01/04–02/12–3.

[758] Katanga and Ngudjolo Trial Chamber, Decision on the Implementation of Regulation 55 and Severing the Charges, November 21, 2012, ICC-01/04–01/07–3319.

[759] Katanga Trial Judgment, March 7, 2014, ICC-01/04–01/07–3436.

Pre-Trial Chamber's Confirmation of Charges decision; followed by a second, more free-wheeling phase, driven by a split judicial bench. The toned-down conviction carried a sentence of twelve years. Recognizing that Katanga would soon become eligible for early release, his Defense team decided not to challenge this whole uncharted process, on appeal. The Prosecution likewise demurred, perhaps realizing that the Trial Chamber had rescued an otherwise lost cause.

Following his acquittal and sudden release, Mathieu Ngudjolo pondered his next steps. Upon arriving at the bustling Dutch airport for the flight back home, he declared his intention to apply for asylum, aiming to resettle in Belgium. Now under detention by Dutch police, he waited while the Dutch government twice rejected his application. In May 2015, he was returned to the Congo, where he may have melted into the national army. The Court granted Germain Katanga early release for January 2016; but he remained incarcerated in the Congo, where he had asked to serve out the final months of his ICC sentence – facing a multitude of domestic charges related to his days in Ituri. In April 2016, the ICC Presidency gave its consent for these local charges to proceed.[760] His sudden release (along with Lubanga) in mid-March 2020 came as a surprise, reportedly the result of peace discussions in Ituri.

Narrowing the Case

As the Prosecutor pondered his first country-wide *situations*, and then suddenly gained access to a few Congolese suspects from Ituri, he wanted to cut through the dark complexity of unconventional armed conflicts. To launch his battle against impunity for mass crimes, he constructed cases against three figures offered up by Kinshasa. With the help of industrious NGO contacts on the ground, his case narratives rose up to match the moral ambitions of the new ICC. Lubanga, Katanga, and Ngudjolo were all seen as leaders – indeed as "supreme commanders," even if the forces reporting to them remained ill-defined, and the pressures under which they operated seemed too obscure to calculate.

In a conspicuous display of neutral balancing, the Prosecution drew his three suspects from opposing camps in a supposed binary struggle, defined by ethnic conflict between Hema and Lendu. His search for accountability in

[760] ICC Presidency, Decision Pursuant to Article 108(1), April 7, 2016, ICC-01/04–01/07–3821-Red. Amid further concerns about Congolese due process, lack of legal aid, and whether the government would honor its pledge not to seek the death penalty, the Presidency affirmed its decision in 2019. Decision on Defence Application for Reconsideration, June 26, 2019, ICC-01/04–01/07–3833.

Ituri was restricted to single individuals, following the historical trajectory of international law. But they must also be leaders in tightly run organizations, operating under imposing acronyms. The Prosecution's narrative about all three individuals placed them at the epicenter of events, pulling the strings, orchestrating the criminal deeds that befell legions of victims. In theory, victims on both sides of the struggle would have their voices heard within the courtroom.

To streamline the legal proceedings, supreme commander Lubanga was charged with just a single offense involving child soldiers. On the opposing side of the conflict, supreme commanders Katanga and Ngudjolo would be charged jointly with offenses occurring on a single day – February 24, 2003 – in a civilian attack that fit the legal definitions of killing, pillaging, rape, sexual slavery, and other offenses. Simplifying the charges (Lubanga) and the number of attacks (Katanga and Ngudjolo) would shorten the process, giving the ICC a chance to find its footing.

On the first day of the trial, Prosecutor Moreno-Ocampo and Deputy Prosecutor Bensouda delivered ceremonial remarks on the importance of a guilty verdict for advancing the ambitions of the Court. It was left to Senior Trial Attorney Eric MacDonald, a proudly bilingual Canadian, to articulate the case. Katanga became the supreme commander for the Lendu militia from the southern part of Ituri (the FRPI), while Ngudjolo played the same role for the northern Lendu militia (the FNI). These acronyms were believed to put the Lendu military campaign on an organizational par with Lubanga's Hema-dominated UPC.[761] But just as the history and leadership of the UPC became a matter of controversy in the Lubanga trial, even greater doubts arose about these organizations cited by MacDonald.

These two commanders had formed a common plan "to wipe out" the village of Bogoro, which was the site of a UPC military camp, as well as home to civilians. The attack was planned and executed between the two militias – and them alone. MacDonald described the FRPI as cropping up sometime in "late fall" 2002, possibly November. The FNI seemed to originate sometime in early 2003. Already, one wonders how organizations with such slim track records could have produced a master plan to bring off the February 24 attack. MacDonald had witnesses prepared to confirm these stories. And the important HRW publication *"Covered in Blood"* had established the solidity of the acronyms.[762]

[761] Katanga and Ngudjolo Trial Chamber, Prosecution opening statement, pp. 34–36.

[762] HRW, *Ituri: "Covered in Blood": Ethnically Targeted Violence in Northeastern DR Congo* (July 2003), p. 17. The report was written by Anneke van Woudenberg.

Missing from MacDonald's narrative was any reference to links with larger armed networks, such as Mbusa Nyamwisi's RCD-ML rebel group. Although Nyamwisi and his front-man Governor Lompondo had been chased out of Bunia in August 2002, his Nande network was powerfully settled across the provincial border in the North Kivu town of Beni. His alliances with Lendu self-defense groups continued to deepen, and his strategy was now aligned with Kinshasa national forces, Mai-Mai irregulars, and other random groups. Also absent from the Prosecution's master narrative was the continuing role of Uganda and Rwanda as powerbrokers inside a volatile Ituri.

These omissions were pointed out in opening statements by lead counsel for both Katanga and Ngudjolo.[763] Katanga's counsel David Hooper tried to keep his remarks short and simple, since it was the Prosecutor's version of events that would be tested at trial. But even that first day, the whole master narrative was perched on a dangerously narrow base of assumptions about the structure of Ituri violence. Rounding off all the rough edges made for an appealing narrative, but it provided little support as pieces began to fall away.

The Prosecution's master narrative followed a template crafted by international NGOs, who swept into Bunia in March 2003, looking to make sense of the violence from preceding months. With an emphasis on tightly organized, hierarchical military organizations, led by supreme commanders, this template was perfectly designed to match up with legal theories of responsibility, particularly the *control over the crime* theory of liability. Such massive atrocities could have happened only through powerful, highly disciplined military units, guided through careful planning from the top.

The Prosecution template contrasts with more nuanced field reports by Africanist experts, like those cited in earlier chapters of this book. The political-military networks in eastern Congo were in fact precarious, struggling to survive in a crowded field among national interlopers and regional freebooters. In particular, the Lendu village self-defense groups were lightly commanded and loosely connected.[764]

For some experts on social violence, the narrow NGO focus became a target of ridicule. Among the critics was political economist David Keen, of the London School of Economics. Writing in 2000, his comments anticipated the cramped vision that would dominate the Congo prosecutions in the new ICC:

[763] Katanga and Ngudjolo Trial Chamber, Defense opening statements, p. 53 (ENG p. 49).

[764] See Koen Vlassenroot and Timothy Raeymaekers, "The Politics of Rebellion and Intervention in Ituri: The Emergence of a New Political Complex?" *African Affairs* 103 (2004), 385; Henning Tamm, *FNI and FRPI: Local Resistance and Regional Alliances* (London: Rift Valley Institute, 2013). Other sources are discussed in Chapters 3 and 4.

> The idea of a war between 'sides' (usually two, often 'ethnic') is easy to grasp; it helps to make complex events digestible and (apparently) comprehensible .... Much contemporary coverage of violent conflict ... follows [a] 'sporting' model. Who is it between? Who is going to win? What are the tactics? And who (if we are delving really deeply into the matter) are the goodies and baddies? Again, we may be left with little idea of the complex issues behind the conflict. For those who do wish to know what is at stake in a conflict, the parade of warring initials is likely to leave them frustrated. For those who might wish to ask about the (diverse) reasons why (diverse groups of) people are orchestrating, funding and carrying out acts of violence, the perfunctory reference to a conflict's 'underlying causes' may be similarly unenlightening.[765]

As the trial wore on, the Prosecution's grip on its grand narrative would falter. In October 2011, in the final days of testimony, when Prosecutor MacDonald opened his cross-examination of Germain Katanga, his first (and unsuccessful) goal was to force Katanga to describe the conflict in Ituri as a binary battle between the Hema UPC and the unified Lendu militias. But Katanga, holding his own in a high-pressure exchange, explained that the UPC did not attack Lendu groups until the latter joined forces with the remnants of Mbusa Nyamwisi's RCD armed troops – the UPC's primary foe. It was a larger conflict, he explained, with multiple angles and interests.[766]

Chasing Down Facts from Ituri

The ICC investigating team found witnesses who would corroborate their preferred story. One such witness, said to be an abducted child soldier forced into militia service, described close contacts between supreme commanders Katanga and Ngudjolo, leading up to the Bogoro attack. There were even some poetic touches: immediately following that attack, the two sat together "under the mango trees" in the center of a devasted Bogoro, celebrating their victory.[767] Later investigations by the Defense questioned whether this witness was in fact a militia member, noting that he had misrepresented his age and was in no position to observe relevant

765 "War and Peace: What's the Difference?" *International Peacekeeping* 7 (2000), 1.

766 Katanga and Ngudjolo Trial Chamber, testimony of Germain Katanga, October 11, 2011, ICC-01/04–01/07-T-320-FRA, pp. 19–26 (ENG pp. 18–25). Judge Cotte had to intervene twice, urging Prosecutor MacDonald to tone down the aggression (pp. 22, 26). Later references will cite "Katanga Testimony" with the appropriate date, document registration number, and page citation to the French and English transcripts.

767 Katanga and Ngudjolo Trial Chamber, testimony of witness P-250, February 1, 2010, ICC-01/04–01/07-T-94-Red2-ENG, p. 51.

events. His school records showed that he was enrolled during this time at some distance from the battle.[768]

Despite some local investigations in Ituri, the Prosecutor's evidence about master planning between two supreme commanders was surprisingly thin. This was the central premise of the entire narrative, but it came down to just six Prosecution witnesses, including three presumed child soldiers abducted into the militias heading for Bogoro. In an eerie reprise of testimonial troubles in the Lubanga case, all three child witnesses (including the one who remembered the mango trees) were evasive or untruthful about their ages, as well as about other material matters. The Trial Chamber could not rely on their testimony.[769] Two more adult witnesses were also deemed unreliable by the Trial Chamber,[770] leaving only a single witness, a Westerner connected with MONUC, who observed both accused in Bunia, but only after the Bogoro attack.

As in the Lubanga case, the Defense conducted its own investigations into the backgrounds of key witnesses, looking for school records and speaking with family members and villagers. Two of the child witnesses may have colluded, possibly through one of the Intermediaries exposed in the Lubanga trial – Intermediary 143, whose identity became the main point of contention in the second shutdown of the Lubanga trial in June 2010.[771]

At the end of the trial, after a series of Defense witnesses had undermined the Prosecution's core narrative, the Chamber was forced to apply its "cautious approach" to assessing witness testimony.[772] In painfully detailed discussions, case-by-case, the judges looked to salvage whatever pieces they could find. Even the witness who spoke about the mango trees, for all his inaccuracies and contradictions, presented himself with "the undeniable ring of sincerity."[773]

768 Ngudjolo Trial Judgment, paras. 157–59. For the Katanga Defense view on this witness, see Katanga and Ngudjolo Trial Chamber, Defence Closing Brief, Second Corrigendum (Katanga), June 29, 2012, ICC-01/04–01/07–3266-Corr2, paras. 95–150.

769 Ngudjolo Trial Judgment, para. 343.

770 Ibid., paras. 254, 283. In the case of witness P-28, the Trial Chamber excluded his evidence only with regard to Mathieu Ngudjolo and kept its options open for salvaging parts for its deliberations on Germain Katanga. An additional witness, P-159, who had contact with the notorious Intermediary 316 (from the Lubanga investigation) had his testimony withdrawn by the Prosecutor, based on later background investigations. See Katanga and Ngudjolo Trial Chamber, Defence Closing Brief (Katanga), paras. 21–24.

771 Concerning witnesses P-279 and P-280, see Katanga and Ngudjolo Trial Chamber, Defense Closing Brief (Katanga), paras. 25–94. In its own closing brief, the Prosecution withdrew claims that P-279 and P-280 were child soldiers. Katanga and Ngudjolo Trial Chamber, Corrigendum du mémoire final, July 3, 2012, ICC-01/04–01/07–3251-Corr-Red, paras. 781, 788.

772 Ngudjolo Trial Judgment, para. 56.

773 Ibid., para. 137.

No one was lying all the time, and some statements could either be rescued or assigned to a liminal range of facts that were not compelling but also not impossible. To be sure, there were some outer limits: another child witness, who had told an improbable story about abduction, was dismissed as "overly inaccurate and contradictory."[774] Even then, he seemed remarkably articulate in the courtroom when describing the use of exotic fetishes – a topic that intrigued the Trial Chamber.[775]

In detailed studies of fact-finding in the ad hoc tribunals, a pair of authors had documented the challenge for international judges in assessing the demeanor and credibility of witnesses from distant cultural backgrounds.[776] In the Katanga and Ngudjolo trial, in addition to judges from France and Belgium, there was also a judge from Mali, who might have provided some assistance to her European colleagues. This may explain some of the Trial Chamber's tone of confidence, for example in calling out witnesses for "surprising behavior" and "overly long silences."[777] And one more witness was caught lying outright about a phone conversation with Germain Katanga (then in ICC detention) that had been recorded by ICC authorities and contradicted the witness's declarations.[778]

A telling moment in the trial had to do with Mathieu Ngudjolo's alibi for February 24, 2003. No one disputed that Ngudjolo was a trained nurse, active in health services affecting his home district and pursuing his studies in Bunia in August 2002, when Governor Lompondo and Mbusa Nyamwisi were kicked out. At that time, he returned to his home village of Zumbe in Bedu-Ezekere *groupement*, where it becomes more difficult to trace his movements. In Court, he explained that on February 24 he was not in Bogoro – certainly not lounging under the mango trees – but rather in another village assisting with a difficult childbirth.[779] This version of events seemed to counter the main Prosecution case, which was based on testimony by five eye-witnesses that Ngudjolo was a supreme commander co-directing the "wiping out" of

774 Ibid., paras. 173, 189.

775 Ibid., para. 170. The Chamber regretted not hearing more about fetish-priests (para. 122).

776 Nancy Amoury Combs, *Fact-Finding without Facts: The Uncertain Evidentiary Foundations of International Criminal Convictions* (Cambridge: Cambridge University Press, 2010); Tim Kelsall, *Culture under Cross-Examination: International Justice and the Special Court for Sierra Leone* (Cambridge: Cambridge University Press, 2009).

777 Ngudjolo Trial Judgment, paras. 241, 183.

778 Katanga Trial Judgment, paras. 176, 179 (concerning witness P-219).

779 Ngudjolo Trial Judgment, para. 417. For Ngudjolo's own testimony on the matter, see transcript, October 28, 2011, ICC-01/04–01/07-T-328-ENG, p. 16. Later references will cite "Ngudjolo Testimony" with the appropriate date, document registration number, and page citation to the English transcripts (Ngudjolo testified in Lingala).

Bogoro. As the Prosecution's testimony was being undermined, it was offset by Defense witnesses who backed up Ngudjolo's story of being engaged at the distant hospital.

The weary Trial Chamber was not persuaded by these Defense witnesses, who were forgetful about other parts of their lives but uncannily fluent about Ngudjolo's nursing activities on February 24. At most the Chamber could assign "great circumspection" to the least suspicious Defense witness.[780] But even if one accepts Ngudjolo's alibi, it would not necessarily preclude his status as a militia commander, especially when his mode of liability was that of indirect co-perpetrator. Although the Prosecutor had not managed to prove much of anything about Ngudjolo's involvement in Bogoro, the nursing alibi would not pass as proof of innocence.[781] The Defense observed that it had no obligation to prove anything but was focused instead on raising reasonable doubts about the Prosecution's case.[782]

Under pressure of Defense revelations, the Prosecution eventually gave some ground. It conceded that the organization of Lendu militias was more complicated than what was imagined at the pre-trial stage, and it finally stopped identifying Katanga with the FRPI and Ngudjolo with the FNI. Instead, the Trial Chamber dove into the micro-geography of Ituri, identifying the relevant "militias" as coalitions of smaller village-based groups. This shift might be just enough to conserve the normative template for individual responsibility. Thus, Katanga was still the supreme commander of "the militia from Walendu-Bindi" and Ngudjolo was supreme commander of "the militia from Bedu-Ezekere." The Trial Chamber accepted this switch as something that did not exceed the *facts and circumstances* contained in the Confirmation decision of the Pre-Trial Chamber.[783] But it was a noticeable change, as FNI and FRPI suddenly faded from the record.

The Prosecution's lapses put the entire case in jeopardy, even as the Lubanga trial was similarly teetering on the edge. In its Trial Judgment, the Katanga and Ngudjolo Chamber expressed its disappointment diplomatically: "In all probability, the Prosecution would have benefited from a more thorough investigation of these issues, which would have resulted in a more

780 Ngudjolo Trial Judgment, para. 421.
781 Ibid., para. 423.
782 Katanga and Ngudjolo Trial Chamber, Conclusions finales de Mathieu Ngudjolo, deuxième corrigendum, November 8, 2012, ICC-01/04–01/07–3265-Corr2-Red, para. 945; but the brief goes on to summarize the evidence on Ngudjolo's activities during February 2003, paras. 947–55.
783 Ngudjolo Trial Judgment, para. 350. The switch in identities came only in the Prosecution Closing Brief.

nuanced interpretation of certain facts, a more accurate interpretation of some of the testimonies taken and, again, an amelioration of the criteria used by the Chamber to assess the credibility of various witnesses."[784] The investigators never visited some essential Ituri locations, staying rather in Bunia and getting local details from informants. They interviewed few of the alleged military associates of Katanga and Ngudjolo – indeed did not interview these two suspects themselves, closer to the events. They had not vetted their witnesses carefully enough, and they were overshadowed in this respect by the industry of the Defense.[785] Remarkably, the Chamber lamented the dearth of facts about Ituri culture and society, something the Chamber tried to pursue within the cramped confines of the courtroom: "In fact, much of the sociocultural framework was discussed in response to the Chamber's questions. In the Chamber's view, this material should have been discussed at the beginning of the Prosecution's presentation of its evidence so as to prompt a more informed debate from the start."[786] Where, then, did the Prosecution look for guidance when conducting its investigation? The team in Bunia inherited some of the same intermediaries who had worked on the Lubanga case.[787] The stories coming from a handful of witnesses seemed to touch all the main points of the Prosecution's case. This overlooks, however, the obligation of the Prosecution to search with equal diligence for evidence that is exculpatory, as well as incriminating.[788] Such concerns were raised in all the Defense summary statements.

Coming to Terms with Uncertainty

One remaining witness seemed to have information that tied it all together. Sonia Bakar was head of the investigations unit in the Human Rights Section of MONUC. She had arrived in Bunia in December 2002, before the onslaught of international NGOs, during the period of extended turmoil. In March 2003, after Uganda turned against the UPC and helped drive Thomas Lubanga out of Bunia, she found a procession of displaced and ambiguous figures descending on Bunia to try their chances with local UN/Kinshasa-brokered peace

784 Ibid., para. 123. For a critique of investigations in the first two Congo trials, written by a member of Katanga's Defense team, see Caroline Buisman, "Delegating Investigations: Lessons to be Learned from the *Lubanga* Judgment," *Northwestern Journal of International Human Rights* 11 (2013), 30.

785 Ngudjolo Trial Judgment, paras. 115–21.

786 Ibid., para. 123.

787 Katanga and Ngudjolo Trial Chamber, Defense Closing Brief (Katanga), paras. 460–504.

788 Article 54(1)(a).

negotiations. There were former combatants, as well as travelers from local villages with vague hopes of promoting personal ambitions and local security. The Bogoro attack had happened some weeks prior.[789]

In this environment, she encountered Mathieu Ngudjolo, from whom she heard the story retold by Prosecutor MacDonald on the opening day of the joint trial. Sonia Bakar was a witness who could not be dismissed as one more evasive combatant. If she heard Ngudjolo say, in his own words, that he had personally "organized" the attack on Bogoro, that admission gave the Prosecutor exactly what he needed. Ms. Bakar was further able to document Ngudjolo's association – in the context of Bunia peace talks in March 2003 – with the FNI. (Although something was still fishy here, because he also claimed to be leader of the FRPI, as well as the FNI/FRPI, depending on the occasion.) Katanga was seen signing documents on behalf of FRPI. These acronyms would suddenly gain attention; they served as credentials for two men (among others) seeking new roles in a new environment.

Even though the Prosecution conceded the problems in tracing these organizations back much before March 2003, the attack on Bogoro still seemed to have at least one self-confessed perpetrator.[790] The attack must have been planned; and here were the masterminds, joining forces between their home districts of Walendu-Bindi and Bedu-Ezekere. It might be difficult to say exactly who did what during the preceding six months in Ituri, but someone must have planned the February 24 attack on Bogoro. The remaining elements could then be established by inference.

The Trial Chamber agonized over Sonia Bakar's testimony. The Prosecution had brought six witnesses to establish its position on the joint role of Katanga and Ngudjolo in crafting the plan "to wipe out" Bogoro. Five of them were not reliable – so it came down to Sonia Bakar.

She was a witness to whom the bench could easily relate. "She expressed herself with authority and demonstrated much aplomb and ease during both the examination-in-chief and the Defence team's cross-examination."[791] Compared to the slippery Ituri witnesses who had difficulties recalling their true birthdates, Sonia Bakar gave the Trial Chamber information they could easily digest. They had "no reason to doubt the objectivity and sincerity of the

789 Her testimony (from early December 2011) is summarized in the Ngudjolo Trial Judgment, paras. 284–95.

790 There were additional reports from 2004 that Germain Katanga had boasted of leading the February 24, 2003 attack on Bogoro. See the Katanga Trial Judgment's discussion of witnesses P-12 and P-160, who testified in the joint trial prior to Sonia Bakar (paras. 180–97). Their testimony about Katanga will be discussed in Section 8.3.

791 Ngudjolo Trial Judgment, para. 289.

witness, who is an outsider to the conflict and lacks evidence indicating any bias whatsoever on her part against Mathieu Ngudjolo."[792] Like themselves, Ms. Bakar was not part of Ituri life and culture. At this moment, had the Chamber desired to know more about the socio-cultural framework, it would not be from her. Instead, her reports resonated with the legal categories advanced by the Prosecution. It was virtually all they had left for evidence.

The Chamber could rely on her testimony.[793] But what could they make of her report that Ngudjolo had told her he organized the Bogoro attack? They would treat it "with circumspection"; but without any further corroborating evidence, it was just not enough.[794] Ngudjolo was similarly quoted by another source (the local Congolese State Prosecutor's Office) as claiming credit for a different Lendu attack on March 6, 2003, in Bunia.[795] But why would this Congolese Prosecutor not have heard the separate Bogoro claim? And why did Ms. Bakar not pick up the claim about Bunia on March 6? These anomalies were grounds for "circumspection," and for ultimately concluding that both statements from Ngudjolo could have been a form of posturing.[796] At least, this alternative could not be ruled out.

This section of the Ngudjolo Trial Judgment tries to comprehend the chaotic events in Bunia, following the ouster of the UPC in early March, leading up to the signing of a toothless peace document on March 18. There were videos showing Ngudjolo in various military costumes; records of meetings in which he was respectfully addressed as "doctor" or "colonel"; and his signature on documents purporting to represent the FNI, FRPI, and even the FNI/FRPI. Western sources found it difficult to sort through the dynamics of such kaleidoscopic moments; one might instead have looked at social research field studies of pacification efforts on the edge of conflict.[797] Precisely here is where the Trial Chamber could have used the socio-cultural assistance it

[792] Ibid., para. 291.

[793] Ibid., para. 295.

[794] Ibid., paras. 497, 499.

[795] Ibid., paras. 455, 497. During the Lubanga Trial, the lead investigator for the Prosecution testified that the local Congolese prosecutor was being paid (and paid well) by international NGOs, not by the Congolese government. See Lavigne's oral deposition, Lubanga Trial Chamber, November 16, 2010, ICC-01/04–01/06-Rule68Deposition-Red2-FRA, p. 70.

[796] Ngudjolo Trial Judgment, para. 497 ("circumspection"), in contrast to still further testimony about Ngudjolo's role, which it would treat "with the greatest circumspection" (para. 496).

[797] A useful source is Jason Stearns, Judith Verweijen, and Maria Eriksson Baaz, *The National Army and Armed Groups in the Eastern Congo: Untangling the Gordian Knot of Insecurity* (London: Rift Valley Institute, 2013), p. 22. See also Séverine Autesserre, *The Trouble with the Congo: Local Violence and the Failure of International Peacebuilding* (Cambridge: Cambridge University Press, 2010); and Alex Veit, *Intervention as Indirect Rule: Civil War and Statebuilding in the Democratic Republic of Congo* (Frankfurt: Campus, 2010).

found missing in the entire Prosecutorial narrative. Lacking any plausible narrative frame, the Trial Chamber's description of events in Bunia during March 2003 comes across as a Gallic transcription of scenes from Gilbert & Sullivan – complete with strange hats, pompous military titles, and participants with multiple agendas playing some unknown kind of charade.

But Was the Prosecution Necessarily *Wrong?*

From a legal perspective, the Trial Chamber was precise in saying that it could not credit the original charge that Ngudjolo was individually (jointly, indirectly) responsible for the Bogoro attack. While some relevant facts could perhaps be substantiated, they allowed no secure inference to the conditions for proving guilt. The Chamber's conclusions are replete with negative assertions, even chains of negations, as found in the emphasized statements below:

> Whilst the Chamber notes that the Accused wore a military uniform from the time of his first public appearance in March 2003 . . ., it also noted that the rank of colonel was only mentioned during the signing of the 18 March 2003 Agreement to End Hostilities. Besides, the Chamber is *possessed of no other reliable evidence* previous to this date supporting a finding beyond reasonable doubt that Mathieu Ngudjolo was the commander-in-chief of the Lendu combatants from Bedu-Ezekere. Furthermore, *it cannot necessarily be entirely discounted that as a soldier operating within the prevailing political and military context of the time, Mathieu Ngudjolo was able to position himself as a key figure after the battle of Bogoro, but not before* . . . . [H]is appointment to a very senior position within the FNI/FRPI alliance *does not necessarily prove* that he was already a senior military leader prior to the appointment and, in particular, before 24 February 2003.[798]

This hedged language reveals a Trial Chamber twisting to maintain its strictly legal focus. What seems plausible from this paragraph is that Mathieu Ngudjolo's military elevation came sometime after the Bogoro attack, in the context of March 2003 peace discussions held in the capital Bunia. But the Chamber says only that this conclusion "cannot necessarily be entirely discounted," using modal logic to distance itself from positive assertions. Assuming that he was some kind of commander in mid-March, it does not prove anything *necessary* about his status in late February. These awkward formulations are a way of leaving open the possibility – somewhere in the interstices of strict "necessity" – that the original Prosecution case *was* true, or

[798] Ngudjolo Trial Judgment, para. 500 (emphasis added).

something like it was true. It just wasn't *necessarily* true based on the evidence before the Chamber.

At the outset of its Ngudjolo Trial Judgment, there was similar hedging:

> It is the Chamber's position that the fact that an allegation is not, in its view, proven beyond reasonable doubt does *not necessarily* mean that the Chamber questions the very existence of the alleged fact. It simply means that it considers that there is insufficient reliable evidence to make a finding on the veracity of the alleged fact in light of the standard of proof. Accordingly, finding an accused person not guilty does *not necessarily* mean that the Chamber considers him or her to be innocent.[799]

Why bother with these obscure formulations? In the broad statement just cited, the Chamber goes out of its way to sidestep the legal principle of *presumption of innocence*. Under that principle, innocence is the default position, unless and until the case for guilt has been made *beyond a reasonable doubt*.[800] According to this rhetorical scheme, the presumption of innocence *does necessarily* prevail in the absence of sufficient proof of guilt. The Majority judges in the Ngudjolo case were searching for other default possibilities, sowing confusion.

Picking up these themes, fourteen months later, a Minority of the Ngudjolo Appeals Chamber tried to articulate that alternative set of logical defaults.[801] Things that are not necessarily true may still *possibly* be true; and if enough of them can be assembled into a "synchronized system of evidence," they might support *reasonable* conclusions of guilt (or at least *not unreasonable*, on appeal). Section 8.5 will explore this bold attempt to deconstruct the *beyond reasonable doubt* standard, and to protest against extreme or *unreasonable* degrees of doubt. Manifestly, there are parts of the Ngudjolo Trial Judgment that gave the Appeals Chamber Minority some encouragement. "The [Trial] Chamber cannot discount the possibility that, at the time of events under consideration, [Ngudjolo] was one of the military commanders who held a senior position among the Lendu combatants from Bedu-Ezekere *groupement*, but emphasizes that it is not in a position to establish this fact beyond reasonable doubt."[802] The Trial Chamber is careful to say that it makes no *affirmative* findings of fact (or of law) in the case of Mathieu Ngudjolo – only that the Prosecution's case does not, on

799 Ibid., para. 36 (emphasis added).
800 Article 66 enshrines the presumption of innocence.
801 Ngudjolo Appeals Judgment, Joint Dissenting Opinion of Judges Trendafilova and Tarfusser, February 27, 2015, ICC-01/04–02/12–271-AnxA. This dissent will be discussed at length in Section 8.5.
802 Ngudjolo Trial Judgment, para. 501.

the whole, persuade them: "the Chamber made no findings beyond reasonable doubt, either in fact or in law, with respect to the crimes charged in this case, given that such issues have no impact on [this] judgment. This approach seems all the more justified as such findings could affect the continuation of the trial against Germain Katanga."[803] And *here* is the clue to what drove the Trial Chamber's convoluted rhetoric: the wider search for grounds on which to convict Germain Katanga. Despite the collapse of the Prosecution's case in this initially joint trial, the mere lack of evidence is not proof of innocence. The Trial Chamber seeks to open up a wide field of residual possibilities, situated between two extremes: (1) the maximal claims made by the Prosecution's master narrative, and (2) an imagined opposing state of complete, doubt-free certainty as the required measure of proof. With respect to the first extreme, as the main Prosecution witnesses faltered, there was no hope of maintaining the original narrative. But with regard to the second extreme (sometimes attributed to the Defense position), some ICC judges wondered whether the standard of proof beyond reasonable doubt is too exacting for the field of international justice – at least as used in practice. At least, if judges had the freedom to revise the original narrative, based on all the evidence available at the end of a trial, perhaps they might salvage some path to legal accountability – approaching the case with their own fresh perspective on the crimes and modes of criminal responsibility. The Trial Chamber in this second ICC trial would experiment by holding onto Germain Katanga's case, reconstructing the original charges on the basis of what it learned during the trial.

8.2 CHANGING THE LEGAL CHARACTERIZATION OF FACTS

Invoking Regulation 55

In proceeding with Germain Katanga's case, the Trial Chamber turned to this problematic section of its judicially adopted *Regulations of the Court*. Regulation 55 had already figured in the Lubanga trial, where it was successfully applied to change the characterization of armed conflict in Ituri.[804] But its broader use was rejected by the Lubanga Appeals Chamber, when two trial judges contemplated adding more crimes to the charges against Lubanga, midway through the trial.[805] All three Congo trials gave the judges open

[803] Ibid., para. 112.
[804] Lubanga Trial Judgment, March 14, 2012, ICC-01/04–01/06–2842, para. 566.
[805] Lubanga Appeals Chamber, Judgment on Appeal from Trial Chamber Notice under Regulation 55, December 8, 2009, ICC-01/04–01/06–2205.

laboratory space to explore the contours of this intriguing principle. The Katanga case may have been the most ambitious experiment of all: exposing deep fault-lines in the Rome Statute, venturing into the outer regions of legality.

The joint trial against Katanga and Ngudjolo had gone badly for the Prosecution, as the Trial Chamber judges were not fully persuaded that both men had jointly masterminded the attack aiming to "wipe out" the village of Bogoro on February 24, 2003. Nevertheless, something appalling actually happened on that day in Bogoro, even if someone else planned the deed. Were Katanga and Ngudjolo involved in some less dominating way? Any role for Ngudjolo remained obscure, based on hazy witness accounts placing him everywhere from a distant hospital maternity ward to a victory spot under the mango trees in Bogoro.[806]

For Katanga, however, there was something more immediate to hang onto. In the final days of the trial, waiving his right against self-incrimination, Katanga gave sworn testimony over the space of thirteen days. On the final two days, answering questions from the Presiding Judge, he discussed his role in "coordinating" the delicate relations among Lendu groups and allies.[807] On trial for masterminding, he spoke openly about his modest background role in local combat preparations. No one thought too much about it at the time. Prosecution and Defense filed closing briefs; the Trial Chamber retired to deliberate – a process that generally takes more than a year.

Six months later, alarm bells starting ringing as the Trial Chamber (now split into factions) alerted the parties that it was recalibrating the whole case against Katanga.[808] It would not alter the list of crimes committed against civilians in Bogoro – a mix of crimes against humanity and war crimes – but it could apply a new mode of individual responsibility linking Katanga to those crimes. The mastermind with *control over the crime* had to be abandoned; but Katanga himself had inadvertently offered the Chamber an intriguing alternative: Katanga the *coordinator*, contributing in some way to the Bogoro crimes, which were presumably planned and carried out by others. It meant lowering Katanga down the hierarchy of Article 25, reaching the bottom mode

[806] As Ngudjolo explained it on cross-examination: "Counsel, a man cannot be everywhere, except God." Ngudjolo Testimony, October 28, 2011, T-328, p. 26.

[807] For examples, see Katanga Testimony, October 18, 2011, T-324, pp. 68–70, 81 (ENG pp. 74–76, 89) and October 19, 2011, T-325, pp. 19–20 (ENG, pp. 22–23). The questioning by Judge Cotte begins on p. 59 (ENG p. 66) of T-324, with an explanation of judicial neutrality.

[808] Katanga and Ngudjolo Trial Chamber, Decision on the Implementation of Regulation 55 and Severing the Charges, November 21, 2012, ICC-01/04–01/07–3319.

not previously tested in ICC trials: Article 25(3)(d) "contributing in any other way" to the commission of crimes against humanity and war crimes.[809]

It was now quite clear what was lurking beneath all those double negatives in the clotted prose of the Trial Chamber's judgment on Ngudjolo. The main case could not be proved beyond reasonable doubt; but this did not necessarily mean that the accused was blameless on all conceivable accounts. Within this wilderness of indeterminacy, Katanga himself had shown the judges a path to resurrecting the case.

Would it be possible for a Trial Chamber to pull off such a major transformation? After a flurry of court filings, the Appeals Chamber declared that it might well be possible; at least it was *not impossible*, provided it was ultimately done in a way that protected the fair trial rights of the accused.[810] The Appeals Chamber too was playing a subtle game, not showing its hand entirely, clearing space for something creative to emerge from the Trial Chamber. In the end, Katanga was found guilty under the new mode of liability (although for a reduced number of crimes). Guilty as he was, the Trial Chamber came up with a short enough sentence that Katanga decided not to risk an appeal. Thus, the Appeals Chamber never had a chance to deliver finished judgments on whether this spectacular use of Regulation 55 met the high standard of legality.[811]

Tensions in the Rome Statute: Ending Impunity

At a minimum, Regulation 55 was meant to rescue cases that could be lost because of technical mistakes in the pre-trial phase. Most everyone would agree on this bedrock view, along with the idea that trials should be streamlined with a closer focus.[812] But the same flexible tool might have wider applications. In the words of the Lubanga Appeals Chamber, Regulation 55 reduces "the risk of

809 Ibid., para. 19. In the eventual Katanga Trial Judgment, the Majority disclaims any notion that Article 25(3) contains a hierarchy of liability modes (para. 1387), weighing into a controversy already established during the Lubanga proceedings.

810 Katanga Appeals Chamber, Judgment on Trial Chamber's Proposed Use of Regulation 55, March 27, 2013, ICC-01/04–01/07–3363, paras. 44–58. The Appeals Chamber used phrases such as "not ... obviously impermissible" (para. 57) and "not immediately apparent" that changes were impermissible (para. 56).

811 The Appeals Chamber adopted a relaxed standard of review for a Regulation 55 notice, asking only whether it was blatantly impermissible on its face, and promising a more exacting standard of review after the final trial judgment (ibid., para. 47), when it would weigh the impact on Katanga's fair trial rights.

812 Hans-Peter Kaul, "Construction Site for More Justice: The International Criminal Court after Two Years," *American Journal of International Law* 99 (2005), 370.

acquittals that are merely the result of legal qualifications confirmed in the pre-trial phase that turn out to be incorrect, in particular based on the evidence presented at trial. This would be contrary to the aim of the Statute to 'put an end to impunity.'"[813] True enough – but the appeals judges were talking about only *some* acquittals, not *all* – or else Regulation 55 would undermine the very purpose of an adversary trial. Their dominant message was that Regulation 55, while pointing in multiple directions, was nevertheless an integrated whole. The rights of the accused could not be diluted, even at the price of acquittals[814] This controversial Regulation would not cure the tension at the heart of the Rome Statute: balancing the mixed goals of ending impunity and ensuring fair trials. But it seemed to provide some precious breathing room for complex cases. Facing extreme pressures in all three Congo trials, some ICC judges hoped to manage their way out of courtroom crises through the lifeline of Regulation 55. Was this rule designed to fix only narrow, technical glitches; or might it be used to offload a sinking ship?

For victims in the Katanga and Ngudjolo trial, as for the larger NGO community, saving at least one conviction was greeted with no more than "two cheers."[815] The downgrade in liability was regrettable, as the Court missed its target of prosecuting those "most responsible" for atrocious crimes. Especially disappointing was the failure to convict Katanga for crimes of sexual violence – which were ultimately dropped from the list of original charges.[816] But yes, the Trial Chamber had avoided the ignominy of dual acquittals in just the second trial at the ICC – a trial whose opening moments had been filled with declarations of confidence in the crusade against impunity. It had taken seven grinding years to reach this tired victory.

Apart from mixed relief felt outside the courtroom, the Katanga conviction left gaping holes in the Rome Statute.[817] The founding treaty entrusted the ICC's moral mission to the impartial discipline of legal procedure, which includes the fundamental principle that the accused shall be informed promptly about the precise charges for which he or she must then prepare a defense.[818] But potentially conflicting rules were being woven into this legal

813 Lubanga Appeals Chamber, Decision on Regulation 55, para. 77.

814 Ibid., para. 88.

815 See Olivia Bueno "In Ituri, Katanga Verdict Viewed as a Limited Success," *International Justice Monitor*, March 21, 2014. On May 23, 2014, the Women's Initiatives for Gender Justice posted a note on its website objecting to the "unexpectedly lenient" twelve-year sentence.

816 See the website e-letter from the Women's Initiatives for Gender Justice, "Legal Eye on the ICC: Special Issue," May 2014.

817 Carsten Stahn, "Justice Delivered or Justice Denied? The Legacy of the Katanga Judgement," *Journal of International Criminal Justice* 12 (2014), 809.

818 Article 67(1)(a).

fabric. The *Regulations of the Court* were not an original part of the Rome Treaty. They were envisioned as a way for judges to codify specific rules surrounding their "routine functioning."[819] But in the Congo trials, those routines included a share of extraordinary surprises. To that end, Regulation 55 was the place where seismic tensions rose to the surface.

The Rome Statute creates an adversary process, but it appoints judges as something more than neutral umpires. At key moments, they are summoned to serve the interests of *truth and justice*, and to guide others toward the same ambitious goal. This is the sentiment that constrains the Prosecutor to search equally for incriminating and exculpatory evidence.[820] It empowers judges to manage evidentiary flows within the trial process.[821] It creates a space at times for judges to manage witnesses.[822] Rising out of the Rome text, *truth* is that lofty vision, which – like the moon – stands at the end of every vista.

More than anywhere else, trials at the ICC are full of surprises, spread over vast reaches of time.[823] It is clear enough why judges might want flexibility to change the parameters of the trial during the proceedings themselves. There is even the notion that judges should simply decide for themselves – at the end of robust trial proceedings, after all the evidence has been introduced and cross-examined – *which crimes* should now be charged, and through which particular mode of liability. A relevant maxim, recalled from the Lubanga trial, insists that *jura novit curia* – "the court knows the law" – and generally the court knows precisely what it needs. Let all the facts and evidence flow in, and then let the court select the most suitable legal categories.[824]

While this approach could be encouraged in some alternative legal universe, it is not what the Rome Statute provides. Put into this larger context, Regulation 55 restricts the freedom of judges to discover their own legal charges, in favor of overriding principles of balance and fairness. Defenders of Regulation 55 emphasize its enabling role in the battle against impunity. In

819 Article 52(1). For the argument that Regulation 55 exceeds this statutory mandate, see Kevin Jon Heller, "'A Stick to Hit the Accused With': The Legal Recharacterization of Facts under Regulation 55," in Carsten Stahn (ed.), *The Law and Practice of the International Criminal Court* (Oxford: Oxford University Press, 2015), pp. 982–84, taking issue with para. 67 of the Lubanga Appeals Chamber Decision on Regulation 55.

820 Article 54(1)(a).

821 Article 69(3).

822 Article 65(4); Regulation 43(a).

823 Recalling the quotation from Judge Fulford, "there are great successes and not a few problems, and the unexpected occurs almost on a daily basis . . .." "Reflections of a Trial Judge," *Criminal Law Forum* 22 (2011), p. 215.

824 For applications of this principle in civil law jurisdictions, see Carsten Stahn, "Modification of the Legal Characterization of Facts in the ICC System: A Portrayal of Regulation 55," *Criminal Law Forum* 16 (2005), 12.

the Katanga case, two members of the Trial Chamber were fully enlisted in that larger battle. But ICC trials are not like Truth Commissions. In the end, the truth-seeking functions of judges are balanced by other concerns, expressed in fundamental principles of legal process.

Facts and Narratives

During the Lubanga trial, these competing concerns were acknowledged by the Appeals Chamber, which left the precise balance undecided. That Chamber welcomed initiatives by trial judges to fill impunity gaps – if it meant curing classification mistakes made at the pre-trial stage, before the case had been fully elaborated. Some of these early "mistakes" would rise to the surface only after the evidence was scrutinized at trial; but new evidence could not transform the original basis for the case. The Lubanga trial judges could not liberate themselves from restraining *facts and circumstances*, as contained in the pre-trial documents.[825]

The Rome Statute mandates that the Trial Chamber's final decision "shall not exceed the facts and circumstances described in the charges and any amendments to the charges."[826] The identical constraint is repeated in the first subsection of Regulation 55. The rogue Majority of the Lubanga Trial Chamber had thought that they could escape this limitation by carving off subsections (2) and (3) of Regulation 55; but they were roundly corrected by the Appeals judges.[827] There would be no detours around the pre-trial *facts and circumstances*; although the Lubanga Appeals Chamber shed no further light on these basic terms: exactly *which* facts and *which* circumstances?[828]

Interpreting the phrase *facts and circumstances* remained contentious in the second and third Congo trials. In time-honored legal fashion, this battle was conducted largely through formalistic debates over legal language, writing on the blank slate of ICC caselaw. Relevant terms were located in Regulation 52, which enumerated three components of the "document containing the charges" (one of the core documents produced during the pre-trial phase).[829] These components include:

825 Lubanga Appeals Chamber, Decision on Regulation 55, para. 109.
826 Article 74(2).
827 Lubanga Trial Chamber, Decision on Notification concerning Regulation 55, July 14, 2009, ICC-01/04–01/06- 2049, para. 27. Lubanga Appeals Chamber, Decision on Regulation 55, para. 88.
828 Lubanga Appeals Chamber, Decision on Regulation 55, para. 100.
829 Article 61(3)(a).

> (b) A statement of the facts, including the time and place of the alleged crimes, which provide a sufficient legal and factual basis to bring the person or persons to trial, including relevant facts for the exercise of jurisdiction by the Court
> (c) A legal characterization of the facts to accord both with the crimes under articles 6, 7 or 8 and the precise form of participation under articles 25 and 28.[830]

The crux of Regulation 55, in formal terms, is that item (c) can be changed, but not item (b).[831] Note that item (b) is distinct from evidence produced at trial, which is what motivated the Katanga judges to fiddle with item (c). Courtroom evidence may prompt changes in legal characterization, but any changes are boxed in by pre-trial *facts and circumstances*. Some commentators have expressed approval of this formal distinction, arguing that it sets the proper balance point between useful change and preserving the rule of law.[832] Others have taken a more skeptical view.[833]

Beyond these formal distinctions, the pragmatics are quite slippery, starting with the sheer mass of background facts spread throughout multiple pre-trial documents. Facts of all kinds are stated and restated with multiple degrees of generality. For example, general references to *Ituri* as an arena for mass killing meant that events in other specific locations, beyond *Bogoro*, could arguably become relevant in various recharacterized scenarios. Actions attributed to *Lendu armed groups* could refer variously to the *FRPI*, or (later on) to *the militia from Walendu-Bindi*. These core actions might even implicate some Lendu allies: the rebel faction RCD, or the national Congolese armed forces, or the supporting rogue generals from Uganda. The bigger question was whether references to master plans and masterminds, in the pre-trial hearings, might be construed broadly enough to incorporate facts about contributory actions by lesser figures – those with lesser degrees of responsibility.[834]

830 *Regulations of the Court*, Regulation 52(b) and (c).
831 As the Lubanga Appeals Chamber put it, basing its analysis on the three parts of Regulation 52: Regulation 55 refers only "to a change in the legal characterization of the facts, but not to a change in the statement of the facts" (Decision on Regulation 55, para. 97).
832 Stahn, "Modification of the Legal Characterization of Facts," p. 12 (on the connection with Regulation 52).
833 Heller, "'A Stick to Hit the Accused With,'" p. 1006 (ICC practice encroaches on both prosecutorial independence and fair trial rights for the accused).
834 This line of argument was developed by Katanga Trial Chamber Judge Van den Wyngaert in successive dissents to her colleagues' deployment of Regulation 55. See Katanga Trial Judgment, Minority Opinion of Judge Christine Van den Wyngaert, March 7, 2014, ICC-01/04–01/07–3436-Anx1, para. 26.

The scramble to find stable, disembodied, bedrock facts in the pre-trial record was doomed. Even Regulation 52(b) describes a legal function for the purest facts. Nearly all facts in pre-trial proceedings are bound into *narratives* of some kind, where they make themselves available for legal classification. In the Congo trials, judges seeking to change the legal characterization of *facts* were really looking to change factual *narratives*, rebuilding them so that they might fit more securely into different legal categories. The hair-splitting definitions of *facts and circumstances* tend to ignore this discursive link between facts and narratives. It is always possible to find stray nouns and descriptive terms (Aveba was the home village of Germain Katanga; Lendu self-defense groups started to form in 1999). But this did not give the Trial Chamber free rein to create new narratives about anything connected to Aveba, or about any actions by the evolving Lendu militias. The shift in regarding Katanga now as a *coordinator* was a shift in the core narrative, even if the geographic and temporal frames were kept within their broad pre-trial parameters. It would also entail new narratives about alternative plans and planners.

Facts in legal proceedings are not the atomic building blocks of empiricist epistemology, the kind of bedrock realities found in classic works of realist philosophy.[835] Legal facts are dynamic and variable; they are functional – they *do* things. In ICC cases, most background facts are already *legally characterized*: through narratives, they are assigned to statutory categories, bringing the statute to bear on a particular case. Changing the legal characterization of facts goes all the way down to the core identity of facts. Looking for pure facts, independent of legal categories, is itself a highly speculative venture.

Changing the factual narrative might still fall within the spirit of Regulation 55. In the Lubanga trial, Judge Fulford acknowledged the bond between facts and narratives, and allowed that Regulation 55 permitted modest changes in narrative – provided they did not go too far. These outer limits are to be judged on a case-by-case basis, providing ample room for judges to manage the definitional ambiguities of the law through their oracular decision-making power.[836] The pragmatics of Regulation 55 submerge *facts and circumstances*

835 Even here, the philosophical problems were substantial, reaching back to Bertrand Russell's *Our Knowledge of the External World* (New York: Routledge, 2014 [originally published 1915]). The elusiveness of bedrock facts became obvious in Karl Popper's *Logik der Forschung* (1937), translated in 1954 as *The Logic of Scientific Discovery* (New York: Routledge, 2002). Since this time, fact-realism has become an ethical campaign as much as an ontological doctrine.

836 See Judge Fulford's dissent to the implementation of Regulation 55 in the Lubanga case, saying that narrative changes were the natural result of implementing Regulation 55, and

into narrative streams, reducing them to a judicially measured degree to which the surface narrative may change.

To what degree, then, did the Majority of the Katanga Trial Chamber propose a change in the prior narrative surrounding the confirmed charges? In their view, several key elements in the original story remained in the picture: there was an attack plan, and the plan was carried out by groups (or parts of groups) that overlapped with local armed groups in Katanga's home village. It was a matter of taking certain elements out of the background (the fighters who executed the attack plan) and making them central – their lethal actions suggesting, by inference, the prior existence of a plan for "wiping out Bogoro." Only now it was not Katanga's plan, but a plan presumed to have been hatched by the actual attackers, inferred after-the-fact from the events themselves.[837]

In addition, prior elements at the very center of the case (the mastermind thesis) would be tucked into the underbrush. "It is a matter of bringing to the fore (*mettre en relief*) the commission of crimes by some of the physical perpetrators identified in the Decision on the confirmation of charges . . .." The Majority would shine the spotlight on Katanga, revealing him lurking now in the background shadows. No longer the lead actor in the drama, he was admittedly a supporting player, making some kind of contribution to those militia members who had been moved to center stage in delivering the Bogoro attack.[838]

The dissenting Trial Chamber judge concluded that this maneuver "fundamentally changes the narrative of the charges."[839] In her view, the *facts and circumstances* behind the original charges are not a mere collection of names, places and events that can be enlisted or discharged at will. Instead, the charges are embedded in a relational grid, with determinate places for specific actors and their contextual roles. Everything about the attack – the master planning, the general purpose of the plans, the intent of actors at all levels, the foreseeable consequences – all these narrative aspects had been altered. Referring to the abandoned narrative of Katanga as mastermind, Judge Van den Wyngaert noted: "The Ngiti fighters of Walendu-Bindi – formerly members of the hierarchically structured FRPI – are promoted from being

whether they violated the terms of Article 74 was a question of "fact and degree." Lubanga Trial Chamber, Minority Opinion on the Decision on Regulation 55, July 17, 2009, ICC-01/04–01/06–2054, para. 19. See the discussion in Judge Van den Wyngaert's Minority Opinion in the Katanga Trial Judgment, paras. 29–31.

837 Katanga Trial Judgment, paras. 1654, 1665.

838 Ibid., para. 1476.

839 Katanga Trial Judgment, Minority Opinion, para. 26.

Germain Katanga's blindly obedient subordinates to independent and autonomous actors."[840]

Judge Van den Wyngaert takes a dramaturgical view of the *facts* behind the charges, seeing them as more than a summary list of potential actors and activities.

> Indeed, the reason why facts are included in the *facts and circumstances* is precisely because of how they are relevant to the narrative in a particular way. Taking an isolated fact and fundamentally changing the relevance by using it as part of a different narrative would therefore amount to a "change in the statement of facts . . . ."[841]

In the high stakes of the Katanga case, the debate over *facts and circumstances* was played out across a range of metaphors and declarative judgments. Back when the controversy first emerged over Regulation 55, the Appeals Chamber declined to offer guidance for how these tensions should be resolved, insisting that it would say nothing more until the Katanga Trial Judgment had been issued in final form. It attacked a strawman by rejecting the view "that a change in the narrative exceeds *per se* the facts and circumstances described in the charges." Regulation 55 is subject to limitation, but defining that limit is a situational judgment, to be made only after the case is completely done. "Whether the change of narrative is of such an extent or nature that it does, in fact, exceed the facts or circumstances is something on which the Appeals Chamber will only be able to rule if and when the Trial Chamber has changed the legal characterization in its decision under Article 74 of the Statute."[842] It is, in short, just one more fact to be "found": whether the new legal characterization has breached the boundaries of pre-trial *facts and circumstances*. And, of course, the judges themselves are empowered to declare these found-facts. Appeals Judges would then face the question of how much deference to give these complex judgments about the integrity of the legal process.

Regulation 55 and Fair Trials

Attempts to resolve the tensions within Regulation 55 proved elusive, to the extent that they relied on formal analysis of the terms *facts and circumstances*, as well as the more transactional analysis of facts as narratives. Allowing some degree of narrative change enables judges to get around qualitative or

840 Ibid., para. 31b.
841 Ibid., para. 32.
842 Katanga Appeals Chamber, Judgment on Regulation 55, para. 58.

quantitative limits bound up with the rigors of *facts and circumstances*. But Regulation 55 embodies a more fundamental limit, based on the legal principle of fair trial rights for the Defense. It imports verbatim the statutory guarantee that the accused has a meaningful opportunity to build a Defense with regard to time, resources, and strategic opportunity.[843] Necessary considerations include: additional trial delays, timely notice of charges, the opportunity to prepare a defense, and whether an altered narrative undercuts strategic options already used by the Defense. The Appeals Chamber had deferred any response to these objections, postponing judgment until after ("if and when") the Katanga Trial Chamber had issued its final decision.

In the case of Germain Katanga, the requirements for an effective defense were not only a question of time and resources. As the dissenting trial judge pointed out, Katanga had closed off his strategic Defense options when he testified on his own behalf. Speaking to the confirmed charges in the Prosecution's original narrative, Katanga managed to undercut the mastermind mode of liability. His role in local armed groups was completely different, he told the Court, providing examples of his more modest involvement. His testimony about being a *coordinator* was an effective defense under Article 25(3)(a); but it would be potentially incriminating under Article 25(3)(d) – the mode of liability that covers "assisting in any other way."[844]

It was Katanga's courtroom exchange with Judge Cotte that guided the Trial Chamber Majority's new factual narrative, based on a different standard of individual responsibility. One year after testifying, facing the prospect of recharacterization under Regulation 55, Katanga no longer had any meaningful opportunity to revise his Defense. The replacement narrative, created by the judges themselves, had been tailored to statements he made in open court.

> [T]he Defence could not possibly have foreseen how the Majority would use its own evidence, as well as that of the co-accused – which was presented to disprove the charges under Article 25(3)(a) – in order to prove the charges under Article 25(3)(d)(ii). The significance of this point can be seen from the fact that the Majority relied heavily on several Defence witnesses and exhibits ... as well as Germain Katanga's own testimony. Had the accused been given adequate notice of how the Majority planned on using this evidence against him, the Defence may well have decided to recall some of these witnesses to clarify a number of points.[845]

[843] Regulation 55(3) draws on Article 67(1)(b).

[844] The Confirmation of Charges decision had explicitly declined to consider liability modes under Article 25(3) other than 25(3)(a), Katanga and Ngudjolo Pre-Trial Chamber, October 1, 2008, ICC-01/04–01/07–717, para. 471.

[845] Katanga Trial Judgment, Minority opinion, para. 83.

The strategic impact of Regulation 55 was tied to the late timing of the notice about recharacterization. The Trial Chamber signaled its intentions some six months after all the evidence had been submitted in the joint trial. As it clung to Katanga's case through the period of deliberations, it released piecemeal information about its fresh imaginings of the case – functioning more like a prosecutor during the pre-trial phase. Adding to the mystery of their intentions, the Trial Chamber acquitted Mathieu Ngudjolo. Why not Germain Katanga?

The timing of its recharacterization drew heated controversy in the Katanga trial. Regulation 55 authorizes the procedure at "any time during the trial." It also suggests that, if required by fairness, the accused might be allowed to recall some witnesses. In this instance, the notice was delivered to the Defense one full year after the last witness had been heard inside the courtroom. It was nearly a year since the Court had made a field trip to Ituri to inspect various locations. Now, it seemed, the security conditions in those areas had worsened, leading the Defense to protest that it had no meaningful opportunity to go back and prepare a new case, with new witnesses and new evidence. Why had the Trial Chamber waited so long – and was it now too late to invoke Regulation 55?

Answering these questions meant deciding whether the phrase "anytime during the trial" includes the deliberation process following the close of evidence. The Appeals Chamber saw no violation based on timing alone in its determination to allow the case to go forward with new characterization, while reserving its powers to decide, later on, whether fair trial rules had been stretched too thin. On the question of timing, academic critiques have explored definitional arguments pro and con,[846] while common sense might straddle yes-and-no, depending on what was at stake. As Judge Van den Wyngaert indicated, moving the Regulation 55 process into the deliberation stage creates problems for the ability of the Defense to respond. Some problems are practical, such as the lack of security in Ituri. But the more important problems are strategic: how could Katanga withdraw parts of his original testimony, which was given under waiver of his right against self-incrimination?

In justifying its eccentric Regulation 55 timing, the Trial Chamber asserted that the Defense had only itself to blame for not anticipating this change, back at a time when it had an opportunity to present and shape its own evidence. As

[846] See Heller, "'A Stick to Hit the Accused With,'" pp. 992–93. In his later article on the Katanga trial judgment, Carsten Stahn takes a more critical stance to the implementation of Regulation 55, "Justice Delivered or Justice Denied?" pp. 829–32.

for the Chamber itself, there was no need to hear anything further from the Defense in order to deliberate under the new mode of liability. Yes, it was relying in great part on Katanga's own testimony, but he (and his trial team) should have anticipated just this kind of change in the basic theory of the case.[847]

There was a crisp rejoinder to this notion that the Defense should have expected some turn to Regulation 55. What should have been so terribly obvious to the Defense should have been still more obvious to the Trial Chamber itself.[848] Indeed, both timeliness and transparency from the Trial Chamber are integral to the balancing calculus built into Regulation 55. In the event, the Katanga Trial Chamber let most of a year slip by before facing up to the collapse of the trial's master narrative. At that point, the Chamber Majority's statement seemed tone-deaf in its protestations of fairness. The Majority struggled to demonstrate that its proposed changes did not exceed the *facts and circumstances* from the pre-trial phase. It stretched this argument to the extreme in altering the mode of individual responsibility. At the very least, it ignored one part of the Pre-Trial Confirmation decision that declared moot any other mode of liability besides Article 25(3)(a).[849]

By invoking Regulation 55, Judges Cotte and Diarra decided to appropriate the particular narrative volunteered by Katanga and relate it to a previously unused part of the statute – the mode of individual responsibility that covered "any other contribution" to the underlying crimes. They did so for the purpose of closing impunity gaps – avoiding a demoralizing second acquittal in a high-profile ICC trial. But the provisions in Regulation 55 are balanced between that goal and the interests of the rights of the accused; just as the Rome Statute speaks to both interests. In the eyes of many observers outside the courtroom, the search for truth and justice needed to be strengthened. The two judges in the Trial Chamber Majority had no way to know that the Appeals Chamber would never get an opportunity to second-guess the results.

This twist in the Katanga case fundamentally changed the character of the Court's role, shifting the emphasis away from fair trial rights for the accused, and launching a voyage in search of the truth, based on all the evidence introduced at trial. Moving to the opposite end of the spectrum from the reductive mastermind analysis, the Katanga Majority surveyed the whole web of causation involving many hundreds of players. It spent little effort reconciling this expansive approach with the requirement not to exceed the *facts and*

[847] Katanga Trial Judgment, para. 1531.
[848] Katanga Trial Judgment, Minority Opinion, para. 66.
[849] Katanga and Ngudjolo Pre-Trial Chamber, Confirmation of Charges decision, para. 471.

circumstances contained in the pre-trial documents. After all, those documents spoke in loose and general terms about all sorts of military activities and preparations in the Lendu areas of Ituri. While the case was originally focused on the master planners of the Bogoro attack, there were other topics lurking in the background, including the natural assumption that an attack so severe must also have had a fleet of accessories. The legal category of contributing in "any other way" to the crime was included in Article 25, waiting to be used if it best fit certain facts uncovered in the course of judging the conflict in Ituri. The Majority had new facts handed to them by the accused himself; and they duly placed them into this residual legal category.

Judge Van den Wyngaert's dissent identified the weakness in the Majority's treatment of *facts and circumstances*. This repository of pre-trial constraints would be meaningless, she argued, if creative judges could find their own meaning anywhere within the broad sweep of contextual events.[850] True, it would be going too far to convict Katanga of committing some newly discovered crime in the CAR, if the *facts and circumstances* dealt only with the conflict in Ituri. But within Ituri's many-sided conflicts, during the specified time period, one could find implied references to just about anything that happened. The only way to restore some sense of constraint to the *facts and circumstances* standard was to treat it as a specific narrative thread – the master narrative itself. If there is a change in that master narrative, then the obvious question is whether it undercuts the opportunity for the accused to prepare a Defense. If it does, then the change exceeds the *facts and circumstances* laid down in Pre-Trial proceedings.

Judge Van den Wyngaert's functional analysis of these key variables has gained considerable attention from academic commentators, even though it was just a dissenting voice in the Katanga trial.[851] The Majority's expansive practice was unstoppable in the Katanga case, but later Trial Chambers and Appeals Chambers may find some countervailing force in this dissent.

Several points of contention were left over to future cases. One point was the timing of the Trial Chamber's notice about deploying Regulation 55. Another was the role of the Trial Chamber over against the Prosecutor's authority to determine or amend the original charges. And a third point was the role of the Trial Chamber as steward of the accused fair trial rights, which was asserted

[850] Katanga Trial Judgment, Minority Opinion, para. 26, pointing out that the accused would somehow have to anticipate an infinite range of new readings in the aftermath of any Pre-Trial Confirmation Decision.

[851] Stahn, "Justice Delivered or Justice Denied?" pp. 829–32.

proudly by the Lubanga Trial Chamber in the "abuse of process" controversy. The second Congo trial punted on answering these questions.

8.3 WHY WAS KATANGA CONVICTED BUT NGUDJOLO ACQUITTED?

The Lion and the Leopard

After September 2008, after the Pre-Trial Chamber confirmed charges against Katanga and Ngudjolo, the ICC communications office prepared reference sheets on both accused, to be consumed by thousands of public visitors. Alongside the dry details about legal charges and procedural milestones, the first-time ICC visitor learned that Katanga was also called "Simba," meaning *lion*, while Ngudjolo was called "Chui," meaning *leopard*. It made immediate sense to novice global observers that warlords from darkest Africa should carry such *noms de guerre*, with connotations of exotic prowess. Even when other contextual matters were glossed over, these intriguing names were earnestly impressed upon visitors.

During the last days of their joint trial, both Katanga and Ngudjolo put aside their procedural right to silence and chose to testify at length – under oath. Their respective attorneys sought to humanize their clients before the Chamber, eliciting details about families and upbringing. Katanga was only twenty-four years old in February–March 2003 when the key events in his district took place. In hundreds of pages of testimony, he came across as highly impressionable, with a desire to please his elders in accordance with local custom. (It was at the end of this testimony, in over-eager exchanges with Judge Cotte, that Katanga unwittingly gave the Presiding Judge a legal handle for salvaging the prosecution, turning to a new theory of liability.) Katanga's usefulness in his home district was enhanced by his gift for languages. In detention in The Hague, he built on early exposure to French language in school, to the point where he offered his high-stakes testimony entirely in French, gaining the full attention of the Francophone bench.[852] While everyone gave him high marks for trying, his exuberance, his sense of his own innate potential, and his eagerness to win praise could all be seen, in retrospect, as contributing to the twisted outcome of his case.

The language that still gave him some trouble was Kingiti, which was the mother tongue among Lendu groups living in southern Ituri, known as

[852] Katanga Testimony, September 27, 2011, T-314, pp. 11, 22–23 (ENG pp. 13, 26); September 28, 2011, T-315, pp. 9–10 (ENG p. 10).

Ngiti.[853] Katanga had been raised in wider ethnic and linguistic communities, speaking both Lingala and Congolese Swahili, in addition to the schoolroom French to which he was exposed.[854] Despite hearing all these details, the judges who convicted Katanga simply stated his ethnic classification as Ngiti.[855]

According to Katanga's testimony, the Ngiti villages in the area of Ituri southwest of Bunia, known as Walendu-Bindi, were each led by groups of elders who came into frequent conflict with one another. The original Prosecution template projected a unified formal military structure stretching across these communities, naming their organization "FRPI." Later on, when the actual history of FRPI was cast into doubt, the Prosecutor loosened this rubric to become the "unified command of combatants in Walendu-Bindi."[856] Although the Katanga conviction clung to this notion, during the trial there was little direct evidence to show that any such monolithic force existed. The diverse elders spread across the district were clearly jealous of their authority, reinforced through fetishes and prophecy (to the intense interest of Judge Cotte[857]). The younger people were engaged in village self-defense units, each led by a so-called "commander," even for groupings as small as twelve. Katanga thrived within this system by bridging fraught social relations within his extended community and beyond. His wider cultural experience allowed him to reach out to larger alliances, using his Swahili to become a liaison or *coordinator* with the rebel RCD alliance in North Kivu, which in turn was actively supported by the national Congolese government.[858]

The name "Simba," it turns out, was not a nickname, but rather a given name at birth – the name of his maternal grandfather. His primary school

[853] Katanga Testimony, September 27, 2011, T-314, p. 22 (ENG p. 25).

[854] Katanga Testimony, September 28, 2011, T-315, pp. 19–21 (ENG pp. 20–22). Katanga did not claim any specific ethnicity and pointed out that he was friends with members of Thomas Lubanga's extended family. Katanga notes that in the detention facility, he and Lubanga conversed in Swahili. Katanga Testimony, September 27, 2011, T-314, p. 23 (ENG p. 27).

[855] Katanga Trial Judgment, para. 1247, citing Katanga himself as their source. But Katanga's testimony was more nuanced, noting the cultural fact that ethnicity would have been formally determined by his father, in this patriarchal society. Katanga Testimony, September 27, 2011, T-314, p. 21 (ENG p. 24). Until he actually met up with his biological father in 1998 (at age twenty), he did not know his own ethnicity (Katanga Testimony, September 28, 2011, T-315, p. 20 (ENG p.22)).

[856] Katanga and Ngudjolo Trial Chamber, Prosecution Closing Brief (Corrigendum du mémoire final, July 3, 2012), para. 304. See also Ngudjolo Trial Judgment, para. 345.

[857] Judge Cotte makes a final return to this subject near the end of his questioning of Katanga. Katanga Testimony, October 19, 2011, T-325, p. 27 (ENG p. 30).

[858] The main points in this paragraph emerged from Katanga's testimony on the first two days of questioning by his own counsel, Katanga Testimony, September 27, 2011, T-314, pp. 41–57 (ENG pp. 47–64); September 28, 2011, T-315, pp. 21–50 (ENG pp. 23–51).

records listed him as "Germain Katanga Simba."[859] While the ICC never fully sorted out these Congolese proper names (despite calling an expert on this topic to testify[860]), the communications office may have thought that "Simba" would grab the attention of visitors. As a child, Katanga was separated early from his biological parents, being raised by a revered uncle and aunt – only at the age of twenty coming to terms with his father, as armed violence drew closer to their region.[861] What comes through personally is less his leonine temperament than his strong ambition to make something of himself, in an environment where ordinary men were largely destined to remain stuck in poverty and isolation. In Katanga's early youth, the region and the world were changing; fluid power-sharing arrangements were being negotiated at the national level; and these changes were not far from his doorstep in turbulent Ituri. Eventually that ambition led him to integrate with the Congolese army, a career cut short by an arrest in 2005 for supposed involvement in the deaths of UN peacekeepers in Ituri, followed in late 2007 with a further arrest under the ICC warrant.[862]

Mathieu Ngudjolo was eight years older than Katanga and projected a more elusive persona in his trial testimony. Although geographically still close to the Ngiti (Southern Lendu) village of Aveba, where Katanga moved to in 1998 to be with his father, Ngudjolo's village of Zumbe was in the separate district of Bedu-Ezekere, extending along different linguistic and cultural dimensions associated with Northern Lendu. Like many witnesses brought to The Hague, Ngudjolo's school records assigned him the wrong age, after his father persuaded school authorities to trim off two years, as compensation for time lost when young Mathieu was held back.[863] To make something of himself in the 1990s, even as the Mobutu regime was already in tatters, Ngudjolo signed up for training with the civil police. The Prosecution would treat this experience as military training for a hardened soldier, and indeed it was true that the civil police were drawn into battle as the eastern Congo fell into anarchy in the late 1990s.[864]

Ngudjolo's fallback plan for advancing himself drew on his early schooling in public health and nursing. As the Mobutu regime collapsed and Ngudjolo

859 Katanga Testimony, September 27, 2011, T-314, p. 18 (ENG p. 21).

860 "Names and Other Social Conventions in the Democratic Republic of Congo," commissioned during the Lubanga trial by the ICC from Professor Kambayi Bwatschia (Université Pédagogique Nationale de Kinshasa), Lubanga Trial Chamber, August 3, 2009, ICC-01/04–01/06–2025-Anx1.

861 Katanga Testimony, September 27, 2011, T-314, pp. 21–30 (ENG pp. 24–34).

862 Katanga Testimony, October 10, 2011, T-319, pp. 61–65 (ENG pp. 55–58).

863 Ngudjolo Testimony, October 27, 2011, T-327, p. 25.

864 Ibid., pp. 33–34.

returned to Bedu-Ezekere, he received classroom instruction and practical training in nearby health schools. And when Governor Lompondo was chased out of Bunia in August 2002, Ngudjolo had just started a major internship at one of the Bunia hospitals. He retreated to his home village and built a small health center in nearby Kambutso, desperately hoping to continue his practical training.[865]

Ngudjolo practiced modern, Western medicine. When Judge Cotte tried to question him about fetishes and traditional Congolese healing methods, Ngudjolo cut him off abruptly, saying that he did not spend much time on superstition.[866] (This was in contrast to Katanga, who had proudly discussed his ritual scars from traditional cleansing ceremonies.[867]) While there were contested reports of Ngudjolo's participation in armed local clashes, he insisted that his role was essentially medical.[868] The only time he trained any grassroots armed groups, he said, was in teaching them first-aid.[869]

Throughout his testimony, there remained a mystery surrounding Ngudjolo's manner of finding a way in the world. In March 2003, after the key battle in Bogoro, and after the UPC was driven out of Bunia, Ngudjolo seemed to catch a bit of luck. On his trek into Bunia in early March, he testified, he met by accident the key Ugandan general who retained military authority over the town.[870] Ngudjolo showed his readiness to advance smartly within this highly fluid situation – signing documents, donning stray uniforms, inventing and accepting whatever honorifics fell upon him, always calculating his chances for joining the Congolese national army in the coming demobilization. In his blunt style of speaking, Ngudjolo freely admitted his opportunism at a moment of transition in Ituri. He was not about to miss his chance. The Prosecutor marveled that a mere nursing student could advance so quickly in this environment, accusing Ngudjolo of hiding his deeper role as a military mastermind.[871]

865 Ibid., pp. 50, 37–38.

866 Ngudjolo Testimony, November 11, 2011, T-333, p. 68.

867 Katanga Testimony, September 28, 2011, T-315, p. 32 (ENG p. 36); October 4, 2011, T-316, p. 26 (ENG p. 30).

868 Ngudjolo Testimony, October 28, 2011, T-328, p. 5. According to Ngudjolo, the armed groups in his home district of Bedu-Ezekere were all local self-defense groups (pp. 68–72) and not "militias" (November 11, 2011, T-333, p. 27). He told the Prosecutor on cross-examination that the Bedu-Ezekere self-defense groups were led by grassroots committees – not by "commanders" such as he was imagined to be. He provided details on these grassroots structures in tense exchanges with Prosecutor MacDonald (November 8, 2011, T-330, pp. 63–69).

869 Ngudjolo Testimony, October 28, 2011, T-328, pp. 37–38.

870 Ibid., pp. 30–38. The Prosecutor expressed incredulity at this coincidence.

871 Ngudjolo Testimony, November 8, 2011, T-330, p. 75.

Throughout his ICC trial, case documents gave Ngudjolo's formal name as Mathieu Ngudjolo Chui. But as he started his lengthy courtroom testimony, he explained through his counsel that the name Chui was neither a nickname nor a given name. Rather, it was a corruption of his given name Tchulo, derived from his grandfather, which appears in all his school records. During the March confusion in Bunia, the Ugandan general who sponsored Ngudjolo could not understand this Kilendu name, so gave it a Swahili twist – converting Tchulo into Chui, the common word for "leopard."[872] It is a clue to Ngudjolo's manner of advancing himself that he simply absorbed this new name, which he embraced from March 2003. Both the Lion and the Leopard were not quite the creatures they were made out to be in ICC case publicity.

"Men Who Allow Themselves to Become Nothing"

Nobel-prize-winning author V.S. Naipaul published his big Africa novel in 1979, loosely based on events in Mobutu's Zaire. His chiseled opening sentence captures the stark personal challenge for everyday people caught inside post-colonial struggles: "The world is what it is; men who are nothing, who allow themselves to become nothing, have no place in it."[873] For men of Katanga's and Ngudjolo's age, when Mobutu was pushed aside and the Congo state collapsed, it was radically unclear where opportunities might be found. The main power center had broken into rebel groups like the RCD, along with Bemba's MLC. Uganda remained the key power broker in Ituri, even after Lubanga's UPC made its discreet opening to Rwanda in late 2002. From early 2002, the drawn-out national peace talks with diverse rebel groups, under the rubric of an Inter-Congolese Dialogue, bowed to international pressure by promoting broad power-sharing in a future Congolese state. For men who were already connected to powerful factions, such as the RCD-ML's Mbusa Nyamwisi, these negotiations opened a path to personal advancement in a uniquely transitional moment.

For ambitious men lower down the chain in rural Ituri, it was no small task to find a toehold amidst sweeping changes. By February 2003, the outlines of a national power-sharing agreement had been hammered out, incorporating those rebel leaders able to "shoot their way" to the negotiating table.[874] The

[872] Ngudjolo Testimony, October 27, 2011, T-327, p. 14. Ngudjolo explained that "Tchulo" meant "many people" in Kilendu, which was Ngudjolo's first language.

[873] V.S. Naipaul, *A Bend in the River* (New York: Knopf, 1979), p. 3.

[874] See Emeric Rogier, "The Inter-Congolese Dialogue: A Critical Overview," in Mark Malan and João Gomes Porto (eds.), *Challenges of Peace Implementation: The UN Mission in the Democratic Republic of the Congo* (Pretoria: Institute for Security Studies, 2004), p. 39.

fallout from this process hit Ituri in March 2003 in a sidebar process supported by Uganda and MONUC forces, called the Ituri Pacification Commission.[875] For any man of ambition, this month meant the opportunity of a lifetime, as the constraints of war and local hierarchies were suddenly upended. It was a time for free invention of interest groups, for claiming extravagant personal titles within upstart organizations, and for competitive boasting about past military experience.

The Prosecutor's master narrative in the second ICC trial was constructed from reports gathered during this period of flux, especially by UN staff and international NGOs like Human Rights Watch (HRW). Thus, the story about FRPI and FNI as powerful Lendu militias led, respectively, by Katanga and Ngudjolo was hatched amid the postures and ambitions of men scrambling for recognition under fluid circumstances. Reasoning backwards from March 2003, certain men and their titles were presumed to be the main drivers of events during the preceding year, up to the key battle in Bogoro on February 24. Western observers brought their old paradigms about how military battles were organized, based on older European models, overlying some stereotypes about African violence.

Some local informants, eager to please (and to settle old scores), were ready to reinforce these paradigms, which fit all-so-neatly into emerging doctrines of criminal responsibility in the Rome Statute. Others were ready to point out the emptiness of these sudden organizations: "I am alluding to those who are loosely grouped under the label FNI, but who are really a bunch of independent groups under the leadership of no one." The speaker here was Thomas Lubanga, in an interview with the United Nations News Service in late summer 2003.[876]

Ngudjolo's personal moment of opportunity (according to his testimony) came less than two weeks after the Bogoro attack. In early March 2003, a chain of events saw the expulsion of Lubanga's UPC from Bunia, the return of RCD armed forces with the blessing of the national Congolese government, and the sudden union of Uganda and MONUC to provide a counterweight to possible Rwandan interference. Walking back toward Bunia ten months after abandoning his nursing internship, Ngudjolo's fate was shaped by that encounter on the road with the Ugandan general. Some

[875] The Ituri Pacification Commission was included as part of the September 6, 2002 agreement between the DRC government and Uganda, known as the Luanda Agreement. See Veit, *Intervention as Direct Rule*, pp. 119–20.

[876] *IRIN News*, "Interview with Thomas Lubanga," August 29, 2003.

two weeks later, on March 18, Ngudjolo was signing documents listing his title as Deputy Chief of Staff for Operations for the combined FRPI/FNI.[877]

It was a sham position and a nonexistent organization, and it would all collapse in a matter of weeks.[878] One might understand it simply as a bluff move for personal advancement, in a local environment that had suddenly been turned upside down. But the story of Ngudjolo's ascent to high military titles elicited a sarcastic response from Prosecutor Eric MacDonald, who taunted Ngudjolo with his remarkable turn of fortune. It was simply beyond belief, he announced:

MR MACDONALD: . . . you were only a trainee nurse. You had no military training. You had nothing – you were nothing on the 16th of March. You were nobody. And yet, and yet, you were chosen by [FNI President] Floribert Njabu because he was your friend.

MR NGUDJOLO: Mr. Prosecutor, all the members of the self-help groups in Ituri, if they became soldiers it was by improvisation almost. Nobody amongst any of these people were really soldiers. It was because of the situation that was prevailing that people became soldiers. Without the war nobody would have thought of becoming a soldier.[879]

The Trial Chamber could make no coherent sense of March 2003, when men emerged from small Ituri villages to brandish the stripes of high military rank.[880] The template rigidly maintained by the Prosecution stipulated that the Bogoro attack of February 24 had been carried out jointly by tightly organized militias commanded respectively by Katanga and Ngudjolo. But the Trial Chamber realized, by the close of testimony, that this story (especially about Katanga and Ngudjolo) could have been a retrospective construction, based on extraordinary dynamics at the

877 Ngudjolo Testimony, October 28, 2011, T-328, pp. 33–40.

878 Ibid., pp. 41–43. Ngudjolo emphasized in this testimony that the FRPI/FNI "did not function in reality." See also Ngudjolo Testimony, November 8, 2011, T-330, p. 58.

879 Ngudjolo Testimony, November 8, 2011, T-330, p. 75. Immediately after this exchange, MacDonald apologized to the Court for getting carried away in his questioning (p. 76). Earlier that day, Ngudjolo had explained the situation with his usual bluntness: "Prosecutor, you have to realize what the context was" (p. 51). And Ngudjolo explained several days later (under redirect questioning by his counsel) that he left the hollow FNI/FRPI and branched out into other improvised groups, hoping that he would find sufficient status to make it into the Congolese army (November 11, 2011, T-333, p. 81).

880 Ngudjolo said that he was given his uniform by a minister from the [former "enemy"] UPC (Ngudjolo Testimony, November 11, 2011, T-333, p. 67).

March pacification meetings. Within this massive cloud of doubt, Prosecutor MacDonald's skepticism made little impression.

In the judgment acquitting Ngudjolo, the Chamber treated these March events as indecipherable chaos, following no discernible rules of military procedure. On the surface, it seemed closer to musical comedy; while the real truth must have been deeply hidden behind all the posturing. In Ngudjolo's case, after the Chamber rejected as unreliable the local witnesses for the Prosecution, there was nothing left to say. The Chamber resisted the Prosecutor's most desperate surmise: that the improbable events of March 2003 were themselves compelling proof of Ngudjolo's prior military status. Without some credible witness testimony, Prosecutor MacDonald's sarcasm would not be enough to support a finding of guilt, beyond reasonable doubt.[881]

Both Ngudjolo and Katanga had reportedly boasted to others about their role in planning and executing the attack on Bogoro. The UN human rights worker who spoke to Ngudjolo in March or April was a reliable witness, said the Trial Chamber; but the opaque circumstances of March 2003 raised enough doubts to sideline this semblance of a full confession to the ICC crimes.[882]

The supposed confession of Germain Katanga came a year later, in February 2004, after he fell under the influence of a sketchy Congolese figure now operating as an intermediary agent of Ugandan President Museveni. There was a fresh Ugandan scheme to round up eager Congolese to rejuvenate the mysterious FRPI, in alliance with some other splinter groups (including former allies of Lubanga's UPC) who were still searching for a way forward after all the 2003 changes. Offered the post of President of the new FRPI, the young and eager Katanga was readily seduced – figuratively and literally – by the Museveni agent and his willing girlfriend, who lured Katanga into four fruitless trips to Kampala, including meetings with Museveni and his ministers, offering Katanga a quick path to upward mobility.[883] Years later, when brought to The Hague to testify for the Prosecution, this enigmatic pair recalled a 2004 dinner conversation, when Katanga larded his credentials with claims about Bogoro.[884] But the two witnesses differed between

[881] Prosecutor: "Why sign a peace agreement if you had nothing to do with the conflict?" Ngudjolo: "A community is one thing and armed forces are something else. Please do not confuse the two, Sir" (Ngudjolo Testimony, November 9, 2011, T-331, p. 42).

[882] Ngudjolo Trial Judgment, para. 42. Ngudjolo denied the whole conversation (November 9, 2011, T-331, pp. 58–64).

[883] Katanga Testimony, October 10, 2011, T-319, pp. 27–46 (ENG pp. 24–41).

[884] Ngudjolo Trial Judgment, para. 441; Katanga Trial Judgment, paras. 195–97. The Chamber was unclear on the extent to which it accepted parts of P-12's testimony concerning Katanga's

themselves on key details – and, in any case, the Trial Chamber was ready to abandon the main prosecution theory that Katanga was the Bogoro joint-mastermind.

What intrigued the Bench was Katanga's proud description of his self-created role in 2002–03, growing out of the decentralized Ngiti self-defense groups in his immediate district. In Katanga's telling, these groups were mere "combatants," which he defined as untrained village volunteers, emerging from the grassroots self-defense network spread out across local villages; they were farmers, not trained soldiers.[885]

In an environment where communications occurred through drums and whistles,[886] and without advanced weapons, Katanga described to the Court his resourcefulness in military upgrading. The main event came in November 2002, when Katanga accompanied some village elders on a trip to RCD-ML headquarters in Beni (North Kivu).[887] Their meeting took place against the backdrop of the Inter-Congolese Dialogue, in which the Congolese national government began strategic cooperation with Mbusa Nyamwisi's RCD-ML to pose a counterweight to Ugandan influence in Ituri.[888] It was also a preemptive step to block Rwandan cooperation with Lubanga's UPC, once the Ugandans might have departed.

The strategic military plan to change power alignments in Ituri came from this Beni group. In the short term, the Beni alliance wanted to use the airstrip in Katanga's village of Aveba to funnel more substantial weapons to RCD troops closer to Bunia. In the context of these larger military plans, as Katanga explained to the Court, Bogoro was a tactical military target – a known stronghold for the UPC that was blocking the main road route into Bunia. The eager young Katanga saw personal opportunity in this larger campaign, although he held no overarching military rank or control.[889]

"confession" (para. 197). Katanga rigidly denied these claims in his testimony (October 13, 2011, T-323, pp. 62–63 (ENG p. 60)).

885 Katanga Testimony, September 28, 2011, T-315, pp. 41–43 (ENG pp. 47–48). In this exchange, Katanga noted that the term "militia" had no counterpart, except to designate a group of gangsters, or a term used by fathers to quell unruly children (pp. 44–45 (ENG p. 50)).

886 The communications setup in Ituri was explored in Ngudjolo's testimony, October 28, 2011, T-328, p. 27.

887 This visit is covered in Katanga's testimony, e.g. September 28, 2011, T-315, p. 62 (ENG p. 69); October 4, 2011, T-316, pp. 12–14 (ENG pp. 14–15).

888 Katanga testified that the Ugandans in Walendu-Bindi were largely replaced by new RCD-fighters in mid-2002, who remained in conflict with Lubanga's UPC and his wavering Ugandan protectors. September 28, 2011, T-315, pp. 22–26 (ENG pp. 24–29).

889 Katanga described at length these meetings and plans, providing the Court with information that had been entirely missing from the Prosecution's narrative. October 4, 2011, T-316, pp. 25–65 (ENG pp. 28–75).

It was in Beni that Katanga first heard the initials FRPI, invoked by an older Kinshasa-based Lendu opportunist, who had invented his own organizational shell as a way of winning attention from the RCD.[890] Katanga also imbibed the military strategy that would play itself out over the next three months, including an assault on Bogoro, on the way to making a play for Bunia.[891]

In its final judgment on Katanga, the Trial Chamber Majority concluded that Katanga must have been something more than a passive bystander. Katanga did not help his case by boasting, in talking about the trip to Beni, that "I led the delegation of combatants from Aveba" to this meeting. He also said, "I was like one of the commanders from Aveba," but the first formulation left a lasting impression on Judge Cotte.[892] There were also some documents surrounding this Beni visit that listed him with the title "leader of Aveba combatants."[893] Under cross-examination from Prosecutor MacDonald, Katanga was confronted by further documents (some as early as January 2003, but most coming after March 2003) where Katanga was addressed formally by more exalted titles: Commander of the self-defense groups from Aveba, President of the Movement in Aveba, Commandant Auditeur des FRPI des Walendu-Bindi, among others. (These documents were culled from caches of materials confiscated by MONUC in the months after March 2003.) While the Prosecutor offered each example to insist that Katanga must be lying about his modest role in the larger conflict, Katanga's consistent answers held to a common theme: titles were made up on a whim to suit rough-and-ready needs. They were mere pretensions; and everyone knew it.[894]

890 Ibid., pp. 46–52 (ENG pp. 53–59). On the history of FRPI, based on testimony of Defense witnesses, see Katanga Defence Brief, Second Corrigendum, paras. 585–94.

891 Katanga Testimony, October 5, 2011, T-317, pp. 4–20 (ENG pp. 5–22).

892 Katanga Testimony, October 4, 2011, T-316, p. 58 (ENG p. 66). See also October 13, 2011, T-322, p. 19 (ENG p. 18). Katanga suggested a smaller number of combatants on this mission, in contrast to the "over 60 combatants" accepted by the Trial Chamber Majority (Katanga Trial Judgment, para. 581).

893 Katanga Testimony, October 5, 2011, T-317, pp. 20–23 (ENG pp. 22–25); October 11, 2011, T-320, pp. 3–4 (ENG pp. 3–4).

894 Katanga Testimony, October 14, 2011, T-323, p. 35 (ENG p. 36). About the earlier use of titles prior to March 2003, Katanga responded: "People were just creating names for themselves, giving free rein to their imagination. It was fantasizing they were strongmen . . ." (October 5, 2011, T-317, pp. 23–24 (ENG p. 27)). Also: "People gave themselves any name they wanted" (October 19, 2011, T-325, p. 47 (ENG p. 54)). At the Bunia signings on March 18, 2003, Katanga said that he had not even read the document, but he had signed it because he respected two other signers from his district who were "intellectuals" (October 14, 2011, T-323, pp. 2–4 (ENG pp. 2–4)). In the same exchange, he reported being paralyzed by the attention of video cameras – having previously never been caught on camera (p. 4 (ENG p. 5)).

The ultimate surprise came later in 2005, when Germain Katanga was finally inducted into the national Congolese army at the rank of Brigadier-General – the youngest man to be given that title. This last title carried real benefits: it meant that Katanga had truly made something of himself. But it was also to be understood as situational and opportunistic. And it lasted only a few months before Katanga faced domestic arrest.[895]

Questions from the Bench: Katanga the Coordinator

In his lengthy courtroom testimony, Katanga offered up to the Trial Chamber the self-awarded title of *coordinator*, following the November 2002 trip to Beni. The word had no standard military meaning and was subject to multiple interpretations. Describing these functions in his own words, he was a conflict manager, someone who promoted harmonious relations between the Beni military force and the tension-filled local self-defense groups. Months of conflict within these Congolese districts brought out rivalries at all levels – something Katanga prided himself in managing. His eagerness to describe his accomplishments produced a decisive turn in his trial.[896]

Germain Katanga was barely twenty-four years old as armed conflicts closed in on his newly adopted village of Aveba, in the Southern Lendu (Ngiti) area of Irumu district, ten kilometers outside Bunia. How did it happen that such a young man, recently arrived, came to be trusted by the wise men of his village, then by other elders in the same district, and finally by the expansive alliance of political-military groups based in Beni, across the provincial border in North Kivu?

This was a radically different question from the one framed for Katanga by the Pre-Trial Chamber, and advanced at trial by Prosecutor Eric MacDonald. But it emerged fully during the thirteen days in which Katanga was questioned by his own counsel, by two Legal Representatives of Victims, and by MacDonald on cross-examination. On the final day, Judge Cotte unleashed a series of questions from the bench, testing a line of inquiry that would salvage a conviction based on reworked theories of liability.

The questions from Judge Cotte differed in tone and direction from the overheated cross-examination by Prosecutor MacDonald, who was playing a weak hand as his overall case lost credibility. Most striking is the genial tone

[895] Katanga Testimony, October 10, 2011, T-319, pp. 57–64 (ENG pp. 50–58).

[896] Judge Cotte suggested that his self-described role as a mediator was perhaps overly modest, and that, for someone without formal authority, he always seemed to play above his weight (October 18, 2011, T-324, p. 61 (ENG p. 67)); and later that day: "... you were a young man, and they respected you even though you were a young man?" (pp. 69–70 (ENG p. 76)).

and almost conversational interchange between two French speakers – one a supremely accomplished courtroom questioner, the other making his high-stakes début as a French conversationalist. Given Katanga's core distinction of propitiating his elders – his evident desire to come across as both knowing and enterprising – it was a mismatched dialogue. Nor was dialogue the main goal for Judge Cotte, who repeatedly drew Katanga deep into the Judge's train of reasoning, coloring the responses.[897]

For Katanga, all his badges of status were carefully scrutinized. In small cases where Katanga managed to persuade a village elder to bend some rule or practice, Judge Cotte pressed to know how such a young man could exert so much influence.[898] When Katanga mentioned facilitating cooperation with the real military leaders of RCD, Judge Cotte yearned to know who was superior in rank. (The answers denied that military rank was a factor.) When Katanga talked about managing the munitions supplies arriving at the Aveba airstrip, his collaborative role in distribution raised the presumption that he must have operated from somewhere high up the formal hierarchy.[899]

Katanga maintained steadily that his effectiveness depended on "trust," not on rank. His testimony in these passages provides a rich commentary on decentralized, low-wattage structures, embedded in a network of traditional relationships – the kind of connections at which Katanga excelled. Faced with this exotic counter-narrative, Judge Cotte acknowledged the unexpected frequency with which Katanga turned to the word "trust" ("confiance").[900] Ultimately, however, Judges Cotte and Diarra remained dubious that

[897] Judge Cotte was quick to "lead" Katanga into making affirmative nods to the Judge's elaborate verbal formulations. At one point he offered a metaphor for Katanga's *coordinator* role that prefigured the Judge's eventual conclusion that Katanga was an "accessory" to the Bogoro attack: "Q. So if we understand ourselves well and if we talk in terms of mechanics, you had to put oil into the equipment for it to function well? A. Yes." (October 18, 2011, T-324, p. 69 (ENG p. 75)). Following up the next day, he put words into Katanga's mouth, while confusing the terms Hema and Hima, the latter term referring to wider regional groups associated with Rwandan Tutsi. These similar-sounding words evidently confused Katanga, but this exchange would later contribute to Judge Cotte's conclusion that Katanga himself accepted an anti-Hema ideology; October 19, 2011, T-325, pp. 9–11 (ENG pp. 10–12). But soon Judge Cotte broke the pattern: "Please, you don't have to say yes if you don't agree with what I am saying. I don't want to deform what you are saying" (p. 16 (ENG p. 18)).

[898] Katanga Testimony, October 18, 2011, T-324, p. 70 (ENG p. 76).

[899] Ibid., pp. 60–81 (ENG pp. 66–89).

[900] Ibid., p. 63 (ENG p. 69). It was also the case that Ngudjolo explained his miraculous elevation to high military status in March 2003 because the nominal head of the FNI (Floribert Njabu) "trusted" him – an explanation that was received with skepticism by Prosecutor MacDonald. Ngudjolo Testimony, November 8, 2011, T-330, p. 75. In the accounts by both accused, relationships of "trust" were described as under continual pressure from local ambition and competition.

traditional relationships could explain Katanga's protean efforts. Their thinking turned on familiar concepts of military hierarchies and unified command.[901] Meanwhile, the Prosecutor clung tenaciously to his original view, allowing no deviation from his chosen hierarchical model of perpetration – with Katanga at some kind of apex.[902]

Although the formal announcement waited another twelve months, there evidently came some point when Judge Cotte started to weave Katanga's fascination with military life into a different scenario, anticipating a different mode of legal responsibility. The Chamber revealed its split decision in November 2012, with two judges preparing to embark on a voyage of discovery guided by the magic compass of Regulation 55. It happened after all the evidence was submitted (November 2011), after the Court's field visit to Ituri (early 2012), and after closing arguments (May 2012). It explains why the Chamber agreed to sever the joint trial into two separate cases, and it presaged the coming acquittal of Ngudjolo (December 2012).

For all its vagueness and obscure cultural context, the word *coordinator* implied contributing in some fashion to the recurring conflicts. It was clear that Katanga had understood the larger military state of play as early as his November 2002 trip to Beni. In subsequent activities, he relished the role of facilitating a web of relationships to advance that strategic mission. It was a sea change in the whole posture of the trial, in a Court that otherwise strove to prosecute those "most responsible" for the worst atrocities. Changing the mode of liability to that of a residual contribution meant abandoning the prosecution of a mastermind perpetrator. Given the ambiguity surrounding Katanga's material efforts, there was a mode of individual responsibility lurking down in the nether regions of Article 25(3) – part (d), "contributing in any other way" to the crimes perpetrated by others.

The procedural rupture surrounding this recharacterization has already been discussed. The Regulation 55 issue went immediately to the Appeals Chamber, which coyly opined that the Trial Chamber's initiative was not unreasonable in general terms, provided it ultimately upheld the fair trial rights of the accused, and provided it observed the inscrutable legal standard of not exceeding the facts and circumstances laid out in the Pre-Trial Chamber's

[901] In the Katanga Trial Judgment, the Majority was unable to pinpoint Katanga's military authority, but nonetheless asserted that he "outranked" other commanders, at least de facto (para. 1305); that he "was vested with a certain authority" (para. 1319); that he was a "key figure" (para. 1353); and, by inference from para. 1343, that he was "a particularly seasoned and well-known combatant" (para. 1258).

[902] These assumptions dominated the intense cross-examination on October 12, 2011, T-321, pp. 31–73 (ENG pp. 28–67).

Confirmation proceedings.[903] The Katanga Trial Chamber Majority felt empowered to move forward, converting as many legal issues as possible into findings of fact settled by the power of judicial assertion, while expecting a relaxed standard of review on appeal. As it happened, the Trial Chamber Judgment on Katanga was not appealed by either side – and the whole gambit with Regulation 55 would escape higher scrutiny. The existence of a Trial Chamber dissent, however, provided an "insider witness" for articulating strong doubts about the Majority's ends and means.

In the eyes of many friends of the Court, all the stuttering over Regulation 55 was a distraction from the moral mission that inspired the ICC. Putting aside some of the procedural niceties, taking a broader view, why should Katanga have any grounds for complaint? Assuming that his testimony itself was credible, it pointed the Chamber toward a larger truth about the violence in Ituri, even if it left him facing legal jeopardy. Although Article 25(3)(d) had not been previously tested, it offered precisely the right label to cover his behavior, as the newly energized Trial Chamber Majority now saw it.[904] After surviving legal objections to the technical process of moving the case to this new stage, Judges Cotte and Diarra believed that it brought the Court closer to the truth – which was, after all, an ultimate goal of Hague prosecutions.

8.4 CONSTRUCTING A CONVICTION (AND DROPPING THE SEXUAL CRIMES)

Creating a New Narrative

Katanga's story about the February 24, 2003 attack on Bogoro departed sharply from the Prosecution's original narrative. It was not a plan by ethnic militias "to wipe out Bogoro," he testified, but a tactical effort to dislodge UPC soldiers. It was carried out by a mix of professional RCD troops and local combatants from various districts. The masterminds were based in North Kivu. Katanga himself did not take part, as his presence was demanded back at the village to confront a local troublemaker.[905]

903 Katanga Appeals Chamber, Judgment on Regulation 55, para. 98.

904 Katanga Trial Judgment, para. 1691. Prior discussion of this provision took place in pre-trial proceedings for Callixte Mbarushimana, for whom charges were not confirmed. Mbarushimana Pre-Trial Chamber, Confirmation of Charges decision, December 16, 2011, ICC-01/04–01/10–465, paras. 269–84. Questions have been raised as to real or imagined differences with the ICTY's doctrine of JCE III. See Jens David Ohlin, "Joint Criminal Confusion," *New Criminal Law Review* 12 (2009), 406.

905 Katanga Testimony, October 5, 2011, T-317, pp. 54–55 (ENG p. 62).

Katanga's Defense team knew that there are always risks when the client takes the stand. But he had been charged under the liability mode of masterminding an ethnic attack on Bogoro civilians. It seemed like an effective defense for Katanga to provide details about the real strategic planners – about the heavy role of RCD troops in his local district – while narrowing his own personal role in the events of early 2003.[906] The Defense team did not consider that the Chamber might seize on Katanga's disarming description of this coordinating role, and that it might reframe the entire legal case accordingly.

As for the real masterminds, the Beni alliance (identified by the new acronym EMOI) centered on Mbusa Nyamwisi's RCD rebel group, which had gotten a foothold in national peace talks through the Inter-Congolese Dialogue. The RCD-ML faction in Beni offered an eastern base for the national Congolese army, which hoped to regroup in the eastern districts during the course of 2003. According to Katanga, this alliance of political and military forces developed a strategic vision for regaining control over Ituri: seeking to drive out Lubanga's UPC, to blunt any influence from Rwanda, and to work with Uganda to ease them back home across the border. The EMOI alliance regarded Bogoro as one of several interim targets, as they took aim at UPC strongholds along the main transportation route to Bunia. From their side, the Ugandans also saw Bogoro as important militarily, for impeding their escape path should they need to beat a quick retreat from Bunia to Uganda. Bogoro, with its UPC military camp, thus became a target for military opponents of the UPC in early 2003, given revived prospects for national power-sharing in a rebuilt Congolese state.

After November 2002, villages like Aveba and another dozen or more small localities nearby started cooperating with the military arm of the RCD, allowing fully trained professional troops to be garrisoned in several locations within Walendu-Bindi.[907] As the Katanga Defense unfolded, the main parties would disagree about the meshing of these disparate forces, with the Prosecution suggesting that RCD members had somehow melted into the ranks of a unified, well-honed Ngiti militia army (originally labeled as FRPI).[908] Katanga insisted that the two groups maintained strict differences in structure, command, and training, with the Ngiti fighters still locked into decentralized patterns under a dispersed field of local commanders, who frequently

[906] Katanga Testimony, October 4, 2011, T-316, pp. 57–65 (ENG pp. 65–75); October 5, 2011. T-317, pp. 4–24 (ENG pp. 5–25).

[907] Katanga Testimony, October 5, 2011, T-317, pp. 19–24 (ENG pp. 21–27).

[908] Katanga Testimony, October 12, 2011, T-321, pp. 61–64 (ENG pp. 55–57).

quarreled among themselves and with powerful village wise men.[909] As already noted, Katanga reserved the term "combatant" to describe these untrained, volunteer, local irregulars, in contrast to the fully trained "soldiers" of the RCD. Commanders were the individual leaders who held the personal allegiance of twelve or more combatants.

Personal names and titles remained a fixation for the Prosecution and the bench. MacDonald pressed Katanga on the use of conventional military titles, including terms like S4 through S1. But Katanga explained that these were just loosely assigned names, not technical ranks. Judge Cotte joined in this inquiry and was told the same thing. In some exasperation, Katanga explained that his group might refer to someone as "S3" (in charge of "operations") because he had a bike and knew how to repair it. "Sometimes it happened that he would accompany [RCD] soldiers on the bike. That is all."[910] Similar terms borrowed from Western military hierarchies functioned as casual nicknames in a small group of hardscrabble local fighters. Thus, the title "chargé de front" was used to designate the one who collects leaves and roots to prepare protective fetishes.[911] In the Katanga Judgment, the Majority nonetheless accepted these references to "S" titles as evidence of tight military organizations: "this description of precise, regulated structure in the camps is an initial clear indication of the organized nature of the group."[912]

Apart from personality-driven conflicts within the Ngiti self-defense groups and with village elders, Katanga spoke of larger tensions between these combatants and the trained RCD forces, whose assigned leaders might sometimes balk at their long-distance chain of command.[913] The growing presence of RCD troops from late 2002 meant that village forces got new access to firearms to supplement their bladed weapons.[914] But local commanders of the self-defense groups were further burdened with random orders coming from the patronage of village elders – "wise men," occasionally characterized in the trial as *féticheurs* or even "witch-doctors."[915] The presence of a separate, professional, offensive military force added to these frictions.[916] In telling his story before the Court, Germain Katanga took pride in his track record as a mediator among these disparate forces.

909 Katanga Testimony, October 5, 2011, T-317, pp. 24–47 (ENG pp. 27–53).
910 Katanga Testimony, October 11, 2011, T-320, p. 57 (ENG p. 55).
911 Katanga Testimony, October 14, 2011, T-323, p. 44 (ENG p. 43).
912 Katanga Trial Judgment, para. 672.
913 Katanga Testimony, October 5, 2011, T-317, p. 24 (ENG p. 27).
914 Katanga Testimony, October 18, 2011, T-324, p. 37 (ENG p. 40).
915 Katanga Testimony, September 28, 2011, T-315, p. 32 (ENG p. 36); October 4, 2011, T-316, p. 26 (ENG p. 30).
916 Katanga Testimony, October 19, 2011, T-325, pp. 2–5 (ENG pp. 3–6).

After presenting this counter-narrative about the configuration of armed groups in Walendu-Bindi, Katanga was asked relentlessly about his place within this complex system. His self-portrait portrays someone who earned distinction by commanding trust rather than troops[917] – although he began as one of many local commanders leading his own Aveba followers, who numbered as many as sixty by early 2003.[918] At times, he chose his words unwisely, as when he gushed that he had become an important hub of communications ("I was almost at the center"[919]).

Katanga meant to describe his role in practical terms as someone who resolved conflicts, someone who mediated to ease tensions, when highly diverse fighters tried to mesh their efforts.[920] Conflicts arose from natural rivalries among and within local communities, resulting from both the diversity of commanders and wise-man patronage. As Katanga described his role, resting on customary norms of trust and respect for tradition, he claimed success in resolving some disputes among the local forces – but not all. In network theoretic terms, he was a local hub, a broker among distributed sections of larger networks. It was a far cry from the unified chain of command presumed by the Rome Statute notion for a mastermind perpetrator, with complete *control over the crime*. In the final days of the trial, the Chamber's attention was captured by this massive gap between hierarchical models of armed combat and the Ituri pattern of customary, tradition-based and trust-based *coordination*. It was a confounding perspective on armed conflict, forcing the Chamber to consider taking bold steps.

Putting aside the Regulation 55 controversy, the Trial Chamber Majority's voyage of discovery ventured into turbulent seas. While purporting not to deviate from the original *facts and circumstances*, it suddenly needed to make a radical change of course. It needed to construct a new chain of events that would link Germain Katanga's *coordinator* role, beyond reasonable doubt, to the crimes actually charged. He could be no more than a supporting actor in a criminal drama whose leading roles would now be taken up by someone else. It was first and foremost a drama about civilian casualties in Bogoro, a toll that cried out for action from the Hague tribunal. It meant resuscitating the old

[917] Katanga Testimony, October 18, 2011, T-324, p. 63 (ENG p. 69).
[918] Katanga Testimony, October 5, 2011, T-317, p. 28 (ENG p. 32).
[919] Katanga Testimony, October 19, 2011, T-325, p. 19 (ENG pp. 21–22). This comment came in the last hour of his thirteen days on the stand. Elsewhere he had pointed out that none of the multiple commanders had authority over the others (October 18, 2011, T-324, p. 80 (ENG p. 89)), a position rejected by Trial Chamber in Katanga Trial Judgment, para. 195. According to the Trial Chamber Majority, it was up to the Defense to establish this point (para. 680).
[920] Katanga Testimony, October 18, 2011, T-324, pp. 70–71 (ENG p. 75).

plan "to wipe out Bogoro" – but whose plan was it now? The Trial Chamber Majority was ready to enlist – as both planners and perpetrators – the local combatants from Katanga's home district, now transformed back into a tightly organized, hierarchical fighting force.

Katanga told the Court about his coordinating role in a very different kind of military effort. He invoked the strategic military plan coming from the EMOI group in Beni, in alliance with Kinshasa, aimed to expel the UPC from its military base in Bogoro. It was a plan directed at military targets, not at civilians – not a plan to "wipe out Bogoro." On these terms, there was nothing criminal about the EMOI plan, assuming that Katanga's low-level support had contributed in some way to its implementation. Katanga's testimony did not yet give the Majority enough of what it needed.[921]

Katanga was now being measured up by the Trial Chamber Majority as a contributor – but to *which plan*? If it was just the strategic military plan (the plan reportedly hatched in Beni by the EMOI), then any accessory to *this particular plan* might well avoid responsibility for ICC crimes. Associating Katanga with this plan could easily produce an acquittal – as the Minority judge pointed out in her dissent.[922]

So, it had to be the *other* plan: a criminal plan like the one first alleged by the Prosecution, steeped in ethnic hatred, carried out by armed fighters from Katanga's district. It was still *Hamlet*, but without Katanga as the (joint, indirect) Danish Prince. The planners and perpetrators of the Bogoro crimes were not on trial; but, still, Katanga had to be linked to them in some way – now as a contributor.

New Context – Same Criminal Charges

The second ICC trial was supposed to focus on the civilian victims in Bogoro. The Prosecution goal was to convict those most responsible for a series of criminal acts: murder, rape, looting. The charges fell under crimes against humanity (Article 7) and war crimes (Article 8), going well beyond the narrow war crimes charges in the Lubanga case. But once the testimony started and cracks showed up in the Prosecution's joint mastermind theory of responsibility, the trial emphasis shifted to modes of liability and managerial powers of

[921] Judge Cotte elicited some pieces to work with, but the gaps remained. Katanga explained that his role as coordinator meant keeping ammunition from Beni out of the hands of unreliable local forces (Katanga Testimony, October 19, 2011, T-325, p. 15 (ENG p. 18)). The planning he was aware of – coming from Beni – was written down and highly detailed (ibid., pp. 15–16 (ENG pp. 18–20)).

[922] Katanga Trial Judgment, Minority Opinion, paras. 133, 217.

the judiciary. The topics covered across this entire chapter reflect the Court's serial struggles to fulfill its mission, in the face of endless complexities in Ituri.

After MONUC forces were increased in Bunia in late 2003, the United Nations and other organizations reconstructed a series of attacks in small Ituri villages, leading up to the bloody ouster of the UPC from Bunia in early March 2003. In their telling, these were ethnically driven outbreaks of violence directed against civilians, understood as tit-for-tat revenge attacks, commonly described as pitting Hema against Lendu. The memories of genocidal massacres in Rwanda (understood as Hutu against Tutsi) doubtless influenced this framing of the situation, especially as the Kivu provinces to the south were coping with the violent spillover of Rwandan Hutu refugees in conflict with indigenous Congolese Tutsi. The ethnic mix in Ituri was nonetheless different from that in the Kivus, and some of the bloodiest attacks studied by UN investigators included further ethnic factions like the Bira. In addition, even the NGOs who were most focused on ethnic conflict acknowledged the incendiary role of Ugandan forces, of Congolese rebel factions like Nyamwisi's RCD and Bemba's MLC, as well as the vengeful national Congolese troops directed from Kinshasa. All these groups were identified as instigators of civilian violence in Ituri.[923]

Instead of exploring these complex intersections, the Prosecution chose to narrow its first trials by selecting imagined leaders of Ituri *militias*, classifying the violence as *non-international* conflicts (even when they might be understood as nested within international dynamics) and stressing ethnic motivations as the driving force. When the Katanga Trial Chamber Majority needed to cobble together a new scenario for salvaging Katanga's conviction, they fell back on these original templates. Despite all the complexities revealed in the first two Congo trials, the Trial Chamber Majority gave a judicial performance filled with simplifying paradigms, bold presumptions, reductive inferences, and manipulation of proof burdens, with the acknowledged goal of allowing the ICC to fulfill its destiny in the fight against impunity.

Nearly 300 pages into its much-awaited Katanga Judgment, the Majority began to address the actual crimes that had been confirmed five years previously by the Pre-Trial Chamber.[924] In keeping with the facts and circumstances of that original process, the Judgment addressed crimes tied to the single event of February 24, 2003 in Bogoro. But the dramatic change of

[923] UN Secretary-General, *Special Report on the Events in Ituri, January 2002–December 2003*, S/2004/573, issued July 16, 2004. This material supplemented the influential July 2003 report from HRW, *Ituri: "Covered in Blood": Ethnically Targeted Violence in Northeastern DR Congo*, written by Anneke van Woudenberg.

[924] Katanga and Ngudjolo Pre-Trial Chamber, Confirmation of Charges decision, paras. 574–82.

narratives (denied by the Majority as crossing the boundary line within Regulation 55) shook up many of the background assumptions. And while crimes involving murder and pillaging were upheld, those involving sexual crimes (rape and sexual slavery) were mysteriously dropped, along with charges about child soldiers.

The specific charges were drawn from Articles 7 and 8, which must be read to include a set of background conditions as described below:

Article 7 Crimes against humanity

1. For the purposes of this Statute, "crime against humanity" means any of the following acts when committed as part of a widespread or systematic attack directed against any civilian population, with knowledge of the attack:
   (a) Murder
...(g) Rape, sexual slavery ....

2. For the purpose of paragraph 1:
(a) "Attack directed against any civilian population" means a course of conduct involving the multiple commission of acts referred to in paragraph 1, against any civilian population, pursuant to or in furtherance of a State or organizational policy to commit such attack ....

Article 8 War crimes

1. The Court shall have jurisdiction in respect of war crimes in particular when committed as part of a plan or policy or as part of a large-scale commission of such crimes.
2. For the purpose of this Statute, "war crimes" means:
   (a) Grave breaches of the Geneva Conventions of 12 August 1949 ...:
   (i) **Wilful killing**;
   ...(b) Other serious violations of the law and customs applicable in international armed conflict ...:
   (i) **Intentionally directing attacks against the civilian population** as such or against individual civilians not taking direct part in hostilities;
   ...(xiii) **Destroying or seizing the enemy's property** unless such destruction or seizure be imperatively demanded by the necessities of war;
   ...(xvi) **Pillaging** a town or place even when taken by assault;
   ...(xxii) Committing **rape, sexual slavery** ...;
   ...(xxvi) ... **using [children under the age of fifteen years] to participate actively in hostilities**;

Accompanying this list of ten specific crimes, spread across two Articles, was pre-trial confirmation that the mode of liability fell under Article 25(3)(a) in the novel formulation of *indirect co-perpetration* (crimes "jointly committed through other persons").[925] Under this mode, several of the crimes were charged as being committed by the accused *with intent*; and the others *with the knowledge that the crimes would occur in the ordinary course of events*.[926] These terms derive from Article 30 concerning the "Mental element" of crimes (known generally as *mens rea*), which codifies the forms of *intent* and *knowledge* required for finding individual criminal responsibility.

The pre-trial judges did not agree among themselves on these requisite elements of intent and knowledge. One of the three judges dissented on the charges of rape and sexual slavery under both Articles 7 and 8, on the grounds that there was insufficient evidence to show that Katanga and Ngudjolo had the requisite knowledge that these specific sexual crimes would occur "in the ordinary course of events" during the Bogoro attack.[927] This was an early preview of doubts surrounding the rape and sexual slavery charges – which were ultimately dropped in the final Katanga Judgment (for reasons to be explained below). Additionally, the Pre-Trial Chamber declined, on the basis of insufficient evidence, to confirm the charges of "other inhumane acts" under Article 7 and "inhumane treatment" and "outrages upon personal dignity" under Article 8.[928]

How many civilians were killed in Bogoro on that day, and by whom? The numbers accepted by the Trial Chamber Majority were lower than the original 200 confirmed by the Pre-Trial Chamber. With no forensic analysis to draw on, the accuracy of such estimates was left mostly to witness testimony, discounted by the usual factors of credibility and lack of corroboration. The Trial Chamber Majority would count a minimum

[925] For an analysis of this concept, see Thomas Weigand, "Indirect Perpetration," in Stahn, *Law and Practice of International Criminal Law*, chapter 22 (including discussion of "indirect co-perpetration").

[926] Katanga and Ngudjolo Pre-Trial Chamber, Confirmation of Charges decision, para. 574.

[927] Ibid., Partial Dissenting Opinion of Judge Anita Ušacka, para. 22, which challenges her colleagues' willingness to infer Katanga's and Ngudjolo's intent and knowledge from the general proposition that the crimes of rape and sexual slavery were committed routinely in Ituri conflicts. Even though the *Elements of Crimes* provides that intent and knowledge "may be inferred from relevant facts and circumstances," in this case Judge Ušacka thought that the Chamber's inferences were based on a particular kind of risk analysis (*dolus eventualis*), which the Pre-Trial Chamber had explicitly declined to use (para. 12). It was a preview of interpretive controversies unresolved in the Lubanga case.

[928] Ibid., paras. 364, 377, 465,

of thirty civilian deaths, while believing that there must have been more. The number of confirmed rapes and acts of sexual slavery was three.[929] Even within this group of victims, the Majority was unable to attribute any secure subset of victims to actions specifically by Ngiti militia from Walendu-Bindi, which was the moral link to Katanga's individual responsibility. Other fighters were present, they acknowledged, including the Lendu from Bedu-Ezekere, ethnic Bira fighters, in addition to the cadre of professional soldiers from the RCD.[930]

Finding the Necessary Facts

The general language introducing Articles 7 and 8 allows that international crimes must surpass a certain threshold of magnitude and organizational complexity. These structural requirements are additional to the criteria used to establish the individual criminal responsibility of perpetrators and others. Crimes against humanity must be carried out by states or state-like organizations, acting on the basis of some policy, in a manner that is either widespread or systematic.[931] Similarly, war crimes are actions that violate particular norms associated with the Geneva Conventions and other relevant treaties and customs of war. These norms apply to only those armed groups that exhibit degrees of internal organization and effective command, operating in conflicts that are more intense than mere civil unrest or mob violence. War crimes norms may be assessed differently depending on whether an armed conflict is international in nature, or non-international.[932]

For the casualties in Bogoro to count against Germain Katanga as crimes against humanity, the Court needed to certify the strict hierarchical structure of fighting forces, the broad scope of their actions, their coherence as an organization, their pursuit of a unified policy, and the strategic context of their engagement with enemy forces. Knowing what all it needed, the Trial

[929] Katanga Trial Judgment, paras. 999, 1023.

[930] The Katanga Trial Judgment loosely describes the perpetrators as "amongst others, the Ngiti combatants of Walendu-Bindi *collectivité*" (para. 849). Elsewhere they are simply described as "the combatants" (para. 817), although it notes some particular acts for which the evidence was insufficient to decide which of the diverse groups was responsible (para. 844).

[931] Kai Ambos, "Crimes Against Humanity and the International Criminal Court," in Leila Nadya Sadat, *Forging a Convention for Crimes Against Humanity* (Cambridge: Cambridge University Press, 2011), chapter 12.

[932] Christopher M. Ford and Winston S. Williams, *Complex Battle Spaces: The Law of Armed Conflict and Dynamics of Modern War* (Oxford: Oxford University Press, 2019), Part I (on the complexity of using legal categories in unconventional armed conflict).

Chamber Majority went back and found it in the tattered remnants of the Prosecution's main case, making sweeping assumptions about events, deftly improvising around the lack of the original mastermind. Their facts came from the same witnesses whose statements about Katanga's mastermind role were deemed unreliable. Their conclusion was a bold leap of faith: "Though they were stationed at different camps under different commanders, received logistical assistance from the [RCD] and formed a somewhat rag-tag collection, all of these combatants, who communicated and could have moved between camps, nonetheless worked together, as part of a single armed militia, in pursuit of a common objective, to attack the enemy located in Bogoro."[933] Unless the Court declares these rag-tag forces to be "a single armed militia," there can be no crimes against humanity. By definition, these crimes apply only to actions taken by state or quasi-state organizations. The Trial Chamber Majority was driven by an urgent call to stipulate these and other essential predicates of crime, on the way to ensuring a conviction. Its purpose was plain enough from the cascade of presumptions and inferences throughout its Judgment; but it was also proudly declared as a moral imperative. In tortured prose, starting from the "purpose and object" of the Rome Statute, the Chamber

> [u]nderscores that a restrictive conception of the organization requiring that it possess quasi-State characteristics, would not further the Statute's goal of prosecuting the most serious crimes. To so conceive the organization would in effect exclude any entities that may have undertaken a[n] ... operation involving the multiple commission of acts under article 7(1) of the Statute pursuant to or in furtherance of the policy, on the sole ground that they are insufficiently hierarchical to be considered in theory, as capable of pursuing or enforcing a policy whose aim is such an attack.

The reasoning here is circular, assuming the very point in question: that the Bogoro attack just naturally belonged under Article 7. The Majority starts from the presumption that it did, and then proceeds to find all the facts necessary for meeting Article 7 criteria.

Certain presumptions were necessary to meet minimum conditions for war crimes. The degree of organization and hierarchy might not be quite so high as in Article 7, but it still needed to cross a critical threshold, for which the convenient term "militia" begged all the important qualities. Echoing the language of Article 7, the war crimes scenario includes cryptic language that it applies "in particular when committed as part of a plan or policy or as part of

933 Katanga Trial Judgment, para. 681.

a large-scale commission of such crimes."[934] In addition the Trial Chamber wrestled with the task of classifying the conflicts as *international* or *non-international*. The particular war crimes confirmed by the Pre-Trial Chamber fell under the first category; whereas the Trial Chamber used its Regulation 55 powers to change the classification to *non-international*. This meant shifting all the war crimes charges into a different segment of Article 8:

Wilful killing under Article 8(2)(a)i was shifted to Article 8(2)(c)(i) **Violence to Life and persons, in particular murder of all kinds;**
Intentionally directing attacks against a civilian population under Article 8(2)(b)(i) was shifted to Article 8(2)(e)(i);
Destroying or seizing the enemy's property under Article 8(2)(b)(xiii) was shifted to Article 8(2)(e)(xii);
Pillaging a town or place under Article 8(2)(b)(xvi) was shifted to Article 8(2)(e)(v);
Rape and sexual slavery under Article 8(2)(b)(xxii) were shifted to Article 8(2)(e)(vi);
Using [children under the age of fifteen years] to participate actively in hostilities under Article 8(2)(b)(xxvi) was shifted to Article 8(2)(e)(vii).

These changes made no discernible difference in the substance of the war crimes charges.[935]

Under the stress of constructing a conviction, the Majority seemed relieved to retrieve enough facts to render its presumptions reasonable, or reasonable enough to survive deferential appellate review. Its formula included ritual declarations of "caution" and "circumspection" in all the usual places, as well as periodic reports on internal states of *intime conviction*. It used the techniques of leveraging allegations by some conflicted witnesses through "corroboration" from other conflicted witnesses, borrowing bootstrap mathematics from the Lubanga Trial Judgment. It rejected alternative explanations of events coming from the Defense, on the grounds that the Majority was simply "not persuaded," and that the Defense had not proven the superiority of its alternative. All these techniques can be found in Trial Chamber Judgments in all the Congo trials. Here, they stand out most conspicuously, seen against the improvised case narrative.

934 Article 8(1).

935 One difference related to child soldiers, with the original charge (Article 8(2)(b)(xxvi)) applying to conscripting or enlisting underage children in "national armed forces." The Lubanga Pre-Trial Chamber had shown the way for determined judges to work around this restrictive term. Lubanga Confirmation of Charges decision, January 29, 2007, ICC-01/04–01/06–803, paras. 275–85.

Katanga's Individual Responsibility: A Flurry of Presumptions

The only way that the ICC can channel humanitarian outrage for documented crimes is by finding someone accountable. If there is a deeper truth to be discovered under the power of law, the time comes when ICC judges must unleash some bold surmises. In the battle against impunity, there is no role for the timid. The Lubanga case had stumbled in what should have been a swift and routine trial. And now the second trial had been threatened by the collapse of the core narrative.

This was the spirit in which the Katanga Trial Chamber Majority tackled its greatest challenge: closing the conviction loop by confirming Germain Katanga's individual responsibility for the crimes – or at least some of them. In this effort, the Majority's arguments offer an extreme example of the presumptive style of reasoning used in other Congo trial convictions. For the vital pivot from the plight of victims to individual criminal responsibility, the Chamber applied a series of paradigms and presumptions to the deeply compromised evidence brought by the Prosecution. These inferential leaps allowed the Chamber to link the Bogoro civilian casualties to a presumed (but otherwise opaque) group of perpetrators. In turn, these perpetrators would be linked to a presumed (but unarticulated) plan, one characterized as criminal in nature (on the retrospective basis of how it worked out). Further presumptions would need to embed this supplemental criminal plan inside the primary lawful plan carried out simultaneously, "in perfect concordance"[936] by the Beni-based EMOI. Once this first round of presumptions was locked in with some factual flourishes, there would need to be still further inferences to establish Katanga's personal knowledge and intentions.

For the first stage of this process, the reasoning pattern was disarmingly simple. The all-important starting axiom was the bare fact of thirty-three-plus civilian casualties in Bogoro. This fact itself would support all the major inferences needed to advance the conviction:

(a) the existence of some group that meant to commit these atrocities;[937]
(b) the pre-existence of some group common purpose or plan to carry them out;[938]

[936] Katanga Trial Judgment, para. 1672.
[937] "In the Chamber's view, the manner in which Bogoro was attacked and that Hema civilians, who had no part in combat, were pursued and killed confirms the existence of a common purpose of a criminal nature vis-à-vis the population of the village" (ibid., para. 1657).
[938] "Proof that the common purpose was previously arranged or formulated is not required. It may materialize *extemporaneously* and be inferred from the subsequently concerted action of the group of persons" (ibid., para. 1626, emphasis added).

(c) that this group with the common purpose or plan had a strict hierarchical structure;[939]
(d) that its structure was that of an organization capable of sustained, widespread attacks like the one in Bogoro;[940]
(e) that this organization must have acted on some "policy," according to which the Bogoro attack was intended as revenge in the ongoing ethnic struggle between Lendu and Hema.[941]

In essence, the civilian violence must simply be enabled to speak for itself. Everything follows by presumption from these core facts. The raw data on victims "presuppose" the criminal purpose of whatever group had done it.[942] To be sure, that group's purpose does not have to be overtly criminal, as long as it "entails" criminality; and it can be in the "extemporaneous" execution of the crime that a group is actually constituted as acting with a common purpose.[943] And even if the group does not explicitly mean to cause the criminal consequences, it is enough for it to be aware that these consequences will occur in the ordinary course of events. "Some shared intent may be established by ... the group's collective decisions and action, or its omissions."[944]

A second group of presumptions provides a similar short link between the civilian violence and Germain Katanga's actions as a "coordinator." The Trial Chamber Majority's first batch of presumptions thus connects to the new mode of liability adopted under Regulation 55. Article 25(3)(d)(ii) applies to someone who "[i]n any other way contributes to the commission or attempted commission of such a crime by a group of persons acting with a common purpose. Such contribution shall be intentional and shall ... (ii) Be made in the knowledge of the intention of the group to commit the crime ...." The

939 "[I]t cannot be reasonably argued that the Ngiti combatants who were in Bogoro and committed crimes did not belong to the group of Ngiti commanders and combatants from Walendu-Bindi *collectivité*" (ibid., para. 1668).

940 "The Ngiti combatants of the *collectivité* demonstrated that they were capable of conceiving and executing large-scale attacks [including] the attack on Bogoro in February 2003 .... In the Chamber's view, these facts suffice to determine that the Ngiti combatants of Walendu-Bindi *collectivité* constituted an organization within the meaning of Article 7(2) of the Statute" (ibid., paras. 1140–41).

941 "The Chamber further considers that ... the ultimate modus operandi of the attack demonstrates that the Bogoro operation ensued from the design harboured specifically by the Ngiti militia to target the predominantly civilian population of Bogoro" (para. 1150). "Accordingly the Chamber finds that the attack ... was executed pursuant to an organizational policy to attack it with a view [to wipe out] first and foremost the Hema civilians who were present ..." (ibid., para. 1155).

942 Ibid., para. 1626.

943 Ibid., paras. 1626–27.

944 Ibid., para. 1627.

"group of persons acting with a common purpose" was presumed to be the local Ngiti fighters from Katanga's district.[945] While Katanga had testified that his coordinating activities were aimed at the lawful military campaign against the UPC soldiers in Bogoro, this was not enough to avoid liability.

> Admittedly, not all assistance lent in preparation of a military operation perforce and as a rule constitutes a contribution to crimes committed by the members of an armed group taking part in the operation. Nonetheless, it must be underscored that the fact that the Accused's conduct constituted a contribution to the military operation which was decided in Beni does not preclude that his conduct may also constitute a contribution to the commission of crimes by the Ngiti militia, within the meaning of article 25(3)(d) of the Statute.[946]

In the Majority's view, the Ngiti force was a kind of time-bomb lurking inside the military attack organized by the Beni group, with the two synchronized plans acting "in perfect concordance" in the run-up to February 24.[947] Katanga had known about the Beni plan since November 2002. The Chamber then presumed another critical point of knowledge: that "Germain Katanga was fully aware of how war was being waged in Ituri at the material time . . .."[948] "Accordingly, the Chamber must find that Germain Katanga knew that the attack on Bogoro would proceed as it did and that the Ngiti militia would commit the crimes of murder, attack against civilians, destruction of property and pillaging."[949] And because Katanga would have known these things from the moment he returned to his home village as a *coordinator*, "[t]he Chamber takes the view that as of December 2002, Germain Katanga knew of the intention of the Ngiti militia, as a group, to commit during the 24 February 2003 attack, each of the aforementioned crimes, which formed

945 For a general discussion of "common purpose" as a basis for liability under Article 25(3)(d), see Marjolein Cupido, "Group Acting with a Common Purpose," in Jerôme de Hemptinne, Robert Roth, and Elies van Sliedregt, *Modes of Liability in International Criminal Law* (Cambridge: Cambridge University Press, 2019), chapter 10.

946 Ibid., para. 1673.

947 Ibid., para. 1672. The dissent found this plan-within-a-plan theory to be "totally unpersuasive" (Minority Opinion of Judge Christine Van den Wyngaert, para. 220).

948 Ibid., para. 1685.

949 Ibid., para. 1689. This characterization of knowledge imports a camouflaged risk factor, along with a shift in the burden of proof to the Defense to demonstrate otherwise. The implicit theory behind this presumption was discussed in Chapter 7, in relation to Mark Osiel's supplement to the *control over the crime* paradigm. Osiel, "Ascribing Individual Liability within a Bureaucracy of Murder," in Alette Smeulers (ed.), *Collective Violence and International Criminal Justice: An Interdisciplinary Approach* (Portland: Intersentia, 2010), chapter 5.

part of the said group's common purpose."[950] He knew these things because he knew how Ituri violence unfolded in the normal chain of events. It was enough to bring him under the "knowledge" standard of Article 30: knowing what "will occur in the ordinary course of events."[951] And while this sounds like the element of risk that was flirted with by the Lubanga Trial Chamber, it loses any sense of contingency if one presumes that events in Ituri happen in "ordinary" ways. Without that presumption, the Court would have gotten tangled up in degrees of risk that might be difficult to reconcile with Article 30(3).

Beyond Katanga's knowledge, it was also required that the Chamber show that his contributions to the crimes were "significant" in scope. In the Chamber's view, Katanga's contributions to the non-criminal Beni plan should count equally as contributions to the criminal Ngiti plan, since the former was but the logical precondition for the latter to take place. "It was indeed his activities as a whole and the various forms which his contribution took that, in the circumstances, had a significant influence on the commission of these crimes."[952]

The Chamber concludes its exercise in presumptive reasoning by announcing that "all these findings establish beyond reasonable doubt that Germain Katanga's intentional contribution to the crimes ... was significant and made in the knowledge of the intention of the group to commit the crimes."[953] Two of the three Trial Chamber judges were persuaded of all these inferential findings – in the depths of their moral consciences.

End of the Presumption Chain: Dropping the Sexual Crimes

Back at the time of the Ngudjolo acquittal, the Trial Chamber had expressed serious doubts about the credibility of most of the trial witnesses. It decided that the joint mastermind mode of liability could not be proved beyond reasonable doubt. But the Trial Chamber in that earlier judgment also went on to say that it could not exclude the possibility that other parts of the original narrative might survive.[954] In particular, it seemed not to buy most of the Defense position, most notably the notion that the Bogoro attack was essentially a military venture planned by someone in North Kivu. While it was impossible, beyond reasonable doubt, to link Ngudjolo and Katanga to each

950 Katanga Trial Judgment, para. 1690.
951 Article 30(3).
952 Katanga Trial Judgment, para. 1681.
953 Ibid., para. 1691.
954 Ngudjolo Trial Judgment, see, for example, paras. 112, 501.

other and to planning the Bogoro killings, other parts of the story might still have legs. The enigmatic Ngudjolo was too far removed from any preparatory action and was canny enough in his testimony to focus on his practical work as a nurse. But Katanga seemed rather to immerse himself into the life and spirit of local armed groups in Walendu-Bindi. It was not much of a stretch to link his protean activities as *coordinator* to some kind of support for these separate Ngiti fighters.

The imperial logic of broad presumptions runs counter to the inductive inquiry of fact-finding based on critical scrutiny of courtroom evidence. While the presumptions create the main scaffold for the Chamber's arguments, the whole structure still needs to incorporate at least some factual elements from evidence produced at trial. The Trial Chamber Majority ran back through its summaries of all the witnesses and other evidence, finding just enough credibility to confirm what the presumptions had already foretold. While nearly all of the Prosecution witnesses had been compromised in some fashion, the Majority would extract only what it needed from each person's testimony – and from Defense witnesses as well. The results meant to project a tone of reasonableness, at least sufficient to survive the deferential scrutiny of an Appeals Chamber.

As dissenting Judge Christine Van den Wyngaert pointed out, the Majority relied heavily on Katanga's own testimony – the witness cited most often at critical points. Katanga covered a lot of ground over thirteen days in the witness box; but the Chamber embraced those particular parts that confirmed its own presumptions, while discarding much larger parts that could have exonerated Katanga.[955] Judge Van den Wyngaert noted further what other critics of the Judgment later emphasized: that Katanga's testimony made out an effective Defense under the original mastermind theory, but it suddenly became incriminating when scrutinized under the presumptions built into the new theory.[956]

Here, then, was a self-described *coordinator* "contributing in any other way" to an ethnically motivated attack, carried out by a well-organized militia, waged against a civilian population. The Majority's underlying paradigm featured a fixed *modus operandi* for Ituri attacks, all motivated by the same ethnic hatred. It was a broad factual generalization that was never explicitly put to the test in the courtroom; it just subsisted in the ether of judicial presumption. It was enough to persuade two members of the Trial Chamber that Katanga knew what was coming, because he knew all too well how warfare

955 Katanga Trial Judgment, Minority Opinion, para. 168.
956 Ibid., paras. 34, 58. See also Stahn, "Justice Delivered or Justice Denied?" p. 830.

actually works in Ituri. He assumed the risk that the Bogoro attack would work out the same as all the other attacks.[957] It was this special chain of logic that supported the Majority's finding, beyond reasonable doubt, that Katanga's contributions were significant enough to link him to some of the crimes charged.

Some of the crimes – but not *all*. Conspicuously missing from the list was the crime of using child soldiers, and also rape and sexual slavery. At the pre-trial level, the child soldier offenses had been charged against Katanga as a direct perpetrator, on the expectation that witnesses would say that Katanga used underage youth in his personal bodyguard. When the main child witnesses proved unreliable, as did other alleged eye-witnesses, the Majority abandoned this particular charge.[958]

The rationale for eliminating the sexual crimes relied on a spontaneous risk calculus conjured up by the Trial Chamber Majority. Knowing the way that warfare was conducted in Ituri, Katanga assumed the risk that the Bogoro attack would follow the usual path. But not all the Bogoro crimes were equally foreseeable, even though they were carried out under the same set of circumstances. It was reasonable to say that Katanga assumed the risk that the Ngiti militia would kill, attack, and pillage. But not so with rape and sexual slavery. The Majority was not prepared to hold that these offenses were fully baked into the pattern of Ituri violence. They occurred, tragically, on February 24 in Bogoro; but the Chamber lacked confidence that Katanga could have foreseen them.

> [A]lthough the acts of rape and enslavement formed an integral part of the militia's design to attack the predominantly Hema civilian population of Bogoro, the Chamber cannot, however, find, *on the basis of the evidence*

[957] The Trial Chamber Majority left obscure the kind of risk analysis bound up with this presumption: whether Katanga's actions fell into categories like gross negligence, or some lesser form of negligence tied to foreseeability of the events. In the jargon favored by the Court, there is a distinction between *dolus directus of the second degree* and *dolus eventualis* – with the former fitting more properly into the "mental element" requirements in Article 30. This vocabulary lends a false precision to the matter, but in this instance the Majority disclaimed using the looser form of negligence (Katanga Trial Judgment, para. 777). In her dissent, Judge Van den Wyngaert nonetheless detects the drift toward *dolus eventualis* in their Judgment (Minority Opinion, para. 292). The key point is that the Majority's position presumes that Katanga was facing an environment where events unfold predictably, normally, "ordinarily." Without that presumption, the risk factor becomes far more speculative and problematic.

[958] The Trial Chamber Majority was unable to find any "direct nexus" between Katanga and children known to be under the age of fifteen (Katanga Trial Judgment, para. 1085), but pointedly noted that they also could not rule out some connection (para. 1088). They concluded by dropping the charges (para. 1483).

> *put before it*, that the criminal purpose pursued on 24 February 2003 *necessarily* encompassed the commission of the specific crimes proscribed by articles 7(1)(g) [rape as a crime against humanity] and 8(2)(e)(vi) [sexual slavery as a war crime]. Accordingly, and for all these reasons, the Chamber cannot find that rape and sexual slavery fell within the common purpose.[959]

With this breathtaking paragraph, the sexual crimes vanished from the conviction. The obscurity in this result is ensured by the two rhetorical phrases emphasized in the quotation. The first phrase says that there was not enough evidence to make the connection, blaming the result on evidentiary grounds. But the whole exercise of presumptive reasoning took place in speculative terms: everything leading up to Katanga's conviction (including the contours of the common purpose) was justified, first and foremost, by inferential logic, leaving the facts to play a supporting role in confirmation. The key questions of who did it, according to what plan, and with what intent, were all decided by logical inference; not by induction from the facts. The pivot to Katanga's individual responsibility operated likewise according to inference: everything followed from the Majority's presumption that Katanga understood how war always worked out, and that he evidently assumed the risk.

Were rape and sexual slavery "necessarily" part of the package? Yes, they occurred; but were they as entirely predictable as the other crimes? The term "necessity" is misplaced here – because, in the conduct of war by Ituri militias, none of it happened *necessarily*. The notion of an "ordinary course of events" is a rhetorical device, not a generalization from experience.

In the end, the Majority was unwilling to extend the chain of presumptions beyond murder and pillaging to the crimes of rape and sexual slavery. That unwillingness could not have been driven by lack of evidence, because the trial did not entertain *any* direct evidence about the typical way that Ituri wars were conducted. To be sure, the Prosecutor had referenced a series of Ituri attacks, leading up to Bogoro, which were presumed to provide incentives for ethnic revenge, and which the Prosecution portrayed in monotonic terms. But the presumption of an "ordinary" mode of Ituri attack, falling into a pattern of ethnic payback, was derived from NGO reports like "*Covered in Blood*" – and not subject to courtroom scrutiny. It was only the raw beginning of a critical review, not the conclusion. Without more than this presumption, the Majority left itself open to the charge of imposing cultural stereotypes on African events.[960]

959 Katanga Trial Judgment, para. 1664 (emphasis added).

960 This whiff of cultural stereotyping was detected by Judge Van den Wyngaert in her dissent (ibid., Minority Opinion, para. 318).

Why two members of the Trial Chamber lost their nerve, in this final step, cannot finally be gleaned from their voluminous Judgment. They made heroic efforts to transform the case, leading up to a conviction. The whole performance was sustained by presumptive reasoning, intersecting with a responsive *intime conviction*. But in the final pages they fell short of where NGO supporters most wanted them to go.[961]

Reasonable Doubt and Reasonable Alternatives

The Majority undertook a survey of trial evidence meant to back up its chain of presumptions. Its search should not be mistaken for an inductive inquiry starting out from facts. The logical order was just the reverse: starting from presumed conclusions, and only then looking for corroborative evidence to render those conclusions plausible, or at least reasonable – or perhaps just "not unreasonable."[962] Some of the facts might not stand up on their own, but they gained greater stability as part of a consistent pattern, held together by a structure of presumptions. While some factual determinations might seem contestable in isolation, it was the final result that brought everything together, earning the designation of proof *beyond reasonable doubt*.[963]

It was no longer the Prosecution's case – which had long-since collapsed, despite efforts by the Prosecution to stay afloat to the bitter end. Rather, it was an exploratory journey through Regulation 55, requiring the serious reshuffling of evidence under a new theory of liability, at a point well after the parties had made their final arguments. That journey was prompted by a nagging feeling within the judicial psyche that parts of the Prosecution's narrative were not

961 The Women's Initiatives for Gender Justice issued an immediate statement calling this part of the Judgment "a devastating result for the victims/survivors of the Bogoro attack . . .. We are extremely disappointed that the judges appeared to expect a different level of proof regarding Mr. Katanga's contributions" to the sexual crimes, as opposed to the other charges. Press Release, "Partial Conviction of Katanga by ICC: Acquittal for Sexual Violence and Use of Child Soldiers," March 7, 2014, www.iccwomen.org/images/Katanga-judgement-Statement-corr.pdf.

962 Katanga Trial Judgment, Minority Opinion, para. 262.

963 Judges Cotte and Diarra wrote a separate concurrence in response to their dissenting colleague's rejection of virtually the entire Judgment. They stressed two main points (addressed in Section 8.5): the method of interpreting facts "holistically," and the idea that proof beyond reasonable doubt applies to only the composite final determinations, rather than to constituent case facts that are not in themselves "indispensable" for a conviction (Katanga Trial Judgment, Annex II, para. 4.) One might consider their two points together: as a plea for holism in bundling facts in an additive way when it comes to reaching a conviction, while disaggregating those bundled facts when it comes to applying the standard of proof. These points are discussed in Section 8.5 in the context of the Ngudjolo Appeals Judgment, leading up to the major reckoning in the Bemba Appeals Judgment.

necessarily wrong . . . and thus might perhaps be partly true. The extent to which the Majority resolved the matter through presumptions and inferences reflects its daunting challenge: reimagining the evidence while remaining faithful to original *facts and circumstances* in the pre-trial confirmation documents.

The trial record gave only a thin layer of cover for important presumptions that were guiding the recharacterized case. As the dissent observed about the final Judgment, "the entire decision is very short on hard and precise facts and very long on vague and ambiguous 'findings,' innuendo and suggestions."[964] Such problems surround the Majority's bedrock belief in the existence of a coherent, cohesive Ngiti militia, an essential premise for salvaging a conviction under the Rome Statute. As the dissent points out, the Majority itself had "to admit that there is no evidence to suggest that the 'Ngiti militia' was under a centralised chain of command or that Germain Katanga (or anyone else for that matter), possessed any real authority over all the Ngiti fighters of Walendu-Bindi."[965] For her part, Judge Van den Wyngaert saw no evidence during the trial for anything more than "a loose coalition of largely autonomous units."[966]

Without solid proof either way, this contrasting notion offered a reasonable alternative to the Majority's presumption. It represents the kind of doubt that ought to matter for the high standard of proof. Reasonable alternatives were likewise available to balance the Majority's insistence that this overriding group purpose was sheer ethnic revenge. The evidence for that position was never more than circumstantial. The main hypothesis came from a September 2002 attack in Nyankunde, for which NGOs had alleged massive reprisal killings of civilians.[967] Although the Prosecution could not prove its assertion that Germain Katanga had taken an active part in this prior battle, the Majority believed that there was some possible overlap in the local Ngiti commanders involved in both events. Yet there was "not a single item of direct evidence" to back it up, in the judgment of its dissenting colleague.[968] These events do not speak for themselves: "Whether these [combatants] were motivated by ethnic hatred, a thirst for revenge or purely opportunistic reasons, it is clear that their conduct cannot be relied upon to draw any inferences whatsoever about the purpose of the [Bogoro] attackers under Article 25(3)(d)(ii) of the Statute."[969]

964 Katanga Trial Judgment, Minority Opinion, para. 172.

965 Ibid., para. 205, referencing the Majority Judgment, paras. 675, 1306, 1365.

966 Ibid., Minority Opinion, para. 206.

967 An awkward fact about this attack was that a significant proportion of Nyankunde victims were of Bira ethnicity; and the transfer of ethnic bitterness to the Hema was based on an alleged temporary alliance between the two groups (see ibid., paras. 245–50).

968 Ibid., para. 226.

969 Ibid., para 5. The Trial Chamber Majority wavered in its assessment of attributing such rigid ideological coherence and purpose in constituting this group (Katanga Trial Judgment, para.

Judge Van den Wyngaert offered a contrasting interpretation of the Bogoro killings, for which she thought the available evidence could provide equal if not greater support. Her alternative version abandoned the theory of a criminal plan (Ngiti-led) wrapped up in a non-criminal military plan (EMOI-inspired), suggesting how the civilian casualties might nonetheless have happened:

> Considering the clear and preponderant role of EMOI, and in light of the total absence of reliable evidence about any planning activities – e.g. meetings or other forms of communication among local commanders – at the level of the Ngiti fighters of Walendu-Bindi, it is my considered opinion that the evidence indicates that there was only one plan. Indeed, I think that the authorities in Beni took the initiative to regain control over Ituri, enlisted the Ngiti fighters of Walendu-Bindi (as well as others) to that end, provided them with weapons and tactical coordination, and carried out a joint operation with them, which ended up causing a number of civilian casualties because the troops were insufficiently trained and disciplined and went on a rampage once the military operation was over.[970]

The Majority sidestepped as "not persuasive" a series of alternatives proposed by the Defense. But cognitive dissonance, while undoubtedly sincere and psychologically honest, was not a *sufficient* response, in legal terms, when these alternatives raised reasonable doubts about what actually happened.[971] With such alternatives on hand, the reasonable doubt standard cannot be satisfied by a tight chain of logical inferences, no matter how deep an acceptance they gain in the judges' personal will to believe.

> In order to satisfy the evidentiary standard, the inference that the Bogoro attack was aimed at the civilian population should be *the only possible inference on the evidence produced at trial*. Whereas I do not claim that it is unreasonable to think, from a first look at some of the evidence about what happened in Bogoro, that the attackers made no distinction between UPC

718), but nonetheless settled on this premise as a necessary presumption for its desired conclusions (para. 1144). A pillar of the Majority's position came from one more opaque document that was seen by the Majority to speak for itself – the *lettre de doléances* – which was a letter written in late 2002 by Lendu elders to local, national, and regional authorities, expressing their grievances, including harsh language about ethnic rivals. Katanga distanced himself from these views in his testimony (Katanga Testimony, October 11, 2011, T-322, pp. 13–16 (ENG pp. 12–15)); and the context of the letter is summarized by Judge Van den Wyngaert in her Minority Opinion (paras. 234–40, 251).

970 Katanga Trial Judgment, Minority Opinion, para. 219.

971 Ibid., paras. 299, 145.

> combatants and civilians, I strongly reject that this is the only reasonable interpretation of the evidence.[972]

The Majority approached it differently, rejecting alternative explanations that could not pass its subjective test of conscientious persuasion. One might leave the matter at the level of individual psychology, if the authority of law were purely a matter of decisional weight in which two judicial votes cancel out one dissent. But the standard of proof in ICC cases promises a good deal more than this. The Majority represented its view not just as persuasive to itself but also as meeting the legal standard of *beyond reasonable doubt*. While hueing to presumptive building blocks that remained surrounded by doubt, the Majority would boldly assert its final conclusion in ultimate terms. Anything else would have meant another acquittal – abandoning the Bogoro victims and ignoring the possibility that Katanga might have lent some kind of support to the whole outcome, even if the details were not fully manifest. Having seen weaknesses in the first liability mode brought by the Prosecutor, the Majority may have considered it its duty to salvage something from the shards of evidence that survived.

The dissenting judge saw the result as the Majority's determination to avoid an acquittal at all costs.[973] In her view, the Court's long-term integrity required the Chamber to admit when the outcome of a case could not be determined either way by the evidence:

> Let me be clear, I do not claim to know more about the facts of this case than my colleagues or to have a better understanding of the situation in Eastern-DRC in 2002–2003. On the contrary, I am keenly aware of the limitations of the available evidence, which makes it impossible, in my view, to form a balanced and complete picture of what really happened during the weeks and months leading up to the attack on Bogoro or indeed on that day itself. Accordingly, the only thing I pretend to know is that we do not know enough to convict Germain Katanga of the charges against him, be they under article 25(3)(a) or 25(3)(d)(ii).[974]

An important long-term issue for the ICC trials will be the significance of acquittals. Given the small number of cases before the Court, acquittals burden the particular faith in impunity, stirring fears of an overly skeptical judicial view of the evidence. On the other hand, convictions like the Katanga Judgment burden the particular faith in neutral legal principles, weakening

972 Ibid., para. 4 (emphasis added); see also para. 149.
973 Ibid., paras. 314, 310, 311.
974 Ibid., para. 319.

the presumption of innocence and spreading skepticism about the value of legal principles in the larger humanitarian battle.

8.5 JUDICIAL REFLECTIONS ON MODES OF JUDGING

Appealing an Acquittal

It's a "very delicate process," to be sure – determining the merits of the case. It requires a critical application of the judge's "appreciation skills," which cannot be reduced to simple formulas or stale exercises.[975] Sounding the alarm about judicial reasoning were two skeptical judges, dissenting from the five-judge Appeals Chamber decision that narrowly upheld the acquittal of Mathieu Ngudjolo. The Majority had relied heavily on the same deferential review of trial reasoning laid down by the Lubanga Appeals Chamber, less than three months before.[976]

But the dissenters were in no mood for deference, in the face of a Trial Chamber acquittal. Their dissent was an occasion for sharpening the jurisprudential debate, exposing tensions in judicial styles coming out of the first two Congo trials. So much had been said about fairness to the Defense in those trials: but what about fairness to the Prosecution? And wasn't it more important to find the truth than to obsess about procedural rights? Finding the truth was the whole purpose of a trial, and yet the Ngudjolo Trial Chamber had tied itself up in rhetorical knots. It was time to stipulate best practices for judicial deliberations. At the end of that process, it was also time to apply some restraints to the *reasonable doubt* standard of proof, which had been allowed to reach hyperbolic levels. Not all doubts are reasonable enough to produce an acquittal. It was now time for judges to search their souls, bringing final decisiveness to the battle against impunity. Deference to the trial judges depended on whether they had done their jobs properly in the Trial Judgment. The Ngudjolo acquittal was instead filled with obscurities and distractions.

So much had happened in the second Congo trial, with attention shifting to the Trial Chamber's voyage of discovery under the flag of Regulation 55. Two trial judges had rescued the Katanga conviction, and Katanga's case would never reach the Appeals Chamber. But through it all, the Ngudjolo case lived

[975] Ngudjolo Appeals Judgment, Joint Dissenting Opinion of Judge Ekaterina Trendafilova and Judge Cuno Tarfusser, ICC-01/04–02/12–271-AnxA, para. 45.

[976] The composition of the Appeals Chamber was different now from three months previously in the Lubanga Appeals Judgment. Gone was the lone dissenter, who would have overturned Lubanga's conviction, replaced by a judge prepared to overturn Ngudjolo's acquittal.

on, even as the newly liberated accused pursued his futile request for asylum in the Dutch courts.

For both high-profile cases, it was a sobering ordeal, in contrast to the extravagant hopes expressed by the Prosecutor and Legal Representative of Victims on the opening day of the joint trial. Katanga's conviction came at the price of a reduced mode of liability. In the larger battle against impunity, that conviction missed its rendezvous with history by dropping charges specifically tied to crimes of sexual violence. The Ngudjolo Appeals Judgment offered a final critical forum for judicial reflection on these tumultuous events. And it previewed the reckoning, three years later, by another divided Appeals Chamber in overturning the convictions of Jean-Pierre Bemba.

Faith and Skepticism about Reasonableness

It was not as if the Ngudjolo Trial Chamber had proclaimed his innocence. With its grudging and convoluted prose, the Judgment made perfectly clear that it was not exonerating Mathieu Ngudjolo.[977] All it meant was that the judges – all three of them – could not reach a level of subjective belief that the evidence met the standard of proof beyond reasonable doubt.

In the rhetorical shadows of this perplexing Judgment, much was said (using conditional verbs and modal qualifiers) about what else might have been true in the confusing circumstances of 2002–03. And so much remained unknown about the events in Ituri, especially during that critical month of March 2003, following the battle in Bogoro and the sudden ouster of the UPC from Bunia. Doubts about the Prosecution's main case – about the insistence that Ngudjolo had jointly masterminded the February Bogoro attack – seemed to morph into a dense cloud of ignorance, as the Trial Chamber could discern no rational pattern to the parade of would-be militia leaders, with everyone sporting impressive uniforms and hailing each other with exalted military titles, all ready to sign peace documents on behalf of organizations dignified by acronyms – all transcribed into the handy chart later compiled by HRW. Perhaps it was this cloud of ignorance that prompted the trial judges' wistful

[977] Problematic on appeal was the Ngudjolo Trial Chamber's linguistic contortions, as when it declined to find Ngudjolo's military rank confirmed by his later public appearances. It would not infer his prior rank from later circumstances because "it cannot necessarily be entirely discounted" that there were completely different reasons for his subsequent status (Ngudjolo Trial Judgment, para. 500). The Ngudjolo Appeals Judgment wades into this formulation, gently rebukes the Trial Chamber's "somewhat cursory analysis," but concludes that it was "not unreasonable" (para. 117).

desire for more evidence about the social and cultural background of the region.

The Ngudjolo appeal raised an important jurisprudential question: whether the passive style of appellate review for Lubanga should prevail when the Prosecution was appealing an *acquittal*. If the struggle against impunity might someday prevail on its chosen battlefield of the courtroom, perhaps there should be more energy at the level of appeals. In this way, the deferential approach laid down by the Lubanga Appeals Chamber suddenly came under close scrutiny. The Lubanga Appeals Judgment called for deference with respect to the Trial Chamber's factual findings and its use of broad presumptions and paradigms for establishing modes of liability.[978] In that first review of an ICC Trial Judgment, the Appeals Chamber announced that it would not relitigate judgments of facts that were supported by some reasonable basis. Only if the judgment in question seemed unreasonable, after applying a generous margin of appreciation – only in that case would a factual determination be rejected. Even then, to overturn the whole decision, the impugned conclusion must have played a substantial role in determining the outcome of the trial.[979]

On its face, the skeptical turn by the Ngudjolo appeal dissenters was opportunistic. Even if the Ngudjolo Trial Chamber seemed haunted by its own doubts, it was unable, finally, to accept the testimony of virtually all the witnesses who placed Ngudjolo at the nerve-center of the Bogoro attack. It decorously suggested that even some witnesses with credibility issues nonetheless conducted themselves honorably for some parts of their testimony. But it didn't add up to a conclusion of guilt beyond reasonable doubt. The ICC statute endorses the *presumption of innocence* in Article 66, placing the onus of proof on the Prosecutor and adopting the *beyond reasonable doubt* standard as obligatory on the Court.

If the deferential style of appellate review were to face deeper skepticism, it might have happened instead in the Lubanga case, which was an appeal from a conviction. Of the two judges raising skeptical doubts in the Ngudjolo appeal, Judge Cuno Tarfusser took no part in the Lubanga appeal; but Judge Ekaterina Trendafilova had endorsed the deferential approach in that earlier case. For the Prosecutor's appeal in Ngudjolo, she moved from the style of faith to the style of skepticism – albeit a mode of skepticism aimed at certain principles of legality.

978 Lubanga Appeals Judgment, December 1, 2014, ICC-01/04–01/06–3121, paras. 21, 27.
979 Ibid., paras. 18–19.

Fair Trial Rights for Whom?

The two Ngudjolo appeal dissenters needed some sturdy legal principle for support: a principle strong enough to counter the presumption of innocence. They needed to find legal values elsewhere in the Rome Statute for setting limits to the Defense-leaning standard of proof – some kind of "balancing" principle to achieve the "delicate process" of judging in international courts. Later on, when yet a third Appeals Chamber released its Judgment overturning the convictions of Jean-Pierre Bemba, the narrow appeals Majority would raise similar questions about the deferential style of review; but in that case it would rely fully on the presumption of innocence. The discussion in that third appeals case would further deepen the dialogue within fractious appeals benches about the proper modes of fact-finding and determinations of guilt.

The Ngudjolo appeal dissenters approached this debate about judicial styles by mustering forces on behalf of the prosecutorial mission. In an audacious move, they advanced an oblique reading of the Rome Statute's provision on fair trials. Article 64(2) provides: "The Trial Chamber shall ensure that a trial is fair and expeditious and is conducted with full respect for the rights of the accused and due regard for the protection of victims and witnesses." Although the concept of fair trial rights is normally seen as tipping the scales in the direction of the Defense, the Ngudjolo appeals dissent speaks broadly of fairness rights for the Prosecution and for the victims. The appeals Majority declined to wade into the fair trial issue "in the abstract," reducing its analysis to the more practical question of whether the Prosecution was given adequate opportunity to present its case.[980]

But it wasn't clear whose vision of the fair trial should prevail. In the Lubanga trial, the Defense had wanted to seize control of the fair trial principle. Notably in its "Abuse of Process" application, the Lubanga Defense insisted that the Prosecution's testimonial evidence had been hopelessly corrupted by intermediaries. In this context, however, the Lubanga Trial Chamber designated *itself* as the custodian of the accused's fair trial rights, pledging that it would not falter in safeguarding that fairness, in part by exercising its fact-finding power with supreme skill and insight.[981] The sweeping fair trial issues in the Lubanga case included disclosure of the Prosecution's exonerating evidence, as well as disclosure by the Prosecution of identities for the impugned intermediaries – with the Trial Chamber on

[980] Ngudjolo Appeals Judgment, para. 256; Joint Dissenting Opinion, para. 6.

[981] Lubanga Trial Chamber, Redacted Decision on the Defence Application Seeking a Permanent Stay of the Proceedings, March 7, 2011, ICC-01/04–01/06–2690, paras. 197–98.

both occasions prepared to abort the trial in Lubanga's favor, if the Prosecution failed to comply with judicial orders.

The cumulative drama of the Lubanga case strengthened the notion of Defense fair trial rights; but it leaned even more heavily on the principle of judicial supremacy. Trial judges (backed up by interlocutory appeals decisions) would protect the Defense by taming the excesses of the Prosecution. But those same judges would also ensure that the trial did not fall apart in the end. Defense rights would be fully protected by judges acting as impartial assessors of facts and guilt, serving not just one of the parties but all interests involved in the trial process.

Article 64(2) does not explicitly address the Prosecutor's claim to some measure of fair treatment during the course of a trial. Indeed, by entrenching the presumption of innocence, the Rome Statute ensures special solicitude for the Defense as the primary beneficiary under fairness standards. It came as a surprise, then, when the Ngudjolo appeal dissenters insisted that the Prosecutor might assert, as a procedural error on appeal, a violation of its own fairness rights under Article 64(2). The dissenters invoked a legal precedent from the Yugoslav Tribunal's famous Tadič Appeals Decision, for the notion "'that the right to a fair trial . . . covers the principle of equality of arms,' which 'means that the Prosecution and the Defence must be equal before the Trial Chamber.'"[982] If equality of arms is inherently reciprocal, then the Prosecution should not be placed at a disadvantage over against its adversary. That may not be the only inference from what Tadič said, but it became a point for leveraging further notions.

What was the precise disadvantage befalling the Prosecution in the Ngudjolo case? Exactly what kind of unequal treatment took place? The answer may look contrived, but it meant to elevate the reciprocity notion to a more powerful principle. It seems that the Trial Chamber withheld some vital materials from the Prosecution, abusing its power of managing courtroom evidence. The Prosecution wanted specific access to certain administrative records, held tightly by the Trial Chamber, relating to Ngudjolo's alleged corrupt communications with witnesses, in phone calls recorded at the ICC detention facility. The Ngudjolo appeal dissenters championed the Prosecutor's complaint that withholding this specific information "prevented the Prosecutor from conducting a proper and effective presentation of her case in order to meet her statutory obligations."[983]

[982] Ngudjolo Appeals Judgment, Joint Dissenting Opinion, para. 6, n. 6.
[983] Ibid., para. 7.

But what were these vital "statutory obligations"? Nothing less than the all-important search for *truth*, for which the Prosecutor demanded an independent privilege.

Fairness and the Search for Truth

For the Ngudjolo appeal dissenters, the argument from Article 64(2) was not quite enough, reaching no farther than strict parity between the two sides. The fuller argument is that such equality requires allowing the Prosecutor to meet her unique statutory responsibilities under Article 54(1)(a): "The Prosecutor shall: In order to establish the truth, extend the investigation to cover all facts and evidence relevant to an assessment of whether there is criminal responsibility under this Statute and, in doing so, investigate incriminating and exonerating circumstances equally." To achieve equality on the neutral playing field of fair trials, the Prosecution demanded access to materials it deemed necessary for its truth-seeking mission. By blocking full disclosure about Ngudjolo's unauthorized communications, the Trial Chamber prevented the Prosecution from conducting its larger functions, rising to the level of a procedural violation of Article 64(2) – the Prosecutor's fair trial rights. These rights are underwritten by the higher mission of truth-seeking.[984]

As with the "equality of arms" concept, this reference to *truth* carries the Ngudjolo appeal dissenters further out onto a weak interpretive limb. Article 54(1)(a) puts truth-seeking into a subordinate clause, subservient to facts and evidence relevant to the assessment of guilt, stipulating that the Prosecutor shall operate in an impartial manner at the stage of investigations.[985] The thrust of the article is to impose on the Prosecutor a duty of achieving balance in the pursuit of truth. But there is no denying the talismanic power of the word *truth* at moments of greatest anxiety for prosecutors, victims, and the judges themselves. Its magical qualities pose a counterweight to *fairness* for the Defense, limiting the discretion of courtroom judges managing the flow of information. The Ngudjolo appeal dissenters invest this word *truth* with sufficient authority to challenge the hard-won dominance of courtroom judges as custodians of fairness and truth – the legacy of the shutdown crises in the Lubanga case.

984 Ibid., para. 15.

985 Article 54(1)(b) speaks further of requiring the Prosecutor to take all "appropriate" measures to ensure the effectiveness of investigations, and is consistent with allowing the Trial Chamber to determine "appropriate" rules for disclosing its own confidential sources of information.

There are further echoes of prior Lubanga battles, especially the crisis surrounding the charge that intermediaries had corrupted the testimony of key child-soldier witnesses. In that instance, the Lubanga Trial Chamber waged a high-stakes battle to compel the Prosecution to disclose the identities of the intermediaries, and to bring two of them to The Hague to testify in open court. Despite strong suggestions from the bench that the Prosecutor should consider bringing criminal charges against the two men for impeding the administration of justice (under Article 70), no charges were eventually brought.[986] It was in that same episode that the Lubanga Trial Chamber justified its demands on the Prosecution under the Chamber's power to "request the submission of all evidence that it considers necessary for the determination of truth" (Article 69(3)). The upshot of the whole Lubanga crisis was to underscore the dominant power of the Trial Chamber's truth-seeking responsibilities.[987]

Despite this stream of empowerment, the Lubanga Trial Chamber overplayed its hand by embracing Regulation 55, for purposes of augmenting the charges against Lubanga at the conclusion of the Prosecution phase. For all their powers to seek truth and to manage the evidence flowing through the courtroom, the trial judges could not abandon their duty to respect the fair trial rights of the accused (Regulation 55(2)) or to obey the statutory injunction to issue a final judgment that did not exceed the *facts and circumstances* contained in the original charges.[988] Even though this last constraint remained difficult to define, the contest over managerial powers of the trial judges continued through all the Congo trials. In this respect, the Prosecutor's appeals strategy in the Ngudjolo case highlighted important tensions inherent in the Rome Statute. And now two judges on the Appeals Chamber were prepared to strengthen the hand of the Prosecutor over against the Trial Chamber, realigning authority within the ICC Statute.

The Ngudjolo appeal dissenters asserted these broader arguments with rhetorical panache. Even if their arguments fell short on the level of principle, they were searching earnestly for some systematic limit on the Trial Chamber's powers to control the flow of evidence and disclosure.

[986] Lubanga Trial Judgment, March 14, 2012, ICC-01/04–01/06–2842, para. 1361. The Prosecutor later reported commissioning an external review, on the basis of which she decided to take no further action under Article 70. But there was no public access to that review, and a Defense motion to disclose it was denied by the Appeals Chamber. Lubanga Trial Chamber, Decision on the Defence Request in Relation to Investigations Pursuant to Article 70, June 17, 2014, ICC-01/04–01/06–3114.

[987] Lubanga Trial Chamber, Redacted Decision on Intermediaries, May 31, 2010, ICC-01/04–01/06–2434-Red2, para. 150.

[988] Lubanga Appeals Chamber, Judgment on Regulation 55, para. 88.

But the dissenters did not remain at the level of general procedure. They went on to challenge the Ngudjolo Trial Chamber's distrust of the main Prosecution witnesses, whose testimony was vital to the original case against Ngudjolo as a joint mastermind of the Bogoro attack. All but one of these witnesses were found to have serious credibility issues, causing the Chamber to arrive short of its exacting *beyond reasonable doubt* standard of proof. And yet the Ngudjolo trial judges seemed haunted by the possibilities of a *larger truth* lurking somewhere in the shadows of doubt. On appeal, the dissenters faulted the Trial Chamber's judicial style – filled with conditional verbs that added up to nothing – for abandoning these traces of important truths.

The Prosecutor lodged a specific appeals argument concerning witness P-250, the purported child soldier who remembered seeing Ngudjolo and Katanga relaxing, under the mango trees, in post-battle Bogoro on February 24, 2003. P-250's testimony was rife with conflicts, retractions, and mysterious deviations – perhaps because (as several Defense witnesses eventually pointed out) he was formally enrolled as a student in a distant school and could not possibly have been a child solder, let alone witnessed anyone lounging about in Bogoro on that date. But on appeal, the Prosecutor strongly contested this counter-narrative, pointing out that these Defense witnesses had their own credibility problems – which should not have been overlooked in a "fair trial" based on equality of arms between the two sides. At the time P-250 testified, the Prosecutor had realized this witness's many weaknesses and had asked the Trial Chamber for permission to quiz P-250 about possible intimidation, or other cultural sources of his apparent confusion. By denying this request, the Trial Chamber showed further disregard for equality of arms and trial fairness. But the appeals Majority noted that the Trial Chamber provided a full account of credibility issues involving P-250 and the Defense witnesses who spoke against him. In the Majority's view: "The Trial Chamber is not required to find a witness to be credible simply because other evidence appears to confirm the content of aspects of his or her testimony."[989]

The Deeper Strategy of Holism

To follow the spirited debates within the Ngudjolo Appeals Judgment, bear in mind that the Prosecution never gave up on its original narrative.[990] Despite

[989] Ngudjolo Appeals Judgment, para. 170; see also para. 152. Among the further issues regarding P-250 (after he finished testifying and left the ICC Witness Protection Program), Ngudjolo claimed that P-250 issued death threats back in Ituri against members of Ngudjolo's family (ibid., paras. 37, 39).

[990] Ibid., para. 35.

the obvious breakdown of the courtroom case, the Prosecution opposed the Regulation 55 maneuver to recharacterize the charges against Katanga. On appeal, it emphatically clung to its position that Ngudjolo was a supreme military leader, leading up to the attack on Bogoro, for which he was a joint mastermind.

The Trial Chamber, as it prepared to abort the Ngudjolo prosecution, seemed to lose patience with the elusive details of Ngudjolo's Ituri career. It dutifully marched through the evidence, pointing out prodigious gaps and conflicts in testimony, concluding with some wistfulness that the credible parts did not add up to proof beyond reasonable doubt. At least, this was the tone from two trial judges who then went on, in a burst of judicial boldness, to salvage the Katanga conviction. The third judge, who dissented at length in the Katanga judgment, had already noted profound weaknesses in the Ngudjolo case.[991]

The Ngudjolo trial ended with an acquittal. But the judgment managed to send mixed signals, offering the two appeal dissenters valuable talking points. The acquittal judgment went out of its way to separate its findings on evidence from any relation to the *truth* of what really happened surrounding the Bogoro attack. This pointed detachment suggested, with palpable regret, that the Court limited its own role to handicapping the trial evidence through discrete credibility scores, moving witness-by-witness, point-by-point, and document-by-document. Like educators marking after a grueling examination, their scores overall mainly fell short of the passing mark. For each witness, the weaknesses were plainly noted. Not everyone scored a zero, to be sure; but the total enterprise added up to nothing approaching the requisite standard of proof. The Prosecutor's narrative was not *necessarily* wrong, in some perfect-world way of thinking. After all, the case began with recollecting common facts that many considered to be general knowledge, including the all-too-real atrocities befalling Bogoro civilians. But the idea of a trial was to determine, inside the courtroom, whether the proffered evidence could substantiate that common knowledge, with sufficient confidence to meet the burden of proof. Only then could it overcome the presumption of innocence.

The Prosecution appeal challenged this dry method of scoring evidence. In effect, it demanded partial credit for witnesses who fell short of a passing score. The evidence from Ituri was never going to reach standards of perfection. As successive witnesses began to hemorrhage credibility, especially under cross-

[991] Ngudjolo Trial Judgment, Concurring Opinion of Judge Christine Van den Wyngaert, December 18, 2012, ICC-01/04–02/12–4.

examination about basic matters like birthdates, family members, and school attendance, the master narrative came under increasing pressure.

The remedy for all this dithering, according to the Ngudjolo appeal dissenters, was *holism*. For a Court dedicated to ending impunity, there should be adjustments in the judicial calculus, looking beyond just the numerous flawed testimonies. The word "holism" took on heroic qualities. By contrast, the Trial Chamber had used a flawed "piecemeal" methodology in calculating its sums. The alternative was to consider "the totality of the evidence." By compiling all the pieces of partial credibility, there would be a corresponding boost to each judge's level of internal conviction, reassured by thematic repetition and cross-witness consistency. Until this buildup of confidence could be achieved, it was pointless to consult the standard of proof for each step in a long journey. It was better to postpone the highest standard of proof until all the pieces could be compiled and aggregated. Proof beyond reasonable doubt would apply only to the final stage of judging composite facts – those facts that go directly to the central elements of crimes and modes of liability. These final holistic judgments, based on a proper judicial methodology, were the only determinations that merited appellate review – and only then should the standard of review grant full deference to the Trial Chamber.[992]

The insistence on this methodological point was hard to miss in the Ngudjolo appeal dissent:

> The finder of fact has to assess each piece of evidence in light of all evidence bearing on the element of the crime or the mode of liability in question, and give preference to the item *which best fits into the system* established by that evidence. It is our categorical understanding that only by conducting a holistic evaluation of the evidence can a trial chamber ensure that potential inconsistencies arising within or among individual items of evidence are overcome, if and to the extent possible.
>
> Only when the trial chamber does not confine its assessment to each individual piece of evidence in isolation will the trier of fact be in a position to make an accurate determination on the merits of the case.[993]

992 Ngudjolo Appeals Judgment, Joint Dissenting Opinion, paras. 33–40 (summarizing these elements of holism). On the matter of considering the totality of the evidence, this approach had already been endorsed by the Lubanga Appeals Judgment (para. 22). Indeed, Trial Chambers in all the Congo trials professed to embrace holism, welcoming the interpretive leverage for granting credit to evidence that was also subject to particular care, caution, and other metaphors of circumspection.

993 Ibid., para. 39 (emphasis added).

> Only when the evidence at trial is evaluated in its entirety can the accurate determination of the subject-matter of the case and, accordingly, the *truth* be achieved.[994]

Adversarial trials will always be littered with conflicting evidence and counter-narratives. All the more important, then, for Trial Chambers to reduce friction across witness accounts by using a rubric of mutual support, building up a "*synchronized system of evidence* adduced as a basis for the final determination on the merits of the case."[995] These outpourings of jurisprudential advice reveal the special mode of skepticism employed by the Ngudjolo appeal dissenters. It was a strategic skepticism, designed for questioning an acquittal, after members of the Trial Chamber found themselves short on evidence to achieve their joint and several moments of personal conviction about legal guilt. This particular form of holism operated on two levels: it salvaged otherwise deficient forms of evidence, and it produced its salutary effect by boosting the subjective confidence of the judge – which would reach its peak intensity at the final moment of decision. Holism was a top-down process: starting from some vision or *system*, it searched far and wide for confirming supports; and its summative features arose in the soul of each judge, where they were no longer open to scrutiny by others.

The word "holism" has a long career in theoretical discussions about courtroom evidence across multiple legal systems. In these academic debates, holism is often the victor in a ritual dichotomy with the strawman "atomism," said to apply mainly in common law systems, where bits of evidence molder in interpretive isolation. These debates tend to recycle the same rhetorical arguments, even footnoting the same references.[996] Almost as common is the weary assurance by common lawyers that masses of evidence are normally considered both individually and cumulatively. The same response comes in ICC debates, where judges faulted for insufficient holism continually reassure their critics that a judicious dose of holism was naturally applied to the case at hand.

What is at stake in this espousal of holism is not simply the logical distinction between whole and part. It is more the mechanics of aggregation. Holism's strategic design starts from a mental *gestalt* or prescribed pattern, serving as a magnet for stray bits of evidence that tend to fit the pattern. This is

994 Ibid., para. 35 (emphasis added).

995 Ibid., para. 48 (emphasis added).

996 Mirjan Damaška, "Atomistic and Holistic Evaluation of Evidence: A Comparative View," in David S. Clark (ed.), *Comparative and Private International Law: Essays in Honor of John Henry Merryman on his Seventieth Birthday* (Berlin: Duncker & Humblot, 1990), pp. 91–104.

what the Ngudjolo appeal dissenters mean by a *synchronized system of evidence* that allows the judge to search for evidence confirming the model of the whole. This method fits especially well with the jurisprudence of paradigms and presumptions, without which it would be difficult to support clear findings of individual criminal responsibility. While holism appears to be self-contained within a unified *system* constructed by judges – it is also fortuitously linked to the faith in some deeper *truth* outside the courtroom. With this leap of faith, the dissenters' initial skepticism has come full circle.

Holism in Practice: Mango Trees and Soap Powder

These general characteristics of holism can be gleaned from the passages cited above. But more helpful are the applications presented by the Ngudjolo appeal dissenters. We return once more to Prosecution witness P-250, the would-be child soldier who reported seeing Ngudjolo and Katanga in repose under the mango trees in Bogoro. The Trial Chamber disregarded this key witness for the Prosecution's narrative of joint masterminds, partly because of doubts raised by P-250's reported attendance at a distant school – far from the mango trees of Bogoro. Several other reasons for rejecting P-250's testimony were laid out by the Trial Chamber. But on appeal, the Prosecutor urgently pointed out that two additional witnesses had mentioned the mango trees shading the Bogoro victors: P-219 and P-28. P-219 was another critical witness, who also said he heard Ngudjolo take credit for the Bogoro attack. The question on appeal was whether some indication of a larger truth might be salvaged from all three witnesses – each with credibility issues – who all shared overlapping recollections about the mango trees. Using holism, there might be a greater truth lurking in the sum of these parts.[997]

But the Ngudjolo appeal Majority saw something quite different. Both P-219 and P-250 had been analyzed extensively by the Ngudjolo Trial Chamber and judged not credible for the entirety of their testimony. In both cases, the Trial Chamber had already applied some spontaneous holism to compare evidence from still other witnesses, who might salvage any portion of their stories – only to conclude not.[998] On this basis, the appeal Majority concluded: "It was *not unreasonable* for the Trial Chamber to disregard evidence that may have potentially corroborated witness P-219's testimony as no corroboration is possible when a witness's credibility is impugned to such an extent that his or her

[997] Ngudjolo Appeals Judgment, para. 191, citing the Prosecutor's Appeals Brief and noting drily that three witnesses who all lack credibility cannot corroborate each other.
[998] Ngudjolo Trial Judgment, para. 269.

testimony is entirely devoid of any reliability."[999] From a mathematical perspective, two times zero is still zero.

In the Trial Judgment, P-28 had been granted low credibility for multiple reasons, including lying about his age and his involvement with intermediaries (including the intermediary from the Lubanga trial who had occasioned the crisis over disclosure). All this would have left the mango trees in some doubt as well. But P-28 received ambiguous marks in the final Trial Chamber reckoning, when he reported being close to Germain Katanga from at least February 2003, with the result that he "may be of interest to the Chamber with regard to Germain Katanga."[1000] So it was not a total zero with respect to *both* accused. And yet P-28 was likely never in a position to observe Ngudjolo, let alone those famous mango trees.[1001] As far as Ngudjolo was concerned, it was still difficult to link P-28 to a *synchronized system of evidence* composed of two other sums amounting to zero. In this case, the strategic faith in holism was not sufficient to reveal any larger *truth*.[1002]

Among the memorable parts of the second Congo trial was the judicial reckoning with the *lettre des savons* – or "the soap letter." It was an ordinary letter sent from a group in one Ituri village addressed to a second group in a different village, mentioning a visit of several weeks for the purpose of laying in basic household supplies, including soap.

If ever a piece of evidence needed to find some larger context, this particular letter required the strongest possible dose of holism to perform at all well for the Prosecutor. In the Prosecution's view, this letter was a coded message, sent by Group Z, traveling from Ngudjolo's home village (Zumbe), to Group A living in Katanga's home village (Aveba), noting the occasion of their three-week presence in Aveba. Hiding its true message behind an innocent cover story was, to be sure, consistent with having guilty motives, such as planning the upcoming attack on Bogoro. Instead of soap, the traveling delegation must have been picking up ammunition from the air depot known to be in Aveba. The coded aspects may seem strained; but this was not just more oral testimony; it was a written document that could be encouraged to speak for itself. A secret message fit right into the Prosecution's *synchronized system*.

To "seal" the argument, the courtroom could see plainly on the letter a seal with the initials FRPI and a return address from a group that could have been

999 Ngudjolo Appeals Judgment, para. 192.
1000 Ngudjolo Trial Judgment, para. 253.
1001 Ibid., para. 254.
1002 In the Katanga Trial Judgment, Minority Opinion, Judge Van den Wyngaert thought all of P-28's testimony should have been dismissed, with the only corroboration coming from sketchy sources – an example of misplaced holism (paras. 156–63).

a forerunner of the FNI. Here then was evidence that might link the two masterminds, perhaps working by stealth through allies from their respective villages, but memorializing their joint venture with the symbols of their respective military organizations. This story was not just some retrospective guesswork, growing out of the confusion of March 2003. The soap letter was dated January 4, 2003, placing the visit some ten weeks prior to the attack on Bogoro, and potentially linking the two military structures contained in the Prosecution's master narrative. The Prosecution kept this soap letter near the top of its list of supports for the master narrative – and never abandoned it. If there was to be a *synchronized system of evidence* for leveraging some of the more doubtful witnesses, the soap letter formed a kind of nucleus. Its own power as evidence seemed to approach the legal standard of "speaking for itself."[1003]

Of course, the Defense teams for both Ngudjolo and Katanga found a counter-story for the famous letter, even though many details remained contested. The author of the letter (a man from Ngudjolo's home village) testified before the ICC that it was a letter about soap, written for the benefit of a local Aveba vendor who was thereby willing to release some funds for the group's household purchases. Soap or no soap, the seal on the letter caused the most controversy; with the letter's author saying that he hadn't seen or used such a seal at the time he sent it. In extended testimony on these points, witnesses for the Defense noted that the preparation of seals was a flourishing home industry, with new seals being concocted all the time.[1004]

For the Ngudjolo appeal, the advocates of holism asserted that the soap letter provided support for the testimonies of P-250 and P-28, both of whom reported seeing delegations from Zumbe visiting Aveba. Based on challenges from the Defense, it appeared that neither witness was actually present in Aveba at the time of the soap delegation's visit. P-28's roster of visitors was different from the names invoked in the soap letter. The real strength of the soap letter as a catalyst for credibility was its documentary status: the letter (with some interpretive help) was invited to speak for itself, especially through its all-important seal. In the Ngudjolo Trial Judgment, any synergies here were

[1003] The existence of a physical letter, taken as self-evident, might have shifted the burden of proof onto the detractors of the letter, in the manner of the legal doctrine *res ipsa loquitur*. But the Ngudjolo Appeals Judgment (Majority) aligned its approach with the larger presumption of innocence and found the Trial Chamber's treatment of the soap letter "not unreasonable," notwithstanding the overlap with P-250's testimony (para. 143).

[1004] In his own testimony, Ngudjolo stated simply that a group from his village went to the marketplace in Aveba to purchase wash powder (Ngudjolo Testimony, November 9, 2011, T-331, p. 32); and that seals were commonly concocted for all kinds of purposes (ibid., November 10, 2011, T-332, p. 61).

downplayed; and P-28 was discounted as a credible witness. But when it came to the Katanga conviction, P-28's credibility was suddenly elevated. And in the Katanga Trial Judgment, the soap letter was read holistically by the two judges voting for conviction.[1005]

The third Katanga trial judge, dissenting from the Trial Judgment, questioned the contrived holism of her colleagues in their determination to convict Germain Katanga:

> What is even more striking with respect to this instance of alleged corroboration is the selective manner in which my colleagues have chosen to rely on P-28's testimony. Indeed, as the Majority recognizes, the composition of the delegation mentioned in the "Lettre des savons" is different from the composition of the delegation mentioned by P-28. One would assume that this immediately puts an end to any suggestion of corroboration. However, the Majority resolves this obstacle by simply discounting those parts of P-28's testimony that are incompatible with the contents of the "Lettre des savons" and simply concludes that there was "a" delegation from Zumbe. With all due respect, this is like saying that if one witness states that she saw an eagle and another witness states she saw a parrot, then it is safe to conclude that there must have been a bird.[1006]

If holism is just another term for seeking corroboration from multiple sources, then it is a common judicial practice embraced on all sides. Fact-finding is never restricted to atomistic bursts, starting each time from a totally clean slate. But there is some deeper strategy at work when judges or prosecutors impute *synchronized systems of evidence*, and then proceed to confirm them by searching far and wide among the remains of discounted court testimony (or mysterious documents). The holism–atomism dichotomy was a red herring: the legal process requires elements of both. What matters is precisely when to be holistic and how far (an exercise of faith); and when rather to disaggregate and to cash in your chips (an exercise of skepticism). In the second and third Congo trials, split rulings by judicial benches brought these tensions into the dialogue on ICC jurisprudence.

Holism promotes the reduction of judicial decisions to moral certainty, deep within the judicial soul. There is a well-known psychological attraction to coherent stories, along with a common tendency to fit new bits of information into existing patterns of thought or perception. Cognitive psychologists have been studying *confirmation bias* for the past five decades; but it is also something that most people recognize from simple introspection. It correlates

[1005] See Katanga Trial Judgment, paras. 614–16.
[1006] Katanga Trial Judgment, Minority Opinion, para. 160.

on a subjective level with the role of default structures in all levels of argumentation. It dovetails with the use of paradigms and presumptions in applying legal doctrines of criminal responsibility. The judicial debate over holism brings this same mode of practice (holistically, as it happens!) to the hard judicial task of fact-finding. In the view of the Ngudjolo appeal dissenters, the holistic judge brings a *synchronized system of evidence* to the evaluation and comparison of like-minded facts. Significantly, judicial conclusions reached holistically come wrapped in the declaratory authority of the judge's satisfied conscience. And they will be received on appeal with great deference. As further elements of the holism strategy become clear, they reach their final target by reframing the legal standard of proof.

Reasonable and Unreasonable Doubt

The persistence of the soap letter stems from the conviction that some bits of evidence speak for themselves – so much so that further doubts can be laid aside. Because it is theoretically possible to form doubts about the most obvious facts, there is such a thing as overzealous doubting. The standard of proof in criminal trials – *beyond reasonable doubt* – must be read in its entirety. It does not say "beyond all doubt," where doubts might include the hyperbolic doubts that swirl around spirited Defense arguments. Taken seriously, the word "reasonable" restricts the modes of doubt that must be overcome to gain a conviction. The battle against impunity wants to play out on level ground, living in a common-sense world.

The Ngudjolo Trial Judgment created a twisted narrative around reasonable doubt. In reporting its inability to meet the required standard of proof, it went out of its way to distance its conclusions from possible real-world truths, refusing to venture beyond the evidence presented (and rejected) in court. But it also invoked certain improbable, speculative events to justify its failure to accept the Prosecution's original narrative. This opened the way on appeal for the Prosecution to charge the Ngudjolo Trial Chamber with raising the standard of proof to impossible levels.

A striking example for the Prosecution was the Trial Chamber's unwillingness to believe fully in the status of Ngudjolo as a supreme commander prior to the attack on Bogoro. For the Prosecution, this assessment was but a tiny inference from testimony that went unchallenged in Ngudjolo's trial: that Ngudjolo had signed various peace documents in March 2003 using high military titles, with the notable encouragement of other active commanders from Ituri. It was simply impossible, argued Prosecutor Eric MacDonald, that Ngudjolo could be hailed as a military hero in mid-March, while being nothing more than a back-country nurse in the months prior. In his cross-examination of Ngudjolo, MacDonald used his full rhetorical toolbox to ridicule Ngudjolo's denial on this point. It came as close to a self-confirming inference as MacDonald could imagine.[1007]

How could the Ngudjolo Trial Chamber remain unconvinced? Here was their finding on this central point in the Prosecution's collapsing case (as quoted in Section 8.1 (see footnote 798)):

> Whilst the Chamber notes that the Accused wore a military uniform from the time of his first public appearance in March 2003 . . ., it also noted that the rank of colonel was only mentioned during the signing of the 18 March 2003 Agreement to end Hostilities. Besides, the Chamber is *possessed of no other reliable evidence* previous to this date supporting a finding beyond reasonable doubt that Mathieu Ngudjolo was the commander-in-chief of the Lendu combatants from Bedu-Ezekere. Furthermore, *it cannot necessarily be entirely discounted that as a soldier operating within the prevailing political and military context of the time, Mathieu Ngudjolo was able to position himself as a key figure after the battle of Bogoro, but not before* . . .. [H]is appointment to a very senior position within the FNI/FRPI alliance *does not necessarily prove* that he was already a senior military leader prior to the appointment and, in particular, before 24 February 2003.[1008]

But reasonable proof may not be the same as "necessary" proof. The final sentence of the quote takes an inference considered obvious by the Prosecution and faults it for lacking strict logical necessity. Yet even some minimal orientation in the real world tells us that logical necessity is not a requirement for warranted belief. The doubts that matter here are only "reasonable" ones. Besides, elsewhere the Trial Chamber had accepted that the March events were "somewhat indicative" of Ngudjolo's prior status.[1009]

1007 MacDonald's certainty may simply have reflected his fixed assumptions about how military operations worked, based on his own background. In his response, Ngudjolo commented that the only way to know was to have been there yourself: "Prosecutor, you have to realize what the context was" (Ngudjolo Testimony, November 8, 2011, T-330, p. 51). In his direct examination on these events, Ngudjolo offered no pretenses, emphasizing that people assigned themselves useful ranks for purposes of advancement (October 28, 2011, T-328, p. 56); and further: "So the only reason was to give some significance to myself because, in fact, at the time I was not even a true soldier" (October 31, 2011, T-329, p. 18). In his cross-examination of Katanga, MacDonald cited the HRW report "*Covered in Blood*" as the source of his assurance about these events (Katanga Testimony, October 12, 2011, T-321, pp. 60–64 (ENG-pp. 54–57)).

1008 Ngudjolo Trial Judgment, para. 500 (emphasis added).

1009 Ibid., para. 434.

Another troubling reference to *necessity* appears in the next-to-last sentence. Lacking direct evidence on the point, the Trial Chamber says that it is logically possible to imagine that Ngudjolo's behavior in mid-March could have been caused not by his prior military status but rather by his opportunism during a strangely fluid moment in Ituri history. In response to this claim, the Prosecutor insisted on appeal that there was likewise "no reliable evidence" to back up this invented alternative explanation. In the contested landscape of a criminal trial, serious doubts should be based on some kind of evidence. But here the Chamber resorted to counterfactual speculations about things that are logically not impossible.

The Ngudjolo Appeals Chamber, both Majority and Minority, accepted the basic premise that "reasonable" doubts are a smaller class than any and all speculative doubts. Quoting the Appeals Chamber of the Rwanda Tribunal, the Majority endorsed the position that "[t]he reasonable doubt standard in criminal law cannot consist in imaginary or frivolous doubt based on empathy or prejudice. It must be based on logic and common sense, and have a rational link to the evidence, lack of evidence or inconsistencies in the evidence."[1010] But within the Ngudjolo Appeals Chamber, any common agreement was short-lived. In the view of the dissenters (echoing the Prosecution), there was an affirmative duty for the Trial Chamber to demonstrate the reasonableness of its doubts.[1011] Here, on the brink of final decision, the burden of proof shifts over to the Defense (and to the Trial Chamber) to show that its doubts are sufficiently reality-based. By mentioning the very category of hyperbolic doubt, the Prosecution hoped to shift some part of its own evidentiary burden back onto the doubters. When the evidence (such as the prior military status of Ngudjolo) speaks for itself, then these perverse doubters should have to defend their case.

The Ngudjolo appeal Majority was ready to make the case for the reasonableness of the Trial Chamber. With regard to Ngudjolo's confused military status, there was in fact quite a lot to draw on in the trial evidence. To be sure, the Trial Chamber stated its position awkwardly and mysteriously, turning Ngudjolo into a cipher while already shifting its attention to Katanga. But at least Ngudjolo himself told a coherent story about upstart alliances and the free invention of military titles, focusing on the tumultuous days in

[1010] Ngudjolo Appeals Judgment, para. 126, quoting from *Prosecutor* v. *Rutaganda*, May 2003.

[1011] Ngudjolo Appeals Judgment, Joint Dissenting Opinion, para. 65, using the example that the Ngudjolo Trial Chamber had not fully justified its reasonable doubt about the credibility of Ngudjolo's "confessions" to being the commander of the Bogoro attack. The Majority had already addressed this episode, resisting the shift of proof burdens onto the Trial Chamber to prove the reasonableness of its doubts (Ngudjolo Appeals Judgment (Majority), para. 103).

March 2003.[1012] The Prosecution was clearly not persuaded by these observations. It would have preferred to ratchet up the onus of proof to cash in on the Trial Chamber's own wariness.

The Prosecution was also lamenting the loss of its only incriminating witness whose credibility had not been rejected by the Ngudjolo Trial Chamber. Sonia Bakar (P-317) was the UN human rights official who heard (in March 2003) Ngudjolo take credit for leading the attack on Bogoro weeks before. Of all the witnesses who claimed any kind of knowledge about Ngudjolo's actions as a military leader, she was the only one considered credible and forthright. In the spirit of holism, her testimony might have provided enough weight to secure the general inference about Ngudjolo's active role in Bogoro. In the face of such evidence, the Trial Chamber's doubts surpassed the Prosecutor's understanding. Here is what it said:

> Although . . . there is no reason to doubt the credibility of this witness' [P-317] statements, it cannot be presupposed that the Accused actually assumed those military responsibilities imputed by the Prosecution. . . . [I]t cannot be ruled out that akin to others in Ituri at the time, [Mr. Ngudjolo] had wanted to claim responsibility for an attack so that he would be given a higher rank if integrated into the regular Congolese army."[1013]

In short, Ms. Bakar may have accurately heard what Ngudjolo said, but that doesn't establish its truth beyond reasonable doubt. On appeal, the overall reasonableness of this doubt was confirmed by a 3–2 vote. More strictly, the appeals Majority found that this *reasonable doubt* was itself *not unreasonable*, mainly because the Trial Chamber had articulated its ultimate judgment in subjectively sincere terms – even if tinged with ambiguity.

But deciding what it means to be *rational enough*, or *not unreasonable*, was itself a kind of oracular performance. Everyone understood that a majority of an Appeals Chamber had the final word; but now the full process of judgment was coming under the microscope. The standard of proof *beyond reasonable doubt* could not, without further analysis, resolve all doubts in favor of the Defense. Coming out of the second Congo trial, the *beyond reasonable doubt* standard was linked to other fundamental concepts of fair trials, equality of arms, and the overriding search for truth.

[1012] On cross-examination, Ngudjolo emphasized that his signature on the peace documents was meant to represent his community, not his militia (Ngudjolo Testimony, November 9, 2011, T-331, p. 42). During his separate testimony, Katanga made the same point (Katanga Testimony, October 14, 2011, T-323, p. 27 (ENG p. 26).

[1013] Ngudjolo Trial Judgment, para. 434.

The power of *reasonable doubt* would figure heavily in the Bemba Appeals Judgment, where another split bench continued the debate, offering new variations on faith and skepticism. In that next decision, the Appeals Chamber built on Judge Van den Wyngaert's observation in her Katanga dissent that a finding of guilt "should be the *only possible inference* on the evidence produced at trial."[1014] A Trial Chamber can rely on the incriminating version of events only "if all alternative explanations can be rejected for being unreasonable." It is not enough for the Trial Chamber to say, subjectively, that it was "not convinced" by the Defense position: "With all due respect, this is not the appropriate approach. Instead, the Chamber must convincingly explain why the alternative explanation is considered to be unreasonable."[1015]

This was not a subjective test but a protocol for weighing alternative hypotheses coming out of an adversarial trial, structured according to the presumption of innocence, and allowing public scrutiny of a discursive argument. The jurisprudential battle lines were rapidly taking form.

1014 Katanga Trial Judgment, Minority Opinion, para. 4 (emphasis added).
1015 Ibid., para. 145.

Jean-Pierre Bemba receives his eighteen-year sentence on June 21, 2016. ©ICC-CPI

9

The Trial of Jean-Pierre Bemba

9.1 IN THE FOREST, LOOKING FOR SOME TREES

A Hard Look from the Appeals Chamber

The ICC's third trial was even more tortured than the first two, lasting almost seven years past the pre-trial Confirmation of Charges. But Jean-Pierre Bemba's convictions for multiple crimes, including rape, were short-lived. Two years on, in June 2018, a divided Appeals Chamber erased his convictions and eighteen-year sentence, freeing Bemba after more than a decade in ICC custody.[1016] In doing so, the Appeals Chamber Majority also raised broad questions about patterns of reasoning used by trial judges, which had been permitted to stand with the timely deference of appeals judges. The third Congo trial was an ordeal for the accused, for the broken victims, and for legal counsel. It was also a clear moment of reckoning for the Court, approaching the twentieth anniversary of the Rome Statute.

This trial differed from the two earlier Congo trials in important ways. Jean-Pierre Bemba was a prominent Congolese political figure, a major power-broker possessed of wealth and continuing political influence at the national level. But the criminal charges stemmed from actions outside the Congo – a thousand miles away in the CAR.[1017] For the Court, it was a different *situation* from the first two trials, based on different politics and fresh prosecutorial calculations, even though it was yet another self-referral by a member state. Initially, the Prosecution tried to use the standard liability paradigm:

[1016] Bemba Trial Judgment, March 21, 2016, ICC-01/05–01/08–3343; Bemba Appeals Judgment, June 8, 2018, ICC-01/05–01/08–3636.

[1017] This distance, often cited in the legal briefs, is the overland route, with bad roads and few bridges. A plane ride between the CAR capital Bangui and Bemba's headquarters in Gbadolite would be closer to 150 miles.

defining Bemba as a mastermind-perpetrator of violence. But the Pre-Trial Chamber recognized important differences in this case, sending the trial into uncharted waters under the liability rubric of *command responsibility*.

The alleged crimes were committed in the context of a political coup, which ousted CAR President Ange-Félix Patassé. In late October 2002, members of Bemba's MLC militia crossed the border to help save the doomed leader, reprising their role from 2001, when their efforts had been more successful. According to humanitarian agencies on the ground in the capital city of Bangui, MLC troops were at the center of extreme violence carried out against innocent civilians, even as their supreme commander was tending to other matters back home.

Bemba's MLC movement was no longer just the rebellion that began in 1998, during the Second Congo War, when the Bemba clan rose up in solidarity with the ousted dictator Mobutu Sese Seko.[1018] Acting in alliance with Uganda, Bemba's forces opposed the Rwanda-backed RCD rebels, consolidating their stronghold in northern Équateur province. By late 2002, under the watchful eye of international peace brokers, conditions were changing, as Bemba came to play a dominant role in the Inter-Congolese Dialogue.[1019] Factional rivalries within the RCD only strengthened Bemba's stature, leaving him as the presumptive alternative to the weak national leadership of Joseph Kabila. From mid-2003, he became one of four transitional Vice-Presidents, setting himself up for a second-place finish in the 2006 Presidential elections. After losing to Kabila, and then losing an appeal before the Supreme Court, Bemba was subject to retaliation, and in 2007 he finally took his family and wealth into European exile.[1020]

Despite all this statesmanship, there had also been reports of MLC atrocities committed in Ituri in late 2002 and early 2003, in the western regions of that troubled district, near the lucrative gold fields. Operating alongside Ugandan strongmen, and fending off RCD forces from North Kivu, Bemba garnered a share of the mineral wealth then being plundered – even while, further east,

[1018] On the origins of Bemba's MLC and its early development, see Jason K. Stearns, *Dancing in the Glory of Monsters: The Collapse of the Congo and the Great War of Africa* (New York: Public Affairs, 2011), chapter 15.

[1019] See Emeric Rogier, "The Inter-Congolese Dialogue: A Critical Review," in Mark Malan and João Gomes Porto (eds.), *Challenges of Peace Implementation: The UN Mission in the Democratic Republic of the Congo* (Pretoria: Institute for Security Studies, 2004), pp. 25–44.

[1020] Filip Reyntjens, *The Great African War: Congo and Regional Geopolitics, 1996–2006* (Cambridge: Cambridge University Press, 2009), pp. 273–77 (on the election and Supreme Court challenge); Séverine Autesserre, *The Trouble with the Congo: Local Violence and the Failure of International Peacebuilding* (Cambridge: Cambridge University Press, 2010), p. 234 (on the post-election attacks and move into exile). Reyntjens mentions reports that an election oversight group of international ambassadors threatened Bemba with ICC prosecution if he persisted with his electoral challenges (*The Great African War*, p. 277, n. 111).

local Ituri networks were caught up in separate armed conflicts. The MLC campaign in western Ituri was decried by the UN and other groups, amid lurid charges of cannibalism carried out against the local pygmy population. The reported MLC motto was "*effacer le tableau*," and Bemba allegedly erased the competition when it came to sharing the region's wealth.[1021] It was during these same months that other units in Bemba's military force were engaged in the losing battle to save the CAR President. In November 2002, Bemba took a short break from his Congo affairs to visit his troops on-site in the CAR.

From the CAR came reports of appalling civilian treatment during the overthrow of President Patassé, including widespread sexual violence against women, children, and men. The Paris-based human rights organization FIDH began investigating in November 2002, completing its report in mid-February, just about the time Bemba was signaling his troops to withdraw.[1022] FIDH was eager to identify those "most responsible." When the organization received an inquiry from Bemba himself, asking for an assessment, FIDH denounced him as complicit in the violence – a co-conspirator with Patassé. For the NGOs, Bemba was a mastermind-instigator, not an innocent bystander. The FIDH report ended up at the ICC and helped guide Prosecutor Moreno-Ocampo toward the superior commander of the offending MLC.[1023]

A key novelty in the Bemba trial was the mode of liability. It was the ICC's chance to test the language in Article 28(a), aimed specifically at high military leaders for failing to control the actions of troops under their command. The legal doctrine of *command responsibility* had been evolving since World War II and was developed further at the Yugoslav Tribunal just when the ICC was drafting its own legal code. In the Bemba case, the ICC Prosecutor had started down a different path, framing the case with the same paradigm as the two Ituri trials: focusing on a supreme commander-mastermind, cast as the main *perpetrator* by way of the *control over the crime* theory. But the pre-trial judges rejected that familiar storyline, for reasons to be explained below, forcing the Prosecutor to rebuild the narrative around the idea of a supreme leader who

[1021] See MONUC, *Report of the Special Investigating Team on the Events in Mambasa, 31 December 2002 to 20 January 2003* (July 2, 2003), which puts Bemba's forces into that region between October 2002 and January 2003. Another commonly cited source is HRW, *Ituri: "Covered in Blood": Ethnically Targeted Violence in Northeastern DR Congo* (July 2003), which incorrectly locates MLC troops in Mongbwalu, fighting alongside Lubanga's UPC (pp. 23–27). For discussion, see Ntaganda Trial Chamber, testimony of Anneke van Woudenberg, June 23, 2016, ICC-01/04–02/06-T-108-ENG, pp. 14–21.

[1022] Fédération Internationale des Ligues des Droits de l'Homme (FIDH), *When the Elephants Fight, the Grass Suffers: Report on War Crimes in the Central African Republic* (February 2003).

[1023] FIDH Press Release, "War Crimes in the Central African Republic: FIDH Formally Brings Its First Case before the International Criminal Court" (February 2003).

wantonly failed to control his troops, thus abandoning his leadership duties. Notwithstanding this novel approach to individual criminal responsibility, the Bemba Trial Chamber stumbled over many of the same impediments as the first two Congo trials. In the final assessment of the Bemba Appeals Chamber, the evidence of Bemba's personal criminal responsibility was not strong enough, even if serious international crimes had been committed in the CAR.

The divided Appeals Chamber questioned the judicial strategies used for prior ICC convictions. While two appeals judges filed a vigorous dissent, a delicate coalition of views among the other three judges overturned Bemba's conviction and sentence. Later parts of this chapter will examine these developments in close detail. Along with the startling reversal of fortune for Bemba himself, the Appeals Chamber Majority faulted past trial practices (including those examined in previous chapters of this book, in the first two Congo trials). They challenged the method of fact-finding based on circumstantial evidence, weak corroboration of compromised testimony, subjective belief as the root of judicial decisions, reversals of proof burdens, and limits to the *reasonable doubt* standard of proof. They raised questions about extensive use of paradigms and presumptions in the determination of individual criminal responsibility, supported by fortuitous reliance on weak testimony. And for the conduct of appeals, the Majority announced a more exacting level of scrutiny for Trial Chamber findings of fact, in contrast to the deferential standards used for the first three accused. As the two most determined members of this Majority summed it up, in their separate opinion in the Appeals Chamber Judgment: "... proof of the forest requires proof of the existence of a sufficient number of trees."[1024]

It remains to be seen how future appeals bodies will respond to this critique advanced by the Bemba appeals Majority. The dissenting judges in this hard-fought decision connected their views to a contrasting judicial style spread across all three Congo trials, including the passionate dissent in the Ngudjolo Appeals Judgment. (But now, of course, that style was being relegated to appeals dissents, leaving its status in some doubt.) At the very least, these cumulative debates reveal a fundamental clash of judicial strategies that may be difficult to resolve in the heat of future adversarial trials.

In addition to prompting strong jurisprudential debates, the Bemba Trial Chamber endured its own sobering crises. Most dramatically, toward the end of the main Defense case, the Prosecutor formally accused Bemba, his lead counsel, and three others of bribing witnesses and fabricating documents. She launched a separate prosecution under Article 70 (crimes against the

[1024] Bemba Appeals Judgment, Separate Opinion of Judges Van den Wyngaert and Morrison, June 8, 2018, ICC-01/05-01/08-3636-Anx2, para. 60.

administration of justice). Arrest warrants in this special proceeding were enforced in Belgium, the Netherlands, France, and the Congo against four of the accused; Bemba himself was already in detention.[1025] After a halt in the main proceedings – amid concerns that the Prosecution's eighteen months of surreptitious eavesdropping on Defense communications might have compromised Bemba's fair trial rights – the case soldiered on, left to surviving members of Bemba's depleted Defense team. The four arrestees joined Bemba in detention for some eleven months, each one engaging a separate team of Defense lawyers (also new special counsel for Bemba himself). The four were conditionally released during the course of the special trial – which ended in five convictions but no additional time in detention.[1026] The story of this proceeding will be told in Section 9.4.

And yes, Regulation 55 made still another controversial appearance, in a Trial Chamber announcement made five weeks into the Defense presentation of its case.[1027] The threatened change in legal characterization of facts expanded the mode of liability under Article 28(a), beyond what had been specifically confirmed by the Pre-Trial Chamber. It meant another halt in proceedings while the Defense considered its limited options for making strategic changes. The tensions in this episode built on familiar controversies from the first two Congo trials, and featured yet again the managerial ambitions of trial judges, straining against the bonds of pre-trial *facts and circumstances*, raising all the familiar fair trial issues for the Defense. In its final Trial Judgment, the Chamber decided not to change the liability standard, instead sticking with the original formula from pre-trial confirmation. But the final word came from the Bemba Appeals Chamber, which adopted a more robust view of the *facts and circumstances* constraint, proposing new limits on judges and prosecutors seeking to change pre-trial stipulations during the course of a trial.[1028]

Upon release in mid-2018, Bemba emerged from detention with immediate thoughts of becoming a candidate in the October Congolese presidential election. But the electoral commission ruled him ineligible, and so Bemba did not become part of yet another closely fought and controversial electoral

[1025] ICC Press Release, "Aimé Kilolo Musamba, Fidèle Babala Wandu, and Jean-Pierre Bemba Gombo make first appearance before ICC," November 27, 2013.

[1026] Bemba *et al.* Pre-Trial Chamber, Decision Ordering Release, October 21, 2014, ICC-01/05–01/13–703; Bemba *et al.* Trial Judgment, October 19, 2016, ICC-01/05–01/13–1989; Bemba *et al.* Appeals Judgment, March 8, 2018, ICC-01/05–01/13–2275.

[1027] Bemba Trial Chamber, Notification under Regulation 55, September 21, 2012, ICC-01/05–01/08–2324.

[1028] Bemba Appeals Judgment, para. 115 on *facts and circumstances*.

outcome.[1029] His network of supporters remains largely in place, and it seems likely that Bemba will remain a force in Congolese politics.

What remains of his personal wealth is difficult to assess. Unlike the other Congolese accused, who were declared indigent and provided with legal aid, Bemba had parked his considerable fortune in Portugal, where the ICC could freeze his assets. Although he was expected to pay for his own Defense, the Court had to advance the up-front costs while figuring out how to manage the Portuguese funds.[1030] This arrangement raised expectations for the more than 5,000 accredited victims in the case, as any court-ordered reparations would likewise come from Bemba's personal fortune. Following the earthquake of his acquittal in 2018, Bemba filed a financial claim against the ICC for mismanaging his wealth, seeking millions of euros in damages.[1031] For the shocked victims, who were not prepared for the dramatic reversal on appeal, any hope for individual reparations was abandoned. But in the same instant, the ICC's innovative TFV announced a special program of benefits.[1032] It was a powerful reminder of the mission of the Trust Fund, with its orientation to humanitarian relief and restorative justice.

Chaos in Bangui

In early March 2003, President Ange-Félix Patassé congratulated himself – a bit too soon – for surviving the second coup attempt of his decade-long administration. As the first democratically elected leader of the CAR, Patassé had squelched the first rebellion, led by a former autocratic President back in May 2001. In that struggle he had needed outside help, including armed troops from Jean-Pierre Bemba, as well as from Libya and Chad. Then in October 2002 came a second attempt, this time led by Patassé's former army Chief of Staff, François Bozizé, who had been dismissed months before, and now returned from his temporary refuge in Chad. In late October, the same outside forces

[1029] "Congolese Court Bars Bemba's Presidential Candidacy due to ICC Witness Tampering Conviction," *International Justice Monitor*, September 6, 2018. In the meantime, Bemba has sought (so far unsuccessfully) to overturn his conviction under Article 70 (Bemba *et al.* Appeals Chamber, Decision on the Scope of the Bemba Appeal, August 20, 2019, ICC-01/05–01/13–2337).

[1030] Tjitske Lingsma, *All Rise: The High Ambitions of the International Criminal Court and the Harsh Reality* (Utrecht: Ipso, 2017), pp. 242–43.

[1031] That claim (apparently upwards of US$70 million) continues in 2019, as Bemba's lawyer seeks to join Belgium, Portugal, the Congo, and the United Nations as responsible parties. The standard under Article 85(3) is a steep one for the claimant to meet. See Bemba Pre-Trial Chamber, Redacted Filing of Bemba's Reply to Prosecution and Registrar's Filings on Compensation, July 17, 2019, ICC-01/05–01/08–3687.

[1032] See Bemba Trial Chamber, Final Observations on Reparations following the Bemba Acquittal (Trust Fund for Victims), July 6, 2018, ICC-01/05–01/08–3648.

returned and dug in around Bangui, with the blessing of the African Union,[1033] occupying the surrounding districts while the President hung on, and as Bozizé was driven back to northern CAR regions. But on March 15, as Patassé was returning from a brief state visit to Niger, his plane was greeted at the airport by gunfire – as Bozizé had made a lightning second strike. Patassé's plane rose back up and flew him off to Cameroon, on his way to exile in Togo.

The stand-off around Bangui coincided with alarming reports of widespread pillaging by both occupying troops and the rebels. Local CAR human rights organizations started collecting stories in October 2002, and discovered a pattern of brutal rapes and murders, including rapes of male community leaders that were clear acts of humiliation, seeking to intimidate the local population.[1034] The armed forces surrounding Bangui included CAR Presidential loyalists and the coalition of outsiders, but many victims described their attackers as "Banyamulengues," a derogatory term pointing to Congolese nationals.[1035] The victims' stories included reports of Lingala-speaking attackers, yet another indication of Congolese identity.

Sorting through the patterns of violence, local human rights activists around Bangui took immediate efforts to identify victims. In cooperation with religious leaders and local journalists, they concluded that the pillaging had been common on both sides of the conflict, but that the rapes and murders came primarily from the Patassé defenders. Local leaders notified their international federation, the Paris-based organization FIDH, which sent a fact-finding mission after the first burst of violence in October 2002. In its February 2003 report, it named both Patassé and Bemba as among those primarily responsible and sent the results directly to the ICC Prosecutor. Local CAR organizations were aware that the ICC Statute had come into force the preceding summer, motivating their efforts to document what had happened. With the final success of the coup in March 2003, another wave of violence accompanied the withdrawal of support troops back to the Congo and other home countries.[1036]

[1033] The intervention in 2001 had been approved by the Community of Sahel-Saharan States (CENSAD), in support of a democratically elected leader threatened by a coup. The move was endorsed by the African Union and a UN Special Representative. For background, see Press Report, "CEN-SAD Wants Peacekeeping Force in Bangui," March 7, 2002 (Panapress News Service).

[1034] FIDH, *When the Elephants Fight*, pp. 21–29.

[1035] Ibid. The term (spelled slightly differently) literally refers to "people of the Mulenge hills," designating Congolese of Tutsi ancestry living in a region of South Kivu. The FIDH report simply uses this name as a descriptive term.

[1036] FIDH Report, *Rule of Law, Respect of Human Rights, Fight against Impunity: The Essential Acts Still Have to Be Taken* (June 2004).

Under the guidance of FIDH, local activists continued to organize the victims. A UN-sponsored program in 2004 provided humanitarian assistance for the survivors of sexual violence, and a contingent of doctors from Spain brought further attention and structure to their plight. The Bozizé government encouraged these efforts, appointing one of the local human rights organizers to a state post to facilitate a formal referral to the ICC – which came at the end of 2004.[1037] Months earlier, the CAR judiciary reported that it would be "unable" (in the words of the Rome Statute) to prosecute the key perpetrators of the 2002–03 violence, who were inaccessibly situated in Togo, Chad, and the Congo. FIDH followed up in 2006 with yet another report emphasizing sexual violence,[1038] and the ICC Prosecutor finally opened an investigation in 2007, four years after receiving the initial reports.[1039]

Also in 2007, a political scientist from the University of Amsterdam conducted extensive interviews with civil society groups in Bangui. She interviewed the organizers of victim groups, digging into the hopes and anxieties of people whose lives had been unalterably changed. The pillaging had been relentless in occupied neighborhoods around Bangui. But the rapes (the victims included children and men) had been especially devastating, destroying community structures and leaving a burden of disease and despair. Approaching the ICC had brought them hope of recognition, and perhaps assistance in the form of reparations.

> Victims ... have invested tremendous hope and faith in the Court, but are generally very poor, sometimes ill, sometimes homeless, and often hungry. Some victims expect great personal satisfaction from the process: "When I myself heard the arrival of the people doing the inquiry, I had courage. I had courage seeing them. Thank God. To have justice."
>
> ... At the same time, while expressing a theoretical willingness to participate in trials, many victims also express concern about how they will survive to do so. According to an HIV-infected victim:
>
> "It's true that I want a trial. But they should at least bring little things so that I can eat. Because I am sick. I need to have strength to continue to wait. And we also want to do little activities that bring us more income to survive."[1040]

[1037] ICC Press Release, "Prosecutor Receives Referral Concerning Central African Republic" (January 7, 2005).

[1038] FIDH Press Release, "The Civilian Population in Northern Central African Republic Is in Great Danger" (March 1, 2006).

[1039] ICC Press Release, "Prosecutor Opens Investigation in the Central African Republic" (May 22, 2007).

[1040] Marlies Glasius, "'We Ourselves, We Are Part of the Functioning': The ICC, Victims, and Civil Society in the Central African Republic" *African Affairs* 108 (2008), 55.

Given the high degree of organization on the ground, the ICC recognized more than 5,000 victims as the Bemba trial progressed. But, as the interminable proceedings wore on, it was painful to imagine how the survivors coped with poverty and disease. It seems doubtful that many of Glasius's informants were still following the trial when the Appeals Chamber overturned Bemba's convictions in June 2018.

François Bozizé stood for election in 2005 and prevailed in a chaotic contest against opposing factions. There had been a series of rural uprisings and armed opposition groups, coalescing into what was referred to as the Central African Bush Wars. Further uprisings in the northeastern parts of the country (next to Darfur) brought down harsh retaliation from the Bozizé government.[1041] During this time, Bozizé was gently reminded by the ICC Prosecutor that ICC investigations in the CAR situation could include scrutiny of ongoing international crimes.

The CAR opposition grew even stronger during the years when the Bemba trial was being launched in The Hague, after a coalition of groups united behind an agenda pushing Muslim interests.[1042] After another troubled election in 2011, the Muslim-based coalition was accused of inflicting its own wave of violence on the ravaged country. Bozizé himself followed the well-worn trail of exile to Cameroon and was subsequently indicted by his successors for genocide and crimes against humanity. Christian militias joined the battle against the Muslim interim government, carrying out their own brutal attacks on civilians in Muslim communities.[1043] In 2014 there was a de facto partition of the country, with Muslim leaders declaring their own autonomous northern region in late 2015.

The level of violence caused a fragile new Christian-based government to make a second national referral to the ICC in May 2014, singling out the post-2012 wave of violence against civilians.[1044] In 2015, the government created a Special Criminal Court, with jurisdiction retroactive to 2003, integrated with the CAR judiciary but with a mixed bench of national and international judges.[1045] In early

1041 HRW, *State of Anarchy: Rebellion and Abuses against Civilians* (September 14, 2007).

1042 Muslim ideologies had emerged as a driver behind insurgencies in the last years of the Cold War and proceeded to spread. See Paul Thomas Chamberlin, *The Cold War's Killing Fields: Rethinking the Long Peace* (New York: HarperCollins, 2018), part III. The 2002–03 conflict between Patassé and Bozizé had little hint of ethnic components; but this was an exception to the later pattern of violence.

1043 HRW, *"They Came to Kill": Escalating Atrocities in the Central African Republic* (December 2013); *"I Can Still Smell the Dead": The Forgotten Human Rights Crisis in the Central African Republic* (September 2013).

1044 Press Release, Statement of the Prosecutor on Opening a Second Investigation in the Central African Republic, September 24, 2014.

1045 Patryk I. Labuda, "The Special Criminal Court in the Central African Republic: Failure or Vindication of Complementarity?" *Journal of International Criminal Justice* 15 (2017), 175.

2019, two suspects were apprehended and brought to The Hague, accused of a range of crimes committed by the anti-Muslim forces during the period 2012–14. The international community sees in this second round of prosecutions a new opportunity to bring justice to the CAR. Meanwhile, the population of civilian victims has swelled to new proportions, adding both hope and despair to the spirits of those who bear the brunt of political turmoil. Recent surveys of poverty and health conditions in the CAR confirm that the country sits near the very bottom of all 188 countries under review.[1046]

Confusion in The Hague

No one was sure why it took the Prosecutor so long to react to reports coming his way from the CAR. The flow of information started with the FIDH report in February 2003, which was followed up by a similar on-site visit from AI later that year.[1047] The self-referral was no surprise when it came in December 2004, as the Bozizé government brought on board the principal local human rights advocate to help manage the domestic judicial response. Most alarming in the materials sent to The Hague were the deeply researched reports on sexual crimes, confirmed by extensive victim interviews, suggesting a systematic pattern of intimidation carried out during the 2002–03 coup. The CAR judiciary had examined the evidence and certified its inability to prosecute the cases internally. That domestic judicial decision was later confirmed in April 2006.[1048]

Yet the Prosecutor didn't actually open an investigation until May 2007, more than four years after the alleged crimes were committed, when eyewitness accounts were growing stale. There was always the expense of pursuing cases in a new situation, at a time when Uganda, the Congo, and Sudan (Darfur) were soaking up resources. Perhaps Moreno-Ocampo was keeping an eye on the 2006 Congolese presidential elections, where Jean-Pierre Bemba had emerged as the leading challenger to the incumbent Joseph Kabila.[1049] International peacebuilders had invested moral capital in rebuilding the Congolese state – constricting Moreno-Ocampo's options in the Congo itself. But eventually the pressure from global NGOs proved overwhelming, in a situation where sexual crimes would necessarily become the central focus. At a time when the Lubanga prosecution was being criticized for its charges

[1046] United Nations Development Program, *Human Development Indicators Report*, 2019.
[1047] AI, *Central African Republic: Five Months of War against Women* (November 2004).
[1048] IRIN News Organization, "CAR-DRC: ICC Reviewing Suit against ex-President, Official Says," April 26, 2006.
[1049] See David Bosco, *Rough Justice: The International Criminal Court in a World of Power Politics* (Oxford: Oxford University Press, 2014), p. 142.

limited to child soldiers – with no particular recognition of the sexual travails of girl soldiers – organizations like the Women's Initiatives for Gender Justice added their voice to FIDH and others.[1050]

The Bozizé regime, too, was growing impatient. In September 2006, it lodged a plea with the ICC Registrar, urging the Prosecutor to "provide information on the alleged failure to decide, within a reasonable time, whether or not to initiate a [formal] investigation." The Prosecutor responded that the preliminary examination was moving along, rejecting the notion that there was any kind of strict timetable for deciding on the next phase. A team from the Prosecutor's office had traveled to Bangui and been in touch with local informants. A decision would result in the fullness of time.[1051]

Perhaps the unresolved questions had more to do with identifying the perpetrators than with confirming the crimes themselves. This was a critical moment for making the legal pivot from the crimes to the question of individual criminal responsibility. For human rights groups, both local CAR groups and global organizations, the focus was on victims and what they endured. It was their suffering and willingness to speak out that drove the campaign to take their cause to The Hague. But to bring a case before the ICC, there needs to be one or more suspects, and the crimes have to be linked to the individuals on trial.

The investigators closest in time to the first round of violence were from FIDH, conducting interviews in November 2002, just weeks after the events. Their report favored criminal responsibility for the commanders of three separate armed groups: the CAR loyalists reporting to President Patassé, mercenaries under the Chadian warlord Abdoulaye Miskine, and MLC troops reporting to Jean-Pierre Bemba. The suggested mode of liability was Article 28(a), which recognized the "superior responsibility" of military commanders.[1052]

The CAR criminal justice system determined in 2004 that it would not be possible to conduct domestic trials against the likely suspects. In addition to the three commanders listed by FIDH, it also considered accusations against the French mercenary Paul Barril, who had been working as an advisor to President Patassé, and two other aides of the ousted President. The range of possible suspects depended on the choice of liability theories, and the CAR

[1050] Women's Initiatives for Gender Justice, *Gender Report Card on the International Criminal Court*, 2007, p. 41. See also Katy Glassborrow, "CAR Case to Focus on Sexual Violence," Institute for War and Peace Reporting (May 24, 2007).

[1051] Benjamin N. Schiff, *Building the International Criminal Court* (Cambridge: Cambridge University Press, 2008), pp. 242–44.

[1052] IRIN News Organization, "CAR-DRC: ICC Reviewing Suit" (April 26, 2006) mentions a press briefing with Moreno-Ocampo in The Hague, indicating the ICC Prosecutor's awareness that the CAR courts had weighed legal charges against a larger group of suspects.

courts did not confine their scope to the "superior responsibility" mode recommended by FIDH.

As far as is publicly known, the only arrest warrant sought by the ICC Prosecutor was for Jean-Pierre Bemba. In May 2008, Belgian authorities arrested him and packed him off to The Hague.[1053] Authorities in Portugal had been monitoring his financial accounts. There could have been multiple reasons for narrowing the focus of the CAR situation to just a single case. The Prosecutor had already shown a marked selectivity when it came to the Congo, another self-referral where the Prosecutor omitted to confront more prominent suspects, whether those taking part in the Inter-Congolese Dialogue, or the intervening leaders in Uganda and Rwanda. Patassé had grown restless in his Togolese exile, and in 2008 had entered into reconciliation talks with his former rival, preparing to run again for elected office in the CAR. Pursuing Patassé in 2008 could have upset this delicate process. Removing Bemba from future Congolese politics would likely ingratiate the Prosecutor further with Joseph Kabila and his government in Kinshasa. There was also the matter of expense in mounting multiple cases. The wealthy Bemba might even have been self-financing as an accused. Other possibilities include the distractions of preparing individual warrants in the situation in Sudan (Darfur): in July 2008, the Prosecutor applied for an arrest warrant against President al-Bashir.[1054]

Two political scientists have suggested that the focus on Bemba was calculated to ensure CAR cooperation in the ICC's investigation prior to trial. It was obvious that Bozizé himself was not a propitious target (although his forces, too, had been accused of committing crimes during the original five-month stand-off with Patassé). In the further CAR turbulence that continued in 2008, Bozizé would be admonished to conduct his military actions according to the book.[1055] His steadiness would allow the ICC to carry out its business. For Bozizé, ridding himself of any potential threat from across the border in northern Congo was well worth his efforts in cultivating the ICC – a process of constraining potential opposition that the authors call "the international legal lasso."

> Cooperating with the ICC helped Bozizé in three ways. First, cooperation showed Western partners and donors that Bozizé was committed to accountability and the rule of law. Second, the ICC's prosecution offered a mechanism – the international legal lasso – to get rid of one of Bozizé's

[1053] ICC Press Release, "ICC Arrest Jean-Pierre Bemba–Massive Sexual Crimes in Central African Republic Will Not Go Unpunished" (May 23, 2008).

[1054] ICC Press Release, "Prosecutor's Statement on the Application for a Warrant of Arrest against Omar Hasan Ahmed al Bashir" (July 14, 2008).

[1055] Glasius, "We Ourselves, We Are Part of the Functioning," p. 56.

> potential challengers. Third, working with the ICC to prosecute Bemba helped Bozizé distract from and delay any possible investigation into his own troops' wrongdoing. International courts can take years – as with Bemba – to open, hear and adjudicate a case.
>
> Our research suggests that when violence is two-sided, the victors are more likely to cooperate if they can ensure that the ICC tries their opponents first. The victors calculate that a full decade could lapse before the court tried another party in the conflict. At that point, they can threaten to suspend cooperation.

The authors mention another example of the international legal lasso: the cooperation offered by President Ouattara of the Ivory Coast in the ICC prosecution of his electoral opponent Laurent Gbagbo. When pressure eventually came for the ICC to investigate the Ouattara group's involvement in electoral violence, the authors suggest, the regime reduced its level of cooperation.[1056]

Both the first CAR self-referral and the case against Jean-Pierre Bemba would not have happened without the strenuous efforts of local civil society groups in Bangui, in alliance with international NGOs. As Marlies Glasius notes:

> The manner in which the ICC investigation entered the socio-political life of the Central African Republic has been substantially different from other cases. In the DRC and Uganda, the prosecutor invited state referrals. The situation in Darfur was referred to him by the UNSC. In the CAR, on the other hand, some very small local human rights organizations first alerted their international counterpart for the possibility of soliciting an ICC investigation. When their report failed to attract the prosecutor's attention, they appear to have engineered a state referral . . ..
>
> As a result, rather than being seen as barging in without prior consultation, which was the perception of many civil society figures particularly in Northern Uganda, the ICC is seen as having come in, after much persuading, at the initiative of civil society figures, with lukewarm support from the state.[1057]

With such high levels of involvement in launching the case, the patience of the victims would be tested over the years in which the Bemba trial blundered on. But there was no alternative:

[1056] Courtney Hillebrecht and Scott Straus, "Last Week, the International Criminal Court Convicted a War Criminal. And That Revealed One of the ICC's Weaknesses," *Washington Post*, March 28, 2016. The news story is based on a subsequent article, "Who Pursues the Perpetrators? State Cooperation with the ICC," *Human Rights Quarterly* 39 (2017), 162.

[1057] "We Ourselves, We Are Part of the Functioning," p. 62.

> With no prospect of redress at the national level, the ICC is for [victims] a *deus ex machina*. They construct the ICC either as coming to do a trial "for them," or as being on their side through the mediation of "their lawyers," or "their NGO," led by a charismatic fellow-victim. Another motivation for victims to be involved ... is the expectation that the ICC will "look after them" in economic terms.
>
> ... [T]hey ... fully expect the Court to help them survive during and perhaps also after the trial, and sometimes conceptualize this as part of the "justice" that is to be done. A man who was raped and mutilated, and had seen his house destroyed explained: "I now live like a parasite at people's houses. So justice is needed. Because of my arm. So I can be rehabilitated. So that I can build a house to replace my house."

A teenage girl said:

> We prioritize justice. We wait for justice. But if justice occurs, we strongly wish to be supported so that we can really recover because, for example, currently, we cannot go to school .... So we want the Court to think about justice but also to support us to redo our life. Everyday, they talk to us, to ask us to interview us. We will wait for justice eternally without eating? We are hungry.[1058]

Facing hopeless challenges, the CAR victims' hopes were lifted in these brave initiatives taken up by local civil society. Professor Glasius conducted her interviews nearly five years after the wave of violence, just before still another tumultuous rupture for the citizens of this most unfortunate of nations. From The Hague, the Prosecutor selected a single individual to bear the burden of criminal responsibility in the context of several thousand victim-claimants. Eleven years later, when Bemba was suddenly acquitted, the only remaining beacon of hope from the ICC would come from the TFV.

As happened in the other Congo trials, the courtroom's attention-span was deeply divided between the crimes themselves and the proof of individual criminal responsibility for those crimes. In the Bemba case, there was no doubt that extensive violence had taken a large toll on civilians caught up in the central African political struggles. Victims' stories were extensively featured at trial and fully acknowledged in final judgments. But the Bemba trial was especially disjointed, as the proceedings focused intensely on the oblique relationship between the undeniable toll of human misery and the responsibility of Jean-Pierre Bemba. The next two chapter sections (9.2 and 9.3) follow this pivot away from the underlying crimes.

[1058] Ibid., pp. 62–63.

9.2 COMMAND RESPONSIBILITY

The Lure of Leadership

In all three Congo trials, the quest for criminal responsibility looked upwards to the heights of *leadership*. On closer scrutiny, this fixation on leaders faced serious obstacles, falling back on stereotypes and imputations that were then used to filter complex facts on the ground. Apart from all four suspects being Congolese, their roles and concrete actions as "leaders" were utterly diverse. They all carried titles of presidents or commanders (at various times), but with different practical significance. Among the four, Jean-Pierre Bemba had by far the greatest scope and power; and yet his judicial link to responsibility was also the most tenuous, looking more to what he *failed* to do than to any positive steps. In his case, too, the Trial Chamber mobilized factual evidence to defend its core presumptions, using a paradigm of leadership dating back to World War II.

In its first three trials, the ICC tested two different leadership models. The first (originating with the Lubanga Pre-Trial Chamber) was the model of a leader-mastermind, standing at the apex of an efficient organization, through which the leader's intended criminal plan is implemented. The efficiency level is so high that the plan encounters no friction, as it passes through the organizational structure. The physical crimes are carried out by foot-soldiers at the coalface of conflict.[1059] Under the *control over the crime* theory, the perpetrator who "commits" the crime in a primary sense stands at the top of the organizational chart. It is a model that failed to match the armed groups operating in Ituri during the period 2002–03, as the first two trials discovered. It fell apart completely in the cases of Germain Katanga and Mathieu Ngudjolo. In Lubanga's case, it survived with the approval of two out of three Trial Chamber judges, using strategic presumptions, supported by circumstantial evidence, about what Lubanga, as President of his UPC organization, knew, intended, and contributed to, in essential ways. There were further presumptions about Lubanga's power to prevent the offenses involving child soldiers, combined with an inference, from circumstances, that he must have failed to use that power, or simply accepted the risk that crimes would occur.

[1059] On the emergence of this important doctrine at the ICC, see Neha Jain, *Perpetrators and Accessories in International Criminal Law: Individual Modes of Responsibility for Collective Crimes* (Oxford: Hart, 2014), pp. 81–93. See also Miles Jackson, "Command Responsibility," in Jerôme de Hemptinne, Robert Roth, and Elies van Sliedregt (eds.), *Modes of Liability in International Criminal Law* (Cambridge: Cambridge University Press, 2019), chapter 15.

The second model of leadership made its appearance in the trial of Jean-Pierre Bemba. In contrast to *control over the crime*, this second model stresses what one might call *control over the prevention of crime*. It is codified under Article 28(a) in the Rome Statute with the rubric "Responsibility of Commanders."[1060] It imagines a military leader who does not openly direct the commission of international crimes by the foot-soldiers under his general command. The trigger for responsibility comes not from the leader's intent but from his degree of *knowledge* about those crimes – whether carried out in the past, present, or future. A leader with operational *control* over the rank-and-file is assigned a duty to react in some appropriate way: to punish past crimes, or to mitigate present ones, or to prevent future ones. This duty to eschew inaction is built into the legal definition of command leadership. In the CAR, where Bemba's troops had traveled to prop up the besieged President, the alleged crimes carried out by these troops had to be linked to their distant commander, a thousand miles away across the Congolese border. Under *command responsibility*, that link would come through this distinctive model of *leadership failure*.

Both ICC models stem from the same profound concern behind the Rome Statute: a desire to hold accountable those "most responsible" for international crimes occurring in complex mass violence. In such cases, the large toll of victims demands from criminal law new formulas for accountability. As Guénaël Mettraux noted in his comprehensive study, "... the focus of international criminal justice upon high-ranking individuals has prompted a search for legal mechanisms capable of capturing the conduct of those who, though not physically involved in the commission of the crimes, played an important part in the realization of these crimes or who bore responsibility for their remaining unpunished."[1061]

The mechanism of command responsibility brings strengths and weaknesses to this challenge. Although the ICC Prosecutor started out with the familiar mode of liability from his first two Congo trials, the Bemba Pre-Trial Chamber redirected the case toward Article 28(a). That Chamber's assessment of the pre-trial evidence fit the contours of Mettraux's definition of the command responsibility doctrine:

> *Stricto sensu*, "command responsibility" is concerned not with the criminal responsibility of a leader or commander who is personally and directly involved in the commission of criminal offences and who can be shown to have planned, ordered, committed or aided and abetted the crimes of others.

[1060] There is also an Article 28(b) dealing with superior leaders other than military commanders, who face slightly more exacting liability standards.

[1061] *The Law of Command Responsibility* (Oxford: Oxford University Press, 2009), p. 17. Mettraux became a formal member of the Bemba defense team.

> Rather it is concerned with criminal liability for a culpable omission to prevent or punish crimes of individuals who are in a position of subordination *vis-à-vis* the accused. Under international law, the doctrine of superior responsibility thus developed, not as a separate criminal offence, but as a form of liability for omission in relation to crimes of subordinates.[1062]

A more practical consideration, as noted by former ICC official Alex Whiting, is that command responsibility may provide a quicker route to conviction, in contrast to the complications (abundantly demonstrated in the first two Congo trials) of proving masterplans and "essential" contributions to the crimes from on high. "In some cases, [command responsibility] can be easier to prove than a charge of direct involvement in crimes and it offers an important avenue to promote deterrence." Coming from a seasoned coordinator of investigations and prosecutions in the ICC Prosecutor's Office during the period 2010–13, this strategic observation must be taken seriously. Following Bemba's conviction in 2016, along with the stiffest sentence yet imposed by the Court (eighteen years), there was a clear moment when this choice of mechanism earned due respect.[1063]

Ever since its inception in a landmark Japanese war crimes tribunal following World War II, the legal doctrine of command responsibility has produced a nagging anxiety about fairness. It runs the recurring risk of making military leaders accountable strictly because of their place at the top of the command structure. While its function is to foster accountability for war crimes, its origins seem closer to the law of torts: a socially imposed duty of care owed to unknown strangers. In the field of torts, with only civil penalties not extending to criminal punishment, the notion of "strict" duties for unintended acts has been readily accepted.[1064] But for assigning criminal responsibility to military commanders, the sense of justice says there must be something more than just the leader's high military title.

The notorious war crimes case against General Tomoyuki Yamashita, following World War II, is recognized as the first prosecution using some version of the command responsibility doctrine. The charge against General Yamashita was unclear as to whether *his* crime (as opposed to the atrocities carried out by his

1062 Ibid., p. 18.

1063 "Commanders Put on Notice," *Just Security*, June 28, 2016. (Two years later, after reversal on appeal, new doubts were raised about the future efficacy of this mechanism.) Whiting had previously served as a senior Prosecution attorney at the ICTY, where the doctrine of command responsibility was used extensively, starting from a different statutory base.

1064 The classic examples in Anglo-American tort law include strict liability on persons who engaged in ultrahazardous activities, such as handling explosives. For a policy-oriented description, see Fowler Harper, Fleming James, Jr., and Oscar S. Gray, *The Law of Torts*, 2nd ed. (Boston: Little, Brown, 1986), chapter 13.

troops) was anything more than being a high commander with a strict duty to prevent or punish the crimes committed by soldiers under his command. Stern judicial dissents from his case have been amplified by later commentators, challenging later courts to articulate additional factors (besides mere rank) to qualify command liability.[1065] Chief among these elements is some kind of knowledge on the part of the commander – an awareness of what happened (or would soon happen) as the trigger, if not a measure, for the obligation to punish or prevent the harm. In this case, culpability (what criminal law means by *mens rea*) comes exclusively from knowledge, not from any accompanying intent.[1066]

According to Mettraux's history, pervasive ambivalence about the "strictness" of command responsibility led to an unstable doctrine during the active years of the ICTY. That tribunal started with a bare-bones legal standard of liability, augmenting the Yamashita precedent with the stipulation that the commander "knew or had reason to know" about the criminal acts, and further that the commander's failure consisted in omitting "to take the necessary and reasonable measures to prevent . . . or punish . . . ."[1067] This language captures the two central themes of knowledge and feasibility, as supplementing the strictness of command liability. In multiple ICTY cases, the implementation of an emerging legal standard saw wide variation in practice, owing partly to the subtle use of presumptions to pre-select facts necessary for successful convictions. Mettraux confirmed this practice: "[T]he stated legal standards are effectively diluted by stealth through evidential inferences, which have the practical effect of reshaping – and lowering – the standard relevant to establishing the accused's liability under the doctrine."[1068]

When the Rome Statute received its final shape in 1998, several moderating conditions had arisen from the diversity of ICTY cases, addressing (at least at

[1065] Mettraux allows that "The *Yamashita* precedent stands out in the history of international criminal law as a warning against the unrestrained temptation of making law to fit a preferred judicial result." *Law of Command Responsibility*, p. 8. For a full history of the case and its admonitory effects, see Allan A. Ryan, *Yamashita's Ghost: War Crimes, MacArthur's Justice, and Command Accountability* (Lawrence: University Press of Kansas, 2012). For the post-World War I discussion of related concepts, see William A. Schabas, *The Trial of the Kaiser* (Cambridge: Cambridge University Press, 2018), pp. 310–11.

[1066] In the burst of enthusiasm that surrounded the Rome Statute's early days, some historical qualms about command responsibility were dampened, as proponents saw a powerful new liability tool in the fight against impunity. See Jenny S. Martinez, "Understanding *Mens Rea* in Command Responsibility: From *Yamashita* to *Blaškić* and Beyond," *Journal of International Criminal Justice* 5 (2007), 638.

[1067] Statute of the International Criminal Tribunal for the former Yugoslavia, Article 7(3). Following the Yamashita case, an intermediate definition was included in the 1977 supplement to the Geneva Conventions, Additional Protocol I §§86–87.

[1068] Mettraux, *The Law of Command Responsibility*, p. 11.

a formal level) the anxiety about balance and fairness. Issues of balance came from the mixed aims of international criminal law: putting an end to impunity while conducting fair trials under principles of legality. Issues of fairness grew from a sense of hardened battlefield realism, raising questions about what can be expected from commanders operating under wartime conditions. The Rome delegates placed three main burdens on prosecutions under Article 28(a): proving that a commander exercised "effective control" over subordinates who went on to commit crimes; that he possessed sufficient knowledge of such actions; and that he utilized mitigating options that were "reasonable" and "necessary."

These three elements of command responsibility provide some buffer to the natural regression of the concept toward strict liability. The Bemba judges (at all phases) approached liability questions through these several categories. But for each element, the evidence was largely circumstantial, requiring broad inferential leaps, pivoting off the ideal model of a chain of military command. In the Trial Chamber, controversies arose about the evidence used to establish various types of knowledge. The Appeals Chamber focused on evidentiary weaknesses in the finding that Bemba failed to pursue "reasonable and necessary" measures in mitigation. For all these doctrinal elements of command responsibility, the ICTY had drawn up lists of factual "indicia," or typical kinds of facts that might variously be used – in a purely case-by-case analysis – to decide whether each element had been properly established.[1069] Trial chambers differ in applying such wide-open fact-finding methods; and appeals chambers also vary in their deference to such judgments. As Mettraux noted in regard to the ad hoc tribunals: "There is often a fine line, and one that experienced judges do not necessarily agree upon, as to where the difference lies between applying an existing principle to a new set of facts and making new law."[1070]

Article 28(a) did resolve, still, a separate question: whether *command responsibility* defines a unique crime consisting of dereliction of military duty, or whether it is yet another mode of liability for the underlying crimes themselves – such as the murders, rapes, and pillagings alleged in the Bemba case. Article 28 (a) says (about itself) that it is a mode of criminal responsibility "for crimes within the jurisdiction of the Court." Those crimes, of course, are committed by others, while the Commander failed to control them. But Article 28(a) means that Bemba's conviction was "for" the proven crimes against humanity and war crimes. He neither committed them nor acted as an accessory; nor did he need to manifestly intend for them to happen: but he was "found responsible for" them. It is neither its own special crime nor any contribution to the commission

1069 Ibid., pp. 214–15, 237–38, 240–41, 260.
1070 Ibid., p. 9 n. 23.

of substantive crimes. The safest label is to call Article 28(a) cases *sui generis.*[1071] A further puzzle was the question, left unresolved in the Bemba case, about whether language in Article 28(a) required some proof of a causal connection between the commander's omissions and the actual crimes.[1072]

The Pre-Trial Chamber Takes the Lead

It wasn't the prerogative of the Bemba Pre-Trial Chamber to set the charges. The Rome Statute assigns that responsibility to the Prosecutor – who must, nonetheless, seek confirmation of charges through a pre-trial judgment. At an earlier stage, before the arrest warrant was requested for Jean-Pierre Bemba, the initial Pre-Trial Chamber hassled the Prosecutor about his long delay in responding to the detailed reports sent by FIDH and other global NGOs, reinforced by the formal referral from the CAR Bozizé regime. The frosty response was that the Prosecutor governs the pace of his own investigations. But at some point along this path to trial, the pre-trial judges hold veto power over the criminal charges and mode of liability. In the Bemba case, they used that power effectively to shape the case, steering it away from the paradigms used in the first two Congo trials.

During the first half of 2009, as the Bemba confirmation process advanced, the Prosecution was not yet in a position to learn from the weaknesses of its chosen narratives surrounding Lubanga, Katanga, and Ngudjolo. Indeed, it would survive serious ruptures and courtroom reversals to win a conviction for Lubanga; and it would never abandon its discredited theory about Katanga and Ngudjolo as joint masterminds of Ituri violence. The Lubanga Pre-Trial Chamber handed the Prosecution a powerful boost with the *control over the crime* theory, which was designed to redirect the criminal blame upwards, through complex organizational structures, to attribute primary responsibility to the highest leaders. While the theory itself purported to impose strict burdens on the Prosecution – a demonstrated pattern of planning, control, criminal intent, and essential contributions – the Lubanga Trial Chamber would show how these burdens can be lightened through the generous use of presumptions and inferences. Pre-trial hearings for Katanga and Ngudjolo anticipated these expeditious methods, six months prior to the Bemba pre-trial process.

The Bemba Pre-Trial Chamber had something different in mind. It wasn't the lack of a suitable organizational structure; Bemba's MLC group was a far

[1071] This phrase was echoed in the Bemba Trial Judgement, para. 174. For the ICTY background of this rubric, see Mettraux, *The Law of Command Responsibility*, pp. 37–38.

[1072] See Otto Triffterer, "Causality, A Separate Element of the Doctrine of Superior Responsibility as Expressed in Article 28 Rome Statute?" *Leiden Journal of International Law* 15 (2002), 179.

more developed political/military machine than any of the Ituri "militias." But it also didn't match the scenario of a tightly regimented army, especially in its CAR deployment, with MLC troops operating at a distance from their commander. Nor did it seem likely that Bemba could be assigned the kind of clear criminal purpose and intent required for holding him responsible as a co-perpetrator. By contrast, under Article 28(a) he did not have to be anywhere near his troops; and any criminal intent on his part to commit the crimes was superfluous. The pre-trial judges allowed AI (which had investigated the CAR crime scene in late 2003) to submit observations strongly commending Article 28(a) as a more fruitful path to convicting Bemba.[1073] After the oral confirmation hearings, the Pre-Trial Chamber formally requested the Prosecution to change the mode of liability to *command responsibility*.[1074]

The Prosecutor resisted. There was a clear strategic advantage in binding together two masterminds of violence – Jean-Pierre Bemba and embattled CAR President Ange-Félix Patassé – as co-perpetrators, even if Patassé was not present as a live suspect in The Hague. While the injuries to victims might be clearly established, the precise identity of perpetrators for each case might be hard to prove beyond reasonable doubt. The NGO reports from 2003 found evidence of violence implicating not just Bemba's MLC troops but CAR loyalist forces as well. Indeed, the same could be said about the Chadian mercenaries also called in by Patassé, not to mention the rival forces from the coup leader François Bozizé, now the elected CAR President, whose cooperation was welcomed for the ICC investigation. Under the legal doctrine of co-perpetration, Bemba (as one of the creators of the "common plan with criminal implications") would be held equally responsible for the reported murders, rapes, and pillagings, whether carried out by MLC troops, by Patassé troops, or by their other allies in crime. Provided the Prosecutor could meet the other rigors of the *control over the crime* theory, he would be relieved of disentangling contested facts about who caused specific incidents during the 2002–03 violence. It was worth the trouble to meet some other prosecutorial burdens: proving criminal intent and proving Bemba's "essential" contributions to the outcomes. These hurdles, in the final judgment, could be cleared by a Trial Chamber willing to invoke the requisite presumptions and inferences.[1075]

1073 Bemba Pre-Trial Chamber, Amicus Curiae Observations on Superior Responsibility submitted pursuant to Rule 103, April 24, 2009, ICC-01/05–01/08–406.

1074 Bemba Pre-Trial Chamber, Decision Adjourning the Hearing Pursuant to Article 61(7)(c)(ii), March 3, 2009, ICC-01/05–01/08–388.

1075 Bemba Pre-Trial Chamber, Prosecution's Submission of Amended Document Containing the Charges, March 30, 2009, ICC-01/05–01/08–395.

The Prosecution was anticipating a flow of jurisprudence that would have smoothed out all the rough narrative edges. As further parts of this chapter will acknowledge, there were reasons to expect that ICC trial judges might continue to cooperate. But there was also growing resistance; and in the Bemba case clear objections arose with the pre-trial confirmation. When advised initially by the Pre-Trial Chamber to redraft the Document Containing the Charges, the Prosecution simply added a further mode of liability as a secondary option. It persisted with Article 25(3)(a) as the primary mode, interpreting the suggestion of appending Article 28(a) as a fallback option. The Pre-Trial Chamber responded by killing the primary option, leaving the participating counsel – Prosecution, Defense, and Legal Representatives of Victims – with a different kind of case.[1076]

The Chamber was able to block the Prosecution's preference for its favored narrative. All it took was a willingness by the judges to interrupt the chain of inferences that tied everything together: common plan, intent to implement the plan, knowledge of its criminal purpose, unwillingness to stop it. In its Confirmation decision, the Pre-Trial Chamber made its point by challenging the Prosecution's evidence on criminal intent, with reference to Article 30 of the Statute. The Chamber was also dubious about the common plan itself: whether a plan "to save a president under threat" could be presumed to contain an associated criminal purpose of attacking local civilians. "Even assuming" there was evidence for that original plan, the Chamber would not allow criminal intent to be smuggled in under that assumption.[1077]

There was no need for the Pre-Trial Chamber to challenge every element in the original narrative, when the glaring omission in the Prosecution's case was precisely this intentional component of individual liability as a main perpetrator: the combination of knowledge and intent. Under the original theory, Bemba's awareness that the common plan would lead to criminal attacks could always be used to infer his intention that these attacks should happen. But the Chamber was "not convinced" that Bemba's intent could be "simply inferred from his continuing to implement the common plan."[1078] Some inference along these lines might be intuitively appealing, but it must also be backed up by evidence. At this pre-trial phase of proceedings, the standard of proof was not "beyond reasonable doubt" but the more relaxed standard of "substantial reason to believe." Even so, the Prosecution's pre-trial evidence

[1076] Bemba Pre-Trial Chamber, Confirmation of Charges decision, para. 401.
[1077] Ibid., paras. 389, 374.
[1078] Ibid., para. 400.

did not measure up.[1079] The Chamber explained at length why it would not accept an inference to Bemba's criminal intent, despite the Prosecution's offer of some nine assorted fact-bites:

> The Chamber considers that the Prosecutor's arguments to prove Mr. Jean-Pierre Bemba's intent are again based on the idea of past events. The Chamber has underlined ... that past conduct is not a sufficient factor to rely upon in order to infer the suspect's intent within the meaning of article 30 of the Statute. In particular, the Chamber finds it difficult to accept the argument put forth by the Prosecutor that because Mr. Jean-Pierre Bemba possessed an allegedly pillaged vehicle from the 2001 intervention in the CAR, he must have intended that the crime of pillaging would occur with certainty as a consequence of sending his MLC troops to the CAR in 2002.[1080]

Showing intent is never easy in such complex cases. Inferences of some kind may well be inescapable, when building a case from testimony of eye-witnesses. Part of the problem here was the limited scope of witnesses presented to the Pre-Trial Chamber, long before the Prosecution had developed its full case through evidence at trial. Much of the investigation was built on previous findings of local and global NGOs, which had made unprecedented efforts to interview victims and to make sure their stories were heard. But the pivot from victims to perpetrators is a more perilous maneuver. The Pre-Trial Chamber had already indicated that NGO reports would be treated at the level of hearsay and given "low probative value."[1081] There were Prosecution witnesses who spoke to the abhorrent inhumanity of their treatment by armed groups during the period of the coup. Some of them had opinions about Bemba's accountability; yet the Pre-Trial Chamber was careful to resist their expansive suppositions.

> At the hearing, the Prosecutor argued that "despite [Mr Jean-Pierre Bemba's] full knowledge of the commission of crimes in 2001, he sent the MLC troops to the CAR in 2002 and placed them in a permissive environment with '*carte blanche*', allowing them to rape, kill, torture and pillage with impunity." On reviewing the evidence presented the Chamber realizes that the Prosecutor's assertion was based on a sole witness statement .... The context ... does not support the Prosecutor's inference that Mr. Jean-Pierre Bemba had the requisite intent.[1082]

The Chamber was especially cautious about Prosecution inferences regarding Bemba's knowledge of criminal acts carried out by his MLC troops in the

[1079] Ibid., para. 401.
[1080] Ibid., para. 384.
[1081] Ibid., para. 51.
[1082] Ibid., para. 387.

CAR. These inferences were based on the bold stipulation that Bemba must have understood all too well how things worked in the CAR: that sending his troops in for a second tour of propping up the President would virtually ensure that they would commit crimes against civilians. This type of inference would succeed later on in respective Trial Chamber findings for Lubanga and Katanga. But the Bemba Pre-Trial Chamber would not accept this argument under the language of the Statute.

> As the disclosed Evidence indicates, the most that can be inferred is that Mr Jean-Pierre Bemba may have foreseen the risk of occurrence of such crimes as a mere possibility and accepted it for the sake of achieving the ultimate goal . . .. In the Chamber's opinion, this does not meet the required standard for article 30 of the Statute . . ..[1083]

This hard look at witness statements, Prosecution inferences from past behavior, and presumptions about plans, intentions, and knowledge meant the end of Article 25(3)(a) for purposes of the Bemba trial. Perhaps it was so definitive because the Pre-Trial Chamber had already revealed its fallback mode of liability in *command responsibility*. Under that approach, there was no requirement to show the accused's participation in a common plan, nor the kind of intent and knowledge needed to support the subjective elements of the crime. All those elements might pertain if the actual perpetrators were to be placed on trial. But under Article 28(a), there was a much-reduced checklist of conditions that would allow the ICC to find a distant military commander "responsible for" the crimes.

Article 28(a) may sidestep *intent*, but it contains a capacious definition of *knowledge* about the underlying crimes. In this regard, the ICC statute offers Prosecutors an unusual degree of leeway. The commander found "responsible" under this theory needs to have only an attenuated kind of knowledge about the crimes themselves. Instead of "knowing" that the crimes have occurred or "will

[1083] Ibid., para. 400. The Bemba Pre-Trial Chamber noted the language in Article 30(3): "'knowledge' means awareness that a circumstance exists or a consequence will occur in the ordinary course of events." Borrowing language familiar to civil law jurisprudence, that Chamber ruled that Article 30(3) is restricted to *dolus directus of the first or second degree*, but excludes *dolus eventualis* – or what might be loosely termed *recklessness or negligence*. Both the Lubanga and Katanga Trial Chambers pushed the other way, stretching the boundaries of risk awareness to support a finding of criminal knowledge. For commentary, see Mohamed Elewa Badar, "*Dolus Eventualis* and the Rome Statute Without It?" *New Criminal Law Review* 12 (2009), 433. The Bemba Trial Chamber suggested that the negligence-tinged *dolus eventualis* concept might be included in the knowledge component for Article 28(a)(i), even if not for Article 30(3). For commentary, see Gerhard Werle and Florian Jessberger, "'Unless Otherwise Provided': Article 30 of the ICC Statute and the Mental Element of Crimes under International Criminal Law," *Journal of International Criminal Justice* 3 (2005), 35.

occur in the ordinary course of events" (the standard for knowledge under Article 30(3), which must be applied to all main perpetrators), the commander's more limited knowledge has to do with what he knows about the actions of his distant subordinates (either pending or past actions): whether he "(i) … knew or, owing to the circumstances at the time, should have known that the forces were committing or about to commit such crimes …."[1084] There remains no requirement for "intent" to commit the crimes directly or through others. Rather, this provision defines the commander's duty to control his wayward forces, based on what he actually *knew* about them, or on what he is duty-bound to know (*should have known*). This element of command responsibility was the main lever of the Bemba Pre-Trial Chamber's efforts to bend the Prosecution to a different mode of liability.

The "knew or should have known" language contained in Article 28(a)(i) was a departure from previous formal versions of command responsibility, notably the one used by the ICTY. In that tribunal, the literal standard was "knew or had reason to know," which placed greater burdens on Prosecutors.[1085] In Mettraux's view, the looser ICC standard of liability "might have been motivated by a desire for … facilitating prosecution – and conviction – of military commanders."[1086] It "was expressly rejected as a basis for liability by the nations which negotiated the terms of Additional Protocol I to the Geneva Conventions and by the ad hoc Tribunals."[1087]

This controversy raises the important question of precisely what it is that commanders *should* have known about their wayward forces – and how that duty is tempered by unspecified "circumstances at the time." The Bemba Pre-Trial Chamber sidestepped this issue by confirming charges against Bemba, under Article 28(a)(i), based on only what he *knew*, and not what he *should have known* under the circumstances.[1088] The Chamber confirmed the charge that Bemba possessed some kind of actual knowledge, although it appeared to distinguish this kind of knowledge from the standard definition in Article 30(3). "Actual knowledge" under the terms of *command responsibility* had its own distinct meaning. This would make it easier for the Prosecution to draw inferences about knowledge from Bemba's past behavior. These same

[1084] Article 28(a)(i).

[1085] While commentators like Mettraux insist on the novelty (and danger) in the ICC "should have known" standard, in practice trial courts, using case-specific facts, can narrow the distance between "had reason to know" and "should have known." Mettraux remains critical of these elisions, but they are embraced by Martinez, "Understanding *Mens Rea* in Command Responsibility."

[1086] *The Law of Command Responsibility*, p. 27.

[1087] Ibid., p. 31.

[1088] Bemba Confirmation of Charges decision, para. 489.

inferences could otherwise be blocked, according to the Pre-Trial Chamber, under the grander co-perpetration theory.

The Confirmation Decision clearly rejected the liability mode as a co-perpetrator; and it just as clearly confirmed the mode of command responsibility. But it left unexplained details about how this doctrine works in practice, especially in the degree to which it deviates from the knowledge requirements developed by previous courts. The Trial Chamber inherited these unsolved problems, especially the enigmatic concept of what commanders "should have known under the circumstances."

In closing this discussion of pre-trial judicial activism, it is also important to note the Chamber's general concern with simplifying charges, eliminating alternative forms of charging. The Prosecution would have liked to keep both modes alive for the trial, retaining Article 25(3)(a) as the primary mode, with Article 28(a) as insurance. The Pre-Trial Chamber rejected this redundancy. The Chamber might also have allowed the Prosecution to retain all its leeway under the Statute regarding Bemba's knowledge; but instead it confirmed only the charge that Bemba "knew" what his troops were doing, ignoring the more expansive option of whether, under the circumstances, he "should have known." This preference for limiting Prosecutorial options extended also to the actual crimes confirmed by the Chamber. The Chamber declined to confirm the charge of torture as a crime against humanity (Article 7(1)(f)), as it seemed merely to duplicate the Article 7 charge of rape.[1089] The Chamber's opposition to "cumulative charging"[1090] would not be followed by some later pre-trial panels, which may have noted problems encountered by trial judges seeking mid-trial flexibility through the controversial Regulation 55.[1091]

Regulation 55 Meets the Question of Knowledge

Five weeks after the Bemba Defense started presenting its case, the Trial Chamber issued a notification that it was considering the use of Regulation 55.[1092] That move would lower the goal posts for the Prosecution, by expanding the dimensions of knowledge for liability under command responsibility. The

[1089] Bemba Trial Chamber, Confirmation of Charges decision, para. 70.

[1090] Ibid., para. 209.

[1091] See Ntaganda Pre-Trial Chamber, Confirmation of Charges decision, June 9, 2014, ICC-01/04–02/06–309, para. 100. The Chamber confirmed eighteen specific criminal charges distributed across six modes of liability (para. 97).

[1092] Bemba Trial Chamber, Decision Giving Notice of Possible Change in Legal Characterization of Facts under Regulation 55(2), September 21, 2012, ICC-01/05–01/08–2324.

proposed change would measure Bemba's criminal liability according to not just what he *actually knew* about the criminal actions of his forces but also what (under the circumstances of the time) he *should have known*. The change was not a complete shift in the mode of liability, such as occurred in the Katanga Regulation 55 controversy. Article 28(a)(i) already includes both kinds of knowledge. The Trial Chamber was signaling it might use the full scope of that statutory provision, rather than limiting the case to the narrower category confirmed prior to trial.

Regulation 55 had already seen a mixed reception in the first two Congo trials. In the Thomas Lubanga trial, at the conclusion of the Prosecution's main case, two judges wanted to include criminal charges for sexual offenses. Their request was interpreted by the Appeals Chamber as an amendment to the original charges, and as such impermissible.[1093] Regulation 55 had a more limited purpose – introducing a new legal characterization, allowing the trial judges to place important trial evidence into a new set of legal categories. Yet there were limits to this power to change the direction of an ongoing trial. Legal categories were tethered to specific elements in the pre-trial Confirmation decision: *after* that phase, there could be no amendments to the criminal charges (not, at least, without reverting to pre-trial proceedings), nor other adjustments of legal standards exceeding the confirmed *facts and circumstances* underlying those original charges. The Lubanga Trial Chamber was not permitted to impose new criminal charges midway through the trial.[1094]

The Germain Katanga case needed rescuing, after the collapse of the Prosecution's theory about the mode of liability, and the acquittal of co-accused Mathieu Ngudjolo. When all of the trial evidence had been submitted by both parties, the Trial Chamber wanted to change Katanga's mode of liability, shifting him from a master perpetrator to someone who "contributed" in some residual way to the attacks committed by others. While the timing of this move was itself controversial, the Appeals Chamber allowed the change to go through, provided that Katanga was given a meaningful opportunity to prepare a Defense.[1095] When Katanga was convicted under the lesser mode of liability, there was no appeal from either side, and thus no appellate scrutiny of the trial rupture engineered by Regulation 55.

The Bemba Trial Chamber was not proposing to add whole new criminal charges. It was also not planning to change the mode of liability from one type

[1093] Lubanga Appeals Chamber, Judgment on Appeal from Trial Chamber Notice under Regulation 55, December 8, 2009, ICC-01/04–01/106–2205, para. 94.

[1094] Ibid., para. 109.

[1095] Katanga Appeals Chamber, Judgment on Trial Chamber's Proposed Use of Regulation 55, March 27, 2013, ICC-01/04–01/07–3363, paras. 44–58.

to another. Five weeks after the Defense made its opening arguments, the Trial Chamber warned that it might utilize the full scope of the particular knowledge requirement for command responsibility, that Bemba "Article 28 (a)(i) . . . knew or, owing to the circumstances at the time, should have known that the forces were committing or about to commit such crimes . . . ."

The Bemba Pre-Trial Chamber had handcuffed the trial by confirming only the first half of this provision: that Bemba "knew" what his forces were doing (or about to do); while saying nothing about liability for what he "should have known." In its Regulation 55 notification, the Bemba Trial Chamber wanted to make full use of the liability standard laid out in the Rome Statute.

It was an intriguing counterpoint to the judicial activism shown earlier by the Pre-Trial Chamber, which had forced the Prosecution to change its headline narrative from "mastermind-perpetrator" to "errant military commander." The reason given during pre-trial was that the evidence seemed a better match with a different mode of responsibility. Similarly, at the trial stage, the Trial Chamber was saying that it thought the evidence (at this point, mostly from the Prosecution) was a better match with the "should have known" language. These changes purported to serve the interests of fair labeling – finding the best legal terminology for characterizing the evidence in the case. They were also both designed to prevent possible acquittals, if in the end the evidence did not match up with the original legal theory.

But the time for this kind of flexibility was back at the pre-trial stage, where the judicial purpose was to frame and to freeze the charges and circumstances on which the trial will then be fought out, and to provide the Defense with necessary information about those charges, allowing for a properly informed Defense. By contrast, such changes, during the trial itself, will likely surprise the Defense with new allegations, without sufficient time to prepare new responses.

Regulation 55 is thus balanced between two goals with clear potential for conflict.[1096] The Trial Chamber's flexibility confronts the imperative to respect the fair-trial rights of the Defense. Regulation 55 holds that the Trial Chamber's final judgment cannot alter the basic facts and circumstances confirmed by the Pre-Trial Chamber, which sealed the understanding with the Defense about the kind of case it would need to conduct.[1097]

The Bemba Trial Chamber that issued this Regulation 55 notice was not the original panel of judges, back in 2009, when the Chamber was first appointed.

[1096] See Carsten Stahn, "Modification of the Legal Characterization of Facts in the ICC System: A Portrayal of Regulation 55," *Criminal Law Forum* 16 (2005), 12.

[1097] For applications in ICC cases, see Kevin Jon Heller, "'A Stick to Hit the Accused With': The Legal Recharacterization of Facts under Regulation 55," in Carsten Stahn (ed.), *The Law and Practice of the International Criminal Court* (Oxford: Oxford University Press, 2015), chapter 39.

Two of the original judges stepped down four months before opening arguments, pleading overwork (they were also on the bench for the Lubanga trial), and were replaced in late July 2010.[1098] On their final day as a team, the original panel of Trial Chamber III issued a lengthy ruling on a series of Defense challenges, all based on the argument that the Prosecution's amended Document Containing the Charges (DCC) was rife with facts and circumstances exceeding those confirmed by the Pre-Trial Chamber. (The issues raised here would persist into the appeals process, where they received intense scrutiny.)

In a decision more than 100 pages in length, the first Bemba Trial Chamber issued dozens of micro-decisions about the Prosecution's restatement of *facts and circumstances*: whether it was consistent with the Pre-Trial Chamber's authoritative version. There is little rhyme or reason to this compilation of decisions. When the Prosecution listed the time frame for the alleged crimes as "between approximately 26 October 2002 and 15 March 2003," the Trial Chamber required it to change the language back to "on or about 26 October to 15 March 2003."[1099] But alongside this trivial literalism, the Trial Chamber generously allowed the Prosecution to insert "additional background evidential details," provided they were "consistent" with pre-trial facts: incorporating only minor inferences, or adding new examples of the same kind as already confirmed.[1100] On the whole, the Trial Chamber's document reads like a dry accounting statement, shining a spotlight on some few small fudges, while passing on much darker practices that would lead to reversal on appeal – notably the proliferation of alleged "criminal acts" beyond those discussed at the confirmation stage, and the non-specific times and places for criminal events.

On two important matters, however, the first Trial Chamber was definitive. First, the Prosecution went offside by asserting that Bemba's *mens rea* (culpable intent and knowledge) could be *inferred* from statements made by MLC soldiers and reported by CAR civilians. While the process of fact-finding is riddled with inferences – both tacit and explicit – in this case the first Trial Chamber found no authority in the confirmation decision for the Prosecution's claim.[1101] More important, the Prosecution was ordered to excise all references to what Bemba "should have known," as matters that clearly exceeded the facts and circumstances

[1098] Judges Fulford and Odio Benito were replaced by Judges Steiner and Ozaki, comprising an all-female bench. ICC Presidency, Decision Replacing Judges in Trial Chamber III, July 20, 2010, ICC-01/05–01/08–837.

[1099] Bemba Trial Chamber, Decision on the Defence Application for Corrections to the Document Containing the Charges, July 20, 2010, ICC-01/05–01/08–836, para. 75.

[1100] Ibid., paras. 46, 67, 78, 141, among other examples.

[1101] Ibid., paras. 205–06.

confirmed at the pre-trial level.[1102] For the three judges writing this document, the gap was obvious to the naked eye, requiring no special analysis.

While Judge Aluoch remained a member of the new panel – which would push the Regulation 55 initiative – she and Judges Steiner and Ozaki were ready to argue, some two years later, that the *should have known* standard was *not inconsistent* with the Confirmation decision. The Regulation 55 Trial Chamber never explained how it squared this proposed change with the Pre-Trial Chamber's silence on the matter of *should have known*. In one defensively worded ruling, the Regulation 55 Trial Chamber quoted the Confirmation decision as finding some overlap in factual indicia for demonstrating both kinds of knowledge.[1103] This statement was troubling in itself, as it anticipated the solution ultimately used in the Bemba Trial Judgment: that artful judicial interpretation of the same facts might find liability under either standard.

The Bemba Defense was denied leave to appeal the Regulation 55 notice, despite the fact that earlier notifications about Regulation 55 had gone to appeals in both the Lubanga and Katanga cases.[1104] The Trial Chamber pointed out that the Prosecution planned to call no additional witnesses or present new documents related to the "should have known" standard. All the relevant evidence was already there; the plain language of Article 28(a)(i) embraced both standards; and it was no significant breach of the pre-trial Confirmation foundation. Despite all this bravado, when it came time to write the Trial Judgment, the Chamber relied solely on the *actual knowledge* standard.[1105]

No clear definition of pre-trial *facts and circumstances* came out of the first two Congo trials; and nor did that happen during the Bemba trial. In its final Judgment, the Bemba Trial Chamber seemed to retreat from its Regulation 55 gambit. There was no speculation about what Bemba "should have known, owing to the circumstances of the time." But this surprising result left key jurisprudential questions unanswered. At the appellate stage, the Majority

[1102] Ibid., paras. 121, 169.

[1103] What the Pre-Trial Chamber says concerns overlap between the "had reason to know" standard from the ad hoc tribunals and "should have known" in the ICC Statute. Bemba Confirmation decision, para. 434. It is important to mention, as well, the overstatement by the Bemba Defense, which held that the Pre-Trial Chamber had "refused" to confirm the "should have known" grounds for liability. (Bemba Trial Chamber, Defence Request for Leave to Appeal the Regulation 55 Decision, December 18, 2009, ICC-01/05–01/08–2483-Red, para. 1.) The Pre-Trial Chamber did not outright refuse; it simply confirmed the charges with the tighter language, in a spirit of confirming charges that were as spare as possible, seeking to avoid unnecessary duplication.

[1104] Bemba Trial Chamber, Public Redacted Version on the Defence Request to Appeal Temporary Suspension of Proceedings Pursuant to Regulation 55(2), January 16, 2013, ICC-01/05–01/08–2487.

[1105] Bemba Trial Judgment, para. 718.

articulated an exceptionally narrow interpretation of how pre-trial *facts and circumstances* may work in practice. By then the whole Regulation 55 question was no longer the main point; instead, the appeals analysis of pre-trial limits was used to overturn nearly half the counts on which Bemba was convicted.

Was the Bemba Regulation 55 interlude a tempest in a teapot? After all, the Trial Chamber seemed to back down. The sheer drama of the announcement, midway through the trial, may have rattled the Defense for a period of time. But in the end, there was no change from what was expected from the very outset of the trial. How miraculous, then, from the standpoint of gaining a conviction, that the evidence (which may have seemed a bit slim, measured by the standard of what Bemba *actually knew*), turned out to be strong enough to meet that higher standard. Perhaps the Trial Chamber simply overreacted, if the evidence was really strong enough all along. Or perhaps it was no miracle, but rather a skillful manipulation of factual evidence, allowing the Trial Chamber to enlist the evidence according to the requirements of its liability theory. It was this second possibility that burst into the open, two years later, on appeal.

9.3 DEBATES IN THE BEMBA APPEALS CHAMBER

A Jurisprudential Reckoning for the Congo Trials

The Appeals Judgment came as a thunderbolt in June 2018.[1106] The reversal of all Bemba's convictions brought an abrupt end to a legal process that had lumbered on for more than a decade. It freed Bemba to reinvent his career as a Congolese political figure and economic magnate.[1107] It was the worst possible outcome for the thousands of CAR victims for whom the Court's torchlight had long been failing – sustained only by the ICC's TFV.

The Appeals Judgment was also a moment for stocktaking on the Court's own future. Like no other event in any of the Congo trials, it exposed the deep conflicts built into the Court's practice. It was comparable in drama to earlier cases that were aborted at the end of the Prosecution's evidence – in the Kenya situation, with the cases of William Ruto and Joshua Arap Sang[1108]; and in the Ivory Coast situation, with the cases of Laurent Gbagbo and Charles Blé

[1106] Bemba Appeals Judgment, June 8, 2018, ICC-01/05–01/08–3636.

[1107] He wasn't quite free to leave the detention facility pending a final ruling on the status of his sentence in the trial-within-a-trial: Bemba *et al.* Trial Chamber, Decision on Mr Bemba's Application for Release, June 12, 2018, ICC-01/05–01/13–2291.

[1108] Ruto and Sang Trial Chamber, Public Redacted Version of Decision on Defence Applications for Judgments of Acquittal, April 5, 2016, ICC-01/09–01/11–2027 (a split decision by the three-judge Trial Chamber).

Goudé.[1109] The Bemba appeal carried far more than drama. It was a piercing review of internal conflicts and tensions that had roiled previous Congo proceedings, pitched at a sober jurisprudential level. Inevitably, it was a split decision, with excruciatingly detailed arguments from two minority judges trying to maintain continuity with past practices. Somewhere among the three-judge Majority, Judge Chile Eboe-Osuji agreed "in essence" with the conclusions of his two other colleagues, but issued his own thoughtful musings on wider legal implications. Three months before this ruling, Judge Eboe-Osuji had been elected President of the Court for a three-year term. During the remainder of that term, he and his seventeen fellow judges will have more occasions to ponder these important questions.

The breadth and detail of the appeal were predictable from the special hearing called by the Appeals Chamber in January 2018. Months after all the standard briefs had been submitted, the parties and Legal Representatives were invited to address five sets of legal puzzles, derived from the six grounds of appeal filed by the Bemba Defense. Some of these issues were specific to Article 28(a) liability, while others raised more general points about pre-trial *facts and circumstances*, about judicial fact-finding, and about the strategies behind standards of proof. All counsel participated in this three-day dialogue, responding to one another and to questions from all five Appeals Chamber judges. Counsel were given an opportunity to follow up with further written comments, as the Appeals Chamber continued to hammer out its internal differences. Although the Legal Representatives made their best efforts throughout this process, the discussion floated up into the jurisprudential ether, leaving behind the current agonies faced by CAR victims. This regrettable consequence was acknowledged by the appeals Majority.

In a major departure from the other Congo trials, the Bemba appeals Majority took an active critical approach to findings of fact reached by the Trial Chamber. The Lubanga Appeals Chamber had followed a more standard routine of broad deference, questioning only those trial findings that struck the appeals judges as unreasonable. While there was no appeal in the Katanga conviction, the contentious appeal over Ngudjolo's acquittal found a majority of the split appeals panel extending the same deference to trial-level findings of fact. The dissenters in the Ngudjolo case focused on trial-level management of facts – stressing the need for "holism" and related techniques, which might have led to a conviction. And while earlier cases had things to say

[1109] Gbagbo and Blé Goudé Trial Chamber, Reasons for Oral Decision of 15 January 2019 on the Requête de la Défense de Laurent Gbagbo afin qu'un jugement d'acquittement, July 16, 2019, ICC-02/11–01/15–1263 (another split decision).

about the standard of *proof beyond reasonable doubt*, its relationship to fact-finding had been left rather hazy.

The Bemba appeals Majority did not abandon the notion of deference. But it relegated appellate deference to an ancillary role, insisting that findings of fact must first be formulated in reviewable terms. Trial Chambers should not simply declare the facts as personal beliefs, but should present them discursively, with emphasis on the process of *reasoning*, as opposed to oracular conclusions passing as *reasonable*, or *not unreasonable*. The lesson for the legal process was that findings of fact are *judgments*, not declarations, and not reports on judicial inner psychology. A Trial Chamber must present a pattern of reasoning, and not simply reveal its own soul.[1110]

And if these "found" facts are really judgments, then they can be subject to norms of reasoning, subject especially to the master norm supplied by the standard of *proof beyond reasonable doubt*. Fully articulating factual judgments becomes a procedural necessity, opening up to appellate scrutiny. Deference does not enter the picture until that process has been justly followed. When an appeals body identifies "injustice" in trial court reasoning, it has no choice or discretion: it *must* intervene and take remedial action.[1111] Such was the revisionist take on appellate judging announced by the Bemba appeals Majority.

Enumerating the Trees

What were Jean-Pierre Bemba's crimes? What precisely was he convicted of? In the artful language of Article 28(a), he was found "responsible for" several international crimes: murder, rape, and pillaging, drawn from Articles 7 and 8 of the Rome Statute. No one said that he had physically carried out these crimes himself. Nor that he nurtured the intentions or masterplans associated with criminal perpetrators or accessories. Others carried out the crimes; others conducted any requisite planning for them. His responsibility was based on the legal theory that he failed to prevent, mitigate, or punish these crimes.

But the appeals Majority required something more specific: which particular murders, rapes, and acts of pillaging? Was it a pervasive crime wave in the areas where MLC troops were present, or were there particular crimes associated with his troops? If Bemba was aware of something (or perhaps "should have been" aware), was it all these murders, rapes, and pillagings *in*

1110 Bemba Appeals Judgment, para. 44.

1111 Ibid., para. 3. The reference to "justice" in para. 40 is confusing but makes the point that a procedural injustice in finding facts should not be allowed to constrain the exercise of justice at the appellate level.

general? The appeals Majority found itself stranded in a forest of criminality, looking for the individual trees: particular criminal acts, as opposed to generic crimes. It seemed that both the Pre-Trial Chamber and the Trial Chamber were overly casual about the timber count.

When asked for clarification, in the Appeals Chamber hearing of January 2018, the Prosecution came up with two sets of answers. What were the precise charges against Bemba; and for which of these charges was he found guilty, beyond reasonable doubt? The first answer invoked the whole forest: murder, rape, and pillaging carried out by MLC troops "in the CAR during the period on or about October 26, 2002 to March 15, 2003."[1112]

The Trial Chamber found Bemba guilty beyond reasonable doubt, under these general terms. But there were also individual cases – indeed, lots of cases: some of them were mentioned, in varying degrees of specificity, back at the pre-trial phase, in auxiliary documents following the Confirmation decision, and again in courtroom evidence produced at the trial. The charges "included, but were not limited to" these specific acts. In an excess of tidiness, the Trial Chamber enumerated some twenty-nine acts, based on trial evidence, for all of which they found Bemba criminally responsible *beyond reasonable doubt.*

Both answers provoked a response from the Bemba appeals Majority. Putting aside momentarily the first answer (the "forest"), the appeals Majority gave immediate attention to the second answer, and then worked its way backwards from the trial process, back to pre-trial proceedings. Of the twenty-nine acts that seemed to constitute the "trees" included in Bemba's conviction record, only eleven of them had been summarized in relevant pre-trial documents. With that, the appeals Majority dismissed the other eighteen convictions, on the procedural grounds that the Trial Chamber had exceeded its powers under the Rome Statute.

The Trial Chamber is expected to rule on the criminal charges (murder, rape, and pillaging); but in doing so it cannot exceed the underlying "facts and circumstances described in the charges," which mention eleven specific acts. To the extent that the conviction decision strayed beyond these acts, anything extra had to be dropped. It was not an acquittal on the merits. This particular subset of convictions was simply vacated – and there was no going back.[1113]

[1112] Bemba Appeals Chamber hearing, January 9, 2018, ICC-01/05–01/08-T-372-ENG, p. 54. In fact, the forest cliché was first introduced into these hearings in stray Prosecution remarks, quoting a learned academic article, and meaning to provide some lift to the Prosecution's big-picture outlook (Appeals Chamber hearing, January 11, 2018, ICC-01/05–01/08-T-374-ENG, p. 52). It was seized on by some members of the bench, who tendered obvious follow-up questions about the trees. It became a gentle mocking theme in the hearings, and then returned with a vengeance in the Appeals Judgment.

[1113] Bemba Appeals Judgment, para. 116.

Which Facts? Which Circumstances?

The phrase *facts and circumstances* had previously roiled all three Congo trials. In each trial there were moments when the Trial Chamber invoked Regulation 55 for the purpose of changing the dynamics of a sputtering trial – while professing not to exceed the Chamber's limited powers. Those limits are laid down in several places, foremost in Article 74(2), which constrains the Chamber's scope in its final trial judgment: "The Trial Chamber's decision shall be based on an evaluation of the evidence and the entire proceedings. The decision shall not exceed the facts and circumstances described in the charges and any amendments to the charges . . . ."

"Charges and any amendments to the charges" are determined in the pre-trial Confirmation process.[1114] They are compiled by the Prosecutor in a "document containing the charges" (DCC), which may be revised after Confirmation to reflect changes required by the Pre-Trial Chamber. This document, which must be approved by the Pre-Trial Chamber, plays a key role in the fair trial regime of the Court, setting the legal parameters that control the scope of the trial – operationalizing the limits quoted above from Article 74(2).

The Document Containing the Charges consists of three sections, according to Court Regulations. Regulation 52(a) starts with the name and identity of the accused. The next two sections provide important details that became critical in the Bemba appeal:

(b) A statement of the facts, including the time and place of the alleged crimes, which provides a sufficient legal and factual basis to bring the person or persons to trial, including relevant facts for the exercise of jurisdiction by the Court;
(c) A legal characterization of the facts to accord both with the crimes under articles 6, 7 or 8 and the precise form of participation under articles 25 and 28.

In the final trial judgment, the Trial Chamber cannot exceed the limits stipulated in Regulation 52(b), which define "the facts and circumstances described in the charges." In addition to Article 74(2) cited above, the constraining power of *facts and circumstances* is repeated in Regulation 55(1), which permits the Trial Chamber, under certain circumstances, to change the

[1114] Article 61 covers the Confirmation process. Article 61(9) specifies that amendments to the confirmed charges must come from the Prosecutor and must then be approved by the Pre-Trial Chamber; with any additional charges subject to another Confirmation procedure.

legal characterization of facts mentioned in part (c), but not the *facts and circumstances* mentioned in part (b).

The clear innovation of the Bemba appeals Majority was to require the Prosecutor and future Chambers to specify alleged crimes *at the level of individual acts*. They derived this requirement from Regulation 52(b), interpreting the language "sufficient legal and factual basis to bring the person to trial" as requiring something more concrete than a vast expanse of time and place. To be sure, in both the Confirmation decision and the Trial Judgment, the broader forest-based concept of generic crimes included a time parameter (on or about October 26, 2002 to March 15, 2003) and a place parameter (in the CAR).[1115] But this gesture at narrowing was not enough to give the Defense a "sufficient legal and factual basis." Merely designating one quadrant of "the forest" does not reach down to the level of specifying trees.

The appeals Majority prescribed these severe interpretations at the level of formal language drawn from the Statute and Regulations. It was a strikingly spare discussion, in which the Majority made all its points in just one-third the space used by the dissenters. This economy included disposing of the entire appeal on only two of the six grounds pleaded by Bemba, using the narrowest possible arguments needed to dispose of the appeal. While the Majority provides short footnotes referencing other ICC cases,[1116] there was no litany of jurisprudential citations, including the vast repository of ICTY judicial decisions. (Both Judge Van den Wyngaert and Judge Morrison served as ICTY judges and were fully aware of similar discussions held in that tribunal.)

One must suppose that the Majority had some purpose in mind, in pressing for such concreteness in the charges. In the separate opinion by Judges Van den Wyngaert and Morrison, there is mention of fairness to the Defense, but also the practical need for stricter guidelines for trial management, and even clarity on reparations. By 2018, it is likely that the appeals Majority was mindful of newer Prosecution strategies, following the weak record of the first two Congo trials and all the angst over Regulation 55. These new strategies included larding the pre-trial record of facts and circumstances, and pressing multiple charges and alternative liability

[1115] When pressed on this point, the Prosecution pointed to language in pre-trial documents that narrowed the places to troop corridors in and around the CAR capital Bangui. Bemba Appeals Chamber hearing, January 9, 2018, pp. 78, 84.

[1116] In the Lubanga Appeals Decision on Regulation 55, with respect to *facts and circumstances*, the Appeals Chamber had defined "facts" as "the factual allegations which support each of the legal elements of the crimes charged," indicating that the standard of sufficient detail came from Article 67(1)(a). December 8, 2009, ICC-01/04–01/06–2205, para. 90, n. 163. See also the main Lubanga Appeals Judgment, December 1, 2014, ICC01/04–01/06–3121, para. 123.

modes for new cases.[1117] This penchant for abstract forestry allowed the Prosecution much needed scope. Without mentioning these parallel developments, the Bemba appeals Majority simply insisted that the accused must receive "sufficient" details in order to prepare a proper Defense; and the trial judges needed "sufficient" details to keep the trial under stricter management.[1118]

When it came to fair trial concerns, in the face of expanding allegations of criminal acts, the appeals Majority rejected the Prosecution's view that any disadvantages to the Defense could be cured, in real time, by timely notification – after the trial phase had begun. As it turns out, the Bemba team acknowledged that it had been fully notified about the eighteen post-Confirmation criminal "acts," even before the opening day of trial. Back at the January 2018 Appeals Hearing, there had been discussion about whether the Prosecution's use of notification had become a license for expanding the charges.[1119] Bemba's ground for appeal was not based on lack of notice, but rather on the formal conception of pre-trial facts and circumstances, as a source of long-term predictability. And it was on these grounds that the appeals Majority based their decision.

The debate about fixed charges versus flexibility-with-notification was a recurring theme across all three Congo trials. A similar issue had interrupted the Lubanga trial, when two members of the Trial Chamber sought to expand the criminal charges to include sexual crimes, midway through the trial. In their view, so long as Lubanga was notified of the new charges (and perhaps given more time to prepare more Defense), what could be the complaint? But that initiative was rejected by the Appeals Chamber, which ruled that adding completely new crimes was a breach of the *facts and circumstances* constraint.

In the second Congo trial, the Trial Chamber made its expansive move after all the evidence was submitted, and when the Chamber was deliberating the fate of both Katanga and Ngudjolo. The notification came in surprising fashion, as Ngudjolo was acquitted, while two members of the Trial Chamber indicated that they were looking at Katanga's criminal responsibility under a new mode of liability. The third judge in that case – Judge Van den Wyngaert – pointed out in her dissent that the notification was delivered long after the Defense had argued its case under the original liability mode. A valid Defense under the old charge, she said, might well be incriminating under the

1117 See Ntaganda Pre-Trial Confirmation Decision, para. 97.

1118 Fair trial issues dominated the lengthy discussions at the Appeals hearing. See Bemba Appeals hearing, January 9, 2018, pp. 82–90.

1119 Ibid., p. 86.

new legal characterization; but at that point it was too late to withdraw the prior arguments. In the Katanga case, while the Appeals Chamber allowed the Regulation 55 process to unfold, there would be no appeal from the Trial Chamber Judgment.

The Bemba appeals Majority's decision was a call to freeze the pre-trial charges, while holding to a narrow construction of the underlying *facts and circumstances*. Additionally, it associated these underlying facts with specific criminal acts, insisting on counting the number of trees within the dark forest of pre-trial suspicions. On the level of "acts," all parties agreed that a raft of new alleged acts had been introduced after pre-trial Confirmation, as part of the Prosecution's amended version of the Document Containing the Charges. Even before the trial began, the Bemba Defense objected to this process on the same grounds that ultimately succeeded on appeal. In February 2010, nine months before the first witness was to be called, the Defense launched a comprehensive challenge to that amended Document.[1120] The Bemba Trial Chamber's response was discussed briefly in the last section of this chapter: it was a mixed set of directives to the Prosecutor, requiring some minor changes to conform to precise wording in the pre-trial Confirmation decision. Along with these minor adjustments, it also ruled out the Prosecution's bid to extend Bemba's mode of liability to include what he "should have known" about the underlying crimes. But when it came to the *supplementary* criminal "acts" added on by the Prosecution, the Trial Chamber readily acceded to the changes. These new acts were further "examples" that fit entirely within the generic charges approved by the Pre-Trial Chamber. Adding more examples of criminal acts was just more evidence to back up the charges framed at the broad level of "murder, rape, and pillaging." And in any case, the Defense was fully notified of the new information.

The Bemba appeals Majority acknowledged that this broad framing of the charges originated with the Pre-Trial Chamber, which meant to capture an indefinite number of crimes within a five-month period, anywhere in the territory of the CAR. But the appeals Majority also seized upon an early version of the Prosecutor's Document Containing the Charges, mentioning those eleven particular criminal "acts." The appeals Majority chose to construe these eleven acts as the operative content of the facts and circumstances, thus restraining the Prosecution and the Trial Chamber for the duration of the

[1120] Bemba Trial Chamber, Requête aux fins d'obtenir une Décision ordonnant la correction et le dépôt du Second Document Amendé Contenant les Charges, February 12, 2010, ICC-01/05–01/08–694.

trial. The Pre-Trial Confirmation should have framed the charges more narrowly.[1121]

The Strategy of Specifics

The focus on trees is a judicial version of philosophical nominalism. Wherever it occurs, nominalism (whose favorite blade is Occam's razor) seeks to reduce complex notions to simpler, more practical levels, and to avoid confusion based on arid distinctions. It provides a critical rejoinder to generic modes of thought: the preference for broad generalizations that omit to touch the ground. In this way, the Bemba appeals Majority's position on facts and circumstances – objectifying "facts" as specific criminal "acts" – was part of a larger thrust. In crisp and iconoclastic terms, the Appeals Judgment took strategic aim at developments across all three Congo trials, not to exclude the inchoate and aborted ICC trials that overlapped this same period. Their critique went beyond the specificity of charges. It included the opaque methods of reasoning displayed in Trial Chamber Judgments, beholden to paradigms, rife with inferences and presumptions, insulated by a fact-finding subjectivism that avoided appellate review

An example of the generic strategy was the familiar Prosecution distinction between "material facts" and "subsidiary facts."[1122] This distinction made it possible to work around the fixed pre-trial constraints – the *facts and circumstances* – by broadening them out into "material" facts: those big-picture, generic issues that provide the headlines for international criminal trials. In the Bemba context, the "material" facts were the composite realities of crimes like murder, rape, and pillaging, seen as a whole pattern of criminality (a *modus operandi*). If the Trial Judgment stayed focused on these larger realities, they alone should bear the weight of *proof beyond reasonable doubt*, deep down in the judicial conscience, with its affinity for higher realities.

By contrast, lesser or "subsidiary" facts concerned minor details. Included in this category were particular criminal acts of murder, rape, and pillaging – serving as mere examples of bigger realities. Constructions like "common plans" were what mattered, not the discrete activities of individual actors. Other "subsidiary" facts include the testimonies of individual witnesses, which

1121 Bemba Appeals Judgment, para. 110.

1122 This topic figures in the discussion of "facts and circumstances" (Bemba Appeals Chamber hearing, January 9, 2018, pp. 59–62, and again in the discussion of contextual elements of Article 7 (ibid., January 11, 2018, pp. 50–62).

become meaningful only when linked to a "synchronized system."[1123] For the generic mode of thinking, proof beyond reasonable doubt should not get lost in these concrete details – and should always be directed to the composite notions.

Something like this more expansive, generic view can be found in both the lengthy Bemba appeals dissent and the wide-ranging Appeals Chamber hearing from January 2018. The distinction between "material" and "subsidiary" facts was familiar to many of the judges and advocates from days at the ICTY.[1124] Such distinctions create useful flexibility for judges, allowing some issues to fade, while others loom large. The art of assigning any given "fact" to one category or the other can be a powerful strategic move. In the context of command responsibility, for example, it could be said that particular criminal acts are relatively minor details: what truly matters is the occurrence of crimes within broader categories. In the context of the Bemba *facts and circumstances* debate, at least, a fresh strategy of judicial nominalism began to chip away at a series of judicial practices.

Doing All that Is Necessary and Reasonable

The Bemba appeals Majority accomplished its task in two relatively simple stages. First, by interpreting the conviction as a discrete number of criminal acts, it determined that the majority of those acts should never have been considered by the Trial Chamber. They fell outside the scope of pre-trial *facts and circumstances*, having been added to the mix by the Prosecutor and improperly allowed to remain (over the objections of the Bemba Defense) to become part the final Trial Judgment. This was a remarkable approach, given that none of the other players – Prosecutor, Pre-Trial Chamber, or Trial Chamber – understood the case in terms of bare criminal acts. For them, the case was about the larger wave of murder, rape, and pillaging, drawing on Article 7 crimes against humanity and Article 8 war crimes. Within this forest of criminality, the appeals Majority suddenly decided to count the number of

[1123] Ngudjolo Appeals Judgment, Joint Dissenting Opinion of Judge Ekaterina Trendafilova and Judge Cuno Tarfusser, ICC-01/04–02/12–271-AnxA, para. 48.

[1124] In a narrow application to the organization of facts in pre-trial "facts and circumstances," this distinction between "material facts" and "subsidiary facts" has gained a toe-hold in ICC practice. See the *Chambers Practice Manual* (May 2017 ed.), p. 12, which is cited hopefully by the Prosecution in the Bemba Appeals Chamber hearing (January 9, 2018, p. 59), as it launched into a much broader use of these terms. The *Practice Manual* is prepared and revised periodically by ICC judges, and "is not intended as a binding instrument on ICC trial judges. Rather it contains general recommendations and guidelines reflecting best practices" (p. 3).

trees, reducing the trial dramatically. The implications of this nominalism would become clear as the Appeals Judgment unfolded.

After this first-stage elimination of eighteen criminal acts (or clusters of acts), there remained just eleven more. The Trial Judgment was trimmed down to just this subset, which encompassed one murder, twenty rapes, and five acts of pillaging allegedly committed by Bemba's MLC troops in the CAR. It was his troops who had committed these criminal acts, and not Bemba himself. Bemba's liability derived from his duty as a military commander to prevent, mitigate, or punish these criminal acts of soldiers under his command. His liability did not strictly follow from the number of such events, under the concept of *command responsibility* codified in Article 28(a). Instead, his liability was conditioned on Bemba's knowledge about what happened, and on the feasibility of his taking appropriate steps in response. Working with this set of concepts, the Bemba appeals Majority found fundamental errors in the Trial Chamber's analysis, and acquitted Bemba on the charges derived from these eleven criminal acts. By disposing of this second cluster of acts, the second stage of the Appeals Judgment was completed; nothing remained of the Trial Chamber's convictions.

In keeping with its spare nominalism, the appeals Majority's analysis of criminal liability was crisp and intense, rather than comprehensive. The statutory tests for knowledge and feasibility encompass three large categories, from which the appeals Majority drew just one. It put aside the knowledge test, which had figured heavily in the Trial Chamber's use of Regulation 55. In the end, the Trial Chamber never carried through on its proposal to expand the scope of knowledge to include (beyond what Bemba actually knew) what he "should have known." It found instead that Bemba possessed *actual knowledge* of the crimes. The other statutory tests concern the feasibility of Bemba's preventing, mitigating, or punishing those crimes. First, was he really the commander of these troops, and did he exercise "effective command" to a degree sufficient to allow for remedial action? And if so, second, did he then fail to assert control? According to the Statute, his duty, given knowledge about the commission of these crimes, was "[t]o take all necessary and reasonable measures within his or her power to prevent or repress their commission or to submit the matter to the competent authorities for investigation and prosecution."[1125]

The Bemba appeals Majority based its acquittals on the Trial Chamber's failure to meet this specific condition, focusing on the terms "necessary and reasonable measures." The Majority judges admitted to holding comparable

[1125] Article 28(a)(ii).

doubts about the Trial Chamber's handling of the other two essential statutory tests: the knowledge test and the "effective control" test. There had already been much discussion of all these statutory issues back in January 2018, at the three-day interactive hearing before the Appeals Chamber. But to complete its task of acquittal, the appeals Majority needed to consider only the matter of *necessary and reasonable* measures.[1126]

The appeals Majority took its nominalist strategy to the next level. First came the reminder that this whole case was about certain trees, not the whole forest. These *necessary and reasonable* measures had to be considered with respect to particular criminal acts, not the whole complex of criminality as imagined by the Prosecution, relying on NGO analysis. Second, the Prosecution was handed a forensic duty to have specified, in advance, precisely *which* concrete steps Bemba might have taken, under the circumstances, to control these particular eleven crimes. In other words, it had been the Prosecution's job, all the way back at the pre-trial stage, to operationalize the general statutory language of "all necessary and reasonable measures." It was a duty that the Prosecution failed to meet.

There was no apparent irony in the appeals Majority's creation of a legal "duty" falling on the Prosecutor, in a case that centered on the duties falling on military commanders in time of war. The source of the Prosecutor's duty of specificity was found partly in Regulation 52(b) ("a sufficient legal and factual basis to bring the person or persons to trial") and partly in the Rome Statute compendium of "Rights of the Accused," leading off with the right "[t]o be informed promptly and in detail of the nature, cause, and content of the charge . . . ."[1127]

At the level of abstract law, everyone could agree that the general terms *necessary and reasonable measures* could not be reduced to a rigid checklist. They should be interpreted case-by-case, following deep immersion in the facts of the particular matter.[1128] The Prosecution regarded this process as an exercise in "holism," which meant grasping the singular gestalt, rising out of

[1126] There was a fourth connected issue raised in Bemba's appeals petition, regarding whether Article 28(a) also included a causal requirement, requiring some kind of causal connection between the commander's failure of duty and the underlying crimes. This matter was discussed extensively in the January hearing, and was also taken up in the dissent and in Judge Eboe-Osuji's lengthy concurrence. See Bemba Appeals Judgment, Concurring Separate Opinion of Judge Eboe-Osuji, June 8, 2018, ICC-01/05-01/08-3636-Anx3, Part VII.

[1127] Article 67(1)(a).

[1128] Bemba Appeals Judgment, paras. 170–71, challenges the case-by-case strategy of the Trial Chamber for failing to take into account unique circumstances of the case and for shifting proof burdens onto the Defense to persuade the Trial Chamber to compose its judgments in different concrete terms.

the many parts – and holding it firm in subjective belief. There would be specific examples during the trial, as evidence piled up about what corrective measures, if any, Bemba had undertaken. Adding up all the evidentiary details (subsidiary facts) was a major task for the Trial Chamber, leading up to a finding about the material fact of whether Bemba had done all that was necessary and reasonable, taking everything into account.

The Bemba appeals Majority scrutinized this determination by the Trial Chamber, challenging both the process and the result. In the first place, the scope of the trial had been allowed to widen beyond any list of specific measures stipulated in the pre-trial *facts and circumstances*; meaning that the forest of potential measures (extending to *all* that were necessary and reasonable) was simply unmanageable. Second, the outcome was revealed in the oracular finding of "material fact," but was not sufficiently transparent for appellate review. It was a declaratory statement that Bemba had not taken all necessary and reasonable measures; but unpacking that judgment on appeal was simply not possible. The judgment was described as a summation of evidence which the Trial Chamber was persuaded to accept – faults and all – compared to the pool of evidence on which the Chamber was unpersuaded. While a great deal of evidence was mentioned in passing, what mattered was the personal level of conviction reported by each judge – and by all in their combined judgment.

The appeals Majority rejected this approach, faulting it for lack of discursive reasoning. The trial testimony had included large amounts of evidence requiring judicial "caution," including circumstantial evidence. The holistic strategy played with this mix of weights and fractions assisted by inferences and assumptions – some explicit, some tacit. The combined product was a report on the satisfied conscience of each judge but not analyzable on review. The appeals Majority was not prepared to defer to oracular judgments of this type, even when described as *beyond reasonable doubt*.

In reviewing the finding on necessary and reasonable measures, the appeals Majority showed its teeth. In scarcely a dozen pages, it rejected this ponderous finding, ordering an acquittal for Bemba for the remaining eleven criminal acts. The appeals Majority began with a list of small omissions: mainly Defense evidence that was variously ignored, disregarded, not addressed, not taken into account, granted insufficient weight, or otherwise slighted. The list included Bemba's personal efforts to gain information and investigatory assistance from CAR authorities, from the United Nations, and from FIDH. When the Prosecution failed to challenge such exculpatory evidence directly, the appeals Majority placed the burden on the Trial Chamber to provide "clear and convincing reasons" for discounting the value of that evidence. The

Majority's reprimand for "disregarding" certain evidence sparked a vigorous protest in the appeals dissent. But the appeals Majority saw it as the Trial Chamber's failure to provide discursive reasons sufficient to establish that it had explored all truth possibilities. This burden falls on the Trial Chamber because of the presumption of innocence; it is not up to the Defense to persuade the Trial Chamber that this Defense evidence was compelling.

The same appellate skepticism applied when the Trial Chamber questioned Bemba's motives for reaching out to international bodies.[1129] The Trial Chamber focused on Bemba's motivation in concluding that he failed to meet his commander's duty to take necessary and reasonable measures. But the Chamber's wholesale disregard of Bemba's evidence suggested rather that "in effect the Trial Chamber appears to have treated the motives as determinative, in and of themselves, of the adequacy or otherwise of the measures."[1130]

Whatever Bemba's motives and degree (or lack) of diligence, the Prosecution's case narrative showed that civilian attacks nonetheless occurred. From the violent results, it was easy to presume that Bemba could not have taken "all necessary and reasonable measures." But reasoning by presumption is no substitute for a full reckoning of evidentiary facts, including facts presented by the Defense.

The Trial Chamber appears to have lost sight of the fact that the measures taken by a commander cannot be faulted merely because of shortfalls in their execution. The word "merely" captures the strictness of review being carried out here by the appeals Majority. Other linguistic formulations include pointing out that some Trial Chamber conclusions were not "necessarily" correct, or did not give consideration to "particular circumstances," or did "not" show that Bemba's version of the facts were "not" correct.[1131] The fact that Trial Chamber judges were "unpersuaded" by Defense evidence could not be the end of the story, but called instead for the judges to provide their own compelling reasons – keeping in mind the presumption of innocence.

From one point of view, the fact and extent of rampant criminality in the war zone could be said to speak for themselves: that such things happened may demonstrate that Bemba failed to do enough to prevent or mitigate. Surely the requirement of "all" *necessary and reasonable* measures invites such a presumption. The commander must have failed; unless the commander can prove otherwise.

[1129] Ibid., paras. 170–82.
[1130] Ibid., para. 178.
[1131] Ibid., paras. 180, 173.

The kind of scrutiny used by the Bemba appeals Majority meant to challenge this presumptive style and to shift the forensic burden onto the Prosecution – a burden then inherited by the Trial Chamber in meeting the standard of proof for conviction. The Prosecution should have notified Bemba, in advance of trial, which specific measures, under the circumstances of the case, he was expected to take that were *necessary and reasonable*. Bemba could then have provided a more focused Defense, leaving the Prosecution to prove its specific allegations *beyond reasonable doubt*. Without this level of specificity, the matter left to the Trial Chamber floats along at a general level of abstraction.[1132] The appeals Majority treated the Defense fair trial rights as leading, axiomatically, to the demand for timely specifics about Bemba's alleged failures: "It follows that the accused person must be informed of the factual allegations on the basis of which the Prosecutor seeks to establish this element."[1133]

Of course, later on the trial evidence would eventually come down to specifics. What did Bemba say to his commanders on the ground during his early November 2002 trip to Bangui? When Bemba took some positive steps to punish a handful of soldiers for pillaging, did he do so in good faith – or was it just a cover-up? At the end of the trial, the Trial Chamber made a composite judgment, overall – arising from subjective belief, and declaring *beyond reasonable doubt* that Bemba had failed "to take all necessary and reasonable measures." But appellate review should be able to disaggregate that judgment, piercing the veil of subjective belief. In order to scrutinize the forest, the Appeals Chamber must be able to scrutinize the individual trees.

It was not enough that the Trial Chamber, in its final Judgment, provided its own retrospective list of specific preventive measures that Bemba could have taken, but did not.[1134] In an ICC trial, the pre-trial stage was the time for operationalizing the legal standard, and not in the final Judgment. These specifics should have been part of the *facts and circumstances* accompanying the charges, prior to Confirmation. Additionally, the particular measures belatedly compiled by the Trial Chamber bore no relationship to the eleven specific criminal acts, which (in the view of the Appeals Chamber) constituted the full extent of Bemba's conviction. The retrospective list of *necessary and reasonable* measures was constructed with an assumption that Bemba's responsibility extended to mitigating the entire wave of criminality, which the Trial Chamber saw as the scope of Bemba's conviction.

1132 Ibid., para. 186.
1133 Ibid.
1134 Ibid., para. 729.

> [T]he Appeals Chamber notes the apparent discrepancy between the limited number of crimes for which Mr Bemba was held responsible under article 28 and the Trial Chamber's assessment of the measures Mr Bemba should have taken, which appears to have been based on the much broader and more general 'finding' by the Trial Chamber concerning widespread MLC criminality in the CAR. Indeed, a finding that the measures deployed by a commander were insufficient to prevent or repress an extended crime wave, for example five hundred crimes, does not mean that these measures were also insufficient to prevent or repress the limited number of specific crimes, for example 20 crimes, for which the commander is ultimately convicted.[1135]

The defect lurking in the Trial Chamber's Judgment was more than just substituting the forest for the trees. The Appeals Chamber demanded a more detailed analysis, backed by compelling reasons, providing a public standard of proof. The lack of specific referencing, whether from the Prosecution or from the Trial Chamber, was a failure to meet evidentiary burdens placed on criminal convictions. Rather than creating a prima facie burden on the accused to show that, under the circumstances, this retrospective list of measures would not have been successful, the burden of proof constrains the Trial Chamber, should it try to use that list to justify a guilty verdict.

> The trial chamber must specifically identify what a commander should have done *in concreto*. Abstract findings about what a commander might theoretically have done are unhelpful and problematic, not least because they are too elusive to disprove. Indeed, it is for the Trial Chamber to demonstrate in its reasoning that the commander did not take specific and concrete measures that were available to him or her, and which any reasonably diligent commander in comparable circumstances would have taken. It is not the responsibility of the accused to show that the measures he or she did take were sufficient.[1136]

The fact that certain crimes were committed by the subordinates of a commander does not show, given the standard of proof, that the commander acted unreasonably at the time.

The inspiration for the Appeals Chamber's implacable nominalism is the presumption of innocence, enshrined in Article 66 and standing high in the pantheon of legal principles governing criminal trials. In dismantling the Bemba convictions, the appeals Majority took exception to tacit presumptions that shift the onus of proof onto the accused. While the standard in Article 28 (a)(ii) says that military commanders must take *necessary and reasonable* steps,

[1135] Ibid., para. 75.
[1136] Ibid., para. 170.

a guilty verdict demands articulate reasons, sufficient to meet the standard of proof beyond reasonable doubt.

The appeals Majority exercised particular scrutiny in reviewing procedures for fact-finding. It singled out for particular criticism those occasions on which the Trial Chamber ignored, discounted, or found disingenuous some key items in the Defense case. While the appeals Majority restricted its review to the question of *necessary and reasonable* measures, similar weaknesses could have been drawn from the other legal elements of *command responsibility*: questions about the commander's knowledge, and about his "effective command" of his forces.[1137]

The law of command responsibility lives in dread of strict liability. The contextual elements contained in the Statute are supposed to provide enough realism to combat any gravitational pull toward that unfair standard. It is an act of politeness to call this mode of responsibility *sui generis*, considering its serious internal tensions. The legal standard concerns the commander's failure to assert control, but only if he retains enough capacity to be in a state of "effective control." It is a moral duty based on omissions, calculated against a field of active measures deemed necessary and reasonable ... but only if actual circumstances allow. With so many legal angles and perspectives, the facts of a particular case can be variously assembled to reach a wide range of outcomes. In his study of *command responsibility* cases in the ad hoc tribunals, as previously noted, Guénaël Mettraux described the subtle use of evidential inferences to dilute legal standards "by stealth."[1138] Unless the reasoning process is fully disclosed in each case, it is virtually impossible for a reviewing court to monitor legal rules. The conclusions stay hidden behind the curtain of appellate deference to trial-court declarations of fact.

The ad hoc tribunals sometimes generated lists of hypothetical factors – *indicia* – that could be used to assess a commander's knowledge, or the existence of "effective command," or whether *necessary and reasonable* measures were used in mitigation. These indicia ensured a kind of uniformity and robustness to the respective liability elements. It was possible to see them as a kind of legal checklist, standardizing the judicial determination of particular facts, case-by-case, related to the determination of guilt.[1139]

[1137] These elements were all discussed at length in the January 2018 Appeals Chamber hearing. The Bemba appeals dissent discussed them all, but the appeals Majority remained selectively focused on the single element of *necessary and reasonable* measures.

[1138] Mettraux, *Law of Command Responsibility*, p. 11.

[1139] On the status of indicia, a question arose in the Bemba Appeals Chamber hearing whether the Trial Chamber's list of remedial measures was simply "inherent" in the scope of Article

The Bemba appeals Majority saw jurisprudential weakness in this orientation to formulaic standards applied generically across a range of criminal investigations, situated in different times and places. According to the Majority's critique, the larger risk came from shifting the Prosecution's proof burdens to the Defense. Whether these *indicia* are fully articulated, or especially if they remain inchoate, they raise a series of default expectations – things any responsible commander should do – against which the Defense would have to find dispelling evidence.

The Bemba Tipping Point: The Congo Trials in Retrospect

The Bemba appeals dissent, in addition to disagreeing forcefully with the Majority opinion, was the mirror opposite in style and substance. It was more than three times the length, obviously concerned to address an audience of future appellate judges, if any might be tempted by the new departure shown by the appeals Majority. It addressed all six Defense grounds for appealing the Bemba Trial Chamber Judgment, pursuing every conceivable legal element and angle.

The dissenters began their long odyssey through the legal thicket by defending the orthodoxy of appellate deference to Trial Chamber fact-finding. In their view, no other Appeals Chamber at the ICC had yet questioned this practice, whether for interlocutory appeals or appeals from final judgments. The Majority's radical departure was likewise unprecedented in light of the practice in ad hoc tribunals. Failing to see any irony in the Majority's pledge to exercise "extreme caution" in extending deference to the Trial Chamber, the dissenters embraced the oracular style of fact-finding, going back to the Lubanga conviction decision.[1140]

In a document running fully three-quarters the length of the original Trial Chamber Judgment, the dissenters found nothing that struck them as unreasonable. In their view, the onus was firmly on the Bemba Defense to demonstrate any lack of reasonableness.[1141] As the Prosecution had argued previously at the January 2018 Appeals Chamber hearing, it was the Trial Chamber alone that heard live witnesses, observed cross-examinations, and detected whatever

28(a). The Prosecution responded: "It may go a little far, and we don't need to rely on that proposition, but if you look at the measures that the Chamber found that Mr Bemba should have taken, they are the basic things that a commander should – are inherent in his duties." January 10, 2018, ICC-01/05–01/08-T-373-ENG, p. 122.

1140 Bemba Appeals Judgment, Dissenting Opinion of Judge Sanji Mmasenono Monageng and Judge Piotr Hofmański, ICC-01/05–01/08–3636-Anx1, para. 8.

1141 Ibid., para. 16.

demeanor might be used to assess credibility. True, different trial judges might reach opposite results in assessing complex factual issues; but either result could still be reasonable. The Appeals Chamber should stick with more technical legal questions on appeal, so long as the settled facts were not unreasonable, "unless you are satisfied that no reasonable trier of fact could have made those findings or that they are wholly erroneous, that is you cannot work out – you cannot discern how the Trial Chamber's conclusion could have been reasonably reached from the evidence before it."[1142] To be sure, in appealing a conviction, the Defense will always challenge the facts as unreasonable. But in reality, it was merely expressing a preference for its own take on the facts, which had already been fully considered, and properly rejected, during the trial.[1143]

The debate over deference can also be seen as a red herring. The key test for deference came three years earlier in the Ngudjolo case, where the Prosecutor was appealing the Trial Chamber's acquittal. As discussed in Chapter 8, two members of the Ngudjolo Appeals Chamber took vehement exception to the fact-finding practices leading up to that acquittal. They faulted the Trial Chamber for failing to interpret the evidence holistically, and for succumbing to premature doubts about Ngudjolo's case, rather than reaching around those doubts to seize the full truth of the matter. The question of deference never arose for these Ngudjolo dissenters, when the Chamber below had so clearly failed to use proper methods of fact-finding.[1144]

Looking back over the Congo trials as a whole, the Court struggled for well over a decade to meet the challenge of fact-finding in the rugged conditions of Ituri and the CAR. The issue was not whether atrocities occurred: exploitation of child soldiers, and the murders, rapes, and pillagings carried out against civilians in the midst of large-scale unrest. But the trials encountered difficulties in sorting through complex modes of liability, and in applying certain definitional criteria for international crimes – such as the organizational auspices for crimes against humanity.

The Court entered its first country-wide situations facing limits on investigations, and then, with hindsight, it paid a price in the courtroom. Witnesses turned out to behave differently from informants interviewed by NGOs and local intermediaries. Each side found a basis for complaining about the lies of the

[1142] Ibid., p. 16.

[1143] Bemba Appeals Chamber hearing, January 9, 2018, pp. 13–16 (Prosecution).

[1144] Note that the only judge participating in both appeals, Judge Monageng, helped form the majority upholding Ngudjolo's acquittal, and dissented in the Bemba case, where she would have upheld Bemba's conviction. In both cases, she subscribed to the practice of deferring to the respective Trial Chambers in their fact-finding roles.

other's witnesses. There were broader concerns about witness corruption, continuing themes that had been ignited during the Lubanga trial. Whatever the reasons, facts that seemed to be taken for granted at the outset of trials turned out to be difficult or impossible to demonstrate inside the courtroom. The experience of the child soldier witnesses in the Lubanga case made this plain. Problems continued when the Prosecutor's master narrative for Katanga and Ngudjolo collapsed under pressure. And the conceptual subtleties of command responsibility ensured further controversy in the Bemba trial, when the available facts had to match up with legal theories about *actions that did not happen*.

During the Court's first two decades, the Congo trials were not the only experiments conducted in the ICC laboratory, although they were the only proceedings to reach the final appeals level. By late 2019, there was one more Ituri-based convicted-accused awaiting appeal, and also another ongoing trial in the Uganda situation. Prominent cases from Kenya and the Ivory Coast had been aborted at the trial phase, based on alleged weaknesses in the Prosecution's case. Several more cases had stopped with pre-trial deliberations. In all these individual cases, the methods of fact-finding created significant challenges. What unfolded in the completed Congo trials was a more extended version of these controversies. The exception was a single case from Mali, where the accused pled guilty without contesting any facts behind the charges.

The Bemba Appeals Judgment can be understood as a reaction to this troubled history. The pressures on the Court arose from deep tensions within the mission endorsed in Rome in 1998. The ICC was expected to play a powerful role in countering the "unimaginable atrocities that deeply shock the conscience of humanity." But it must also follow strict legal principles, including the presumption of innocence. No one thought it would be simple. But the particular hurdles to implementation became clear only with the completion of the initial trials. The Congo trials were, in this sense, a necessary experiment to test the mixed and nuanced goals laid out in the Rome Treaty.

With their stunning acquittal of Jean-Pierre Bemba, the appeals Majority delivered several important messages. Their efforts pushed the outer limit of their mandate as appellate judges, starting with decentering the practice of prior Appeals Chambers, which had extended a broad "margin of deference" to the respective Trial Chambers findings of fact. The core issues at stake were not simply disputes about facts but debates about jurisprudential methods. With some interpretive license, the Bemba appeals Majority can be put in direct dialogue with the Ngudjolo appeals dissenters: both felt that the determination of facts at trial was surrounded by competing pressures from lofty legal principles. The Ngudjolo appeals dissent wanted to recast the legal concepts of *trial fairness* and *proof beyond reasonable doubt*, in the interest of finding the larger truth about civilian atrocities in Ituri. In the Bemba case, the appeals Majority interpreted the presumption of innocence as the overriding procedural mandate, displacing the margin of deference on appeal, and challenging the way trial chambers made use of common presumptions and inferences in reaching opaque, declaratory findings of guilt.

Beyond the Forest: Dialogues for the Future

The appeals Majority's jurisprudential gambit comes into sharp focus in the exchange that took place between judges and Prosecution during the January 2018 Appeals Chamber hearing. On the final day of this three-day session, in an intense discussion of lower chamber fact-finding, the parties were asked to discuss some of the key legal elements for crimes against humanity. According to the framework definitions in Article 7, these crimes must have occurred in a structural context surrounding a sustained "attack": "'Attack directed against any civilian population' means a course of conduct involving the multiple commission of acts . . . pursuant to or in furtherance of a State or organizational policy to commit such attack."[1145] The Prosecution's train of thought in this dialogue may explain the vehemence of the reaction delivered by the appeals Majority.

Crimes against humanity (Article 7) are distinctive international crimes, different from waves of civil violence that may also produce a toll of murders and rapes. They are distinct from international war crimes listed in Article 8, which applies to armed conflicts that rise above the level of domestic unrest – where the results may still be murders, rapes, and acts of pillaging. The Bemba charges straddled both Articles 7 and 8, with murder and rape coming from each distinctive category of crime. Along with the crimes themselves, the special conditions for crimes against humanity must be proved by the Prosecution.

The reference to "a State or organizational policy" recalls Nuremberg, where the particular evils from mass murder were distinguished by connection to a state policy of extermination.[1146] In the ad hoc tribunals for the former Yugoslavia and Rwanda, there were state-like entities with articulated policies of ethnic cleansing. But how did this structural concept apply to the civilian

[1145] Article 7(2)(a).

[1146] This history is richly told by Philippe Sands, *East West Street: On the Origins of "Genocide" and "Crimes Against Humanity"* (New York: Knopf, 2016), mentioned in the Bemba Appeals Chamber hearing, January 11, 2018, p. 42.

violence in the CAR in 2002–03? In addition to proving some accumulation of criminal "acts" to support Bemba's conviction, could the Prosecution also prove that the attack was linked to a formal policy?

This part of the Bemba Trial Judgment began with an elaborate inference. Bemba's MLC was clearly not a state body, and as an "organization" it produced no documents declaring a policy of murder and rape (the two Article 7 crimes fitting under this rubric). But the Court was ready to presume the existence of such a policy, inferring it from general circumstances in the CAR. Exactly which circumstances? The inference traveled through a postulated *modus operandi* imputed for the MLC troops: a unique pattern of behavior that emerged as the Trial Chamber constructed its synoptic view of diverse events.

This is where "holism" proved its value. It was a composite judgment based on a combination of direct testimony and large amounts of hearsay. This generic construct meant to factor out any similar cases, perhaps with the same *modus operandi* but carried out by non-MLC groups reporting to different commanders. The grand abstraction from overall circumstances to "policy" had to finesse myriad details: some crimes might have been committed by MLC troops independent of a "policy"; while other crimes, committed under the same pattern, might have come from someone else. Through it all, the presumptive "policy" displayed bold constructive power. Much of the hearsay evidence came from press and NGO reports, which by sheer accumulation compensated for the low "weight" attached to each single report.

This "holistic" pattern of legal evidence was strangely isomorphic with the postulated pattern of MLC behavior, on the basis of which the Trial Chamber reached its inference for an existing "policy." The collective finding that such a policy existed was deemed a *material fact*, earning the subjective belief of the Trial Chamber as proved *beyond reasonable doubt*. The underlying evidence was a mass of subsidiary facts. Individually these intermediary facts carried doubts and question marks in their wake; and they did not meet the strictest proof standards, taken in isolation. What mattered was the total sum at the end, as it accumulated in the mind of the beholder.

MR GALLMETZER: The Chamber looked at the whole .... What the Chamber needs to be satisfied here is that there is the existence of a forest. In order to be satisfied that there is a forest, you don't need to zoom in and make individual findings in relation to every single tree. In other words, you can look at it from a bird's eye perspective as it were and find that based on all the

> evidence that you find to be credible and reliable, there is an attack, like there is a forest, without slicing it up and looking at every single tree individually before you come to the conclusion . . ..
>
> Our position is that the legal element [i.e. the attack pursuant to an organizational policy], if we keep talking in this context, the legal element is: Was there a forest? Right? So the Chamber's application of the standard beyond a reasonable doubt applies to was there a forest?
>
> How do you find it? Well, it is a question of evidence. But in terms of methodology, the existence of individual trees in that particular context to the threshold of beyond a reasonable doubt is not a prerequisite as to the existence of the forest. The element to which you apply the beyond reasonable doubt standard, the element or the core fact that needs to be established is whether there is a forest and that is a question of evidence.[1147]

This rush of words and hopes could have driven the Bemba appeals Majority to its embrace of nominalism. Judge Morrison responded with words to the effect that "zero plus zero equals zero." Presiding Judge Van den Wyngaert had been sticking with the metaphor:

> I agree with that. You have to prove a forest, not the trees. But how can you prove a forest without proving trees? You don't need to prove all the trees in the forest, but at least a substantial amount of trees . . .. So if you have to prove your forest, I think you have to prove a substantial amount of trees beyond a reasonable doubt.[1148]

But a few lone trees don't make the difference, because the component facts were assigned discrete weights by the Trial Chamber, in a process of aggregation that passed seamlessly into mutual corroboration of each part by all the others. The result is now a composite *fact* at a higher level of generality. As Mr Gallmetzer breathlessly pointed out, it was all explained there in the Judgment, in paragraph 563 to be specific. But the Presiding Judge recalled that this paragraph 563 buries its component facts in a long footnote. The individual facts were themselves so sketchy as to require some basic forest

[1147] Bemba Appeals Chamber hearing, January 11, 2018, pp. 52–54.
[1148] Ibid., p. 53.

management. "And so my question then is, in that footnote, the quality of the evidence, not only the quantity but quality, to what extent in making a finding beyond reasonable doubt on crimes against humanity can the Trial Chamber rely on NGO reports, press articles, possibly anonymous hearsay?"[1149] The answer came swiftly and confidently:

MR GALLMETZER: Now the Trial Chamber in that one paragraph that you have just indicated, there is a very important footnote, and that footnote refers – first of all, it includes some evidence, yeah, but then it also refers to a much broader pool of evidence.

Now whether some media articles, whether some hearsay evidence is credible and reliable is a determination for the trier of fact. Nothing in law prevents a trial chamber from relying on this evidence under certain circumstances. It is a factual determination. This case, the evidence was corroborated.[1150]

Much of the evidence in this footnote could not be assigned independent credibility. It included, for example, raw data about attacks reported in a CAR magistrate's investigatory dossier. It came close to the "zero" rating mentioned in Judge Morrison's comments. But one of the charms of holism was its bootstrap capacity to assign positive weight to previously weightless facts. If these empty reports in the footnote could be "corroborated" by a larger pool of evidence, then they can acquire a positive factor, and start contributing density to the emerging forest.

MR GALLMETZER: The Chamber did not rely on individual items of evidence. Let's assume there was a piece of hearsay evidence, it did not rely on this in isolation. Was it corroborated? Was it consistent with others? Was there any proof of the context of the evidentiary basis as a whole that the Chamber could find it credible and reliable? In this case the Chamber determined yes, that was the case and therefore it added it to the pool of broader evidence to inform together with the evidence that established beyond

1149 Ibid., p. 56.
1150 Ibid., pp. 56–57.

a reasonable doubt the acts of which Mr Bemba was convicted. This is a sufficient evidentiary pool to conclude that an attack existed; i.e. that there was a forest.

PRESIDING JUDGE VAN DEN WYNGAERT: This is based on the footnote in paragraph 563. So are you saying that the Appeals Chamber has to accept that and does not need further explanation about what the evidence is? You say for example mutually corroborating evidence, but how do we know that if we don't know what the evidence is?

MR GALLMETZER: Well, your Honours . . . the footnote critically refers to a large, significant pool of other evidence in which the Chamber makes factual findings in relation to acts of murder, rape, pillaging that inform its ultimate decision. And that other evidence that is then expressly referred to in that footnote corroborates it. They corroborate each other.[1151]

And what about those magistrate's reports, which would not have been considered as admissible evidence in civil law countries? According to the Prosecution, the ICC rules of admissibility need to remain generous, to ensure a rich pool of possibilities for the process of mutual corroboration, keeping in mind that a finding of credibility for any single item can itself be based on the broader pool. What matters is the overall pool strength, the aggregate collective "material" fact (such as the legal element of "organizational policy" for crimes against humanity), which is the proper level for proof beyond reasonable doubt. And the judgment that this standard has been met *is itself a matter of fact*.

MR GALLMETZER: . . . [A]bsolutely, everything that the Chamber admitted in this proceeding as evidence can be properly considered to inform its decisions . . .. In this context here, everything, everything that the Chamber finds to be credible and reliable can be admitted . . . in order to constitute the basis for a Chamber's decision under Article 74(2).

[1151] Ibid., pp. 57–58.

PRESIDING JUDGE
VAN DEN WYNGAERT: Beyond reasonable doubt?
MR GALLMETZER: That then remains a matter of fact of, you know, how strong is the evidence as a whole. If your initial document that was taken, say, by a Preliminary Judge is credible and reliable, judged on the totality of the evidence as a whole, not judged in isolation, then yes, that can contribute, that can contribute to informing the overall conclusion of the Chamber.[1152]

On appeal, some of that evidence in the footnote was objected to by the Defense. What were the Appeals Judges supposed to do with this Defense argument: ignore it?

MR COSTI: Not ignore it, but dismiss it . . . because we believe that the Chamber properly relied upon this evidence and assessed their credibility.

Judge Eboe-Osuji asked about the role of the Appeals Chamber – can it look at that holistic judgment of fact from the Trial Chamber and confirm that it was correct? Or should the Appeals Chamber not look at it, because the Trial Chamber has already made a determination, "in other words, the much-bandied concept of deference?"

MR COSTI: I think deference is the answer.[1153]

And finally, what about specific documents (such as unattributed press reports), many of which entered into the trial record with little more backing than face value?

MR COSTI: Your Honour, I'm not – it's difficult to say what is the forensic stance for a specific document . . . . [T]hat assessment has to be made in connection with the other evidence, unless this evidence should be excluded also altogether. But the assessment of the credibility of this document has to be done in the context with the others. I wouldn't take one document in isolation and ask myself "What is the value of this? Unless I read it in the context with the other.

[1152] Ibid., p. 59.
[1153] Ibid., p. 62.

JUDGE MORRISON: Well, if you don't do that, how can you see whether it has any relevance at all to the other evidence so as to give it evidential weight?

MR COSTI: And I go back to the same point over and over again, I think it's by reading it in context. I'm sure this answer probably doesn't satisfy you.[1154]

And indeed – at the end of the process – it did not. The reaction from the Bemba appeals Majority to the Prosecution's view of facts and standards of proof would find dramatic expression five months later, recoiling from this deep insulation of Trial Chamber findings from detailed review. As Judge Eboe-Osuji explained at the Appeals Chamber hearing, "we are now in the early stages of the jurisprudence of this Court in these matters we're discussing even on questions of standards of appellate review."[1155]

The Bemba Appeals Judgment did not resolve these complex matters. But at least it helped to clarify the larger jurisprudential options for future ICC cases. Judges Morrison and Van den Wyngaert began their separate opinion with the observation, regarding their dissenting colleagues, that there "appears to be a fundamental difference in the way we look at our mandates as international judges."[1156] Just as the three judges in the appeals Majority were not bound to follow the appeals philosophy used in the Lubanga case, the next appeals panel after Bemba will not be bound to the spirit of nominalism found in the jurisprudence of three appeals judges. Across all three Congo trials, several options came into focus, emerging from sharp differences in a range of dissents and concurrences, and not just in majority or unanimous decisions.

The Bemba Majority's approach is centered on the standard of proof beyond reasonable doubt. Expanding the relatively passive *reasonableness* standard practiced by the Lubanga Appeals Chamber, the Bemba Majority believed that it "must ensure that the trial chamber reasonably reached a conviction as to guilt beyond reasonable doubt."[1157]

In their separate opinion, Judges Morrison and Van den Wyngaert wrote further:

> We are indeed deeply concerned about the Trial Chamber's application of the "beyond reasonable doubt standard." Under this standard, the Prosecution's

[1154] Ibid., p. 65.

[1155] Ibid., p. 66.

[1156] Bemba Appeals Judgment, Separate Opinion of Judge Christine Van den Wyngaert and Judge Howard Morrison, June 8, 2018, ICC-01/05–01/08–3636-Anx2, para. 4.

[1157] Bemba Appeals Judgment, para. 41.

> narrative must not only be the best possible explanation of the evidence that is in the case record, it must be the only plausible explanation. As long as there are other plausible explanations, taking into consideration what the evidence has proved and what is still unknown, it is not possible to enter a finding beyond a reasonable doubt. With the greatest respect for our colleagues of the Minority, we are firmly of the view that many of the findings in the impugned Conviction Decision fail to reach this threshold, despite the fact that the Trial Chamber correctly defined the standard when setting it out in the abstract. We strongly believe that the Appeals Chamber cannot turn a blind eye to such obvious evidentiary problems on the basis of a deferential standard of review.[1158]

The main concern was "conditions under which a trial chamber may establish facts on the basis of circumstantial evidence and inferences." The two judges found particular weaknesses in the many situations where the Bemba Trial Chamber relied on its pool of "holistic" evidence. Regarding the required legal element of an "organizational policy" for crimes against humanity, the Trial Chamber Judgment had listed eight circumstantial factors that "holistically" were taken to prove the existence of the required policy.

> This brings us to the key problem we have with the Trial Chamber's finding of an undefined policy, which is that it does not come anywhere near to being the only possible inference that can be drawn from the eight factors to which the Trial Chamber refers. The fact that senior MLC officers did not do enough to stop the troops from misbehaving can also be explained in several ways and certainly does not compel the conclusion that they deliberately did not intervene so that the troops would engage in criminal conduct. Incompetence, cowardice, indifference (or, most likely, a combination thereof) could reasonably offer an equally plausible explanation for the officers' passivity.[1159]

[1158] Ibid., Separate Opinion of Judges Van den Wyngaert and Morrison, para. 14. The same thought with slightly different wording was cited approvingly in the Bemba Majority decision: "Where a factual finding is based on an inference drawn from circumstantial evidence, the finding is only established beyond reasonable doubt if it was the only reasonable conclusions that could be drawn from the evidence. It is indeed well established that it is not sufficient that a conclusion reached by a trial chamber is merely *a* reasonable conclusion available from that evidence; the conclusion pointing to the guilt of the accused must be the *only* reasonable conclusion available. If there is another conclusion reasonably open from the evidence, and which is consistent with the innocence of the accused, he or she must be acquitted" (para. 42, citing from Bemba *et al.* Appeals Judgment, March 8, 2018, ICC-01/05-01/13-2275, para. 868).

[1159] Bemba Appeals Judgment, Separate Opinion of Judges Van den Wyngaert and Morrison, para. 13.

Judges Morrison and Van den Wyngaert ended their separate opinion on a somber note, aware of the disappointment awaiting the Bemba trial victims:

> Today's acquittal will disappoint many who have been waiting for years for someone to be held to account for the crimes that were committed against the population of the Central African Republic. Such disappointment is understandable, especially because the ICC was established precisely to bring justice to situations that would otherwise fall beyond the reach of the rule of law. However, this desire to bring justice should never come at the price of abandoning the basic principles of the rule of law . . ..
>
> Today's Judgment is thus neither a victory, nor a failure. It is the conclusion that a dispassionate application of the Statute compels us to accept. This does not mean that emotionally we do not empathise with the pain and loss of the victims. However, even if Aristotle's dictum that law should be reason, free from passion, may strike us in the 21st century as somewhat inhuman, it remains true more than two thousand years later that, as humans we can only hope to establish the rule of law if we discipline ourselves to be guided by rationality and resist the urge to allow emotions to determine judicial action.[1160]

9.4 THE TRIAL WITHIN THE TRIAL

Allegations of Corruption

Over a weekend in late November 2013, an ICC Pre-Trial Chamber authorized a series of arrests, carried out simultaneously in Belgium, France, the Netherlands, and the Congo. The Prosecutor's investigation had been secret; and there had been no announced situation. It had nothing to do with crimes against humanity or war crimes. The suspects rounded up were Bemba's lead counsel, his case manager, a Bemba ally serving in the Congolese Parliament, and a freelance associate of the Defense team living in France (after fleeing Cameroon and his native CAR). Bemba himself was served with a warrant in his detention cell, labeled as the criminal mastermind. The charges against all five were "offenses against the administration of justice," including soliciting false testimony, presenting false evidence, and bribing witnesses.[1161]

The Bemba Defense had just presented its final witness in a rambling, stuttering case. For nearly a year and a half, the Prosecution had been

1160 Ibid., paras. 77, 79.

1161 Article 70. See ICC Press Release, "Bemba Case: Four Suspects Arrested for Corruptly Influencing Witnesses," November 24, 2013.

monitoring Bemba's personal phone calls, from detention. In the final two months, Dutch police approved phone taps for the lead counsel and the case manager.

The larger Bemba trial had opened three years before the November 2013 arrests. It began with a series of CAR victim-witnesses presenting stories of unimaginable terror and trauma. The wave of rape and sexual violence reached not just women and young girls but men and boys, too. Much of the trial took place in closed sessions, making it difficult for court watchers to keep track of courtroom dynamics. A little over a year into the trial, Bemba's first lead counsel died of natural causes in the Congo. A Bemba family lawyer with little criminal experience, he was originally paired with a succession of well-known Hague defenders. Promoted into his place was Aimé Kilolo, a Congolese member of the Brussels bar; supplemented by the seasoned British barrister Peter Haynes and Australian Kate Gibson.

The Defense had started presenting witnesses in August 2012 when, five weeks into its case, the Trial Chamber gave notice under Regulation 55, forecasting a likely change in the knowledge standard associated with command responsibility.[1162] The trial slackened and finally jolted to a formal halt in December as the Defense team pondered its options; was denied leave to appeal; and reconciled itself to continuing under protest.[1163] After a nearly three-month gap, the Defense continued with witnesses; but the overall schedule was riddled with lapses, including one witness from the Congo who simply disappeared in The Hague.[1164] By mid-2013 the Trial Chamber was putting pressure on Kilolo to wrap it up.

The Trial Chamber's haste at that moment was understandable. Three months previously, it had received secret intelligence from the Prosecutor about her nine-month-long solo investigation of the Defense team, which included monitoring messages from the ICC detention center where Bemba was housed.[1165] Based on a tip-off in June 2012, her investigation overlapped the

[1162] Bemba Trial Chamber, Notification under Regulation 55, September 21, 2012, ICC-01/05–01/08–2324.

[1163] Bemba Trial Chamber, Decision Lifting the Temporary Suspension of the Trial, February 6, 2013, ICC-01/05–01/08–2500.

[1164] Tjitske Lingsma puts the time during September 2012. See *All Rise: The High Ambitions of the International Criminal Court and the Harsh Reality* (Utrecht: Ipso Facto), p. 178.

[1165] The notification to the Presiding Judge occurred on March 20, 2013. See the Prosecutor's timeline on the investigation, Bemba *et al.* Trial Chamber, Public Redacted Version of Request for Judicial Assistance to Obtain Evidence for Investigation under Article 70, February 12, 2014, ICC-01/05–44-Red (originally submitted May 3, 2013). For Article 70 offenses, the Prosecutor has much wider scope for conducting investigations, free of oversight conditions (under Article 53) that apply to standard criminal investigations. See *Rules of*

entire period of the Defense's presentation of its main case, relying on her office's self-imposed restraints to keep the potential criminal conversations separate from the strictly privileged attorney–client deliberations.[1166] Whatever she might uncover about corruption, the Trial Chamber understood the potential conflicts of interest that could jeopardize the main case. As quickly as possible, the Presiding Judge saw the matter deflected to a separate Pre-Trial Chamber. An independent counsel was engaged (still secretly) to somehow separate the criminal and non-criminal phone intercepts; but questions would later be raised about the unreviewable conflicts behind these arrangements.[1167] It might be fairly said that the fair trial rights of the accused do not include criminal corruption of the court system. But even in that regard, there was a further presumption of innocence to be taken into account.

The new corruption-focused Pre-Trial Chamber functioned with a single judge, who involved himself more closely in the investigation than would have happened in a normal country-wide search for war crimes. Judge Cuno Tarfusser approved the request for Dutch and Belgian authorities to release phone logs and recordings, followed later by Dutch phone taps of live conversations.[1168] All this was happening as the Defense case was lurching to a close. On Friday, the Defense team had run out of witnesses. By Sunday, Kilolo was arrested in Brussels and sent to the Hague detention center, where he and Bemba would soon be reunited with case manager Jean-Jacques Mangenda, apprehended in the Netherlands. They were quickly joined by the Congolese Parliamentarian (the alleged financier) and the CAR/Cameroon field rep (accused of enlisting fake CAR former soldiers).

Procedure and Evidence, 162–69, especially Rule 165 on investigations, and the suspension of procedures used in standard investigations.

[1166] Moreno-Ocampo had previously told the Court that any potential conflicts of interest in prosecuting Article 70 investigations against the Defense were controlled by internal division of labor within his Office. See Lubanga Trial Chamber, Prosecution Observations on Article 70, April 1, 2011, ICC-01/04–01/06–2716.

[1167] The Bemba Trial Chamber rejected that challenge, placing the burden on the Defense to specify instances of harm to its overall legal positions, while also disclaiming any jurisdiction over the conduct of the Article 70 investigation or prosecution. Decision on the Defence Request for Interim Relief, March 2, 2014, 01/05–01/08–3059, paras. 20, 24. These arguments came to a head, prior to Judgment, in the abuse of process request, which was denied. Bemba Trial Chamber, Decision on Defence Request for Relief for Abuse of Process, June 17, 2015, ICC-01/05–01/08–3255.

[1168] On obtaining the phone records, see Decision on Prosecutor's Request for Judicial Order, February 3, 2014, ICC-01/05–01/08–52. Judge Tarfusser's role was broadly challenged. Bemba *et al.* Pre-Trial Chamber, Defence Request for Disqualification of Single Judge Cuno Tarfusser, May 1, 2014, ICC-01/05–01/013–372. Through the Presidency, the ICC judges rejected this request, Notification of Decision on Defence Requests for the Disqualification of a Judge, June 23, 2014, ICC-01/05–01/13–511 with Annex.

This improbable story became one more kaleidoscopic phase of the Congo trials, adding a further arc to the ICC's steep learning curve – leaving a host of awkward questions. For a long time, information about the corruption cases was closely controlled, with just a few ICC press releases that shocked other trial participants (other than the Prosecutors) and the professional legal community.[1169] So much of the ensuing process was held in closed session that it was impossible for outsiders to get any grasp of the whole. The Confirmation of Charges hearing was conducted in secrecy.[1170] Ultimately, in 2016 as a Trial Judgment came down in the corruption case (which came to be called "Bemba *et al.*" to distinguish it from "the main case" of Bemba himself), and as sentences were passed and appeals taken, there remained a broader mystery about this extraordinary legal cycle.[1171] The Prosecutor issued her own timeline of events in February 2014,[1172] but it has been left to resourceful journalists to reconstruct the full episode. An especially vivid account was published by Tjitske Lingsma, one of the intrepid corps of professional ICC commentators.[1173]

The corruption investigation unfolded at a hectic moment for the Court and for the Prosecutor. The tip-off hit the Prosecutor's desk on June 14, 2012, the day before Fatou Bensouda formally took her solemn oath as the Court's second Prosecutor. She had been Luis Moreno-Ocampo's deputy from 2006 and was anointed by the ASP the preceding December. Thomas Lubanga had been convicted in March, after a fractured first ICC trial, and was awaiting sentencing. The second trial of Katanga and Ngudjolo was about to fall apart at the deliberations stage, although the Prosecution was in

1169 ICC Press Releases: "Aimé Kilolo Musamba, Fidèle Babala Wandu, and Jean-Pierre Bemba Gombo Make First Appearance before ICC," November 27, 2013; "Bemba, Kilolo *et al.* Case: Appeals Chamber Dismisses the Appeals of Messrs. Kilolo, Babala and Mangenda," July 11, 2014.

1170 See Bemba *et al.* Pre-Trial Chamber, Transmission to Presidency of the Full Record of the Proceedings, including the Confirmation of Charges, January 27, 2015, ICC-01/05–01/13–803. The single judge had denied the accused leave to appeal the confirmation decision, Joint Decision on Applications for Appeal of the Confirmation Decision, 23 January 2015, ICC-01/05–01/13–801.

1171 Bemba *et al.* Trial Judgment, October 19, 2016, ICC-01/05–01/13–1989; Bemba *et al.* Trial Chamber Sentencing Decision, March 22, 2017, ICC-01/05–01/13–2123; Bemba *et al.* Appeals Chamber Judgment, March 8, 2018, ICC-01/05–01/13–2275.

1172 Bemba *et al.* Trial Chamber, Public Redacted Version of Request for Judicial Assistance to Obtain Evidence for Investigation under Article 70, February 12, 2014, ICC-01/05–44-Red (originally submitted May 3, 2013).

1173 The expanded English version of *All Rise*, published in 2017, updated her well-received Dutch monograph of the same name, adding later details about the cases of Bemba and Bemba *et al.* Lingsma has been a steady contributor to the *International Justice Monitor*, tracking developments at the ICC over a period of years.

stubborn denial. The Kony craze was in full-swing worldwide,[1174] but the Prosecutor was still empty-handed in Uganda – and more pointedly in Darfur, after Sudanese President al-Bashir defied the Court's arrest warrant.

The Kenyan cases were meeting strong headwinds in 2012, after pre-trial judges rejected two of the six cases at the confirmation stage.[1175] The highest profile case against President Uhuru Kenyatta seemed to mock the Court's weakness in the face of a non-cooperative member state. The case against his co-accused was dropped in early 2013.[1176] But the agony persisted through successive trial postponements, until the Kenyatta case was abandoned in late 2014, amidst allegations of Kenyan witness tampering and bribery.[1177] Six weeks before revealing the corruption charges against Bemba and his team, the Court had unsealed another arrest warrant, alleging Article 70 offenses against a Kenyan journalist, Walter Osapiri Barasa.[1178] Barasa had worked as an intermediary for the ICC Prosecutor before going rogue (according to the allegations) and bribing witnesses to withdraw their testimony. Barasa, Gicheru, and Bett remained at large in 2019.

The Return of Victors' Justice?

The years 2012 and 2013, when the Bemba *et al.* investigation was gaining steam, were especially rocky for the Prosecution inside the courtroom. The whole Office had taken a beating in the Lubanga case, including the spectacular failure of the Prosecution child-witnesses. Amidst allegations of false testimony, corrupt intermediaries, and botched investigations in Ituri, the Office had been defiant – taunting the Defense in a press interview, resisting

[1174] The video *Kony 2012* had been released in March 2012 and had gone viral. Every twelve-year-old on the planet knew about Joseph Kony – so why couldn't they catch him?

[1175] The cases rejected at the pre-trial stage were Henry Kiprono Kosgey, January 23, 2012, ICC-01/09–01/11–373; and Mohammed Hussein Ali, January 23, 2012. ICC-01/09–02/11–382. Dissenting Judge Hans-Peter Kaul would not have confirmed charges against any of the six suspects.

[1176] See Prosecution notification to the Trial Chamber of withdrawal of charges against Francis Kirimi Muthaura, March 11, 2013. ICC-01/09–02/11–687.

[1177] The Prosecutor gave notice of withdrawal of charges on December 5, 2014, under pressure from the Trial Chamber. These closing moves are reviewed in the Trial Chamber's formal Decision on the withdrawal of charges against Uhuru Kenyatta, March 13, 2015, ICC-01/09–02/11–1005. The Trial Chamber terminated the joint case against William Samoei Ruto and Joshua Arap Sang on April 5, 2016, ICC-01/09–01/11–2027, in a 2–1 split vote, following the presentation of the Prosecution's case.

[1178] Warrant of Arrest, October 2, 2013, ICC-01/09–01/13–1. The warrant had been issued under seal on September 26, 2013. Two more Article 70 warrants were unsealed in September 2015 against two Kenyans, Paul Gicheru and Philip Kipkoech Bett (Pre-Trial Chamber, Order Unsealing the Warrant of Arrest, September 10, 2015, ICC-01/09–01/15–11).

the Trial Chamber's disclosure order concerning the intermediaries. The Lubanga Trial Judgment advised the Prosecutor to consider using Article 70 against his own impugned intermediaries, a suggestion that was quietly buried.[1179] Witness lying in the Katanga/Ngudjolo trial was traced to some of the same corrupt intermediaries – although the Prosecution team was in denial about the integrity and plausibility of its evidence. Ngudjolo's acquittal in late 2012 marked the collapse of the Prosecution's entire case narrative. In Bemba, the Pre-Trial Chamber had redrawn the Prosecutor's original case by consigning it to a different mode of liability. During these early trials, all three Ituri accused were the subject of rumblings about inappropriate phone contacts from the detention facility. When the tip-off came about Bemba's communications, the Prosecutor followed the tip.

Did the Prosecutor's efforts come from sheer frustration, or even vengeance? Obviously, the public message was about constant vigilance in the battle against impunity. But the Prosecution put itself in a delicate position, listening to the accused's phone conversations with his lead counsel for a period of nine months, before alerting the Trial Chamber. Even with the most scrupulous efforts, it would be impossible for the Prosecutor's office to dispel the suspicion that the Prosecutor had used her power with a heavy hand. When Bensouda finally went to the Bemba Trial Chamber, the investigation gained some measure of external oversight; but eavesdropping on Defense communications would still look bad for any organ of the ICC. Unless the matter was quietly dropped, the only vindication would be to prosecute the case as aggressively as possible: sounding the alarm of rank corruption, expanding the circle of conspirators, and using the categories of Article 70 to stigmatize their behavior. It was all or nothing. Prosecutor Bensouda's public comments in the ensuing years would reflect her strong feelings.[1180]

While following her passion, the Prosecutor faced potential costs in proceeding to a second-level trial of an accused and his chief counsel, beyond just

[1179] Lubanga Trial Judgment, March 14, 2012, ICC-01/04–01/06–2842, para. 1361. The Prosecutor later reported commissioning an external review, on the basis of which she decided to take no further action under Article 70. But there was no public access to that review, and a Defense motion to disclose it was denied by the Lubanga Appeals Chamber (Decision on the Defence Request in Relation to Investigations Pursuant to Article 70, June 17, 2014, ICC-01/04–01/06–3114). In March 2014, the Office of the Prosecutor released a policy paper on the use of intermediaries, perhaps an acknowledgment of past problems.

[1180] Lucy Richardson cites comments from 2016 to 2017, in which Bensouda "referred to an 'epidemic of witness interference,' and stated that Article 70 offenses are 'becoming a common feature when cases are brought to the trial phase,' and they affect 'almost all cases.'" "Offenses against the Administration of Justice at the International Criminal Court: Robbing Peter to Pay Paul," *Journal of International Criminal Justice* 15 (2017), 742 (includes citations).

the expense of bringing charges against five individuals. As Gerry Simpson has written: "In war crimes trials, bad men are tried for gross crimes but, at the same time, the prosecuting party often is attempting to clear itself of tyranny."[1181] In the evolution of war crimes tribunals, the cry of victors' justice was a constant refrain. The Nuremberg strategy was to stay the hand of vengeance – and to make an elaborate display of procedural neutrality. That strategy worked more convincingly in Nuremberg than in Tokyo.

In building the ICC, the battle plan was laid out for ending impunity and vindicating victims. But here the victim was the Court itself in all its majesty. In an Article 70 case of "offenses against the administration of justice," any larger notion of victimhood became highly diffuse. This sense of the Prosecutor herself as victim boiled over in Bemba filings, recalling frustrations from the Kenya debacle.[1182] Without the moral ballast of victims' interests represented inside the courtroom, the Prosecutor may instead look self-serving and heavy-handed. Whether that charge is fair or unfair, it is one that the Prosecutor cannot easily disprove.

The Prosecution's control over Article 70 investigations increased the perception of unchecked power. As Lucy Richardson summarized the applicable law:

> While an ICC chamber can communicate information to the Prosecutor, it has no powers under Article 70 or the [Rules of Procedure and Evidence] to direct the Prosecutor, or anyone else, to investigate or prosecute. This remains the case even where the Article 70 offenses are alleged to have been committed by the prosecution, by an intermediary acting on its behalf, or by a prosecution witness.[1183]

Back in the Lubanga case, the Trial Chamber fought successfully for dominance on matters of disclosure. But for investigating serious misconduct, it deferred to the Prosecutor.[1184] And the Defense, when it senses witness corruption by the Prosecution, has even less chance of initiating anything under Article 70.[1185] The record of the first two Congo trials, rightly or wrongly,

[1181] Gerry Simpson, *Law, War and Crime* (Cambridge: Polity, 2007), p. 89.

[1182] Bemba *et al.* Trial Chamber, Public Redacted Version of Prosecution Submission on Sentencing, December 8, 2016, ICC-01/05-01/13-2085, para. 130.

[1183] Richardson, "Offenses against the Administration of Justice," pp. 750–51.

[1184] On confirming that Article 70 investigations were entirely within the scope of Prosecution authority, see Lubanga Appeals Chamber, Decision on Defence Request in relation to investigations pursuant to Article 70, June 17, 2014, ICC-0104-01/06-3114, para. 19.

[1185] The Bemba Defense complained about conduct involving two Prosecution witnesses who testified in February 2011. P-73 testified that he was asked by investigators to misrepresent the value of stolen goods, among other inducements to lie; Bemba Trial Chamber, transcript,

makes it especially difficult for the Prosecution to "clear itself of tyranny."[1186] Unclean hands come to resemble the hands of vengeance – unstayed.

Tu Quoque

And what if the dodgy Defense practices in Bemba turned out to be similar to steps taken by the Prosecution? The Bemba *et al.* controversy reopened debate about ICC witnesses in general, applicable to both adversarial parties. In the midst of fractured societies, how do the parties find proper witnesses in the field? And then how to vouch for their credibility? Or to orient them in the culture of the courtroom, let alone the legal context of the case in which their testimony plays a role? And what about covering expenses, and coping with issues of witness protection? Even among authentic witnesses, in the midst of high-stakes litigation, some will self-present as troubled, erratic, greedy, eccentric – conflicted in various ways. Such witnesses were evident on both sides of all the Congo trials. It was hinted that the source of the June 2012 tip-off was just such a rogue witness.[1187]

Deflecting the inevitable pressure to vindicate her own practices, the Prosecutor found that her clear option was to demonize the Defense. And yet doing so underscored the inequality of arms separating Prosecution and Defense.[1188] These strategic inequalities are substantial in field investigations,

February 28, 2011, ICC-01/05–01/08-T-76-Red2-ENG, pp. 7–11. Earlier that month, witness P-42 reported talking with another Prosecution witness in the airport, on his way to The Hague, in a violation of witness protocols; Bemba Trial Chamber, transcript, February 15, 2011, ICC-01/05–01/08-T-66-ENG, pp. 53–61. In rejecting Defense requests to launch an Article 70 investigation in the P-42 matter (also alleging inconsistencies in P-42's testimony), the Trial Chamber noted its inability under Rule 165 of the Rules of Procedure and Evidence. Citing a similar request from the Katanga and Ngudjolo trial, the Chamber indicated that the only available remedy lay with the Chamber itself, when it came time to evaluate the evidence of all witnesses; Defence Application Concerning Witness Evidence, October 16, 2013, ICC-01/05–01/08–2830, paras. 15, 18.

1186 During the Lubanga trial, Moreno-Ocampo argued that any potential conflicts of interest were controlled by internal division of labor within his Office. See Prosecution Observations on Article 70, April 1, 2011, ICC-01/04–01/06–2716. During the Bemba trial, in an interlocutory Appeals Chamber ruling, Judge Ušacka (the lone dissenter) would have upheld the Bemba Defense motion to disqualify the Prosecutor's continued involvement in the remaining part of the main case. Bemba Appeals Chamber, Décision relative aux requêtes aux fins de récusation du Procureur, du Procureur adjoint et de l'ensemble du personnel du Bureau du Procureur, October 21, 2014, ICC-01/05–01/08–648-Anx2. Her argument summarizes the concern about conflict of interest.

1187 Bemba *et al.* Trial Chamber closing arguments, remarks by Christopher Gosnell, representing Jean-Jacques Mangenda, June 1, 2016, ICC-01/05–01/13-T-49-ENG, p. 20.

1188 See Charles Chernor Jalloh and Amy DiBella, "Equality of Arms in International Criminal Law: Continuing Challenges," in William A. Schabas, Yvonne McDermott, and

where the Prosecution has a clear time advantage, in addition to its own resource budget. In the absence of a dedicated Office for the Defense, the ICC Registry assists with legal aid for Defense costs.[1189] But Bemba's situation was unique: his wealth meant that he did not qualify as indigent, but his assets had been frozen by the Court, and were still being sorted out. At the start of his trial, he needed to borrow funds from the Court, but the budget covered little more than core expenses.[1190] Covering costs of locating witnesses and transporting them to The Hague emerged as a crisis.[1191]

Bemba's long-time associate in the Congo, Fidèle Babala, was industrious in tapping fresh funds; but, of course, the transfers through Western Union became exhibits in his trial on bribery charges. Babala's defense was to explain the charges as covering normal costs of fielding witnesses – at least as far as he knew and intended. Why else would he risk sending funds in such a public manner? "I am not an imbecile," Babala said in his personal statement before the Chamber. It turns out that Babala had previously voted, in the Congolese Parliament, in favor of ratifying the Rome Treaty. He was doubly incensed by the demeaning circumstances of his arrest by Congolese authorities, acting on ICC initiative. Why did the Court not contact him more openly?[1192] In the end he was convicted of sending illicit funds to two witnesses. His ultimate sentence was approximately half the amount of time he had already spent in detention.

The accused in Bemba *et al.* based their defense on the venerable principle of *tu quoque* – which amounts to turning the tables on the accuser, maintaining that "they all do it." What is it that everyone does? Some actions are common to any trial team dealing with central African conflicts: searching for witnesses, assessing their value for the litigation, solving problems of security and expense. In these conditions, the use of intermediaries was already part of the Prosecution's toolkit. Also common to both sides: wide-ranging strategy

Niamh Hayes (eds.), *Ashgate Research Companion to International Criminal Law: Critical Perspectives* (Abingdon: Routledge, 2012), chapter 11.

1189 A different model was used in the Special Tribunal for Lebanon, where the Office of Defence is a separate organ of the Court.

1190 See the discussion of Bemba Defense finances in the closing arguments before the Bemba *et al.* Trial Chamber, May 31, 2016, ICC-01/05–01/13-T-48-ENG, pp. 117–18 (statement by Aimé Kilolo); p. 78 (remarks by Melinda Taylor, representing Jean-Pierre Bemba).

1191 The total sums authorized by Kilolo were surprisingly modest – averaging a few hundred euros each for some two dozen witnesses, often tied to specific trial-related expenses. See the summary in Lingsma, *All Rise*, pp. 242–43.

1192 The context was closing oral statements before the Bemba *et al.* Trial Chamber, June 1, 2016, ICC-01/05–01/13-T-49-FRA, p. 53, and generally pp. 52–59. The French transcript quotes Babala as saying "Je ne suis pas un intellectuel," but his sarcasm was not nearly this subtle; and observers in the room heard "imbecile," as did the English interpreter.

discussions among members of the litigating team. For any eavesdropper, determining precisely when such discussions crossed a criminal line could have been possible only in retrospect. The sharp line for purposes of surveillance was a legal fiction.

Both sides have to work around the ICC's policy against "proofing" witnesses.[1193] To be sure, some kinds of witness preparation are entirely proper under ICC rules; but there are guidelines for avoiding telling witnesses what to say (coaching), not to mention asking them to lie. Some of the lines are clear, such as limits on communications in close proximity to live courtroom testimony.[1194] Other limits may require some interpretation: orienting a witness within the party's main case, but not telling them what to say. In selecting witnesses, it is entirely reasonable for strategists on either team to calculate whether the witness's testimony fits the case and advances the case at that particular moment. By the time such calculations are hashed out collectively among team members, tracking criminality would have been a speculative game.

In dealing with potential witnesses from Ituri or the CAR, all sides would have experienced the problems of preparing witnesses who had no conception of what happens in Western courtrooms. The notion of legal strategy and context would be hard to explain. And in cultures where official connections often entail bribes, handling the payment of normal expenses might test the parameters of Western sensibility. Part of the bargaining may include providing security assurances, and in some cases costly relocation expenses and logistics. As one Defense-oriented investigator has noted, these arrangements can provide potential witnesses with powerful incentives to say whatever is necessary.[1195]

[1193] Sergey Vasiliev, "Proofing the Ban on 'Witness Proofing': Did the ICC Get It Right?" *Criminal Law Forum* 20 (2009), 193; Kai Ambos, "'Witness Proofing' before the ICC: Neither Legally Admissible nor Necessary," in Carsten Stahn and Göran Sluiter (eds.), *The Emerging Practice of the International Criminal Court* (Leiden: Nijhoff Brill, 2009), pp. 599–614. The ICC policy was formulated (initially intended for a single pre-trial witness) in the Lubanga Pre-Trial Chamber, caught in the rhetorical cross-fire between common law and civil law ideologies; DRC Pre-Trial Chamber, Decision on the Practices of Witness Familiarisation and Witness Proofing, November 8, 2006, ICC-01/04–01/06–679. It was later extended to trial practice in the Lubanga Trial Chamber; Decision Regarding the Practices Used to Prepare and Familiarise Witnesses for Giving Testimony at Trial, November 30, 2007, ICC-01/04–01/06–1049.

[1194] For the Bemba Trial Chamber (as for other ICC trials), the ICC Victims and Witnesses Unit produced versions of a "Unified Protocol on the practices used to prepare and familiarise witnesses for giving testimony at trial"; see document "submitted on 22 October 2010" and issued on December 12, 2010, ICC-01/05–01/08–1081 with Annex.

[1195] Caroline Buisman, "Delegating Investigations: Lessons to be Learned from the *Lubanga* Judgment," *Northwestern Journal of International Human Rights* 11 (2013), 60–63. Buisman was on the Defense team for Germain Katanga and conducted investigations in Ituri.

The offenses in Article 70 address the categories of preparing false testimony, presenting false evidence, and bribery – but only when they are "committed intentionally."[1196] This element of *mens rea* (comparable to the default standard under Article 30) requires the investigator and judge to draw vital inferences, in circumstances where witnesses report being told what to say, where evidence has been altered, or where witnesses are paid unusual sums. Such second-order judgments would have made virtually impossible the early surveillance of raw communications among the group of suspects. Potentially compromising episodes were well represented across all the Congo trials, falling somewhere along a spectrum of egregiousness. But even at the far end of that spectrum, unless the accused under Article 70 intends the results, there is no violation. Equality of arms between the parties would require an equal degree of strict scrutiny for deeper intentions of both sides, when it comes to handling witnesses under difficult conditions.[1197]

A Show Trial for the Regime of Legality

There is no more alien image for international criminal law than the show trial. The term is commonly applied to the Moscow purge trials of the 1930s, which were grimly echoed in Eastern Europe during the early 1950s. Compared to trials conducted under the rules of legality, the show trial is the stark antithesis. The outcome has been scripted in advance. The defendant's guilt has already been decided by other means, leaving the trials to make a public display of criminality itself – ideally featuring a compliant perpetrator.

It is a perversion of legality. And yet, as Gerry Simpson has written, the show trial as an image has haunted the movement for international criminal tribunals. "Law's anxiety" – to avoid the lurid spectacle of show trials – has never been far from the dramaturgy of international courts, going back at least to the days of Nuremberg.[1198] Insisting on that binary opposition is part of the "rhetorical clarification" for international trials, underwriting the faith in legal neutrality.[1199] Without the strictest adherence to procedure, law is degraded, and it loses its detachment from overriding political and moral imperatives. But the fact that

[1196] Article 70(1).

[1197] Alternatives to the Article 70 regime, which is driven by the Prosecutor, could help correct this imbalance. Lucy Richardson provides an overview of contempt systems used in other tribunals, as well as possible alternative approaches under the Rome Statute. Article 71, for example, provides for lesser sanctions that the Court can apply to witnesses and legal counsel. Other possibilities might work through the ASP, or by delegating prosecutions to member states. "Offenses against the Administration of Justice at the International Criminal Court," pp. 763–74.

[1198] Simpson, *Law, War and Crime*, chapter 4 ("Law's Anxieties: Show Trials").

[1199] Ibid., p. 110.

legality also serves political and moral aims casts a shadow of doubt over international trials. The defendants can be expected to denounce the process as a mockery of justice. They sense a presumption of guilt and view skeptically any gestures or rituals designed to disguise an outcome that looms as inevitable.

Simpson acknowledges the anxiety of law's defenders, noting that war crimes trials "often share some structural similarities" to their despised contrary. It is wrong to collapse the distinction, but also naïve to ignore points of similarity. One may regard international trials "as spectacles in which the machinery and symbolism of the show trial is sometimes visible." For some trials, "the legitimation strategies and imperatives of the prosecuting state or community often are a key purpose or effect of the trial."[1200]

The Article 70 prosecutions of Bemba and his associates were not a show trial in the classic sense. Of course, among surviving members of the Bemba Defense team, the Prosecutor's secrecy and zealotry produced outrage. The team pushed its complaints vigorously in submissions to the weary Bemba Trial Chamber.[1201] All these challenges were considered and confidently rejected; and the original Bemba trial was propelled to the final Trial Judgment in March 2016, nearly seven years after the Confirmation of Charges.[1202]

Just seven months later, a completely different Trial Chamber issued its Judgment in the Article 70 proceeding known as Bemba *et al.* It was a striking vindication of the Prosecutor's narrative, finding all five accused guilty of individual counts totaling more than 120 criminal acts.[1203] The *tu quoque* defense was rejected – the idea that both parties to the Bemba case engaged in roughly similar practices with regard to preparing and paying witnesses. The Chamber found the accused guilty of coaching witnesses to lie and corrupting them with bribes, acting with both knowledge and intent. In all, their criminality tainted fourteen Defense witnesses. Bemba was the mastermind of the campaign, working jointly with his lead counsel and his case manager, while the other two accused played supportive roles. The common plan tying all these events together was energetically inferred from the outcomes.[1204] In a Judgment of more than 450 pages, the Prosecution's case was accepted with no serious exceptions.

1200 Ibid., p. 111.

1201 Bemba Trial Chamber, Public Redacted Version of Defence Request for Relief for Abuse of Process, November 25, 2014, ICC-01/05–01/08–3203-Red2.

1202 Bemba Trial Judgment, March 21, 2016, ICC-01/05–01/08–3343.

1203 The Bemba *et al.* Trial Judgment had accepted cumulative charges but rejected some liability modes, October 19, 2016, ICC-01/05–01/13–1989, para. 956.

1204 In the opening minutes of oral closing statements, Judge Perrin de Brichambaut asked the Prosecutor for clarification on this inference, which (on his reading) seemed to be taken as implicit across some 120 pages of description. Bemba *et al.* Trial Chamber closing arguments, May 31, 2016, ICC-01/05–01/13-T-48-ENG, pp. 4–5.

In this spectacle of inevitability, the big surprise came at the moment of sentencing. The same Trial Chamber that had produced a thick compendium of culpability came down with a group of featherlight sentences that notably excluded any further time in detention, beyond the eleven months spent by the four co-conspirators. Bemba himself was given one additional year beyond his eighteen-year sentence in the main case.[1205] The punishments for Kilolo and Mangenda could have required additional detention, but the Chamber suspended portions of their sentences, setting minimal conditions.[1206]

The response from court watchers was mixed. The sober commentator in an American legal journal of record offered this critical perspective:

> Finally, a few words about sentencing. Considering the vast and systematic scope of the criminal enterprise carried out by the conspirators, the leniency of the sentences appears remarkable. The Trial Chamber found (upheld by the Appeals Chamber) that an accused and members of his defense team engaged in an operation to falsify vast amounts of evidence over an extended period of time with the purpose of misleading a Trial Chamber. If this does not warrant the highest sentences provided for in Article 70(3) of the ICC Statute, it is difficult to imagine what would.[1207]

Indeed, the Prosecution had recommended longer sentences, even exceeding the statutory maximum of five years under Article 70, based on consecutive terms.[1208] Back at the time of arrest, Bemba's four associates had been brought to the detention center and held for eleven months, until the single pre-trial judge changed his mind and allowed for conditional release.[1209] While there

[1205] In its first sentencing decision, the Bemba *et al.* Trial Chamber pulled no punches in recalling its findings in the Trial Judgment. But in a mitigating spirit, at the time of sentencing, the Chamber noted that "the actual contributions of Mr. Bemba to the implementation and concealment of the common plan, as listed above, were of a somewhat restricted nature. This is certainly owed to the fact that Mr Bemba was detained during the relevant time and his capacities to interfere with the 14 Main Case Defence Witnesses – in contrast to Mr Kilolo and Mr Mangenda – were limited. While his actions, as explained in the Judgment, still amount to offences against the administration of justice, the Chamber will give some weight to Mr Bemba's varying degree of participation in the execution of the offences." Decision on Sentencing, March 22, 2017, ICC-01/05–01/13–2123, para. 223.

[1206] Suspension was not mentioned in Article 70 but might have come from inherent judicial power. But this claim was later rejected by the Bemba *et al.* Appeals Chamber, Judgment on Appeals from Trial Chamber Sentencing Decision, March 8, 2018, ICC-01/05–01/13–2276, para. 80.

[1207] Jonas Nilsson, "International Criminal Court: Offenses against the Administration of Justice," *American Journal of International Law* 112 (2018), p. 473.

[1208] Bemba *et al.* Trial Chamber, Prosecution Submissions on Sentencing, Part VII.

[1209] Bemba *et al.* Pre-Trial Chamber, Decision Ordering Release, October 21, 2014, ICC-01/05–01/13–703. The Appeals Chamber later ruled that this release was based on legal error, but it declined to have them brought back to detention in "the interests of justice." Bemba *et al.*

were clearly divergent views on the pattern of incarceration, the post-conviction sentences were noticeably lenient. The compounding principle was rejected by the Trial Chamber, even as the sentences were contrived to require no additional detention time (for all but Bemba).[1210]

The same pattern persisted in the wake of an Appeals Chamber Judgment upholding the bulk of the convictions. In a gargantuan ruling, the Appeals Chamber made basically one adjustment. It corrected the legal interpretation of the crime of "presenting false testimony," essentially removing it from the mix of offenses in this trial.[1211] But otherwise it upheld virtually each and every charge, using its 700 pages to affirm the reasonableness (or "not unreasonable"-ness) of the Trial Chamber's Judgment against scores of challenges, big and small. But the sentences were also appealed and sent back to the Trial Chamber – which adjusted them downward.[1212] It was the same result even for Bemba himself, whose convictions in the main case were unexpectedly overturned in June of 2018. His additional year's sentence in the Article 70 case was quickly reviewed and counted against time already served – his ten years in detention. Bemba was also free to leave.[1213]

The Prosecutor had been militant on the topic of sentencing. In her view, the sentences against Bemba and his team were necessary to send a clear signal to future litigants before the Court. The Prosecutor's Sentencing Brief to the Trial Chamber contained a litany of past grievances, focusing heavily on Kenya but referencing nearly all the cases coming before the Court.[1214] For her, it was not enough just to gain a trial judgment of guilt, putting paid to the odious *tu quoque* argument: there would also need to be a high personal price extracted. The Prosecutor had vigorously opposed release of the four team members after eleven months in detention. And on the day the Trial Chamber delivered its Trial Judgment in the case, the Prosecutor had already signaled the judges that

Appeals Chamber, Decision on Appeal of the Decision to Release, May 29, 2015, ICC-01/05–01/13–969, para. 57.

1210 Bemba *et al.* Trial Chamber Decision on Sentencing, March 22, 2017, ICC-01/05–01/13–2123.

1211 Bemba *et al.* Appeals Chamber, Judgment on Appeals from Sentencing Decision, March 8, 2018, ICC-01/05–01/13–2276, para. 710.

1212 The Appeals Chamber questioned the Bemba *et al.* Trial Chamber's use of suspended sentences, which are not explicitly provided for in the Rome Statute, and was not willing to accept "inherent powers" in this regard. Appeals Chamber Sentencing Judgment, March 8, 2018, ICC-01/05–01/13–2276, para. 80. In response, the Trial Chamber found reasons to reduce all the previous sentences to periods no longer than time already served (and in two cases, less time than was already served). See the courtroom summary of the revised Trial Chamber sentences, transcript of September 17, 2018, ICC-01/05-01/13-T-60-ENG, pp. 7–9.

1213 Bemba *et al.* Trial Chamber, Decision on Mr Bemba's Application for Release, June 12, 2018, ICC-01/05–01/13–2291.

1214 Bemba *et al.* Trial Chamber, Prosecution Submissions on Sentencing, paras. 127–31.

she would demand that all four be immediately returned to custody, pending the appeal. It was a surprise move, seen by the newly convicted accused as uncompromisingly aggressive. They collectively asked the Chamber for twenty minutes' time to prepare a rebuttal motion; and when the Chamber reconvened, the judges agreed to allow the four to remain free on release.[1215] At the re-sentencing hearing before the Trial Chamber, the Prosecution raised as an aggravating circumstance the alleged role of Article 70 offenses in leading to the Appeals Chamber's dramatic acquittal in the main Bemba case. This theory was categorically rejected by Presiding Judge Schmitt.[1216]

The resemblance to a show trial must be put in strictly limited terms. This was not a case where the accused would be carried out and immediately shot (although the Prosecutor had a clear mind to deal harshly). It was not a case, like Eastern Europe, where the defendants stood and cheered hysterically as the death sentences were read out.[1217] The consequences were certainly severe for them, disrupting their lives and professional careers. But the true spectacle of this case was limited to the Judgment, which was upheld scrupulously on Appeal. This remarkable trial-within-a-trial was a symbolic affirmation of the rule of law. At stake was the sacred principle of legality, on which the legitimacy of the ICC rests.

In upholding the Prosecutor's criminal charges, the trial judges and appeals judges enabled an extravagant display of devotion to legal process. It was not a moment for them to get into the fine points of impartial investigations; and certainly not an occasion to dwell on the ambiguities of the *tu quoque* defense. An exclusive focus on Defense excesses was a natural feature of the case. But, as the American commentator noted in puzzlement, what stands out here is the high seriousness of the offenses, over against the light sentences. If it functioned as a show trial, it was all for noble principles. That display did not require sacrificing the lives of the accused – or at least subjecting them to further cost and humiliation.[1218]

The grand principles were celebrated. But the question remained, for all the Congo trials, what the Court and its agents had learned from two decades of turbulence, outside and inside the courtroom.

[1215] These events are documented in the Trial Chamber transcript of October 19, 2016, p. 10. Lingsma was in the courtroom and tells the story first-hand, *All Rise*, pp. 254–56.

[1216] Bemba *et al.* Trial Chamber, Summary Remarks on Re-sentencing Decision, September 17, 2018, ICC-01/05–01/13-T-60-ENG, p. 5.

[1217] Simpson, *Law, War and Crime*, p. 109.

[1218] In his courtroom summary of the Bemba *et al.* Trial Chamber Re-sentencing Decision, Judge Schmitt said that the deterrent effect of this case had been fully accomplished with the arrest and prosecution of members of a Defense team. The Prosecutor had pushed for full five-year terms on re-sentencing, but the Trial Chamber judges saw this as overkill. "Maximum prison sentences are not necessary for this case to matter." September 17, 2018, ICC-01/05–01/13-T-60-ENG, p. 10.

Observations

Could you kindly wake up our guard?
ICC Judge Robert Fremr
Ntaganda Trial Chamber

LABORATORY RESULTS

At any given moment, it could all be quite tedious. And looking back, more than twenty years after the Rome Treaty was signed, the overall tempo was glacial. Judges came and went. The Court's second Prosecutor was just entering the twilight of her nine-year term. There were three completed trials, memorialized in judgments running many hundreds of pages. The trials lasted seven years or more, hearing hundreds of witnesses, pondering thousands of documents – all with long identification codes announced in ritual tones. Motions were filed seeking extensions to the page limits for so-called "briefs" submitted by the parties. (Upon deliberation, some of those motions were denied, some not.) Much of it took place with curtains lowered in the public gallery, beyond the scrutiny of observers. Inside the courtroom, things moved at a stately tempo, as speakers tried to achieve an unnaturally slow pace, to lessen the number of interpretive errors that surfaced inexorably – requiring real-time correction and bogging things down still more. Even the guards would occasionally tune out, and who could blame them?

But it was too easy to emphasize all the wrong things. Speed and efficiency were never part of the bargain that gave the ICC its power to pass judgment on the "unimaginable atrocities that deeply shock the conscience of humanity." For the countless victims of global violence, for whom even small mitigations are painfully scarce, the prospect of justice provides a flash of transcendence. In its daily operations, the Court displays a quiet heroism, honoring one of its ancestors by "staying the hand of vengeance": breaking the cycle of mass violence; submitting hard questions of responsibility to the judgment of law; bending power to the force of reason. The time frame for achieving these goals must be realistic. Twenty years is a microsecond, measured against such ambitions.

Similar visions had been tested in the ad hoc and hybrid tribunals. But expectations ran even higher for the ICC, as the first round of stress tests took on the complexities of central Africa. The Congo trials marked the initial stage of a long-term legal experiment. The higher norms of justice, engineered in Rome, building on prior experience and bearing all the hopes and limitations of human endeavor – all of it was being sent to the laboratory.

Although it is tempting to stand in rapt contemplation of the Rome ideals, the focus of this book has been the testing process of active trials. With so little courtroom traffic, commentary about the ICC has often focused on inchoate trials, aborted trials, or even the imagined trials of idealized suspects, anticipating confrontations with errant states. There was a guilty plea (after a brief pre-trial hearing) in a case involving destruction of historic monuments in Timbuktu. And now a fourth Congo trial has reached the appeals stage, as will be discussed here.

The justice laboratory needs completed trials for scrutinizing the whole dynamic spectrum. Because the legal process consists of a set of interlocking and reflexive stages, one must observe the entire range of self-commentary. With the Congo trials, this breadth now includes a series of judgments, dissents, reversals, concurrences, and acquittals, alongside the convictions. In this way, "the law in the books" becomes "the law in action," opening up new possibilities for critique and evaluation.

The chapters in this volume are one observer's report on what transpired over many years. This report seeks to capture what emerged from the testing procedure, without getting lost in the details. It is a report about patterns and trends, which others might well describe in different terms. There are many ways to read the overall results: the scorecard of convictions, the record on sexual and gender crimes, the impact on victims, and the long-term contributions to restorative justice in the conflict zones, among other perspectives. For this observer, what stands out are the expanding debates and tensions within the legal process. The experimental conditions from central Africa were the catalyst enabling these tensions to rise up out of the Rome system.

The topics themselves needed to emerge from the process of experimentation. Recalling the words of John Dewey (see the start of the book):

> The object of knowledge is not something with which thinking sets out, but something with which it ends: something which the processes of inquiry and testing . . . themselves produce.

> And so it is with mathematical knowledge, or with knowledge of politics or art. Their respective objects are not known till they are made in course of the process of experimental thinking. Their usefulness when made is whatever, from infinity to zero, experience may subsequently determine it to be.

An approach through *experimental logic* differs from the normal pulse of legal analysis. What we know comes into view at the end of our inquiry, in different guises from the formal doctrines and static principles of textbook law. As objects of knowledge, these topics include:

1. *The contested practices of fact-finding*, encompassing investigations in the field and judicial analysis in the courtroom. The facts entering into the Congo trials were generally bathed in caution and circumspection, when not contaminated by outright lying. Tensions rose across the trials, prompting a judicial debate over the mode of reasoning deemed *holism*, which was met by counter-modes emphasizing transparency and fair trial notions. Behind this struggle loomed the deeper mystery of judicial authority: whether final judgments are validated in the private conscience of the judge (inscrutable on review) or laid bare in discursive reasoning, regulated by proof burdens derived from the presumption of innocence.
2. *The contested protocols for attributing individual criminal responsibility*, which were measured against the resistant features of Congolese social structures. In international criminal law, this step represents the pivot from actual crimes to the process of holding individuals accountable. Tensions accompanied this pivot, which relied heavily on paradigms and presumptions inserted into the mix by judges determined to draw full normative power out of the ICC modes of liability (Articles 25(3) and 28). Key elements of these liability modes (also the contextual elements of Article 7 crimes) had to be linked to case facts, often relying on inferences from circumstantial evidence. Sometimes the result was a conviction; sometimes not. Sometimes the conviction fell short of all the potential charges. And the results were subject to dissents and reversals.
3. *The mystery of final judicial authority*, which reappeared in relation to the main principles of legality – particularly the presumption of innocence and the standard of proof beyond reasonable doubt. The trials revealed stark differences in the management of legal presumptions and burdens of proof, suggesting that the ICC was struggling, after its first cases, to bring these highest principles down to the level of implementation.

4. *The crisis of faith within the legal process*, under pressure to preserve its autonomy in such close proximity to global politics and humanitarian fervor. Trial proceedings had trouble escaping the gravitational pull of politics in pre-trial investigation and case selection, notably in the weakness of Prosecutorial narratives. And the risk of acquittals instilled moral panic among outsiders, only slightly muted in the judicial turn to Regulation 55. The judges' interpretive freedom with modes of liability likewise reflected the existential pressures of moral resolve.

At the end of inquiry, these practices and puzzles have now emerged, along with other important topics for future exploration. They came out of the trials themselves, as the Rome Statute was suddenly set into motion. These topics (among others) mark out fault-lines and tensions buried within the Statute, but which are now part of the reality of everyday practice. Future trials will need to look for solutions. And future experience will need to judge the value of those solutions.

THE NEXT CONGO TRIAL

It was a surprise when Bosco Ntaganda showed up in The Hague in January 2013, via American transport out of Rwanda. While there had been some hesitation about his arrest warrant back in 2006, it was still valid – although a hasty second warrant was needed to expand the criminal charges. The Court was recently exhausted from the Lubanga case; and putting Ntaganda on trial, years later, meant going back over old and troubled territory. While strong rumors had circulated about Ntaganda's later involvements with a string of armed groups in eastern Congo, the Prosecutor stuck with the same time-and-action frame used in the first two Congo trials. The fourth Congo trial would once again focus on Ituri during the period 2002–03, seen now through the behavior of a figure lower in the presumed hierarchy of Lubanga's UPC organization. The same senior Prosecutor would direct the Ntaganda case, starting from the same investigations and NGO reports used for Lubanga.

Looking at the Prosecutor's chosen narrative for Ntaganda, there were some notable changes from the first two Ituri trials. It was a return to the old narrative of masterminds and ethnic hatreds, while avoiding prior risks from narrow framing of crimes or modes of liability. The Prosecutor charged Ntaganda with as many crimes (under Articles 7 and 8) as the legal imagination could conceive, encountering little resistance from the Pre-Trial Chamber. And with prior battles over Regulation 55 well in mind, the charges included virtually all modes of liability under Articles 25(3) and 28(a) – perpetration (of numerous sub-types), plus ordering, aiding, and assisting in any other way; also command responsibility.

To the extent that the Prosecutor found room for improvement from the first two Congo trials, her solution was to spare no legal implements of battle provided in the Rome Statute. No more meekness or streamlining: here was a chance to show the world the deeper virtue in the Prosecution's whole Congo strategy. And with the Bemba experience under Article 70 also well in mind, the Prosecutor is said to have monitored every phone call placed by Ntaganda himself from the detention facility, including calls with his Defense teams.

Another feature of the case was direct testimony from the accused. Like Katanga and Ngudjolo (but unlike Lubanga and Bemba), Bosco Ntaganda decided to tell his own story under oath, subject to cross-examination. He sat on the stand for more than 100 hours. During this marathon, the world would gain an inside perspective on the circle of actors associated with the UPC, including the mutineers who rebelled against Mbusa Nyamwisi and drove out Governor Lompondo, down to the fraught connections with Ugandan generals and the secret liaisons with Rwanda.

Ntaganda's professional identity was hardened in military endeavors. He was a loyal staffer, not the man in charge. From this position, he gave an account of the UPC that supported much of the Prosecutor's original story about tight chains of command and levels of planning – although specifically directed to conventional armed conflicts with Nyamwisi's RCD-ML and their Lendu allies, with Uganda, and ultimately with MONUC. In Ntaganda's strict disciplinarian worldview, war crimes and other atrocities either hadn't occurred, or someone else did them, or (if UPC personnel had done them) no one reported it to Ntaganda. (Ntaganda pointed to a handful of exceptions, which, he assured the Court, were swiftly followed by punishments.) Although much of the Prosecution's evidence was based on dubious witness testimony and circumstantial information, Ntaganda's rigid account of these events offered the judges an unlikely alternative. In nearly every circumstance, the Trial Chamber believed the Prosecution's view, and deemed Ntaganda's version unpersuasive and unproved. Their personal convictions were deeply anchored in the judicial soul.

The Prosecution charges were consistent with allegations found in HRW reports, starting with "*Covered in Blood*" and including a 2005 report, *The Curse of Gold*. The motivation of greed was added to the standard view of ethnic hatred. Ntaganda himself was a Congolese Tutsi, who did not fit the pattern of the Hema ideologue. But he allied himself with the organization, and he shared in its criminal actions through the matrix of indirect co-perpetration. At all times he knew how events would unfold: that legitimate military attacks would ("ordinarily") turn into ethnicity-driven civilian massacres. Because he knew this generic pattern of Ituri violence, he was presumed to know and accept the criminal results.

Once again, the criminal purpose in these endeavors was tied to ethnic hatred – coming not from the perpetrator himself, but rather endemic to the milieu in which he operated. The evidence behind this inference was equally indirect as in the Lubanga case. It was said to be obvious from the events themselves, which point ineluctably to a collective mind steeped in ethnic myths and ideologies. One salient fact behind this massive inference was a Swahili combat slogan recorded in videos of chanting UPC recruits at the training camps. Its literal meaning was an exhortation "to hit and to (re)charge," but the Trial Chamber accepted the views of insider-witnesses that it really meant "to kill and pillage Lendu civilians without mercy." With this interpretation, the slogan was permitted to speak for itself.

Ntaganda's cross-examination was a clash of worldviews. After Ntaganda provided evidence that he was present at neither of the two armed attacks singled out in the master narrative, the Prosecution stuck with its insider-witnesses and NGO-inspired version of events. At one point, the Prosecutor failed to get Ntaganda to acknowledge that Germain Katanga and Mathieu Ngudjolo had been the joint masterminds of the Bogoro attack – still looking to vindicate the collapse of the second Congo trial. In response, Ntaganda denied even meeting them until June 2003, and he professed not to know about the Bogoro attack until weeks after it occurred.

After all testimony was completed and closing briefs were submitted, the Defense heard intriguing news about one of the three judges in the Trial Chamber. It seemed that she had accepted an appointment as Japanese ambassador to Estonia, and was looking to minimize her workload on this case and at the Court generally. Once this news became public, the ICC Presidency (and all the ICC judges) huddled to determine whether it meant some kind of mistrial. Judge Ozaki promised no lack of zeal in deliberating with her Trial Chamber colleagues, and she eventually abandoned the ambassadorial appointment. For whatever reason, the Ntaganda Trial Judgment was delivered with record speed, less than a year after submission of final briefs. Several ICC judges linked to the Appeals Chamber abstained from expressing their views on any judicial conflict of interest; and, predictably, Judge Ozaki's near encounter with Estonia became Count 1 of the appeals petition submitted by Ntaganda's Defense team.

On appeal, the big questions from earlier Congo trials are once again opened up for appellate scrutiny. It remains to be seen if the style of appeal will resemble that of the Lubanga case. The ICC's first conviction was sustained by a mix of holism, subjectivism, the use of presumptions and paradigms, and a malleable approach to the reasonable doubt standard. The Bemba appeal (from a divided chamber) took issue with these practices. The likelihood is that these debates will continue across future cases.

TRIALS OF FAITH AND SKEPTICISM

Serious stocktaking is nearly impossible in the heat of battle against impunity. But now the Congo trials, as a group, have yielded a broad sample of experience, enough to allow the Court, its constituencies, and its critics to scrutinize the results, and to begin the process of assessment.

A laboratory experiment puts faith to the test – in this case, an ongoing test of implementing the mandate of a new international court. Such tests open up space for skepticism; but the testing process does not endorse unqualified doubt. Indeed, that process projects its own separate faith in procedural approaches to higher truths. The two kinds of faith work together at the junction of ends and means.

By codifying humanitarian ideals, the creators of the ICC committed their faith to a cycle of implementation, reaching across barriers of geography and culture. The original purity of concept would thus engage with real-world complications. There were serious risks, first in the negotiations around legal codes, but even more in allowing prosecutors and judges to turn the wheels of implementation. The means would be practical but principled, and their wise administration would remedy some of the worst abuses against human rights. The legal process would take custody of the higher faith, earning its authority to declare final judgment. Stumbles and demurrals in that process would reawaken skeptical fears among defenders of the original faith.

The legal shift from ends to means accepts the risk that skeptical doubts will be encouraged and yet contained. An ICC trial invites questions and complications, and it expects a full share of surprises. The adversary structure of proceedings encourages the articulation of doubt – even doubt about matters otherwise presumed as common knowledge. It then falls to neutral judges to declare the just results. In the Congo trials, anxiety rose to a peak at this moment of final reckoning. It wasn't simply that two out of four accused were acquitted – but that the reasons behind the convictions and acquittals were heavily contested among the judges themselves. Skepticism surrounding this moment of decision strengthens all the other skeptical forces: those seeking to preserve moral faith, and those convinced that the whole exercise reduces to mere politics.

In the laboratory of global justice, both ends and means must endure rigorous tests. The historic encounter with the Congo leaves no doubt that the ICC faces critical challenges in its next generation of trials.

Postscript

The Second Generation of ICC Trials

. . . we accept that it is a fact of judicial life that judges do not always agree. . . . The ICC statute is full of "constructive ambiguities" that have displaced the discussion from the political level (the drafters of the Rome Statute) to the judicial level (the judges of the ICC). Unsurprisingly, some of these discussions remain alive and explain why it is sometimes difficult to reach unanimity.

Judges Christine Van den Wyngaert and Howard Morrison, Bemba Appeals Judgment

OVERVIEW

The three trials examined in this book became the first generation of ICC prosecutions, all focused on Congolese suspects. Those proceedings yielded constant surprises, uncharted delays, and daunting complexities. Across all phases of the Congo trials, the network of judges remained fairly constant, until the slow pattern of rotations began to take effect. Those first trials could not avoid speaking to each other – and *past* each other, as rising dissension coalesced into opposing judicial styles. A mixed record of two convictions and two acquittals underscored emerging splits. Fault-lines in the Rome Statute reached the surface in courtroom practice, culminating in the multiple opinions issued by the Bemba Appeals Chamber.

By mid-2021 we can discern a second generation of prosecutions, building on the legacy of the Congo trials. Of these next four trials, two continued the Court's early focus on parochial violence in central Africa, covering the same distant time period as the Congo trials. Starting from arrest warrants tied to the first generation, these trials were launched after 2013 and 2015, respectively, when two fugitive suspects surrendered themselves to the ICC. Bosco Ntaganda's trial marks the last of the Congo cycle (and was briefly summarized in the closing section of this book). In March 2021, the Appeals Chamber upheld Ntaganda's convictions, in yet another fractured decision that broke differently from Bemba. Also in early 2021, the Trial Chamber convicted

Dominic Ongwen of Uganda, whose appeal is now pending. His trial focused on the destructive path of the notorious Lord's Resistance Army (LRA), of which Ongwen is the only member to face international trial. His personal culpability remained a topic of intense debate at the sentencing stage, where Ongwen was described as both perpetrator and victim – having been abducted at age nine into the life of the LRA.

Rounding out the four trials comprising this second ICC generation, two additional clusters of prosecutions dealt with post-election violence in the distinct circumstances of Kenya and the Ivory Coast. In both situations, the trials were terminated at the end of the Prosecution phase, when the respective Trial Chambers found the evidence too weak to go forward. These abandoned trials revealed further splits among judges, with pluralities shining a strong skeptical light on the Prosecution's investigations and case presentations. While the Ntaganda and Ongwen cases ended in convictions, the cases from Kenya and Ivory Coast ended in preemptive acquittals, inviting another round of condemnation from victims' representatives and the NGO community.[1]

CHARACTERISTICS OF THE ICC SECOND GENERATION

The mixed record of the Congo trials prompted widespread reflection among Court stakeholders – but any lessons learned seemed to widen the gaps. Both Prosecution and Defense repositioned themselves in tactical ways, seeking to avoid prior hazards. Judges in all phases were unable to hide the rifts that surfaced in the Bemba appeals process, while remaining as decorous as possible in their disagreements.

1. *The Prosecution multiplied charges and modes of liability.* In contrast to the simple charges and single events tested out in the Ituri trials, the Prosecution now asserted all of its charging options at the pre-trial confirmation stage. The next trials would encompass multiple criminal charges, all modes of liability, and a proliferation of criminal events or attacks, swelling the "facts and circumstances" controlling the scope of proceedings. This kitchen-sink gambit opened up maximum space for broad case development, reducing the need for judges to employ Regulation 55.

[1] There was also a 2016 conviction for Ahmad al-Faqi al-Mahdi from Mali, who pleaded guilty to charges of attacking cultural monuments in the city of Timbuktu, during a period of Tuareg-Islamist occupation. The evidence included videos of al-Mahdi swinging the destructive crowbars. Al-Mahdi Trial Judgment and Sentence, September 27, 2016, ICC-01/12–01/15–171. His original nine-year sentence was recently shortened, now ending in September 2022.

2. *The Prosecution submitted mountains of evidence*, confident of avoiding early filters of admissibility, and hopeful that the mantra of holism would leverage the weaker parts – including quantities of anonymous hearsay and circumstantial evidence. The moral energy behind this approach had become clear by the time of the Bemba appeals decision, and doubtless contributed to that majority's countervailing judicial "nominalism" (seeking evidence of specific trees within this impenetrable forest).
3. *The Defense spread itself thin to meet these shape-changing master narratives*, while searching for some overarching doctrinal backstop. For Ntaganda, that line of defense was standard military necessity; for Ongwen, it was the embattled doctrine of psychological duress. Both were unable to block the evidentiary flood. In the two abandoned trials, by contrast, the trial judges themselves articulated fatal weaknesses in the Prosecution's case, establishing a new judicial practice of inviting/accepting "no case to answer" motions from the Defense, at the close of the Prosecution phase. Those motions were denied in Ntaganda and Ongwen, but successful in the Kenya and Ivory Coast cases.
4. *The dogma of judicial deference disguised the lack of harmony*. Following the drama of the Bemba appeals majority, the rhetoric of appellate deference failed to stabilize judicial conflicts. The core Bemba controversy remained just below the surface: how judicial deference was to be framed by principles of legality – most especially the presumption of innocence. The Prosecution, while appealing the Ivory Coast acquittals, tried to avoid undermining the deference shield that might protect the next trial conviction.
5. A *dialectic between truth-seeking and principles of legality became entrenched.* In debates projecting a sense of rivalry between civil law and common law judicial models, the Prosecution and sympathetic judges found the fulcrum for balancing Defense rights. By extolling the counterweight of *truth*, some judges would endow the Prosecution with its own fair-trial claims. This full dialectic emerged in appellate dialogues on acquittals.
6. *Retreating from the discursive requirements of the Bemba appeals majority*, judges reverted to psychological metaphors for measuring evidence, implanting inscrutable truth deep within the judicial soul. The path to criminal convictions, after winding through tangled fields of evidence, opened up into a forest enchanted by holistic visions. But these same metaphors hobbled the Prosecution's efforts to overturn acquittals – when trial judges insisted they were unpersuaded by the evidence, and appeals judges deferred to these conscientious declarations.

KENYA AND IVORY COAST: THE ELECTION-VIOLENCE TRIALS

Collapse of the Kenya Cases

During the long decade of the Congo trials, the first ICC Prosecutor wanted to bring additional cases from Uganda but was unable to capture any members of the Kony gang. He had delayed action in the Central African Republic before turning to Jean-Pierre Bemba (then in European exile after losing the 2006 Congolese Presidential race). Both these situations, like the Congo situation, grew from self-referrals by ICC member states. Both Ntaganda and Ongwen were holdovers from these early ventures – late, second-generation surprises, when each suspect unexpectedly surrendered.

Soon after these self-referrals, the Prosecutor exercised his authority derived through the United Nations Security Council. In 2005, the UNSC referred Sudan (a non-ICC member), restricting the scope of ICC investigation to the Darfur region. While the Prosecutor ultimately prevailed with including the crime of genocide in the ICC arrest warrant for Sudanese President al-Bashir, he failed to bring his preferred Sudanese suspects to The Hague.[2] Nor would the Court gain custody over suspects following a second UNSC referral for Libya in 2011.

There remained the prosecutorial "trigger" of *proprio motu*, which allowed the Prosecutor to investigate (with Pre-Trial Chamber approval) the ICC member state Kenya, following the post-election violence of 2007. Another *proprio motu* initiative focused on (then) ICC non-member Ivory Coast, where the winner of the 2010 Presidential election neatly surrendered his defeated rival, following a wave of post-election violence. Both situations would end poorly for the Prosecution, even as Prosecutor Moreno-Ocampo's initiatives were picked up by his successor, Fatou Bensouda, from June 2012.

The Kenya cases tested the Court's political acumen by pitting the Prosecutor against a proud member state with no intention of cooperating with investigations. The six Kenyan suspects showed up voluntarily in The Hague, even as government resistance hardened behind the scenes. The Prosecutor's master concept was to confront two opposing ethnic groups, taken as the underlying source of conflict, and to issue summonses for three men from each group. In a

[2] Some lower-level suspects briefly passed through The Hague: Bahar Idriss Abu Garda, for whom charges were rejected by the Pre-Trial Chamber in 2010; and Abdallah Banda and Saleh Mohammed Jerbo, who appeared under summons in 2010 and then returned to Sudan, where Jerbo reportedly was killed, and Banda remains at large. Then in 2020, Ali Muhammad Ali Abd-Al-Rahman surrendered to the ICC through the Central African Republic, and his was set to begin in early 2022, considering charges from the period 2003–04.

stunning rejoinder, the most prominent men from each side, Uhuru Kenyatta and William Ruto, combined forces to run for President and Deputy President in the 2013 elections – which they won, in part, by running against the ICC. Both continued to take voluntary part in pre-trial proceedings, while being uniquely able to quiet the spirit of Kenyan cooperation.[3] When these cases were finally abandoned, the Court took a heavy blow, and the new Prosecutor was quick to blame Kenyan authorities for blocking her investigations, and for condoning private violence against potential witnesses.[4]

The six Kenya cases were abandoned in three stages.[5] First, in early 2012, pre-trial confirmations were declined for two suspects; and a third case was dropped the following year. This left Kenyatta standing alone for one proposed trial, and Ruto and the broadcast journalist Joshua Arap Sang for a joint second trial. Next, the Kenyatta case was dropped in late 2014, before the trial opened, when the Prosecutor came up short in her investigation – an outcome widely anticipated by close Court watchers. Finally, the joint trial for Ruto and Sang was abruptly terminated in April 2016, at the close of the Prosecution's case presentation. Prodded by the Defense, the Trial Chamber majority declared the case was too weak to proceed.

This mechanism for abandoning the only active Kenya trial would resonate in later second-generation trials, opening the door for judicial innovation. The Rome Statute and the Rules of Procedure and Evidence make no formal provision for judges to terminate trials mid-stream. But, pushed by the Defense, two judges in the Ruto/Sang Trial Chamber brought the case to a sudden halt. It was not an official acquittal, and it was hedged by assurances that unspecified future evidence could bring the trial back to life. But it was an unmitigated loss for the Prosecutor, who opposed the dismissal strenuously. The accused – never in the formal custody of the Court – took the next flight home. There would be no appeal.

TERMINATING THE IVORY COAST TRIAL: "NO CASE TO ANSWER"

This trial was slow to begin as the Pre-Trial Chamber initially hesitated, suspending the confirmation process in 2013 to give the current Prosecutor

[3] This resistance was masterfully understated, if carefully articulated, including instances where the Kenyan Attorney General lectured the Hague courtroom on local bureaucratic hurdles for accessing official information.

[4] The Prosecutor obtained arrest warrants for at least three men charged with violating Article 70 (see main text, p. 437). From this group, Paul Gicheru is currently in The Hague facing charges.

[5] For references to relevant ICC documents, see main text, p. 437.

more time to come up with stronger evidence against ex-President Laurent Gbagbo. Her predecessor had begun investigating Ivorian violence in 2011, under a provision of the Rome Statute that allows non-member states to invite selective ICC intervention through the route of *proprio motu*.[6] It was another doomed venture into internal politics; but here the main suspect was the *losing* candidate – not (as in Kenya) the current head of state.[7] Prosecutor Bensouda assured the Court that her investigations were continuing, hinting that further cases could be brought against Gbagbo's victorious opponents, who had reciprocated the post-election violence.[8] But no such cases have been brought. Charges against Gbagbo were finally confirmed in 2014, and his case was joined with that of his young protégé Charles Blé Goudé, who had likewise been bundled off to The Hague, facing accusations of implementing his mentor's criminal plans.[9]

How weak was the Prosecution's case? Three years after the trial began, in language scarcely imaginable in an ICC judicial document, the Presiding Judge offered a scathing assessment. Judge Cuno Tarfusser was in his tenth year as an ICC Judge, having previously spent a long career on other benches. From his position in the Trial Chamber, he explained, he saw:

> the Prosecutor's case unravelling before my eyes in the courtroom, where witness after witness, from the humblest of victims to the highest echelons of the Ivorian Army, systematically weakened, when not outright undermined, the case they were expected and had been called by the Prosecutor to support. For almost four years, I have also been sifting through mountains of documents purportedly supporting that case, none of which could confirm it in the slightest, whether taken individually or as a whole, many . . . of doubtful authenticity and/or containing significant anonymous hearsay . . . .
>
> . . . Day after day, document by document, witness after witness, the Prosecutor's case has been revealed and exposed as a fragile, implausible theorem relying on shaky and doubtful bases, inspired by a Manichean and simplistic narrative of an Ivory Coast depicted as a "polarized" society . . ., a

6 A non-member may accept ICC jurisdiction by special request under Article 12(3), a step taken by the Ivory Coast first in 2003, and then eagerly reaffirmed in late 2010 and early 2011. The Prosecutor can decide *proprio motu* (with approval of a Pre-Trial Chamber) whether to launch an investigation. The Ivory Coast ratified the Rome Statute in 2013.

7 Two political scientists have explored opportunistic strategies behind ICC referrals in highly partisan national contexts, coining the phrase "international legal lasso" (see discussion and references, pp. 386–87).

8 See her remarks on the opening day of the joint trial, Gbagbo and Blé Goudé Trial Chamber, January 28, 2016, ICC-02/11–01/15-T-9-ENG, pp. 42, 50.

9 The ICC also sought to prosecute Laurent Gbagbo's wife Simone, but the Ivorians have not surrendered her.

> caricatured, one-sided narrative, built around a unidimensional conception of the role of nationality, ethnicity, and religion . . . in Côte d'Ivoire.[10]

Judge Tarfusser's splenetics reached all facets of the Prosecutor's presentation: the questioning of witnesses, the constant shuttling among junior prosecutors, and the utter rigidity of the Prosecution's master narrative, which failed to adapt even as the trial imploded. And the Defense comes off little better: getting caught up in tactical details and failing to note that the ship was sinking. It took an invitation from the bench to elicit the Defense teams' motions for summoning the lifeboat of "no case to answer."

Voting along with Judge Tarfusser, Trial Chamber Judge Henderson submitted a 1,000-page dissection of the Prosecution's case presentation, a level of detail regretted by his colleague, who despaired that such gargantuan ICC documents were themselves contributing to overall trial complexity and opacity. Dissenting here, as she had also done in the prior termination of the Ruto/Sang trial, Judge Herrera Carbuccia opposed the "no case to answer" motion, arguing for the case to continue, albeit with some sober judicial guidance.[11]

BUILDING LIFEBOATS FOR THE FUTURE

Following the Ruto/Sang experience, Trial Chambers and individual judges held a range of views about the legitimacy of terminating trials in midstream, in addition to the practical mechanics. Some denounced it as a power-grab by common-law bench-sitters, while others embraced it as a fundamental human right for the accused. And, if used successfully, what were its exact consequences: acquittal, mistrial, vacated charges? Would double jeopardy principles prevent future retrials on the same basic facts? And could Trial Chamber decisions be appealed by the losing party?

Answers to most core questions were spelled out in the Appeals Judgment of March 2021, upholding (by majority) as "acquittals" the termination of the joint trial of Laurent Gbagbo and Charles Blé Goudé. The appeals decision formally reconciled the "no case to answer" process with the Rome Statute,

10 Gbagbo and Blé Goudé Trial Chamber, Opinion of Judge Cuno Tarfusser, July 16, 2019, ICC-02/11–01/15–1263-AnxA, paras. 4, 12 (some internal quotation marks omitted).

11 She suggested that command responsibility would be a more likely mode of liability than the Prosecutor's favored Article 25(3) choices. While command responsibility had not been confirmed by the Pre-Trial Chamber, it was resurrected by Regulation 55 notice at the outset of the trial. But the Prosecutor paid little regard to it during her case presentation. Dissenting Opinion, July 16, 2019, ICC-02/11–01/15–1263-AnxC, paras. 5, 17.

tying it firmly to principles of legality. Students of judicial innovation will appreciate the array of learned opinions on these fundamental matters, both on and off the bench, in the flow of commentary following Ruto/Sang.[12] Here it is enough to describe the end result and to note implications for future cases, following the second generation of ICC trials.

1. The "no case to answer" procedure connects with Article 74 of the Rome Statute and is thus one form of "decision" ending the Trial Chamber's deliberations in the case.
2. A successful motion leads to acquittal and requires the immediate release of the accused, subject only to restrictions listed in Article 81 (3)(c).
3. Decisions based on this procedure must follow requirements in Article 74: must be in writing, must contain full and reasoned findings on the evidence submitted, may allow for dissents, may be summarized in open court but followed by full written documentation.
4. The question for judges is whether the evidence thus far presented is sufficient in law to sustain a conviction on one or more of the charges.
5. The evidence standard comes from Article 66(3): proof beyond reasonable doubt; and judges may weigh the credibility and reliability of evidence in applying this standard of proof.[13]

In process terms, the Prosecutor can demand an appeal if the motion is granted (Article 81(1)(a)). If the motion is denied, the trial simply proceeds as scheduled, and the Defense may decide separately whether to mount a case. An appeal by the Defense is not automatic, and the Trial Chamber's decision whether to consider the "no case to answer" motion is discretionary.[14]

These rulings put an end to six years of uncertainty about mechanics, standards of proof, and the depth of evidentiary scrutiny open to trial judges at this stage. As with other such innovations, the next generation of ICC cases will stimulate further questions.

[12] A starting point could be the lucid concurrence in the Ruto/Sang trial decision, where Judge Eboe-Osuji embarks on another world tour of lesser-known judicial caselaw, specializing in Commonwealth appellate jurisdictions, and including references to John Rawls and P. G. Wodehouse. Reasons of Judge Chile Eboe-Osuji, Ruto and Sang Trial Chamber, Decision on Defence Application for Judgments of Acquittal, April 5, 2016, ICC-01/09–01/11–2027.

[13] Gbagbo and Blé Goudé Appeals Judgment, March 31, 2021, ICC-02/11–01/15–1400, paras. 1–7.

[14] The Gbagbo Appeals Chamber accepted an Ntaganda interlocutory appeals decision, leaving it to the Trial Chamber's discretion whether to act on Defense motions for "no case to answer." See Judgment on the Appeal of Mr. Bosco Ntaganda against the Decision on Defence Request for Leave to File a "No Case to Answer" Motion, September 5, 2017, ICC-01/04–02/06–2026.

POST-BEMBA DEBATES ON EVIDENCE AND PROOF

The Gbagbo acquittal, midway through the trial, was another blow to the Prosecutor, and prompted a lengthy, strenuous, and ultimately losing appeal. But the rulings of the Trial Chamber and Appeals Chamber were not unanimous. All the major jurisprudential questions raised in the Bemba appeals decision (June 2018) continued to flourish in this dramatic Gbagbo trial decision (January 2019) and its appeal (March 2021). Despite efforts by the Gbagbo appeals majority to codify the "no case to answer" process, their rules can be changed by future panels, with just a simple tilt in the balance of judicial visions and methods. The fault-lines observed in the Congo trials have not been erased. Indeed, the counterweight to the election-violence cases can already be seen in the subdued splits lurking in the Ntaganda appeals decision, issued the day before the Gbagbo appeals decision.

The best vantage point for observing these judicial splits comes from appellate debates on acquittals. Thus, the Ngudjolo appeals decision provided a key rehearsal for the arguments found in the Bemba appeals decision, where a conviction was overturned, but with dissenting views. Smaller-scale versions of these debates occur as far back as several Pre-Trial Chambers declining to confirm charges, and in Trial Chamber dissents in the Ngudjolo and Katanga cases. In the second generation of ICC trials, these themes surfaced in the election-violence cases: first in the Kenya case dismissals, then in the Ivory Coast grand reckoning.

Out of the mob violence that swept the main cities of the Ivory Coast, the Prosecutor selected four or five key moments: snapshots that froze the action sufficiently to compile a record of killings, rapes, beatings, and mass persecutions – the core manifestations of crimes against humanity. Under pressure at the pre-trial phase to submit more evidence, the Prosecutor referenced an additional forty-one incidents, along with thousands of documents and dozens of videos. Included were chilling personal statements from victims, using the anonymous style familiar from international NGO reports. These were disturbing documents, even if courts would treat them as low-level hearsay. Back in the Gbagbo pre-trial confirmation decision, the dissenting judge remarked on this mix of evidence, noting that the Prosecution's quantitative product outpaced its quality.[15]

The Gbagbo master narrative broke down with the pivot to individual criminal responsibility. Going back to the Congo trials, the prosecutorial

15 Dissenting Opinion of Judge Van den Wyngaert, Gbagbo Pre-Trial Confirmation decision, June 12, 2014, ICC-02/11–01/11–656-Anx, para. 2.

template emphasized leadership responsibility, using modes of liability designed to implicate supreme leaders in the mayhem surrounding their obscure plans and policies. Regarding an ex-President resisting the transition of power, the narrative declared that violence carried out in Gbagbo's name must be attributed to his actions. But the Prosecutor had learned from previous cases that these links may be difficult to prove, and so included in the pre-trial materials alternative liability modes listed under Article 25(3), as well as command responsibility.

Both the Kenya and Ivory Coast trials foundered on this question of culpability. The case narratives posited loose networks of planners – allies of the political leaders, who conceived the common plan with its criminal elements. In neither trial, however, was it possible to establish the existence of such a group, let alone its common plan – unless by employing heroic presumptions and inferences. Here the scattered evidence for these malign structures simply did not add up when the inferential links to leaders at the top failed the reasonable-doubt test. The same skeptical approach questioned links between the documented crimes (killings, rapes, persecutions) and a controlling "State or organizational policy" guiding such crimes – a statutory requirement under Article 7(2)(a). President Gbagbo's public refusals to concede the election, combined with the actual violence that ensued, were not enough to underwrite the chain of backward inferences.[16]

This skeptical turn came as a sharp contrast to the more pliant methods found previously in the Congo trials. This contrast was noted by dissenting Judge Herrera Carbuccia in the Ruto/Sang termination decision, who cited with approval the bold inference patterns used to convict Germain Katanga. The Katanga Trial Chamber majority undertook its own search for a fresh mode of liability and was prepared to infer the existence of relevant groups, common purposes, and requisite "knowledge" (bordering on negligence or *dolus eventualis*) – based squarely on the documented

[16] The impact of this "organizational policy" requirement remains at the center of judicial debates. It was this statutory condition that prompted Judge Hans-Peter Kaul's dissents in the confirmation hearings for all six Kenyan suspects (and, before that, dissents to the pre-trial requests for all six summonses to appear). See Dissenting Opinion by Judge Hans-Peter Kaul, Muthaura, Kenyatta, and Ali Pre-Trial Confirmation decision, January 23, 2012, ICC-01/09–02/11–382, para. 7. Contrasting views emerged through the legal rhetoric of rejecting rigid "formalism," seeking to instrumentalize the statutory language in alignment with broader ICC humanitarian goals. These options, moderated by cautious gestures toward statutory purpose, are analyzed by Judge Eboe-Osuji ("Reasons," Part VI), including the importance of fair trial rights for the Defense (para. 328). He developed this emphasis still further in his concurrence in the Gbagbo / Blé Goudé appeals decision, with echoes of the intervening Bemba appeals decision.

mortality toll.[17] When it came to confirming the criminal responsibility of the accused, other Congo trials used similar inference chains. Why not in the Ruto/Sang case?[18] And then why not in the Gbagbo / Blé Goudé case?

Judges who embraced these inferences in the Congo trials were guided by precepts of *holism* – an ingenious method for counting up evidence, which generates large total sums in a ledger packed with fractional values. In those early trials, when many key witnesses were compromised, some portions of their testimony supplied just enough leverage to instill firm beliefs about culpability, deep inside the inner consciences of trial judges.[19] The controversy over holism became central to the Bemba appeals decision, where the majority demanded a more public accounting. Historically, the recourse to holism had been pushed by the Ngudjolo appeals minority; was then picked up by dissenters in the Bemba appeal; and again embraced by dissenters in the Gbagbo Trial Chamber and Appeals Chamber. The term itself became a commonplace, with all judges professing to evaluate trial evidence "as a whole" rather than piecemeal. For the Gbagbo dissenters, it offered hope for boosting the available evidence, by synchronizing the scattered parts so as to capture the inner beliefs of trial judges.[20]

Beyond holism, and beyond the selective bundling of evidence in support of presumptions of liability in the election-violence cases, the dissenters' passions were further directed to *truth* – in at least two forms. First was the truth registered by the inner conscience of the judge, corresponding to states of belief that subjectivized the standard of proof beyond reasonable doubt. This type of truth attaches to the conclusions of long inference chains, rather than to medial facts leading up to final judgment. Second was the very pursuit of truth in criminal trials, serving such ultimate ends as victims' justice and historical justice, and not to be denied by instrumental legal hurdles like the presumption of innocence. Such larger truths were imperative for the Gbagbo appeals dissenters, who were adamant that the trial should continue (under different trial judges), and confident that better-synchronized trial evidence would empower the ICC to fulfill its destiny: spreading justice to the victims, while sending clear messages to future perpetrators that the end of impunity was drawing closer.[21]

[17] On the Katanga trial, see main text, pp. 342–49.

[18] See the Dissenting Opinion by Judge Herrera Carbuccia, Ruto and Sang Trial Chamber decision, paras. 44–46.

[19] This practice was scrutinized by dissenting Judge Van den Wyngaert in the Katanga Trial Judgment, August 1, 2014, ICC-01/04-01/07-3436-AnxI (see paras. 169, 299–314).

[20] On holism and synchronized evidence, see main text, pp. 242–46, 360–68, 425–33.

[21] See the Dissent by Judge Ibáñez Carranza, Gbagbo and Blé Goudé Appeals Judgment, paras. 60, 126–28.

NTAGANDA AND ONGWEN: CONVICTING MID-LEVEL COMBATANTS

Ntaganda showed up unexpectedly in March 2013, followed by Ongwen a couple of years later. They appeared like ghosts from the first Prosecutor's earliest self-referrals and were clearly not the supreme leaders of their respective armed groups. Ntaganda's original arrest warrant had been questioned by the Pre-Trial Chamber because of his medial status in a military staff. Ongwen's name had entered the pool of original suspects from the Lord's Resistance Army, but almost nothing was known about him and his circumstances, let alone the structure of the LRA. As with other former child soldiers turning up in The Hague, the Prosecution could not vouch for Ongwen's birthdate with any accuracy.

In the second generation of ICC trials, the convictions of both men present a clear contrast with the aborted election-violence trials from Kenya and Ivory Coast. Those trials were cut short when trial judges deemed the evidence too weak to continue, measured against principles of legality such as the burden of proof and the presumption of innocence. In response, the dissenters looked to evidentiary practices of holism to boost the sums from weak evidence; and they asserted the overriding moral priority of victims' justice and the service of *truth*, to offset the weight of mere legality. The same divergence of legal styles had already appeared in June 2018, when a differently configured Appeals Chamber issued its split decision overturning the convictions of Jean-Pierre Bemba. The Bemba case tilted the jurisprudential scale briefly in the direction of the narrow majorities that would support acquittals for Gbagbo and Blé Goudé, in both the 2019 Trial Chamber and the 2021 Appeals Chamber.

INFERRING STRUCTURES OF VIOLENCE

What was different in the convictions of Ntaganda (2019) and Ongwen (2021)? In neither case was the Trial Chamber willing to consider the "no case to answer" motion. One factor was simply the magnitude of separate charges and modes of liability. The number of confirmed charges for Ntaganda was eighteen; and for Ongwen over sixty – along with a mix of liability modes from the full menu of statutory options. But the sheer quantity and complexity of these cases would not have distinguished them from the Gbagbo case, where complexity was read as chaos by two skeptical trial judges. Counsel for both Ntaganda and Ongwen pointed to comparable evidentiary failings – but, instead, the judicial balance tilted back in the direction of a robust holism. It was a weary replay of jurisprudential tensions inherited from the first generation of Congo trials. And those tensions remained just below the surface for Ntaganda on appeal, where his convictions and sentence were upheld – and where judicial splits were strangely muted. One day later, the same Chamber upheld the Ivory Coast acquittals, this time with two sharp dissents. Ongwen's appeal remains to be heard by a new roster of appeals judges.

Perhaps the main difference between the two pairs of second-generation trials stems from the basic organization of armed violence, as inferred from background events. Ntaganda could not avoid the same presumptions and inferences already accepted in the Lubanga trial, since he was part of the same armed group – the UPC in Ituri. Early on, international NGOs led by HRW ascribed a strict coherence and military effectiveness to the UPC, modeling inferences to the existence of common plans, criminal purposes, and leadership responsibilities. And just before Ntaganda's surrender, his reputation in other eastern Congo insurgencies had been extensively noted by the same NGOs, popularizing his field moniker as "the Terminator." Perhaps Ntaganda was just a violent man, who would gravitate to lawless groups known for committing civilian atrocities. The Prosecution's case theory was virtually unchanged from the Lubanga trial, and the same presumptive chains had the full benefit of inertia.[22]

And, while little in fact was known about the operational structure of the Lord's Resistance Army, a popular video in 2012 made Joseph Kony and his gang famous around the world. Any group associated with atrocities summarized in this video would have to be taken seriously, encouraging trial judges to make the necessary inferences about who was responsible. Even so, it remained unclear whether this pattern extended to Dominic Ongwen, given his particular history of abduction into the LRA. Putting aside that question of personal responsibility, perhaps the notorious LRA was self-evidently the kind of group whose heinous crimes required a firm ICC response.

By contrast, the skeptical judges in the Ruto/Sang and Gbagbo / Blé Goudé trials rejected the inferential patterns necessary to impute common plans and criminal enterprises led by the respective accused. In Kenya, the Prosecution posited the existence of a non-state "Network" for carrying out election violence associated with the Ruto faction; and in Ivory Coast, it was President Gbagbo's "Inner Circle" allegedly performing this key function. But such presumptive structures, despite holistic treatment of scattered evidence, were not enough to complete the pivot to individual criminal responsibility.

Overarching structures for election violence were also essential for meeting the statutory condition for crimes against humanity: that they be carried out

[22] See main text, pp. 252–73.

"in furtherance of a State or organizational policy to commit" attacks. This last provision has been softened to serve the ICC's broader moral mission, but that mission itself favors confronting the most effectively organized modes of violence, which "shock the conscience of humanity." Judges in all phases of the Ntaganda and Ongwen trials faced this essential question: could atrocities associated in any way with entities like the UPC and the LRA fall short of attribution? Manifestly not – in the wake of the Lubanga trial, and the world-wide condemnation of the LRA. As mid-level combatants, both men were immersed in concrete operations, presumed to be guiding as well as implementing organizational policy.

PRESUMPTIONS OF GUILT AND INNOCENCE

Although it ended seven years after the Lubanga trial judgment, Ntaganda's trial followed the standard Prosecution template from all three Congo trials. According to that template, civilian deaths were presumed to be the intentional, criminal goals of ethnically driven militias, masterminded through common plans by ruthless leaders. The liability mode of co-perpetration kept stretching to reach even Bemba's venture into the Central African Republic – although in that case the Pre-Trial Chamber knocked it back to "command responsibility." From this experience, the Prosecutor came ready to plead all forms of liability from the outset, while swelling the pre-trial cache of "facts and circumstances" with a few well-focused attacks, surrounded by a large halo of "contextual" attacks, from which evidentiary threads might still be holistically drawn. There must be enough threads, at least, to satisfy the inner convictions of trial judges, whose personal sincerity would then receive appellate deference.

As the Ntaganda trial opened in September 2015, the models for Trial Chamber reasoning were the first two Congo trials – both from Ituri. In both those cases, the Chambers had used breathtaking presumptions and inferences to pivot from civilian victims to individual criminal responsibility of the accused. In both cases, Defense teams had pushed back with the reasonable-doubt standard of proof. But there had been no appeal from the Katanga conviction, and the Lubanga appeal yielded only one of five judges willing to challenge the Trial Chamber's reliance on broad inference chains.[23] Yet jurisprudential rumblings were being heard, and soon would come the abrupt halt of the Ruto/Sang case, followed by the Bemba appeal reversal (just

[23] On Lubanga, see main text, pp. 249–50. While the Ngudjolo acquittal referenced the standard of proof, it nonetheless managed to cast doubt on his actual innocence (see ibid., pp. 302–04).

at the point when closing trial arguments were taking place for Ntaganda). The Ntaganda Defense was constructed not simply for the Trial Chamber, but for an Appeals Chamber that might follow the direction marked out by the Bemba appeal.

Closing down the Ruto/Sang trial would have encouraged later Defense teams to lean harder on principles of legality. In particular, Judge Eboe-Osuji's analysis offered a new kind of calculus, which would be further elaborated in the Bemba appeals ruling. Both judges in the Ruto/Sang majority understood the critical importance of broad judicial inferences for sustaining the Prosecution's main case. But, pushing against those inferences, in the context of a "no case to answer" motion, was the presumption of innocence.

> A proper appreciation of the question of law . . . must . . . take into account . . . the value of the presumption of innocence – a notion that must always be given real significance for purposes of a conviction – and the level of evidence required to shake it. In circumstantial cases, the presumption of innocence takes on a substantial value as a veritable barrier that obstructs triers of fact from engaging in leaps in the name of inferences that would justify a conviction. The height of that barrier in specific cases will depend, on the one hand, on the viability of any other hypothesis that is consistent with innocence and, on the other hand, the nature, quality and viability of any other independent evidence such as would assist the trier of fact in making sure of their entitlement to draw the particular inference urged in the direction of guilt.[24]

Here, then, was a jurisprudential response to the Court's earliest trials. It was aimed at the bootstrap practices associated with holism, reaffirming limits derived from core legal principles. In Judge Eboe-Osuji's analysis, the *presumption of innocence* erected a barrier to what might be called the *presumptions of guilt* – inferences like those on display in the Congo trials, without which the leap to individual responsibility would have been impossible. His critique was broadened further in the dramatic reversal by the Bemba Appeals Chamber, which addressed a trial record of unreviewable findings of fact, declared to reside within the inner conscience of trial judges. By psychologizing the reasonable-doubt standard, this practice failed to articulate public grounds for accepting the result as the only reasonable interpretation of contested trial evidence.[25]

[24] "Reasons of Judge Eboe-Osuji," para. 74.

[25] See Bemba Appeals Judgment, separate opinion of Judges Van den Wyngaert and Morrison, June 8, 2018, ICC-01/05-01/08-3636-Anx2, paras. 14 (on reasonable doubt) and 15–16 (on holism).

Seeing how the first Congo trials unfolded, the Ntaganda Defense built the logic of these legal principles into its alternative theory of the case. It meant conceding the high degree of planning and leadership behind the UPC's actions in Ituri during the critical period of August 2002 through May 2003, and several months beyond. But, otherwise, the two case theories were diametrically opposed, and never wavered during the entire conduct of the trial.

According to the Defense, UPC actions were lawfully conducted military campaigns against an alliance of Ugandan, Congolese, and North Kivu forces (the remnants of the RCD-ML that fled Bunia in August 2002), fought under guerrilla-like conditions in parts of Ituri populated by ethnic Lendu villages. The Lendu were not the target of UPC military action, according to the Defense, except when informally organized Lendu combatants integrated themselves with the broader alliance forces. As a Congolese Tutsi born in Rwanda, Ntaganda was not part of any rogue faction directing hatred toward the Lendu. Further, Ntaganda's extensive personal testimony in this case revealed several initiatives by the UPC to cooperate with Lendu combatants, seeking to turn them against Ugandan usurpers (with expected support from Ugandan rebel groups sheltering in Ituri). The violence against Lendu civilians was neither part of the UPC plan nor passively condoned by the UPC and was likely the work of random village-based combatants, who lurked opportunistically during conventional attacks, ready to move in with bladed weapons, intent on looting and exacting revenge for similar attacks against Hema civilians. If Ntaganda got wind of such behavior by men under his command, he made inquiries and exacted punishments.

Was it too good to be true? Truth was not the precise purpose of this rejoinder to the Prosecution's master narrative. In the context of a trial, the aim was to create reasonable doubt about the main charges, and to block the stream of inferences and presumptions based on circumstantial evidence, mixed with insider-witness testimony. It would not be enough for trial judges to construct the usual inference chain, unless they could also show that theirs was the only reasonable interpretation of events – meaning that the Defense case was not just unpersuasive, but ultimately unreasonable. And if the Trial Chamber would not deploy the presumption of innocence in this manner, then the Appeals Chamber should not extend its deference.[26]

A similar gambit, based on the presumption of innocence, was applied to standard questions of fact – when Ntaganda found himself on the witness stand for some 120 hours, under oath and with cross-examination. During this time, he addressed all aspects of UPC operations in Ituri, from secret meetings with

[26] See Bemba Appeals Judgment, Separate Opinion of Judge Eboe-Osuji, para. 17.

Lendu leaders down to details of military operations. Whenever he directly contradicted prior testimony from Prosecution "insider" witnesses, would his particular views merely join the holistic evidentiary mass? Or would they alter the calculus by introducing "reasonable" alternatives into the record, thereby obligating the Trial Chamber to justify its contrary findings as the *only* reasonable alternative?

Two examples are enough to show the futility of this approach. First, on the broader level of inference, the Chamber looked for evidence to confirm its grand presumption that UPC efforts were driven by ethnic hatred. Beyond the scope of circumstantial evidence – primarily the toll of civilian casualties – was there something more concrete? What should they make of Ntaganda's unflagging story of a tightly focused military, directing its efforts to lawful targets? While exercising great care and caution, they decided not to believe it. Although Ntaganda's testimony was articulate and consistent, they would discount it because he had a self-interested motive to distort the real facts.[27]

Instead, they based their ethnic-centered presumptions on reports that UPC troops were taught to sing songs directed against the Lendu, with emphasis on a particular Congolese Swahili battle cry: *kupiga na kuchaji*. Literally, it meant something like "strike and (re)charge." Ntaganda and some other witnesses testified that it exhorted UPC fighters to attack and then reclaim enemy weapons. But instead the Chamber accepted the word of still other insiders, who insisted it meant "attack and kill all the Lendu civilians."[28] A broad holistic net was able to collect such incriminating views, as long as judges were persuaded in their innermost consciences. Another pillar of this finding was some quasi-hearsay about anti-Lendu declarations at a Ugandan training camp in June 2002, months before the UPC evolved into a governing coalition. The Trial Chamber believed there was enough concrete substance in these reports to affirm its key presumption: that the UPC had a common plan with a criminal purpose. And the Ntaganda Appeals Chamber let it stand as "not unreasonable."[29]

There was also the matter of whether Ntaganda personally shot and killed the civilian Abbé Bwanalonga, in the aftermath of the November 2002 UPC military venture in Mongbwalu. This charge was supported by the testimony of a single witness (a disgruntled insider, about whom Ntaganda provided details behind the disgruntlement) who said he heard the shot and saw the corpse. Ntaganda's testimony to the contrary was discounted, and the charge of

27 Ntaganda Trial Judgment, July 8, 2019, ICC-01/04–02/06–2359, paras. 257, 258, 262.
28 Ibid., paras. 799–803.
29 Ntaganda Appeals Judgment, March 30, 2021, ICC-01/04–02/06–2666, paras. 386, 394, 425.

direct perpetration for murder was confirmed (and upheld on appeal as "not unreasonable"). And, for the sake of holism, there was a 2010 Ntaganda field interview with an HRW analyst, in which she raised the question of the Abbé's death – a subject she thought Ntaganda was too quick to deny. Her report was considered low-level hearsay, but it nonetheless played some incalculable part in the holistic calculus of overall evidence.[30]

Putting everything together, the Appeals Chamber left in place Ntaganda's thirty-year sentence – the statutory fixed-term maximum, and the longest issued so far by the ICC.

SPLITTING DIFFERENCES

The Ntaganda Appeals Chamber was a different panel from the Bemba Appeals Chamber. Only two of three judges in the Bemba majority continued, both of whom filed concurrences with no trace of the broad nominalist revolt that overturned Bemba's conviction. There was to be no shocking upheaval in the Ntaganda case, unlike what happened on appeal in Bemba.

The bigger ICC news came one day later, when the same appeals panel upheld the acquittals of Gbagbo and Blé Goudé. It was another split decision, this time with two spirited dissents along the same lines as the Bemba appeals dissents. The Gbagbo appeals majority upheld these acquittals with standard tools of appellate deference: two trial judges had made certain findings; they were deeply conscientious in their beliefs; and their conclusions were "not unreasonable."[31] Protected by this façade of appellate restraint, the Appeals majority seized the moment to solidify a host of new practices surrounding "no case to answer"

[30] Ntaganda Trial Judgment, para. 533, and note 1596 on the HRW interview. The Appeals Chamber saw no reason to challenge what the Trial Chamber concluded (Ntaganda Appeals Judgment, para. 679); moreover, it was not unreasonable for the Trial Chamber to favor the single witness testimony over that of Ntaganda since the trial judges had worked systematically and conscientiously (para. 662).

[31] This strong version of judicial deference laid out in the Gbagbo Appeals Judgment erected a virtually irrebuttable presumption that trial judges act in good faith (para. 177), adding that any party challenging their findings inherits the burden of proving them not reasonable (paras. 69, 74). This forceful stance was enough to defend some sketchy practices surrounding the impugned "no case to answer" motion, including the fact that formal written "reasons" were not supplied by the majority until six months after acquittals were announced in open court. But was this same deferential fortress appropriate for Ntaganda's appeal of a *conviction*? It left no scope for Ntaganda's position that a defendant should not be required to carry the burden of proving that trial findings were weakly articulated (let alone "unpersuasive"), in confronting the repertoire of holistic practices. The Appeals Chamber concluded, with no apparent irony, that "Mr Ntaganda has not demonstrated that the Trial Chamber violated the presumption of innocence or reversed the burden of proof in assessing his testimony. His arguments regarding the manner in which the Trial Chamber evaluated his testimony are therefore rejected" (para. 605).

motions, aligning them closely with principles of legality, including the presumption of innocence. Compared to Bemba, it was a quieter revolution for the appeals judges. The Prosecutor had evidently feared the activist results behind this display of deference and grounded her Gbagbo appeal on supposed errors of law and procedure, and not errors of fact. But it was a thinly disguised feint, especially when the supporting briefs argued that there should have been more holism in the trial judges' mid-case assessment of evidence.

Considering this strategic display of judicial deference in the Gbagbo appeal, the same deferential posture may have been unavoidable for Ntaganda's appeal. Besides, the Lubanga Appeals Chamber had already upheld similar presumptions about the UPC. Clearly, there were insufficient votes now to attempt anything as ambitious as the Bemba appeals reversal.[32] In fact, the lively Bemba debates were barely in evidence across both 2021 appeals decisions, except for the two dissenters in the Gbagbo appeal, with their call for holism in pursuit of higher judicial truths.

The two concurrences in the Ntaganda appeal came from Judges Morrison and Eboe-Osuji – both of whom had joined the activist majority in the Bemba appeal.[33] Here they preferred to play a longer game. Both readily accepted Ntaganda's culpability, but then went on to launch broad critiques of the Court's working model of leadership liability, imported from German criminal law. Their critiques were pitched at the level of textbook theory, loftily abstract, with no suggestion that this model's erratic career at the ICC had anything to do with concrete realities of armed groups operating in Ituri.[34]

There was no need to say much at all about Ntaganda, whose guilt was sufficiently obvious.[35] But both judges insisted that *future* cases should not have to endure the same contorted inferences about common plans, essential contributions, and other paradigmata built into the Germanic doctrine. The Ntaganda Defense had challenged real-life presumptions and inferences, both

[32] In his separate Gbagbo appeals concurrence, Judge Eboe-Osuji pointed out that the shape of judicial deference may be different for appeals from acquittals and convictions (para. 220). But that difference was nowhere evident in the Ntaganda appeal.

[33] In the Bemba Appeals Judgment, see Judge Eboe-Osuji's attack on deference as "the virtual reign of judicial infallibility by another name," in the face of holistic practices ("giving bloated significance to available evidence in ingenious ways"), when trial judges make adverse inferences without "eliminating all other inferences consistent with innocence" (Separate Opinion, paras. 23, 18, 17).

[34] See main text, pp. 260–66.

[35] Judge Morrison found enough strength somewhere within Article 25(3) to support the convictions (Separate Opinion, para. 2). Judge Eboe-Osuji rejected the thirteen charges based on indirect co-perpetration, but accepted the overall outcome on the strength of direct-perpetration charges surrounding the murder of Abbé Bwanalonga (Partly Concurring Opinion, para. 164).

at trial and on appeal – but virtually none of that was addressed here in these abstract concurrences. And, indeed, both judges suggested that abandoning the Germanic model could ease the Prosecutor's burden next time, saving everyone a lot of trouble.[36]

AS GENERATIONS PASS

Across the Congo trials, tensions within the Rome Statute rose to the surface in controversies over trial procedures, witness integrity, patterns of judicial inference, holistic evaluation of evidence, the preemptive status of judicial belief, and even the free pursuit of judicial *truth*. Gradually, these practices came under scrutiny from core legal principles (including the presumption of innocence and proof beyond reasonable doubt), emerging into full-scale debates in the Bemba appeal. Against this background, a second generation of ICC trials has now receded without finding any new direction. Many judges involved in past trials have left the Court, and time will tell how their successors will pick up these jurisprudential threads. In June 2021, a third Prosecutor took office for a nine-year term, opening up possibilities for new situations, new case narratives, and new controversies. Several trials are now just starting up, based on events in Sudan, Mali, and the Central African Republic.

Left over from the second generation is the Ongwen appeal. His sixty convictions will receive extensive analysis, even if most everything passes through as "not unreasonable." His appeal will ponder the same mix of holism and presumptions accepted in the Ntaganda appeal. More challenging will be the 25-year sentence, which caused the trial judges some agony, as they finally reckoned with Ongwen's ambiguous status as both perpetrator and child soldier victim – a conundrum emphasized from the start by his Defense team. Not to be forgotten is Ongwen's remarkable speech at his sentencing hearing.[37] Delivered without notes and lasting almost two hours, in it Ongwen presents a wealth of raw data about his childhood, his LRA experiences, and his entry into the modern world and contemporary consciousness as a detainee in the ICC facility. It leads to untimely questions about whether his case was ever a proper match for the ICC apparatus. Similar questions about the Congo trials hang over the Court's next phases.

36 Both concurrences cited similar critiques by Judges Van den Wyngaert and Fulford.

37 His remarks were not under oath or subject to cross-examination. Ongwen Trial Chamber, Sentencing Hearing, April 15, 2021, ICC-02/04–01/15-T-261-ENG, pp. 3–37. The agony at sentencing came also from the wrenching views of more than 4,000 victims in this brutal conflict.

Index